The History and Expressive Cultures of the Acholi of South Sudan

FIRST EDITION

Saturnino Onyala

The History and Expressive Cultures
of the Acholi of South Sudan
Saturnino Onyala

Translated by Okidi George
a Translator for Makerere University (Uganda)

Picture by: Joseph Lagu

First published in 2018
Address
Web address
Email

September, 2018
Melbourne, Australia

ISBN: 978-0-6484367-0-6
Printed and bound by

About myself

Saturnino is a South Sudanese Australian who came to Australia as a refugee in 2003. By obtaining a Master degree in Social Science, specializing in International Development from RMIT University Melbourne, the author was exposed to global cultural trends. This in turn, inspired him to create conversations around hidden and undocumented aspects of African cultures and historical milestones. 'The History and Expressive Cultures of the Acholi of South Sudan' is a reflection of valuable knowledge gained through a number of research and conversations with elders in the community. Saturnino is currently exploring the cultural frameworks of South Sudanese Lou people and these untold stories will be published as a book in the near future.

About this book

Saturnino used to hear traditional history and cultures of Acholi of South Sudan from elders at the fireplace. Among the Acholi, such stories, which are cornerstones of history, are conveyed verbally from generation to generation. Interestingly, most of the knowledge produced around Acholi culture only managed to cover one group of Acholi that is the Acholi of Uganda. The lack of resources around Acholi of South Sudan prompted Saturnino to document the rich history and cultures of this community by producing this book. He interviewed more than a hundred elders and conducted several focus groups to create an accurate reflection of historical events and cultural frameworks of these minorities.

Acknowledgments

I started writing this book of The History and Expressive Cultures of the Acholi of South Sudan in 1986. I want to tell you readers that without the help and mercy of God, I think writing this book would not be successful. Truly, there are four things which made writing this book difficult to me. They are:

First, I could hardly find Acholi elders who had the knowledge of Acholi history and cultures because most elders had already died. Secondly, the elders who are alive have bad attitude. They want you to give them sitting allowance when you want information about the history and cultures which, at that time, I could not afford. Thirdly, it was the time John Garang De Mabior's war was at its peak and bombs could be heard everywhere. Anya-nya threw bombs almost everyday in Juba. Gun shots rocked Juba from 7:00am to 6:00pm. Women and children stayed out of Juba town. Everybody's ear was kept open. But I want to say that the people's being out of Juba town at that time gave me the opportunity to write this book. When rebels were bombing Juba people took refuge at the bank of River Kiir (River Nile) and at the foot of Mount Jebel Kijur. These two places gave me access to Acholi elders. Fourthly, it became hard for me to get money to pay for computer and a typist. Getting money from Acholi people was difficult because most of them were not employed. The few Acholi people who were employed had meager salaries which could not buy for them food and clothing.

I am very grateful to those who gave me advice and other forms of assistance that enabled me to write this book. In this book, I objectively present the information as I obtained from my informants. Therefore, I want to thank and pray to the Creator for these people: Paterno Abak, Marcello Ogana, Kadensyo Jada Adinya, Anthony Otoo Stephen, Jovita Ayang and Ben Oywak of Pajok. Afulunaro Acire Odano, Matia Aburi Lolori, Marcello Odiyo, John Ongee

Kassiba, Firmo Ondwong, Avelino Alia Ouna, Felix Okot Tibursio, and Anthony Bongomin of Obbo, Kabaab and Julius Okeny of Palwar. Disan Ojwee Olweny, Palacido Langoya Yugu, Cerbolo Okiya, Gerelimo Mamur Odolfere and Andrea Alimu of Panyikwara. Lapwony Alexander Oyet, Mario Wani Atanga, Richard Signal and Jacob Oryem of Agoro. Rwot Anthony Onek Otoo, Simplicio Obwoya and Alex Oringa of Omeo. Justine Oboma, Abraham Paulino Atare and Moise Peter Angabolo of Ofirika. Domasio Otoo Obbo (Palimu), Tokwaro Otoviano, Daniel Ocola, and Rebecca Aran (Palimu) of Magwi and many other people whose names I cannot include in this list.

Secondly, I am indebted to Acholi Literacy Committee: Bernard Oringa, Khalifa Mattia Marcello, Patrick Okot Lamson, Olga Eunice Odera, Paul Otoo, Mwaka Emmanuel Lutukumoi and Father John Oryem for keenly reading the manuscript and helping to put this information in fluent Acholi Language. Without their help, this book may not have come out. Thirdly, my appreciation goes to Mrs. Camila Ayet John and Teddy Angee Purtancio for typing this work. I am optimistic that this book will help the Acholi people to remember their history.

Glossary

1. Adayo = The clan of a man's wife.
2. Aconya = Old tradition.
3. Acwer nyo Wir = The central pole of a hut.
4. Akara-jami = A forked pole which supports the small pole which are nailed on the central pillar to make the hut strong.
5. Alem = A person without sin (offense).
6. Abila = Altar for offertory to God.
7. Auma = A paternal spirit kept under the pot.
8. Boro = A hole in rock into which human or animal can sleep.
9. Bur-lee = A pit which men dig in the wilderness to trap animals.
10. Canga= Small pieces of broken ostrich egg threaded ion a string (spirit beads).
11. Camooput = Drinking the back of oput tree for cooling down ager to reunite antagonised clans/children.
12. Ciriba = A person chosen by the community to perform ceremonial rite on the hunting ground.
13. Coboko= An animal skin sheath for the blade of spear.
14. Cola = a piece of black cloth or a rope which a widow wears or ties around her neck in memory of the deceased.
15. Dak-buk = A billy goat of a grandfather. (repetition 55)
16. Gibegu = Animal skin sewn into a bag for keeping things.
17. Gipyer = Payment for the father of a girl's sperm.
18. Golo = Tree stem (animal hide or papyrus mat) for lying at the evening bonfire on the compound.
19. Gwenobuk = A hen which a grandmother waves on people for blessing when one's mother's kin leave the funeral ground.

20. Gulo = A pot-like hole on a flat rock.
21. Jokodano = One of the gods worshiped.
22. Katala = A long stake or bamboo stem of about two metres or eight feet, which the village leader (chief of the hoe) together with the village members have agreed to use for measuring the portion each member will dig in a garden during communal garden work.
23. Kecabongo wang dako (latin) = The worst kind of famine (farting is worse than excrement) -A man gets up at night to to feel the face of his wife with his hand to ascertain if she is asleep. If the woman is asleep, the man just makes straight for the for the food pot.
24. Kika = Bamboo or reeds woven and used as door shutter by Acholi of the olden time.
25. Kibuka = A hut erected outside the compound for treating patients.
26. Kokoteka = Investigation of the cause of somebody's death through ciko teka.
27. Kweteangaci = Acholi unfiltered millet or sorghum beer.
28. Kwot/okwott = Buffalo hide which is sewn into shield to protect oneself from stroke of spear during war or mock fight.
29. Laa-logoyi = It is an animal hide.
30. Layoyo = Goat droppings which are collected from a goat pen.
31. Longoya= It is a kind of dress that the bereaved wear to mourn their departed dear one.
32. Laliko/lalibo = A person who stealthily stalks another person or an animal to kill.
33. Lapii = A blessing which clears misfortune or mishaps from the way of warriors or hunters during war or hunting expedition.
34. Lawiibol = A lad who has been chosen to command the warriors.
35. Lyero = A piece of land without vegetation cover.
36. Marin = Soldier or warriors.
37. Ngato = The chief's affection/love for a girl.
38. Ngurlatin= The vagina of a young girl.
39. Nagala/kitara = A bed used for carrying a sick person or the body of a person who died in the wilderness.
40. Nyuka = Porridge made from millet or sorghum flour, usually taken before the main meal to reduce hunger.

41. Orwanga = Initiation of boys into manhood.
42. Ocoka = A tree with rough back and long leaves.
43. Oducu = The payment that a boy/man makes to the family of the girl with whom he has been sleeping with before marriage.
44. Od'akar = A place where people pitch camp.
45. Oliemu = Boys who have just been circumcised to be initiated to qualify for initiation to manhood. (repetition 29)
46. Otoko = A hut in which a boys or a man sleeps.
47. Olet = A grazing ground for cattle or goats.
48. Ocodowaya = A woman who eloped with a man and later they got separated from.
49. Owic = A knotted string tied on a bamboo twig used to ensnare rats and other wild animals by setting it in their track.
50. Ojaru = An altar on which offertory is made to God.
51. Orede yat wat = (Family tree)
52. Paneo = A person who lives with his mother's kin.
53. Pawego = A person who lives with his father's kin.
54. Puno = Salty clay soil which animals flock to eat.
55. Peke = Packed food prepared to be used on a journey.
56. Pita(nyo Opita) = A special feeding to women to fatten them so that men can be interested in them.
57. Tana = The food for celebrating gods.
58. Taya = A place where people gather or a crowd.
59. Teng =. Part of a place (land, home, etc.).
60. Telemete = Ululation to call people together at the time of problem, or at the time of war.
61. Tim = A place where a person who serves the government lives.
62. Tir = A long stick which boys play *lawala game with.*

Saturnino Onyala, the Man

"Autobiographical sketch"

I was born on the 01/01/1951 in Licari-Obbo. Licari is situated on a plateau. People settled here because the soil is very fertile. Secondly, there is a good number of games which provide meat for the inhabitants – food staff in Laciri is adequate. There are no schools in Licari. All children study in a 'Bush school' in Oyere, which is about four to five miles from Licari. My father was a great hunter and farmer. He also worked in coffee farm at Obbo between 1960 and 1962. Later, he went to work as a game ranger in Kasese-Uganda.

I started Primary One in a bush school in 1960 when I was already ten years old. Joining school was a problem to me because teachers said I was above the age of starting school. Fortunately, the God of my father had "lain stomach up". A police officer, Lazario the brother of Adik-Diko-moi, of Licari, who headed the police who were keeping peace at the time of enrolling school pupil told the teachers to register me in Primary One. With the authority of Lazario, I was enrolled in Primary One. Although my father was working in coffee farm at Obbo, we did not have a bicycle. So I always walked to school. Sometimes I met elephants and buffaloes on my way to school. My 'Bush school' teachers were Opeko of Obbo, and Teodoro Lo-um, (he was often called by his nickname, Otyien) of Pajok. As the Acholi said, it is the children from poor families are the ones who are brighter in class. Truly, I was a bright child and all my teachers liked me.

In 1963, I passed the examinations which were for the pupils of Palwar, Pajok, Obbo, Magwi, Omeo and Panyikwara. At that time, Acholi children from different families completed their primary two from village schools, after which they did the examinations to join Palotaka Elementary School.

From every bush school, teachers chose forty five Primary Two pupils who scored high marks to join Palotaka Elementary School. I studied in Palotaka Elementary School for six months. Later, government transferred one teacher from Juba to Palotaka. This teacher had two boys who were in Primary Three. That year, Mr. Labuk was the headmaster of Palotaka Elementary School. Shortly, the new teacher asked the headmaster to remove two pupils from Primary Three so that there was space for his boys in the class. I do not know how the headmaster's eyes functioned! His sight fell on me and one of my friends, Michael Oyuru of Pajok Paitenge. The headmaster called both of us in his office and informed us that each of us should go back to study in the village schools. Michael Oyuru went back to study in Pajok village school while I went to Oyere village school.

The Mwony Anya-nya rebel had started in 1962. In 1964, my mother, Laura Onek, fled with my two sisters and I to Palabek Akeli-kongo in Uganda. Refugee life was not easy. A short while later, the Palabek people started calling us *Agono ki Lokung* (I came via Lukung). In 1964, I resumed Primary Three in Palabek Kal Primary School. All the same, life was hard because the wife of my Uncle, Dr Mario Tokwaro, with whom I lived, used to deny me breakfast every morning. She did not want me to wash my face with the water in her pot. At the same time, I was also a mass boy at Palabek Mission. When it was time for me to go to school or church, I washed my face from a bore hole, or with dew using cassava leaves. In 1965 I went to study in Palabek Padwat where I lived with my mother's sister called Mrs. Imerigiana Lalaa. When I realised that I may not have a good place to study from, I joined *Pakele Minor Seminary* in 1966 when Father Leopoldo Anywar of Amika Magwi was the Rector of Pakele Minor Seminary. When Father Father Leopoldo identified me as a bright boy, he appointed me as a storekeeper of student's food store. Later, Father Hillary Loswat Oboma of Lokoro, realised that the Parish Priest of Pakele Mission wanted to remove me out of the seminary because I gave food to students whom he wanted to punish by starvation. It is true that when the Parish Priest ordered that there was no food for students the following day, I gave much food staff to be prepared for their meals because I thought that if they eat much today, they would not feel very hungry the following day. In 1967 Father Hillary Loswat Oboma, transferred me to *Nadiket Minor Seminary* in Moroto, where I completed Primary seven. In 1969, I went to study in *Lacor Senior Seminary* Gulu-Uganda. It was from there that I began to think of writing a book. I wanted to write a book titled *All Acholi Traditional Names Have Meanings*. In this book, I wanted to explain the meaning of Acoli names like Okeny, Onen, Opiyo, Acen, Olum, Oryiem, Acayo, Abalo, Akwero, Onek and many others that I cannot list all here. I found that I had a lot of academic work, so I suspended the writing project because I wanted to score high marks at the seminary.

In 1973, when the Government of Sudan and the leaders of Anya-nya One rebel group signed a peace deal at Adiss Ababa in Ethiopia, Bishop of Sudan said that all Sudanese seminarians who were in Uganda should go back to Sudan. In 1973 I started studying Philosophy in *Juba St Paul National Major Seminary*. Father Joseph Nyekindi, who later became a Bishop of Yambio, was a Rector. I completed Philosophy in 1975, and in 1976 I joined *St Paul National Seminary* in *Bussere National Major Seminary*, where I studied Theology. Eventually, I discovered that academic victory was not in the classroom because we were only three theologians in the class. For this reason, we wrote to the Bishops to allow us to study at *St. Thomas Aquinas National Major Seminary* in Kenya. Unfortunately, the lecturers at Bussere National Major Seminary were Italian and American fathers. They looked at our request as disrepute to them. One evening the fathers talked this issue over their supper. They said I was the one who enticed the other two students to think of going to study at St. Thomas Aquinas National Major Seminary. As a result, they resolved and sent me on a one year probation. Bishop Gabriel Ziber, who headed Wau Diocese, came to the Seminary to investigate the matter. He found out that I was innocent. He then asked the lecturers if they could allow me to resume studies at Bussere. Unfortunately, none of the lecturers agreed with the Bishop. In 1977 they sent me on the one year probation in Juba so that I could stay out of the seminary. When I was on probation, I asked Bishop Ereneo Dut of Juba Diocese if I could look for a job so that I could take care of my welfare before going back to the seminary. He did not object to my request. I was employed in the Ministry of Finance as an Office Clerk.

I worked in the Ministry of Finance for six months before the government appointed me Community Development Officer in the Regional Ministry of Cooperative and Community Development. The government transferred me to Torit District where I lived with Father Julius Igaa in *Torit Mission*. The one year probation elapsed but the Rector of Bussere National Seminary did not call me back to the Seminary. Subsequent to this, I left Torit Mission and rented a house in Malakia. In 1978, I married my senior wife, Mrs. Margarete Ayaa of Oruku (Madi). In December 1978, God blessed us with a child whom we named Emmanuel Onen (which means, behold God is with us). I served in Torit from 1978- to 1982, and then the government sent me back to Juba as Assistant Director of Community Development. In that year, *Agency for Cooperation and Research Development* (ACORD) began to work in partnership with Department of Community Development. The government saw my efficiency at work and promoted me to Coordinator of Community Development Support Unit where I supervised Community Officers of Equatoria Region, Upper Nile Region and Bahr El Ghazal Region.

In 1986 I started writing the book, *The History and Expressive Cultures of the Acholi of South Sudan.* The Dr. John Garang de Mabior, insurgency did not give me time to visit Acholi informants in different places. In 1990, when I was piecing up my work, my Uncle (my father's brother), Justice John Onge Kassiba observed that the book I was writing "would be useful to future generations." unfortunately, I did not know where I could get the money to publish the book.

In 1991 when the war in Juba intensified, I took refuge in Khartoum together with my family. Because of my good work record and efficiency CONCERN SUDAN (Irish International Organisation) employed me as a Refugee Program Manager at Kosti where I worked from 1991 to 1994. Unfortunately, before I finished writing the book, my wife, Mrs. Margarete Ayaa passed away in 1993 from Kosti. I had five children with her one daughter and four sons. But one of the sons called John Onge, later died from Juba. My second wife Santa Alal was in Juba, South Sudfan, when we were in Kosti. In 1996 I went to Khartoum, and worked as Logistic Assistant Officer with Action Contra La Faim (ACF) at Jaborona Regugee Camps in Omdurman. In 1996 I married the third wife, Mrs. Faima Doka. I had the first child with her and called her Anna Achiro Olaa. In 1999 I went to study Diploma Primary Health Care at Halliah University Omdurman.

In 2001, the security situation in Khartoum grew tense. The soldiers of President Omer El Bashir were secretly killing them. Many people lost their lives. I then fled to Cairo-Egypt. Before I reached Cairo, I thought Cairo would be a resting place, but when I reached there I found life in Cairo as hard as sitting on fire. Sudanese traveled fearfully. Refugees slept in fear.

The Egyptians stated calling us *Chokoleta*. Egyptians also increased rent for Sudanese refugees up to LS 500 for a three room house. Yet an Egyptian rented it at only Ls 20 to 30. In addition to that, most UNHCR workers were Egyptians. As a result, passing interviews in the office of UNHCR became very hard for Sudanese refugees. To get out of Egypt, refugees must for the decision of UNHCR for two or seven years. If they allowed you to go, they conditioned you to go to America, Canada, Finland, and Australia. Some Sudanese have never got their way out of Egypt. Some people went back to Sudan, but those who realised that there was no peace in Sudan are still in Egypt.

In 2003 I came to Australia, and I thought it would be easy for me to get a job here because of my vast experience. Unfortunately, Australian government did not recognise degrees of Sudanese universities. This made it a little difficult for me to get a job here. In 2004 I began to study Community Development in Dandenong TAFE, and graduated with Diploma in Community Development in 2005. From 2006 to 2008, I obtained B.A. in Human Services, Victoria University. When I was studying at Victoria University, I worked with Migrant Information Centre, Eastern Melbourne, on the terms of three days a week. On completion of the course, the Manager of Migrant Information Centre gave me Case Management job which was on the basis of five days per week. Although most of the employees of Migrant Information Centre were women, there was high level of solidarity among them. This made my work at Migrant Information Centre easy. When I was searching for other jobs from the Internet, I discovered that most employers wanted people with Master Degree. For this reason, I began to pursue Master in International Development at RMIT University-Melbourne campus. I completed this course in 2012 since I was a part time student and, at the same time, working to support my children.

In 2010, when I was sending the manuscript of this book, *The History and Expressive Cultures of the Acholi of South Sudan* to Mwaka Emmanuel Lutukumoi, I thought of writing another book in English. It will be titled *The Short Social Anthropology of the Northern Luo of South Sudan*.

Introduction

M any people have been writing about the history of Lwo. Among them we have D. Wosternmann (1912), W. Hofmayer (1925) and B.Z. Seliman (1932). In their writing, they say that Lwo came from a big lake in the east called Great Lakes. However, another writer, Crazzolara (1950) said that Lwo originated from Rumbek in Bahr el Ghazal. But Onyango says Lwo came from a lake, which he does not know its location. All these writers relied on guess work in their attempt to trace the Lwo Cradle land. The history of the Lwo is very important. People should continue tracing it. In this book, I will not generally talk about Lwo, but I will talk about the history and expressive cultures of the Acholi of Sudan only though I will briefly talk about the Lwo of Kenya, Tanzania and Uganda.

When I talked to Acholi of Sudan, I realised that many people did not know where the people who inhabit the present Acholiland (the Acholi people themselves) came from. They also did not know the culture of the Acholi. Culture is very important. I discovered that it only those who know the culture well were the ones who could handle it. I also learnt that little knowledge about culture was bringing a lot of conflict among the Acholi people. These conflicts would arise during discussion of bride price or funeral issues, wilderness or mountains, between a woman and man and many others.

Unfortunately, the Acholi of South Sudan have not been interested in writing their history which would be of value to their progeny. They orally transmitted information they learned from their elders to their children. I think this is not bad, but the culture may completely die if it is not written down. The children who have not been close to their elders may begin to do things they have seen. Not only that, the Acholi children of today reject their culture outrightly, especially those who have been to places like America, Australia, Canada, Britain, Holland, Norway and Finland.

This is the main premise for which I have written this book. I also know very well that Acholi people are usually well known, among other ethnic groups, for respecting their culture. If culture is used well, I am sure, it can help us to guide children who may digress from the expectations of the people. This is why I want to know the culture of the Acholi of South Sudan as one of the Lwo groups. In this book I will write about the culture of Acholi and their way of marriage according to the information I obtained from Acholi elders without adding anything to it. Secondly, I will look at how British divided the Acholi people into Acholi of Sudan and Uganda.

From what I read from other people's writing about the culture of Lwo, I found out that they wrote about the Acholi of Uganda (Central Lwo) and Lwo of Kenya and Tanzania (Southern Lwo), but they wrote very little about the Acholi of South Sudan. Some writers did not say anything about them. For me to present this information correctly, I will use what Acholi elders told me, and what I read from different books.

In 1986 I dedicated my time to collecting data about Acholi history and expressive cultures from heads of clan of Acholi of South Sudan. I then started putting down background information. The data I obtained include the following: feeding the dead, the origin of the Acholi of Sudan, Acholi proverbs and land and wilderness. I got this information from John Ongee Kassiba, Mathia Aburi Lolori, Marcello Odiyo, Mamur Odelfere, Disan Ojwee, Paterno Abak and Ben Oyak. The informants provided the facts objectively. I obtained some of the information from *laraka-raka* and *bwola* because this is one of the ways elders transmit culture to the younger generation. These songs which were sang between 1890 and 1960 are laden with message for the audience.

Unfortunately, the John Garang de Mabior insurgency separated me from the elders before I finished writing this book. In 2001 he Sudan army wanted to kill me, I fled to Egypt and took refuge in Cairo for two years. I continued searching for information from Acholi elders who were exiled in Cairo. In 2003 I obtained a Humanitarian Visa (Visa 202) from Australia where I later relocated as a refugee. I continued compiling information for this book. Written history can be very accurate when it is compiled by a native because he is able to distinguish between facts and myths. So, the history of the Acholi of Sudan can be best written by an Acholi native because he knows the history better than a foreigner.

Most of the contemporary Acholi people do not know the origin of Lwo in spite of the fact that they are the offering of Lwo. But if you ask a Lwo from Uganda, Kenya, and Tanzania that "Where did you come from?" they will tell you straight that "We came from Sudan." That means if the cradle land of Lwo is Sudan, it cannot be in Rumbek as Crazzolara asserts, but it should be in Kassala because other writers such as Onyango, they say Lwo people migrated from shore of a water body, but there is no water body in Rumbek. As Onyango (1976) maintains, water body east of Sudan. The water which is east of Sudan is Red Sea. This is in keeping with what the Acholi elders have told me that Lwo came from Kassala, near a water body called Red Sea. The Acholi elders such as Paterno Abak and Mamur Odelfere told me that the contemporary Lwo occupy the land which begins from Malakal up to Dinka land and it stretches along River Kiir (River Nile) to Lake Victoria in Uganda and Kenya and it expands to Musoma in Tanzania. So, if we put the Lwo land together, it is as large as 1,000 square Kilometer (i.e. from Malakal to Musoma).

Acholi culture had been intact until the time when our youths began to intermarry with other ethnic groups. Foreign cultures infiltrated Acholi culture. This brought a lot of changes in Acholi culture. In the past Acholi people did not marry outside their tribe. However, with the novelty of modernity, Acholi children, especially boys, began to marry foreigners like Madi. For example, when Madi man followed his daughter in Acholiland, he used Madi culture. If an Acholi man followed his daughter in Madiland, he also demanded to use his culture together with Madi culture. Eventually, some elements of Madi culture were borrowed into Acholi culture as we will read in this book.

Long ago, people did not need many things to feed the dead (pay the uncle of the deceased. They asked only for five things which did not cost as much as they do today. This time, clan leaders have turn death into a money raising event. Parents have also turned their daughters into shops or income generating objects. Today people ask for things which were not asked for in the past for marriage and funeral. Bride price used to be very low in the past, unlike today where parents of the groom may be unable to pay the very high bride price. This is one of the reasons why many girls now take very long to get married. Consequently, an easy way to find a wife is to impregnate a girl and take her home. This is because in Acholi culture, a girl who gets pregnant in the house of her father must take the pregnancy to the man responsible for it. The boys from poor families take advantage of this custom to get a wife.

We will also look at Acholi religion in this book because foreign /white teachers of religion think that, in the olden days, Acholi people did not know God. They also said Acholi people worship devils. To us Acholi, the religious teaching of the whites is not correct. Acholi people know God and they call Him Jok. But the God whom Acholi people know is not in heaven as the white religious teachers proclaim. The God of the Acholi is on earth and He found in many places such as mountains, caves, under big trees and at streams, and wells. What I want readers of this book to understand well is that in the olden days Lwo people did not call the Creator *Rubanga*, but they called Him *Jok*. Up to today, people of Shilluk still call God *Jok*. Unfortunately, the foreign religious teachers say Jok is evil, which they call *Satan*. We did not have Satan in Acholiland. This does not mean that Acholi people could not differentiate between good and bad – they were able to.

Another thing which I will discuss into detail is land and wilderness in Acholi, and then we will look at how Arabs entered South Sudan. I think if we want people to know many new things which foreigners brought to Acholiland, we cannot talk about Arabs only, but we also need to discuss the British rule in Sudan. Some people say there is no development in Acholiland because Arabs oppressed them. However, if we look at it carefully, we find that it is British who made the place undeveloped. They handed over administration of Sudan in the hands of Arabs and yet the owners of the place were there. Secondly, when the British masters still ruled Sudan, they developed Northern Sudan at the expense of Southern Sudan. Although we blame the British for the poverty in South Sudan, we also blame the Arabs because they added more problems on South Sudan. Lastly, we talk about the significance of initiation rite to other Acholi groups. We will also look at birth and proverbs which are used among the Acholi people.

Table of Contents

Chapter One

LWO (LUO) GROUPS

The Lwo people are found in many places in Africa. Some of them are in South Sudan. Others are in Northern Uganda, Eastern Democratic Republic of Congo, South western Kenya and Northern Tanzania. All the groups of Lwo speak the same language, Lwo Language though some groups may not be very intelligible to others. Some Lwo elders and some writers say that the Lwo people are sometimes called *River Lake Nilotes or Western Nilots*. The Lwo language group includes Dinka and Nuer, the groups that speak more proto-typical Lwo are the Acholi of Sudan and Uganda, who live in Magwi District, Gulu District, Luo of Kenya and Tanzania. Others include Shilluk in Malakal District of Sudan, Anywak of South Sudan and Ethiopia, Jo-Luo or Jur Chol in Wau Distrct of South Sudan, Lango in Lira and Apac Districts in Uganda. Palwo people live in Gulu and Kitgum District in Uganda. Balanda live in Wau District of South Sudan, Alur live in Nebbi District of Uganda and some are in Democratic Republic of Congo, Padhola or Badama are found in Tororo District in Uganda, Lokoro are in Torit District in South Sudan and Kuman or Ikumama at Kaberamaido District in Uganda.

Lwo Came from Sudan

The writers of history and Lwo traditional leaders claim that the Lwo people lived in south eastern Sudan at a place which is now called Kassala. The Lwo separated from the people of Kassala around 300BC and eventually settled in Barh El Ghazal at *Sue River* South in Sudan. Lwo people lived in Barh El Ghazal for more than eight hundred years. Around 1200 AD and 1450 AD the Lwo had a number of migrations at Sudan Uganda border. We do not know the reason why Lwo left Barh El Ghazal. But some people say they left the place because there were too many people, and there was not enough space for them. In 1600 AD Acholi of South Sudan migrated from Barh El Ghazal and they settled in the land they occupy today in South Sudan. In 1600 AD, the Acholi and Alur of Uganda moved away from Barh El Ghazal, and they entered and settled in Uganda. Fr. Crazzolara said the cradle land is at Bahr-el-Ghazal (P.32) but he did not know that the first settlement of the Lwo was actually at Kassala.

According to B.A. Ogot *nilotes* (people of the river) divided into three groups. That is, people in the north, central and south. The nilotes who are in the northern group are the Dinka, Nuer, Shilluk and Anywak, Atwot, Pari, Bor and Lwo of Barh El Ghazel (Wau). The central Lwo are the Acholi, Lango, Alur and Palwo. The Southern Lwo are the Lwo of Kenya, Padhola and some Bantu. We can now divide the *nilotes* into two groups. One group comprises Dinka, Nuer and the peole who speak Lwo. However, the recent writers of Lwo history divided the nilotes into two. The first group is the people of Shilluk, Anywak, Acholi, Lango and Palwo. The second group consists of Alur, Padhola and Jo Lwo of Kenya – all these are Lwo-speaking people. The home ground of the nilotes stretches from Bahr-El-Ghazal up to Bar-el Jebel "Juba-Sudan", which is between 2,000 and 6,000ft. Others are in northern and north-western Uganda, while others are in eastern Kenya (B. A. Ogot, 1967, PP, 3133).

Northern Lwo-Sudan

Acholi: Acholi elders contend that Acholi of South Sudan and Acholi of Uganda came from Shilluk. They are the grand children of Omara. Omara had a son called Kolo. Kolo begot Mol, Mol begot Okwa. When Okwa grew up, he married two women. The senior wife was Dumo's mother and the junior wife was Nyikang's mother. Acholi elders and some writers claim that Acholi of Sudan are the offspring of Dumo (read chapter two of this book), and they came to Sudan around 1550 A. D. They were first under the administration of the D.C. of Gulu. Thereafter, they were under the D.C. of Torit District. A few years after, they were under Magwi District.

The people of Shilluk, or Chollo has about one hundred clans. Chief Nyikango was the leader of Shilluk after his separation from his brother, Dumo over the beads. (Read chapter two to find out more about what took place between these two brothers). The people of Shilluk occupy Malakal, and in

Sudan, they are the smallest group after Dinka and Nuer respectively. Long ago, the Shilluk were led by Reth who was said to have come from Omara (descendants of Omara). Like the nilotes, Shilluk were cattle keepers. They also kept sheep and were great cultivators.

The Anywak people settled at the river bank, and they also kept domestic animals. They are in two groups; one in Sudan and another in Ethiopia at a place called Gambela. Oral sources claim that the Anywak of South Sudan are 52,000, and those in Ethiopia are 26,000. Therefore, the Anywak of both South Sudan and Ethiopia have a population of 78,000 people.

The population of Jur Chol is between 60,000 and 80,000 people -they live in Wau, Tonj, and Aweil Districts of South Sudan. However, most of the Jur Chol are in Wau, Mapel, Udici, Alel, Thony, Barmayen and Umbili. The people of Jur Chol are cultivators and they also keep domestic animals such as goats, sheep and cattle. According to oral sources, Jur Chol are also the progeny of Dumo.

Lokoro or Pari also migrated from Barh El Ghazal around 1600 A.D. They eventually settled at the foot of Lafon Hill in six different groups. They lived at the foot of this hill from 1600 A.D. up to 1993, when Arab soldiers burnt down their huts. Subsequent to this, Pari people scattered and settled in many different places but still around mount Lafon. In the census of 1982 the population of Lokoro was 11,000 people.

Central Lwo — Uganda

Around 1500 A.D. Acholi of Uganda, who were called *Biito-Luo*, split from the Central Luo, the Acholi of Uganda today. Biito-Luo moved away from Barh El Ghazal and were led by chief Labongo to the land of Baganda (Bantu) in Bunyoro. Biito-Luo lived in Bunyoro land where they later founded *Babiito Dynasty*. Biito-Luo lost both their culture and language in Bunyoro and were assimilated into Bantu.

In 1600 AD some Acholi and Alur of Uganda left Barh El Ghazal and inhabited their present home in northern Uganda. Some Alur went and settled in Congo or Zaire, Chad and Niger. Acholi of Uganda settled in Gulu, Kitgum and Pader Districts. The 1991 *census* shows that Acholi people who were in Uganda were 746,796, but about 45,000 Acholi people were out outside the country as refugees.

Oral sources claim that Lango migrated from Lotuko in 16 00 AD and found a place to settle at the shore of Lake Kyoga. When Acholi and Alur reached Uganda, they had some internal conflict. Although Lango people speak Lwo, they are not Lwo by ethnicity, but they came from Lotuko and Ethiopia.

However, other oral sources claim that Lango are true Lwo people. They left Barh El Ghazal around 1600 AD and went to the land of Anywak in Ethiopia where they moved on until they reached Uganda. From Uganda, Lango split up into two major groups. One of the groups settled at the shore of Lake Kyoga, and the other group which was called Ateker, later split up into four groups: Karamojong, Iteso, Kuman and Lango Omiro. Other Lango moved to Kenya and are now called Kalenjin and Massai. The oral sources assert that Lango people found Kumam people at *Lake Kyoga, and that some Kumam people came from Teso and Karamojong though they speak Lwo.*

Between 1600 AD and 1700 AD Chief Adhola took his people (Jopadhola) from Barh El Ghazal to central Uganda where they lived for a few years before settling in Budama in eastern Uganda. The fact that the place was forested made it hard for Bantu to penetrate it to fight JoPadhola.

As we have read above, people did not move together, but in different groups and at different times.

Southern Lwo — Kenya and Tanzania

Between 1500 A.D. and 1800 A.D. some groups of Lwo left Barh El Ghazal, entered Uganda and proceeded to Kenya, where Jo-Luo of Kenya are. Some of them moved on to Tanzania, and are now Lwo of Tanzania. The Lwo people of Kenya and Tanzania are found at the shore of Lake Victoria which is between 4,000 ft. and 5,000 ft. away from the water (B. A. Ogot, 1967, P, 37). We cannot separate the movement of Lwo from that of Acholi, Palwo, Alur and Lango, because the history of Lwo says that they all came from Anywak.

Chief Ramogi Ajwang led the Lwo of Kenya and Tanzania from Barh El Ghazal. They first went to Nimule and proceeded to Pakwach in Uganda. The history of Lwo states that these people rested for a few months at Pakwach before they separated and some went to Alur while others moved on to Palwo, Lango and Teso in Uganda from which they continued to Lake Victoria (Victoria Nile).

Like other Lwo, the people of Joka-Jok came from Anywak, entered into Barland and proceeded to River Kiir (River Nile) where Lwo people again split up. Some of them moved southwards while others moved to the east. Others moved west and followed River Kiir and eventually settled at Pakwach or Pubungu as it was called in the old days (Crazzolara, 1950, P, 53). The Lwo who went eastwards to Pajok and proceeded to Agoro passed via Gulu and Soroti. From there they moved on to Bugwere, Mbale and Tororo, and they continued to Samia in Bukangala. They farther moved to Nyanza between 1590 and 1670 A.D. This group did not reach Pakwach and Bunyoro. It seems around 1590-1750 had a number of migrations between Acholiland and Alurland. The people from whose places they passed did not fight them. That is why today we have names such as Gem, Koc, Puranga and Nam among Acholi, Alur, Padhola and Nyanza in Kenya and Tanzania. The history of Joka-Jok states that they entered Nyanza without fighting the people they found there (B.A. Ogot, 1967, PP, 55-60).

In my investigation of the history of Acholi of Sudan, I discovered that the history of Acholi of Sudan does not spell out if Joka-Jok moved together with Kor people of Pajok and does not tell us if Joka-Jok met Kor of Pajok at the foot of Agu Hill. However, according to Bethwell A. Ogot, Joka-Jok of Kenya are akin to Kor of Pajok. The history of Joka-Jok maintains that Joka-Jok people came from Ywaya-Pajok (B.A. Ogot, 1967, P, 148).

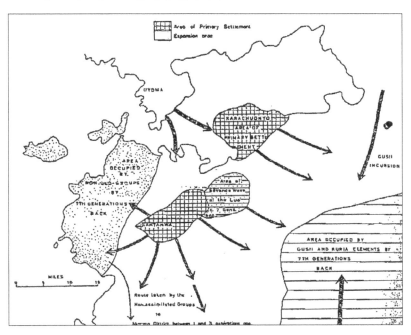

Figure 1. The home of Lwo in Nyanza

5

According to Westerman, the people of Alur, Palwo, Lango and Lwo of Kenya split up from Acholi from Pakwach (B.A. Ogot, 1967, P, 48). All of them settled at the shore of *Lake Victoria*. We cannot tell if Ramogi Ajwang moved together with Lwo of Kenya or with Lwo of Tanzania. It appears the Lwo people arrived in this place in the month of *curi*, dry season, and oral sources assert that they immediately began to cultivate millet, sesame and sorghum. They also began to keep cattle, sheep and goat, and later started making spear and shield. Four different groups, Joka-Jok, Jok Owiny, Jok Omolo and group which comprises Suba, Swaka, Asembo, Uyoma and the people of Kano, entered in the Lwoland of Kenya at different times. The history of Lwo states that Joka-Jok were the first group to enter Nyanza followed by the other three groups (B.A. Ogot, 1967, PP, 143-144). One elder from Kenya told me that "Lwo of Kenya were the third largest ethnic group in Kenya after Kikuyu and Luhiya in 1994. The population of the Lwo of Kenya was 3,185,000 people. The Lwo of Tanzania were 280,000 in 2001. Jo-Lwo of Kenya have twelve clans. They are Jo-Gem, Jo-Ugenya, Jo-Seme, Jo-Kajulu, Jo-Karachuonyo, JoNyakach, Jo-Kabundo, Jo-Kisumu, Jo-Kano, Jo-Asembo, Jo-Uyoma and Jo-Sakwa. If you want the details of the movements of Lwo, see the map on the last page of this book.

In reality, the story of Lwo of Kenya and that of Tanzania began when Lwo settled in Nyanza because before this there were no people called JoLwo. As we have seen above, Chief Ramogi Ajwang, was the one who led the Lwo from Anywak. History also maintains that all the Lwo have their roots in the house of Chief Ramogi.

What is the etymology of the name Acholi?

If you ask the Acholi people the meaning of the word "Acholi" some of them will tell you that "Acholi is Acholi," while others will tell you that "Acholi means people who live in Acholiland." These answers do not tell us what Acholi means. Explaining the meaning of Acholi is a problem to many people as we will see three attempts made to explain the same.

To answer this question well, let us first look at where Acholi came from. If we understand where Acholi came from, it will help us to answer the question. Different writers have varying ideas about the cradle land of *Acholi*. Some think that Acholi came from Anywak and others argue that they came from Shilluk while others say Acholi came from Lwo. However, if we follow the history we find that it is not possible that Acholi originated from three different groups as some writers have stated above. That means Acholi could have come from one of the groups of Anywak, Shilluk or Lwo.

This indicates that people who have been writing about Acholi have been guessing where Acholi came from because no Acholi elders gave them correct information about it. In my sharing with many Acholi and Shilluk elders, they told me that Acholi came from Shilluk, and they think that is the right information. They also told me about clans in Acholi and Shilluk.

Long time ago, in Shilluk, there was *river cow of God*. Dyiang kulu married *Nikia* (which means *the sister of crocodile*) and they begot Omara, Omara begot Kolo, Kolo begot Mol, and Mol begot Okwa. Okwa grew up and married six women. The senior wife was the mother of Dumo, Okwa's first born. The junior wife was the mother of Nyikango, the second child to Okwa. Oral sources maintain that the other four wives begot Gilo, Anywak, Luo and Achol, a daughter among sons of Okwa.

Acholi elders contend that Lwo people originated from Okwa's six children. Dumo fathered the following clans: Balanda, Jur Chol of Wau, and Jur Chol in Chad. Nyikang fathered the people of Shilluk, and Gilo fathered Anywak and Lokoro (Kor), Anywak begot Anywak clan, and Luwo fathered Lwo (Luo) who are in Kenya and Tanzania, and Acol fathered Acholi. This indicates the origin of Acholi. The name Acholi was derived from the name Achol. That tells us that Acholi means children of Acol.

In the old days Okwa's people did not have names of tribes and clans. The six children were the ones who named the different tribes we have today. Oral sources state that since people were moving a lot, the children of Okwa split from one another and others remained in Bahr El Ghazal in Sudan, but Dumo and Nyikango settled at "KAL KAARO". The elders of Shilluk told me that the base of *Kaaro* is close to Lake Victoria in Uganda. They said that many children of Shilluk had fear to go to Kaaro, thinking that they would die if they went there.

THE SEPARATION OF DUMO AND NYIKANGO

(Spear and Beads Separated Lwo for the first time at Kaaro)

After the death of Okwa, Nyikango (Divine King) inherited the throne of his father. He lived well with his brother. But this makes us ask ourselves why Okwa's children did not live together if there was no conflict among them.

The Shilluk elders believe disagreement over beads separated the two sons of Okwa, Dumo and Nyikango. According to oral sources, one morning when Dumo was threading his beads on his compound. Nyikango's wife came to her brother-in-law to chat with him. She sat next to Dumo and unstrapped her child, who was still in a crawling stage, to play around.

Just a short while after, the child picked Dumo's bead and threw into the mouth and swallowed it. When Dumo saw that his brother's child swallowed his bead, he went to his brother, Nyikango, and told him that, "My brother, your child has swallowed my bead. I do not want anything else apart from my beads.

Figure 2: Nyikango's child swallowed a bead

Just a short while after, the child picked Dumo's bead and threw into the mouth and swallowed it. When Dumo saw that his brother's child swallowed his bead, he went to his brother, Nyikango, and told him that, "My brother, your child has swallowed my bead. I do not want anything else apart from my beads.

When Nyikango heard this statement, he politely answered his brother, "My brother, as my child has swallowed your bead, I kindly request you to wait until tomorrow in the morning and search the child's feces and I will give it back to you." Dumo rudely answered his brother that "I cannot wait up to tomorrow. I want my bead right now."

Nyikango listened to his brother with deep sorrow. He entered his house,

8

picked a spear and lain his child in front of Dumo where he ripped the child's stomach open. He took the bead from the child's stomach and told his brother, "There you are.

Figure 3: Nyikango ripped open the child's belly

Take your bead. I have already killed my child because of your bead.

Dumo received his bead while laughing and walked back to his home. One thing that Dumo did not remember at this time is that he was a lone stalk-hunter, and he had only one spear. It did not take many days when Dumo took his spear and went out on a hunting expedition. In the wilderness, Dumo found a herd of elephants under a big tree. He drew closer to the elephants and speared a mother elephant. Unfortunately, the elephant did not die. It ran with the spear in its body. Dumo was left without any spear in his hands.

One day, Dumo wanted to go hunting. Since he had no spear at that time, he went to his brother Nyikango and asked for a spear from him to use on his hunting trip. He told his brother that, "My brother, animals have run with all my spears. Could you help me with one so that I go to hunt with? I will give it back to you went I return from the wilderness." Nyikango did not object to his brother's request. He gave him the spear which he used to open his child's belly.

Dumo took the spear and off to the wilderness he went. He did not go very far in the wilderness. He found a herd of elephants. Dumo was very happy. He raised his hand high and let the spear go. He speared one elephant, but the elephant did not fall down. It ran with the spear in its body.

Figure 4: Dumo speared elephant

When this elephant reached home, its brother asked, "Who has speared you?" The elephant responded that, "A short small bodied man speared me." Dumo returned home and pleaded to his brother, Nyikango, "My brother, forgive me. I speared an elephant with your spear and it ran away with it."

Nyikango immediately answered him, "My brother, I do not want to talk much. I killed my child because of your bead. I also want my spear. Nothing else, but my real spear." Dumo could not do anything. The following morning, he set out for the wilderness. After a long walk, he saw a herd of elephants. He did not know how he got there. Then, stranded, he sat under a big tree.

It is said that, in the olden days, elephants spoke the same language with humans. Therefore when Dumo sat for a long time under the tree, elephants sent a young elephant to ask Dumo what he wanted. "Man, what do you want here?" the little elephant asked him.

Dumo said, "I want my spear which I speared with one of your brothers." The little elephant reported to the other elephants that, "The man wants his spear with which he speared one of our brothers."

One elephant took one spear from among other spears they had, and gave it to little elephant who took it to Dumo. Dumo was very happy to see his brother's real spear. He trudged back home. He called his brother and gave his spear back to him. "It is okay, my brother. I have brought back your spear which elephant had carried away in its body. Here, take your spear."

Nyikango received his spear and immediately told his brother, "It is okay, my brother. To avoid this kind of sad occurrence between you and I, I want you to know that from today on, I will leave you here on this land of Kaaro".

That evening Nyikango gathered his people together (together with the people of his brothers, Anywak and Gilo), and told them what happened between him and his brother, Dumo. After telling this story, he told his sad audience, "From today onwards, I am going to leave for Dumo and his people this home of Kaaro. Whoever wants to go with me should pack their food."

Anywak's and Gilo's people accepted to go with Nyikango, and he also told his people, "Tomorrow, in the morning, we will move to the north until we find a place to settle in."

Early in the morning, Nyikango and his people began to trek to the north. Nyikango looked back when he heard his brother's call. Dumo hurled a stick (a sharp-headed one, the type that, up to now the people of Shilluk sow with their seeds) after Nyikango, as he cursed his brother's people, "I throw this stick to show you that since you have left us in Kaaro (where there is no death) you and your people should find death in the new place of your settlement. This stick is for digging Nyikango's grave."

Nyikango moved back, picked the stick and told Dumo, "It is alright my brother. I will go, but none of us will die. Some may die, but those left behind should multiply and fill the land on which I will settle."

Turtled by the exchange of words, one man ran after Nyikango and told him, "Nyikanyo, I beg you to change your mind and do not go."

When Dumo saw the man talking to Nyikang he told him, "You choose either to go with Nyikang or remain with me," Nyikango told the man to go back to Dumo.

Nyikango left Kaaro around 1550 A.D. He moved with his two sons, Bur and Shall together with his wife, Ungwedo and three of his uncles, Moiny, Nywado and Juok and three of his workers: Ubogo, Ujul and Mielo. Some elders say that Nyikango did not go with the people named above only. Many people followed him.

Nyikango moved to Pothethura near Wau in Bahr El Ghazal State. At this time it was Chief Dimo who ruled Bahr El Ghazel. Lwo elders maintain that Chief Dimo was a miracle man. It was a short while that Nyikango had lived here when he married Chief Dimo's daughter whose name we do not know. This woman gave birth to a baby boy and named him Dak. Elders say Dak was a very notorious boy. He often fought other children. Although he was labeled bad, he had great respect for his grandfather, Dimo.

One day Chief Dimo despised Nyikango and said, "You are a dull man. Your son, Dak is brighter than you." The following morning Chief Dimo miraculously hid fire from the whole place so that nobody could cook. It was said that God gave Dimo's power of miracle to Dak. When Dak saw his grandfather's atrocity, he also made all the subjects of his grandfather blind. Chief Dimo knew very well that it was Dak who blinded his people.

The only people who were not blinded were Chief Dimo and his wives and Nyikango's people. The people who became blind cried to the chief, and he asked his wife, "Why has Dak made my subjects blind?" This issue brought conflict between Nyikango and his son, Dak.

Chief Dimo called his grandson and asked him, "I know that you are the one who blinded my people. If that is the case, I bring back fire for people for cooking." Dak saw what his grandfather did then he also cured the people he had blinded.

Dimo could not learn from this incident. Three days after, Dimo stopped rain from falling in the gardens of Dak and Nyikango. Dak paid Dimo back in his own coin by blinding all his cattle.

The animals could not see pasture, and they became emaciated. Secondly, the cows could not produce milk.

Dimo asked his wife, "Why have Dak and Nyikango blinded my animals?" His wives also asked him, "Why did you stop rain from falling in the gardens of Dak and Nyikango?" In the subsequent evening, it rained in the gardens of Dak and Nyikango.

When Dak saw this, he cured all the animals he had blinded. It became a serious competition between Chief Dimo and his grandson, Dak. As a result, life became hard for Dimo. He called his palace elders to come and settle the matter. All the elders came and assembled under a big tamarind tree in the chief's palace. The chief thanked the elders for turning up for the meeting and told them, "Nyikango is a dull man, but Dak is very bright. I therefore want to kill Dak. I have called you here so that you can tell me how I can kill him." All the elders agreed that Dimo should kill Dak in the evening after blowing Dak's tortoise cell bugle. The elders did not want the chief to soil his hands with blood, so they offered to take Dak's life by themselves.

When the elders were discussing how to kill Dak, there was a man who pretended that he was a Jur man though the elders knew as a very close friend to Dak. Convinced that the man was a Jur, the elders entrusted him to kill Dak from his home. The man did not refuse the task given to him, but before it was time to accomplish the task, he went to Dak's place and disclosed everything the elders said about him and the plot to kill him. That evening Dak made statue that looked like him, and he dressed the statue in the dress he often wore, placed it in his house and he sat a distance away from the house and blew his tortoise cell bugle. As he blew the bugle, he watched the path to his house.

When they heard the bugle, the elders thought he was now going in the house. They sent four men to go and kill Dak from his house. They wasted no time to reach Dak's house. When they were close to the house, they saw someone siting in the house and they thought that that must be Dak. All of them hurled their spears on the statue and it fell down at the strokes of the spears. The elders pleased themselves that they had killed Dak. They went back to inform the chief and other people that Dak was already dead.

The chief's subjects called a dance to celebrate the death of Dak. Dimo was very happy for the death of his enemy. He told the people who were dancing, "We are moaning Dak."

Oral source has it that everybody in the arena was happy that Dak was dead. So, they all sang in one voice:

My grandchild my daughter's child
Dak Nyikango's son has died.

At the peak hour of the dance, Dak appeared in the arena. On seeing Dak, the dancers went cold. Their legs could barely hold their weight. These people thought that it was God who appeared to them, not Dak. Secondly, they thought that if this was Dak, where they would run to.

Ubogo told Nyikango that "Pothethuro" (Tura) was not a good place to live in. What Dimo did to Dak angered him very much. Ubogo asked Nyikango to move ahead as he talked to him. He told Nyikango, "Your two sons, Bur and Shall hold the blessing for this matter. If it turns to war, it is you and Dak who will face it rough, and Dak may die."

Nyikango heed to Ubogo's advice. The following morning, he took his children, wives and animals and left Tura. They walked for thirty days before reaching River Kiir (Blue Nile). They had many boats, but were unable to cross the river because of the elephant grass which had thickly grown in the river.

Ubogo asked Nyikango to kill one person as a sacrifice so that the river would open for them to cross. Nyikango asked Dak if they could sacrifice one of his workers. This proposal did not please Dak. He asked his father, "Are my workers chicken to be slaughtered on the way?"

Ubogo then told Nyikango that "Not to cause conflict between you, I offer myself to be killed for the sacrifice to the river. When you kill me you should take care of my children."

Figure 5: Ubogo's throat cut

Nyikango did not object to Ubogo's offer. He sent people to cut Ubogo's throat so that his blood would flow into the river. Once that was done, the thick elephant grass cleared and the river open for the people to cross safely.

They crossed River Kiir and moved to Kofal, the present Kodok. They settled in Kofal for a short time. Nyikango eventually noticed that Bur and Dak could not get on well together because both of them were very authoritative.

To separate his two sons, Nyikango gave Dak's mother to Bur as a wife. After this Bur left Kofal to look for a place to settle. When Dak heard that Bur was looking for a new place for a home and that his mother was given to Bur for a wife, he was hurt so much that he could not contain his temper. He began to follow Bur with the intention of killing him. Elders say that it seems Dak knew that his mother and her new husband were leaving Kofal. On the way, Dak's mother carried Bur at her side like a child. However, it is questionable how a grown up man like Bur could be carried at the side of a woman. Dak feared spearing Bur from his mother's side for fear that he would injure his mother. Dak decided not to kill Bur and returned to Nyikango and asked him, "Why did you give out my mother?" In an attempt to quell down Dak's anger, Nyikango offered some of his wives to Dak (Dak's step mothers), but Dak turned down the offer. Secondly, Nyikango offered Dak heads of cattle, which he also rejected.

After trying all these options, Nyikango asked Dak, "What do you want?" Dak told his father, "I want one of your daughters."

Nyikango handed over one of his daughters whom he begot with another woman to Dak. Dak became a son-in-law to his own father. But Acholi custom did not allow siblings to marry among themselves. Nyikango accepted to give his daughter to Dak because he thought Dak would fear to sleep with his sister. If he slept with his sister, they would not even be able to have children since they had the same blood (children of the same man). Nyikango's thinking was wrong. A few months after, the girl conceived and they had a son. Nyikango was very surprised to see the girl pregnant.

One day Nyikango told Dak, "Child, I thought you would fear to sleep with your sister whom I gave to you." "Do you think that your daughter is a woman or no?" Dak asked his father. This marriage caused a lot of complaints from the Lwo clan elders, and they later agreed that the children of chiefs should marry children of other chiefs.

However, Nyikango and his people continued their trek along River Kiir. They made twelve makeshift settlements in different places: Papwoja near Malakal, Nyalwal, Wau, Ocor, Otiko, Akurwa —Nyikango's most important home, Moro, Oriang, Ogik, Ala-Adwai. Chual and Kawii near El Duem

But some elders say that Nyikango's twelve homes were Pothe Thuro (Wau), Tonga (Acieta gwok), Nyilwal (Nyikango camped at Dedigo and Dak camped at Falol "Fanyidwai Pac"), Demoth, Maban (where Nyikango was flown by wind to heaven), Ocoro, Otiko, Okurwa, Moro, Ogik, Chual, and Kawii -here he put a long bar/stick which is still there up to today.

From Kawii Reth Nyikango moved to Malakal where he met the owners of the place, and fought and defeated them. As elders say Nyikango had few people, so when he took over Malakal he realised that land was too large for them. For this reason, he looked for people from other clans to live with him.

Getting people for Reth to add to his people was not a simple thing to do because he had fought people who lived in and around Malakal. We cannot tell which people exactly he asked to live with him. Nyikango brought very many people, women, men and children, under his rule. Unfortunately, the people Reth Nyikango brought under his governance used to sleep like wild animals. He divided these people into many groups to add to the clans of Shilluk, and he appointed one man whom he came with from Karoo to be their leader. The elders of Shilluk said that the people whom Reth captured in war, and brought home to live with him, were more than the people with whom he came with from Karoo.

The captives, together with the people Nyikango came with, made up seventy clans of Shilluk who are in Malakal today. Segregation found its way among Reth's people. They said the people who came with Reth right from Karoo were the true people of Shilluk. Those who brought there through war were called foreign clans.

Rev. D.S. Oyler explained very well how Nyikango brought his people when he says,"One day Nyikango sat under a big tree at the bank of the river when he a saw a very big fish swimming in the river. He thought that that was not a fish. It must have been a human being who had just disguised himself. He drew nearer to the fish and tried to catch it, but he discovered that he could not.

After failing to catch the fish, Nyikango asked Dak to catch it. Dak entered the water and caught the fish. As Dak was coming ashore, the fish first turned into a snake and later into a human being. Nyikango put this man who came from fish under his leadership.

One evening Reth Nyikango was moving around an anthill near his compound. As he was passing by the anthill, a termites bit his toe. He bent down to see the termite but he did not see it. He called Dak and told him, "My child, termite bit my toe. Help me look for it. If you find it, give it to me."

That evening Dak went and sat at the foot of the anthill. He waited for termites to come out. Just a short while after, many termites got out to converse. Dak caught many termites and put them in a gourd and took them home. When he poured them out of the gourd, they all turned into human beings.

Another day Nyikango went hunting far away from home. In the wilderness, he met some strangers who were hunting with dogs. Nyikango walked closer to them, but they all entered the ground together with their dogs. A few minutes after they reappeared a distance ahead of Nyikango, he found it difficult to reach them.

Nyikango asked Dak to help him bring these people to him. The next morning, Dak took three dogs with him and began to track those people. When Dak drew close to the people, their dogs came to fight Dak's dogs. They killed all the three dogs Dak went with.

Dak went back home in low spirit, but did not give up. He went back to the people with a large land-boat. When they saw him, the people together with their dogs disappeared in the ground. He ran very fast to the point where they entered the ground. He sat down at the spot and waited. It did not take long, these people came out. Dak captured all of them and put them in his boat. Dak discovered that the dogs these people moved with were their wives. It is said that the women often turned into dogs.

The elders of Shilluk said that one day Nyikango went to fish in the river. He threw hid hook into the water and caught a man instead of a fish. "Why do you catch a man but not a fish?" the man asked him.

Nyikango answered, "If I do not catch human being, with what will I fill this land?" The man changed in different ways. First he turned into a snake. He later turned into a crocodile, lion, leopard, hyena then later a human being. This did not scare Nyikango.

Other people say that Nyikango went to the river twice. On the first day he killed a rhinoceros. On the second day, he also killed a rhinoceros. When they were celebrating the killing of the two rhinoceros people danced and sang to Nyikango, "If anyone begins to fight you, we are ready to lose our life for you."

Nikango answered, "That is not true. If a battle begins, you will all run away."

These are the different ways through which Reth Nykango increased the population of his people at Malakal. There are many other ways of explaining how Nyikango added more people to the people he came with from Karoo.

After these incidents, Nyikango told his people that "I will give my royal spear to Dak." After saying this, the elders of Shilluk say, Nyikango mysteriously disappeared, and up to now nobody knows where he went.

The people of Shilluk believe that Nyikango did not die. Some people say that Reth Nyikango went back to his father's land. Others say that he went to heaven, while others say he disappeared in the air. Others believe that he went under water and still lives there up to now.

After the death or disappearance of Nyikango, Dak, his son inherited his throne. Dak died around 1845 and Reth Kwadhker inherited the throne. Reth Kwadhker did not take long on the throne. When Arabs slave traders came to Shilluk to look for slaves around 1850, Reth Kwadhker was still on the throne.

The leader of Arab slave traders was El Fiki Mohamed Kheir. Around 1867 the government of Sudan appointed Mr. Ali Bey Kurdi the first *mudir* of Fashoda District. A few years after, Mr. Ali Bey Kurdi removed Reth Kwadhker from the throne and replaced him with Ajang Nyidhok.

The administration of Mr. Ali Bey was good, but the change he made did not please people. This brought division among the people of Fashoda. People of Northern Fashoda were behind the Commissioner of Sudan that Ajang should become *mudir* of Fashoda, but the people in the south wanted Reth Kwadhker to continue holding the throne.

War subsequently broke out between the two conflicting groups. After a few years of war, Kwadhker invited Mr. Ali Bey Kurdi to meet him at Lul. Mr. Ali did not turn down the invitation because he did not know why Kwadhker asked him over to the place. When Mr. Ali Bey Kurdi arrived at Lul, Reth Kwadhker arrested and imprisoned him at Kodok.

Mr. Ali Bey fell sick and died in prison around 1879. Around 1879 British appointed Rashid Bey to be the *mudir* of Fashoda. Reth Ajang tried to collect guns from the hands of the people to hand over to the government. Reth Ajang brought many guns to thegovernment. Despite this effort, government did not appreciate who later arrested and killed him at Kodok.

According to elders, when Nyikango and his brother, Dumo, vacated Karoo, some of their brothers who remained there died of thirst. Those who survived sold their sister, Acol to Olum Banya for water. Eventually, the people who remained in Karoo also vacated the place. Acol who then became the mother of Acholi people had a number of children with her husband, Olum Banya. This is the etymology of the name *Acholi*. We can now answer the question, *"What is the meaning of word 'Acholi'?* Acholi means CHILDREN OF ACOL.

Many people including Acholi elders have attempted to explain the meaning of "Acholi". They have given three different definitions. Some of them define Acholi as black people. But there are many ethnic groups of black people in Africa. Do we also call them Acholi? The second definition has it that the word *Acholi* was derived from COLO, given by Lwo to Shilluk. To date, the people of Malakal call themselves "Colo". Some historians who tried to write the history of Acholi was said the word Acholi was derived from Colo. The Arab traders were the ones who talked of *Colo*.

The Egyptian Arab traders left their place in 1860. They migrated to Sudan and later moved to Malakal (Upper Nile Region) in South Sudan. When Arab traders arrived at Malakal, they asked the people they found there who they were. These people said, "We are Colo people." It was heard for Arabs to articulate the word "Colo", so they pronounced it as *"Shulli"*.

The Arab moved farther south and reached Acholiland. They found that the people spoke a language similar to Colo. The Arab traders subsequently called the people in Acholiland *"Shulli"*. Because the sound "sh" did not exist in Acholi, they articulated the word as *"Culli"*.

Mr. M.E.C.Pumphrey maintains in his book that, "The people of Shilluk called Acholi, "Colo". The name *"Culli"* was used for a long time, and eventually Acholi speakers changed it to "Acolli". Later on the whites who were writing about Acholi added letter *h* (which did not exist in Acoli) and the word "Acoli" became "Acholi". Some people assert that the name came from the name of a woman called Acol, who was the mother of Acholi people.

According to Akena p'Ojok Kodok Gilo, the brother of Reth Nyikango parted from his brother and moved to the south untill he reached River *Sobat River, and the* Anywak people also in three different places near Ethiopia Gambella. The places are Baro, Pibor and Akobo. Anywak is a very small tribe among the Lwo. Today, it is said that they are 100,000 people only. However, we cannot tell the exact number of Anywak people because the Sudan census was not accurately done. But we know that the Anywak people live at Akobo, Pibor and Pochala in

Jonglei Region. Some of them are found at Gambella in western Ethiopia. Nasir is Anywak district in South Sudan. The people of Anywak are both cattle keepers and cultivators. They cultivate sorghum, sesame, rice, peas and tobacco. The population of Anywak declined drastically due to the frequent war of cattle rustling between them and Nuer people. Nuer stole their cattle many times.

The worst war fought between Anywak and Nuer was in 1880 in which Nuer killed Anywak in a large number and burnt their homes in Ukadi. The Nywak survivors of this war fled and camped in Ubaa while others settled at the foot of a sacred rock-pools called Abula (Agula), southeast of Anywak.

The Anywak people began to buy guns and slaves from Ethiopia with ivory. This indicates that Anywak were the first Lwo to learn to fight with gun. Eventually, Anywak acquired more sophisticated weapons than Nuer who used spear and shield.

Weapons gave Anywak great power. They had so many friends and spies that they were able to protect themselves from massive killing as it happened in the past. They all united under one leadership called *Ocwak (weaver bird)* which means bringing hands together at the time of problem. (It is the royal emblems of the Anywak people)Anywak became great soldiers and trades-men in Jongolei Region and Ethiopia Gambella. They sold guns, ivory, bangles (copper bracelets), beads, slaves and ostrich feather. They traded with Nuer of Ethiopia Gambella, Nuer of Sudan and people of Mbale in Uganda. Oral sources state that it was through this trade that the Acholi of Uganda acquired guns. Clan elders maintain that in 1911 the subjects of Chief Ogwok of Padibe had 2,000 guns. In 1902 British government of Sudan signed *Anglo-Ethiopia* Abyssinia *Treaty* and divided Anywak into two – some in Sudan and others in Ethiopia.

In 1911 Anywak fought Lau and Jikany of Nuer. They defeated and scattered these people away from their territories. This scared the British, the adminis-trators of Sudan. They tried to control Ethiopia arms trafficking. For this reason, British sent DC Postlethwaite (Bwana Gweno) to Kitgum to get 120 Nuba soldiers to be taken to fight the people dealing in guns at the foot of Lakwar Hill and Orom Hill. At this time, Anywak was ruled by Chief Akwei-wa-Acam.

Chief Akwei-wa-Acam died in 1920 and his son, Sham Akwei succeeded him. In 1921 British fought Anywak with the intention of making them develop fear for the British government. British went up to a place called Adonga where they discovered Anywak's very strong belief in circumcision. British were astonished at the culture of circumcision of Anywak. British arrested Chief Sham Akwei from Ethiopia and took him to Sudan because they did not want the headquarters of Anywak to be in Ethiopia.

British disturbed Chief Sham Akwei a lot and they divided his people (divide and rule). This resulted in a lot of confusion on how to rotate Ocwak leadership among the Anywak people. Although the British had controlled Anywak, in 1931 Anywak fought Nuer of Gaajak. They also fought Burun and Koma. Some sources state that in 1932 groups of Anywak of Sudan and Ethiopia, in unison, attacked Murrle. Italians took over Ethiopia in May 1936. In December 1936 Italians extended their territory to Gambella. Elders contend that Anywak lived in both Sudan and Ethiopia up to 1956. When Sudan got political independence, British removed Gambella from Sudan and gave it to Ethiopia.

THE FIRST HOME OF ACHOLI

Some people like Onyango-ku-Odongo do not agree that Acholi are the progeny of Dumo. Although Onyango claims that Acholi in Uganda did not descent from the house of Dumo, he has not explained where the Acholi of Sudan came from. However, as we know the Acholi of Sudan and the Acholi of Uganda descended from the same house. Not to argue too much, I leave it to the readers. Onyango-ku-Odongo also maintains that all the Lwo groups speak the same language though they call certain things differently. The custom and tradition of the Lwo are different from those of other people such as Murule, Karamojong, Dinka, Abuluyia, Nuer, Lugbara, Lotuko and Bantu.

Although Acholi people say that they are one people, they live in different places (i.e. different regions and countries). As we saw before, Lwo of Uganda are at the shore of Lake Victoria and Acholi are in the northern part of the country and South Sudan. The Alur occupy north-western part of Uganda, near Lake Albert. Jur Chol, Balanda, Anywak, Shilluk and Lokoro are in South Sudan. Another Anywak group is in Ethiopia and Lwo of Tanzania are at Musoma. The Lwo people in different places are still aware that they are the offspring of Dumo. To say that some groups of Lwo do not belong to the house of Dumo is not correct.

In his *"The Central Lwo During The Aconya"* Onyango-ku-Odongo (1976) mainly relied on his grandmother, Alunga Lujim who told him that the name *Lwo* was derived from the name of a great grandfather called Lwo. In the past, Lwo people did not call themselves "Lwo," but "Didinga" or people of Didinga. This makes us as if Lwo are related to Didinga because once called themselves Didinga. To date, Lwo people do not know whether they are related to Didinga or not.

The first chief of Didinga was Chief Kuku Lubanga. The chief was called Lubanga because he did so many miracles that he was likened to God. Acholi elders say that Chief Kuku Lubanga could make it rain even during dry season. Secondly, he could dig a hole on flat rock using a stem of sorghum. Thirdly, he was able to cleave a hair into two.

Kuku Lubanga had three sons: Olila, Boni and Koma. Among the three sons, Koma was the youngest. Boni and Olila were arrogant and liked fighting, and they had no fear for death. The chief thought that Koma was a coward – fearful like a woman. As a result, his father abused him, "Look at him, a coward. You are a coward like a woman." Chief Lubanga's spitefulness worried Koma. However, Koma knew that he was not a coward. He had manliness lurking behind his apparent cowardice. He wanted to show his father that he was not a coward, neither was he a woman.

One day Didinga went to raid cattle from Lango. Chief Lukok of Lango and his people fought Didinga. Didinga tried with all their might to break into the kraals of Lango, Chief Lukok did not give them time. As the fight was on, Lukok was in the main home whetting his spear. Girls and women were sounding yodel over him. No Didinga worrier could go close to Lukok at that time. The sun was already setting when the Didinga warriors decided to go back because raiding cattle from Lango became difficult for them.

Surprisingly, Koma attacked Chief Lukok like a lion. His spear stroke the chief below the stomach and it sent him sprawling on the ground. When a Lango girl quickly ran to help save the life of the chief, life had already left him.

Koma who was standing by the dead body, held the girl by her wrist and threw her hard on the ground, and he continued piercing the chief with his spear. Lango warriors went cold when they saw what Koma was doing to their chief. Lango opened their rare gate which Didinga did not know and they ran away and left their homes to Didinga. Left alone in the home of Lango, Didinga broke into their kraal, but did not find any animal. They immediately set out for home. Koma captured a daughter of Chief Lukok and took her home to Chief Kuku Lubanga.

As soon as they reached home, Didinga warrior reported to their chief that Koma killed Chief Lukok. Chief Lubanga was ashamed by the great militant ability his son had exhibited. Although it was the custom of the Lwo that when a man captured a girl or a woman in the battle filed the woman should be given to the chief, when Koma presented the girl he captured to Chief Lubanga, the chief told him, "My son, take this girl for a wife. You are a man. I thought you were a woman."

Many people showed their gratitude to Koma, but he told them, "Don't respect me because I am a coward. I fought Chief Lukok because of the insults which were heaped on me" (Onyango-ku-Odongo, 1976, p.39).

Three months later, Koma's wife conceived. She gave birth to a boy whom they named Lwo. Koma named the child Lwo in memory of his father's insult on him that he was a coward "Lwo" in Acholi means cowardice. The second reason why Koma named his son Lwo was because he wanted to show his father and his subjects that he was actually not a coward.

When Chief Kuku Lubanga died, Koma became the chief. When he died, his son Lwo was enthroned. It is said that Chief Lwo was a very intelligent man and knew how to manage his subjects. To show their respect for the new chief, Didinga people began to call themselves Lwo.

Chief Lwo had two wives. The senior wife was called Alipere. This woman had only one son whom they named Olum. The rest of her children were girls. Lwo's junior wife was called Amolo. She had two sons. The first born was called Okang and the second born was Dermor. The two boys were very peaceful. Elders say that there was no single day that they were found quarreling.

A serious famine broke out in Chief Lwo's territory, near a water body. Foodstuff became very scarce. Onyango-ku-Odongo asserts that, "It is not known where this water body is" (read Onyango-kuOdongo, 1976, p.40). But we think that the water body is "Red Sea" which tells us that the home near a water body was "Kassala" which is in Sudan.

Since there was serious lack of foodstuff, Chief Lwo was felt hopeless. He also thought he was going to die. Lwo called his three sons in a family conference to discuss their family affairs. He told them, the sea is annoyed because someone has soiled this place by shedding blood. You take away the people of

Didinga from here to a new place." As soon as he finished talking to his sons, he lay his head down and his life left him immediately.

After the death of the chief, his sons decided to divide the people of Didinga into two groups. As a first born son, Olum was enthroned to replace his father, and he consulted a diviner priest to find out which place was safe for him to take his people. The diviner priest told Chief Olum to take his people to south of Red Sea. Olum told his wife what the diviner priest told him to do, but she outrightly rejected the priest's divination. She went to another diviner priest who told her, "If Olum wants to go to the south, do not allow him to go with your sons because there is death on the south of the sea. You and your sons should go to the north if your husband insists on going to the south. He will just take his body to the mouth of death." This brought a lot of rope-pooling arguments between the two diviners.

After a hot debate between the two priests, Okang and Dermor led a group of Didinga to the north as the diviner priest of their mother advised. They walked for about a month before they finally reached a place called "Wipaco". *Wipaco* in Acholi means "the children who grew up after the death of their father." Some people interpret *Wipaco* as people who survived the spear/ war. The people who followed Olum were more than the followers of Okang and his brother. Before Olum left the sea, he married another woman called Lagilo. Olum and his people moved to the south until they reached Ogili Hill in Agoro, also referred to as Tekidi, which means "at the foot of a hill." When they reached this place, they ran short of food. They began to eat fruits. It did not take long before it began to rain.

Having seen that the land at the foot of Ogili Hill was very fertile, Olum and his people decided to settle here. His subjects were very happy with the chief's decision for they had also realised that the land was very fertile. They wished Okang's people death.

A few months after, Olum's people discovered that there were some people called Muru living near them. Olum was afraid because he thought the Muru people would kill his subjects. One day Chief Olum told his wife, Lagilo, that he wanted to meet the chief of Muru to discuss with them how to live with them peacefully, and he met the elders of Muru. He told them everything in his heart. When the elders of Muru heard him talk of peace, they accepted everything he said.

After the meeting, the elders of Muru assigned some of their young men to escort Chief Olum to his home. On his return, Chief Olum told his elders all the matters they discussed with the elders of Muru. He told them that, "The elders of Muru agreed with him that they should live in peace with the people of Didinga."

When they were still at the foot of the hill, Lagilo had four sons and one daughter. The first born was named Ocola. The boy was given this name because he was born before his father had untied the mourning string, called *cola* in Acholi, from his head. Chief Olum was still mourning his father who died at the sea.

In Acholi culture, a child who is born before *cola* is untied from his parents is usually named *Ocola* if it is a boy and *Achola* if it is a girl. The second child was named Luru because his mother had serious diarrhea when he was still in the womb. Olum used to cover her watery excrement with dry fine soil called *luru* in Acholi. The child was named Luru because his mother used to instruct his father, "My husband, gather for me *luru* whenever she wanted to go for a call. Lagilo's third child was a girl. She was named Kipwola, which means misfortune. The fourth child was Lwo to remember the grandfather of Didinga who was also called Lwo.

Lwo was born at the time when Olum wanted to meet his father's people who were at Wipaco Dwong. He wanted to go there and ask over his father's people to his new home at the foot of Ogili Hill, where crop yield was very good. Olum was not certain if he could go to Wipaco and return alive to his home, Tekidi. He thought the people at Wipaco might kill him. This is the reason why he named his son after his grandfather, Lwo. This idea reached the Didinga in Wipaco and both the people at Tekidi and Wipaco began to call themselves Lwo, or the people of Lwo.

One time, after harvest, Olum set on a journey to visit the people of Wipaco. He started the journey in the morning and walked seven days and seven nights to reach his destination. Okang and Dermor very warmly received him. Okang and his brother had thought that their father was already dead because before their separation from the sea, Amolo's diviner priest said that "If Olum insisted on going to the south he would die because death was in the south."

One messenger told the elders Olum had come to Wipaco. As soon as they received this message, the elders said Olum should not step on Okang's compound unless an appropriate customary ritual was performed. The messenger went back and gave Olum a stool to sit on under a tamarind tree which was near home. Elders immediately gathered before the main shrine in front of Okang's house. One elder took an egg on the way for Olum to step on before entering the compound. Olum stepped on the egg, entered the compound and stood before the shrine where elders continued to perform other rituals on him.

After the rituals on Olum and Okang were performed, the people of Wipaco asked Olum how his people moved to Tekidi when they separated at the sea. He told them how they traveled and how he met the people of Muru to talk about peace. Thereafter, Okang stood up and told his father how he traveled with his people too, and how they finally settled at Wipaco Dwong.

The following morning, the elders continued with the preparation to reunite the two people. In the same morning, Olum asked if they could migrate to Tekidi. He told them that the land at Tekidi was better than that at Wipaco because it was fertile. The people of Wipaco did not accept to migrate and told Olum that, "We will remain here, and we ask you people to migrate to us if they can."

They debated on this issue for three days. When he saw how hard it was for the people to accept his invitation, Olum accepted before the elders that it was his people who would move to Wipaco. The elders did not know that Olum was deceiving them. When he returned to Tekidi, Olum did not tell his people anything about migration to Wipaco. A few months after, Lagilo conceived and had a son whom they named Coope. The name means "There are no tough men now," or "There are no heroes now." This name is still found among Acholi people up to now.

Much as Olum lived at Tekidi together with Muru, they called themselves Lwo. The people loved and trusted him very much.

One dry season, some Lwo from Wipaco went to Tekidi. The first person to meet these people was Lagilo who was gathering firewood in the bush near home. The three people from Wipaco were very tired and thirsty. Lagilo took them home and gave them coagulated milk. They felt rejuvenated after taking the milk. They rested and told Olum about the famine which had broken out at Wipaco. They said what brought them to Tekidi was famine.

Olum listened to this people and immediately thought of going back to Wipaco to visit the people there because he had not dropped his plea to Okang and his people to migrate to Tekidi. Luru asked his father if he could go together with him to Wipaco. Olum did not object to his son's request. Six Muru boys also asked Chief Olum to allow them move together with him. This too, he did not turn down.

Olum packed some food and they set off for the journey he following morning. They spent seven days and nights on the journey. It was already a rainy season, but food staff was still very much lacking. People were informed of Olum's visit and they came to meet him. The people of Wipaco saw that Olum and his people were plump, unlike them who were lean.

After his rest, Olum met the clan elders of Wipaco to discuss their family matters. He insisted on the people of Wipaco joining his people at Tekidi where there was abundant food. This time he was able to convince many people of Wipaco, and they accepted to migrate to Tekidi. Three days after, Olum set out for Tekidi together with the people of Wipaco who made up their mind to go with him to the south. They took seven days to reach Tekidi. The Lwo and Muru people happily received the visitors, and they raised food stuff, for the visitors, from every household.

The people from Wipaco built next to Chief Olum. As a result, Olum had more people than the Muru people. Olum's children realised that, owing to their growing population, there was shortage of land. Olum's sons therefore acquired settlements outside Tekidi.

The bead spear conflict was the cause of the separation. Olum was already aged by the time the conflict erupted among his children. I asked elders where Tekidi was, but I discovered that nobody knew where it was. For that matter, I agree with Onyango-ku-Odongo that no one knew the location of Tekidi, but he assumed that the place must have been the place we now call Agoro in Uganda (Onyango-ku-Odongo, 1976, p. 48).

Although the population of Olum's people was higher that of Muru people, their population also increased. Despite the increase in their population, the Muru people at Tekidi learned Acholi language and later were assimilated by the Acholi people.

There were a number of visits between the people of Wipaco and Tekidi. They were all aware that both groups were actually descendants of one person. This idea kept the relationship between the people of Wipaco and Tekidi very strong. Elders put tough rule that the children at Tekidi and Wipaco should not marry among themselves.

Chapter Two

THE ORIGIN OF SUDAN

God created the Africa, but British created Sudan. Sudan was baptised about one hundred years ago (i.e.1930). Before 1930, the place which today we called Sudan had no name. Before the naming of Sudan, people would just move about without saying, "This is Uganda, and that is Sudan." The people of today's Uganda came to trade in Rajaf (Juba) and Sudanese also went to trade in Uganda. In 1930, the places which are now called Equatoria, Bar-El-Ghazal and Upper Nile were not there. People identified themselves with the languages they spoke.

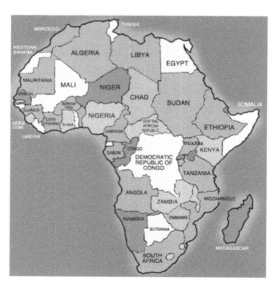

Figure 6: God created Africa, but British created Sudan (Figure No 6)

In 1898 when British and Egyptian took over the administration of Mahdi (at Omdurman), they brought a new governance system which they called "CONDOMINIUM GOVERNMENT" under the control of British. When they had just exerted their control in the place, British had problem in drawing boundaries because they did not know the place well.

In 1899 British did not treat the people of Equatoria, Bahr El Gahzal and Upper Nile as one people, but as separate regions. They also stopped the Arabs in northern Sudan from teaching Islam in southern Sudan. This policy was called "Closed door". They closed the Arab traders out.

Figure 7: Sudan as a country

Fortunately, countries such as Kenya, Uganda and Tanganyika were under British rule. Ethiopia, the neighbour of Sudan was under Italian rule, and Congo was under Belgium/France. The leaders of the places which today we call Uganda and Kenya met several times to discuss the borders of Kenya, Uganda and Sudan, and in 1930 they agreed on the borders of Sudan, Kenya and Uganda. The British immediately came up with "Southern Policy" which stated that Southern people of Equatoria, Bahr El Ghazal and Upper Nile should get ready to be part of East African countries which were under the British rule.

The British rule divided Sudan into two: Northern Sudan and Southern Sudan. Eighty percent (80%) of northern Sudanese were Muslims. The remaining 20% were Christians. Speaking Arabic was compulsory to all Muslims because all their prayers were in Arabic, and Allah did not listen to any other language apart from Arabic. Whoever did not know it must learn.

However, all the people of Southern Sudan were Africans, and 90% of them were Christians. All Christian prayed in Latin, the language which all Christians did not even understand. Eventually, when the Christian leaders learned the local languages, they began to pray in their respective indigenous languages. The oral sources maintain that the use of the local languages started around 1967. From 1905 when Christianity reached Acholi of Sudan up to 1966, all Christians prayed in Latin which was only understood by the Reverend Fathers who lead the prayers. All Christian converts did not understand even a single Latin word.

On their entrance in Sudan, to make their administration easy, the whites divided Sudan into nine different regions. In the norther part of the country, they created Khartoum, Kassala, Darfur, Kordofan, Gezira and Northern Province. In the southern part there were Equatorial, Bar El-Ghazal and Upper Nile.

These nine regions were later divided into smaller parts called districts. They assigned a D.C. for each district to make sure that everybody abides by their rules. Since Sudanese had not yet received formal education, they assigned only white people as D.Cs. Equatoria region was divided into six districts: Juba, Torit, Kapoeta, Yei, Yambio and Maridi. In this book we will not talk about other districts apart from Torit since our interest is in Acholi, the occupants of this district.

TORIT DISTRICT

Before British created a boundary between Sudan and Uganda, the district of the Acholi of Sudan was Dufele (i. e. West Nile in Uganda). Dufele District was one of the thirty districts under the rule of the D.C. of Gulu. The Ugandan who were in Dufele district were not under the rule of Executive Officer who ruled Dufele District because Deufele was the district of Acholi of Sudan. This district included the people of Latuko, Lolubo, Lokoya, Lokoro, Lopit, Lango, Madi, and Dongo-tono.

Before long, the D.C. of Gulu realised that Dufele District was far away from the people who should work for them. As a result, between 1906 — 1907, they transferred this district headquarters from Dufele to Nimule. This was the first action that drew a boundary between Sudan and Uganda. Although they transferred the district headquarters to Nimule, they forgot to appoint a Paramount Chief much as people were under chiefdoms. The white man put all the chiefs under their rule though each chief led his people.

In deed at the time the district headquarters was shifted to Nimule, the Acholi chiefs worked without a Paramount Chief. In 1910 the district headquarters was taken from Nimule to Opari. It was at that time that the white man appointed Chief Oceng Anyoda of Pajok – Bura as the first Paramount Chief of Acholi. As we have already read, there were many clans in Equatoria region, which were under one D.C. Hence, Chief Oceng Anyoda became a County Chief and headed the chiefs of Madi, Acholi, Latuko, Lolubo, Lokoya, Lokoro, Lopit, Längo and Dongo-tono.

People respected Chief Anyoda, but some Pajok people did not like him. In 1912, Pajok people reported to the white administrators that it was Chief Anyoda who ordered people to set fire in the hunting ground, and many wild animals were burnt in the fire. The white man was not happy about the death of the animals. They were already looking for the person who ordered for the burning of the bush. When the white man was told that Chief Anyoda ordered for the burning of the bush, he wasted no time to send his security men to arrest the chief. The security men brought the chief before court, which found him guilty and sentenced him for about ten years in prison. The people of Opari district were without a Paramount Chief for two years as Chief Anyoda served his sentence.

In 1914, Chief Aburi Kassiba was appointed a Paramount Chief of Acholi. At this time when Chief Milla was heading Madi and Lotuko had his headquarters at Terangore. Chief Aburi was a very strong Paramount Chief. He presided over a number of meetings between the Acholi of Sudan and the Acholi of Uganda. For example, the meetings which were held in Kitgum and Padibe at the time of Chief Lacito Obol and Chief Andrea Olal were under his steward-ship. He was respected for the good pieces of advice he gave the two chiefs. In 1914, Anglo-Egyptian Sudan and Protectorate of Uganda converged in Gulu to discuss the border between Sudan and Uganda. In this meeting Mr. Tufell wanted all Acholi people to be under one leadership, which would mean that all Acholi would be in Uganda, and other clans such as Lotuko, Madi, Lolubo, Lokoyo, Lokoro, Lopit, Lango would remain in Sudan. However, Mr. Kelly, who led the Sudan delegation, aware of the intelligence of Acholi, and that they were more civilised than Lutoko, he realised that no one would be there to help Lutoko people to become civilised if all Acholi were to be in Uganda. Members agreed with Mr Kelly and Acholi was divided into Acholi of Uganda and Acholi of Sudan.

In 1919 British appointed Captain Wallace D.C. of Opari, but he did not take long in the office (i.e. 1919 -1920). Later, in 1926 Brtish appointed Mr. Oboke Bay the second D.C. of Opari. Chief Aburi was in office from 1914 to 1942. The people of Opari district liked Aburi very much. This was for two reasons. Firstly, it was because he did not segregate any of his subjects. Secondly, he was very generous and was able to feed his people well.

The Sudan government shifted the District Headquarters from Nimule to Opari in 1914, and then in 1928, the headquarters was transferred to Torit. In 1942, when Chief Aburi left the office of the Paramount Chief, the government appointed Chief Joseph Olaa to take up the office. But some people say that it was Chief Aburi has handed over office to Joseph Olaa because Olaa was his son-in-law. He married Rose Ayironga (mother of Odii), the daughter of Aburi. However, people learned that it was the government who appointed Olaa a Paramount Chief because they knew him very well since he was the secretary of D.C. of Opari. Chief Joseph Olaa was in office for five years (1942 — 1947).

In 1928 the government transferred Opari District to Torit, and later divided Torit Local Government Centres (LGC) into five. In 1948 they found it unneces-sary for them to appoint Paramount Chiefs. They gave the people the liberty to elect their paramount chiefs according to their interest. The people were pleased with the government for granting them the opportunity. Every L.G.C. elected the people they deemed fit as their paramount chiefs. The division of L.G.C. and election of chiefs are as follows:

LOCAL GOVERNMENT CENTRE No.1- LOA

O'DUPWEE LEFT LOLUBO

The O'dupwee clan, which is now called Boro kwac was one of the members Aru family who lived in Lolubo. The great grand father of O'dupwee was Ba'da. Ba'da had many children. Jukiri was one of his children. One morning, O'dupwee boys gathered under a tree on the compound, waiting for elders. The elders of O'dupwee and other clans came and stood near the boys and asked them to leave for them the shade, but the boys did not. No one knew why the boys did not show respect to the elders. This brought conflict between O'dupwee and other clans. It is said that Jukiri was one of the O'dupwee boys.

Many people said that Jukiri was very bright. When the conflict between the clans intensified, he decided to leave Lolubo. In the evening Jukiri called his brother, Nyikwaro and told him about his plan to leave the place. Nyikwaro keenly listened to his brother and told him, "As you go, I do not want you to go and die alone. I will go with you because I too do not like conflicting with brothers or clans."

Early in the morning, Jukiri took Nyikwaro and one of their younger brothers, and moved towards Acholi. Oral sources say that Jukiri left Lolubo around 1685. When they reached Acholiland, Nyikwaro remained to live with Acholi people. We do not know if Nyikwaro came with a wife, but it is said that he married an Acholi girl with whom he had children. He was a hospitable person who gave space for many people to settle. It did not take long that the people Nyikwaro received built all round him and his children. They then called themselves "The people of Nyikwaro," and they gave rise to the clan which is today called Panyikwara.

O'DUPWEE TOOK OVER LUKAYI CHIEFDOM

Jukiri and his brother moved farther to the west for three days and met Chief Vuri of Lukayi. The chief welcomed them very well, but later made them his slaves. The people of Lukayi were Madi. They inhabited six different places which included Mugali, Nimule, Loa, Arapi, Pageri and Nyongwa. Other Madi joined Lukayi without a chief of their own. The people who came without their chiefs are five places in Madi, which include Opari, Kerepi, Moli Tokuro, Moliandu and Iyii.

Jukiri worked for the chief so well that the chief and Madi elders were pleased with him. Eventually, Jukiri married the Lukayi's daughter with whom he had a son called O'du. O'du grew up and had a son whom he named O'du. The boy grew up and had a son called Folo, Folo begot Kado and Kado begot Alimu Dengu.

In the past the rain stone of the chief was handed over to one child in the royal house. It is not clear if Chief Vuri had children. When he saw Jukiri's intelligence, he gave the authority of his rain-hill to him. This is why Jukiri of O'dupwee became the Chief of Lukayi. Since he had the control of rain, the people of Lukayi respected him. When Jukiri died, his son, O'du had the control of rain. After the death of O'du, the authority was successively passed to Folo, Kado and Alimu Dengu.

In (1919-1937), when the district headmaster was at Opari, Chief Alimu Dengu was the chief of Madi. Chief Alimu liked his people. This made the people of Lukayi (the father of Bufura) to elect him to serve as a chief three times. However, in 1938 Lubayi became the chief of Lukayi and ruled from 1938 to 1944. In 1945 people elected Cirino Odego son of Chief Lobayi, who lived in Loa Mission. Chief Lobayi did not give Odego the rain-hill, but he gave it to his junior wife. Chief Cirino married his father's junior wife so that he could also have the power of the rain. He then ruled from 1945 to 1951.

Chief Odego was a good leader, but he did not know Arabic and English. In 1948, the government told the people of Torit district to elect their Paramount Chief. Madi people refused to elect a paramount chief because they wanted Cirino Odego to continue serving them. The issue of election brought a lot of confusion among the people. Some of them said, "Cirino should stand for the position with other interested persons, among whom was Alimu Dengu. If he passed the election, Cirino was going to continue ruling. If he failed, he would leave the throne to the winer." In the end, no election was conducted. Chief Cirino Odego continued leading the people of Torit District. This shows us how O'dupwee took over the chiefdom of Lukayi.

O'DUPWEE LOST THE CHIEFDOM

In 1952, when the D.C. of Torit District realised that Chief Cirino did not want to learn Arabic and English, he ordered the people to elect some one who knew Arabic or English because information was interpreted to Chief Cirino in Madi.

But the D.C. did not want a chief to whom information was just interpreted. He wanted to receive information directly from the chief.

In response to the order of the D.C., in 1954, the people of Madi elected Chief Sabasio Okumu Abdallah who became the first Madi chief who spoke Arabic and English. Sabasio Okumu served for thirty one years (i.e. from 1954 to 1984). Okumu died at Loa in 1984. The D.C. of Torit then appointed Alexandro Moigo, who was leading Nimule and Mugali, an acting paramount chief.

In 1984, the D.C. of Torit asked the people to elect a new Paramount Chief. In particular, he wanted Alexandro Moigo to become the next paramount chief, but the people objected to his idea and they nominated three other candidates to compete with Alexandro Moigo. The three candidates were Marcelo Cube of Bori, Mateo Drani of O'dupwee and Joseph Longa of Moli Andro. Fortunately, when Chief Moigo was acting as a paramount chief, he exhibited high competence and diligence, so Alexandra Moigo defeated the other two candidates. Alexandro was chief of Madi for four years, from 1984 to 1987. Later, John Garang De Mabior's (SPLA/SPLM) insurgency put an end to the reign of Chief Moigo. Moigo fled to Uganda with some of his subjects. The Madi people who remained in Sudan were left without a chief for three years. However, in 1990, the Madi in Juba, elected Silvestro Otoo their paramount chief.

*LOCAL GOVERNMENT CENTRE No.2- MAGWI

In 1948 Acholi elected Chief Oteno Awontur of Pajok their first paramount chief in Acoliland. Chief Oteno's reign ran from 1948 to 1961. The chief's administrative centre was created in Magwi in 1960. Therefore Oteno left Pajok and resided in Magwi. Oteno died in 1961, and Severino Odur, also from Pajok, replaced him and his reign ended in 1973. In the same year, Anyanya rebels and the government of Sudan signed a peace accord at Adisababa in Ethiopia. On their return from wherever they had fled, they chose Otaviano Oyat Akut in 1974 as the next paramount chief, and he served up to 1998.

President Jafar Mohammed Nimeiri visited Magwi in 1974, and Sudan Government built an army barracks at Wii Kaolo, and later transferred it to Kimoru. In 1980, the government promoted Magwi to a district status (i.e. Acholi district). In 1990, Magwi became a Province Headquarter of Acholi and Madi, and they appointed Okot Omer of Pajok the first Commissioner of Magwi Province. In 2000 SPLM/A instituted their office in Magwi (Santo Ongin, 2005, P, 2).

Under the British rule, Magwi Centre 2 had four paramount chiefs. These included chief of Obbo, Magwi, Pajok and Palwar. At that time the people of Panyikwara, Omeo, Agoro and Ofirika were under the chief of Magwi. Immediately Sudan obtained political independence from British rulers, the new government gave Panyikwara chiefdom. The first chief of Panyikwara was Chief Wani who was the father of Ambrozio of Goloba (Lolubo). Abrozio took up his father's office after his death. The government also asked the chief of Panyikwara to rule over the people of Kit and Owiny-ki-bul as well. However, the people of Omeo, Agoro and Ofirika remained under the leadership of the chief of Magwi.

The chief of Obbo lead his people together with southern Iyire, Koyo and Ngabara. The chief of Pajok led the people of Pajok only. The chief of Palwar led Palwar, Lobone, Isore and Paduro.

*LOCAL GOVERNMENT CENTRE No. 3- TORIT

The people chose Mr. Peter Icaro in 1948 as their paramount chief.

*LOCAL GOVERNMENT CENTRE No. 4- KIYALA.

In 1948 Loturo Mohamed Morhum was chosen by the people as a paramount chief.

*LOCAL GOVERNMENT CENTRE No. 5- IMEHEJEK.

In 1948 Lopwonya of Ikotos was also chosen to be the paramount chief of Imehejek.

Chapter Three

THINGS WHICH MAKE ACHOLI STAND OUT FROM OTHER TRIBES

The Acholi people can tell who is and who is not an Acholi. There are nine things with which an Acholi person can be identified:

Creation
God created Acholi people in a way that they appear distinct from other people (the head, long legs, sunken eyes, the ear and the style of walking).

Language
An Acholi person distinctively articulates other languages such as Arabic and English. Their pronunciations are different from the pronunciations of other ethnic groups. For example, letter **s** does not exist in Acholi. So, in a foreign word which has the letter **s**, an Acholi would pronounce the **s** as **c** as in cukul in place of school. The language the Acholi people speak is Acholi.

Nomenclature
Most masculine Acholi names begin with the letter **o**. Olaa, Okeny, Okulu, Odera, Odwar, Opiyo and Omwony are a few examples of such names. Most feminine names start with the letter **A**. Some of the names are Akwero, Alal, Acii, Aciro, Abalo and Amoyo.

Culture
The Acholi people have the culture which includes birth and funeral

ceremonies. This culture is not exactly the same with the cultures of other people. Secondly, every Acoli person and anybody who marries an Acholi must live by the culture.

Songs

The Acholi people like singing very much. An Acholi sees what you are doing and composes a song about it immediately. When you hear such song in Sudan today, the next day you will hear it among the Acholi of Uganda.

Dress and Decency

Acholi are the most decent people in the Equatorial region. They cherish cleanliness, well cooked food and balancing diet. They also have many traditional dances which include Larakaraka, Otole, Bola, Dingi-dingi, Lokeme, Adungu, Apiti, and Goyo longo. Before the white man brought clothe, all Sudanese walked naked. Some Acholi people were equally naked, but that does not mean they did not have their traditional dress. They had their traditional dresses though not all wore it.

Captain E.T.N. Grove, wrote that Acoli people walked naked, but when they got a dress they loved to be in it very much, and they did not want their cloth to be dirty. In Acholiland, elders wore dresses made from goatskin antelope skin, duikar skin, or leopardskin (it is only the chief who wore leopard skin in Acholiland. No other person did).

In a distant past, men and elegant boys wore *layamo-okwe* but girls walked naked with beads round their necks. They also wore bungles on their wrists and ankles. There were also girls who wore nothing on them – they were just stark naked. Acholi elders wanted a girl in her puberty to wear beads round the waist, and some lines of beads were worn hanging down on the front lower part of the body to cover her pubic region. After a girl's first child, she is allowed to wear apron skirt *cip* which covered the pubic area. This was a descent dress which kept women's private parts out of sight.

Differentiating wives of poor men and rich men was very easy among Acholi. Wives of poor men wore only the front cover (i.e. cip in Acholi), but wives of rich men wore both *cip* and a sheet that covered the buttock (i.e. ceno in Acholi). Wearing the apron skirt ended between 1940 and 1945 when wearing clothe entered Acholiland in a considerable quantity. However, older men continued wearing animal skins up to 1960 to 1964.

Acholi elders said that in the past Acoli boys and girls liked shaving their heads clean. Boys shaved all the hair on the head but left some hair in the middle of the top of their head. However, girls just clean shaved their head without leaving any hair. A boy or a girl who did not shave frequently was considered a dirty person, and such a person found it difficult to socialise with other people. Women loved removing their lower front teeth and tattooing their forehead. None of the woman would be able to tell why they tattoo themselves, but a few of them would just say it was their culture. Boys also used to remove their teeth. A boy who did not remove his teeth was not wanted by any girl for a boyfriend. So a boy who refused to remove his teeth would die a bachelor.

We have already looked at the culture in relation to the life of boys. Let us also explore how culture worked among Acoli girls and housewives. In the past, women pricked open their lower lip and inserted a split of sorghum neck in the opening created. Elders contend that men also used to pierce the the lobe of their ears and insert bangle or a small piece of well shaped iron in it for decoration. At that time, a boy who did not wear bungle was not the son of man. Pricking the lip and the ear ended around 1920 to 1930. The end of these decorations gave way to new innovations. Girls started tattooing their forehead and their waist. This gave girls confidence because the tattooing was done by elderly women. The women used needle to prick and pull the skin of the forehead and cut with razor blade. In the Acholi culture, a girl undergoing this process of decoration should not cry.

Hunting

Acholi had different types of hunting which included setting the bush on fire, group hunting covering a vast hunting ground, hunting with net, hunting smaller animals like edible rats. The hunting artifacts were spear, bow and arrows. Acholi elders say that hunting with bow and arrow was recent among Acholi people. It was boys who liked hunting edible rat with bows and arrows though some of them would accompany elders in bush burning hunting where they would remain behind for fear of shooting people with their arrows. Therefore in this kind of hunting people used spear because there were many bigger animals such as elephant and buffalo. Once in a while, some hunters went to hunt with guns because the government did not want people to possess guns. So, whoever had a gun would always keep in out of sight. If a hunter's enemy saw him with a gun, he would report him to the government. As a result, he would be arrested by the police who would remove his gun and put him in jail for one or more years.

Some Acholi hunters liked amulet very much. They wore it on their arms and their neck. Some of them put it together with beads on their horns for decoration. Acholi believed that amulet brought for them luck of killing animals, but hunters who did not have amulet listened to bats singing. Every bat sound has a meaning to Acholi. Men could tell the bat song which would bring luck and that which could bring death in the hunting expedition. The bird whose song Acholi people did not want to hear was woodpecker. They believed that woodpecker was a bird of bad luck. If it sang when hunters were on a hunting expedition, wild animals would attack them. The interpretation of the song of woodpecker in the contemporary time varies from the interpretation in the past. For instance, Mr. T.E.N. Grove wrote that at a certain time in the past, "Woodpecker was a good bird to Acholi. If it sang on the left of the hunters, they would kill a female animal, and if it sang on the right they would kill a male animal." Why do the contemporary Acholi do not interpret the song of woodpecker in the same way with their predecessors? No Acholi elder was able to answer this question.

Building and Home

In the past, the Acholi people lived in group. They built their houses in enclosed clusters, unlike the scattered homes among the present Acholi. They used to live in a community of one clan. Every clan would have their own settlement in one place known as theirs. Some people built among big trees to prevent their enemies from penetrating their settlement. The settlement had only one opening to let people in and out. Some of them had two openings – one was an inlet and the other was a security exit to be used at the time of attack on the settlement.

The contemporary Acholi do not build in an enclosure, and they do not build among big trees because there are no primitive wars as it used to be in the past. This time people build anywhere they find good for them, but it must be among or close with their clan members. The most important factor that determines where to build is the fertility of the land. The Acholi people usually do subsistence cultivation and they plant crops such as rice, potato, banana, paw paw, yam and cassava. A person who visits a family is free to take this kind of foodstuff without asking the owner.

Children's Play House

During dry season, boys and girls of five to ten years of age build a hut in a burnt bush away from home. This is how children learn family responsibilities. Here girls learn how to cook, how to brew *kwete* (a local alcohol), house hygiene and listening to a man. In Acholi it is the man who builds the hut and controls the family – his wife listens to him. The children often steal flour, salt, meat and fermented flour for brewing alcohol from home. Elders say that the hut is not only a place for learning family responsibilities, but they also a place for learning about sex.

Children get to know that in a family there is a man a woman and children. Therefore, before building a hut in the burnt bush, a boy chose a wife from among the girls they plaid together with. The boy then instructs his wife to choose two or three playmates to be their children, and the children must be between three and five years old. The children would build many huts and divide themselves in different huts which had to be at least five to ten meters away from one another.

In this play, the children knew the right time to go to the garden, to go for a dance and to go to bed. At bed time, everybody enters the hut and closed the door with twigs. Two children would act the cock. When it came to "down," they would crow like a cock, "*Kung-ku-luru kuuuk! Hooo! Kung-ku-luru kuuuk! Hooo!* This would be done three times, at an interval of five minutes, before daybreak. Then everybody rose and started to do their work. Women would sweep the compound and men would carry their spears, hoe and seeds and set out for the garden. The hoe was not the real hoe but some forked tree branch that looked like hoe, and they used sand for seeds.

After sweeping the compound, women would prepare food and take to the men in the garden. This is one way of assessing a woman's diligence. A woman should be able to take food to the garden by 12:00 noon. She would keep the food under a tree where it was already cleared by the men. At this time the man must have already been tired, and he would not take long to wash his

41

hands and go to eat. After eating, the man would continue up to 1:00 pm or 2:00 pm. If there was any digging for alcohol that day, the man would leave his garden and proceed for it.

The Acholi culture does not allow any child aged fourteen and above to engage in the kind of play described above. Boys of fourteen and above should have their own huts at home. It is also important to note that even grown up men have their sleeping huts. Every boy must build his own hut. Boys do not share huts. Every boy must have his own sleeping hut. Acholi boys liked sleeping with girls very much. If there were boys sharing a hut, and one of them was going to host his girlfriend, he would tell other boys to sleep else where. In an Acholi home there was sleeping hut of the head of the family, kitchen, sleeping hut for girls and each boy's sleeping hut and a goat kraal.

A boy's sleeping hut (Figure No 8)

In Acholi sleeping hut was built on four forked poles fixed in the ground. This was to avoid attack by fierce wild animals like lion and bear. It is said that bear used to scratch people in the night. At the time of going to bed, people would enter the hut by climbing a ladder. The last person to climb must pull the ladder up so that wild animals and enemies could not climb after them. The sleeping hut has a very small door, but enough for one to pass. Entering the sleeping hut was never easy. One would start by pushing his head followed by the chest, waist and finally the legs. Boys made exit door on the floor for their girlfriends to pass from. When a girl visited her boyfriend for sexual relation, her brothers would sometimes follow her if they discovered her whereabouts. So if her brother climbed up the sleeping hut of her boyfriend, the boy would open for her the door on the floor and she slid out before her brothers entered the hut. We are aware that other boys knew that every sleeping hut of a boy had such emergency exit, but why couldn't they wait for the sister from the outlet? No elder was able to answer this question. Another thing which I did not understand well is the claim that the brothers of a girlfriend would climb up to her boyfriends hut, yet the ladder would always be pulled up to avoid such people climbing up. How did the girls' brothers climb up their boyfriend's house?

Hospitality

Acholi elders told me that Acholi people welcomed everyone, a trader, a poor person or a government agent. When someone comes home as a visitor or a trader, Acholi people would serve him food, help him with water for bath and give him space to sleep. In Acholi culture, it was important that a visitor is given food, alcohol, water for bath and a place for sleeping. Since they did not have extra huts for visitors, visitors were slept in the kitchen. If the visitor was a girl, she slept together with the girls in the home.

Cultivation

Acholiland was very fertile. This was one thing which made Acholi proud because the cultivated a number of crops. Other tribes like Lotuko, Madi and Bar bought foodstuff from Acholi. Most of the neighbours of Acholi did not know how to welcome visitors. Most of the time their visitors slept hungry, or they were not given where to sleep at all. But in Acholi, people knew how to receive visitors very well. Acholi liked dancing laraka-raka. During harvest, they danced to give thanks to God for giving them rain which made their crops to yield well. (look at the picture below).

Cwiri

Acholi dance during rainy season to thank the Creator (Figure No. 9)

Orphans were raised at the bond fire on the compound

In every Acholi home there was a point for bond fire. Some people think that bond fire is only a place for family members to gather in the evening, but in Acholi culture, it plays a lot of roles. First it is where members of a family converge in the evening. Secondly, it is a point where children learn from elder their culture and how a man heads his family. Thirdly, it is a place where an orphan finds food.

It is boys who make the fire on the compound. The people who gather at the fire do not sit on chairs or animal hides, but they all sit on reed bed. Sometimes they erect shade at the fire place – as elders contend, is to protect people from drizzles during rainy season. At the side, some dry forked poles are fixed against which men lean their shields and spears. Men did this because at that time people used to be attacked any time. So, the men had their weapons ready to defend their people.

At the time men are at the fire, women remain in the kitchen preparing evening meal. When all the men were at the fire, each woman took her food to them. There was always two or three boys whose work was to receive food from the hands of the women. Before the meal, two boys were sent to bring water. One would carry drinking water and the other water for washing hands. The boy who carried water for washing hands poured the water in

44

a medium size calabash and gave it to elders to wash their hands. In Acholi, elders washed their hands first the children would follow. After washing their hands, the elder who washed first would carry the calabash of bread in his left hand, pinched a piece off and passed the calabash to the elder on his left. The first elder would then carry the bowl of food dipped his bread in it and passed it to the next elder on his left. The elder who received the calabashes would do the same to the elder to his left until it reached the children and circular movement continued until food was over. When the first pair of food and bread was finished, they picked another pair and continued the same process. When they were eating, there was no conversation because they respected food. There are reasons why Acholi people ate at the fire on the compound. Eating in the open gave opportunity to orphans to find food. He ate together with the family members.

Where did Acholi women eat from in the evening? The Acholi culture does not allow women to eat together with men. Women eat together with girls and boys, who are below eight, in front of one chosen hut. Boys of eight years and above usually eat together with men.

There used to be women who were selfish – they thought eating together would not make them satisfied. So, such a woman would put a big lump of bread in her child's hand so that when the child failed to finish it, she would now eat it. This usually happened during famine.

Unlike men, women did not pass calabash of bread and bowl of food from hand to hand. They just put two calabashes of bread and two bowels of food in the centre of a ring of women. When the first pair of food and bread was finished, they kept adding until all the bowels and calabashes were emptied. Since children ate together with their mothers, the mothers cut a reasonable piece of bread and gave to their children. It is this piece that a child ate.

Acholi people ate with their fingers. The use of spoon was introduced by the white man around 1967. However, Acholi people did not like using spoon for eating. Before spoon was introduce in Acholiland, people used shell for taking porridge, but in 1967, they started taking porridge with spoon.

CHAPTER FOUR

THE ACHOLILAND IN SUDAN

Around 1650 Acholi people lived in groups without serious conflict among themselves. At that time, they believed that they were children of one person, so there was no need to live apart from one another. Around 1650 Acholi people were not called Acholi, but they were called Sudanic. The name Acholi came much later as we will see in this book. Between 1698 and 1700 Lwo entered the present Acholiland in Sudan with their chief, and they lived there for a while and some proceeded to Uganda, Kenya, Ethiopia and Tanganyika where they are today.

Okot P' Bitek said it very clearly that "Before British rule, the Acholi of Uganda and Sudan were one. The moment British rulers entered Acholiland, they divided the Acholi into thirty groups who were under the leadership of thirty chiefs. Each chiefdom was autonomous, but later, they were all served under a *District Commissioner (D.C.)* whose administrative headquarters was in Gulu. Therefore, Gulu became Acholi district.

The boundary of Acholi of Sudan today is River Limur between Pajok and Uganda, between Uganda and Palwar, the boarder is at River Liringa, and between Palwar and Lotuko the boundary is at Kidikidi Hill. Between Omeo and Lokoya, it is at Lowai. Between Magwi and Imurok, the boarder is at River Koli. Then between Agoro and Aruu, which is in Lokoya the boundary is at Joseph Lagu's farm which is along Juba Nimule Road. Between Panyikwara and Bar, it is at River Otur, and between Panyikwara and Madi it is along River Iyipii (Buffalo river?). On the side of Owinykibul the boarder is between River Limur and River Aswa.

The land on which both Acholi of Sudan and Acholi of Uganda live, as

William J. House and his friend Kwin D. Phillip Howard put it, "When put together, it totals to 28,112sq.Km. This land stretches to Lake Victoria on the south, Albert Nile on the west and runs to Lolubai, Agoro, Oromo Hill (in Karamoja)- on the east. However, the land of Acholi of Sudan alone is 2,700sq km²."

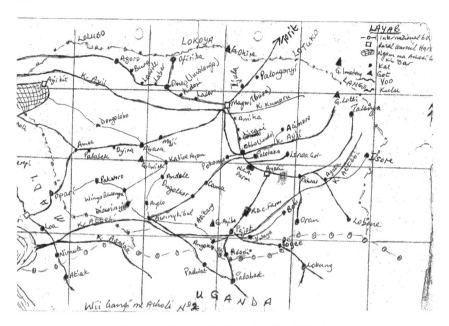

Figure 10: The land of Acholi of South Sudan

THE HOMES OF ACHOLI

The Acholiland in South Sudan is divided into seven parts, but some people say there are five main divisions of Acholiland with the argument that Omeo, Agoro and Ofirika are under Magwi. Nevertheless, in this book we realise that it was the D.C. of Torit who put Omeo, Agoro and Ofrika under the chief of Magwi to ease their tax collection. The D.C. ordered that the three chiefdoms should take the tax; they collected, to the chief of Magwi who was supposed to remit it to the Paramount Chief. This makes us ask the question, "Why did the D.C. of Torit make this order? Did he not know the chiefs of Agoro, Omeo and Ofrika?"

The law had it that if a chiefdom had five hundred tax payers, it could be an autonomous chiefdom. The seven chiefdoms had different demographies. The census of 1983 revealed that Pajok had 6,434 people, which showed that Pajok had the highest population among the Acholi of Sudan. The census also showed that Panyikwara had the lowest population because they had only 3,388 people.

The details of the population of the different Acholi chiefdoms are given in the table below.

Table 1: The population of Acholi of South Sudan

No	Chiefdom	Population
1	Pajok	6,434
2	Obbo	5,307
3	Palwar	4,612
4	Magwi	?
5	Omeo	4,499
6	Agoro	?
7	Ofirika	?
8	Panyikwara	3,388
	Total	24,240

This data was extracted from the 1983 *Sudan Census*, p.3

THE OLD RAIN CHIEFDOM

Traditional chiefdom in Acoli started between 1700 and 1800, and the tradition did not allow shift of chieftain away from the royal house. So, if a chief died, the rain chose one of his sons to become the next chief. We will see how the rain went to the chosen son. The Acholi people respected their chiefs very much, and they believed the chief was the second person after God. Acholi showed respect to their chiefs in many ways: offering their freshly harvested millet, leopard skin and domestic animals like cattle to the chief. The offers were meant to help the chief to take care of his visitors because, in the past, visitors who did not have what to eat and where to sleep would be hosted and accommodated in the chief's home. People respected the rain chief for two main reasons. Firstly, they respected him because he made rain, and secondly because of his good leadership.

OTHER TRIBES NEIGHBOURING ACHOLI OF SUDAN

There are ten tribes which are neighbours of the Acholi of Sudan. On the west is Madi, on the north are Bar, Lolubo and Lokoya. While on the east are Lotuko, Lango, Dongotono, and Logir, and on the south Palabek and Lokung which are in Uganda.

From 1973 when people returned from refuge in different countries, the Acholi, Madi and Bar boarder conflict erupted. In 1986, Madi and Bar claimed that Jokokii was their land. Both Madi and Bar claimed the ownership of the land. Subsequent to the claims, Bar renamed the place Kit. However, Acholi elders know very well that Jokokii (Kit), from a long time ago, the contested land was Acholi's that is why, up to now, Acholi people live on that land. The Acholi people who inhabited this land called it *Ayii Jokokii*. In 2005 Madi again claimed that Opari, Owing-ki-bul and Kit was their land.

Acholi listened to this claim with a lot of pain, and they thought, "If the government did not intervene then it would lead to a serious conflict between Acholi and Madi in future." However, Sisto Otim Oywak (2008) wrote that the Madi in Juba wrote a letter on 11/07/2007 to invite Acholi to discuss the border conflict.

Oywak stated that when the chairperson of Acholi received the letter, he called his people in three different meetings to review the content of the letter. Unfortunately, the Acholi did not have action plan to respond to the letter.

Oral sources have it that the people of Madi sent a copy of this letter to the D.C. of Magwi (H.E. Commissioner of Magwi County). As a result, on the 30/07/2008 the D.C. of Magwi invited delegations of both Acholi and Madi to Magwi, by letter, to discuss how to settle the border dispute. The D.C. asked the conflicting parties to find a peaceful means of settling the conflict about Opari, Owiny-kibul and Kit.

The meeting was eventually held in Magwi Town, and it took four days. It commenced on the 21st and ended on the 24th of August 2008. The meeting was attended by elders of Acholi and Madi whose names I did not obtain. An Member of Parliament of Acholi, whose name was not given, ministers, SPLA commanders, religious leaders, boys, women, clan elders and owners of hunting grounds. The chairperson asked the delegations of Acholi and Madi to tell the meeting what they think about the disputed places, Opari, Owing-ki-bul and Kit -and what their history was in relation to the same. Secondly, they should tell the meeting what each of them called the places (names of hunting grounds), and lastly, they should name the owners of the hunting grounds.

After the submissions of the two conflicting parties, the chairperson divided members into three working groups to discuss the claims of each party. The three groups came up with three significant findings. Firstly, they discovered that Owiny-ki-bul belonged to the people of Pakala who are also people of Panyikwara. Secondly, they found out that Opari was the home of the Gaya people who are also children of Panyikwara. The people of Madi came to Opari quite recently and were hosted by Gaya people. Thirdly, they found out that Kit (Ayii) belonged to Acholi. The minutes of the meeting spells out clearly that Alwala, Maria, Wii Obur, Kotokoto, Layoyo and Deyo which surround Ayii Jokokii are actually the hunting grounds of Acholi. This should help us researchers to recognise Ayii Jokokii as the land of Acholi.

Many Acholi elders told me that the boundary between Acholi and Madi is at River Jubi – River Jubi also belongs to Acholi. The words/name *"kulo"* and *"Jubi"* are Acholi words. "Kulu Jubi" was a name the Acholi people gave the river so that anybody who hears it is able to tell that it belongs to Acholi.

If we analyise the situation critically, we realise that Katakata, Ajuni and Kugi hunting grounds surround Opari. Madi settled on the land much later. When the government found that Madi people were now many, they gave the leadership of Opari in the hands of Madi because it was close to Loa. So, the boarder between Acholi and Madi was moved from Kulu Jubi to *Abongrwot* at a stream near an Oloro man, Lojukoreng's tamarind tree.

But the Madi people said that Chief Milla of Pandike was the one who led the people of Opari and Owiny-ki-bul in 1910. They also claimed that the people of Palabek and Oloro were under the administration of Chief Milla up to 1942, who later handed over the people of Oloro and Palabek back to the chief of Panyikwara. The son of Chief Milla said it rightly, "My father was the administrator, but he did not own the disputed land. My father defended the people of Gaya and Palabek very much against the Kuku (Kajo-Keji) killers." Severino Vuli (of Madi) was the one confusing people in his book, "Reshaping Southern

Sudan." This book explains the movement of Madi, the story of Owiny-ki-bul and the reign of Chief Milla. Although the dispute with Madi was settled, the people of Bar still claim that Kit is their land. Therefore, there is need to settle the dispute between Bar and Acholi.

Chapter Five

. . . .

THE COMING OF ARABS TO SOUTHERN SUDAN

Sudan is a very large African country. It covers a vast area of 2,505,813 km. The struggle for independence of Sudan started during of Kush's (760 BC-350 AD) administration. In 1820 Muhammed Ali of Turkish of *Ottoman sultan* in Istanbul had already occupied Egypt and he was prepared to extend his territory to Sudan. He wanted to take over Sudan for two reasons. He wanted to get slaves for sale, and secondly, he wanted gold.

Muhammed Ali son of Ismail Kamil Pasha sent 4,000 soldiers to fight Sudan. Oral source state that among these soldiers were the people of Albanian, Tarki, Maghri who were all North Africans. It also included soldiers from Egypt. At that time Egypt was dominated by Turkey.

The Ottaman entered Sudan because Sudan did not have powerful weapons. However, Shayqiyya tried to fight, but unfortunately they only fought with swards which could not do anything to their enemies who used guns to fight them. The chiefs or Ja'aliyyin makks (in Arabic) of Berber together with the chiefs around White and Blue Niles offered themselves to Ottaman.

Muhammed Ali immediately ordered the shooting of everyone at the rivers because he did not want a leader to emerge from Sudan. He said that it should take sixty years to get a new leader from Sudan.

Turkey appointed Circassian Manluk a Governor General of Sudan. It is also said that it was Manluk who established Khartoum in 1825, and he trained the slaves he obtained from Nuba Mountains and Upper Nile (Malakal) as Sudanese soldiers. Although Turkey enlisted Sudanese in their arm, after occupation of Sudan, the new administrator of Sudan, Ismail Sudan ordered that people must pay tax in form of human, domestic animals and sorghum.

Between 1821 and 1885 when Turkey ruled Sudan, they did not want to associate with foreigners, and they did not want to listen to religious teaching of
Arabs or the white man. Acholi had their traditional religion as we will read
later in this book.

In 1881 Mohammed Ahmed who was from Dunqula, and was forty years
old, together with Mahdi, fought and pushed Turkey away. Ahmed used a
group of Muslims called ansar to fight Mohammed Ahmed, and Mahdi fought
Turkey for two years. That is from 1881 to 1882 and later defeated the Ottaman
soldiers.

Mohammed Ahmed was an educated man and very knowledgeable in
Islam. After his education, Moammed settled in Aba Island. He went to fight
Turkey from this island. Ahmed promoted himself in three ranks. At first he
said he was the Head of true Muslim community. Secondly, he said he was the
prophet of God, and thirdly, he was the Mahdi who could foretell the future
and the end of the world.

In 1884 he appointed Gordon the second time to be the Governor General
of Khartoum. He immediately realised that peace between Mahdi and Turkey
government and returning Egyptian soldiers to Egypt was not an easy thing
to do. He then decided to control Khartoum until the relief expedition arrived
from Britain.

Later, Muslim took over Northern Sudan. Mahdi and his friend Mohamed
Amed realised that penetrating Southern Sudan was hard. Eventually, Khalifa
Abdullah, an assistant of Mahdi, began to enter southern Sudan.

The first foreigners to enter Sudan were the Turks as we have read above,
followed by Arabs. Oral sources maintain that the Arabs came from three
different places: Saudi, Libya and Egypt. They came to Sudan as traders and
missionaries. They entered from northern Sudan.

The Arab traders married African girls, but it was not easy for them to get
African girls for marriage for it was not permissible in Acholi culture to mix
blood with foreigners. That means Acholi should marry amongst themselves,
but not with foreigners. We cannot tell why Acholi elders accepted Acholi girls
to marry Arabs. The interesting thing about the intermarriage is that the Arabs
married Acholi girls, but no Acholi man married an Arab girl. Some people said
that Acholi men did not marry Arabs because the Arab traders came without
girls and women from their countries.

Marriage built a very strong relationship between Arabs and the black people. This gave Arabs opportunity to teach their Islamic doctrine to the blacks. The Arabs started by teaching their in-laws, and they also took their teaching to northern Sudan. The Islamic teaching spread in southern Sudan after 1905.This was the time Arabs took the trade in southern Sudan. Being a bit hostile, the southern Sudanese did not receive the Arabs traders well and they did not want Arabs and any other people apart from blacks to enter their place. The Arabs found it very hard to live in southern Sudan. So, most of them returned to Khartoum while those who remained in southern Sudan lived together in towns such as Juba, Malakal and Wau.

Acholi was one of the people of southern Sudan who did not want Arabs. They did not give Arabs time to trade in their area until 1932 when Arabs found ways of entering Acholiland. They first went to Magwi and later continued to Obbo. Entering Magwi became easy because it was also on the way to Acholi, and secondly, because it was also the administrative headquarters where the county chief of Acholi resided.

Other places like Palwar, Pajok, Lobone and Panyikwara did not accept Arabs in their areas. Some people said the Arabs went to sell their goods to them but nobody showed interest in them. When they realised that no one was willing to buy their goods, the Arab traders went back to Magwi and Obbo where they had potential buyers. This made it very difficult for Arabs to begin teaching Islam to the people of Acholi.

According to Acholi elders, from the time Arabs came to Acholiland, up to 1987, it is only the people of Pajok and Agoro who joined Islam. The Islamic converts in the two places did not reach thirty. Although Arabs built Mosques in places where their religion was welcomed, up to 2009 there was no Mosque in Acholi. However, that is how Islam spread among the people of southern and northern Sudan.

In 1898 the government of British and Egypt (Anglo-Egyptian) opened another war on Mahadist (Ansar). Ansar was at first hesitant, but later attacked Egypt on the 3/8/1889, it is said that an Egyptian commander called Abd al-Rahman al Najumi led the soldiers to Tushki in Egypt. Ansar lost a number of soldiers. The few who survived went back to Sudan. The British and Egyptian eventually took over Sudan from Arabs Mahadiya, and they established a new government in Sudan.

THE COMING OF BRITISH TO SOUTHERN SUDAN

In 1898, when British and Egyptians took over Sudan, they too found it diffi-cult to enter southern Sudan because the inhabitants of the place were very hostile. After ten years of governance in Sudan, the British eventually crept into southern Sudan though it was not an easy move to make. Arabs entered southern Sudan as traders. They did not fight with the northern Sudanese. It is also said that British entered southern Sudan peacefully. They came gently so that they could enter the land of the black people who were as wild as a lion. The British talked to the blacks about peace and unity.

When the southern Sudanese heard the British talk about peace and unity, they welcomed them because peace and unity were also cherished among them. The British were confident when they came to southern Sudan. They did not exert their power immediately, but they gave all the authority to Chiefs of Rain who were loved by the people. They did this because they wanted to divide the people slowly so that they could easily rule them.

In 1940 British ordered that the Arabs in northern Sudan should not go to southern Sudan. Secondly, southern Sudanese should not go to Khartoum. This was intended to stop Arabs from advising black people against British and stop them from spreading the Islamic doctrine in the area. On the 3/4/1942, a black student wrote a letter to the administrators of Sudan asking them to allow people from northern Sudan and southern Sudan to freely move in and out of the two regions. The student asked the administrators to give black students and students from northern Sudan to study together in Khartoum University. The British considered this letter useless, but after six years, they invited the blacks and Arabs to a meeting in Juba on the 12/7/1948. In this meeting, people accepted that Arab traders could build their business prem-ises in southern Sudan. It was also resolved that the black Sudanese students studying in Makerere University should go to study in Khartoum University. Before this meeting, all black students studied in Makerere University (in Uganda) because Sudan government did not allow them to study in Khartoum University.

British granted Sudan political independence in 1956. The new Sudan government found out that there were six hundred tribes in Sudan, and Acholi was one of them. Although there were many tribes in the Sudan, Sudanese usually stuck together in unity. It was religious difference which brought disunity among them. For example, the Catholic Church did not want its members to mix with Protestants. Islam as well brought great division among the people because they did not want to mix with Christians because they considered Christians pagans. The Islamic segregation was more prominent in northern Sudan where Islam was deeply rooted.

Former administrators of Sudan said the the Sudan population census of 1986 showed the different races in Sudan as follows: Arab had 20%, Nilotics was 9%, Fur was 6% and Nubia or Nilo Hamites had 5%. The government did this to deceive people outside Sudan that the Arabs had the largest population in Sudan. Secondly, since 90% of Arabs were Muslims, it was used to show the outside world that most Sudanese were Muslims. But in reality, the population of the blacks was higher than Arabs'. If the census was well conducted, it would reveal that Arabs had only 39% of the population of Sudan. The blacks, who are the owners of the place, would have 61%. It is only 5% of the black people that joined Islam.

BRITISH RULE AND THE DIVISION OF ACHOLILAND
The British entered Sudan through Uganda. They meet Acholi people who were still primitive, but every Acholi clan had a rain chief. They used the chiefs to talk to their subjects because they were very much respected by their subjects. If they want the people to do something, they talked to the chiefs who in turn talked to the people. People would just follow the order of their chiefs. The British operated with the help of the chiefs for eleven years as they thought of what means to use to begin to rule the people.

According to oral sources, some of the chiefs had very good warriors. If they were attacked by their enemies, these warriors would fight hard until they defeated their adversaries. It is also said that some chiefs did not have strong warriors and were weak chiefdoms. Many times such chiefdom lost their subjects who would migrate to stronger chiefdoms who could protect them.

When British came to Acholiland, they assigned the chiefs to collect tax from their subjects. According to Acholi elders the chiefs were poor, so they accumulated wealth from their subjects as they collected tax from them. Teacher William J. House and his friend Kevin D. Phillips Howard in their book asserted, "Some chiefs became wealthy around 1860 when Arab traders from Egypt came to Acholiland. Other white people also relied on the chiefs for

ivory, rhinoceros horn and slaves. The Arabs and the whites gave the chiefs tokens of appreciation after they helped them to get what they wanted, and the token was given in terms of cattle or guns."

Before long, the Arabs began to raid ivory, rhinoceros horn, slaves and food-stuff from Acholi people, and this reduced the wealth of the chief for the gains they used to get from the traders was no longer there.

When this act was reported to Britain, in 1870, British asked Ismail Pasha and Khedive of Egypt (administrators in Egypt) to top slave trade in order to bring peace in Acholiland. When Khedive of Egypt received this command, he asked Samuel Baker to put Equatorial region under Egyptian rule. Samuel Baker, Charles Gordon and Emin Pasha could not stop slave trade and the rampant raids at that time.

The Britain administrators removed Emin Pasha from Acholi in 1889 — that was the beginning of return of peace in Acholi. In 1902 Mr. F.A. Knowles, a Briton ordered that Acholi people should manage their affairs and control their security by themselves. So, he assigned an Acholi man whose name was not found in the course of the research to lead Acholi. Every chiefdom fell under the leadership of the man. But people like Kevin Phillips and his friend William House said that although British rule brought independence to Acholi, the British did not take Acholi people as one people with one language and culture.

In 1914, Pasteltwaite was assigned a D.C. of Acholi in Gulu (Uganda), Anglo-Egyptian Sudan and Protectorate of Uganda, and they met to discuss boarder line. At that time, Acholi of Sudan and Acholi of Uganda were both under the rule of Anglo-Egyptian Sudan. Acholi elders say that Sudan, in the past, covered up to Soroti on the south, Pakwach on the west (both in Uganda. The administrators, who attended the boarder meeting 1914, were Mr. N. Kelly from Sudan and Mr. Tufnell from Uganda.

The meeting was held at Gulu, the headquarters of Acholi in Uganda. The meeting was not meant to split up Acholi but to separate Lutoko from Acholi. In this meeting, Mr Tufnell wanted all Acholi to be together in Uganda, and Lotuko should be in Sudan, but Mr Kelly knew that Acholi more civilised than Lotuko. For this reason, Mr. Kelly said that it would not be good to have all Acholi in Uganda. Removing all Acholi from Sudan would be of shame to lead-ers of Sudan because Lotuko did not have developmental mind, because they were not as civilised as Acholi. Mr. Tufnell concluded that if all Acholi were taken to Uganda, there would be no other tribe to help Lotuko to get civilized.

Acholi elders believed that Mr. Kelly wanted the Acholi of Pajok and Obbo to remain in Sudan to train Lotuko because Mr Kelly knew very well that people from those two villages were particular about smartness and hygiene, but he also knew that the people of Obbo and Pajok were very hardworking manual labourers. However, Mr Tufnell did not support Mr Kelly's argument, though he later agreed with him. Mr Kelly thought that the people of Obbo and Pajok would provide labour for the construction of Gondokoro Nimule railway.

After the meeting, the delegates of Anglo-Egyptian Sudan and Protectorate of Uganda agreed that the southern boarder of Sudan should be removed from Soroti to Adodi Hill, but the western boarder was to move from Pakwach to Koboko. The leaders of Sudan and Uganda both accepted the boarder agreement. That is why Acholi are in both Uganda and Sudan. According to Acholi elders, after 1914 Acholi people were under the D.C. of Gulu, but now the Acholi of Sudan are under the D.C. of Magwi.

After 1914 the whites stopped working with the rain chiefs, and they assigned sub-county chiefs because they thought the sub-county chiefs would do what they wanted and work well with the people. The white rulers also removed from the people the right to elect chiefs. The new chiefs were responsible for settling disputes among clan members, punishing offenders and collecting tax, which they took to the office of the white rulers. The black representatives of the rulers paid the chiefs with part of the tax collected and remitted the rest to the white man. Under every sub-county chief there was a parish chief and sub-parish chief. As we will see later in this book, parish chief and sub-parish chief were also entitled to settle disputes and helped sub-county chiefs to collect tax. Tax payers who did not have money were allowed to pay their tax with chicken or goat.

Chapter Six

. . . .

OCOLA AND LWO

(Spear and bead separated Lwo the second time at Tekidi)

When Lwo were at Tekidi Chief Olum was on the throne, three of his children migrated away from Tekidi because the population at Tekidi had grown so much that there was not enough land for all. Each of them settled in different places of their own choices. However, Ocola, Olum's eldest son remained at Tekidi where his father had initially settled. Tekidi, where Ocola and his father remained was renamed *Pucola* which means Ocola's place. Where Luru settled was named *Puluru*, meaning Luru's place. The place where Lwo settled was called *Palwo*, and Coope's place of settlement was named *Pacoope*, which also means Coope's place.

These children of Olum lived independently from one another, but if an enemy attacked one of them, all of them would defend their brother against the enemy. The people at Wipaco learned that Olum's sons departed from one another and they also followed suit and the male children left the place and built at different places. Those whose daughters were married at Tekidi migrated to Tekidi, and this led to increase in the population of Tekidi. Ocola's people became more that Luru's, and the clan elders built a shrine in front of his house. Ocola became a chief after the death of his father, and it was required by the elders that the shrine was celebrated every year where all of them gathered at Ocola's. Those who came to celebrate the shrine brought many things as offertory before the shrine. On the day of the celebration, men placed their spears on the shrine and elders blessed them. The spears were supposed to remain at the shrine overnight before the owners picked them back.

One morning after the celebration of the shrine, Ocola took one of the spears, before the owners came to take them, and went to check his wire-trap in the bush. The spear he took was his younger brother's, Lwo. He found a mother elephant had been trapped in his wire. Unfortunately, the wire he set was for smaller animals like antelope and buffalo, so the mother elephant had broken the wire, and it was still standing under *opok* tree near a water point. On seeing how the elephant had damaged his wire, he decided to spear the elephant. Ocola then scooped a handful of sand and pour it in the air. The dust flew to the west. This signified that the wind was blowing to the west. Ocola then changed his position from north to west so that the elephant could not sense his presence by smelling. He stalked the elephant and when he drew nearer, the elephant began to move to the other side of the stream. Ocola increased his pace to catch up with the elephant before it crossed the stream.

When he was close enough to the elephant, Ocola hurled his spear, which stoke the thigh of the elephant. The elephant leapt up so wildly that the shaft of the spear came off leaving the blade in the body of the elephant, and the elephant fled into the forest.

Ocola rushed and took the shaft of the spear from the other side of the stream and went back home with it. People gathered under a tamarind tree on the compound to listen to his story. He told them, "I found an elephant had been trapped in my wire, and it broke the wire. I found it standing under *opok* tree and speared it, but it ran away with the blade of the spear in its body."

Elders picked the rest of the spears at the shrine and followed the elephant. Ocola led them to the place where he speared the elephant, and they searched for the elephant in vain, but they did not even get the spear. When Ocola told the men that the spear was not his, they checked their spear, but when Ocola showed them the shaft of the spear, Lwo realised that the spear was his. Lwo was annoyed and quarreled on his brother. "Why did you spear the elephant with my spear and yet yours was there?"

Ocola gave Lwo his spear, but he rejected it. Clan elders tried to mediate between the two brothers, but Lwo could not listen to them, so Lwo and Ocola exchanged words until sun set. Since Lwo refused to take the spear his brother offered him and could not listen to elders, everybody walked away.

Ocola thought to himself, "Why did I take somebody else's spear and yet mine is there? It has brought me problem and I do not know what to do." He then told his wife to pack for him some dry ration to eat as he followed the elephant up to the meeting point between the earth and the sky.

Early in the morning when bulbul was still singing, Ocola said good morning to his father and told him, "Father, I am going to look for the spear of my brother, Lwo, which the elephant ran with it in its body. I want you to know that if I do not find the spear, I will not come back home."

Olum and Lagilo said, "Even if you have not found the spear, you come back home."

Ocola answered, "I am ready to die of hunger in the wilderness. It is better than coming back without Lwo's spear because he will again pester me about it."

Olum took Ocola before the shrine, dipped *olwedo* leaves in a calabash of water and sprinkled it on Ocola and prayed, "My ancestor's God open for you the way, and you do not stumble on any tree stump."

After Olum's blessing, Ocola made straight for the wilderness. He went with five spears and bow and arrows. He walked the whole night, and the following morning he reached where he had stopped with other people who helped to search for the spear the day before. From here, he tracked the elephant to the east. Eventually, he reached a high hill (we do not know its name), and he walked for ten more days before he found the elephant that ran with Lwo's spear in its body. It was standing in burnt bush. Ocola moved towards the elephant, taking care of the direction of the wind lest the elephant should sense his presence.

The elephant began to walk towards a nearby stream. Ocola blew some dust in the air to determine the direction of the wind. It showed that the wind was blowing to the west, and Ocola decided to reach the elephant when it was still drinking water at the stream. He quickly picked one good spear and bowed down to pray to God. After the prayer, he stalked the elephant and speared it with all his might. The spear damaged the elephant's heart and it fell at the stream and bled to death.

Ocola hurried to search the blade of Lwo's spear in the body of the elephant, and he found it. He removed the blade from the body of the elephant, cleaned it with leaves and sat under a tree to rest. He took his packed lunch, filled his gourd with water and began to walk back to the west. When darkness set in, Ocola slept in a cave.

He set out in the morning, but before long, he realised that he had lost his way. Despite his failure to tell direction, he moved on and in the next night, he slept under a tree. The following morning Ocola saw the sun rising from the west instead of the east. This made Ocola more confused and he kept meandering in the wilderness until his packed lunch was almost finished. He came across many footprints which he did not even recognise. In fact, he did not go any farther from where he slept under the tree.

At sun set, Ocola thought he could not find his way back home. Fortunately, he saw some footprints and he followed the track. He trusted that he would follow the woman up to her home, or if she had not yet returned home, he would find her in the wilderness and she would show him the way to his home.

Ocola went up to the water in which the woman was fishing, but she had already left. He crossed the stream and saw the footprints continued ahead. He followed the footprints up to the woman's home. On reaching a sesame garden, his eyes opened and he was able to tell direction, and he walked back home. But when he was about to reach his home, Ocola sat in the bush because he wanted to reach home at night.

Ocola wanted to reach home at night so that his arrival would be a surprise to others. At night, Ocola stealthily walked into his house, and his wife was very frightened on seeing him enter the house and spoke to her in a low voice. "Don't cry. This is Ocola your husband who has returned. Do not shout with my name so that people do not know that I am back." His wife sighed heavily and regained her strength.

The next morning, Ocola did not come out early. He waited for the moment when elders came to comfort his father since he had refused to eat because he thought his son had died in the wilderness. Ocola unexpectedly emerged from his house and and placed a blade of spear before the clan elders. The elders were very surprised to see Ocola and wondered how he came back. They called Lwo and gave his spear back to him, "Child, your brother has returned the blade of your spear which an elephant went with. Here it is," they told him. Lwo received the spear smiling and went back to his home.

When Lwo left, Ocola told the elders, "Elders, I would like to tell you that I suffered a lot in the wilderness, looking for my brother's spear. I survived by God's mercy. For this reason, I want to call myself *Jur* among other people.

Elders thought Ocola was not serious and they paid little attention to what he said because they considered Ocola a very good person. The elders also thought that there would be no more conflict between Ocola and his brother,

Lwo. Unfortunately, the elders were wrong because they did not know that the anger which would destroy peace in the family had started with the spear incident. Olum, on the other hand, knew that his children would one day separate because he observed a lot of changes in Ocola's life.

Before five months elapsed, a serious conflict erupted between Lwo and Ocola. At mid morning, Ocola sat in front of his house threading his beads when children were playing around. Lwo's brilliant son was also playing among the children. When Lwo's son saw a blue bead among the ones Ocola was threading, he stopped playing and sat next to Ocola. The child watched the bead keenly and later took some of the beads and threw one in his mouth. Ocola asked the child to spit out the bead. Due to freight, the child swallowed the bead, and Ocola became so annoyed that he sent for Lwo to come and see what his child had done. Ocola explained to Lwo everything that happened. The child was nearby, so his father asked him, "Is it true that you swallowed Ocola's bead?"

The child answered, "Yes, father. That I swallowed Ocola's bead, is true."

Lwo pleaded to his brother, "My brother, it is true that my son swallowed your bead. Please, let me pay for it with a cow."

Ocola was a very good person. He did not want his brother to pay for the bead, but he just wanted to scare him to instill discipline in him. He thought to himself, "Even if I do not want to be paid, I want to scare Lwo. So, I should tell him that 'I want my real bead.'"

He did this because he wanted Lwo to have the mental trouble as he had when looking for his spear which an elephant ran with in its body. Unfortunately, Lwo did not understand Ocola's intention. He ripped his son's belly open, took the bead and returned to Ocola. The child screamed loudly, and after a short time, he died.

The death of the child perplexed everybody at Tekidi. Lwo took the body of the child and buried it. After the burial, Lwo refused to have the second funeral rite of the child performed. In Acholi culture, when a person died, the body would sleep in the grave for two days, and then clan members converge to investigate the cause of the death that killed him or her. Lwo did not want to tell people the cause of his child's death, so he refused to have the ceremony done.

Clan elders tried with their level best to reunite Lwo and Ocola, but Lwo outrightly rejected all the attempts they made. The death of the child became an abomination between the two brothers. This means members of the two families were not supposed to eat from the same bowl, or drink from the same water calabash/water pot unless the abomination was cleansed. If the offspring of the two families would like to reunite, elders must perform the Acholi cleansing ceremony between them.

Three days after, Lwo called all his people and told them, "My people, Tekidi is not a place to live in, and for this matter, I want you to get ready. Early in the morning tomorrow, we will leave here and go to look for a new place to settle."

The following morning, Lwo set out with his people and moved southwards. Lwo vowed, "God let me die if I meet Ocola." Because he was very upset, Lwo did not talk to his parents when he was leaving Tekidi.

On their way, Lwo's eldest son asked his father, "Is there peace where we are going?"

Lwo answered him, "Everything is in the hands of God. He holds all the power, but whoever does not trust in God, let him return to the womb and be born the second time." This is why Lwo's people were named Jo-ka-Jok, which means the people who trust in *Jok* (God).

Lwo and his people later settled at Budoma in Uganda. After a short rest, they moved on, but some of them remained at Budoma. Those who remained at Budoma called themselves Padhola. Acoli elders say that the word *Padhola* was derived from the word *adola* (ulcer) which was eventually transformed to Padhola.

From Budoma Lwo went to Nyanza where they lived for a short time and moved to the shores of Lake Vitoria and settled there. The people of Chief Owiny also left Tekidi and joined Lwo at the shore of Lake Victoria. Before long, Chief Omolo of Pawir came and settled with Lwo and the people later called themselves Jaluo.

Luru and Coope were not happy to hear what happened between Lwo and Ocola. They wanted to leave Tekidi but could not follow Lwo to the south because he was believed Lwo was wrong.

Luru and Coope moved westwards to Lake Albert and continued to Pakwach at the onset of rainy season. They settled on the western shores of the lake. They called themselves "Lwak Bong-won," which means "people without father" because they had left their father at Tekidi. This is why they called the place where they settled Pu-Bongo. Then after the conflict between Labongo and Gipiir the word Pu-Bungu was transformed to Pubungu or Karaa.

Chapter Seven

GIPIIR AND LABONGO

(The third separation of Lwo at Pubungu)

The people of Luru and Coope settled at Pu-Bongo (Pubungu) for almost one hundred and twenty years, and because there was plenty of food in this place, there was prolific production of children. As a result, the land became little, and some of them migrated to Pawir, Kacung, Kaberamaido and some people went and settled east of Lake Victoria.

Onyango (1976) in his book, "*The central Lwo During The Aconya*" asserts that after a short time at Pubungu, Ongole, Luru's daughter-in-law gave birth to a baby boy. Luru named the child Gipiir to remember the conflict between Ocola and Lwo, and to remember their first grandfather called Lwo. For a better understanding of Gipiir, we will call this child Gipiir II. This name was derived from the Acholi word *pir*, which means feud. After two initiation rites (generations) from his grandfather, Luru died, Gipiir II became the chief and headed the people of Pubungu. His subjects liked him for his good administration and leadership skills. Chief Gipiir II did not take the people of Tekidi as his adversaries on account of the conflict between Ocola and Lwo. He visited the chief of Tekidi who also had courtesy visits to Pubungu. Although there was strong relationship between Chief Kwor and Chief Gipiir, Lwo's family members were not happy (Onyango, 1976, p.72).

There were exchange visits between the people of Wipaco and Pubungu, in Pubungu, and even after the death of Gipiir II, Okene migrated from Wipaco and settled among the people of Coope. Okene came together with his junior wife, Acara. Three months after, Oyuru together with his sister, left Wipaco Dwong and settled at Pubungu, among Luru's people. Oyuru's sister gave birth to a child whom they named Gipiir III. Oyuru married a girl from the house of Luru. The population at Pubungu increased faster because there was peace and enough food.

Okene's wife, Acara gave birth to a baby boy named Labongo, which implies that Okene came to Pubungu without any of his brothers – he was alone. Acholi people usually give the name Labongo to a child whose father is not there, or one who has no brothers. Others name such a child *Bongomin* which means without father or brothers, instead of Labongo. Labongo grew up among the people of Coope and later became a respectable person. Labongo was more brilliant than Gipiir, but they got on very well with each other (Onyango, 1976, p.72).

The separation of Dumo and Nyikango can be compared to the separation of Gipiir and Labongo. Acholi people say that the separation resulted from a conflict about bead and spear. This story is still confusing. Crazzolara, in his book *"The Lwoo Migration Part One"* says, " The history of Shilluk, Anywak and Lokoro talks about Dumo (Dimo) and Nyikango, but the history of Acholi does not say anything about Dumo and Nyikango, but it talks about Gipiir and Labongo, and elders say he became the grandfather of Alur" (Crazzolara, 1954, P, 560).

Different groups of Lwo tell different version of the story of bead and spear. They do not tell the story in the same way. According to Lacito Okech and Reuben S. Anywar, Acholi of Uganda, the spear bead incident happened between Labongo and Gipiir, while Onyangoku-Odongo, Acholi of Uganda states that the separation due to conflict over spear and bead took place between Ocola and Lwo. The people of Alur believe that the separation happened between Tifool and Nyipiir, and the people of Pajok maintain that it happened between Amuda and Agiri, as we shall see later in this book. However, I discovered that the Amuda Agiri separation happened in a narrower context in Pajok. It does not cover the whole Lwo community. For a better understanding of the bead spear conflict between Amuda and Agiri, read *"Amuda and Agiri"* page77.

Crazzolara asserts that the separation because of bead and spear occurred between Dumo and Nyikango. Despite all the disparities in the setting of the story and the people involved in it, the story still remains the same. I think, although the story of bead and spear separation actually took place, the people give different names of those who were involved in the incident and where it took place. The variation may have been caused by the up and down movement of the Acholi people. The story could have been deliberately distorted or people forget certain things about it since it was not written down. It was transmitted orally from generation to generation, and this is a challenge to us writers. Odongo investigated the history of the Acholi among the people of Acholi and Shilluk between 1950 and 1955. Unfortunately, he lost all the information he had obtained when he was imprisoned (Odongo, 1976, p. 32).We would have got a lot of information about the history of Acholi which Onyango received from elders if he had not lost them during his imprisonment.

To Fr. Crazzolara, the information about bead and spear can be got among the people of Jur-Chol in Wau, Bar in Juba, Pajok and Alur and Acholi in Uganda. He thinks that Lwo people use this story to account for the the different separations because there is nothing more they could use to explain the cause of the separations (Crazzolara, 1950, P. 61).

From the information I obtained from elders of Acholi of Sudan and Shilluk, I agree with Crazzolara's conclusion that it is the bead spear conflict which led to separation occurred between Dumo and Nyikango. Fr. Crazzolara postulates that Acholi people do not know what happened between Dumo and Nyikango, but they know, very well that Olum Banya married Acol who was the sister of Nyikango. God blessed them with four children: Tifool, Kamraci, Gipiir and Labongo.

As far as the story of bead and spear is concerned, Acholi people say that one day, elephant grazed in Gipiir's garden. Gipir ran home and picked the spear of his brother, Labongo and speared the elephant with it. The elephant ran with the spear in its body. The following morning Gipiir told Labongo, "My brother, when an elephant came to graze in my garden last evening, I came home and took your spear with which I speared the elephant. Unfortunately, the elephant did not die. It ran with your spear in its body."

Gipiir speared the elephant (Figure 11)

Gipiir pleaded to his brother to allow him to pay for the spear with cows, hoes or anything he wanted. Labongo did not listed to Gipiir's plea, and he said, " I only want my spear."

Gipiir had no alternative to convince his brother to accept his offer, and he told him, "It's okay my brother, I will go to look for your spear which the elephant ran away with and return to you."

Gipiir asked his wife to pack for him food to eat on his way. He also asked three of his friends to accompany him in the wilderness.

In the evening, Gipiir and his three friends set out on the expedition. They walked for sixteen days and found a herd of elephants. A mother elephant called Nyambongo, turned into a human being when she saw the four men approaching them. When they drew closer to Nyambongo, Gipiir told his friends to remain behind because he wanted to meet the mother elephant alone. Nyambongo asked him, "What have you come to do here?"

"I am looking for a spear which I speared with one of your brothers, who was grazing in my millet garden. He did not die. He ran with my spear in its body."

"Since the elephant is not dead, and you are not wrong to spear him, because it grazed in your garden, this is a simple issue. If it had not been so, you would have offered yourself to death as you followed us up to here," said Nyambongo.

68

Nyambongo told Gipiir and his three friends to enter a hut and be silent there. They should wait there until other elephants returned from hunting.

All the elephants returned home in the evening and immediately made straight to sleep, but Nyambongo remained awake, and brought to Gipiir five bundles of long spears for him to search for his among them. After a careful search, Gipiir did not find his spear, and Nyambngo brought another bundle of spears which Gipiir searched in vein. He did not find his spear. Nyambongo brought two more spears and Gipiir immediately saw that one of them was his. He cried in happiness and told Nyambongo, "This is my spear."

Nyambongo handed the spear to him and told them,"Alright, I tell you. You should return home without sleeping on the way because if the elephants wake up from their sleep and sense your smell, they will follow you. If they find you, they will kill all of you."

People waited for Gipiir and his friends for a long time and thought that they may have died. The father of Gipiir, Olum Banya, and clan members wanted to perform Gipiir's funeral rite. In his explanation of the cause of the death of his son, Olum told the people that wilderness consumed his son.

When he found the spear he was looking for, Gipiir thanked Nyambongo very much and asked her if she could help them with more food because they had finished the food which was packed for them from home.

Nyambongo went into the hut and brought some foodstuff into which she put some beads (Acholi people called it *burjok*) and gave them to Gipiir. She did not tell him that she had mixed the foodstuff with beads.

Gipiir received the package with a lot of happiness, and they walked back home. They spent only one day on the journey as the mother elephant told them.

As soon as the four men reached home, Gipiir immediately took the spear to Labongo and told him, "Here is your spear. I managed to find it."

Labongo was glad to receive his spear back. Two or three days after, Labongo's wife visited her brother-in-law, Gipiir. She went with her child who was still crawling.

Labongo's wife sat at Gipiir's door and unstrapped the child to play around. Gipiir was sorting out the beads Nyambongo gave him. The child saw the beads and moved closer to the winnowing fan in which the beads were. A short while after, the child picked a bead and swallowed it.

Labongo's child swallowed a bead (Figure 12)

Gipiir saw everything the child did, but the mother of the child did not see how the child swallowed the bead. Gipiir told her, "When your child was playing, he swallowed one of my beads. I want him to bring back my real bead."

The mother of the child flashed when she heard what Gipiir said. She searched around and found no bead, and Gipiir repeated to her, "The child swallowed the bead." The woman was worried and she sent for Labongo to come and settle the matter.

"Your child has swallowed my bead, and I want my real bead back," Gipiir told Labongo.

Labongo pleaded to Gipiir, "My brother let me give you cows or anything you want." Gipiir refused the offer and said, "I want my bead only."

Some people said that elders asked Gipiir to give his brother two days so that every morning they could search the child's feces. Perhaps they would find the bead in it. Gipiir gave his brother the two days. Labongo and his wife did the same for two days, but did not find the bead. Some people say Gipiir did not give his brother any time. Labongo then told his brother to open the stomach of the child and remove his bead. Gipiir told his brother, "It is okay my brother, I can do it."

Gipiir spread a leopard skin in a winnowing fan and a black cloth. The leopard skin was to show respect for chiefs. He washed the child with fresh milk

70

to signify his curse and secondly so that the bead could be easily seen. Gipiir opened the stomach of the child and took his bead which he showed everybody who was around so that no one would think he was telling a lie that the child swallowed his bead. His brother and his wife stood by and watched everything he did with the child. They wanted to confirm if the child really swallowed the bead. After removing his bead, Gipiir washed the body of the child with clean water and gave it to Labongo. The grieved Labongo took the body and buried it. Gipiir was happy for he found his bead (Crazzolara, 1950, PP. 62-64).

Gipiir ripped open the child's belly (Figure No 13).

Many Acholi elders maintain that this sad incident occurred between Gipiir and Labongo at the foot of Kilaak Hill in Uganda, in Acholiland. Labongo and Gipiir were still under the control of their father, Olum Banya. Olum named himself Banya because he used to borrow things from people and did not return or pay the owners.

Gipiir told Labongo, "My brother, I do not have anything to do with you now. I do not even want to set my eyes on you. I will leave you here and move to the west."

Gipiir and his people moved away and left some Acholi people at the foot of Kilak Hill. Labongo was deeply hurt by the departure of his brother from him. Two days after, Labongo and Kamrasi began to follow Gipiir. Labongo walked for many days and reached the present day Pakwac (in Uganda). Here they learned that Gipiir and his people had crossed the river two day ago. Labongo had moved with cattle and they drove the animal in the water while holding their tails so that they could pull them across the river but did not find Gipiir. They crossed the river back and returned to Kilaak Hill.

Up to today, the people of Labongo and Kamraci are on the eastern side of River Nile, and Gipiir and his people are one the western side of the river. Labongo and Kamraci fixed an axe at the bank of River Nile and the water opened for them to pass. They also planted tobacco at the bank to remind people of what happened between Labongo and Gipiir. It was also a vow that the children of the chief on either sides of the river must not cross the river to the other side. The vow affects children of the two chiefs only. Other people were free to cross the river and visit one another. The scene of the vow is called "wat-lee" or "wat-latong" (i.e. port of the axe) (Crazzolara, 1950, P. 66).

According to Onyango, Gipiir and Labongo separated because of "Nyarubanga famine". Labongo and Gipiir lived together peacefully and united to help their people grow until "Nyarubanga famine" broke out. Acholi called the famine "nyarubanga" because they thought it was God who sent it to punish them. The famine broke out because there was no rain for two consecutive years. Acholi people still talk about the famine today. People lost their domestic animals to thirst. Many Acholi fishers at the bank of River Kiir died because their staple food was fish (Onyango, 1976, P.73).

By the time rain returned, the people who survived the famine had no seeds for sorghum, sesame, etc because they ate them all during the famine. Fortunately, when rain returned, millet, sorghum and other crops sprout from the previous gardens. They waited for the crops to grow and produce seeds. Close to the harvest time, Oyuru, Gipiir's uncle went to steal seeds from Labongo's garden. Unfortunately, Labongo who was returning from hunting caught him stealing and stubbed him to death. Gipiir was angered by this brutal act of Labongo. He denounced Labongo's action. He would rather Labongo held Oyuru as a thief and made him to pay with a goat or sheep. This resulted in serious conflict between Gipiir and Labongo, and Labongo, together with his people, left Pubungu and moved southwards. They followed River Kiir up to Lake Victoria where they crossed to the western side of the river, to a place called "Atoora" nyo "Atura" (Onyango, 1976, PP 73-74).

Labongo also left Pubungu followed the river and eventually settled at a place they called Pawir, and his people dropped hunting, became fishers. They later vacated the place and moved to the eastern bank of the river because of sleeping sickness which had plagued them. Acholi people, in memory of what happened during the famine, sang a *bwola* song as below:

Eiyee! Acuma yee!	O! Acuma
Ku remo kwedi ye!	O! Wait for the blood
Iyee Acara wan waromo kwedi yee	O! Acara we will meet you
Iyee kec ceng omiyoLabongo ocobo	O! Labongo stabbed Oyuru
Oyuru ki pala yee	because of famine

(Onyango, 1976, p.78)

Every Acholi clan has a praise name and ululation alarm. Each ululation has its own meaning. The people of Obbo, for example has the following praise name which is exclusive to them:

Obbo Yee!
Obbo Yee!
Akara Jubi Yee!

It is only the people of Obbo who declaim this praise name. When it is declaimed, every Obbo person will know that an Obbo person is involved in problem, or has speared an animal and young men rush to the scene.

Chapter Eight

AMUDA AND AGIRI

(The separation of Amuda and Agiri at Pajok)

The people of Pajok moved a lot, as we will see in this book. However, according to Onyango-ku-Odongo, the people of Pajok came from Anywak of Ethiopia. He also maintains that when he visited Sudan in 1955, the people of Pajok told him that the bead spear conflict between Amuda and Agiri happened when the people of Pajok were still living with Anywak. He does not give an account of the occurrence (Onyango-ku-Odongo, 1976, p.31). But in my research among the Acholi elders in Juba and Australia, they told me that the conflict between Amuda and his brother Agiri took place in 1882, when the people of Pajok were at the foot of Polila Hill. Other elders told me that it happened between 1924 and 1928. I cannot tell whether it is Onyango's or the elders' claim which is correct. It needs more research. Fr. Crazzolara did write about Amuda and his brother Agiri. If it is true that the conflict occurred between 1924 and 1928, I think Crazzolara must have written about it in 1950. He must have left it out because it was a minor conflict within a small clan. The bead spear conflict happened in many Lwo communities. Onyango states that the bead spear conflict happened between 1088 and 1112 (Onyango-ku-Odongo, 1976, p. 3); Crazzolara asserts that it took place between 1550 and 1600 (?) (Crazzolara, 1950, pp.37-39).

Amuda and Agiri were brothers, and Agiri was the follower of Amuda. Both brothers married from Pamunda family. According to elders of Pajok, the people of Pamunda did not come from Anywak of Ethiopia, but they came from Cwua in Uganda and were hosted by the people of Bura during the reign of Chief Oceng Lokwor-moi. They did not explain how Pamuda and Panyiagiri are related to P'Anyianga at Padibe in Uganda and Okareng in Agoro of South Sudan. So, Pamuda became one of the clans in Bura. Elders contend that Amuda and Agiri did not get on well with each other. They hated each other. We cannot tell whether the conflict between Amuda and Agiri was sparked by disagreement over spear and bead or they were not in good terms before the issue of spear and bead.

The children of the two brothers usually plaid together,r because they lived on the same compound. One morning, two daughters of Agiri were threading beads on the compound. At that time, Agiri's and Amuda's younger children were playing near the girls. One bead darted out of the small calabash and Amuda's child picked it and played with it. Unfortunately, the child swallowed the bead. The child asked the girls, "I have swallowed the bead. Won't it sprout in my stomach?"

Agiri's child began to cry for her bead. When they heard the cry of the child, Amuda and Agiri rushed there to find out what had happened. Agiri asked his child, "What are you crying for?" The child told his father that Amuda's child swallowed her bead. Agiri asked his brother's child, "Why have you swallowed my daughter's bead? Spit it out and give it back to her." He emphasised that "I want you to return my child's bead right now."

"My brother, my child has already swallowed the bead. I now kindly request you to allow us search the child's feces tomorrow and see if we can find the bead and return to you," pleaded Amuda. Agiri arrogantly responded to his brother, "I cannot wait for tomorrow. I want my daughter's bead now, not tomorrow."

This response angered Amuda very much. He laid his child down and ripped his stomach open. He took the bead, washed it and gave to his brother saying, "Alright my brother. Here is your bead. I have killed my child because of the bead." Agiri received the bead, gave it to his daughter and went back to his house. Amuda's child struggled with death and eventually died. He took the body and buried.

Agiri loved hunting very much. One day he went to hunt with Amuda's spear. In the hunting ground, he saw a herd of elephants under a big tree. He moved close to them and speared a mother elephant. Unfortunately, the elephant ran away with the spear in its body. Agiri came back home and reported to his brother, "My brother, I went to hunt and speared an elephant; unfortunately the elephant did not die. It ran away with the spear in its body. I will pay for your spear with another spear."

Amuda responded to Agiri, "My brother, have you forgotten the bead which made me to kill my child. I also do not want anything much. I have already killed my child because of the bead and I also want my real spear. Agiri pleaded to his brother to allow him pay for the spear with cows, hoes or anything, but Amuda did not accept. "I want my spear only!" shouted Amuda.

Realising that he could not convince his brother, Agiri set out for the hunting ground, the following morning, to look for Amuda's spear. He spent two to three months in the wilderness, and he finished the food he packed, and did not find the elephant. He eventually died alone in the wilderness. After a long waiting, people just knew that Agiri had died of hunger and thirst.

Agiri's children prepared a funeral rite of their father after waiting in vein for him to return. The death of Agiri led to a serious conflict between his children and the children of his brother, Amuda. "We look useless to you," said the children of Agiri to the children of Amuda. "We cannot live together with you." They eventually moved away from Amuda's family and settled elsewhere and called themselves "Panyagiri". Although they settled in different places, they still pay funeral rites contribution, but it seems they do not intermarry among themselves.

The conflict between the children of the two brothers lasted very long. They had a reconciliation rite at the time the white man entered Acoliland. Agiri's eldest child slaughtered a goat, took its liver and cut into halves. He gave one half to the children of Amuda to eat, and he ate the other half. They drank *oput* on behalf of their fathers. If their fathers were alive, they would drink it by themselves.

This is how the bead spear conflict separated the children of Amuda and Agiri. However, this separation does not involve the whole Lwo as it took place at the sea, Wipaco, Kaaro, Tekidi and Pubungu. This separation happened in a small family in Pajok. Up to now, the population of the people of Pamuda and Panyagiri is very low. Fr. Crazzolara asserted that the Pamuda people and P'Anyianga are one big clan in Padibe (Crazzolara, 1954, P. 501).

An elder, Jovita Ayang, told me that Pamuda and Panyagiri are one clan with P'Anyianga which remained in Padibe in Uganda. Pamuda and Panyagiri are also one clan with the people of Okareng who are in Agoro in Sudan. Although it is claimed that Pamuda, Panyagiri, P'Anyinga and Okareng are one clan, we still do not know why they should be considered as one clan. When I asked some elders of Pajok such as Paterno Abak and Kadensyo Jada Adinya, they told me that Pamuda came from Cwua-Uganda.

Chapter Nine

OBBO

THE HOME AT OBBO

Obbo is the name given to the place which stretches from Ayaci up to Licari, from Nyara, where Iyire people are, to Cama where one time Itingo-wi settled. The land of Obbo and Pajok are very important in the history of Acholi of South Sudan. Acholi of Sudan hosted and assimilated other people who were not Lwo, and everybody was happy to see that the foreigners entered Acholiland peacefully without any fighting. Even the Sudan Government commented, in the 1928 Rajaf Language Conference at Juba that the people of Obbo and Pajok were as hospitable as the Zande people who were west of Southern Sudan. Many outsiders joined the people of Obbo, Pajok and Zande because of their peacefulness (Crazzolara, 1951, P. 169). Not everybody who lives in Obbo today is a Lwo, but they all speak Acholi now. The history of the Obbo people states that many people who live in Obbo came from different places such as Tirangore, Imila (Katire) Ifwotu, Imurok, Anywak, Goloba (Panyikwara), Loudo (Torit) Baar-Tingiri, Lango-Uganda, Bilinyang (Bar) Lokoro, Duk-pa-dyer (Dinka), Karamoro and Nya-Rubanga (Bar).

Obbo land is different from other places such as Panyikwara, Pajok, Magwi, Palwar, Omeo, Agoro and Ofirika because any crop yields in the land. On the east of this land is Lotii Ranges and Lomarati (Talang-ga) where grasses grow to the height of up to six feet.

As we will read in this book, Obbo people all came from different ethnic groups. The Acholi history also has it that even the indigenous came from

78

somewhere else. The history of Obbo states that the people of Koyo and Kitaka are the indigenous people here. As we will see in this book, the different people at Obbo came to Obbo at different times.

Before we look at the various clans in Obbo, I want us to answer the question, "What does the word 'Obbo' mean?" Some elders at Obbo maintain that 'Obbo' means "people from a foreign land." The word was derived from Lutoku word, 'Lobo' which means "came from a outside or foreign land."

Other elders say Obbo means "people who believed in their might." This name came as a result of the war Obbo fought with different clans such as Pajok, Magwi (Palimu), Agoro, Omeo and Panyikwara (Pakala and Pajaa). This tells us that Obbo liked fighting because they believed in their mighty war prowess. According to Acholi elders, the only people Obbo did not fight, among Acholi of Sudan, are the people of Palwar. Acholi elders say that Obbo did not only fight Acholi of Sudan, but they also fought Iyire, Imurok and Lokoro. Other elders think Obbo came from Lobona which means "Here are some."

The land we called Obbo, long ago, belonged to Koyo. It became known as Obbo in 1700 when Abong people entered the land. It seems the people of Abong renamed Koyo's land as Obbo when Chief Katula took over chiefdom from Omini of Kitaka (Chief of Koyo). Imayi, Katula's father, did not take the chiefdom because he was already old.

According to oral sources, the population of Obbo was larger than the population of any other Acholi groups, but because of the many wars they engaged in, their population drastically reduced. They lost many lives (women, men and children) in the wars. This indicates that Obbo had a very large population, and they compared themselves with *heaven, elephant hide, akara jani, pele-pele kwang*. Therefore, any son of Obbo, who spears an animal in the hunt, shouts their praise name:

Maa yew!!	*Mother yee!!*
Pele-pele Kwang	*Pele-pele kwang*
Akara jani	*Akara jani*
Del Iyiec	*Elephant hide*
Polo Yeeeeeeeee!	*Heaven Yeeeeeeeee!*
Ocamo kwon ki ngur latin!	*He ate bread with a child's vagina!*

How did the story of eating bread with a child's vagina come about? One day, Chief Aburi of Obbo visited Chief Hidye, father of Kanuto of Imurok. When he entered the compound of the chief of Imurok he was welcomed and given water to drink and a seat. In the culture of Imurok, a visitor did not go straight to the chief. The chief's subjects received the visitor, gave him seat and water. After a few minutes of rest, they sent one person to tell the chief that he had a visitor who wanted to meet him. It was the chief to permit the visitor to come to him, or told him to wait.

After Chief Aburi's rest, one of messengers of the chief told him, Chief Aburi of Obbo is waiting outside. He wants to see you."

Chief Hidye told his messenger, "Take to him bread without sauce, then you take a naked female child, open her vagina for Chief Aburi to eat with the bread as food which I should have served him."

The messenger took bread and the naked girl to the visitor. He placed the bread before Chief Aburi and opened the child's vagina and said, Chief, here is bread, but there is no sauce, so you can tap the child's vagina with bread in place of sauce."

Chief Aburi was angered a lot. He took his spear and returned to Obbo. He just forgot what took him to Hidye.

The people of Imurok remained agape for the visitor's declination to eat. The chief's messenger ran back to him and told him, "Chief, your visitor refused the food and he left in indignation."

Hidye called his council of elders and told them to tell their people to collect cell beads. He ordered that the cell beads should be threaded in three different stakes to be taken to the chief of Obbo to pay for the insult the chief of Imurok levied on him. The elders collected the cells from all household and appointed a few people to thread them. They selected people to take the threaded cells to the chief of Obbo.

The delegation set out for Obbo early in the morning. They respectfully entered the chief's compound. The delegation told Chief Aburi, "Chief, we have brought to you cells from our chief to pay for the wrong that happened when you visited Imurok."

Chief Aburi looked at the delegation of Chief Hidye and told them, "I cannot take the cells. Take them back to your chief." The delegation went back and told their chief, "Chief Aburi refused to receive your offer from us."

Chief Hidye told his delegation, I want you to go back and tell Chief Aburi that I am very upset for what happened to him. Secondly, I do not want enmity to develop between us and Obbo. For this reason I give our hunting ground Holok to Obbo.

Chief Hidye's delegation went back to Aburi and told him, "Chief, we have carried the message of our chief. He says he is not happy for what happened to you when you visited him. He said that since you refused to receive the cells he offered to you, he now gives you Holok hunting ground."

Chief Aburi accepted the hunting ground, Holok, smiling and told the delegation, "Alright, I am grateful for Chief Hidye's offer. You can go back."

The delegation went back and told Hidye, "Chief Aburi happily accepted your offer. This is how Holok hunting ground of Immurok became Abong hunting ground.

The people of Obbo are divided into two: Obbo North and Obbo South. Clan elders made this division so that it is easy to notice which Obbo people one is talking about. *Obbo North* and*Obbo South* have the following clans: *Obbo North* has:- Abong, Kitaka, Loudo, Oyere-Lacam, Oyere Lacam Lokomini, Pokongo, Koyo, Tinggili, Ngabara, Iyire South and Pajombo North. *Obbo South* has: Pajombo, Logolo, Padyeri, Opokomere and Lokide.For a better understating of these clans, it is good to look at the bigger groups one by one.

There are six villages that surround Obbo. They are Pajok, Palwar, Katire (Imila), Imurok, Magwi and Panyikwara. The border between Obbo and Pajok runs from Lianga stream to Atebi stream; Bore, hunting ground where Pajok settled belongs to Koyo (Obbo). The border between Obbo and Palwar is at Lianga stream. The boundary between Obbo and Katire is at Upper Talanga Hill; the border between Obbo and Imurok (or Iyire), some people say that it is at Kapai Hill or Lomolong. Others say that the boundary between Obbo and Imurok is at Tul, and between Obbo and Magwi is at Kimoru Stream. Loudo hunting ground which is now called Ayoko is near Okire Hill in Magwi, but some people say that it is at Pa-Loyomoi Hill in Alworo-Alii (Licari). Between Obbo and Panyikwara (Owiny-ki-bul), the boarder is at Atebi stream, because Ongol-kor hunting ground in which the people of Owiny-ki-bul settled is Pajombo's.

OBBO SOUTH

ABONG:-THE RELATIONSHIP BETWEEN ABONG AND THE CHIEFDOM OF

OBBO

According to Crazzolara, long time ago, Abong lived in a place called Akaaro in Kapoeta where Toposa people are today. Abong took more than eighty years in Kapoeta, and they spoke Lango. One day, Loberete and some of his brothers had a quarrel. Chief Loberete took his people from Akaaro and brought them to Tirangore where he died. Abong people lived in Tirangore for a few years. One year there was a serious drought that destroyed their crops and led to famine which claimed some human lives. When Moronyo, Loberete's son saw that his people were dying of hunger, he took them away from Tirangore and took them at the foot of Kapai Hill, where they lived for many years (Crazzolara, 1951, p.170).

The Abong elders whom I asked how their people moved, do not know if Abong came from Akaaro in Kapoeta. Some of the contemporary Abong contend that they hailed from Kafurere (Tirangore). But Abong elders such as Marcello Odiyo and Justice John Ongee Kassiba, who helped me to write about the movement of Abong, told me that Abong came from the east from a place called *Akaaro* and settled at Kapoeta for a year or two and moved to Kafurere in Tirangore during the reign of Chief Ileregi. The people of Abong settled near Chief Ileregi who was a woman who ruled Tirangore. She bore many children, one of whom was called Imayi. Ileregi was a rich chief. She had heads of cattle, sheep and goats. As in Acholi tradition, "the wealth of a parent is the wealth of their children." Ileregi's children were very passionate about their mother's wealth. The wealth and power conflict between them erupted many times. As a result, Chief Imayi took his people to the south of Tirangore.

According to elders of Abong Chief Imayi took the people of Abong from Tirangore. When Chief Imayi found hardship in living in Tirangore, he decided to leave the place when his mother was still alive. Around 1700 Imayi led the people of Abong and Tirangore towards Lotii Hill. Oral sources state that Imayi left Tirangore because of power conflict. He took part of his mother's wealth (cattle and sheep) and moved *south-west*. When Imayi was still in Tirangore he heard that fertile farm land was in (south west). They moved on, looking for pastures for their animals and land for cultivation. But Crazzolara contends that it is Chief Loberete who took Abong people out of Tirangore and brought them to Acholiland. Because of hard life at Triangore, Chief Loberete decided to leave the place (Crazzolara, 1950, p.171). Around 1700 Loberete led Abong out of Tirangore towards Lotii Hill. Some people say Luberete left Tirangore because of power wrangle. He moved with his people south-west. When Chief Loberete was still in Tirangore he heard that a fertile land for cultivation was on the south west. They moved on looking for pastures for their animals and cultivable land. They reached Iyodo stream from the north and settled there for one year. After harvesting their millet, they moved away and settled at the foot of Ifwotu Hill.

Abong did not take long at the foot of Ifwotu Hill because young men kept looking for a better way out of there. One day they got a track which they followed up to Lomolong. The place became too small since they had many animals in their hands.

Acholi elders maintain that though the place was too small, the people of Abong did not move away immediately. They cultivated their crops there for one year. They saw the smoke raised from the settlement of the Kitaka people, but it was too far away. Some elders say the Kitaka people also saw the smoke at the settlement of the Abong people at the foot of Lomolong Hill but they did not know which people were there.

From Lomolong Hill, the people of Abong moved to Kapai Hill near Kimoru Hill from the north. Kapai Hill is in Lohile Hunting ground. From Kapai, Abong saw Bokoro hunting ground from the other side of Kimoru stream. They lived here for a few months and shifted to a fertile land along Kimoru stream. Secondly, the land was also large enough to graze their animals.

From this place, Abong people saw the smoke from Kitaka people was nearer. They lived at the foot of this hill for many years. Chief Loberete came with a wife from Akaaro. They had a child, whom they named Moronyo, from Tirangore. After the death of Chief Loberete at the foot of Kapai Hill, his son, Moronyo became a chief. Many Obbo elders said that Chief Moronyo led his people very well. Moronyo married and had a son whom he named Katula. After the death of Chief Moronyo, Katula took up the chiefdom. The people of Obbo contend that Chief Katula also led the people well like his father. Chief Katula had a wife with whom they had a son called Lobeta or Lobitak.

When Chief Katula died, his son, Lobeta inherited the chiefdom. He also led the people so well that they loved him a lot. Chief Lobeta married a woman with whom he had a son called Kabeke. When Lobeta died, his son, Kabeke became the next chief. Chief Kabeke also married and had a child called Ogwe.

Chief Kabeke led the people well as Crazzolara reports that one day, in a dry season Chief Kabeke called people to a hunting expedition. When people set the bush on fire, Chief Kabeke followed his people on the hunting ground, together with other people. Unfortunately, because they were late, they did not know where the first group of hunters were. The chief followed a route which took them in an isolated bush in which fire surrounded them. Chief Kabeke and the people who accompanied him were burnt in the bush. After the death of the chief, his son, Ogwe was enthroned. As we have seen above Chief Loberete, Moronyo, Katula, Lobitak and Kabeke all died at the foot of Kapai Hill. This indicates that the people of Abong lived at the foot of Kapai Hill for about one hundred and eight (108) years because at that time the life span of a man was 27 years and a woman's was 35 years.

Chief Ogwe, when he found that life was hard at Kapai and took his people to Kimoru Stream where they lived for a few years. Chief Ogwe kept visiting Imurok when they were at Kimoru Stream where he got a wife, a daughter of Imurok from Lotuko clan. Chief Ogwe died before his wife conceived. So, he did not have any child who could inherit his chiefdom. Therefore, Tokboye or Tok-boye, the brother of Ogwe's father became the chief (Crazzolara, 1951, p.170).

Chief Tok-boye married and had a child called Malakiteng.

After the death of Chief Tok-boye, his son, Malakiteng inherited the chief-dom. It is said the Malakiteng led his people as well as his father did. Chief Malakiteng and his wife had a child whom they named Iliri. After the death of Chief Malakiteng, the chiefdom was left in the hands of Iliri. Chief Iliri and his wife had a child called Imayi. Chief Ogwe, Tok-boye and Malakitang all died at Kimoru Stream. It was Chief Iliri who took the people of Abong away from Kimoru stream and settled with them at Ayii Stream (Crazzolara, 1951, p. 170).

THE COMING OF ABONG TO OBBO

The people of Abong were the third group of people to join the people of Kitaka and Lokide. They followed the people of Pajombo Okwee and Pokongo. The history of the Acholi of Obbo states that Kitaka were the first people to join the people of Koyo, folllowed by Lokide Pokongo and Pajombo respectively.

Chief Iliri spent only a few days at Ayi stream and died. After his death, his son, Imayi was enthroned.When Chief Imayi realised that the land at the stream was too small for his people and their animals, he moved his people to Luul near Lerwa Hill among Koyo people. When the people of Abong were at Luul, Agwinya, son of Imayi, was visiting Koyo, and eventually married daughters of Koyo. The senior wife was called Apuul. She gave birth to Kaciba, and the junior wife was called Acaa. From Luul Abong moved to Ayom Hill where they lived for about two years. Abong left the hill and went back to Kimoru stream where they lived for a few years. Because of the good relationship between them and Kitaka, Abong migrated to Lotii Hill where Crazzolara met them in 1937. Abong moved from Kimoru stream, as elders told me, because one day when some boys were herding their animals, they reach the gardens of Kitaka people. They went back home and told Chief Imayi, "Chief, when we were herding animals, we came across some gardens which are close to us here."

Chief selected ten boys to wait and see if the owner of the gardens would come to their gardens. When they reached there, the boys found Kitaka working in the gardens. Kitaka used to wear animal skin round their waist, but Abong were still moving naked. When the Kitaka farmers saw the Abong boys who were naked and with spears in their hands, they were frightened and they ran away — they left their seeds in the garden.

The Lotuko boys went back home and reported to the chief, "Chief, we found people working in the garden, but they ran away when they saw us."

The Kitaka gardeners also reported to Chief Omini Iliri, "Chief, there are some naked people with spears who got us in the garden. Because we had never seen such people before, we were frightened and we ran away from them."

Chief Omini told the gardeners that "I want some of you to go back to the garden and find out if these people will come back to the gardens."

Chief gave these people spears and clubs and told them, "If the naked people come back to the garden, show them the clubs and point at them with the shafts of your spears with the blades of the spears pointing at you. After this, give them the spears."

Omini instructed his people to do this because in Acholi culture, if you meet people you do not know, you point at them with the end of the shaft of your spear to let them know, "We do not have any problem with you." If you point at them with the blade of the spear, it means there is enmity between you and them. Kitaka was to do this to show Abong that there was nothing wrong between them and Kitaka.

When the Kitaka gardeners reached the gardens, they found six Abong boys standing at the edge of the gardens. Kitaka gardeners drew closer to them, picked the spear which their chief gave them and pointed at the boys as they were instructed. The later, they gave the spear and a club to them.

Pointing at people with the end of the shaft of spear and with the blade was not new to Abong. It seems they knew it because Lotuko also had the same culture. When Kitaka pointed at them with the end of the shaft, they just knew there was no problem between them and Kitaka. So, they were not scared, and they went with the gardeners and met Chief Omini. He was sitting on the compound waiting for the message his people would bring. Omini and gave them food and water. Unfortunately, Abong did not know Kitaka language. They spoke only Lotuko.

Chief Omini communicated to them in body language, and they also responded in body language. Fortunately, they all understood the body communication that went on between them.

"Where did you come from?" Omini asked the boys.

"We were sent by our chief. If you want to know where we come from, you need to talk to our chief because he also wants to meet you," answered the boys.

Chief Omini immediately told his people, "These boys can go back to their place. I also want to meet their chief."

Before the boys set off for their place, the chief ordered his people to give them alcohol, water and food. They brought for the boys *boo* dish which was heavily pasted with sesame paste, but without meat in it.

The boys took water and alcohol and left the food untouched because they did not know 'boo'. Kitaka informed their chief that the boys did not eat the food offered to them. They only drank alcohol and water. Chief did not answer them.

Lotuko boys returned to their home and showed their chief what Chief Omini gave and all he did to them. Imayi was very happy to receive the news.

After one month, the chief of Kitaka sent his messengers to Chief Imayi to tell him that he wanted to talk to him. Chief Imayi welcomed the message and told the messenger from Kitaka, "Go back home and tell your chief that I am visiting him tomorrow."

The Kitaka messengers went and told their chief, "Imayi said that he is visiting you tomorrow." Chief Omini nodded to signify that he understood the coming of the visitor.

The next morning Chief Imayi set out for Kitaka accompanied by twenty to thirty people. When they entered the compound of Kitaka they found Chief Omini waiting for them, surrounded by his people.

Chief Imayi and his people went naked. Women and children were shamed when they saw these people. They all ran in the house. But Chief Iliri and other men remained to welcome the children of Abong.

Before the visitors from Abong sat down, Kitaka people pointed at them with the end of the shaft of spear to communicate to them that there was nothing wrong between them and leaned the spear on a granary.

Chief Imayi's people also did the same to their hosts and placed the spear on the ground. After this, Chief Iliri showed his visitors where to sit. After the visitors had taken water, Chief Omini asked Chief Imayi the same question which he asked the Abong boys, "Chief, where do you come from? What are you looking for?"

"We came from Tirangore. We are looking for land for cultivation and pastures for our animals. We came to your place because we have had serious conflicts with some of our brothers at Tirangore." responded Chief Imayi.

Omini did not respond to the answer of his counterpart. He turned to his people and ordered, "Bring water and alcohol to the visitors. Do not bring sauce and bread because Abong people may not eat them." The chief said this because he remembered that when Abong boys came to Kitaka for the first time, they did not eat *boo* sauce because they did not know vegetable.

Kitaka people served Abong visitors with alcohol in a big calabash and put small calabashes to be used as cups. Alcohol was one of the favourites of Lotuko people. They drank it to their fullest.

After the feast, Chief Omini gave his friend one billy goat and a ram. He led his friend to the grazing ground and showed him the size of the billy goat and the ram by sign language, "I want to give you a billy goat and a ram."

Chief Imayi understood everything his friend told him and told him, "I have enough domestic animals. Thank you for the offer, but I request that you keep the billy goat and the ram in your grazing ground."

Omini did not object to his friend's advice, but his keeping the animals with him did not mean they were Chief Imayi's. Chief Omini of Kitaka therefore kept them as his.

In the evening, some Kitaka people escorted Chief up to the garden where Abong boys, one day, found them cultivating.

After one month Chief Omini sent his messengers to Chief of Abong, and told him, "Chief Omini sent us to tell you that he wants to visit you." Chief Imayi told them, "Go and tell Chief Omini that I have no objection to his visit. My friend can come and see my people."

The messengers went back and told their chief, "Chief Imayi said you can visit his people. He does not have anything against you."

Two days after, Chief Omini selected about twenty to thirty people to go with him, and he told them, "I want to go to my friend's, so I want you to accompany me."

The following morning, Chief Iliri and his retinue set out for Kimoru Stream which they reached in the evening. Before they entered the home of Abong, the chief of Kitaka turned the blade of his spear to point backward to show that he did not have any problem with them. The messengers at the gate received Chief Iliri with a lot of respect and led him to Chief Imayi.

Chief Imayi was very happy to see his friend. He gave his visitors seats and asked one of his messengers to bring water and food for them.

Long ago, the people of Lotuko used to drink alcohol with clay vase and pot. They served their Kitaka visitor alcohol in pots and vases. They sat round the pots and vases with the visitors on the right and the host on the left. The hosts brought a medium size calabash (because in Lotuko people drank alcohol with the medium size calabash). When the Kitaka people saw the calabash, they told their host, "In our culture we do not drink alcohol with medium size cala-bash, but the smallest, called 'abit'." One Abong messenger quickly dashed into the house and brought five small calabashes, which were scrubbed clean with sand. As Kitaka drank with the small calabashes, Abong used the medium size as they usually did.

Before people were drunk, Chief Imayi took his friend to his grazing ground where he offered one billy goat and a nanny goat. Chief Iliri did not turn down his friend's offer. He took them to show gratitude to his friend. Chief Iliri offered his friend three shields and three spears. Acholi shield usually bore a round head called *lalem*, but the one Omini gave to his friend did not have it. After the exchange of gifts, the two chiefs went back to the drinking party.

Chief Iliri thanked Chief Imayi who was also very grateful for Chief Iliri's visit to the people of Abong. He said that kind of visit should continue because it could build trust among people. Secondly, it would make Abong people learn Acholi language faster. The two chiefs shook hands and the visitors set off for their home.

Because of the strong relation between Abong and Kitaka, Abong continued to graze around the Kitaka gardens. Despite the good relationship, Omini was not happy because his friend still walked naked. He did not tell Imayi that it was bad to walk naked, but he prepared a very good goat skin, a month after his visit, and sent it to his friend to wear.

Chief Imayi happily received his friend's offer, but he refused to wear it. He kept it in his house and continued walking naked. He only wore the skin when he was going outside Abong. Abong people eventually liked the skin their chief wore. They also began to make their own and some for their chief. They later realised that it was not good for them to wear skin when going out only, but it was also good to wear it even at home.

Much as Abong and Kitaka were great friends, they did not cultivate in the same place, but during harvest period they took some of their harvests to the Chief Imayi as required by their chiefdom. The first harvest should be taken to the chief for blessing so that the next harvest was good. Therefore, they took the first to their chief and others to the chief of Kitaka. The people of Kitaka, having seen what the people of Abong were doing to their chief; they embraced the practice and began to do the same. The good life that Abong and Kitaka lived, as friends, made Kitaka to remove Abong from the bank of Kimoru stream and to Kitaka. Chief Omini gave them Bokoro hunting ground to settle in. That is why, up to date, Bokoro belongs to Abong. When they found that Bokoro was not a fertile land, Abong migrated to Luul where they lived for a few ears and moved to Alia (Palotaka). They took a short time in Alia before they moved to Lotii Hill where they met the people of Obbo. Together with Obbo, Abong migrated back to Luul. They lived here peacefully for a short while before they moved to Pakwa Hill, and eventually to Malaya Hill, where they lived for about two or three years, and eventually moved to Ayi Stream.

At the time Obbo was looking for a place to settle, according to elders, some of the smaller clans which are today under Obbo were not yet there with them. The existing clans were Kitaka, Koyo, Lukide and Pokongo. Abong was the third group which joined them. When Chief Imayi reached Obbo, he saw that Chief Omini ate on top of anthill. His wife took for him food there climbing. It is obvious that Abong joined Kitaka and Koyo peacefully. They obtained the chiefdom of Obbo because of their peacefulness, and the chief of Abong was very generous, unlike Chief Omini who was selfish. Many times, his visitors slept hungry. On the other hand, Chief Omayi's visitors did not sleep hungry or thirsty because he ate at the fire place on the compound where everybody (children, orphans, etc) ate from. He often invited Omini's people to join them at meals.

When people saw that the chief of Lotuko ate together with people, they said, "It is Chief Imayi who can bring the people of Obbo together. He did not despise visitors and orphans; they sat together with him at the fire place." As a result, Kitaka people began to respect Imayi as their chief, and he later took over Omini's chiefdom. This made him to head the people of Kitaka, Koyo and Abong. In deed he was able to bring the three groups together as one. When he was about to die, the chief of Kitaka strongly instructed his people that after his death, they should be under the leadership of the chief of Abong. He told Padyeri people to hand over their rain-hill to the chief of Abong.

Abong respected their chief as Lotuka respected theirs. They usually collected first harvest and white ants and and took to their chief. They also took to the chief meat when they came back from their hunting expedition. The Acholi tradition did not allow a chief to beat his wife, neither was he allowed to go for hunting because he was the one to gives blessing to his people. The practice of showing respect to a chief by taking food staff to him was not in Obbo. I also agree with Tim's statement, "Collecting food staff for a chief was a very important practice among the people of Palwo, but it seems Obbo did not copy the practice from Palwo, but from Abong because long ago, Lotuko collected foodstuff for their chiefs (Tim, 1985, P.37).

Samuel Baker has it that between 1860 and 1865, though Chief Kassiba was very old, he was respected a lot. Chief Kassiba had high authority over the people of Obbo because he had the power of rain in his hands. If someone annoyed him, or did not want to participate in foodstuff collection for him, he would curse such person's animals to death. The chief also scared his subject that if they did not collect foodstuff for him, he would make their food burn in the garden with drought. This confirms to me the fact that his subjects continued to raise foodstuff for him. Oral sources has it that in 1860s there was no tax among the people, but when he wanted anything, Chief Kassiba asked his people to bring to him any number of goats or sheep he mentioned. Fortunately, he used not to ask for such payment frequently. So, when he asked them to make such payment, his subjects did it without grumbling because they loved him. Chief Kassiba was also a very wise chief, and when there was too much rain, he called his subject and told them, "I want to tell you that I am not happy because of bad things some of you have been showing recently. I want you to know that, that is why I have sent much rain this month. When there was no rain he said it was such reason which made him to withdraw rain from them. You should be aware that this has happened because of your offense. If people do not want to bring for me foodstuff, then what is the reason why I should rain for them? If you don't bring for me goats, forget about rain. This is what we all agreed upon, my people." If some people refused to listen to him, he threatened them. If they remained defiant after the threat, the following day, he sent rain with hailstorm. If Obbo persons wanted to go on visit, they had to obtain their chief's blessing first. This blessing protected them from rain drenching them on the way and from attacks by wild animals such as lions, buffaloes, leopards and elephants. Because of the power Kassiba exhibited, Sir Samuel Baker called him Doctor of Magic. This indicates how the culture of Lotuko was practised in Obbo (Sir Samuel Baker, 1875, PP, 317-318).

When I asked Obbo elders how Chief Imayi came to Obbo, they told me that in the month Chief Imayi entered Obbo, there was a lot of rain, and people collected a lot of white ants. As required by their culture, Abong people collected white ants and took to their chief. The subjects of Chief Omini saw what the people of Abong did and they also raised white ants from every household and took to Imayi to show their respect to him. To continue showing their respect for the chief of Abong, the people of Lokomini accepted to cultivate together with the people of Abong for the chief of Abong, and they learned the new idea from them.

When Chief Omini Iliri was critically ill, he called all the elders of Kitaka and told them, "I think my day is not far now. For that matter, I want you to be united and help our posterities, but before I tell you everything, I want to hear from you. What do you think about the future?"

"We would like you to leave your chiefdom to the people of Abong because we have seen that he is capable of leading well," responded the elders."

Chief Omini had no objection to the elders' advice, but he thought that Chief Imayi was so old that he would not lead Obbo for long before his death. Considering this factor, Chief Omini left his chiefdom in the hands of Tok-boye, son of Chief Imayi to whom he gave the rain-stone, *Nyar-itali*.

Sudanese say different things about the rain-stone of Abong. Some people say that after a few months in Obbo, Chief Omini gave his rain-stone to Chief Imayi. Abong came from Tirangore without any rain-stone. They inherited the rain-stone of the people of Lokomini. Others say that Abong came with their rain-stone.

According to some people, Abong entered Obbo by fighting in which they raided the rain-stone of the Kitaka people. In his *Acholi Decision Making: Paper for Norwegian Church Aid Sudan Programme*", Tim Alley maintains that "Abong entered Obbo by fighting. They fought us and took our rain-stone and our god, Jikiloti" (Mr. Tim, 1985, p.7).

When the elders of Kitaka and Abong were for the coronation of Chief Tok-boye, Chief Omini gave him his royal stool to use. He also gave Tok-boye his spear, knife, crown and a black rope to wear round his neck.

Chief Omini ordained Chief Tok-boye in the presence of Abong elders who guided him how they, Lotuko, ordained their chiefs. Chief Omini did exactly what the elders told him. He rubbed *logoyi oil* in Tok-boye's right and left hands and put some on his forehead and his chest.

In the tradition of Acholi of Sudan, it is only the royal family which can do the coronation of the chief. That is why the royal family of Kitaka coroneted Tok-boye. In the absence of the royalty of Kitaka, the royal house of Pakongo would be called to perform the same because the Lokomini who are in Pakongo came from the royal family of Kitaka. That is why the Pakongo are entitled to coronate the chief in Obbo.

Logoyi oil for anointing the chief was kept in an animal horn in the chief's house. When a chief is being coroneted, a royal man gets the oil from the house of the chief's wife.

Before he died, Chief Omini together with Chief Imayi, called the people of Kitaka and Abong and told them, "You should all live together without segregation. You should consider yourselves one people. If there is any problem, stand together as a people."

Kitaka people and Abong people accepted the idea of the two chiefs. That is why, up to now, Abong and Kitaka move together when going for hunting. The unity among the people of Kitaka and Abong is not only seen in hunting, but also in their building, traditional dances. The two groups of people live in one settlement and also dance together as one people.

The Lotuko whom today we call Abong joined Acholi in the name of Lotuko and later the Kitaka called them "*bong*", which means foreigners. Lotuka usually put the letter "a" at word initial position of most words such as "*mile*," is an Arabic word for salt which Acholi called "*kadomile*". Since "mile' is not a Lotuko word, they added "a" in front of it and it became "amile" among them. "Kubaya" is also an Arabic word which means a small calabash for drinking water or tea, and it has also been transformed by Lotuko speakers into "akubaya" for they added "a" in its word initial position. They have added "a" in front of "cabun," an Arabic word, and made it "acabun" and many others. That is the same reason why Lotuko people added "a" before the word "Bong" and it became "Abong."

Chief Tok-boye and his wife begot a son called Lolori. When Tok-boye died, Lolori, his son inherited his chiefdom. He also led the people well. He had a son called Lojik. Lojik became chief when his father died, and had a son called Agwinya, who inherited the throne from his father. He led the people of Obbo well and never led them to war. The chiefs Tok-boye, Lolori, Lojik ki Agwinya led Obbo when they were at the foot of Lotii Hill (Crazzolara, 1951, p.170).

In the year Agwinya became chief was a bad one to the people of Obbo because of a very serious drought which burnt their crops in the garden. There was hardly any pasture for their animals. Chief Agwinya, consequently brought his people to the foot of Lotii Hill. When the people of Obbo migrated here an elder, Pido-moi, of Koyo decided to move to Ayom Hill in Panyikwara.

Chief Agwinya's leadership also went on well. His first children were twins who were followed by a boy named Okelo. In the month they named the child, chief had a visitor from Bar. The visitor asked the women who were naming the child, "What have you named the child?" The chief's wife told him, "We named him Okelo." The Bar man asked again, "Can I also give the child a name?"

The Abong women answered him, "In our culture, a male child who follows twins is automatically named Okelo. But if the child is a girl, she is named Akelo. Since you are the chief's visitor, we can allow you to name the child." The visitor took *olwedo* twig, dipped in water and sprinkled it on the child and named him Kassiba. Eventually the child's name Okelo was replaced by Kassiba.

CHIEF KASSIBA INHERITED OBBO CHIEFDOM
Crazzolara states that after the death of Chief Agwinya the people of Ngabara and Iyire enthroned Kassiba the chief of Obbo, but I know that Crazzolra's statement is not true because the chiefdom of Abong had already been left in the hands of a child. Chief Kassiba was the first chief in Obbo to object to Arab slave traders who were based in Palodo. Chief Kassiba did not know Arabic, so he made Lawele his interpreter to communicate to Arab slave dealers that he wanted them to leave Obbo. Kassiba realised that the Arabs did not respect his order; they continued with slave trade. One day, around 9:00 am, musketeers announced an illegal entry of some foreigners in Obbo. On receiving this announcement, Chief Kassiba was frightened that Arabs might have come to kill him. He hid himself in a big granary. Later on it was discovered that the foreigner was not an Arab, it was Samuel Baker. Acholi elders maintain that Samuel Baker entered Obbo on 04/05/1863.

Chief Kassiba had a son whom he liked very much. His name was Otoo, he used to call him Olworo, and then later Arabs gave him the name Ibrahim. (Crazzolara, 1950, PP.170-171). Pronouncing the name was hard for Acholi people, so they nativised it to Abarayi. Therefore, in this book, I will often use the name Abarayi or Otoo.

Justice John Onge told me that Chief Kassiba had many wives, but the people of Obbo could remember only two of them: Min Locii, the most junior wife, and Lanaka Ajuc sister of Akut Lowaramoi. It is said that the mothers of Lanaka Ajuc and Akut Lowaramoi came from Bobi (Pajok), but the father of Lanaka Ajuc me Pajombo Obbo. It was Lanaka who was the royal wife of Chief Kassiba. She gave birth to a son called Abarayi Otoo. In Acholi culture when a chief dies, it is his first son, born of the senior wife, who inherits his chiefdom.

According to Sir Samuel Baker, in the olden days, the people of Obbo gave to Chief Kassiba many of their daughters. That is why he had many wives. He had at least a wife in every village in Obbo. Whichever corner of Obbo he went, he was at home. Since he had many wives, Kassiba had 160 children. There was one woman among his wives who was barren. When Sir Samuel Bake came, she thought that a white man might have medicine for bareness. The woman asked Sir Samuel Baker to give her medicine which could make her conceive, because her husband became rude to her and did not like her for failing to produce children for Abong clan. Sir Samuel Baker knew that he did not have the medicine the woman wanted, but to please her, he gave her contraceptive pills. The woman was pleased that Sir Samuel Baker gave her the medicine which would cure her bareness (Sir Sammuel Baker, 1866, Vol 1 PP 316-320)

Lowaramoi was the rain chief of Pajombo when his sister Ajuc Lanaka got married to Kassiba. He also gave rain to Abong. Rwot Lowaramoi gave the Pajombo rain to Abong to pay for Odong god and Odano god.

When Abong received rain from Lowaramoi, Chief Kassiba told him, "Since you have lost your rain together with Pokongo and Lukide (who have rain) we do not have any problem with you. You can look for a piece of land which is good enough for you and settle there." Chief Kassiba told the people of Pajombo, Pokongo and Lokide that if there was any problem with the people of Abong, they should help, and Abong people would also help them if they were in problem.

The history of Obbo states that Sir Samuel Baker reached Chief Kassiba's home on 05/05/1863. By then Kassiba was in Iyele (or Lapiem) which is now called Ayaci. Kassiba was between 58 to 60 years of age, but there was still no grey hair on his head. When Sir Samuel Baker entered Obbo, Kassiba called his people to dance before their visitor for that was one of the ways people could welcome a visitor. It is said that up to one hundred people came for the dance. When they were dancing, the wind began to blow so strongly that it nearly stopped them. Because he had some magical power, Kassiba stopped the wind and told the dancers to go on. This was *bwola* dance which was performed with the male dancers holding a small drum, made of elephant ear skin, in the left hand. They danced to the rhythm of the mother drum (i.e. the big drum). In the past, the Acholi *bwola* dancers wore leopard skin, Columbus monkey skin, antelope skin or goat skin. Girls wore apron skirt which was four inches wide and two inches long. The rest of the body remained naked (Sir Sammuel Baker, 1866, Vol 1 P, 314).

Samuel Baker realised that Kassiba was different from other chiefs whose places he passed via, such as and Lotuko. According to Samuel Baker, the chief of Lotuko liked asking for assistance, but Chief Kassiba liked conversation and was not interested in loftiness. Obbo people liked and trusted Kassiba very much. It is said that they loved him for two things: he was their chief and he cured many sick people. So, no one should annoy him. He cursed to death the goats, chicken, cows of anyone who annoyed him. If he did not want to kill the person's animals, he would scare him that he would make it rain in his gardens. This kind of expression scared them so much that they did not err to the chief (Sir Samuel Baker, 1866, Vol 1 P. 317). When it rained or did not rain during cultivation period, it gave the chief time to show his subjects his power to make rain or bring drought. When there was no rain, he told his people, "I am very unhappy with the crude behavior of some of you which made me to levy this punishment on you, but we should know that this is because of the misconduct of a few of you. If they do not want to raise their share for me, than what is the use of giving them rain. I want you to know that if there is no goat for me, there is also no rain for you."

Sir Sammuel Baker says that when he was in Obbo, Chief Kassiba told him every thing about Obbo. Baker reached Obbo in May, a rainy season. Kassiba knew that Baker wanted to cross Aswa, so he told Baker to first camp at Obbo, or go back to Tirangore to wait for dry season, when the water must have gone down, Sir Sammuel Baker, 1866, Vol 1 P, 322). Sir Sammuel Baker listened to the chief and decided to go to Pajok instead of Uganda. He left his wife and his guards with Kassiba. The history of Obbo states that Chief Kassiba offered a hut of a diametre of 9 ft. to Mrs. Baker. The hut was smoothly smeared with cow dung. He ordered his people to tether one fat sheep on each of the forked pole of the hut in which Mrs. Baker slept. Baker took three men with him and went to Pajok.

Chief Kassiba was aware of the fact that the best dish for a visitor, in Acholi, was chicken. So, one day he collected chickens from his people to feed Mrs. Baker. Kassiba knew his subjects very well. He knew that if he sent his guards to collect chicken from the people in the villages, they would refuse to give them. Chief Kassiba drew closer to Mrs Baker and told her, "My people are not good. If I send my guards to collect chickens from them, they will say that they do not have chicken, but if I go together with guards, people will fear and give the chickens. I therefore request you to give me one of your horses to go on."

The chief made this request, as their history has it, because he used to ride on a billy goat when moving around among his people.

Mrs. Sir Sammuel Baker gave Kassiba a horse called Tetel (hartebeest). Kassiba thought riding a horse was as easy as riding a billiy goat. Mrs. Baker also warned him, "Chief, if you do not ride the horse well, it will drop you and you will break your leg or hand." Chief did not heed to the piece of advice. Mrs. Baker's guards helped chief to mount the horse. After mounting the horse, chief commanded the horse in Acholi, "Eno citi!" (Okay, go now!). Unfortunately, the horse did not understand Acholi language, but only English. So the horse did not move. Then the chief asked it in Acholi, "Pingo pe imito wot?" (Why don't you want to move?). He thought the horse was just pretending and did not want to start walking intentionally. Mrs. Baker's guard told Kassiba, "Tap the horse with a stick if you want it to run." Kassiba hit the side of the horse with his scepter. The horse jerked and began to run, and Kassiba fell down and sprained his hip joint. The Acholi culture did not permit laughter when a chief fell. But at that moment, everybody broke into laughter. Even Mrs. Baker also laughed at him. Mrs Baker's guards held the chief by the hand and helped him to his feet. When he got up, the chief looked at the horse with displeasure. Kissiba was a man who did not keep things to heart. A short while after, he told his wife to bring for him alcohol. After taking *kwete* alcohol, he told the people who were around, "You see, this horse is very high." He again asked Mrs Baker if she could give him a lower horse. But there was no low horse except donkeys. Mrs. Baker's guards helped the chief on the donkey's back. One man held him from the right and the other from the left. In just a minute, Kassiba started moving on the donkey with a smile on his face. He went with one of his wives to carry for him his *kwete* to drink on his way. In the villages, Kassiba collected chickens from his people telling them, "There are thirty visitors in my home. They came from Turkey. That is is why I want you to give chickens. If you do not do so, they will burn all our homes." When they heard about burning their homes, Kassiba's subject willingly gave the chickens to Chief Kassiba. He went back home and told the elders that people gave chickens without any question (Sir Sammuel Baker, 1866, Vol 1 P, 334).

We cannot tell how many days Sir Sammuel Baker spent in Pajok, but he returned to Obbo. The history of Obbo says that when Sir Samuel Baker was about to reach Kassiba's home, he blew a whistle. One of his guards called Saat ran to Mrs Baker and announced to her, "Master has arrived." A while after, Baker entered the compound and found his wife squatting with a calabash in her hands to welcome her husband, just the way Acholi women welcomed their husbands when they returned home. Before he spoke to anyone, Sir Samuel Baker made straight to the chief who also joined in welcoming him. When Baker was resting outside, his wife told him all the good things Kassiba did for her when Baker was on his visit to Pajok. On 21/5/1863, Sir Samuel Baker together with his friend, Ibrahim moved to Tirangore (Sir Sammuel Baker's main camp). Acholi history tells us that, when Baker was leaving Obbo, Kassiba dipped a twig of olwedo in a small calabash of water and ceremoniously sprinkled it on them to bless him, his wife and their guards to reach their destination well. After the supplication, Kassiba gave the twig to his brother whom he instructed to escort Baker and his people. He did this to stop rain from drenching his visitors on their way (Sir Sammuel baker, 1866, Vol 1 P, 337).

ABARAYI BECAME THE CHIEF

Kassiba, as we have seen above, had only one child with his wife Ajuc Lanaka. They named the child Abarayi Otoo who grew up and married nine women.

No	Wife's name	Daughter of	Clan	Mothered
1	Min Akat(Ariyai)	?	Pokongo	Akat(Ariyai)
2	Aber Lokono	Lokono	Omeo (Odongo i Magwi Lobure)	Baki, Felice, Ayaa, Adwar ka Geremia Lodang
3	Ayany Isau	Isau	Omeo,omin Lokono.Odongo i Magwi bene	Aburi
4	Nyacet	Adano, omin Lotwala matidi	Pajok(Bobi)	Onyala ka Bongomin
5	Lamoko	Lotwala	Pajok(Bobi)	Oluc Saberio (onywalo ki Aburi) Ogeno ki Lalum

6	Nyangom	Won Otii	Magwi (Kilio)	Kiyoo, Acee, (Akweroki Ali onywalo ki Baki)
7	Acilo	(Omin Alil)	Obbo (Pokogo)	Ayero ki Alal
8	Apiyo	Loritum	Lokomini (Oyere)	Omon
9	Laker (Lajonga)	Itimo	Obbo (Orak)	Pe onywal

The people of Pajombo Bura and Pokongo were the ones who took Acholi language to Obbo because they were Lwo. Pajombo had their rain chief called Lowaramoi. For this reason, the people of Pajombo and Pokongo did not contribute any collection to the chief of Abong. Long ago, the children of chiefs did not marry anyhow. They married children of other chiefs. The best example is the marriage between Kassiba and Ajuc Lanaka, daughter of Lowaramoi of Pajombo.

In 1870 Chief Kassiba called elders of Obbo and told them, "When I die, I want my son, Otoo Abarayi to take up the chiefdom of Obbo. However, if I die before Abarayi is mature enough, Locii will temporarily take charge of the chiefdom until Otoo Lworo Abarayi has grown up. But if Otoo has grown up, Locii should relinquish power to him because he is the son of my senior wife. As the Acholi people say, "No one can predict the day of death." After his statement, Kassiba became sick and passed away in a few days.

Immediately after the death of Kassiba, the people of Abong enthroned Locii. Abong elders told me that Otoo was not there at the time Kassiba talked to elders about the succession of Obbo chiefdom after him. He did not know what his father told Obbo elders. When Locii was enthroned, Otoo was not pleased because he knew well that, since he was the first born son of his father's senior wife, he was the heir of his father's throne. Subsequently, Otoo killed his brother, Locii as we will look at later in this book (read *The Separation of Abong*).

Some people say that after he killed Locii, Abarayi, was made the chief of Obbo because he was the rightful heir of Obbo. Chief Abaryi lived in fear of the children of Locii because they wanted to avenge the death of their father. Abarayi was a strong man, and he also had guns which he bought from Arab traders. Abarayi's home was fenced and there was only one opening which served as both entrance and exit points.

The wife of Abarayi Otoo was Aber, daughter of Lokono of Omeo, who grew up in Lobure (Magwi). Lokono had a younger brother called Icau. When Aber gave birth to her first son called Baki, Abarayi went for Ayany, daughter of Icau to baby sit Baki. Icau allowed his daughter to go with the chief. Ayany was a very good looking girl. The beauty of Ayang enticed Abarayi into a sexual relationship with her. Abarayi had a child with her and they named him Aburi.

Chief Abarayi was called Otoo Lworo, the name Abarayi came later. One year, Chief Abarayi did not collect ivory as the government wanted. The government arrested and imprisoned him for two years in Gondokoro. From prison, Arab traders gave him a new name, Ibrahim. The name was given to him to join Islamic faith. Acholi language transformed "Ibrahim" into "Abarayi". When he came back from prison, the chief gave all his children Muslem names. Unfortunately, all the names were not popularised.

After killing his brother, Abarayi became very careful with Locii's children. As a result, he migrated to Pajok in his uncle's home at Oryecu — when you are on Ayaci Hill, you can see Oryecu very clearly. From Pajok, Chief Abarayi continued making rain for the people of Obbo.

One evening everybody, including Abarayi's sons, went to bed early because it was drizzling. A short time after, Mandala, son of Locii came to kill Abarayi with gun. He stalked to the compound and set the sleeping huts of Aburayi's sons on fire. People rushed out from their sleep and began to put out the fire from the huts. Before the fire died out a flame landed on the hut of Baki's mother where Chief Abarayi was sleeping. The chief ran out in white jalabia, and began to remove grass from the roof of the hut with a gun in his hands. He began to remove grass from the roof with a gun in his hand. The light of the flames shone on the chief. Mandala who was hiding in pumpkin leaves, shot him. Abarayi cried out loud, and fell down dead. Baki's mother fell on the chief crying. The message of the death of Abarayi spread throughout the village, and the people of Obbo knew it was the house of Locii who killed the chief.

Baki, the first born of the chief, was very annoyed. He went to Nimule to ask the the government to kill Abong and Obbo people with gun. When Baki was still in Nimule, Obbo elders agreed to arrest Mandala and hand him over to the government if they came. The people of Obbo thought that if they did not do that, the government would destroy their home. They arrested Mandala, and when the government came, they just handed him over to them. The government (the white man) did not do anything on other people when they found the criminal. They immediately imprisoned Mandala at Nimule where he eventually died.

However, Crazzolara states that the government remanded Mandala for a short time at Nimule and later transferred him to the main prison at Masindi around 1900, and he later fled from prison. The people of Obbo were not happy with him. As a result he started moving up and down between Atyak and Nimule. Nobody cared about him. He died miserably wandering about (Crazzolara, 1951, P.172).

In 1905, when Mandala killed Chief Abarayi, Baki was already a grown up boy. Aburi was the second child. Although he was the first born, Baki was unable to lead the people of Obbo.

THE CHIEFS OF ABONG (OBBO)

As we have seen, the chiefdom of Abong began and grew as shown below:

I	Chief Loberete brought the people of Abong from Kapoeta in Tirangore, and he begot Moronyo (1730-1745?).
II	Moronyo inherited his father's chiefdom and begot a son called Katuala (1745-1755).
III	Katuala took up his father's throne, and with his wife, had a son called Lobitak (1755-1765?).
IV	Lobitak also became a chief and had a son, Kabeke (1765-1769?).
V	Kabeke became a chief and begot Ogwe (17691773?).
VI	Ogwe inherited the chiefdom of his father and begot Tok-boye 1 (1773-1776?).
VII	Tok-boye 1 became a chief and begot Malakiteng (1776-1780?)
VIII	Malakiteng became chief and begot Iliri (17801785?).
IX	Iliri inherited his father's throne and begot Imayi (1785-1795?).
X	Imayi too became chief and had a son called Tok-boye II (1795-1815?).
XI	Tok-boye II inherited his father's chiefdom and begot Lolori (18151820?).
XII	Lolori became a chief and begot Lojik (1820-1826?)
XIII	Lojik became a chief and had a son called Agwinya (1826-1830?)

XIV	Agwinya inherited his father's throne and begot Kassiba (1830-1835?)
XV	Kassiba inherited his father's throne and begot Abarayi Otoo (1835-1875?)
XVII	Abarayi Otoo became a chief and begot Aburi (1875-1905?).
XVII	Aburi inherited his father's throne and also had a son called Vitto Aburi (1905-1942).
XVIII	Vitto Aburi inherited his father's chiefdom and later handed it over to his brother Mathia Aburi Lolori (1942-1948).
XIX	Mathia Aburi Lolori also handed the chiefdom to his brother, Tubursio Omon (1948-1955).
XX	Tubursio Omon took up the chiefdom and later handed it back to Mathia Aburi Lolori (1955-1957).
XXI	Vitto Aburi had the chiefdom again wen Chief Mathia Aburi fled to Uganda (1957-1975)
XXII	Emillio Ojum took up the chiefdom from Vitto Aburi (1975-1976).
XXIV	Mathia Aburi Lolori took up the chiefdom again (1976-1987).
XXIII	Joseph Otira became chief but worked with the people of Obbo who were in Juba only (1990 — 2002).
XXII	Benjamin Obol, after the death of Chief Mathia Lolori, chiefdom shifted from Obbo to Loudo (to Benjamin Obol). Chief Benjamin entered the office in 2005 and got out in 2009 when I completed writing this book. From long ago, it was only the people of Obbo who were ordained chief. I cannot tell whether it was because there was no Obbo capable of chieftain, or the people of Obbo did not want to keep their culture which started in 1770-1986.

CHIEF ABURI TOOK UP THE CHIEFDOM (1905-1942)

Long ago, there were no violent conflicts over chieftain among children of chiefs. It was the rain-stone which chose the heir of a chief. The chief would call all his sons, and tell his wife to bring for them alcohol. The chief would place the stone in the calabash of alcohol without the knowledge of the children.

One day, when he wanted to determine his heir, Chief Abarayi called all his sons in the house of the mother of Jokoya Felice, his senior wife. Obbo people say that Chief Abarayi Otoo Lworo had eight sons: Baki, Jokoya Felice, Jeremia, Aburi, Onyala, Bongomin, Ogeno, Acee and Omon. Chief Abarayi told the mother of Felice to bring alcohol to his sons. Felice's mother brought a clean calabash of alcohol to the chief. Before his sons began to drink the alcohol, Chief Abarayi Otoo secretly put the rain-stone in the calabash and told them to drink. Since the children of the olden days knew their culture, it is possible that Abarayi's children might have known that, at that time, their father was looking for who was going to be his heir. They also knew that whoever the rain-stone entered his mouth would be the next Rain Chief. It is said that Abarayi trusted that Aburi would be the next chief after him.

God listened to Chief Abarayi's prayer and the rain-stone entered Aburi's mouth. When he felt the stone in his mouth, Aburi spat in in his hand and closed it in his fist, and he continued drinking alcohol. When they finished the alcohol, the boys went out, but after walking a short distance, Aburi came back to his father and told him, "Father, when I was drinking, I found a stone in the calabash." He handed the stone to his father. His father received it without saying a word, then later told Aburi, "Child, go to play." He got out and joined other children who were playing outside.

But Justice John Onge told me that he heard from Baki's mother, the senior wife of Chief Abarayi, that the rain-stone entered Jokoya's mouth, not Aburi's. Jokoya went out and came back to his father and told him, "Father, when we were drinking, I found a stone in the calabash." Jokoya put the stone in the hands of Chief Abarayi who told him, "Child, go to play among your friends."

However, Obbo people know that the chiefdom was left in the hands of Aburi. One thing which we may not understand is why Baki's mother said that the rain-stone entered Jokoya's mouth yet the people of Abong say it was Aburi who received the stone. This claim confused people, and they thought that the woman wanted her son to be the next chief. Other people say that Aburi was ordained a chief, even if his father did not give him the rain-stone. Chief Aburi made rain with stones which people gathered for him.

After two days, Chief Abarayi called his sons in the house of Felice's mother and told his wife to bring for them alcohol. Felice's mother brought alcohol in a clean calabash. Before the boys began to drink, Chief Abarayi Otoo put a rain-stone in the alcohol and gave them to drink. Since Abarayi loved Aburi, he prayed that he drank the stone.

Abarayi's prayer was listened to and it was Aburi who drank the stone. When he drank the stone, Aburi spat it and closed it in his fist and continued drinking. After drinking, the boys, together with Aburi, went out, but Aburi came back to his father and told him, "Father, when I was drinking, I found a stone in the calabash." He handed the stone to his father. His father received it without saying a word, then later told Aburi, "Child, go to play." He got out and joined other children who were playing outside.

Chief Abarayi repeated this test three times, and all the three times, it was Aburi who drank the stone. In the third test, when Aburi brought the stone to his father, Abarayi told him, "Child, sit down." Aburi sat down and his father took the stone from his hand, showing the stone to his son, Abarayi asked, "Child, what is this?" Aburi answered, "Father, I do not know."

Aburi's other name was Ogero, and his praise name was Logicuk-Ton-cwiny. His heroic killer name was Lokicomoi. He was a man of medium height and much hair on his head. His father put the stone under Aburi's hair and asked him, "How do you feel?" Aburi answered, "Father, it is very cold". Chief told him, "That is it, child. Take the rain because the God of my father has chosen you to lead the people of Obbo when I die. Take the rain and give it to your mother and tell her to keep it well. I do not want you to tell anybody about it. Keep it to yourself."

Aburi took the stone to his mother, and did not tell anybody else about it as his father warned. Aburi's mother kept the stone and never told other women about it. However, Abarayi told many Obbo elders what happened in his house – God's choice of Aburi to be the next chief. He also told other people that after his death, Aburi would lead Obbo. When Abarayi died, Aburi's becoming the next chief was a popular talk among the people of Obbo and the white rulers. That is why the government did not agree with Jeremia Lodang as we have seen before.

Some of Otoo's sons said that, before their father died, he left the junior rain-stone with their brother, Felice Lokoya and the senior stone was given to Baki, but most Obbo elders and the people of Obbo know that, before his death, Chief Abarayi left the rain-stone in the hands of his son, Aburi. We have also seen above what Chief Otoo did with his sons to determine who would be his heir. Some Abong people contend that the rain-stone was kept in the house of Baki's mother. When Chief Abarayi died, the stone remained in the house of Baki's mother (the rains are Nyar-itali, Njiki-Njiki, Lobanya-awuru – these are senior rains of Obbo).

In 1905 when Chief Abarayi died, Aburi inherited the chiefdom as Abarayi instructed. Acholi elders of Obbo told me that Abong did not coronate Chief Aburi correctly because elders were not involved in the coronation. When Aburi became a chief, his brothers such as Baki, Felice Lokoya and Jeremia Lodang were not happy with him because Baki also wanted to be ordained a chief as he was the eldest son of Chief Abarayi. Felice Lokoya too wanted to be a chief because he was the second oldest son of his father. Jeremia Lodang, as well, wanted to inherit his father's chiefdom because he was the only son of Chief Abarayi who was formally educated. However, Justice John Onge, son of Londang, told me that when his father completed his education in 1930, the Sudan government recruited him as a teacher. He did not live at home to rival for his father's throne, or to remove Chief Aburi from the throne.

Felice and Jeremia looked at Aburi as a drunkard who was not fit to be a chief. On the other hand, Bakhit Adulla, Abarayi's eldest son, on the compound of whom the Abong shrine was, also did not subscribe to the coronation of Aburi. Some of the people of Abong maintain that the rain-stone contention between Aburi and Jokoya is confusing people. Long ago, the chief did not mention the child chosen by the rain until when he was about to die and was giving his last word. Chief Abarayi did not die of age or sickness, but he was killed.

Some Abong people think that because Chief Abarayi died without giving his last word, Aburi just imposed himself to become chief simply because he was the first sons of Abarayi. Bakhit Abdalla did not show leadership skills. That is why people selected Aburi. Consequently, the children of Chief Abarayi Otoo separated for the second time (the first separation was between Abong Kure and Abong of the chief as we have seen before), which made Onyala Ojuk to migrate to his mother's kin at Oyere (bush school), Obwoya Lomundu moved to his in-laws in Oyere at Licari, Ogeno Ajuko also migrated to his in-laws at Oyere (bush school). From here, Ogeno Ajuko moved to Licari where many Oyere people settled. Ogeno Ajuko left this place and moved to Lobeca where he died in 1977. Omon died in an unknown place. The people of Obbo have not even seen his grave. Other sons of Abong such as Owor Ikubo, Okode Icura, father of Igidio, Olum Gwok, Cura Obele, Imilio Ogum, Bakheit (Baki) and his brothers, Ogwang Okayo-woru all settled among the people of Loudo. Other

Abong: Daudi Olebe, Alwari, Odonga Layolo and Angeleo Okeny, together with his sisters, settled at Alia. The history of Obbo states that other Abong children such as Lomayira and the children of Oketi, son of, Locii who Chief Abarayi killed, moved to Lerwa. For this reason, there is no place said to be Abong's. When Acholi people talk of Abong home, they mean Chief Aburi's home.

Because of this conflict, Chief Abarayi Otoo's children do not visit one another and they do not come together when death occurs in the house of one of them. As we have seen, it was only Geremia Lodang who visited Chief Aburi and Ogeno. Although the sons of Chief Abarayi did not like one another, his daughters at least loved their brothers. An example is their sister Adwar who was in Uganda. When Adwar came to visit her mother in Obbo, she did not forget to visit Chief Aburi. Ogeno was in Torit. When he heard of Adwar's visit to Obbo, he sent words that she should be taken to him immediately.

Acee was a gentleman, and he did not sustain any woman in his house as a wife. Acee wondered among the children of his brothers. I also remember seeing him in the house of my father, Kassiano Otim Onyala at Licari, when I was about five or six years old. After this, there was no home called Abong home, except the home of Chief Aburi.

One Abong man said, "Chief Aburi was not properly coroneted, the way a chief of Abong was supposed to."

Some people said that Abarayi liked Aburi, though he was younger than Baki, because he was married. Baki was still single. In Acholi culture, the man who becomes a chief must be married because all the visitors to the chiefdom would be taken care of by the chief.

The people of Obbo were not happy when they learned that there was power conflict between the children of Chief Abarayi. The Obbo people declared that Baki could not be a chief because he was a killer. One time he brought the whites from Nimule to shoot people with guns. To them, Felice Lokoya was also unable to lead Obbo, but they did not give any reason why they thought he unable to. The people said that since Aburi did not support Baki's idea to kill the people of Obbo, is an indication that he was a good person who was mindful of others. It was therefore right to make him the chief of Obbo, and so it was done. Abong elders contend that there were three factors which propelled Obbo to enthrone Aburi. The first is his declination of Baki's intended avenge of the death of their father. The second is that he had the heart of keeping the people of Abong united. Aburi did not condone the issue of "Abong kure" or "The Chief's Abong." He desired seeing the children of Kassiba living together. Aburi's love for oneness among the people of Abong freed the children of Locii of their burning desire to avenge the death of their father. The third factor is the fact that he paid bride prices of many Abong people who could not afford to pay on their own. Aburi showed his capability by leading Obbo very diligently. However, the problem with Aburi was that he was very authoritative, though he never beat or killed anybody. Chief Abarayi did not drink alcohol and was not an authoritarian like his son, Aburi.

Jeremia Lodang kept accusing Chief Aburi to the white government. One day he wrote to the government, though I did read the letter myself, the elders of Abong told me that Jeremia wrote the following:

"Dear Sir, I have written this letter for a very important issue. I hope that when you read this letter you will advise accordingly. I think, for two reasons, Aburi cannot lead Obbo. Firstly, Chief Aburi is an illiterate. How will he work with you then? Secondly, Aburi is a drunkard. How can he lead the people? I want to suggest that, since I am an educated member of the house of Abarayi, I want you to use your official power and make me the chief of Obbo." When I asked Justice John Onge if it was true that Jeremia wrote the letter, he told me, "This is a lie." I do not know whether Justice John Onge told me the truth or he was defending his father.

A messenger took this letter to the white man. The white man turned down Geremia Lodang's suggestion for the government was aware that Chief Abarayi instructed that when he died, his son, Aburi should be made a chief. Perhaps the government would consider Lodang's suggestion if it was not because of Chief Abarayi's instruction.

Aburi, like his father, was a bright man. That is why the people of Obbo made him their chief. The enthronement of Aburi created a rift among the people of Obbo. The sympathisers of Aburi collected rain stone for him, while sympathisers of Baki also did the same for him.

It was in 1914, when the government was drawing a dividing line between Acholi people, that Chief Aburi was coroneted. The history of the Acholi maintains that the people of Chief Oceng-pa-Anyoda of Pajok who was the first County Chief or Paramount Chief entered office around 1912.

Acholi village dancing place with decorated pole

Descending an outcrop of igneous rock in eastern Acholi Mountains

Aburri, principal chief of the Sudan Acholi, with some of his sons

It is said that when Chief Abarayi died, he left his rain stones in the house of his senior wife, the mother of Baki who later showed her son the stones. In 1942 when the people of Obbo were moving to Loudo from the foot of Pakwa Hill, some rain stones had got lost from Baki's mother. Fortunately, some of the stones were still there, and she moved with them to Loudo. Between 1943 and 1944 Baki went back to Pakwa to look for the stones which his mother lost when they were still at the foot of the hill. He spent about one month at Pakwa, but unfortunately, he did not find any of the stones.

In 1924, the DC of Opari decreed that each Acholi chief should take at least one of his children to school so that when the white government left power in their hands, they would be able to write and read. Chief Oceng P'Anyoda of Pajok sent his son to a Catholic school, but other chiefs took their children to Church Missionary Societies (CMS) School at Opari (Lakanigwa) as follows:

i.   Chief Loteme of Palwar took his nephew, Daudi, but after the death of Chief Loteme power was left in the hands of his son, Paulo Otoo.

ii.   Chief Aburi sent his brother, Geremia Lodang [because his children were still young]
iii. The chief of Magwi, whose name I do not know, took Enoka
iv.   Chief Lokwat of Ofirika took his son, Lofere
v.   Chief Moru Awakoda, brother of Agwaya of Pakala Bule, took his son, Erika
vi.   Chief of Pandiker, whose name I do not know, took his son, Lacito

According to the history of Acholi, in 1924 the government asked Chief Aburi that, if he could, he should take one of the children of Chief Abarayi to school because if he studied successfully, he would become a good chief. This information reached the children of Abarayi, but they did not understand the benefit of education. None of them was interested in education. Wen he realised that the people of Abong did not want to go to school, Chief Aburi took his cousin (the son of his mother's sister), Jeremia Lodang (Jeremia was Baki's younger brother). Some Abong children such as Justice John Onge think that there were two factors which made Aburi to fail to send his children to school. The first is that Abong's children had not reached school going age at that time. Secondly, Aburi, like other Acholi chiefs, did not attach values to education. Lodang, who was a bright child, studied hard. Because of the good advice Aburi gave him, Lodang did not forget the chief. He often paid courtesy visit to Aburi. He completed his studies from Juba High School in 1930. The government eventually appointed him a teacher. Among the children who were sent to study at Lakanigwa, it was only Lofere, son of Chief Lokwat of Ofirika who inherited his father's throne.

Chief Aburi married many women as given below:

1.   Launa Nura, a daughter of Pajok. She was killed in the war between Obbo and Pajok before she had a child.
2.   Lakulo Aliaka, the mother of Vitto and Owang. She was also from Ywaya Pajok.
3.   The mother of Tiburison, the senior wife of the chief. I do not know her name. She came from Lokide Obbo.
4.   Atono, the mother of Mathia Lolori, from Loudo Obbo.

5. The mother of Marko Lojik, Macimino Odum and Ogira (I do not know her name). She was also from Obbo.
6. Mother of Oraca Onde, from Kitaka Obbo.
7. Aringo, mother of Louise Otoo and Fred Owoti. She came from Pokongo Obbo.
8. Ojwiny, mother of Ocilo, a daughter of Koyo Obbo.
9. The mother of Ogeno, whom Chief Aburi inherited from his brother, and they has a son called Saverio Oluc.

Aburi was a friendly and welcoming chief. He usually provided his hosts with food, alcohol and a place to sleep. Many foreigners were hosted in his home. He was a very bright and wise man. He showed his wisdom when his wife, the mother of Tibursio Omon, wanted her son to marry Cibiriana Awot of Kitaka. Many people said Cibiriana Awot was a whore. Chief turned down the marriage because he knew that the girl was truly a whore, and she would not make a good house wife for his son. But Tibursio's mother insisted on paying Cibiriana Awot's bride price. Due to pressure from Tibursio, goats and hoe were taken to Kitaka for Cibirina's bride price. When she knew that her bride price, which would rob her of her freedom, was to be paid, she eloped with Anastasio Okumu, son of Onyala Ojuk, who was courting her. The Abong men were shamed when, after taking the bride price to Kitaka, they learned that the girl had eloped with Okumu.

It was then reported to Chief Aburi that, the bride had eloped with another man.

Chief asked, "Where has the girl eloped?" The messenger told him, "The girl eloped with the son of Onyala Ojuk." Chief responded, "Since you have already paid the bride price, we will not withdraw it because we are one people." The people of Obbo were surprised to hear the chief's decision because they thought he would ask for the bride price back. Some people of Abong did not like Chief Aburi because they thought that Aburi did not like his brothers. He only liked those who surported his enthronement.

Chief Aburi was the first and the last chief who serve both as a rain chief and a paramount chief at the same time. In 1942 when the government terminated Aburi's service as a paramount chief, Vitto was appointed a paramount chief. Aburi continued to serve as a rain chief. When Aburi became the chief of

Obbo, he resided in many places. He first resided at the foot of Lotii Hill, from which he moved to Pamballa at Luul. He later left Pamballa and moved to Lapwode. From Lapwode, he migrated to Lobeca, from which he moved back to Pamballa. The chief lived in Pamballa up to the time when he was taken to Uganda. He died in 1969 from Uganda at a place called Lukung.

When Aburi died, his son, Ocilo was with him, but he did not give Ocilo the rain stones. Before Aburi died, the mother of Tubursyo wanted him to leave the rain stones to her son, but Aburi did not accept her idea. Abong people said that the son of Abong who will bring the skull of Chief Aburi back to Obbo from Uganda will be the one to take up the chiefdom. Due to power tension between Vitto and his brother, Mattia Lolori, up to now the skull of the chief has remained in Uganda.

This shows how Abong people lost their rain making power. No Obbo or Abong child knows where Chief Aburi left the rain stones, though Vitto and Ocilo say they have them. However, many people of Obbo believe that the rain stones were left with Ocilo because, most of the time, when Ocilo says it is going to rain, it does not fail. Around 1984 when the people of Abong wanted to burn Chief Vitto because of the great drought that burned their crops in the garden, in the evening, Ocilo made heavy rain which pleased everybody. Abong stood by Aburi because of the three good ideas he had. Aburi appointed Atele, Oriet Oketi, the father of Firmo, and Logoto to settle minor disputes among the people while he managed the greater Obbo.

CHIEF ABURI GAVE OBBO NORTH TO ONYALA

When Chief Aburi ascended the throne, his brother, Onyala Ojuk, migrated to Oyere. It is said that Southern Obbo and Norther Obbo were both under the leadership of Chief Aburi. Later, Aburi was overwhelmed with the enormous workload and decided to give out Obbo North to his brother, Onyala to handle disputes among them. But if there were disputes which Chief Onyala could not settle, he was to refer them to Chief Aburi. Obbo North begins from Kenya and runs to Lotii Hill, and Obbo South covers Wau, Pajombo, Pokongo, Oyere, Loudo and Licari. The rank of Assistant Chief was not in the government system, but Chief Aburi wanted Onyala to lead Oyere, Loudo, Pokongo, Pajombo and some Oyere who migrated to Licari. The people of Obbo North had great respect for Onyala because he did his work very well. Aburi was now left with Obbo South. The Obbo elders who were advisors to Chief Aburi at the times of settling disputes were Ibura Lodu of Kitaka, Longac, Akilicik, Agalinyang and Owor Ikubo of Abong. That time Aburi was in Pamballa at Luul. In the past, all Acholi chiefs did not know how to write and read. So, they used horns to communicate their messages. Hence, each of them had their horn-blowers, and each note of the horn had its own message. If the chief wanted to talk to his people, he told his horn blower to summon them by blowing the horn. When they heard the horn, the chief's subjects interpreted the note and understood what their chief wanted them to do. Horns were not just blown anyhow on the compound of the chief. It was only when there was something important that the horn blower was instructed to do so:

- ▶ If animals besieged people in the hunting ground.
- ▶ Enemies came to attack the people.
- ▶ They wanted to wage war on their enemies.
- ▶ One of them had killed elephant or buffalo.

It is the chief who chooses his horn-blower, and everyone is made aware of his appointment. Chief Aburi chose Omiya (from the house of Padyeri) to be the horn-blower of Obbo South. Chief Onyala chose Akayi Lokoworo as the horn-blower of Obbo North. Communicating with horn among the people of Obbo started around 1700 to 1948. The chief of Obbo began to send messages with letter in 1948, the time when many children of Obbo were already literates as a result of the school that the Catholic missionaries had opened at Palotaka in 1935. Today, all Acholi chiefs communicate through letter. It is the chief himself or his secretary who writes the letter, depending on the kind of message that the chief wants to communicate.

VITTO ABURI BECAME A SUB-COUNTY CHIEF (1942-1948)

In 1942, the DC of Torit paid a visit to the people of Obbo. He was happily received with a band, and the crowd escorted him to the rest house. It is said that, on that day, Aburi was tipsy, so, before the DC asked Aburi to present the grievances of his people, he just went on to do so without the DC's permission. The DC was not pleased because Aburi was drunk. The DC stopped him from speaking to him immediately. With the kind of boldness of Lotuko, Aburi continued speaking. Since Aburi did not listen and showed no respect to him, the white man shouted at him, "Hi! Aburi, shut up! I do not want to hear your report." When the DC talked to him rudely, Chief Aburi walked out in fright. People thought the white man would give Aburi time to present their voice to him, but the DC did not give the opportunity. The following morning when the DC was returning from Pajok, he made straight for Torit without stopping at Obbo. The history of Acholi has it that when the DC reached Torit, he ordered that Aburi must relinquish his chieftain to his son, Vitto. One Abong man explained to me that Jeremia Lodang, whom Aburi sent to school to become a learned chief, was away. He was teaching in Nuer at a place called Juaibor. It is also said that Lodang did not have any problem with the enthronement of Vitto. Chief Vitto served from 1942 to 1948 when the government sentenced him for two years. The DC of Torit, at this time, wanted Obbo to have a Sub-County Chief.

Because his children were grown ups, Aburi forgot about Jeremia Lodang whom he took to school to become the chief of Obbo. So, he made Vitto a Sub-County chief. Jeremia was at Malakal when Vitto was given the office. Jeremia and Chief Aburi were in good terms, as we will see below. Jeremia also had deep trust in Chief Vitto. For this reason, before he died in 1961, Jeremia instructed that he should be buried in Vitto Aburi's home. It is said that Chief Aburi came to mourn the death.

MATHIA ABURI LOLORI BECAME A CHIEF (1948-1955).

Chief Vitto headed Obbo from 1942 to 1948, but because of his inability to lead well, the people of Obbo chose Mathia Lolori Aburi in 1948 to be their chief. In 1948 Jeremia was taken to teach in Torit, but at the time of election of Sub-County Chief, Jeremia asked for a leave. Chief Aburi wanted his son, Mathia Aburi Lolor, to stand unopposed. Jeremia opposed Aburi's interest, and declared that he would stand together with Mathia. Whoever won would become the chief. The government supported Jeremia's argument, but the people of Obbo did not want to disappoint Aburi since he had already chosen his son for the position. Unfortunately, the government did not buy the opinion of the people. Consequently, they made Jeremia to stand against Mathia, but Mathia Aburi Lolori won the election. Immediately after the election, Jeremia Lodang asserted that Chief Aburi did not want anybody but his children to be a chief.

Jeremia Lodang, as it is said, had been waiting for long to be a chief. This was his first opportunity to work his way to the office through election. In the history of Obbo, this was the first election. Later, the brothers of Bakhit (Baki) complained that that was the second time Baki's children lost in elections for the chieftain of Obbo. From 1948, when Jeremia lost in the election, Baki's brothers were not happy with Chief Aburi because they thought that it was Aburi who campaigned to the people of Obbo to vote Mathia. Jeremia became reserved to visit Chef Aburi.

After the election, Jeremia resumed his work at Torit, but he was discontented with Aburi. During his holiday visit at home, Jeremia did not pay Aburi a visit. In 1957 the government arrested Aburi and imprisoned him for three years in Juba. Because of the unbreakable cord of kinship, in 1959, Jeremia visited Aburi in prison. Aburi was very happy to see Jeremia. This visit repaired the damaged relationship between Aburi and Jeremia, together with Chief Vitto Aburi. On his release from prison, Aburi first spent a few days at Jeremia's in Torit. In February 1960, before Geremia's death, Aburi willed that when he died, he should be buried in Vitto's home at Alia. So, when he died, his body was buried at Alia where Aburi came to mourn his death.

According to Obbo elders, it was Chief Mathia Aburi Lolori who was able to manage the trouble-causing Obbo people. Around 1940 the people of Obbo were very distressing. They waylaid and beat people who came from outside Obbo to Palotaka Mission for catechism, leave alone fighting among themselves. Administrative police arrested such criminals and took them before Chief Mathia who on finding them guilty, mated corporal punishment, and the criminals were punished with ten or more stokes of cane. This instilled in the people of Obbo some sense of discipline and respect.

The history of Abong is a long one, but it is unfortunate that because, long ago, people did not know how to write, the history of the people right from Loberete up to the time of Chief Kassiba was not recorded. However, as we have seen before, Acholi culture did not condone shift of royalty from the house of the chief. Hence, when a chief died, it was one of his sons who took up his leadership position. Abong people told me that Chief Aburi broke the custom and gave the chiefdom to his brother. In the past, when someone became a chief, he was never removed from the office until he died. But when the white man got involved in appointment of chiefs, they said that a chief who was a criminal or did not know his work would be demoted. The government also had the audacity to appoint another chief outside the royal house. One day the government openly asserted that people should not respect a chief because he made rain but because his rank, and that they knew very well that it is God we made rain. The government told the people that continuing to respect a chief because he made rain was useless.

TURBUZIO OMON (1955-1956)

In August 1955 a war erupted between government soldiers and Arabs in Torit government army barracks, and it spread to the whole Equatorial Province. Many Arabs lost their lives during the war. In 1955 an Arab trader called Tahir, who was in Obbo, took refuge at Chief Mathia's in Alia. Chief hid the Arab trader in his ceiling board. It was popularly known that Mathia was hiding Tahir in his house. As a result, one day, Natalino Okwir of Pokongo and Franscesko, son of Alil of Pokongo went to the chief's in a car. Chief Mathia was not at home. Francesko asked the people at the chief's to hand over the Arab to him because he wanted to kill him to avenge the death of his brother whom Arabs killed in Juba. The people told him that, since he was son of a chief, he must have been aware that, in Acholi culture, a person who had taken refuge in the house of a chief was not to be beaten or killed. Natalino and Franscesko did not listen to the people. They vowed to shoot anybody in the chief's home if they did not produce the Arab to them. Everybody on the compound was scared, and they gave Tahir to Franscesko and Natalino who led him about fifty yards from the chief's compound and shot him dead.

People reported the death of Tahir to the government. After two or three days, the government sent their workers to Mathia. These workers told the chief and everybody that there was nothing wrong. So, they should not be scared. They went back after talking to people, but the next morning, they came back and started arresting people. When they saw that the government workers were arresting many people, the chief's subjects told Mathia to run away because he might be arrested too. The chief listened to his people and fled to Gulu in Uganda. This left the people of Obbo without a chief. The people of Obbo chose Tuburzio Omon, Mathia Lolori's brother, and made him the chief of Obbo. Chief Tuburzio Omon led from 1955 to 1956. a short while after, people discovered that Chief Tuburzio was unable to execute his duties as expected. They told clan elders that they wanted another chief.

VITTO ABURI RETURNED (1957-1975)

In 1957 people discovered that Chief Tibursio was not effective, and they asked the government for a new chief. The government told them to do election, and they needed to choose between Vitto and Emilio Ojum who was Vitto's secretary. Emilio Ojum won the election, and people began to grumble about the origin of Emilio Ojum. They doubted his Abongness. Despite the doubt, the government made Emilio a chief. Chief Emilio Ojum was not from the house of Abarayi. He led Abong for a few months and the people of Abong removed him from the office and brought Vitto back in 1975. Chief Vitto Aburi led from 1957 to 1975.

It was during the reign of Chief Vitto that there was a civil war between Anya-nya rebel group and the Sudan government. Many people lost their lives during the warfare. Survivors of the war fled to Uganda between 1964 and 1966, where they met Chief Mathia Aburi Lolori who had earlier fled to avoid government arrest. He was, at that time, selling books at Holy Rosary Catholic Church in Gulu (Uganda). I also saw Chief Mathia in Gulu when I was a student at Lacor Seminary.

EMILLIO OJUM BECAME CHIEF AGAIN (1975-1976)

MATHIA ABURI LOLORI A CHIEF AGAIN (1976-1987)

Mathia came back to office in 1973 after the signing of Peace Agreement in Addis Ababa, Ethiopia in 1972. The government of Sudan called all the Sudanese who had fled the country between 1955 and 1972 to return home and to resume their work. Acholi people who were in diaspora came back including Chief Mathia Aburi Lolori. Since the government wanted those who were working to get back to their work, the people of Obbo reinstated Chief Mathia Aburi Lolori in 1976. At this time, many things changed, and chiefs were not allowed to collect taxes as it was the case with the British. Besides, the salary of the chiefs was very low. But the Acholi chiefs were very ethical. They never asked for or accepted bribes from from their subject. This explains why bribery is not a common practice among the Acholi people.

In 1983 John Garang de Mabior started a guerrilla warfare in Southern Sudan, and it led to internal killings among the people of Southern Sudan. The rebel activities intensified and covered a vast are of Equatorial, BarhEl-Ghazel and Upper Nile. Due to the war, Chief Mathia moved to Juba. Unfortunately, Mathia fell sick and died in Juba in February 1987; in the home of Justice John Onge (John Onge was on leave in Nairobi, Kenya). The chiefdom of Abong in Obbo ended with the death of Chief Mathia Aburi Lolori Otoo.

The death of Chief Mathia nearly caused rift among the people of Abong in Juba. It started with the observation that before filling the grave of a chief with soil, his child must first drop soil in the grave. During the burial of Chief Mathia, none of his biological children was present. I know very well that Chief Mathia was my father's brother (I could also call him my father). The elders of Obbo asked me to drop soil in the grave of the chief on behalf of his biological children, and so I did. After I had performed my duties unto my uncle, an elder, Kornellio Odera rudely asked, "In what capacity does Saturino Olaa Onyala, son of Kassiano Otim Onyala drop soil in the grave of Chief Mathia?" I did not answer him, but walked home as required by Acholi culture that a child who is the first to drop soil in the grave of the chief should walk straight home without looking back. I later talked to Dominic Liling and Falabiano Loum about this disapproval, and all of us were not happy with Kornellio Odiyo complaint.

The second problem was about where to have the funeral rites of Chief Mathia done. Although Chief Mathia died in Justice John Onge Kassiba's home, we are all aware that even if John was in Juba, the funeral of Mathia could not be done in his home. We also know that Marcello Odiyo, Mathia's eldest brother, refused to host the funeral of Mathia in his home. He openly asserted that if the people of Abong wanted to arrange Mathia's funeral, they could do it in any body's home, but not his. Dominic Liling and I, the author of this book, were not impressed by my uncle's carelessness and irresponsibility, and we were forced to talk to Marcello Odiyo and his brother Kornelio Odera. After he was reprimanded, Marcello Odiyo asked the opinion of his wife, Khazisha about it. Khazisha, having realised that Kornelio Odera was on our side, she agreed with us and suggested that Chief Mathia's funeral be shifted from John Onge's home to *Hila Bulluk*.

JOSEPH OTIRA BECAME CHIEF (1990-2002)

In 1987 John Garang de Mabior's insurgency divided the people of Obbo into three. Some of them fled to Uganda. Others moved to Juba and others remained in Obbo taking refuge in the wilderness. Those who went to Juba elected Joseph Otira, son of Oyot-oyot of Logolo in 1990 as their chief since Obbo was without a chief. This provides a clear explanation of the shift of royalty from Abong to Logolo. Abong had the Obbo chiefdom from 1700 to 1986. No family in Obbo is likely to lead this long. This is the reason why the people of Obbo in Juba, in 1995, wanted Fred Owoti (the last born of Chief Aburi) to be their chief. However, we can conclude that the death of Chief Mathia Lolori was the end of Abong chiefdom in Obbo.

BENJAMIN OBOL BECAME A CHIEF

The John Garang De Mabior insurgency started in 1983 and ended in 2005, following the *ComprehensivePeaceAgreement* (CPA) between SPLM and the Sudan Government, which was signed in Nairobi.

In 2006 when the people of Obbo returned from Uganda, they realised that there was no Abong chief to lead them. Hence, they installed Benjamin Obol, son of Abola of Loudo, the chief of Obbo. Chief Benjamin Obol was entrusted with the chiefdom because he was once a parish chief under the chieftain of Chief Mathia Aburi Lolori. The second reason for the enthronement of Benjamin Obol is that he was the only previous parish chief, among many, who was still alive. Abong people appointed Mrs. Marcelina Adyero to be the chief's interpreter. People say Chief Benjamin Obol is still doing his work well, but we cannot tell the future. I think, if a son of Abong shows interest in the chieftain of Obbo, the people of Obbo will return the royalty to Abong as it used to be.

ABONG SPLIT UP

Although he was already married, Chief Imayi left Ayi Stream before he had a child. They had many children when they were at the foot of Lotii Hill. Some of the grand children of Imayi were very good, and they did not segregate anybody. It was Kassiba who split up the people of Abong. How did Kassiba do this? It was a common practice among Acholi chiefs to hand over the chiefdom to the son of queen (the first born son of the senior wife).

One day, in 1870 Chief Kassiba summoned the elders of Obbo and told them, "I want my son, Otoo Abarayi to be enthroned when I die. But if I die before, Abarayi is old enough to be installed on the throne Lucii can be enthroned temporarily so that Abarayi can take the chiefdom from him when he is old enough to lead, because Abarayi is the son of the queen." The Acholi culture demands that it is the son of the senior wife of the chief to inherit his father's throne when his father is dead. Just as Acholi people said, "No one can tell the time death comes". A short time after, Chief Kassiba fell critically sick and died immediately.

Immediately after the death of Chief Kassiba, Abong installed Locii on the throne of Obbo. Abong elders told me that when Kassiba was giving instruction on succession of his throne, Otoo was absent, and did not know what his father said to Obbo. Otoo was not happy because he knew that he was the rightful heir of his father's throne on account of his being the son of his father's senior wife. Because of this lack of information, Otoo killed his brother, Locii as we will see later in this book (the separation of Abong).

In 1900 the people of Obbo wanted to kill Chief Abarayi, but they feared the Acholi belief that if the blood of a chief is dropped in a home, it causes a mishap. But they respected Acholi culture, which condemn shading the blood of a chief on the compound for it causes mishaps to the children and members of the house. Since Chief Otoo killed Chief Locii, the brothers of Locii made up their mind to kill him to avenge the death of their brother as I read from Crazzolara's book that Chief Locii was also called "Adot" (Crazzolara, 1951, p.172).

When Chief Otoo learnt that the brothers of Locii (Adot) wanted to kill him, he fled to Bobi (Pajok) at his mother's kin. I cannot tell if Chief Otoo was killed in Obbo or in Pajok because according to Crazzolara Chief Otoo Abarayi was killed in Pajok, but the people of Obbo told me that Chief Otoo was killed in Obbo. Fr. Crazzolara wrote in his book, "One evening Chief Otoo was playing "nanga", and he had carried his son, Lokoya on his laps. His wives were dancing to the tune he was playing. At the same time, Manadala, son of Chief Adot Locii, had hidden himself nearby with a gun with which he wanted to shoot Chief Otoo. Mandala took care not to shoot Lokoya. It seems Otoo saw Manadala's shadow, and he quickly ran in his house. On seeing this, Manadala set ablaze the house in which the chief's children slept. When Otoo ran out to help his children out of the burning house, Manadala instantly shot him. People reported the chief's killing to the government in Nimule. The government sent their guards who arrested Manadala and remanded him in Masindi in Uganda, but he later escaped from prison.

When Manadala returned home, nobody wanted him. Life became so hard for him that he kept moving up and down between Atyak and Nimule until he died at place that nobody knows. The people of Obbo say, it is the spirit of Chief Otoo that killed Manadala. Chief Otoo willed it that his son Lokoya should inherit his chiefdom, but immediately Otoo died Lokoya fled to Padibe where he worked as a secretary to Chief Ogwok of Padibe. Secondly, alcohol had also ruined Lokoya so much that it seemed he could not make a good chief. For this reason, Chief Aburi was made the chief of Obbo (Crazzolara, 1951, p. 172).

However, the Abong elders such as Marcelo Odiyo and Justice John Onge Kassiba, whom I interviewed, told me, "One day, Chief Locii went for Acholi traditional dance which was usually performed in the evening, before sunset. When a chief participates in a dance, he must lead the dance. No one should cross his way. So when Locii was in the ecstasy of the dance, Otoo Abarayi who was also in the dance, being young and naive, ran in front of the chief. The chief was annoyed with him. The chief caned Otoo three strokes and Otoo ran away in pain. Otoo sat and wept at the side of a granary. When he saw his mother returning from fetching water, he cried so loudly that his mother got scared, and she asked him, "Otoo, what is the problem?" He answered, "Chief Otoo hit my head that I crossed his way in the dance arena."

On this account, Ajuc Lanaka was not happy with the chief. She told her son, "The children of Kassiba do not want you here. I will now take you to your uncle in Pajombo." The next morning, before sunrise, Lanaka set out on a journey to take her son and her daughter to their home in Pajombo.

On reaching her brother, Lowaramoi, Lanaka explained what Locii did to her son. Lowaramoi, son of Akut, was not happy with the maltreatment of his nephew by son of Kassiba. He then told his sister, "Chief Kassiba married you, the Queen of Abong, according to Acholi culture. It is your son, Otoo Abarayi who should inherit his throne; how could Locii whose mother comes from a non royal house of Opokomere become a chief?"

Lowaramoi turned to his nephew Abarayi and spoke to him, "Alright, my sister's son, I know that you are the rightful heir to you your dead father." This happened in 1870 when the people of Pajombo were at the foot of Lwo Hill and the people of Abong were at Iyele (Lapiem), the place which is now called Ayaci where Nicola Obwoya of Pajok cultivated his coffee.

Ajuc Lanaka transferred the rain of Abong to Pajombo, and Chief Locii was left without rain. The people of Obbo waited for rain in vein, between April and May. The people asked their chief, "Why is it not raining and yet it is already time for cultivation?" They also asked him, "Where is your step-mother, Lanaka?"

Locii did not answer the first question. He instead answered the second, "Ajuc Lanaka and her son, Otoo returned to Pajombo because I beat Otoo." When Locii asked the advice of elders, they suggested that he should follow Lanaka at Pajombo so that Chief Lowaramoi could settle the dispute between them. Chief Lowaramoi should allow Lanaka to return to Abong – because Ajuc Lanaka had the rain of the Abong people.

The people of Abong were very serious, and the following morning Chief Locii took his gun and set out for Pajombo. Chief Locii was well received in the palace of Chief Akut Lowarmoi where he spent three days. The first evening, Pajombo elders listened to the matter between Abarayi and Chief Locii. The elders of Pajombo asked Lanaka to go back to Abong after they successfully settled the dispute. On the second day, Chief Akut and Chief Locii spread animal skin in a cool tree shade and began to converse. Chief Locii lay with his gun next to him. Otoo came from the house and lay at the side of his brother, Chief Locii and asked him, "What is this that you have put next to you?" Locii said, "This is a gun called *lobotole*. It protects me." Otoo asked Locii to show him how the gun worked. Chief Locii got up and showed Otoo how to insert bullet in the gun and how to trigger it. Otoo practiced how to use the gun and later returned the gun to Locii.

The next morning Chief Locii shared water with Lanaka and the following day, the chief decided to travel back home. It used to be a practice in Acholi that when a visitor is leaving his host's place he was escorted by girls for two or three miles. Early in the morning, Pajombo elders selected three girls to escort Chief Locii on his way back home. Chief Locii was accompanied by four men who had long spears to protect the chief. The three girls curried *kwete* alcohol in vases, sesame paste and smoked meat for Ajuc Lanaka who was returning to her home. Chief Locii gave his gun to Otoo to hold for him.

After walking a mile away from home, Otoo told Locii that he wanted to go for a call. He entered the bush and inserted a bullet in the gun and came back on the path. He walked after Locii until he drew close to him. He pointed the gun at the back of Locii and shot him in the back. Locii made a feeble groan and fell dead on the ground. Otoo, on seeing blood on Locii, he dropped the gun down and dashed into the bush. In anger for the death of their chief, the four men also speared the three Pajombo girls to death. The information reached the people of Abong who hurried to the scene and carried the body of their chief home in a leopard skin.

The death of Chief Locii is told differently by different people. Some say it was the four men who accompanied Locii who killed the three Pajombo girl escorts. They also wanted to go back and kill the people of Pajombo, but when the people of Pajombo heard the gunshot, they all fled to a nearby hill. Other people say the people of Obbo who were near the scene killed the three Pajombo girls and carried the body of their chief and Ajuc Lanaka home. Another version of the story has it that when the men who accompanied Chief Locii to Pajombo saw that the chief was dead, they ran home to inform the people of Obbo that Locii was dead. The information reached everybody and they went with bows and arrows to attack the people of Pajombo. When they saw Abong warriors from the top of Lwo Hill, the people of Pajombo were very scared and they hid on the hill. Before they reach the hill, Abong warriors met three Pajombo girls, and they killed them and moved on. They did not find anybody at the foot of the hill because the Pajombo people had hidden themselves on the hill. Aware that they could not find Pajombo people, the people of Abong went back to bury Locii. At the time of burial, four sons of Kassiba, Ibura, Labongo, Muki and Aluka swore to kill Abarayi Otoo. Among these four men, Ibura and Aluka were Locii's brothers from the same womb. It is said that after the burial of Chief Locii it rained for three consecutive days.

ABARAYI OTOO INHERITED THE CHIEFDOM

In 1870 Mandala was still below fifteen years of age, but he had understood everything that happened to his father and kept it at heart. One day, after the burial of Locii, the people of Abong held a meeting in which they told Abarayi, "As you have killed your brother, you take up his chiefdom." Aware that he was the rightful son to inherit his father's throne – the son of the senior wife, Otoo Abarayi did not object to the proposal of the people.

Immediately after the death of Chief Locii, the government at Nimule was informed, but before they reached Obbo, the Arabs who were around arrested Chief Otoo and handed him over to the government officials. Otoo was then imprisoned at Patiko in Uganda. After a short time, they transferred him to another prison at Padibe during the reign of Chief Ogwok. Ogwok sent a word for the people of Obbo to bring elephant task to pay for the release of Chief Abarayi Otoo if they wanted him to return home. The people of Obbo raised ten elephant tasks and gave to the Arabs who were at Palodo. Some Arab traders reported to chief Ogwok that Obbo people had brought ten elephant tasks to pay for the release of Chief Otoo from prison, and Chief Ogwok immediately released Otoo from prison. The release of Otoo pleased the Arabs who were at Obbo. The Arabs at Palodo gave Chief Otoo ten guns for the use of his guards to protect him. The Arabs supported Chief Otoo's continuing to serve as a chief. Unfortunately, chief Otoo was a very authoritative man, and many times he did not agree with Arabs. The authoritarianism of the chief caused many problems to the people of Obbo. The Arabs amputated and cut many people of Obbo to death. They also cut the ears and lips of many people for no reasons. For that matter, the people of Obbo did not like Chief Otoo. One day, in a dance arena, Chief Otoo ordered his people to tie the hands and legs of the Arabs who were in the arena and make them to lie on the path, and his subjects just did as they were told. When other Arabs heard what happened to their colleagues, they came and, with guns, shot many people dead in the village. Because the Arabs outnumbered the chief's guards, the guards ran away and left the chief at home with his wives. Chief Otoo then fled with his wives to Magwi. After that, the chief married two women from Koyo. One of the women was called "Ayany," the mother of Aburi. The other was called "Aber," the mother of Baki, F. Lokoya, Aya, Adwar and Jeremiya Lodang (Crazzolara, 1951, p. 171).

Chief Abarayi Otoo disagreed with Arabs because they had no respect for Acholi culture. They did not respect housewives and married men. Arabs slept with girls and house wives. They also slept with black men in cell. It is said that the Arabs killed most of the people they sexually abused. Arab shot Acholi with guns and left Acholi homes depleted of domestic animals and anything good (Onyango, 1976, P, 163).

However, according to Justice John Onge Arab traders arrested Chief Otoo and took him to Gondokoro because he had refused to to collect ivory from his subjects to be given to Arab traders. The people of Obbo did not want the government to imprison Chief Otoo. But the chief said, "Let me go because I also want to know why they are taking me there." Chief Otoo spent two years at Gondokoro before Arab traders learnt that he was actually a very good man. As a result, Arab traders released Chief Otoo, and they taught him Islam and gave him an Islam name, Ibrahim. They also offered him three guns and a band. Being at Gondokoro gave Chief Otto an opportunity to meet Chief Pitia Lugar of Bar. Chief Otoo later offered his friend, Chief Pitita Lugwar, his daughter called Kiyo, and they had a daughter, Keji Lugar. When he returned from prison, Chief Otoo also gave his children Islam names as below:

- He named the eldest child whose first name we do not know, "Kakhit". Acholi called him Baki.
- Aburi was named "Awatchi", but the name was not popularised.
- Jokoyo was also given an Islam name, but elders could not remember the name.
- Jeremia was named "Hakim".
- Onyala was named "Babikir"
- Ogeno was named "Farah".
- And nobody could remember the name given to Omon.

On his return from Magwi, Chief Otoo settled at Luul stream far away from the people of Abong because he thought the children of Locii waned to kill him. That is why he settled with another group of Abong people. He wanted to let people, if he died, know the cause of his death.

During rainy season, Chief Otoo was infected with guinea worm in the leg when he had visited his sister Atwon who was married at Magwi. Atwon, Chief Kassiba's daughter was married to Chief Ruk-Onyang of Magwi. This chief of Magwi had two wives, the senior of whom was Atwon, and a Magwi girl whose name we do not know was the chief's junior wife. Atwon bore two children. The first child was Chief Anga and the younger child was called Ongee. The girl from Magwi girl had a son called Auya Owau. Auya Owau also had two children, Marino Omon and Inoka.

Justice John told me that immediately after the killing of Chief Locii, Abarayi Otoo migrated to his mother's kin at Pajombo when he was not yet married. One day, a man spied and found out where Otoo was living and reported to brothers of Locii Otoo that Abarayi was down with guinea worm. "If you go there, we will just find him." Some men were sent to kill Otoo. When they reached there, they found Otoo lying down and they told him to say out his last words for they were going to kill him. Otoo was scared, but he later asked the men to wait for him outside. After a short time, Otoo threw out chicken incubation cage and the men hurled their spears at it thinking it was Chief Otoo who was running away. Otoo then carefully got out of the house and crawled to the fence and climbed out. As he was jumping over the fence, one of the men speared one of his buttocks, but fortunately, he managed to flee. Otoo treated himself until he fully recovered. Later the people of Obbo called him back among the people of Abong. His home was surrounded with trees. After sunset, Otoo did not move out of his home. Abarayi was a strong tall brown man and he was a *nanga* player. People used to call him *Abarayi Otoo Lworo*, but others called him by his nickname, *"Ottacayom"*, or his killer name, *"Lorenga-moi"*. His killer named was derived from thedescription of the stranger he killed. He was a brown man.

Ibura thought that the best day to kill Abarayi was when he was sick with guinea worm at his sister's place, though he did not know the house in which Atwon was treated Otoo from. Ibura sent his brother, Labongo to spot where Otoo was and report back to him. Labongo went to Magwi and found out where Otoo was being treated. He told the people of Magwi that, "I am Kassiba's son. One of my brothers has guinea worm in his leg and is with our sister, Atwon. I think you, the people of Magwi, know where my sister is treating our brother from."

The people of Magwi did not know that Labongo and Ibura had a plot to kill their brother, Abarayi. They innocently answered, "If you are looking for Chief Abarayi, he is at "kibuka" at the stream." They also directed him how to reach the place. He went and saw the place and went back. When he reached home, Labongo told Ibura, "O! The man is finished. You will just find him straight since he is also down with guinea worm." Labongo described to Ibura how to reach the shelter where Chief Abarayi was being treated from.

Ibura was very pleased with the message Labongo brought to him. He wasted no time to pick his spear and set out for Magwi. When he drew closer to the shelter, Ibura drew his spear at a ready and moved stealthily at the edge of the compound. He stood at the doorway and told Abarayi, "Whoever is in this shelter must come out."

Chief Abarayi recognised the voice of Ibura and answered him, "Alright my brother. If you are a real man, then wait for me outside there. I will not die in the shelter today."

Ibura did not enter, but he was ready to spear Chief Abarayi if he came out.

Chief Abarayi threw out a chicken incubation cage. Ibuka thought that that was Chief Abarayi running out of the shelter, and he speared the cage.

Chief Otoo ran out and fled the place. Ibura took another spear with which he speared one of Abarayi's buttocks as he was fleeing. Abarayi hid at the edge of the gardens of the people of Magwi.

After failing to kill his brother, Ibura did not go to Atwon. He went back to Obbo. After a few hours, Atwon went to check Otoo in the shelter, but she found the door open. There was a chicken incubation cage lying in front of the shelter. Atwon was scared, and she called her brother loudly: — Otoo! Otoo! Otoo! Where are you?

Chief Abarayi heard his sister's call from the edge of a garden where he was hiding and walked to her. Atwon was not happy with what happened to her brother, and she ran to her husband and asked him to help save her brother. Chief Ruk-Onyang made *ogali* fibre and used it to bandage the wound Otoo sustained. Atwon's husband transferred Abarayi to the foot of Kinonuka Hill, in Palongayi, when he realised that the people of Abong wanted to kill him. He wanted Chief Abarayi to treat his guinea worm and the wound Ibura inflicted on his buttock from Palongayi. Rukonyang assigned some Magwi people to guard Chief Abarayi for the six weeks Atwon was treating him at the foot of Kinonuka Hill.

As soon as Ibura reached home, Labongo asked him, "Why are you not shouting your praise name? Why are you not pulling ogali twig?" With shame, Ibura answered, "O! My brother, the thing fled." When they want to obscure something Acholi people call even humans "the thing". The information is not understood by non members. Ibura also did not want people who were with them to know what they were talking about with Labongo. That is why he said "the thing fled" though he meant Abarayi.

Chief Abarayi returned to Obbo when he healed. Alimo, Abarayi's cousin, knew everything Ibura did to Otoo. So when the chief returned, he told him to settle at Pajok. Chief Abarayi followed the advice of his cousin. Alimo was at Lakido, in Aciri. Chief Otoo built next to sausage tree at Lakido (the tree is still there up to today). Abarayi's people fetch Atebi water from the north and Alimo's fetch it from the south.

Chief Abarayi came with six wives. The people of Pajok respected the chief of Obbo, and they built their houses round the chief's. The chief built a large house for each of his six wives and erected a fence with only one gate. He built the sleeping hut of his children close to the gate. All his five sons, Baki, Aburi, Onyala, Omon and Ongee slept in the same hut. Alimo chose a son of Pajok, Aruko to keep the gate of Chief Abarayi. Aruko liked sleeping close to the hut of the boys.

Men and boys slept in their sleeping hut called *otogo* or *jwan*. This hut was built on four legs. To enter the hut one used a ladder to climb up there. He pulled the ladder up on the veranda so that no one could climb after him.

When the children of Chief Otoo were grown ups, they asked their father to return them to Obbo. The chief understood what the children wanted. He told them, "Alright, my children, you have grown up into men! Will you stand by me if any problem arises in the land of Abong? If you cannot, I will not return to Abong. We will continue to live here at Lakido." The children stopped thinking about their return to Abong. But Chief Otoo deeply thought about it and felt pity for the people of Abong. Two days after, the chief called his children and told them, "We will live here at Lakido, but the people of Abong who are at Obbo can visit us. You can also visit them at Obbo." Although he was up to Lakido, the chief had control over the people of Obbo. The people of Abong at Obbo and those at Lakido began to pay visit to each group when they received the message of the chief.

This made the people of Abong to think that there was no conflict among the children of Kassiba any more. That also meant that the people of Abong had no conflict with their chief, Otoo. However, the children of Locii still wanted to kill Chief Otoo. The visit that took place between the people of Kassiba gave the children of Locii opportunity to kill Chief Otoo.

Locii's children consulted a sorcerer to find a way of killing Chief Abarayi. Abong elders told me that the children of Locii sought the help of a sorcerer to kill Otoo, is true. They were flanked by their friends Logoto and Oketi (Firmo's father) to go to the sorcerer. They wanted the sorcerer to blind everybody by the time Mandala would go to attack the chief. The magician tied a goat-skin string on Mandala's wrist to blind people. Mandala stalked the chief two times. Unfortunately, each time he tried, people saw him and asked him, "What are you stalking here?" Mandala wanted to spear the chief secretly. It was unfortunate that all that the sorcerer instructed him to do never worked for him.

One day, Ibure Lodu, the grand father of Anna, Afulunaro Acire's wife, from

Bar but grew up among the people of Abong told the people of Abong, "Your quest for divine intervention is not okay. I just request you to give me time to go to Bilinyang (Bar), and I will be able to make Mandala do what he wants to do."

The children of Chief Locii were very thankful to Ibure Lodu for the good idea he came up with. After three day, Lodu went to Bilinyang. He consulted different sorcerers from Bar and they told him different thing that Locii's children could do to kill Chief Abarayi. Loudu spent about thirty day consulting the sorcerers in Bar before he returned to Obbo.

Lodu came back to Obbo, and he went with Logoto and Okayi to visit Chief Abarayi. He did this to follow the instruction of the sorcerers of Bar. Chief Abaryi welcomed them and slaughtered for them a billy goat and served them alcohol. This visit was meant to cast spell on the chief as the sorcerers instructed Lodu. After the meal, the three went back to Obbo.

That evening, Lodu told Mandala, "Child, I have prepared your way when I went to Bar. Do not worry now. Everything is alright. You can now do anything you want with Chief Abarayi."

Mandala was pleased to listen to Lodu. Although he was told he could do anything with the chief, Mandala did not go to attack the chief immediately. Mandala went after seven days, at night, but he could not tell in which house the chief was. Abarayi had fenced his home very thickly. Mandala knew the chief was around but did not know the house in which he was sleeping. The chief was in Baki's mother's house.

Mandala paced along the fence thinking of what to do so that Abarayi could come out. He did not want to go back. He moved closer to where Aruko slept, close to the sleeping hut of the sons of the chief. Mandala made a grass torch and threw it over the fence. It fell on the hut of the sons of the chief. The boys ran out crying loudly.

The chief dressed up, picked his gun and rushed out immediately. He paced around with his gun in the hand. He put his gun down and began to pull off the burning thatch. Aruko joined the chief in removing the thatch.

Mandala had hidden close to the burning hut. The flames shone on the chief. Mandala aimed his gun at the chief carefully and shot him in the chest. Abarayi fell down crying and died after a few minutes.

Mandala went back pleased for his mission was accomplished. When he was close to his home, Obbo, Mandala shot in the air. The people of Abong, when they heard Mandala's gun shot, also shot in the air.

As Mandala entered his compound, Ibura, Aluka, Muki and Labongo welcome him with gunshots – a sign of happiness for the death of Chief Abarayi.

When Ibura, Aluka, Muki and Labongo were shooting guns, Lomudu's mother, wife of Labongo, sounded yodel three times to appreciate the death of the chief. They later assembled in front of Labongo's house and sang "Akero" three times. The people of Obbo buried Chief Abarayi the following morning. They performed his funeral rites at the home of the mother of Anjelo Olweny. That is how the children of Locii avenged the death of their father.

The children of Chief Otoo were not happy with the death of their father. Baki, Otoo's second son, insisted to his brother that they should report the killing of their father to Nimule so that the whites would shoot the people of Obbo to avenge the death of their father. All his brothers, except Aburi, agreed with him. Aburi said, "Why do the children of Kassiba want to kill the people of Obbo who did not kill the chief – Abong killed themselves."

Aburi's brothers were immediately convinced that it was useless to take the matter to Nimule. The people of Obbo thanked Aburi for his mature judgment.

Although most of the children of Kassiba changed their mind, Baki did not. He went to Nimule and he brought soldiers to shoot the people of Obbo, but the people of Obbo had taken refuse on Lotii Hill. The soldiers arrested Mandala and took people's cattle, goats and sheep, and they burnt houses. Mandala was imprisoned for about two months in Nimule and later transferred to Masindi in Uganda.

The death of Locii and Abarayi Otoo brought division among the people of Abong. People thought that if Kassiba had temporarily given the chiefdom to one of his brothers, Chief Locii and Chief Abarayi would not have died. This is where the elders of Abong went wrong. The people blamed Kassiba. The death of Locii and Abarayi split up Abong into two: the royal Abong and the ignoble Abong. The offspring of Locii called themselves ignoble Abong and they called the rest of Abong people plainly Abong. The people of Obbo later called them Royal Abong, but all of them were children of Abarayi. In Obbo culture, Abong Ignoble and Abong Royal do not marry among themselves. However, some people violated the custom and married from one group. The best example is the marriage between Owang of the noble Abong and his wife Renata of ignoble Abong. However, during hard time like death, the two groups join hands to handle the situation. It was noted that some people did not bother to unite with others even at the time of hardship. The fact that some Abong people marry among themselves is an indication that they think there is no kinship tie between the two groups. It is also said that the people of Abong noble and Abong ignoble do not eat the marriage goat of a girl together. But it seems this is not true because I am Abong royal, and when I was still in Sudan, we used to eat the goat together with sons of ignoble Abong.

WHO KILLED ONYALA?

The elders of Obbo did not have the same story of the death of Onyala Ojuk. Some of them say it was Chief Aburi who killed Onyala because he cursed Onyala. Aburi said that Onyala should be killed by wild animal because he knew that Onyala was brighter than him and could lead the people better. He thought Onyala would rob him of his chiefdom if he lived.

But some people said it was Ogeno, father of Marcello Odiyo, who caused the death of Onyala. They said that Ogeno was angry with Onyala for two issues. First, he was annoyed with Onyala about his sister Lalum whom Aburi used to pay for Onyala's crime of killing to the people of Koyo. Second, he was annoyed with Onyala because Onyala slept with his wife, called Maro-otoo.

To better understand the death of Onyala, let us look at how he led his life. Onyala's mother was Lacet, daughter of Adang, and Adang was a younger brother of Lotwala. They were from the same house of Bobi (Pajok). Lamoko was the daughter of Lotwala. Lamoko and Lacet were cousins. But if Lamoko and Lacet were cousins, why did they both marry Chief Abarayi? The Obbo elders said that Lacet was the woman whose bride price the chief paid, but Lamoko was given in the house of Kassiba because of Atwon.

One time, Lamoko's brother called Bur-Opong lived in Obbo, in the hands of Chief Otoo. Bur-opong became interested in Kassiba's daughter called Atwon. They develop a deep relationship, at that time; Chief Ruk-Onyang of Magwi had already given Atwon an engagement ring. Unfortunately, Atwon did not tell Bur-opong about it. The people of Obbo knew everything about the relationship between Atwon and Bur-opong.

One day, Chief Ruko-Onyang sent a word for the people of Abong that he wanted Atwon to go to live with him at Magwi. The people of Abong sent some people to him, and they told him, "Chief, we have been sent by the people of Obbo. If you delay, a Pajok man called Bur-Opong is already in love with Atwon." Chief Ruk-Onyang was not happy with this message, but he did not think of rejecting his wife.

The people of Obbo also informed Chief Abarayi of the affairs between Atwon and Chief Bur-opong, and the chief immediately sent his messengers to Lotwala. The messengers told Lutwala, "Alright, Chief, Chief Abarayi has sent us to you to let you know that he is not happy with your son, Bur-Opong because he slept with Atwon. The chief of Magwi had already booked Atwon for marriage. What your son had done is not good. If the chief of Magwi learns of this, it might cause him serious problem. For that matter, he wants you to pay a fine for the stealthy affairs your son had with Atwon. If there is any issue from Bura, the chief of Magwi, he will know how to handle it."

Lotwala was equally unhappy with his son. He told the messengers, "I do not have cattle, goats, sheep and hoe to pay the fine to the people of Abong." Lotwala forgot one thing here, for in the culture of Acholi, if a child errs, it is not paid with his father's own wealth, but it is paid with a girl. People made this law because they thought a girl would give birth and replace the dead person. So when Lutwala understood that, he he gave his daughter, Lamoko and paid the people of Abong. When Lamoko came to Abong Chief Abarayi took her for a wife. A few months after, Lamoko conceived and gave birth to Ogeno. Nyacet, the chief's senior wife, on seeing that Lamoko had a baby, she sent her son, Onyala to take care of the baby, Ogeno. Onyala took care of Ogeno for two years and went back home. After Ogeno, Lamoko gave birth to two other children, Lalum and Olul.

After the death of Chief Abarayi the elders of Abong gave Lamoko to Aburi with whom she had a child called Saberio Oluc. It is seems the elders gave Lamoko to Aburi because he was not yet married, but he was already enthroned as the chief of Obbo. Then later, Aburi married four other women. The first of the four women mothered Ayany, the second gave birth to Mathia Aburi Lolori, and the third gave birth to Vitto Aburi and the fourth mothered Marko Lojik. Since Chief Aburi had four young wives, he rejected Lamoko. Onyala and Ogeno were already grown ups. Onyala married six wives:

S/No.	Wife's name	Daughter of	Clan	Mothered
	Ayet		Lokide	Apiyo and Acen
	Lakop Ocol	Ocol	Oyere Palyec	Kassiano Otim, Agengo, Anastasyo Okumu, Genesyo Okelo, Ayaa Eufenia and (Selestiono Otii, fathered by Ogeno)
	Anyeko	Lokoya	Gem-Oyere	Damica, Falabiano Loum, Marcana Igira
	Lalweny	Lokwat	Pajombo	Lokwat Akene, Lobwonyo and Ocen
	Nya P'Akera	Akera	Loudo	
	Latoo		Palio (Pajok)	

ABURI CURSED ONYALA

One day in 1935 Rwot Aburi left Alia to visit Onyala in Obbo. The chief spent two days here. During the chief's visit, leopards killed six goats of Chief Kitara, of Koyo. The people of Koyo informed the people of Obbo that leopards killed the goats of Chief Kitara, and the six leopards were at Obbo East. The people of Koyo asked the people of Obbo if they could help them to kill the leopard. The people of Obbo went to hunt the leopards together with Koyo people. Koyo people came with animal net. They erected the net and set some of Obbo and Koyo people at the net. The rest of the people went to surge the leopards from the small bush in which they were hiding. Just in a short moment, the leopards ran out of the bush and got entangled in the net. Ogeno killed one of the leopards. Loudo people killed one and Koyo wounded one leopard. Three of the leopards fled untouched.

Koyo people suggested that, as the owners of the net, it is the people of Koyo who were the killer of the leopards. The people of Abong and Loudo were the shouters of praise names and ululation. Obbo rejected Koyo's suggestion, and said, "Even if the leopards were caught in Koyo's net, those who speared them should be considered the killers." This resulted in serious conflict between Obbo and Koyo. Abong stood their ground and took the leopard. Koyo took the other kill from Loudo. The people of Loudo fought Koyo and took away the leopard from Koyo. Koyo went to Chief Aburi at Onyala's and narrated the story of Koyo. The chief said Loudo should take the leopard.

Chief Aburi went to rest in his house after people dispersed. Around 4:00 pm Latoo, Onyala's wife, entered his house when he was still resting. When he raised his head up and saw his sister-in-law, he asked her, "Why do you enter the house without talking?"

Latoo thought the chief wanted to sleep with her. She ran out screaming, "Chief Aburi wants to sleep with me!" Everybody did not accept Latoo's claim, but her husband, Onyala, thought it was true that his brother wanted to sleep with his wife because Latoo was a lecherous woman. Onyala was also aware that Aburi was also lecherous. So it could be true that Aburi wanted to sleep with his wife. He entered Aburi's house and began to fight him. In annoyance, the chief cursed Onyala three times, saying, "You my younger brother, why do you fight me in public? Onyala, Onyala if I call the name of my father for you, it can cause problem."

Having expressed his anger, the chief left Onyala's home and went back to Alia in grate anger. He never thought of going back to make up with his brother. It is on this ground that the people of Abong blame the death of Onyala on Aburi because they thought that if the chief had come to terms with his brother, Onyala would not have been killed by wild animal.

The relationship between Onyala and Aburi, in 1935, was not good. Obbo elders said that one day when Onyala was coming from Pajok, Aburi sent his guards to arrest him. Fortunately, the guards knew that Onyala committed no offence, so they left him to go. Onyala was very annoyed when he heard that the chief wanted to arrest him. He told Obwoya, Okono and Olaa Cwer-moi about it. These elders disagreed with Aburi, and they wanted him fought for this. They waylaid him many times, but Aburi never entered any of their ambushes. Aburi learned that these three men wanted to fight him, and he called elders of Obbo to listen to the case between him and Onyala. The chief also asked the elders to settle the case between Onyala and Maro-otoo, the wife of Ogeno. The elders told the chief, in his face, that his hatred for his brother was unjustifiable. They also told Onyala that it was wrong of him to have affairs with Ogeno's wife. The Obbo elders asked Aburi to stop thinking bad of his brother. In the same way, the elders also asked Onyala to stop sleeping with Maro-otoo as if he did not have wives.

OGENO CURSED ONYALA

Between 1933 and 1935, when locusts destroyed the crops of Obbo people, Onyala went to Opari to report to the government how locusts were destroying people's crops. There, he admired a Palio (Pajok) girl called Latoo. People said that Latoo was a loose woman who liked sleeping with men anyhow. She was Alongo's wife. Alongo was a sweeper in the office of the District Commissioner. Because of her easy going character, Latoo acknowledged Onyala's love advance, and on the day Onyala was returning to Obbo, she eloped with him.

In 1935 Ogeno also went to Opari and fell in love with an Obwolto girl called Maro-otoo. Elders said that Maro-otoo was a married woman, but she accepted Ogeno and eloped with him when he was coming back from Opari. Maro-otoo's husband asked Ogeno to pay fine for taking his wife. Unfortunately, Ogeno did not have any money at hand. So, it was Onyala who helped his brother and paid the fine. Unfortunately, both Marootoo and Latoo were barren.

Maro-otoo was passionate about trying her fertility with other men so that she could get a child for Ogeno. One night in March of 1936, Onyala went to converse with his sister-in-law, Maro-otoo in Ogeno's absence, and Maro-otoo was alone at home. Onyala and his sister-in-law happily chatted with a lot of laughter. In the conversation, Maro-too told Onyala, "I am not happy because Ogeno's blood and mine do not match, and we cannot have a child. Because of that, my love for Ogeno has gone down. If God wants me to live with him, then He should allow me to get a child outside my marriage with Ogeno."

Onyala immediately thought that the woman wanted to take her bone back to Pajok. It happened many times that Pajok girls who got married to sons of Obbo went back home, so many Obbo sons did not have much trust that daughters of Pajok would live with them in marriage for ever. Onyala threw away his brotherhood with Ogeno. He told Maro-otoo, "Woman, I understand your ordeal. I am also not happy about your being here without a child. Now I want to ask you: why do you want to look for men from outside? Can't we make it with you?"

Since she wanted to try her fitness with any other man, Maro-otoo did not reject Onyala's proposal. A moment later, she drew near to Onyala and they met. After this, it seemed they continued to meet.

In June 1935 Ogeno fought his wife, and that was not the first time he did it. Marootoo ran to Onyala's place where she spent two weeks before Onyala took her back home. Maro-otoo did this in pursuit of Acholi culture. In Acholi, if a man fought his wife, the woman did not run to any other person, but to her brother-in-law or other close relatives of her husband. The man to whom she ran should take her back after three days. On the day the woman was returned, a meeting was held before the man received his wife back. If it was found that the man threw out the belongings of his wife when he was chasing her away, he was asked to chew sesame and spit on the belongings, or he would slaughter a cock and sprinkle its blood on the woman's belongings which he violently threw out. If the man had performed this ritual more than two times, clan elders asked him to slaughter a ram to cleanse his bad act of throwing his wife's properties out. If a man fought his wife and did not throw her properties out, he did not perform any of the rituals described above because he committed no abomination. After settling the dispute, the woman enters the house without any ritual. I do not know if Ogeno threw his wife's properties out because no elder told me anything about it.

Abong elders told me that all the times Maro-otoo ran to Onyala's home, Onyala's wives gave him time to sleep with her. The people of Obbo said that, Onyala's wives gossiped many times about Maro-too's secret affairs with their husband on nights when he was alone in his sleeping house. It reached a point where Onyala's wives could not stomach this affair anymore. So, one day when Ogeno fought her, Maro-otoo ran to Onyala's place. Onyala's wives, Anyeko and Lalweny, quarreled with her telling her not to sleep with their husband when she was with them. Unfortunately, Ogeno was not aware of the secret affairs between his wife and his brother, Onyala. He eventually learned of the affairs from his friends, and he later called Maro-otoo and asked her, "I have learned that Onyala's wives are complaining that you have a secret affair with their husband. I want to hear from you, is that true or not?"

Marotoo said, "As you have heard, it is true." On hearing this response, Ogeno chased away Maro-otoo at night. Maro-otoo ran to Onyala's as usual, and she returned after three days. We cannot tell now what the woman discussed with Onyala when she was at his home.

The people of Obbo were not happy about Onyala's affair with his brother's wife. They told Ogeno and some clan elders about it.

Ogeno was deeply annoyed with his brother and he thought to himself, "My sister, Lalum was given out to pay for the killing Onyala committed, and Onyala again sleep with my wife? I do not know what kind of death should kill Onyala." This statement, "What kind of death should kill." is a curse according to Acholi people. I think that is why Abong people say that Ogeno killed Onyala. He cursed his brother, and truly Onyala died. Ogeno did not fight his brother, but he fought his wife instead.

One morning Ogeno called the elders of Palyec and Abong to handle the matter between his wife and his brother, Onyala. The house of Palyec was represented by Longiroto and Oloya and the people of Abong were represented by Atele, Opiyo Lonyor-moi and Ibure. The people who converged on Ogeno's compound asked Maro-otoo and Onyala to tell them something about the relationship, and Onyala honestly told the gathering that he slept with Maro-otoo. The elders asked Maro-otoo if what Onyala said was true. She said it was true and she defended herself that she discovered that her blood did not match with Ogeno (she could not have a child with Ogeno). So, she was looking for a child outside her marriage. Although Maro-otoo wanted to get a child outside her marriage, elders told her and Onyala to stop the love affairs between them.

ONYALA KILLED ADUR, A GIRL FROM KOYO, IN A POTATO GARDEN

To separate Ogeno and Onyala, Aburi told Onyala that he was already a fully grown up man, he should migrate to South Obbo. Before Onyala could shift to his new place, the case of Adur cropped up. Elders of Obbo said that one day in 1920 Onyala and his friend Olak, son of Oriet, went to Lerwa (Koyo) Hill to visit one of his friends called Pido-moi. On the day they were coming back home, Onyala picked a gun and they set out on the journey. Pido-moi escorted them up to the foot of Lerwa Hill. At the foot of this hill was a very large potato garden. Olak saw "something" shaking grass in the garden. There were a lot of warthogs at the foot of the hill at that time. So he thought that it was warthogs shaking grass in the garden. Olak turned to Onyala and told him, "Hee! My friend, look! There is a warthog there, eating potato." Onyala also thought it was actually a warthog eating potato, and yet it was Adur, with a child on her back, who was digging up potato.

Without first shouting at it, Onyala shot the spot at which the grass was shaken and his bullet caught Adur who screamed in pain, O! Mother! O! Mother! O! Mother! O! Adur was the wife of Ongom, son of Chief Atany of Koyo. Olak, Onyala and Pido-moi, on realising that that was a human voice, they said, "We have done something wrong." Some Abong people said that when Onyala shot Adur, they were scared and they took refuge on Lerwa Hill. Others said that Onyala and his friend Olak ran to Chief Aburi's, but they did not tell the chief that Onyala accidentally killed somebody.

In 1920 the people of Logolo were the ones residing at the foot of Lerwa Hill. When they heard the gun shot and the cry of a woman, the people of Logolo ran to the garden of potato to find out what had happened there. They found Adur shot with gun, but fortunately the child was not shot. They carried the body of Adur from the garden and reported to Pido-moi because he was also a son of Koyo. The death of Adur was announced to the whole village. Koyo men rushed to the potato garden, the scene of Adur's death. The Koyo men asked the people of Logolo if they knew who killed the woman. The people of Logolo all said that they did not know who killed the woman. I think they did not want to tell the people of Koyo that it was Onyala who killed Adur because they feared to have any association with the killing. The people of Koyo then said to the people of Logolo Logolo, "It is okay if you do not know who killed our wife. We will carry the body home. Acholi people say that 'Even if you fart at the bed of the river, it will still come out.' We will also be able to know who killed Adur." The people of Koyo wrapped the body of Adur, carried it on a stretcher and took it home for burial. That night when the people of Koyo were mourning, one Logolo man whose name we do not know, came to the bereaved people of Koyo and told them, "It is some Abong men who shot Adur with gun." The people of Koyo first doubted the information, but later agreed that it could be true. They resolved that they would attack Abong the following day. Koyo men whetted their spears and cleaned their shields.

In the morning, the people of Koyo set out on the war expedition. They stood in a grazing ground called Pamballa at Chief Aburi's. An Abong man called Ogik was standing close to the warriors ran to Chief Aburi and told him, "Chief! You are still sleeping. A multitude of people are in the grazing ground. They came with spears and shields and with feathers on heir heads."

Chief Aburi doubted Ogik's information. So, he called an old man and asked him, "Lacek, what have you heard?" Lacek answered, "I have not heard anything bad, Chief". Chief Aburi asked Lacek another question, "If there is nothing bad, why has Ogik reported that there are warriors around?"

Lacek was baffled and he got up silently and made straight to the grazing ground where he actually saw the people Ogik reported to the chief. He saw the large multitude and confirmed Ogik's report. He did not go close to the people for he was scared. Lacek came back and told the chief, "Chief, Ogik is right." The chief wanted to know why the people of Koyo came to his place in war attire. He then sent Lacek back to the grazing ground to find out what the warriors of Koyo wanted.

Lacek did not want to risk going alone, so he called Oriet to go with him. When they reached there they asked the people of Koyo, "What do you want in the land of Abong?"

The people of Koyo responded, "We have come to avenge the death of our wife who was killed by a man of Abong. He shot the woman with gun when they were descending Lerwa Hill. The woman was harvesting potato and the Abong man shot her dead with a gun."

Lacek and Oriet listened to the people of Koyo carefully and reported back to Chief Aburi, but Aburi was not happy about it and said, "If that is the issue, why did my brother Onyala hide it from me?"

Chief Aburi immediately went together with Lacek and Oriet to meet the people of Koyo in the grazing ground. The chief told the people of Koyo, "Alright, the people of Koyo. I know what has brought you here. If you did not come, I would also not know what happened. The person who killed the woman actually did something bad. First, he hid himself, and second he concealed the information from me. We do not know where these two people are. I therefore implore you to wait for a moment because I want to talk to elders of Abong." The Koyo people stood angrily staring at Chief Aburi, but they did not refuse to listen to him. They gave him some time to talk to his people.

Chief Aburi went back home and told his drummer to beat the drum to summon elders. The messenger did as he was told. It did not take long, Abong elders converged on the compound of the chief in a large number. Baki and Ogeno joined the elders.

The chief stood up and talked to elders, "Alright, the people of Kassiba, I have called you here because Onyala has caused great trouble. He killed a daughter of Koyo. The people of Koyo have come to fight us to pay for the death of their wife. Right now they are in the grazing ground. As you know, Alal has been used to pay for one death to the children of Opoko-mere. We are left with only two girls, Adwar and Kiyoo. I am asking your opinion, what should we do about this issue?"

Before elders said anything, Baki stood up and said, "I have listened to chief, but I want to tell all of you that Adwar will not get out." This puzzled the chief and everybody else. The chief turned to Ogeno and asked him, "What about you, what do you think? Your brother has erred. Ogeno had the heart of brotherhood, and he told the chief that "If that is the problem, I accept that elders take my sister, Lalum to pay the people of Koyo." All elders commented Ogeno. They then took Lalum from the house of Lamoko Angali and handed her over to the people of Koyo.

After receiving Lalum, the people of Koyo asked Aburi to do two important things. First, the chief should allow them to put a ring on Lalum's finger. Second, the chief should bring a goat for cleansing ritual to reunite the people of Koyo and Obbo Abong. They also said that after slaughtering the goat, they would not drink *oput* (peace pact) with Chief Aburi, but they should bring Onyala himself. Obbo elders sent people to look for Onyala on Lerwa Hill where they got Onyala and brought him before the warriors of Koyo.

The Koyo warriors slaughtered the goat and they split its liver into two. They gave one half to Onyala and the other half to the husband of Adur to eat. In 1920 when this incident occurred, some Abong people were at Luul and others were at the foot of Pakwa Hill. After the peace pact (drinking oput), the Koyo warriors went back home with Lalum. When they reached home, their elders slaughtered a goat to perform a reception ritual on Lalum. The following morning the people of Koyo returned Lalum to Obbo. Chief Aburi happily received her, and the chief called Onyala, Ogeno, Lamoko together with Lalum and told them go and settle at the foot of Pakwa Hill, but he (the chief) and other people of Obbo would continue to live at Luul. I asked why the chief wanted the children and his wife to go to Pakwa and yet he wanted to remain behind at Luul forest, but nobody answered the question. Onyala and the children I have listed above went to live at Pakwa as instructed by the chief.

When everybody cautioned him for killing, Onyala brought a different issue. He said Ogeno was not happy with him not because he slept with his wife, but because of Lalum whom they used to pay for the killing he did. Onyala told elders that if Ogeno is not happy for his sister, he would give Ogeno his eldest daughter called Apiyo. If Apiyo was married, Ogeno would use her bride price to pay back for his sister, Lalum.

In March of 1935 people were preparing for a hunting expedition at Giligili. Immediately after settling the dispute, Onyala took his spear to go and hunt at Gili-gili. Abong elders advised Onyala not to go to hunt since there was still a fresh dispute between him and Ogeno. Onyala heeded to elders' advice and returned his spear in the house.

A few minutes after, Odongo, father of Anna son of Ibure, came to Onyala and told him, "Never mind, it is hard to stay at home. Let's go to hunt at Gili-gili." Onyala forgot what the people of Abong had just told him that morning. He entered the house and picked his knife and three spears: two spears and one "lwiri" spear in his left hand. Onyala and Odongo went to Obwoya Lomundu because they wanted to go together with him. Obwoya had just returned from the wilderness looking for building materials. He welcomed Onyala and Odongo in the house of his wife, Mother of Angiro. Obwoya asked Mother of Angiro to bring Onyala and Odongo one bottle of waragi. Mother of Angiro was busy, so she sent Akongo to take the warigi to them, and she placed it before Onyala.

Before Onyala began to drink the alcohol, Mother of Angiro gave him toasted sesame to eat. Onyala took it from her hand and ate. He then asked her to bring a smaller calabash for taking the waragi (local whisky). Mother of Angiro brought a glass into which she poured the alcohol. The glass immediately broke into two from her hand. When they saw what happened, the people who were in the house were surprised, and they told Onyala and Odongo not to go for the hunting. Onyala answered, "This will not do anything. We will go to hunt without fail."

Odongo and Obwoya did not think deep about this incident. They agreed with Onyala and they went to hunt at Gili-gili. Everything went on well on the hunting ground, but there were very many animals at the converging point. Onyala, Odongo and Obwoya Lomundu found themselves in the middle of elephants which escaped from the fire. Onyala stalked one of them and speared it. Another elephant surged towards him. Onyala took off to take refuge among some trees. Unfortunately, he stumbled on a tree stump and fell on the knife he had worn on his waist. The knife hurt him very badly, and the elephant did not do anything to him.

The hunters made a stretcher on which they carried him home. In 1935 there was still no hospital or medical facilities in Acholi. Bel-got, Olok Olwerete, Ogeno and Lakob Ocol, Onyala's wife took Onyala to Torit Hospital where he took one month. Unfortunately, the medicines did not help him. The wound got worse. Abong people sent a word about Onyala's condition to the people of Tirangore who sent Lomilu, Labaluk and Otuyek and carried Onyala to Obbo (Bush School). Onyala did not take long here. He died. All the same, we can still say that it was Aburi and Ogeno who caused Onyala's death.

SNAKES AND SLEEPING SICKNESS KILLED PEOPLE

In 1920 snakes killed many Abong people at Luul. The chief decided to move his people to Alia in 1921. In 1923 the people of Obbo who were at the foot of Pakwa Hill, migrated to Malaya. Between 1923 and 1927, many Obbo people were recruited in the army. Some of them included Ogeno, Odiyo (the elder brother of Lodofiko Obwoya) and Lodofiko Obwoya. Onyala was also interested in joining the army, but the people of Obbo told him, "Onyala, it is not right for you to join the army because you are already the chief of Obbo North". The sons of Abong who were recruited in the army fought very hard, but unfortunately, Odiya died in 1927 in the fight between the government and Dinka.

In 1925 sleeping sickness killed many people in Pajok, Obbo, Omeo and Agoro. On realising that the disease was not ending, the people cried out to the D.C. of Opari. The D.C. instructed the four villages to migrate and settle on Lotii Hill. In 1927 the people of Obbo who were in Malaya, together with those at Alia's migrated to Lotii Hill. In 1932 when the disease reduced, people moved to the foot of the hill, while some of them settled at Pambala (that is Loudo Hill) and others came back to Alia. In 1934 the people of Obbo left Pambala and moved to Kubiri which is at Jikiloti, Ayii Stream.

THE HILLS AND LAND (HUNTING GROUNDS) OF ABONG

The people of Abong had two expand of hunting ground: *Amalac* which is bordered by *Oloyo-tiko*, Logolo, Lokile, Bokoro and Aba. The second is Lokile. We do not know the name of the first Abong man to blow the horn of this place. However, today it is Felix Otoo, son of Okumu who performs its rite and also mobilises the hunting in Amalac and Lokile. So in this book we take Amalac as Abong hunting ground, but not Kitaka's. I also discovered that Abong has only one god. That is Jokiloti. For more information about the god, read "Jok Jikiloti" on page 393.

KITAKA

Kitaka comprises five small clans: Lokomini Kal, KwendaTing-gili, Lokowor, Abolyero and Irwangi.

The people of *Lokomini Kal* came from Imila (Katire), Lokomini Kal left Katire around 1685. Chief Omini Abinya is the one who led the people of Lokomini Kal to Obbo. Acholi elders said that Chief Omini Abanya and his people moved away from Katire because of conflict between him and his brothers who remained there at Katire. The elders did not tell me the cause of the conflict. By the time the people of Lokomini Kal, reached Obbo, the people of Koyo were at the foot of Lotii Hill. The chief of Koyo, whose name nobody knew, welcomed the people of Chief Omini and gave them the land where they settled. Kitaka elders told me that Chief Omini Abinya came with a scepter and rain stone, and the chief of Koyo also had his own rain stone. The elders of Obbo such as Chief Mathia Aburi Lolori told me that Abinya's rain was stronger than the one of the chief of Koyo. People learnt of this difference because the two chiefs used to make rain on different occasions. When they saw that the rain of Chief Omini was stronger than the chief of Koyo's, the people of Kitaka began to give their offertories to Chief Omini.

When the chief of Koyo realised that his subjects became loyal to Chief Omini, he was not happy though he could not stop his people. The chief of Koyo was a peace-loving man. When everybody showed respect for Chief Omini, he handed over his royal stools and rain stone to Chief Ominini Abinya. As we have seen before, Chief Omini came with his own rain stone. He took the rains stone of the chief of Koyo and added to his. Chief Omini brought all other groups that came to Obbo under one leadership. So, the people of Kitaka were not only a royal group, but also the head of all groups.

Unfortunately, Chief Omini was selfish. He liked eating alone, sometimes he ate on anthill. His wife would take for him food on a ladder. For that matter, Chief Imayi of Abong became the chief of Obbo around 1705. Acholi elders told me that Imayi took up the Obbo chiefdom for two reasons:

[1]   Around 1700, when Abong entered Obbo, the chief of Kitaka used to eat alone on anthill. But the chief of Abong was generous. He invited all men (his neighbours) to meal at his fire place. Therefore, the people of Abong said it was only the chief of Abong who could lead them because he was a generous man.

[2]   Secondly, Chief Imayi was highly respected. Some Kitaka elders like Ogweta Opoka told me that Abong came from Abong Tirangore without rain stone. When they reached Obbo, Chief Omini made Imayi a caretaker of his rain stone. It is for Imayi's good work that Omini gave him his rain stone. But some people say that Abong people came with their rain stone and later Chief Omini gave them another.

KwendaTing-gili came from Iyire when the people of Iyire were still at Imurok. They moved away from Imurok because of famine. The elders of Kwenda Ting-gili, when they were coming to Obbo, were led by Loromo. Loromo brought the people of Kwenda Ting-gili from Iyire, and they found some Obbo people were at Lotii Hill. The people of Lomoro settled among the people of Lokomini Kal.

Lokowor came from Imila (Katire) together with Chief Omini Abinya of Lokomini Kal. Chief Omini was the brother of Owor who was also a leader among the Lokowor. When Lokowor reached Obbo, they settled together with Lokomini Kal. In 1685 when Owor and his brother entered Obbo, Owor eloped with a girl of Koyo, but it was unfortunate that Owor did not have bride price. Owor was aware of the fact that, in Acholi culture, if a boy did not have bride price, his brother could help him to pay the bride price. But he eloped with the girl when he was at his maternal uncle's, so it was his uncle to marry for him the woman according to Acholi culture. So, Owor asked Chief Omini Abinya to marry for him the girl. Chief Omini refused to marry a woman for his brother, possibly because he did not think the girl was fit for their family. Or he was sure that the girl was lazy. I also thought that it could be because the girl did not know how to do household chores well. Perhaps that is why he told Owor, "You should go back to the arena to look for a beautiful and promising woman." In Acholi, if people say you are not smart it means you do not know household work.

Chief Omini annoyed Owor very much because he deeply loved the girl.

Eventually, Owor separated from his brother and settled away from him. He had many children with the woman and they called themselves the people of Lokwor – which means the people of Owor.

Fortunately, Owor was a great hunter. One day he went to check his traps and he found vulture pecking at the carcase of a very huge elephant whose task was five metres long. He drove away the vultures and carefully removed the elephant tasks and skinned the elephant. Owor got some firewood and smoked the elephant meat in one day. After this, he took the tasks home and continued to carry the meat home bit by bit until he finished. Owor sold the meat and the tasks and got a lot of money. He used part of the money to pay his wife's bride price, and his in-laws were very appreciative to him. They wished him and his family good luck.

People reported to Chief Omini that your brother whom you refused to marry a wife for has now married with the money he got from ivory – from his own sweat. That is how the house of Lokwor was founded in Kitaka.

Abolyero migrated from Logolo-pa-Kuka led by Adat Jakwor as a result of a serious conflict between Logolo-pa-kuka and Logolo-pa-Owino. The elders of Kitaka told me three things that explain why Abolyero came to Kitaka. The first thing is that Abolyero people came to teach the people of Kitaka drum beating because the people of Kitaka did not know how to beat the drum. The second explanation is that the people of Abolyero wanted to be the messengers of the chief of Kitaka. The third group told me that it was Olak of Logolo-pa-Owino who chased Abolyero away because of conflict between them. This tells us that Logolo-pa Kuka and Logolo-pa-Wino were under one chiefdom. The chief of Logolo came from the house of Logolo-pa-owino. If this was not so, Adat Jakwor would not send away the people of Abolyero from Logolo. I do not know if when the people of Abolyero came to Kitaka at that time, some Obbo people were still at the foot of Lotii Hill.

Irwangi came from Ifwotu. Most Obbo elders told me that it was famine which made them to leave Ifwotu. An elder, Gira Idyeku was the one who brought them to Obbo. This was also at the time when some Obbo people were still on Loti Hill, and they settled at Lokomini Kal.

HILLS AND HUNTING GROUNDS/LAND OF KITAKA

The people of Kitaka have two hunting grounds called *Lohile, bordered* by *Bokoro*.

The second hunting ground of Kitaka is *Holok.* The elders of Kitaka say, long time ago, Lohile belonged to the people of Koyo-Ting-gili, and they later gave it out to the people of Kwenda because the people of Kwenda were the nephews of Koyo-Ting-gili. What is not clear about Lohile is that at time it is the people of Kwenda who call people for hunting expedition and at other times it is the people of Iyire. Elders say Iyire get blessing from Kwenda to call the hunting expedition. Unfortunately, no Kitaka elder told me why Iyire and Kwenda have authority over Lohide. As an Acholi child, I know that a hunting ground belong to only one house, unlike the one of Kwenda and Iyire. For this reason, I think Kwenda and Iyire must be from the same origin. They are the ones who call people to hunt in Holok, and it is they who are responsible for performing rituals on the hunting ground. When the people of Irwangi entered Obbo, no one owned Holok hunting ground, so they took it up. The people of Obbo and Iyire who attended a meeting which was held on 23-24/12/2007 said that Jackson Ochora was the Kitaka horn blower. This means it was Jackson Ochora who called the hunting expeditions at Holok and Lohile. We do not know the person who performed this function before Jackson Ochora. The people of Kitaka have two hills. One is Lomakwa which is in Lohile and another is Lomolong. The Kitaka people do not have a god.

LOWUDO (LOUDO)

Loudo has seven smaller clans as given below: *Gari, IjulaP'Loremoi, IjulaP'Lowala, Orak, Mararii, Irwangi and Mohoi.*

Gari came from Abong Kure, and they were led to Loudo by Opio Lonyor-moi, father of Kalaudio. They settled among the Ijula people. Gari, Ijula P'Loremoi and Ijula P'Lowala are one people, but we do not know if Gari also belong to Abong Kure who came to Loudo or they are people from Ijula who came long time ago and joined the people of Abong Kure. None of the elders of Obbo knew the reason why they left Abong Kure.

Ijula P'Loremoi came from Imurok and the house of Irenge. It is said that Loremoi was the one who brought the people of Ijula P'Loremoi to Obbo. The people of Loremoi moved together with Lowala's people because Loremoi was Lowala's elder brother. Felix Okot Tibursio, son of Ijula, told me that between 1800 and 1865, there was a conflict among Loremoi, Lowala and some of their brothers who remained behind at Imurok. The cause of the conflict was not known. When he saw that the conflict was becoming serious, Loremoi told his brother Lowala, "My brother, I cannot continue to live here lest it should cause me death." Lowala also told his brother, "My brother, the conflict involves both of us. If you are leaving the place, I think it is proper that we go together." Three days after, Loremoi and Lowala took their families and some Ijula people and moved south-west until they reached Okire Hill (in Magwi). They settled here for a while to allow their children to rest. Before the end of the second day, the people of Ijula who remained at Imurok followed Loremoi and his brother with the intention to attack them. But when they reached Okire Hill, Loremoi and Lowala's people did not take spears against them. When they saw that the people were not interested in fighting, they took Oyoo's grand son, whose name we do not know, tied his legs with rope and threw him down the hill.

The people of Ijula split up into groups and moved to Agoro, Omeyo, Magwi and the followers of Loremoi and Lowala moved to Obbo. Loremoi, Lowala, Aramotuka and Oyoo were brothers. Ijula met the Obbo people on Lotii Hill where the chief of Obbo welcomed them and gave them space to settle. In 1920, when people had returned down from Lotii Hill, some Ijula settled at Lerwa while Loremoi and his people settled at Loudo — on the western side of Ayii stream and the people of Lowala moved to Ngabara. Loremoi people called themselves "Ijula P'Loremoi" and the people of Lowala called themselves "Ijula P'Lowala". P'Lowala were at Ngabara for two or three years and later moved back to Loudo, this is what a Loudo person will tell you when you ask, where the people of Ijula P'Lowala come from? He will tell you, "Ijula P'Lowala came from Ngabara". That is why I have stated in this book that Ijula P'Lowala people came from Ngabara. But as we know, the people of Ijula came from Imurok. The people of Loremoi and the people of Lowala all came from Imurok under one name, "Ijula". They divided themselves in the two families of Ijula P'Lowala and Ijula P''Loremio when they were at the foot of Lotii Hill. The people of Ijula speak Imurok up to today. Secondly, to date, the people of Ijula in Acholi put up with Chief Kanuto of Imurok when they visit Torit. That means there is still strong code of kinship between Ijula in Acholi and the people of Imurok. The people of Gari, Ijula P'Loremoi and Ijula P'Lowala are the same people. They originated from the house of Loremoi, who was older than Lowala and Opio Lonyor-moi.

*Ijula P'Lowala*came from Ngabara was led by Lowala to Loudo. For more information, read Ijula P'Loremoi.

The people of Orak came from Ikolong (Iyire). It was Agunya who brought them to Obbo. They left Iyire because internal conflict about the ownership about rain making power. At that time, the power of making rain was in the hands of Chief Kiteng who was Agunya's brother, and Agunya wanted Kiteng to give him the rain.

Kiteng told Agunya, "I am your elder brother and this power of rain making was left to me by my father. How do I hand over the power to you?" This wrangle sparked a fight between the two brothers. When he saw that his brother wanted to kill him because of the rain, Agunya moved away with his people to Obbo.

Mararii people hailed from Gunyoro (Iyire). Acholi said that the people of Mararii moved together with Irwangi under one leadership of Lowic-cilmoi. We do not know why the people of Mararii moved away from Iyire, neither can we tell whether Lowic-cilmoi was from the house of Mararii or Irwangi.

Mohoi came from Omeo from the family of Murwari. The Acholi elders did not tell me the name of the elder who brought them to Obbo. I did not find time to talk to Mohoi though I was told that it was only a Mohoi elder who could tell me the truth of the movement of these people.

THE HUNTING GROUNDS AND HILL OF LOUDO

The people Loudo have four hunting grounds: *Bong-won* which is bordered by Logolo, Okony-kor and Agongara hunting grounds; *Ladeng-deng* neighbouring Oloyo-tiko, Meri-Lokide and Odik-piny; Ayoko at Kimoru steam on Imurok side; *Agongara* neighbouring the hunting grounds, Meri-Lokide, Bong-won and Abar. Some people say that the ritual of Bongwon hunting ground was performed by Dabuniana Malamu, of Orak, and he was the one who called people to come for hunting on the ground. Today Bong-won hunting ground is the hands of Otebe, some people called him Otori Peke. However, if we look at it critically, we find that Orak people are also found in Pokongo, but they are not found in Loudo. This can make us ask, "Why does Pakongo perform the rites of the hunting ground of the people of Loudo?" We are aware that Ladengdeng and Ayoko hunting grounds are also celebrated by Aliardo from Mararii family, and he was the one who called hunters to hunting expedition on the ground. Agongara hunting ground was celebrated by Andira Onyaluk from the house of Mohoi, and he also plaid the role of calling hunting expeditions on the ground. This tells us one reason why Andira Onyaluk moved and settled at Langor in Agongara hunting ground. The people of Loudo have only one hill, *Koyoro* which is in Magwi, but they (the people of Loudo) do not have a god.

THE LOUDO RAIN POT

The Loudo people have a rain called "late-owak" which is in the house of Ijula, but it should be noted that this is a minor rain which Loudo keeps. The major rain was with the people of Abong. We do not know the name of the person who usually invoked "late-owak" rain. He used to make rain when the chief of Abong delayed to make rain for his people. The "late-owak' rain was very reliable.

OYERE

The Oyere family was divided into five smaller houses such as Omini, Panyibila, Wor-obwoli, Palyec and Gem.

Omini people came from Anywak, led by Ombwoli. We cannot tell which year the people of Omini came to Obbo, but some Obbo elders guessed that they arrived at Obbo when some Obbo people were still at the foot of Lotii Hill. The Acholi elders like Chief Mathia Aburi Lolori did not know why the people of Omini moved away from Anywak, but some elders such as Ogeta Opoka said that the people of Omini left Anywak because of famine which had led to some deaths. When they reached Obbo, the people of Omini found that food was in abundance, they settled in Obbo for good.

Those of *anyibila* came from Imurok led to Obbo by Kobu, the grand father of Adik-Dikomoi. When I asked why the people of Omini left Imurok, elders told me that they left because of famine. When famine began to kill many people, Kobu brought his people to Obbo. Kobu's people at first called themselves "People of Imurok" implying that they belonged to the family of Imurok, but when they moved to Obbo, they called themselves "Panyibila" in memory of Nyibila, the place from which they moved at Imurok. The Acholi elders did not know the year in which the people of Panyibila came to Obbo because there was no written record to refer to. Nobody knows the year in which the people of Panyibila entered Obboland. Some people said that when Kobu came to Obbo with his people, the people of Obbo were still at the foot of Loti Hill, but others said that Panyibila people found the people of Obbo already settled at Pambala. However, by the time Kobu's people entered Obbo, there was also famine in Obbo where they found the Obbo people eating "kinyu" which usually saved the people of Obbo from famines. Kobu's people joined Obbo people in eating "kinyu" though they did not know it. They found "kinyu" as tasty as Torit bread.

Wor-obwoli came from the house of "Nyibila Loyere", and it was Wor-Obwoli who led them to Obbo. Elders told me that the people of Wor-Obwoli entered Obboland around 1850 in the same month that the people of Panyibila entered Obboland. The elders of Lodito Wor-Obwoli told me two reasons that made their people to move away from Imurok. The first reason, they said, was a serious conflict between Wor-Obwoli and Libila. When I asked what caused the conflict between these two people, the Obbo elders told me that at that time Wor-Obwoli and Libla used to cultivate together and separate their gardens with with edge from one another's. One day, a garden which stood in Wor-Obwoli's sesame garden fell and the branches reached Libila's garden.

Unfortunately, Wor-Obwoli and Libila did not know who cut the tree, so Wor-Obwolo thought that it was Libila who did it intentionally; while Libila also thought it was Wor-Obwoli who cut the tree in his garden. This confusion led to conflict which led to the separation between the two brothers and Wor-Obwoli moved to Obbo.

However, some people said that in 1850 the people of Imurok called people to a burning-hunting expedition and many hunters turned up for it though other Imurok and Ifwotu people remained at home. When they saw that fires were about to meet, those who remained at home began to spear Nyibila Loyere women, the aged and children. When the Nyibila Loyere hunters came back they found the place smelling blood. They immediately decided to leave Imurok. The population of the Nyibila Loyere was very large, so they thought it wise not to move in one body, they should divide themselves into four different groups and settled in four different places. They then divided themselves into four groups. The first group moved to Liria, the second group settled at Imotong, the third group moved to Ofirika and the fourth group moved to Ikume Hill which is in Imurok.

Those who remained at the foot of Ikume Hill lived there for about two years. One day, after two years some boys were making drums at a stream which was not used for drinking water. Elders said there were also some girls among those boys. When they felt thirsty, the boys sent two girls to fetch for them drinking water from the well where the people of Imurok drew drinking water from. Unfortunately, the girls did not go to the point where women drew water from, they went to god's drawing point. The god made them to mysteriously disappear. After waiting for too long, the boys concluded that the god must have swallowed the girls up. They immediately went back home to inform elders about what had happened to the girls. The incident perplexed the elders very much.

Three days after, people saw vultures alighting at the god's drawing point. Wor-obwoli, having seen the vultures perching there, said "I am sure the vultures are going there to eat the flesh of the girls who disappeared." Libila was an elder brother of Wor-Obwoli. He was observing all the incidents with an eye of an elder. He told Wor-obwoli, "My brother, this is no longer a good place to live in. I want you to take my people to another place to the south." Wor-Obwoli heeded to his brother's advice, and at night, he immediately informed people to get ready to move to the people of Akara [Obbo]. In 1850 Chief Iliri who ruled the people of Lokomini and his people, warmly received Wor-Obwoli and his people, and Chief Iliri offered them a place a short distance away from the people of Lokomini to settle in.

The following day, at mid morning, the people of Lokomini went to greet Wor-obwoli and his brother, Libila. Libila was a serious looking man who did not smile or laugh anyhow. So, when the people of Lokomini went to greet them, he did not smile. But Wor-Obwoli liked conversation, and he was very jolly. He received the chief's people with happiness and with smile. Simply because Labila did not smile at the time people came to greet them, the people of Lokomini just concluded that he was a bad person. When they went back home, they told Chief Iliri, "O! Chief Wor-Obwoli is a very good person, but his brother Libila still has the dark-hardheartedness of the people of the hills. He does not like people. If you think we are telling you a lie, then you can go and see him by yourself."

The chief decided to meet the man. After two day, the chief went to greet Wor-Obwoli and his brother, Libila. When the chief entered the compound,

Wor-Obwoli and his brother knew that that was the chief of Lokomini and they received him with respect. Libila also received the chief with a smile. When Chief Iliri saw how the two brothers welcomed him, he thought his people might have had the intention of soiling the name of Libila.

Chief Iliri did not spend a night at Wor-Obwoli's. When he was leaving, he told Wor-obwoli, "I invite you to come and meet my people." Wor-Obwoli and Libila welcomed the chief's invitation, and with happiness, they shook hands with the chief.

Three day after, Wor-Obwoli and Libila paid a visit to chief at Lokomini to respond to the chief's invitation. When they arrived at Lokomini, they were thankfully received by the chief and taken on a high anthill at the outskirt of the compound. In the olden day, the chief of Lokomini would wear leopard skin when he was passing time with his visitors, so Chief Iliri also wore leopard skin when he was with Wor-obwoli and Libila. Another custom of the house of Lokomini was that when the chief was with his visitors, the person responsible for keeping the rain stones should take one or two stones to the chief. The elders of Obbo did not tell me the reason why the stone was to be taken to the chief at such moment. But they told me that the chief would cover the rain stone in a leopard skin and give it back to the keeper who took it back in the house. Covering the rain stone with leopard skin tells us the reason why the chief wore leopard skin when he was passing time with his guests. It is just because he would cover the rain stone with it at the end of their time together with his guests.

On that day when Wor-Obwoli and his brother visited the chief, the keeper of the rain stone also took the stone on the anthill as required by their custom. At the end of their time together, the chief removed the leopard skin from his waist and covered the rain stone with it and gave it to the keeper to take care of it. A moment after, the keeper of the stone and the guests got down from the anthill. Chief Iliri asked the keeper of the stone to help him see the guests off, but they ended up taking the visitors up their home. At Wor-obwoli, Chief Iliri told him, "Alright, our people, before I go back home, I want to tell you that I have been very happy because of two things: first, I am grateful that you have come to settle in my territory and secondly, I thank you for the social life which is developing between us. To show you that I am really happy, I give you the following appointments: Wor-Obwoli you will head this people, so even when people go for hunting expedition, I want them to get blessings from you so that they are safe in the wilderness. For you Libila who is the first born, I give you part of our hunting ground, Oloyo-tiko". Right now Oloyo-tiko hunting ground is under the control of the people of Wor-Obwoli. After this, the chief went back home.

The Acholi elders said Wor-Obwoli came from Imurok with two children, Loker and Olem. Loker was the first born and was followed by Olem. When Wor-obwoli was in Obbo, they begot a girl called Jwala. The family tree in Acholi was usually kept by men. In the house of Wor-obwoli, we find that two grand children, Ounda and Omwa are the ones that the people of Wor-Obwoli know that kept the family tree. The family tree of wor-Obwoli is as presented below:

► Wor-bwoli begot Loker and Loker begot Awangole; Awangole begot Ounda and Ounda begot Raymondo Opoka; and Opoka begot nine children who are today in Wor-obwoli. They include Latute, Renata Lakuli, Aryemo Lakuli, Biajo Okuna, Regina Alonyo, Anyek, Langoya Martin, Ligon Mark and Terjina Abalo.

► Wor-obwoli begot Loker and Loker begot Awangole. Awangole begot Omwa and Omwa begot Yak-yak. Yak-yak onywalo Lensio Okulo and Okulo begot six children who are in Wor-Obwoli. The six children are Guido Ojara, Ongwen Celestino, Teresa Acilo, Urbano Taban, Tekila and Julius Lotara.

When Wor-Obwoli came to Obbo they called themselves "Nyibila Loyere" or "Imurok" which means they were people who came from the house of Nyibila Loyere at Imurok. This name was used for quite a long time before the children of Loker and Olem changed and called themselves "Wor-Obwoli," which means they were the people of Wor-Obwoli.

Palyec migrated from Ikotos from the house of Odiya. They were led to Obbo by Pela. It seems the people of Palyec came to Obbo when the people of Obbo were already in Pambala, so they did not settle at Pambala, but they first settled at Ngabara then later moved to a place called Oyere.

Some people said *Gem* came from Madi Opei (Lango-Uganda). Elders told me that when the people of Gem left Madi Opei, they did not enter directly into Sudan. They first went to Palabek Gem in Uganda. But we cannot tell whether the Gem of Sudan are kins of Gem of Palabek (Uganda). As many people contend, we can affirm that Gem came from Madi Opei because of famine which had broken out there, but nobody knows the truth of the matter. Nobody knows the name of the person who led Gem from Madi Opei to Sudan, but they called him "Kwar Icunga" (the grandfather of Icunga), so we can say that it was "Kwar Icunga" was the one who led Gem from Madi Opei to Obbo. When the people of Gem settled at Palabek Gem, they were not well received and they did not take long there before the people of Palabek forced them out of the place. Some obstinate people of Gem remained at Palabek Gem while others trekked farther North and settled in Sudan. They found the people of Obbo at the foot of Lotii Hill and they settled with Wor-Obwoli.

Considering the information I obtained from the different books I read, I am not certain whether the people of Gem really came from Madi Opei in Uganda or from Boori-Madi (Sudan). As Father Crazzolara maintains, Boori was a kingship in the land of Boori-Madi who lived together. However, it seems it was the people of Pajulu who scattered them because of the war they waged on Boori-Madi. The people of Pajulu seriously fought Boori-Madi and divided them into three. A few of them fled to Moyo in Uganda. Others fled to Opari district and some were captured by Pajulu warriors and were made prisoners of war. Boori who escaped to Operi settled there and their population greatly increased there. Today there are up to twelve smaller houses (families) in the main house of Boori in Opari as listed below: Dungu, Latsam, Lira, Logobi, Lolopora, Lolubo, Lomora, Nggaaya, Nyamudhi (Lamudhi), Nyoori, Orobe, Orolo, Oyere, Pa-dombe, Pa-Kala, Palabek, Pandiker, Pa-Rathik, Pa-tibi, Pa-wooro, Pa-Yoko and Pa-Ooryo. A few years after, some of the Boori moved away from Opari, others went to Acholiland, others moved to Aku and others moved to Kavirondo (Crazzolara, 1954, P 367 & 385). Some of us think that the Gem people who are in Obbo today, some of them came from Madi Opei (Lango-Uganda) and some came from Oyere-Boori in Opari. This required more research.

However, people like Mr Urbano Taban, who is also a descendant of Wor-Obwoli, say, *"Our people, who are today called "Wor-Obwoli", when they were still at Imurok, were called "Nyibila Loyere". When they first arrived at Obbo, they called themselves"Omini", and then the name later changed from Omini to "Oyere". The name Oyere was not there in Obbo, the people of Wor-Obwoli were the ones who brought it as they called themselves "Oyere" to remember the place from which they came (or the home they left at Imurok).*

OYERE'S HUNTING GROUND AND HILL

Oyere has one hunting ground called *Oloyo-tiko* which is bordered by Abar, Amalac, Ladeng-deng, Ayoko and Lobela hunting grounds. Many years ago, Oloyo-tiko hunting ground belonged to Lokide. We do not know the first name of the hunting ground, but the people of Lokide later named it *"Mataburu"* in *"Angaji"(buru* is unfiltered alcohol). Lokide named the hunting ground "Mataburu" because that time, every time people went to hunt at least one person would die in the wilderness. Animals were killing many hunters. This made the people of Obbo to promulgate that "Any hunter who wanted to go to the hunting ground should first drink *"buru"* alcohol early in the morning because he was not certain whether he would come back alive or not." That is how the hunting ground became to be named "Mataburu". Lokide paid for this hunting ground to Panyibila because of the Panyibila girl whom Lokide killed.

In the year the people of Lokide gave this hunting ground to Oyere, they gave the hunting ground a new name, "Oloyo-tiko" instead of the old one. Oyere gave this name because if the girl was paid for with beads, only one person would wear the beads. So, they found that a hunting ground was better than beads because when an animal was killed on the hunting ground, every Oyere person had the opportunity to have a share of the meat. This is the reason why Oyere changed the name of the hunting ground from Mataburu to Oloyo-tiko. Jildo Odoch, of Panyibila, is the celebrant of Oloyo-tiko hunting ground. Unfortunately, the people of Obbo could not tell me the earlier celebrants of this hunting ground, and no one knew whether Jildo Odoch inherited the authority of celebrating Oloyo-tiko from someone.

Oyere people have one hill called Inapua Hill. The hill is in Oloyo-tiko hunting ground, near Licari. The Oyere people have a god called "Odikpiny" whose priest is from the house of Panyibila. The elders of Obbo told me that one of the earlier priests of this god, whom they could remember, was Oriya, from the house of Wor-Obwoli. After the death of Oriya, his son called Martino Twanga took over the priesthood. When Twanga died, Angeli, son of Oriya, became the next priest. Up to now, Angeli is the priest of Odik-piny.

POKONGO

Pokongo comprises four smaller houses: — *PokongoBura, Pajang-gi, Omili* and *Lokomini*. All these families came from different places.

154

We know that the people of *Bura* came to Obbo in 1686. When I asked people of Panyikwara in Juba, I discovered that nobody knew where the people of Bura came from. However, some few told me that Bura came from Panyikwara, but they did not know the name of the person who led them to Obbo. The history of Obbo has it that the people of Pokongo Bura and Pajombo Okwee were the second group of people to enter Obbo. They followed the people of Kitaka. As we have seen before, Kitaka were the first people to join the people of Koyo, and they later took up the leadership of the place because of the effectiveness of their rain stone. In 1686, the people of Koyo did not know rain stone. During this time, it was the chief of Kitaka who ruled Obbo, and he was the one who welcomed the people of Bura and showed them where to settle.

Pajang-gi people came from Woroge (in Panyikwara from the house of Globa-Alero) around 1850. Most people think that the people of Pajang-gi left Panyikwara because of famine which was killing people at that time. When he saw his people dying of hunger, Ariko remembered "kinyu' in Obbo. He eventually led his people to Obbo. Ariko was accompanied by his father's brother called Okaca. It seems Ariko came from Globa-Alero without a wife. He later married a woman from Panto (Pajok), whose name we do not know. His uncle also married a woman called Akec, from Panto. The people of Pajang-gi came when the people of Obbo were on Lotii Hill. The chief of Abong warmly welcomed them and gave them a place close to Pokongo Bura to settle in. At this time, Obbo was also ravaged by famine. These people came when the people of Obbo were eating "kinyu". It is said the Ariko and his people walked for about three days without eating and eventually reached Lotii Hill. They were badly emaciated, but "kinyu" helped them to regain strength to begin to build their huts. The people of Pajang-gi came from Panyikwara as a unit. When they reached Obbo, Ariko's people divided themselves into three smaller groups (houses): P'Otwong, Pajang-gi P'Ariko and Lokomini. Other sources contend that Lokomini came much later, in Pokongo. It was the friendship between Lociya-moi and Ariko that made them to come, but we cannot tell how exactly they came. Philimena Ayaa of Pajang-gi, from Sydney Australia, said Lociya-moi of Lokomini also married Lucia Angwec (other people called her Cacaa) from Panto. This is why Ariko and Lociya-moi called one another *Obbaa*, because they married from the same house, Panto.

Omili are people of Omili who came from two different places. Some of them came from Panyikwara [from the house of Ayom]. It was Obalo who brought them to Obbo. Others came from Agoro [from the house of Bura], but we do not know the name of the person who brought them from Agoro. Acholi elders told me that the people of Omili came to Obbo at almost the same time with Pajang-gi. They arrived at Obbo between 1852 and 1860. The Omili people who came from Panyikwara and Agoro were forced out of the two places by famine. Omini people came when the people of Obbo were still on Lotii Hill. The chief of Abong received them and gave them space to settle near the people of Pokongo Bura.

Lokomini hailed from Oyere from the house of Wor-Obwoli (Obbo). They found some Pokongo people on the other side of Ayii Stream. The history of Obbo says that Isongo-reng Lotina was the one who led the people of Lokomini from Oyere. Other sources claimed that Isongo-reng's people left Oyere because of conflict between Otoo, the chief of Abong, and him. It seems Isogno-reng had rain stone, so he did not want to be under the chiefdom of Abong. Others say that the people of Lokomini migrated from Pokongo because of land for cultivating peas. In the whole of the Acholiland, the Pakongo are known for cultivating peas. Pokongo Lokomini left some of their brothers at Oyere. That is, *Oyere* P'Ombwoli. They migrated between 1935-1945. Friendship created very strong relationship between Lokomini and *Lokomini of Pajanggi*. That is why after the death of the famous Lociya-moi of Lokomini his people lived with Pajang-gi.

THE HUNTING GROUNDS AND THE HILL OF POKONGO

Pokongo has three hunting grounds which include *Gili-gili* neighbouring other hunting grounds such as Jom, Ongol-kor, la-oraa Kirimanzi, MeriLokide and Pakwa Hill; *Lalworo-odong*. Others said that Lalworo-odong hunting ground is what is today known as Gili-gili, and there is *Jom* which is bordered by Okony-kor, Gili-gili, Apedo and Akidi hunting grounds. Some of the people of Pokongo contend that Bong-won hunting ground is also theirs; many Obbo people affirm that Bong-won hunting ground belongs to the people of Loudo. The people of Pokongo just built in the hunting ground at the time when people were migrating from Loudo Hill. The people of Pokongo also cultivated in Bong-won, but that does not mean the hunting ground is theirs. When I read about the settlement of dispute that the people of Obbo held at Loudo on the 23-24/12/2009, I learned that people said that Pakongo has another hunting ground called Akidi which extends and meets Giligili, Bongwon, Merilokide, Agongara and Jom hunting grounds. The elder Otori/Peke is the one who celebrates the hunting ground and calls people to hunt on the ground. Pokongo has one hill called *Pokongo* Hill. They also have one god called *Nya-Pido*. Irene Abwo of Pokongo-Lokomini told me from Melbourne that the people of Pokongo think that the first priest of Nya-Pido could be Ariko. After the death of Ariko, the priesthood went to Atiyo after whose death Ayonde-Pa-Atiyo took up the priesthood. Nya-Pido is the god that all the people of Pokongo worship on the day they celebrate it. The people would bring spears, bows and arrows before the shrine of Pajang-gi-Pa-Akiro. The celebration is done after every two or three years. After the blessing of spears, bows and arrows, hunters go on a hunting expedition. In the culture of Pokongo, all animals killed from the wilderness must be brought before the shrine. The meat is smoked on a platform made in front of the shrine. The meat is eaten for two or three days. When it is over, every person now goes back to his home. All these days people dance as they sing:

Waneno Ocaa!	We have seen Ocaa!
Ocaa Pudi Tidi!	Ocaa is still young!
Ayonde Pa Tiyo!	Ayonde of Tiyo!

However, the elders would reward a hunter who killed buffalo with the thigh of the buffalo right from the hunting ground. If it was not given from the wilderness, the hunter would not get anything to take to his children.

KOYO LOKOMINI

The people of Koyo are the owners of Obboland because they are the first to settle on the land. When they arrived at the place there was nobody there. They immediately named the place and hunting ground Koyo. Koyo hunting ground became Obbo's later as we will look at in this book.

Koyo has four smaller settlements: Bira, Pa-tany, Obalo and Ayom. From the four, Ayom was the first to enter Obbo. They came from Lokoya as we will see in this book. When I asked Koyo elders such as Julius Okeny, who belongs to the house of Pa-tany, he told me that the people of Bira, Pa-tany and Obalo came from Toposa. They found Koyo Ayom were on Lotii Hill, but he did not know when and how these people moved to Obbo. As a result, I will not say much about the people of Bira, Patany and Obalo, but I will talk about the houses of Ayom and other groups. The people of Bira, Pa-tany and Obalo have been assimilated to Koyo Lokomini because they settled among the people of Koyo Ayom without a chiefdom of their own.

The people of Koyo, among the Acholi Sudan are in Palwar and Obbo only. I would like to inform my readers that when I talk about Koyo, I mean Koyo Ayom because other people have already written about them. We cannot talk about Koyo of Sudan without talking about Koyo of Uganda because they both have the same origin. When I asked people, I discovered that Father Crazzolara is right when he said, when you ask Acholi men, "Where did you come from?" Many times they answer, "We came from Bar, Olubo, Aruu or Ngangala" (Crazzolara, 1951, p.256). I think this kind of response is because most people do not know where they came from. Secondly, some Acholi elders do not tell the truth to their children because they lack the knowledge of their history and culture. Children often take the information they obtain from elders as absolute truth, simply because it was said by an elder, whom everybody trust is the custodian of the culture and history of the people.

About the movement of Koyo, people have different information. For example, Onyango, in his book says that a person called Alunga Lujima told him that the Koyo came from Anywak. They migrated from Anywak after a separation with Wipaco Dwong. They settled at Tekidi at the hills of northern Agoro. They found the people of Lukwor already settled there. Koyo moved with many heads of cattle. It did not take long before the people learned many things from the people of Lukwor. First, they learned how to make spear, and they immediately made their blacksmith oven. The people of Koyo came to Tekidi when Obira was the chief. Koyo elders asked Chief Obira if they could be allowed to dig iron from the mining site of the people of Lukwor. Unfortunately, Obira did not consult the clan elders of Lukwor. When the people of Koyo asked him about the mining of iron by Koyo, Chief Obira said if they wanted to mine iron they should give him a black hornless bull, with a white perch below its eye. Chief Obira asked for a bull of this description because he had seen one in the kraal of the people of Koyo when they had just come to Lukwor. (The chief was interested in the bull). Chief Obira saw the bull when Koyo were watering their animals at the stream. Koyo gave the chief the bull he wanted because they actually wanted to dig iron for the mining site (Onyango-ku-Odongo, 1976, PP. 67-68).

When he received the bull, Chief Obira immediately allowed the people of Koyo to mine iron from the Koyo mining site without consulting the clan elders of Lukwor.

The Lukwor clan elders, having heard what happened between the chief and people of Koyo, were not pleased. Because of this discontentment, the elders removed Obira from the thrown. The elders did this because they knew their rules did not permit the people of Koyo to mine from their mining site for they would easily deplete the iron deposit. The depletion of the iron deposit meant the end of life of the people of Lukwor because their life was mainly dependent on iron.

After removing Chief Obira from the throne, the elders of Lukwor showed the people of Koyo their rules, after which they asked Obira to return the bull of the Koyo people. Unfortunately, the elders had already used the bull for cleansing Obira's abomination of giving out the mining site. This later led to a serious conflict and fight between the people of Koyo and Labwor, and people were killed on both sides. The elders of Lukwor realised that fighting did not lead to development, so they called the elders of Koyo for a peace talk which was well concluded.

To remember the war between Lukwor and Koyo, one Acholi man from Uganda, called Opelu, sang this song:

Iyee Obira Oneka Yee!
Iyee Obira killed me Yee!
En Obira
It is Obira
Obalo Paco-wa YAee!
Who destroyed our home yee!
Obwot Nekka Yee!
He nearly killed me Yee!
Iyee Eee Iyee Eee! (2)
Iyee Eee Obira (2)
Obalo Paco-wa Yee!

Destroyed our home Yee!

A Koyo man also composed a bwola song to insult the people of Lukwor that they were the ones who started the war. Here goes the song:

Jo Lukwor Dag Kom Lela-gi
Lukwor refused for their mining site
Jo Koyo yam Owilo Lela
Koyo had bought the mining site
Iyee Joni Owilo Lela loyo Awobi
Iyee my people bought the mining site and far better than boys
Oyai Lokwor onekka ma Lango Lok Yee
Oyai Lukwor killed me as Lango
Say Yee
Kom Dyianga
About my bulls

These two songs are very important among the Acholi. Up to now, the songs are still there (Onyango-ku-Odongo, 1976, PP 67-69).

I do not know if Onyango talks of Koyo of Sudan or Koyo of Uganda, or both. He does not show how Koyo of Sudan left Tekidi and how they moved. We know very well that Lukwor are found in Puranga (Uganda), these people do not say they came with Lwo, but their leader was Kwor, Kwanga's son who separated from "Jo-ku-Owiny" when the people today we call Lukwor went back to Sudan after Tekidi was deserted.

When I compared what Crazzolara and Onyango wrote about Koyo of Uganda and Sudan, I found that Crazzolara's writing is clearer, and it makes it easy to differentiate between the two groups. Father Crazzolara said, "The people of Koyo do not know where they came from, but we later understood that all the people of Koyo (i. e. from Sudan and Uganda) came from Aruu in at Lokoya. When asked where they came from, Acholi always say, "We came from Bar, Olubo, Aruu or Ngangala, which is along Liria Juba Highway" (Crazzolara, 1951, P. 256).

Since people had moved a lot, it seems the Koyo people who were in Olubo and Aruu learned that some of their tribemates were in Atyak (Uganda). They then left Lokoya to look for their people in other places. When they left Lokoya, they settled at Ayom, where the Ayom Panyikwara are today. But some elders contend that the people of Koyo got away from Lokoya because a rival over chiefdom. It was the chief's jealousy that dispersed them from there. They divided themselves into different groups. Others remained at Ayom. The chief, in 1936, was Chief Acok. Some of them joined Madi people without their own chief. Let us first look at how the Koyo of Uganda moved before we look at Koyo of Sudan moved, to avoid confusion.

KOYO-UGANDA

Chief Lobii took the people of Koyo, who are in Uganda today, to Ayom Hill in Panyikwara and to Atyak (Uganda). Chief Lobii left some koyo behind at Ayom Hill under the leadership of chief Keny. From Atyak, they proceeded to Payira and settled at the foot of Palee Hill at Alero. They lived here for many years. The chief of Alero called Kiriya married Amono, the sister of Chief Obvura of Koyo when they were still at the foot of Palee Hill. Unfortunately, the woman was loose with men. It seems the chief of Oyuu (whose name we do not know) knew about Amono's looseness. One day the chief despised Amono and insulted her, "Look at her, a whore! A woman who leaves her husband and goes to sleep with other men." People who were present reported the insult to other Pangora people. When Pangora heard the chief's spitefulness they waged a war against the people of Oyuu. After many women and children had died, they removed Amono from the man with whom she was sleeping, and they returned her to her husband, Chief Kiriya. At this time when Koyo were at the foot of Palee Hill, they were under their own leadership. Later, they began to despise the people of Alero, that they were cowards like women. So, their sister, Amono should go back to the Oyuu man with whom she was illegally sleeping. It seems Koyo wanted the Alero to fight the people of Oyuu when the Oyuu man slept with Amono, if they were not cowards (Crazzolara, 1954, P. 399).

The people of Alero were so angered that they waged a war against Koyo of the house of Chief Obvura. They also raided the cattle (Amono's bride price). Alero defeated Koyo and Koyo fled from Palee Hill and moved to Paboo, Palaaro, Agoro and Pajule. A few months after, the chief of Alero died at Lamoola. Immediately, after the death of the chief, Kiriya was enthroned. Chief Kiriya led his people out of Lamoola because of the hardship they had experienced there and continued to fight. When he realised that it was impossible to live at Lamoola, Chief Kiriya moved with his people to Patiko. They went past KijuAjulu Hill and reached Ladwong. From Ladwong, they settled at Awal-Aboro, at an animal-clay pit. They settled there, and they food stuff was over. The people of Parabok had dug a number of trap pits near the cattle-clay pit. There are so many animal trap pits among the Acholi of Uganda and Acholi of Sudan. They used to dig such traps around animal-clay pits because many animals would come there to eat lick clay. Among the Acholi, the pit trap was usually six to nine feet long and six to seven feet deep. This is to prevent an animal that fell in the trap from getting out. The animal would remain in the trap until the owner of the trap got it there.

One morning, Chief Odong-Abok of Parabok sent two of his sons, Bwoc and Lapiny to check his animal traps. The boys found so many people at the animal-clay pit that they were frightened and went back home. When they boys reached home, they told their father, "Chief, we found so many people at the animal-clay pit, and we do not know them. They comprise men, women and children, and they have heads of cattle and royal drum (Crazzolara, 1951, PP. 257-258).

When he heard this news, Chief Odong-Abok called clan elders and told them everything that his two sons had told him. The clan elders advised that their royal drum be sounded to call people to come and go to find out which people those were. The chief instructed a man to beat the drum, and when he did, people gathered in great numbers. A moment later, the chief instructed his people, "I want you to take your bow and arrows and any other weapons you have and move to our animal-clay pit to see if the people who have assembled there came to attack us, or they are looking for a place to settle. When you reach there, I want Lapiny and two others to ask them what they want. If you find that they have come to attack us, let them be the first to strike you" (Crazzolara, 1950, P. 259).

After Chief Odong-Abok finished giving instruction, his subjects made straight for the animal-clay pit. On reaching there, Lapiny took two men with whom they went to the people of Alero and asked them, "Do you live here?" The people of Alero humbly responded, "We are looking for a place where there are many people because we have fought with Koyo and they are still interested in fighting us. So, we are looking for people with whom we can join hands to fight Koyo." Lapiny listened to them carefully and told them, "Alright, let me go back and tell my elder brother to come and talk to you. Let him listen to you and and take your voice to our father, Chief Odong-Abok".

After talking to Alero, Lapiny returned home and told his brother, Bwoc, the interest of Alero. Bwoc wasted no time to go and greet the people of Alero. Everybody was pleased with the warm welcome Parabok gave them. Alero confided in Bwoc the cause of their coming to Parabok. Bwoc listened to them very carefully, and later, Chief Kiriya interjected, "You! Women are almost dying of hunger. They slept without eating. When you reach home, do not forget about porridge and bread." Bwoc sent Lapiny to tell their father to instruct women to prepare porridge and bread for their visitors. He also told Bwoc to inform their father that Alero did not want to attack them. They only fled from a fight between them and Koyo. They were looking for people with whom they could join hands to fight Koyo (Crazzolara, 1950, P. 259).

Lapiny reported to Chief Odong-Abok, and the chief was not happy about what happened to Alero. He instructed elders to tell women to prepare porridge and bread for their visitors. The elders made every household informed of the chief's instruction, and the women did as they were told. The chief told Lapiny to bring the visitors home, and Lapiny asked Chief Kiriya and his subjects over to his father's. Before Alero entered the palace, Chief Odong-Abok took white cock and white ram and went to meet Alero people. He waved the cock at the feet of the visitors as he said, "I am pleased to meet my visitors, be healthy and no evil should cross your way. May God bless your women with fertility so that they bear many children! I, Chief Odong-Abok, bless you from the bottom of my heart. I invoke the spirit of my forefathers, Kwinyo, Labwor and Okelo and the spirits of the elders for my visitors to enjoy health at my place."

Chief Odong-Abok slaughtered the ram and took its dung, which he smeared on the chest and legs of Chief Kiriya. He did the same to some of the Alero people. He threw the remaining dung to the west, which implies that all evil should go with the setting sun, and good things should come with the rising sun.

After the rituals, Chief Odong-Abok, Lapiny and Bwoc distributed the visitors to different households of Parabok. Only three days after, women sent their voice to the chief that food was not enough for them. The chief instructed his subjects to help the people of Alero to build *Abak* (hut) so that they could settle in their own houses. The Parabok men helped the men of Alero with building materials, and the Parabok women also helped Alero to gather thatch. In a short while, Alero households had their shelters ready to migrate in. Parabong continued to take millet to Alero women, and the people of Alero began to cultivate different crops. By November, foodstuff was in abundance; there was only lack of space to store it. Alero and Parabok were so united that life became very enjoyable. Alero also forgot what happened to them at Mutongo animal-clay pit (crazzolara, 1950, PP.260-261). Later, there was a serious fight between Alero and Palaro, but I cannot give all its details here. For more information about it, read Crazzolara, 1950, *"The Lwo Volume 2"* pp 261-285.

KOYO-SUDAN

As we have looked at how the Koyo of Uganda moved, let us turn to look at how the Koyo of Sudan also moved. In the same year when Chief Lobii took part of Koyo Ayom (Panyikwara) to Uganda, Chief Keny and his brother, Obeny also took a section of Koyo who had remained in Ayom and led them to the east. They moved for a few day and came to Lotii Hill. Koyo were the first people to settle at Lotii Hill. When they reached there, there were no people there. For that reason, they called the place and the hunting ground Koyo. Since Koyo did not find anybody in that place, they actually become the owner of the place. However, we will look at how Koyo hunting ground became Obbo's hunting ground.

At the foot of Lotii Hill, Koyo split up into two groups: the Koyo of Keny and that of Obeny. Most Koyo of Keny settled on the top of Lotii Hill. Those who followed Obeny settled at Palwar. Although they were in two groups, both groups at Obbo and Palwar seemed to have been ruled by Chief Keny because he was a senior chief to Obeny. Despite their separate settlements, the people of Koyo kept visiting one another and maintained strong bond among clan members. However, what we do not know is whether the Koyo of Obbo can marry Koyo of Palwar or not.

Nobody knows exactly when Koyo entered the land of Acholi in Sudan, but it is thought that they might have come to Sudan between 1600-1700 (?). Koyo lived on Lotii Hill for many years, and some Acholi elders told me that some Obbo came and found Koyo on Lotii Hill.

The first group of people to join Koyo was Kitaka followed by Pajombo Okwee and Pokongo. The third group was Abong. All these groups came when Koyo was still on Lotii Hill. However, we cannot tell, who was the chief of Koyo, by the time Kitaka joined them on Lotii Hill. Some people said it was Chief Atany who was the chief of Koyo at that time, but Chief Atany's reign was between 1855-1902, yet Kitaka joined Koyo around 1700 (?). So, I can conclude that the chief of Koyo at that time was either Chief Labongo or Chief Angaca.

The Acholi elders whom I asked about the history and cultures of Acholi told me that the first Koyo chief was Chief Keny. When Keny died, the throne was left in the hands of his son, Chief Der-Lubanga. After the death of Der-Lubanga, Labongo became the chief. When Labongo died, the chiefdom was left to Angaca who later died and the throne was given to Lokol Lokomini. Some people said that Chief Lokol was the father of Atany and Atany was Pido-Moi's brother. After the death of Chief Lokol, the throne was left to Chief Atany (1855-1902). Atany left the throne to his son called Lotara-kenyo-moi. Then in 1936 when Chief Lotara-kenyo-moi died, the chiefdom was left to his son called Oneka Lamang. We actually do not know which chiefs followed Chief Oneka Lamang.

PEOPLE MIGRATED TO THE FOOT OF LOTII HILL

As we have seen before, the people who joined Koyo came when Koyo were still on Lotii Hill. Obbo lived on Lotii Hill for many years, but in 1920 they thought of bringing the cattle down at the foot of the hill. Obbo people had very many heads of cattle, sheep and goats. I think the pasture on the hill was depleted and people were forced to bring the animals down at the foot of the hill where there was abundant pasture. Even at the foot of the hill, pastures were not enough for the animals, so people split up. Many people of Koyo remained at the foot of the hill under the chieftain of Chief Atany, and Pido-moi took some of them to the west at the foot of Ayom Hill. Pido-moi's people took about ten years at Ayom Hill 1920-1930 (?). Some people said that, at Ayom Hill, Pido-moi had three sons: Ayom, Bira and Obalo (the father of Lopiribok), but other people contend that Chief Pido-moi begot all the three sons when he was still at Lotii Hill. When the three sons grew up, their father assigned them different duties. Bira and Obalo were to watch out for any approaching adversaries and Ayom was to look after the cattle, goats and sheep. Ayom's mother was still alive, but Bira and Obalo's were no longer alive. The two boys lived in the hands of Ayom's mother, their step mother.

One day, Obira and Obalo went very far on spy mission. They came back home very tired and hungry. Unfortunately, their step mother had given all the food and milk to Ayom alone. The boys were very much upset by what their step mother did to them, and they reported it to their father, "Father, when we came back from the wilderness, we found that Ayom's mother had given all food and milk to her son, yet we are almost dying of hunger. This is not the first time she has done this to us."

Pido-moi was not pleased by what his wife was doing to his sons, Bira and Obalo. The two boys thought that their father did not like them, so they decided to leave Ayom Hill and move back to Koyo (Obbo). One morning, Bira, Obalo and their well-wishers walked back to Obbo at the foot of Lerwa Hill.

Bira and Obalo were warmly received by the people of Koyo whom they had left behind. The two continued with their duty of watching out for enemies as they used to do at Panyikwara (Ayom). Vigilante was very important those days because cattle raiders were common. One day Obalo went to watch the eastern part of their territory. On his way, Obalo met the people of Isore. The people of Isore immediately concluded that Obalo wanted to steal their animals. (They thought Obale had gone to their place to spy on them). The people of Isore abducted Obalo. They later disagreed on whether the boy could be set free or not.

The Isore men brought Obalo home. They asked Obalo many questions when they were still on the way (I do not know what they asked him). Fortunately, Obalo knew the language of Koyo, because they used to speak it from Panyikwara (Ayom). Although they also had their own language, the Isore people also spoke the language of Koyo. Obalo was very wise. He did not verbally answer any of the questions he was asked. He behaved like a deaf and nodded his head to say "Yes" and shook his head to say "No." He used body language to respond to the questions. When the Isore men realised that they could not get any information from Obalo, they told him, "You will not go back to your homeland since you cannot tell us anything that we want."

Isore gave Obalo a beautiful girl so that he could tell them what they wanted from him. Elders instructed the girl to do anything that Obalo wanted, but should not allow him to have sex with her. The girl worked with Obalo for three months, and Obalo kept on asking her to sleep with him but the girl turned him down all the time. But for how many months would the girl keep turning Obalo down. As Acholi say, a leopard does not live together with a goat. Three months after, she could resist Obalo no more. He slept with her and she eventually conceived. The people of Isore were not pleased with their daughter and Obalo. Some of them thought of killing Obalo, but elders disagreed with them. The elders said that Obalo should marry their daughter whom he had impregnated.

One day elders called Obalo and told him that, "Young man, you have impregnated the girl we gave you to work for you. We want you to pay her bride wealth with heads of cattle." Since he had pretended deafness, Obalo responded to elders by pointing to the direction of Lotii Hill. He did this to let the elders know that since they wanted him to marry the girl with heads of cattle, his father's cattle were at Lotii Hill (pointing at Lotii Hill). The elders allowed him to go and ring the animals from Lotii as he was pointing to its direction. However, the elders thought that if they left Obalo to go alone, he might not come back. They selected three young warriors to accompany Obalo to Lotii (Koyo). When he reached home, Obalo told his brother, Bira everything that had happened to him, including the trick he plaid to the people of Isore, which made him to survive and come back.

Bira was very pleased that his brother had got a wife. He instructed his herdsmen to take fifty heads of cattle for the bride price of the woman to the people of Isore. The herdsmen did as they were instructed and handed over the fifty heads of cattle to the men of Isore. However, in the culture of the Isore people, if a girl married a foreign man (a non Isore man) , the girl must not live in the land of the boy because they wanted their girls to be close to their parents. So, after receiving the fifty heads of cattle, the Isore men asked Obalo to go and make his home in the land of Isore. Since Bira did not want to disappoint their brothers-in-law, he gave them the animals and allowed his brother, Obalo to go to live in Isore as their culture demanded. Bira's people escorted Obalo up to Gicenge stream, and they shook hands with him, telling him, "May the Creator be with you, you should be a mediator between the people of Isore and Bira (Koyo)."

Obalo took all the animals to the clan elders of his bride. Obalo then went back and settled at Gicenge. Some Isore people came and settled there with him. All the people of Isore and the children that Obalo begot called themselves Obalo's Koyo. Then after a few years they changed their name to Abee's Koyo. The Koyoo that remained at Obbo called themselves Bira's Koyo, the people of Bira {some people call them Atany's Koyo} and the Koyo people at Panyikwara called themselves Ayom's Koyo (or the people of Ayom). That is the reason why the Koyo of Sudan have three different houses as "Koyo Obalo" or "Abee's Koyo" who are in Palwar, "Koyo Bira" at Obbo and "Koyo Ayom" in Panyikwara.

When Bira returned to Obbo, all Atany's subject fell under the control of Chief Bira. The elders of Koyo told me that when Obalo went to Isore, Atany remained at the foot of Lotii Hill together with Bira. Before Bira came back to Obbo, Chief Pido-moi handed over his rain stone to him, but when Bira reached Obbo, he gave the stone to his brother, Atany. That is why Atany became the chief of Bira's Koyo. We are not sure if Atany was Pidomio's son or Bira's because some people say Atany was not Pido's son but Bira's though others claimed he was Piomoi's eldest son to whom Pidomoi left his chiefdom when he was leaving Lotii Hill to go back to Ayom (Panyikwara).

From Lotii, Bira and Atany moved to Iwala Hill from where they moved on to Loyuru Hill. Bira lived at the foot of Loyuru for a few years and migrated to Loudo. From here people moved to Pambala, but the people of Koyo and Ngabara went and settled at the foot of Lerwa Hill. Koyo people found that Lerwa was not a good place for them, they continued moving and reached Agata, while others went and settled in Lobone and Isore. Atany remained in Lerwa where he became chief. He lived here up to 1902 (?) when he died. After the death of Chief Atany, the chiefdom was left to his son called Lotara-gengo-moi who left the chiefdom to his son called Oneka Lamang, after his death. Chief Lamang took care of the chiefdom up to 1936.

KOYO'S HUNTING GROUNDS AND HILLS

As we have seen before, Koyo are the original owners of this place and they owned the hunting grounds and hill in Obbo. When many groups of people joined them, the people of Koyo gave out some of their hunting grounds and hills to the people they hosted. For this reason, the Koyo of Atany has now remained with only nine hunting grounds. They include Ciri, Oyaa (which the people of RDC/Pajok have cultivated on), Abiri, Lobano-Ayii, Alyebi, Igoli, Lotii,

Apala and Alai hunting grounds. Ciri hunting ground is bordered by Oyaa, Lobano-Ayii and Oloyo-Iweny which ends at Atepi stream. Tim Oyaa bordered by Ciri, Logolo and Borokwac. Abiri is bordered by Acineno (we do not know if Acineno is a hunting ground or a stream. On the other side Abiri bordered by Onek-gwok (we also do not know if Onek-gwok is a stream). Lobano-Ayii is neighboured by Logolo, Balbal and Iluki hunting grounds. Alyebi hunting ground is bordered by Igoli, Lohilim, Lotii, Alai and Ayii stream.

Igoli hunting ground is bordered by Lohilim, Alyebi, Lotii hunting grounds and and Ayii Stream. Apala is bordered by Lobano-Ayii and Alai which is bordered by Alyebi. We actually do not know the person who was the first to perform rituals and called people to hunt on these hunting grounds, but the person whom people know as the one to call hunters to hunt in the nine hunting grounds is Okumu Silva. Koyo did not only give out hunting grounds to the foreigners, but also hills and this made them to remain with only six hills now. They are Abiri Hill, Lotii Hill, Coko Hill, Layuru Hill (?) Ilai Hill and Ciri Hill. Koyo has only one god called Nya-rubanga who is on Abiri Hill. We do not know if Koyo gave out some of their gods to the foreigners who joined them or not.

THE WHITE MAN MOVED PEOPLE TO LOTII HILL BECAUSE OF SLEEPING SICKNESS

Ahamed Bayoumi (1976), in his book,"*The History of Sudan Health Services*" claims that "Long ago, sleeping sickness (Trypanosomes) was in East Africa only. In 1842 the disease first showed up in Guinea. Sleeping sickness had been killing many people in the east from 1842 up to 1887, and in 1887 the disease entered Congo. In 1914 Chalmers and O'Farrel reported the the disease had entered 1888. The disease was clandestinely killing people until 1901 when the health workers in Kampala diagnosed the first patience with it."

Map showing where sleeping sickness were found in Sudan

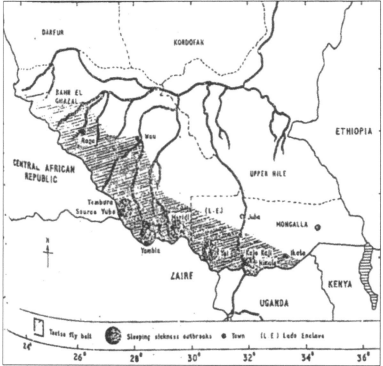

Sleeping sickness entered Sudan from the south through Uganda. The health workers in Sudan said that they discovered the first case, transmitted by animal, in 1904. In 1905 the Sudan Government formed "*Sudan Sleeping Sickness Commission*" to find ways of containing the disease. To help Sudan Sleeping Sickness Commission, the government appointed Lt-Colonel Hunter a Medical Officer in charge of all health units in Sudan. The disease does not cover the whole of Sudan, but it is only found in Yei, Kajo-Kaji, Tombura, Meridi and Yambio. In 1910-1940 the disease killed very many people in Yei, Kajo-Kaji and Tombura. Later, the sickness spread to Meridi and Yambio between 1941 and 1965 (Ahmed Bayoumi, 1976, P. 42). To know the different places which are ravaged by this disease in Southern Sudan, look at Picture No. 17). Although Ahamed Bayoumi claimed that the disease was only in south eastern Sudan, Acholi elders told me that the disease also killed Acholi people in 1925. In 1925 sleeping sickness killed many people in Pajok, Palwar, Obbo, Omeo and Agoro; but we cannot tell which houses exactly in Pajok, Palwar, Obbo, Omeo and

Agoro were attacked by the disease. D.C. of Opari saw that many people were dying and the disease could not be easily controlled, so he ordered the people of Pajok, Obbo, Palwar, Omeo and Agoro to vacate the places and settle on Lotii Hill. In 1927 the people followed DC's instruction and moved to Lotii Hill and settled there from 1927 to 1932.

In 1932, when the disease had reduced, the government told the people who had migrated to Lotii Hill to leave the top of the hill and come to settle on the plains. At that time, some Obbo people settled in Pambala (at the foot of Loudo Hill) and other people settled in Alia. The people of Pajok settled in Tumatuma and later moved to Ayacii. However, the people of Pajok did not find Ayacii good for settlement because there was lack of water there. Women would walk a long distance in search of water. For that reason, in 1936 the people of Pajok moved to Atebi Stream and that is the present place the Pajok people inhabit today. The people of Omeo and Agoro settled where they are found today. Sleeping sickness did not attack all parts of Acholiland. The oral sources have it that Panyikwara and Magwi did not experience the disease, and that is the reason why the government did not ask them to migrate to Lotii Hill. Panyikwara and Magwi remained in their place up to the present.

TING-GILI

Ting-gili is divided into three smaller families: Ileregi, Logoti and P'Ogwee. All the three families came from different places.

Ileregi and Logoti both came from Loudo (Torit). These two groups left Loudo in 1890 because of a serious famine which killed many people. Otherwise, we do not know the name of the person who led this people from Loudo to Obbo. When the people of Ileregi and Logoti arrived at Obbo they found people at Loudo Hill. The chief of Obbo received Ileregi and Logoti warmly and gave them space to settle in.

P'Ogwee came from Baar-Tingiri. According to Fr. Crazzolara, the people of P'Ogwee of Obbo moved together with P'Ogwee who are now in Padibe. They first camped at the foot of Agoro Hill and later moved to Padibe in Uganda. When the people of P'Ogwee entered Padibe, Chief Amot who brought the people of P'Amot and Baar, welcomed P'Ogwee and allowed them to settle among the people of P'Amot as a chiefless people. They settled at a place called Okoora, and later they became the responsible of the coronation of the chief of Padibe (Crazzolara, 1954, P. 500). Crazzolara clearly states that P'Ogwee came from Baar-Tingiri, but he did not make it clear whether the people he talked about were the people of P'Ogwee who are today in Obbo, or he talked about the P'Ogwee in Padibe only. In his book, he did not make it clear if P'Ogwee of Obbo just returned to Padibe or they remained there when the P'Ogwee who are today in Padibe were moving to Uganda.

However, when I asked elders, they told me that the people of P'Ogwee, who are in Obbo, truly came from Baar. It was Ogwee who brought them to Obbo. They found people of Obbo at Loudo. Chief of Obbo welcomed them and gave them a place to settle among the people of Ileregi and Logoti. This is why P'Ogwee became one of the houses in Ting-gili. A few years after, most P'Ogwee did not find Obbo a good place for them to settle, so some of them moved further until they reached Padibe in Uganda. Some of the P'Ogwee people, who enjoyed living in Obbo, remained there among the people of Ileregi and Logoti. That is why we find some P'Ogwee people in Obbo and others in Padibe. These two groups have very strong kinship tie. Consequently, during the Joseph Lagu war between 1963 and 1973, P'Ogwee in Obbo fled to their brothers in Padibe (Uganda) when Anyaya guerrilla and the Sudan government soldiers were killing people in Acholiland in Sudan.

TING-GILI'S HILL AND HUNTING GROUNDS

Ting-gili own five hunting grounds. These include Balbal, Lohilim, Buk-buk, Iluki and Nyara. It is Peter Odok who is the main celebrant of the five hunting grounds and it is him who invites people to hunt on the grounds. However, some oral sources have it that Nyara Hunting ground which is situated north of Ayii Stream belongs to the people of Kitaka, and Jackson Ochara is the one who celebrates it. I think these people are not right because when I was in Juba, I asked many elders of Obbo who told me that Nyara belongs to Ting-gili. So, in this book, we take Nyara to be the hunting ground of Ting-gili. The people of Ting-gili have a hill called Baile which is near Palotaka Mission. Baile Hill and the five hunting grounds of Tingi-gili belong to Ileregi. Therefore, it is Peter Odok of Ileregi who controls all the five hunting grounds. Unfortunately, the people of Ting-gili do not have a god.

Although Ting-gili honours the rain chief of Abong, they also have their own rain chief whose name we do not know. Obbo elders told me that at the time when Ileregi were coming from Loudo (Torit), one elder of the family carried his rain stone along. We cannot tell from which chief the rain making power started, but the ones whom people can remember are Chief Ogoda, who left the power to his son called Alfonsio Ogoda after his death. To date, Alfonsio is the one who makes rain in Ting-gili. He makes rain when the chief of Abong does not want to make rain for the people of Ting-gili. The chief of Tingigili does not make rain often for his people, and the people of Ting-gili are aware that the power of the chief of Abong is stronger than that of their chief.

NGABARA

Ngabara has three houses which are Iriok, Palo-pali and Lotiri. They all came from different places.

Iriok migrated from Ifwotu due to famine which killed people in Ifwotu, and they came to look for where they could find food. Iriok came when Obbo were at Loudo. The chief of Obbo showed them where to settle.

Palo-pali is another group of people who joined Obbo, but we do not know where they came from. Unfortunately, during my investigation, there was no person from Palo-pali whom I could ask. But some Acholi elders told me that one Lopali elder brought the people to Obbo. We think that the name of the people as Palo-Pali was derived from the description of the name of the elder, Lopali. Because of this, the people of Palo-Pali called themselves people of Lopali. It is said that when Palo-pali reached Obbo, the chief of Obbo gave the space to settle among the Iriok. I think that in the second edition of The History and Expressive Cultures of the Acholi of South Sudan, we will look at the history of Ngabara into details.

Lotiri people came from Imila (Katire). According to oral sources, they left Katire because of famine, but we do not know the person who led them to Obbo. They came when Obbo was still at Loudo. The chief of Obbo welcomed them and settled them in Iriok.

THE HUNTING GROUND AND HILLS OF NGABARA

The people of Ngabara have one hunting ground called *Alyebi*; but I would like readers of this book to know that *Alyebi* hunting ground is in two parts. On the left hand side of Fr. Cerida's road, which runs from Palotaka to Lerwa is the hunting ground of the people of Ngabara, and on the right hand side of the road, still from Palutaka to Lerwa, is the hunting ground of Koyo people. We do not know the person who celebrates Alyebi of Ngabara, but the one who celebrates Koyo's is called Okumu Silva.

Ngabara people have two hills. That is Lotii Hill and Gumia Hill. Both hills are Itiok's. The people of Ngabara have no god.

IYIRE

Iyire is divided into smaller houses as Iyire-pa-Lomunya (who are a royal family) and Iyire-pa-Igele. Iyire-pa-Lomunya and Iyire-pa-Igele are both of Lotuko origin, and before they came to Obbo both groups were under Chief Hidye of Ifwotu. That means Iyirepa-Lomunya and Iyire-pa-Igele are Lotuko of Ifwotu. During my investigation on the history and culture of the Acholi of South Sudan, I asked different elders of Obbo that "What brought the people of Iyire in Acholiland?" They gave me four different answers to explain why these people came to Acholi. It is hard to tell which the one is the correct one of the four, or if all the four are correct. To better understand what we are talking about here, I think it is good to look at each of these answers one by one.

The first group of respondents, with the same answer, told me that Iyire had a chief called Igele who was loved by the people of Iyire. They also had a rain chief called Chief Lomunya. Chief Igele was under Chief Hidye. Since Chief Igele was under Chief Hidye, he had the authority to settle only minor disputes among the among the people of Iyire, but if the dispute, though minor, involved people of Iyire and Ifwotu, Chief Igele was not supposed to settle it because that was within the power and authority of the chief of Ifwotu. Chief Igele did not have the power to settle major disputes even among the people of Iyire. Such disputes were handled by Chief Hediye and Igele would attend as one of the council members.

It is said that Chief Hedye and Chief Igele were not in good terms because Chief Igele wanted to have full authority over the people of Iyire, but Chief Hedye was opposed to his opinion. It seems it was because of this disagreement that Chief Igele eventually left Ifwotu and looked for a place where he could have full authority over his people and live in peace with them. Chief Igele and his people joined the people of Obbo when the people of Obbo were still on Lotii Hill. Chief Kassiba welcomed the people of Chief Igele warmly and gave them space to settle in.

The second group of respondents said that it was famine which drove the people of Iyire to Obbo. Long ago, the people of Obbo and Iyire hunted in Logolo Hunting ground together. One day Kitaka called people for hunting in Logolo. That time, different animals such as elephant, buffalo, water backs, rhinoceros and other small animals like duiker, antelope left different hunting grounds and came to Logolo. Both Obbo and Iyire went for the hunt. In Acholi, in a hunting expedition like this, every house has its posts in the wilderness. That day people just stood anywhere and they set the bush on fire. The flames rose and engulfed all the animals and so many animals were killed in the fire. The hunters immediately skinned the animals and realised that the meat was too much for them to carry home. They then made a big platform for and smoked the meat, but it was still too much. The people of Obbo started to carry the meat home bit by bit, but the people of Iyire did not think of doing so, because their hunting custom was that when hunters killed very many animals, people should stay in the hunting ground and eat up all the meat before returning home. So, this made the people of Chief Igele Lomunya who came for the hunt to camp in the wilderness, eat all the meat and go back later. Iyire took three months in the wilderness of Logolo eating the meat. They called their people from Ifwotu to join them. When the Iyire who were left in Ifwotu heard of this and that there was a lot food in Acholi, they all migrated to Logolo. After the three month, the people of Iyire said they would not go back to Ifwotu. Therefore, Igele's people settled in Logolo. When the rains came, the people of Iyire cultivated many crops such as sesame, peas, groundnuts, millet and others. They had a great harvest and they lacked space to store the harvest. The people of Obbo also allowed all the people of Iyire to live in Logolo.

The third group maintain that after the Iyire people migrated from Logolo Hunting ground, Chief Igele made friendship with Chief Kassiba (chief of Obbo); because of this good relationship between the two chiefs, Chief Kassiba told Chief of Iyire, "My friend, if you want to settle in Logolo, I have no objection to it, but I need to first consult the people of Kitaka and other clan elders, who are the owners of the place. If they agree with me, then Iyire can settle in Obbo as brothers, but if my people differ with me then you will go back to where you came from." Chief Igele was very pleased with Chief Kassiba's opinion. He went back to his people and told them what he shared with Chief Kassiba. The people of Iyire were as well pleased to hear Chief Kassiba's opinion, but it was the people of Obbo to determine what would happen. Chief Kassiba consulted the owner of the hunting ground (whose name we do not know) together with Obbo clan elders, then agreed for the people of Iyire to settle in Logolo hunting ground, but elders of Obbo and Kitaka objected to Iyire settling in Logolo. They said if Iyire wanted to cultivate in Logolo, they had no problem with that.

Four days after later, Chief Igele and Lomunya went back to Chief Kassiba and told him that the people of Iyire were all interested in settling in Obbo. They were only waiting to hear from the Obbo. When he saw that the people of Iyire really wanted to live in Obbo, Chief Kassiba, irrespective of the opinions of the elders of Obbo, just allowed Iyire to settle in Logolo at Nyara. He then told Igele, "As my people have accepted that you settle in Obbo, I want you to relinquish your chieftain because Obbo has one people." Igele submitted to Kassiba's chiefdom. The people of Obbo, when they heard that Kassiba had given Logolo to Iyire, were very displeased with him. For that reason, some Kitaka people who were at Nyara migrated to the other side of Ayii stream (where Kitaka presently is). When Kitaka migrated, Kassiba told Igele and elder Lomunya that they should ration to their people the land for cultivation. Igele divided the land as follows: — (1) Nyara (2) Acimoro (3) Lohuba (4) Lomolong and (5) Gunyoro; Igele and Lomunya divided their people in the five pieces of land and each group settled at the edge of each piece. These five places later became five different houses. That is how the third group tried to explain me how Iyire came to Obbo.

The forth group said that Iyire's home was in Ifwotu and were under Chief Hidyej. People said that, most of the time, Ifwotu and Iyire fought, and many of Igele's subjects lost their lives in the fights. These wars soiled the relationship between Chief Hidye and Chief Igele. Eventually, Chief Igele told himself that, "Chief Hidye has over disturbed my people. I have to avenge the deaths of my people." The oral sources state that most of the wars between the two clans took place between 1871 and 1875. Chief Kassiba, at this time, was already dead as we have seen before that he died in 1870. It was Chief Aburi who was the chief, and Chief Igele and Lomunya told Chief Aburi how Chief Hidye had killed the people of Iyire. They then asked Chief Aburi if he could join them to fight the people of Ifwotu. Chief Aburi, because he liked fighting, welcomed Iyire's proposal wholeheartedly. Immediately, Chief Aburi summoned different Acholi clans. First, he contacted Chief Ocieng of Pajok, second was the chief of Palwar (we do not know his name), and third, he called the chiefs of Magwi and of Panyikwara (we do not know the names of these two chiefs) to mobilise their warriors to fight Ifwotu. Chief Aburi also called the people of Obbo to join them in this war. Chief Aburi, on the other hand, asked Acholi of Uganda because Acholi were quite united. So, when they received a call of this kind, they would all make ululation as they went to join hands with their brothers. The Acholi of Uganda who came to fight this war were Palabek, Lokung, Padibe, Kitgum, Patiko and Patongo.

When warriors had converged in Obbo, the Acholi of Sudan and Uganda moved to Ifwotu ladened with bows and arrows, and a coward needed to borrow hare's speed. When Acholi reached Ifwotu, as they were about to enter the place, Acholi instructed Chief Igele to go ahead and tell the people of Iyire to smear themselves with red ochre and tie palm fibre on their heads. This was to make it easy for Acholi to tell the people of Iyire from Ifwotu because it was hard to distinguish the face of an Ifwotu man from that of an Iyire man. God made them to look alike. Secondly, both Iyire and Ifwotu still moved naked. If one of the groups wore clothes, it would be easy to differentiate them. Chief Igele told the people of Iyire what Acholi instructed them to do and they did as they were told.

Acholi elders instructed their people, "We now go to fight Ifwotu, if you see anybody who has smeared his body with red ochre and has tied palm fibre on his head, do not spear him, but if you see anybody who does not have both prescriptions, that is the person to spear immediately."

Acholi planned to move in group of village to village because each village wanted to lead the war. They thought of this strategy because they had learned that Ifwotu had many heads of cattle, goats and sheep. So, being on the lead as they enter each village would give them opportunity to take most of the animals in the villages for themselves.

When the warriors were still arguing over the matter, Pajok warriors started moving and other people followed them. Early morning when people were still sleeping, Aburi's people entered Ifwotu. In a short time, Acholi began to spear the people of Ifwotu who were still sleeping. Each village wanted to lead the war so that if they entered a village, this would give them opportunity to take most of the animals Ifwotu people left behind. The oral source has it that Longulu (this is another name with which Acholi called Ifwotu) were killed in a large number, and there was no space to lie and there was groaning everywhere"*Iyangi yooi iyangi yoo*". ("Iyangi yooi" is how Lotuko cry at times of problem or death). The Acholi warriors defeated Ifwotu. At day break, Ifwoto showed Acholi warriors their heels. They left behind cattle, goats and sheep, and Acholi raided the animals.

Chief Igele thought that, even if Ifwotu fled their homes, they may reorganise themselves and come back to attack them. For that matter, Chief Igele and Lomunya assembled their people and instructed them all to go with Acholi people.

After the fight that took one whole day, Aburi and Igele's people moved to Acholiland. In the early evening, when the people of Igele and the people of Aburi were moving, it rained on them and the red ochre was washed off from Iyere worriers and they also untied the palm fibre from their heads. On seeing naked people walking next to them, Acoli warriors thought that those were Longulu warriors who might have clandestinely infiltrated their group. So, Acholi speared them thinking that they were the people of Ifwotu. Iyire ran back on the hill where they had camped before. Aburi's people even took away Iyire's animals. But later, Acholi realised that they were spearing Iyire whom they had come to liberate from the brutal treatment of Chife Hidye of Ifwotu, and they stopped immediately. The Iyire who survived moved together with Aburi's people to Acholi. When they reached Obbo, the Acholi of Sudan went back to their homes and Acholi of Uganda moved on to Uganda. Chief Igele and his subject settled with Aburi who later instructed Igele and Lomunyo to take their people to settle in Logolo. He strongly warned them, "You can live in Obbo, but you should be aware that you will all be under the chief of Obbo. I want Iyire to treat Obbo as their brothers." We do not know if Aburi consulted Kitaka, because in Acholi, the authority of a hunting ground lies with the owner only. No one could give out a hunting ground without the permission of the owner. This is the forth explanation of how Iyire became the same family in Obbo.

After this, Chief Aburi and Chief Igele took their people to settle in Logolo where they built beautiful huts and, in October, they engaged in cultivation which led to very rich harvest. Before long, Iyire found that life was easy in Obbo than it was in Ifwotu because here they faced no threat and there was abundance of food stuff. Up to now, the people of Iyire are in Logolo hunting ground where if you stand in front of Palotaka Church (Palotaka Mission), you see it on the other side of Nyara stream.

When Igele was critically ill, he called Iyire elders from every family and told them, "It seems I may not live long among you. I want to tell you that when I die, all Iyire people should not split from Obbo. You should accept what the people of Obbo tell you because Chief Aburi freed us from the brutal killing of Ifwotu. If it was not for his effort, we would be no where in this world."

Iyire welcomed Ilege's last word with both hands and they continued to show great respect to the chief of Obbo. But we cannot tell if Iyire also made subscription to Chief Aburi as it was the custom of Obbo people. Although Igele instructed Iyire to remain under Obbo, around 1982/84, two Iyire men, Mark Lotang and Mario Ochilo argued that Iyire should stop following what Igele told them to do long time ago because the world was developing, and Iyire also needed freedom. Mark Lotang and Mario Ochilo proposed that Iyire should break off from Obbo and have their own chief. These two men did not want Iyire to be under the chief of Obbo anymore. They wanted their own chief who was not supposed to be under the paramount chief of Magwi. They wanted their chief to be under the paramount chief of Torit. They asserted that, even if the chief of Iyire would go under Torit, Iyire would continue to live in Obbo. Most Iyire people did not agree with Mario Ochilo and Mark Lotang's argument. All the subjects of Lomunya did not accept the opinion of these two men, but some few of Igele's people bought the idea. It seems the two men hailed from the family of Igele. That is why some of the Igele's people could not oppose them. In 1982, Iyire made Aburi their Parish Chief, but he was under Chief Mathia Aburi Lolori. Aburi, as a parish chief and a government representative, opposed Ochilo and Lotang. He then told the people of Iyire, "If you support Lotang and Ochilo, then you should know that Iyire will split into two. We should stick to what our grandfather, Igele told us." Most Iyire heeded to Aburi's advice. Meanwhile, Obbo were not impressed with Ochilo and Lotang campaign that Iyire should be under the chief of Torit. They said that if Iyire wanted to be under Torit, then they must leave Obbo. When Iyire realised that the issue would cause them problem, they all resolved to remain under the chief of Obbo.

From 23rd to 24th December 2007 in the meeting of "Obbo Community Development Association" (OCDA) to discuss the land occupied by Iyire, Mr. Celestino Oryem Jino, the leader of Iyire people, attended the meeting and reaffirmed Igele's words, "Iyire and Obbo cannot break apart because there is no conflict between them, and Iyire have a story in which their grand fathers said iyire and Obbo should live together. If Iyire wanted to open their own town, people should not think that it is because Iyire wanted to split from their brothers and sisters of Obbo. It should be noted that the population of Iyire was growing very fast, and that is the main reason why they asked for their own chief. As far as the land is concerned, we all know very well that, in Acholi, all land/hunting grounds have their owners, and we know the boundary of each hunting ground. A member of OCDA called the meeting which was held in Obbo in English as *"Obbo/Iyire Peace and Reconciliation Conference"* (Minutes Obbo/Iyire peace and reconciliation, P.4).

IYIRE'S HILL AND GOD

Iyire has one hunting ground called Bokoro which its cleansing rite is performed by a man from the house of Igele, but we do not know the name of the man who did it in the past. Iyire has one hill called Kapai Hill, which people say initially belonged to the people of Tingi-gili before they gave it to Iyire. We do not know if Tingi-gili gave the hill to Iyire to pay for a lost life. Unfortunately, Iyire do not have a god.

CHAPTER TEN

OBBO LEFT(NORTH)

Obbo North has five families namely; Pajombo, Logolo, Padyeri, Opoko-mere and Lokide. For us to better understand these families, I think it would be best to look at them one by one.

PAJOMBO

Pajombo family is divided into three small families; they are Pajombo Bura, Pajombo and Palyec, all of who came from different places as seen below.

Pajombo Bura

In the previous pages, we saw that the second people to enter Obbo north were the Pajombo and Pokongo. The Pajombo Bura came from Lango (Uganda), headed by elder Agoro. They separated from their brothers who remained in Uganda, due to conflicts over their father's cattle. When Agoro realized that the conflict was getting complicated, he decided to leave his brothers in Lango. He then started traveling with those who were willing to relocate with him, and they moved towards Sudan. When and Bura reached Sudan, they settled around Ayiba hill in Obbo land. The followers of Agoro moved with cattle, sheep and goats. But the brothers of Agoro who remained in Lango were unhappy with Bura, because they looted many cattle and fled with them to Sudan, besides, they also left with a royal drum which united the Pajombo Bura and the Lango.

When the Pajombo reached Ayiba Hill, they did not know where the Obbo Pajok people had settled. They then built around Mount Ayiba, thinking that they were the first group of people to reach that land. In the past, many people engaged in hunting wild animals. Each family in Acholi would go hunting alone in any hunting ground of their choice, because in the past, hunting grounds belonged to no particular people. The Pajok, however, loved hunting in Ayiba Hill. One day, the Pajok went hunting as usual in Ayiba hill, and met the Pajombo there. The Pajombo did not know that people had settled there, because from time to time, they would go to hunt in the hill, and not meet anyone. When the Pajok saw all these people and domestic animals, they asked their chief, who they referred to as Agoro chief, if they could go back home with them. The Agoro chief refused to go with the Pajok for two reasons. One, the chief saw that the land around Ayiba Hill was very fertile, and had good pasture for grazing. The second reason was because Chief Agoro had his own rain stone and royal drum. For this reason, he did not want to be under the leadership of another chief. When the children of Pajok saw that the Agoro chief of Bura refused to leave with them, they did not force him. The Pajok then left those who followed Chief Agoro around mount Ayiba.

After a few years, Acura, a nephew of Bura, brought an important message to the Pajombo Bura in Sudan. The message was that the children of the Lango (who are also brothers of Bura who remained in Uganda) wanted to come and take their people and animals back home in Uganda. The Bura waited for the children of Lango for almost two months. Unfortunately, they took long to come because they were still discussing how to travel. This made the Bura to conclude that Acura misinformed them (so he was a liar).

When the Lango did not come as the people of Bura were told by Acura, they forgot all about the issue. They did not imagine that any other issue would arise in future. The Bura used to take afternoon naps in a forest in Atebi. So one afternoon, when the men were taking a nap in the forest, they suddenly saw different animals running very fast towards them, with grass hoppers clacking and buzzing as they flew all over the place.

The Acholi believe that when animals are running and grasshoppers are snapping like this, it means other huge wild animals like elephants and buffaloes are invading the area. When the men saw many animals and grasshoppers all over the place, they woke everybody who had fallen asleep, and headed to Atebi where women and children were. Each of them entered the house and picked spears and shields, ready to defend themselves from whatever or whoever was coming. In a few minutes, the men had sat all around the home, waiting till almost 9:00 pm for the impending attack. After some time, the men and boys decided to enter their houses to sleep since all seemed well. When the men, women and children were sleeping, the Lango came and surrounded them at the break of dawn, when sleep was so sweet, (like the soup of giant edible rat).

Very early in the morning (at sunrise) Lango came to Pajombo, with the ends of their bows violently scraping the ground, (producing loud mm mm mm sounds). When the Pajombo saw that the Langi had come with such violence, they created escape routes behind their home for the women and children to flee to Pajok. The Bura had many animals, that the woman and children could not graze and control them all. For this reason, women and children took only a few animals and left some in the kraal. When Lango entered the home, they engaged in fierce fighting for three days. After three days, Lango defeated the Pajombo. When the Pajombo men realized that they were increasingly becoming powerless, they decided to flee to Pajok. Lango then went to the home of the Pajombo and gathered all the cattle the Pajombo had left behind, and steered them back to Lango (Uganda). Those who had come with Acura again went back to Uganda. Acura however remained, because he saw that there was plenty of meat around Lwo hill, where he later died. That is why the Obbo have (coined) a saying that, "Greed killed the son of Acura in Pajombo hill." But others say Acura died during the fight between the Pajombo and the Lango.

When the Pajok- Ayuu saw many women, children and cattle of the Pajombo heading towards them, they made alarms and all gathered to discuss how to go and rescue the Pajombo from Ayiba hill.

After the discussions, the Pajok-Ayuu caught up with the Lango who were on their way back to Uganda. The Ayuu engaged the Lango in a serious fight, in which many Lango and the Pajok were killed. But the Pajok had a more warriors than Lango did, so they defeated Lango. The Pajombo chased Lango and took back all the animals to the Pajombo.

After the fight, Chief Oceng Lokwor-moi of Pajok put the Pajombo under his leadership. But when he learnt that Chief Agoro of Pajombo also had a rain stone, he decided to appoint chief Agoro leader of the people of Paitenge and Pajombo. The Paitenge easily accepted the decision of Chief Ocieng, and they all lived under the leadership of chief Agoro of Pajombo. But as he was handing over the Paitenge to Chief Agoro, the chief of Pajok summoned all of them and emphasized that, "The children of Pajombo and those of Paitenge are like bothers and sisters; so they should not intermarry. But if a son of Paitenge dies and leaves behind a widow, a Pajombo can inherit her. And if a son of Pajombo dies and leaves behind a widow, a Paitenge can also inherit her."

Before long, the Pajok came asking chief Agoro, "Since we the Pajok saved you from your enemies, Lango, we want you to reward us with seven girls." When chief Agoro heard this request, he asked the Pajok if he could pay them with seven cows, instead of seven girls, but his offer was turned down by the Pajok. Because of this complication, chief Agoro and Ocieng decided to discuss the matter themselves. The chief of Pajombo told Chief Ocieng that "Now that your people do not want seven animals, I will give our hunting ground known as Ayuma to the Pajok." And he added that "This hunting ground should unite the Pajok and Pajombo."

Chief Ocieng reported the matter to his people to seek their views. All the people of Pajok supported chief Agoro's suggestion. Much as the Pajombo gave part of their land to the Pajok, they still had rights to the land. Before going for hunting, the Pajok had to first get blessings from a son of Pajombo Bura, so that they were not attacked by buffaloes. If a son of the Pajok went hunting alone, animals could attack them. The elders of Obbo told me that immediately after the discussions to give the land, the Pajok followed all the terms set by the Bura people. But after a few years, due to their stoneheartedness, they went hunting in Ayuma before getting blessings from a son of Pajombo. At the hunting ground, many people were killed. This made the Pajok to lament; "We have lost more people in this wilderness than those we lost when we were fighting Lango. This wilderness should now be named Oloyo-Iweny (the war champion). This also tells us how Ayuma wilderness has become known as Oloyoy-Iweny.

After a few years, the husband of Aero, of Paitenge, died. Clan elders then started reminding people of what chief Ocieng had stated, that if a Paitenge man died, a son of Pajombo should inherit his widow. The clan elders then chose one young man of Pajombo to inherit Aero. After a few months, she conceived. When the children of Paitenge heard about Aero's pregnancy, they forgot all about the terms set by Chief Ocieng Lokwor-moi. The news about Aero's pregnancy caused a lot of disorder among the Pajombo and Paitenge. Many people from Acholi land kept saying that the Paitenge had accepted the terms of the chief 'just for the sake of it', meaning they had actually not agreed to the suggestions of Chief Ocieng Lokwor-moi.

Because of Aero's pregnancy, a born of Pajok one day decided to whip the cattle of a son of Pajombo, as payment for having their sister impregnated by the son of Pajombo. When the Pajombo saw someone entering his kraal, he picked a bow and arrow, and shot him (the intruder), killing him instantly. The Pajombo did not know that the person in the kraal was a borne of Pajok. He thought he was a thief who had come to steal his animals. In the past, there were many cases of thieves entering the kraal to steal animals. Others could even come from outside to steal cattle. Shortly, news was sent around and both the Pajok and Pajombo gathered and started fighting. It was a win-win battle, meaning both sides lost the same number of people. After three days of fighting, the Pajombo decided to go back to Obbo. They gathered and started moving towards Ayiba hill. This scenario explains why the Pajombo returned to Obbo. When the Pajombo went back to Obbo, they did not live under the leadership of Kassiba, the chief of Obbo. They instead remained under their chief called Agoro. The British, who conquered Sudan, advised chief Kassiba and chief Agoro to live in harmony as brothers, though they were independent. Both Chief Agoro and Chief Kassiba agreed with the British rulers, and lived peacefully.

Pajombo Okwee came from Bilinyang (Bar) in 1695, because of hunger. The elders of Pajombo, among them Afulunario told me that in 1695, Bar was hit by serious famine that killed many men, women and children. While still in Bar, the Pajombo Okwee were led by Olwedo. When Olwedo saw that his people were dying of famine he gathered them and started moving with them towards the East. They trekked for about three days before reaching Panyikwara, at Iwire hill, where they settled for a few months. When Chief Olwedo thought that his people had rested enough, he told them to continue walking. However, some people refused, and remained in Goloba. That is why some of the Pajombo are in Pajombo- Panyikwara.

When some of his people refused to move further, chief Olwedo continued with those who were willing, until they reached Pakwa (Ayiba) hills. We are not sure if it was the people of Pajombo Bura were the first to reach Pakwa hills, or the people of Pajombo Okwee. While other people claim that the Bura were the first to reach Pakwa hill, others say the Pajombo Okwee were the first to settle at Pakwa hill.

The Pajombo Palyec also came from Bilinyang (Bar). They traveled together with the people of Pajombo Okwee. It is assumed that some of the Palyec remained in Goloba, but those who remained in Goloba call themselves 'Pajombo'. They are known by only one name 'Pajombo', because they do not want to distinguish themselves from the (Palyec or Okwee). We also do not know if the present day Pajombo Okwee and the Pajombo Palyec came from the same or different family/ clan in Bilinyang. The elders told me that young girls and boys of Palyec do not marry boys or girls of Bura. We do not know why the children of Palyec and Bura do not intermarry. However, we understand that Bura migrated from Lango (Uganda), and the Palyec came from Bilinyang (Bar). If the two clans came from different places, what now bars them from intermarrying?

HUNTING GROUND AND HILLS IN PAJOMBO

The Pajombo have four hunting grounds; Ongol-kor that borders Okony-Kor and Logolo. A born of Pajombo is the one who blesses this hunting ground. Elder Olwedo was the first to own Ongol Kor hunting ground. We do not know the names of the five members of the Olwedo family who used to bless Ongol-kor hunting ground. After these five people died, elder Itingo-wi, became the owner of the hunting ground. After Otingo-wi's death, his son named Lopit became the owner of the hunting ground. Up-to-date, he still owns ongol-Kor. The second hunting ground of the Pajombo is Okony-kor, which borders Ongol-kor, Akidi, Bong-won, Jom and Oloyo-lweny hunting grounds. The third hunting ground is Amoyo-tonga, which borders Logolo, Ciri, Okony-Kor, Bong-won, Achombo Hill and wang-Lobuchu hunting grounds. The fourth is Pakwa, which borders Merigala (Magwi hunting ground), Oburo (Ogura of Agoro Right), Gili-gili, Acila hunting ground and Kalindiyo Hill of the people of Panyikwara. Okony-kor hunting ground, Amoyo-Tonga and Pakwa hunting grounds are blessed by elder John Ochan Ogaa, who also invites people to go hunting there. We also do not know the first person to invite people to go hunting in this area. The people of Pajombo have one hill known as Pakwa (Ayiba).

LOGOLO

Logolo has two families, Pawino and Pakuka. All these families came from the family of Kor, which is in Lokoro. They came bearing the same name 'Logolo'. Later when they reached Obbo, they divided themselves into two families now called, 'Pawino' and 'Pakuka'. Elder Ayoko led the people of Logolo from Liful. He also came with his two sons named Okuka and Owino. Owino was Ayoko's first born, followed by Okuka. We also do not know if Okuka and Owino were children of the same mother, or not. What we know is that the two children have the same father.

Elder Ayoko left Lokoro with his people because of disagreements between him and his brother who remained in Lokoro. Acholi elders told me that the two disagreed over their father's wealth; because Ayoko's father was a rich man (who had many cattle and sheep). Much as the children of Logolo settled in a new place in Obbo, they never forgot the spitefulness of the people of Kor to them. This is why the people of Logolo speared the people of Kor in 1911, on their way to Pajok, to visit some of their brothers who lived there. Much as the Logodo still hold a grudge against the people of Kor, they share a deep relationship. This relationship is shown by the regular visits the children of Kor paid to Celestino Apire of Pakuka in Obbo between 1950 and 1960. If there were no relationships among them, the people of Kor would not come to Logolo (Obbo).

Elder Ayoko met the people of Obbo at Lotii Hill. He then told chief Koyo that "Chief, we the homeless people are looking for a place to live. If you have any idle hunting ground, please allow us to buy it." Chief Koyo then sold one of the hunting grounds to the people of Logolo, who then named it "Logolo hunting ground". We also do not know what the people of Koyo used to call this hunting area.

After the people of Ayoko had bought Logolo hunting ground from the people of Koyo, they did not settle there. They instead built among the people of Koyo at Lotii. Shortly, it was planting season and everyone who was at Lotii Hill started cultivation. Owino also got some land, where he planted different crops. His crops yielded so much that he did not have where to store all the harvest. However, Okuka was a lazy man. During planting season, he stayed back home in front of other people's doors. In November, when people were harvesting their millet, Okuka had nothing to harvest. As a result, his family was greatly hit by famine. This forced his children to go to their uncle's home to look for food. But they were not always warmly received at their uncle's home. According to their uncle, they deprived his children of satisfaction.

One day, Owino entered his house and found his children and brothers children sharing a meal. He drove out his brother's children, telling them rudely, "Go back to your father's home. Why do you want to add more problems to me when I have mouths to feed? Your father (Okuka) is a lazy man who doesn't want to dig. Who does he think is able to provide food for your family?" On hearing these utterances, Okuka's children stopped eating, and went back to their mother's house. When they reached home, they narrated to their mother what Owino told them. Okuka was unhappy when he heard that his brother denied his children food. He immediately went to his brother's home and started him, "Why do you insult my children at meal as if am not your brother? If that is the case, my brother, we cannot live in the same place." After one month, Okuka left his brother and built a distance away. From here Okuka bore many children, who also gave him grandchildren. They then named their family 'Pakuka', which means the people of Kuka. This also tells us why the family of Logolo separated into two different families.

LOGOLO HUNTING GROUND AND HILL

The people of Logolo have one hunting ground, known as 'Logolo'. It borders Okony-kor, Amoyo-tonga, Amalac and Nyara hunting grounds. The people of Logolo bought this hunting ground from the people of Koyo, after they came to Logolo. A child born in Pawino family invites people to hunt in this hunting ground. We do not know the name of the men who used to invite people to hunt in this land. However, the person who blesses this land and invites people to go hunting in Logolo hunting ground is Samuel Tokwaro, who I know personally. The people Logolo also have only one god named 'Agore', but they don't have a hill.

PADYERI

The Padyeri have only two small families namely; 'Pa-tyeno' and 'Bwola'. Pa-tyeno was born from the family of Duk-pa-dyer, which is found in the land of the Dinka Agar. They came together with the people of Okano-mere. The people of Okano-mere entered Obbo land, bearing the name Dingka Agar. The current name, Okano- mere was started much later, as we shall learn in page 193. Elder Girikon was the leader of the people of Pa-tyeno, and elder Oyat was the leader of Okano-mere. The people of Pa-tyeno, and Okano-mere seem to have left Dinka Agar around 1869, for fights over cattle with their brothers, who remained in Dul-pa-dyer. When the group that followed Girikon and Oyat left Duk-pa-dyer, they settled in Rejaf near the capital city of South Sudan, currently known as Juba. Many people say the people of Pa-tyeno and the people of Okano-mere lived in Rejaf for almost five years, and later discovered that the land was infertile. Hence, Girikon and Oyat led their people out of Rejaf and went to Lotii Hill, where they met other people of Obbo, who first settled there. In this year, chief Kassiba who was the leader of the Obbo, warmly welcomed the Pa-tyeno and the people of Okano-mere Lotii Hill, and gave them land to build their huts. The people of Pa-tyeno built in a different place, and the people of Okano-mere also built in another place and they lived independently, much as they remained under the leadership of chief Kassiba.

The people of Bwola came from Koyo Bira (Ngabara). When they saw that the people of Patyeno had completed building their huts on the land given to them by chief Kassiba around 1870, the people of Bwola separated from the people of Koyo Bira, and build among the Pa-tyeno. They later named these two families 'Padyeri'. We do not know why the people of Bwola separated with the Koyo Bira. The people of Patyeno and Bwola united and became one. The clan elders later set a strong law against intermarriage among the young men of Pa-tyeno and the girls of Bwola. They also warned against intermarriage among the boys and girls of Bwola. Much as the elders set such tough rules, we later see that some children disobeyed this rule, and married among themselves. Up to date the Bwola and Patyeno still intermarry.

PADYERI HUNTING GROUND AND MOUNTAIN

The people of Padyeri have one hunting area named "Abar". It borders Agongara, Amalac, Oloyo-tiko and Ladeng-deng hunting areas. A child born of the Pa-tyeno is the one who blows the flute/horn of Abar hunting ground. We do not know the names of those, who in the past, blessed and invited people to go hunting in Abar hunting area. But elder Masimino Oyonda of

Pa-tyeno is now the person, who is well known by the Obbo for inviting people to hunt in Abar.

When I was asking the people of Obbo, I learnt that the Padyeri don not have any hill or god, because it seems in the year they arrived in Obbo, chief Koyo P'Atany had already divided hills and gods among those who were the first to arrive.

OPOKO-MERE

The family of Opoko-mere has two small families; Opoko-mere and Okano-mere.

The people of Opoko-mere came from Karamoro, in Iyire family. They built in the place now occupied by the Opoko-mere family, located after Ayi stream, to the East of Palotaka mission. Long time ago, the name Opoko-mere was not among the family members of Obbo or the Iyire family members. This name was first used when the people of Okano-mere, which in Acholi means, a good custodian of someone else's property given to him to take care of. Opoko-mere, in Acholi on the other hand means someone to gives away something he has been asked to keep, orensure that it multiplies. This also shows us that it seems elder of Okano-mere, had given goats to the children to two children of these families to keep until he asks for them. Acholi elders liked giving children intelligence tests, to enable know which child is wise, and which one is unwise. If you were defiant, you would find yourself always breaking laws. But if you were obedient, whatever you did would fall into place as the elders expected.

One of the two children, who were given goats by the elder, took good care of its young ones. The other child on the other hand, kept on giving away his goats to his friends, after they had grown. After four years, the elder called them and inquired how many goats each of them had. One of the boys, who took good care of the goats, brought almost nine goats before the elder. The elder was very happy on seeing that his goats had multiplied. He told the boy, "Child, you really know how to keep things, may God take care of you." After this, the second boy, who was giving away goats to his friends brought two goats, male and female that the elder had given to him. The elder then told him, "Child, you cannot keep a home. What will my people eat if famine strikes Obbo land? You are not a good castodian, because you like giving away things that should help the family to your friends, because you do not think about the future." The man who gave away his goats was unhappy about the praise that was heaped on his brother, who had kept his goats well. Before three days elapsed, the issue caused tension between the two men.

Gradually, the man who had given his goats away, became known, together with his children as the people of 'Opoko-mere, while the one who multiplied his goats, together with his people, maintained the family name 'Okano-mere'.

All these events transpired when the people of Opoko-mere were still in Iyire. That is why to this day, Opoko-mere has two families; Okano-mere and Opoko-mere.

Okano-mere

Many Acholi elders I interacted with said the people of Okano-mere came together with the people of Pa-tyeno of Padyeri. They came from the family of Duk-padyer in the family of Dinka Agara. As we saw while learning about the people of Patyeno, we realized that elder Girikon was the leader of the Pa-tyeno, but the people of Okano-mere (Dinka Agar) were led by elder Oyat. What I want readers of this book to understand is that Girikon and Oyat had the same biological father. What we do not know is if they had different mothers. When Oyat left Duk-pa-dyer land, they settled in Rejaf. They lived for almost five years, and later recognized that Rejaf was an infertile land. For this reason, Oyat and his brother Girikon, together with their people left Rejaf and went to Lotii Hill. Here, they met some of the people of Obbo, who went there initially. This year, chief Kassiba, the leader of Obbo welcomed the people or Okano-mere and Pa-tyeno to Lotii Hill. He gave them a piece of land to build their houses. The people of Patyeno built at a distance, while the people led by Oyat (Okano-mere) also built away from the Patyeno, with both groups living independently of each other. They all however, were still under the leadership of Chief Kassiba. A few years after Aburi gave Logolo hunting ground to the people of Iyire, the people of Okano-mere relocated to Nyaka and built among the people of Iyire. We do not know why the people of Oyat decided to relocate and settle among the people of Iyire. We also do not know if there is any relationship between the people of Okano-mere (Dinka Agara). Around 1932, the people of Okano-mere and Opoko-mere built in a place currently occupied by the people of Opoko-mere, over Ayi stream, to the West of Palotaka mission.

THE HILLS AND HUNTING GROUNDS OF OPOKO-MERE

The people of Opoko-mere do not have a hunting ground or a hill, but they have a god named 'NyaRubanga'. As I was reading the minutes of meeting between the Obbo and Iyire that was held on 23-24/12/2007, they stated that long time ago, the people of Opoko-mere had other hunting grounds called Aduce, Lobela and Obeng-monye. The people of Opoko-mere had then given Aduce and Lobela hunting areas to the people of Palwo, and then gave Obeng-monye hunting ground to the people of Imurok. We do not know why the people of Opoko-mere gave away Aduce, Lobela and Lobeng-monye hunting places to the people of Palwo and Imurok (minutes of Obbo/Iyire conference, 2007 p.14).

LOKIDE

The people of Lokide have two small families; 'Lokide Bura' and 'Lokide Kurukak'.

The family of Lokide Bura came from the family of Okulu, in the land of Imurok. The people of Bura moved away from the stream because that year, Imurok was hit by severe famine. When elder Oboyo saw many of his people dying of starvation, he gathered the survivors and started moving towards the south. They settled in a place called Palaya, located in Meri- Lokide hunting ground, where the people of Kurukak had settled. The people of Bura saw that Palaya land was fertile and produced good crop yields. The place also had enough water sources during rainy season, but during dry season, they faced acute water shortage. Women had to walk three to four miles to fetch water. The water shortage forced the people of Bura and the people of Kurukak to leave Palaya and later settled in Otwong. The people of Bura and the people of Kurukak did not take long in Otwong. After a few years, they shifted to Kubiri (Luodo), where they met some people of Loudo.

Lokide Kurukak, however, came from the family of Nya-Rubanga in Biligyang in Bar land. There are claims that the people of kurukak left Bar because of famine. In that year, Bar land was hit by the worst famine scenario. When Aliya Kec saw that many of his people were dying because of hunger, he started moving with them towards South-East. They reached Palaya, where they met the people of Lokide Bura. Elder Oboyo of Bura welcomed the people of Aliya kec and gave them a place to settle in. They became one people, but left Palaya because of water scarcity. They shifted with the people of Bura to Otwong. The people of Kurukak and Bura did not live for long in Otwong. After a few years, they relocated to Kubiri (Loudo), where they met other people of Loudo.

LOKIDE HILL AND HUNTING GROUNDS

Long time ago, the people of Lokide owned three hunting grounds; Meri-Lokide, Lohube and Matabura hunting ground. So around the year 1930, the people of Lokide gave away Matabura as compensation for a girl from Panyibila, who was killed by the people of Lokide. It seems that it the past, if someone accidentally killed a friend, people from other families would repay by giving one of their girls, beads or a hunting ground. This is why the people of Lokide gave their hunting ground as compensation for the death of the little girl from Oyere. In the year the people of have their hunting ground to the people of Oyere, they renamed it Oloyo-tiko (meaning, better than beads). The people of Oyere gave this hunting ground the name "better than beads" because if their girl was compensated using beads, only one person would wear it. However, everybody benefited from or shared the meat that was hunted from the hunting ground. This means the people of Lokide remained with only two hunting grounds: Meri-Lokide and Lohube hunting grounds. But according to some Obbo, the people of Lokide gave away Lohube hunting ground to Imurok. But I learnt from some elders that the people of Lokide did not give away Lohube. Up-to-date Lohube hunting ground still belongs to Lokide. Meri-Lokide hunting ground borders Merigala, Apedo, Agongara, Gili-gili and Ladeng-deng hunting grounds. We do not know the names of those who previously blessed this hunting ground. But all the people of Obbo know that Peter Onge, son of Odur, is the one who invites people to come hunting in Meri-Lokide. (Minutes of Obbo/Iyire Conference, 2007 p.14)

The people of Lokide have one god named 'Muul'. This god lives in Ayii stream, in Meri-Lokide hunting ground, but people of Lokide do not have a hill.

WHY DID FOREIGNERS LEARN ACHOLI LANGUAGE (LUO) SO FAST?

As we have already read in this book, we learnt that many of the Obbo people came from different places like Bar, Dinka, Imurok, Lokoya and Lotuko. This also proves to us that these people do not speak Luo. They also spoke different languages like Bar, Lotuko, Dinka, Imurok or Lukoya. They learnt Acholi language much later. The people who used to speak Acholi were the Pokongo and the Pajombo Bura, because they are Luo. The foreigners learnt Acholi language because of four reasons:-

The first reason is that in the past, everybody who lived in Obbo was under the leadership of one chief, known as Chief Aburi. Chief Aburi of Abong, who also spoke Lotuko dialect, but they learnt Acholi very quickly. Secondly, in case of any matter of debate, they could table the case before the chief, and debated the issue in Acholi. Tim clearly stated that the Pajombo and Pokongo ensured that the people use Acholi when debating an issue before the chief. Besides, the need to preserve the culture of the Lotuko made the foreigners learn Acholi very fast (Mr. Tim, 1985 p.38).

Thirdly, the people of Obbo gathered in the market named 'Te-iduro'. People went to this market every Saturday. All the sellers were expected to speak to their customers in Acholi. The forth reason the foreigners learnt Acholi very fast was because they said the language was very simple. These are the four reasons the foreigners who came to Obbo learnt Acholi. Tim (1985) said that the procedure the foreigners followed to live like Acholi and speak Acholi seems to have been very long. Much as the people refer to their leader as chief, a closer examination shows that the system of leadership of the chiefs did not originate from the Luo speakers or the Acholi. After 1950, Crazzolara wrote in his book that much as the people of Obbo (Mr. Tim 1985 p.38).

Chapter Eleven

THE RAIN POT OF OBBO

The rain pot of Obbo is in these four families; in Abong family, the pot was held by chief Aburi. In the Pokongo family, the pot is kept by Chief Alil Lotara, and in the Pajombo family, chief Lowarmoi Akut keeps the pot. While in the family of Lokide the pot was kept by Lolunya, the father of Lyekmoi Olum.

Much as there are four rain pots in Obbo, we shall not go into the details of each of the pots. We will only talk about rain pot of Abong, because it is bigger than the rest. Secondly, many people in Obbo worship the rain pot of Abong more than the other pots.

Before we go into the details of the rain pot of Abong, I want us to have a look at the three different ways Chief Aburi acquired his rain stone. Chief Aburi got his first rain stone from his father, Otoo Abarayi. Records show that before Abarayi died, he took the biggest rain stone and gave it to Aburi, and the smaller one to Aber Lokono, the mother of Baki. Secondly, when chief Aburi married the mother of Tibursio, the daughter of the chief of Lokide, the father-in-law of Tibursio got a rain stone and gave it to Tibursio's mother who then handed it to her husband. Thirdly, in the past, chief Aburi had messengers in each family in Obbo. Chief Aburi ordered that if anyone in Obbo found a rain stone, they should hand it to the representative of the chief in that home. The representatives would then take it to the chief.

Some people followed this order, but others defied it. Those who obeyed the order took the rain stone to chief Aburi. But those who disobeyed the order did not. They instead gave the rain stone to Aber Lokono, the mother of Baki. The children of Abong said that chief Aburi possessed a rain pot which he placed under a big tree behind the home of Tibursio's mother. Inside this pot, there were nine rain stones. Marcello Odiyo of Abong said that 'among these nine rain stones, eight were male and one was female. Chief Aburi named all these rain stones as seen below:

Lomeet is the rain stone that brings rain in September to shake off the fruits of grass. Lomeet rain always falls so heavily and people could easily tell that it was lomeet rain falling. On the day this rain falls, nobody gets out of the house, and they should have foodstuff in the house for it is not possible to get out picking anything from the granary. Lomeet is a male rain.

"*Omwol/omol cet*" is the rain stone that invokes the rain that falls from January to March. This is also the month when the children of Obbo put on a lot of weight because there is always plenty of food and yet there is little work. Very few people of Obbo have pit latrines, majority of them defecate in the bush behind their homes. Dung beetles do not eat feces passed during dry season. So from January to March, you find dry feces all over in the burnt bushes. At a distance the dry feces look like stones in the burnt bush. Omwol cet rain falls each day in January, February and March, to wash away the feces littered all over the burnt bush. This is also the reason why the rain was named omol-cet (dung washer). The Acholi say this is the period when people make hoes ready for digging. "Omwol cel is a male rain".

Nya logugu is the rain stone that invokes rain that falls from June to August. *Nya Logugu* rain is normally followed by a little sunshine. Afterwards, it rains again and the sun shines. On the day this rain is falling, women do not find time to bring their millet out to dry in the sun. Nya-Logugu rain is female. It is also the one that 'feeds' the people of Obbo. The Obbo people call this Nya-Loggugu "the rain of food".

Opit kic (feeder of orphans) rain stone invokes the rain that falls in March until May. In Acholi, the month of May is called the month of famine. From April to May, people plant fast maturing crops like spider flower, millet and sorghum. These are the crops that save people from starvation. This rain (opit kic) is male.

Nyar Itali (the daughter of Italy) is the rain stone that provides rainfall between the months of June and July. This rain always falls gently but heavily. It is also a male rain.

Loyile is the rain stone that provides rain that falls between June and July. July is the month when millet is ready to be harvested. For this reason, if the women do not hurry with the harvest, then the millet grains will be washed by the rain. Loyile rain is male.

Ongol kor is the rain stone that invokes rain that falls in October until November. Ongol Kor rain falls in different areas on different days. If it falls in this area today, the next day it will rain in another place. This rain makes it easy to harvest groundnuts. Ongol Kor rain is also female.

Kijumbi is the rain stone that provides rain that falls between August and November. This rain makes it easy to plough gardens for the next planting season. It is also a male rain.

Lajiki jiki is the rain stone that invokes rain that falls between March and April. Lajik jiki rain always falls mildly and for many hours. On the day this rain falls, white ants come out of the anthills that very night. This is why the Acholi call this rain "the white ant rain" (kot ngwen). This rain is male.

THE CARETAKER OF OBBO RAIN

The clan elders of Obbo have different opinions about the care taker of Obbo rain. Some people say chief Aburi did not have a caretaker of the rain. If chief Aburi wanted to invoke rain, he would oil the rain stone personally. But occasionally, he would also give the rain stone to his wife, the mother of Tibursia to apply oil on it. The Acholi culture permits the chief to instruct his wife to apply oil on the rain stone on the day he wants to invoke rain. They also said the rain caretakers, chief Aburi used were not genuine. They were the people appointed by the chief as representatives in each family. Their work was to get rain stones from people who found them. If people found rain stones, they would hand them over to the representatives of the chief, who would first take some millet flour and smear it on their face before getting the stone from them.

The practice of smearing the face with millet flour is a sign of pride and happiness among the people of Lotuko.

However, some people said chief Aburi had a rain caretaker. They also said Chief Aburi's first rain caretaker was Ogik of Orak, who was taken from the family of Loudo. After the death of Ogik Lodila, a man named Owor Tongomoi, the son of Alodo of Gari, became the rain caretaker of the chief. In the year 1964, when Owor Tongomoi died, a man named Ayora became the rain caretaker. And in the family of Kitaka, the rain caretaker of the chief was Akilicek. After his death, a man named Agalinyang became the rain caretaker.

Some people of Obbo said that Ayora is not a born of Loudo, but of Lokoro, because in the year 1902, when the people of Lokoro went to fight the people of Obbo, some people captured Ayora's mother, when expecting a child. They took her to Liful, where she gave birth to a child now known as Ayora. According to Acholi culture, even if a woman impregnated by an outsider, the child also assumes the tribe of the the man. And if a woman is impregnated by a member of the clan, the child is taken as a child of the family. This means that even if the mother of Ayora conceived by another man before going to Lokoro, her child is treated as a child of Obbo. This explains why the people of Obbo who are well versed with the Acholi culture, say Ayora is a true son of Loudo (Obbo).

When Ayora had reached puberty, his mother called him one day and told him,, "Child, now that you have become a grown up man, I want to show you that you are not a borne of Lokoro. In the year 1902, when the people of Lokoro went to fight the Obbo, they captured me and brought me here when I was already carrying you in my womb. Your father is Owor Ikubo of Loudo (Obbo). We were separated because of the fight between the people of Obbo and Lokoro. So I do not want you to forget your origin. If future, if you find yourself in Obbo, you should ask where your father is. If I die here, you should look for your father's relatives."

Ayora listened attentively and happily to his mother. He later asked himself, "How can I find my way back home?"

Much as the people of Lokoro fought with the Obbo in the year 1902, from 1930-1940, we found many people of Lokoro selling fish which they called Lokiri fish (this is how the people of Lokoro call their fish) in Obbo. When Ayora saw many children going to sell fish in Obbo, he also joined the other children in the Lokiri fish selling business. He went to sell fish in Obbo for almost two months. This gave him the opportunity to know the clan elders to ask about his father's family. One day, Ayora saw three elders seated with their back turned towards the morning sun. It seems someone had already told him that these elders came from his father's family. He went and sat beside the elders. The elders turned to look at Ayora but said nothing, because they wanted to hear what Ayora had to tell them.

With much respect, Ayora told the elders, "My elders, my name is Ayora. I believe you saw me several times two months ago, among the sellers of Lokoro fish. I want to tell you that my mother came from Obbo. In 1902 the people of Lokoro captured and took her to Liful during the fight between the people of Lokoro and Obbo. My mother told me that the people of Lokoro took her when she was carrying me in her womb. One day, my mother told me that my father is called Owor Ikuno of Loudo (Obbo). I have come, so that you show me where my father's relatives are among the Loudo family.

On hearing this, the elders were grateful to Ayora's mother for having told Ayora the truth about his origin. One of the elders answered him, "Very well child, we have listened to all you have said. It is good the god of your grandfather led you here. As you were told by your people, you are a true child of Loudo. We also want you to know that we are the kin of your father, which you have been looking for. Therefore, we want you to go back to Lokoro and inform your people that you have located your father's kin. We want you to return here immediately after telling your people.

Ayora was very excited after confirming that these were truly his father's relatives. The following morning, he went back to his mother in Liful and narrated to her all that he saw, and what the three elders told him. The news of Ayora meeting the elders of Obbo spread among other Obbo children who were also taken to Lokoro when they were still in their mother's womb during this war. For this reason in 1940, the children who were taken to Lokoro when they were still in the womb started returning to Obbo to trace their fathers. People say the children of Obbo who came back from Lokoro in 1940 were William Onee, Owinyo and Ayora Longirodel, all from Abong. In this year (1940), some people of Obbo were in Reyi and the people of Loudo were in Amalac, the place where all of them are living to date. Chief Aburi, however was in Kenya.

Among the three people who came back from Lokoro, Ayora Longirodel was between 40-45 years old. He came together with his wife and two children. The eldest son was called Apuko Longirodel and the younger one was called Ogila Longirodel. When Ayora Longirodel reached Obbo, he went and built near Chief Abura's home in Kenya. The chief then appointed him caretaker of the rain. Initially Ayora, showed commitment and dedication while performing his duties and the chief was very happy with him. Much as he was a good rain caretaker, he had intentions of stealing the chief's rain stone. Around the year 1942-1944, Ayora requested chief Aburi that "Chief, I want to go and visit my mother in Liful." The chief did not realize that Ayora had intentions of stealing the rain stone, so he accepted his request, but emphasized that he should return immediately after visiting Lokoro.

In the morning, Ayora went under the tree where the rain pot was kept, and took the rain stone named Nya-Logugu (this is the most valued rain stole because it feeds all the people of Obbo). He put the rain stone in a bag and started traveling to Liful. The following morning, chief Aburi also went under the tree where the rain pot was kept, because he wanted to check if all the rain stones were intact. Unfortunately, he found the rain stone named Nya-Logugu missing, but the other eight were there. Chief immediately stated that "No one except Ayora Longirodel has stolen the rain stone and taken it to Lokoro." Later chief Aburi swore that "If this rain stone has really been stolen, may it get lost and never be found. But if this rain stone was given to me in good faith, may it return to me."

Before ten days elapsed, Nya-Logugu jumped from Liful and gradually returned to Obbo. The elders of Abong did not tell me how many days the rain stone took jumping back to Obbo. While in Lokoro, Ayora kept searching for the rain stone in his mother's house in vain. He then concluded that the rain stone must have returned to Obbo. He felt so ashamed, did not return to Obbo immediately as the chief had told him to. He went back to Obbo in 1965, but the chief did not put him back as a rain caretaker.

Chief Aburi did not invoke the rain anyhow because each rain stone had its day and month. If the chief wanted to invite a particular rain, he sent a caretaker to put oil on the rain stone he wanted to use. But some rain stones were not smeared with oil. After the rain caretaker had applied oil on the rain stone, he put it back in the rain pot. He then poured water in the rain pot and stired the pot with his hand. After the caretaker finishing his work, he would go back home. After a short time, dark clouds would cover the sun, and in a few minutes it would start to rain. Many people in Obbo knew each and every rain stone belonging to the chief. Whenever it was raining, they also knew which rain stone brought the rain.

The rain chief is highly respected in Obbo land, so no one is allowed to provoke the chief. Some other people, however, cannot keep this law. Many times people utter words that made the rain chief angry. If the rain chief is angry and does not want rain to fall so that their crops dry up, he picks the rain pot from under the tree and puts it up on a tree so that it dies up. But if the rain chief doesn't put the rain pot it up on a tree, he picks the pot and puts it near the fire place in the kitchen so that heat from the fire place dries it. If he does this, it shines so much that all crops in the garden dry up.

Some elders say during planting season when farmers engage in communal farming, each person must request the chief not to make rain fall when their garden is being ploughed. Whenever the owner of the garden went to request the rain chief not to let rain fall on that day, he would carry infiltered local brew "kwete angaci". The chief would then pick an axe or a tomahawk, and heat its blade on fire. Whenever the chief performed this act, it would not rain. A perfect example of this performance happened at the home of Baki's mother. As we saw in the previous pages the children of Obbo separated into two groups because of conflict over rain issue. Some people after finding rain stones took them to the mother of Baki and other would to Aburi. One day, a group of farmers went to collectively work on the garden of a certain man. The owner of the garden also got local brew early in the morning and took it to Aber Lokono the mother of Baki. Before she had had any means, Aber picked a tomahawk and went ahead to heat its blade. On that day, it did not rain, and the farmers dug their garden to completion. There are many methods a chief can use to stop rain from falling during communal farming. However, I cannot write all of them exhaustively in this book. We should also know that stopping rain from falling is not the sole responsibility of the chief. Ill-minded individuals, who want people to suffer, also acquired skills of stopping rain from falling. If an evil-minded did not want rain to fall during communal farming days, he would pick a millet finger from the previous harvest and bury it in the ground. He would bury the millet finger, making it face the home of the farmer in whose garden he does not want rain to fall.

Whenever a wicked person performs such an act, the rain chief could try to invoke rain in vain. People would get angry at the rain chief whenever it did not rain and their crops begin to wither. But before openly showing their anger towards the rain chief, they would first hold a meeting to figure out if anyone uttered words that annoyed the rain chief. If they discovered that someone annoyed the chief, they would send messengers to the rain chief to request him to forgive them. But if the members found out in, their meeting, that the chief was not angry at them, they would look for the reasons why it did not rain. Elders would instruct tell boys and men to search the surrounding of every home, in case anyone had buried millet finger in the ground. If they found a millet finger buried, they would immediately say someone else committed the abomination.

They would then exhume the buried millet finger and take a ram from the grazing ground, slaughter it to cleanse the millet finger that had been unburied. Later on, a clan elder would throw the unburied millet finger in a river or in a stream near home. When all this is done, the rain chief would then invoke rain without difficulty. The elders of Abong, like John Ongee Kassiba told me that chief Aburi fled the fighting of Joseph Lagu in 1967. He fled to Lokung in Uganda, but unfortunately the rain chief did not flee with his rain stones. All the nine rain stones remained in Sudan. In the year 1968 when chief Aburi died in Lokung, his son named Ochilo Aburi was very close to him, but the one called Vitto Aburi was in Loudo (Sudan). Many people in Obbo kept thinking that after the death of the chief, rain stones remained with his son, Ochilo Aburi. While others said chief Aburi did not take all his rain stones to Uganda, but left some with his son Vitto Aburi. This also proves that until now, the people of Obbo do not know the whereabouts of the rain stones of the people of Abong. While some people say there is rain at Vitto Aburi's, others say rain is available at Ochilo Aburi's. This is how the people of Abong lost their rain.

CHAPTER TWELVE

PAJOK

THE FAMILY OF PAJOK

Pajok is a name given to people who live to the North West of the land of Acholi of Sudan bordering Uganda and Sudan. The land of Pajok is very important in the culture of the people of Sudan, because foreigners came and settled here and started Lwo culture. Everybody was happy after seeing people who came from the other side, came and settled among the land peacefully without waging any war. The matter was mentioned by the government officials of Sudan in a conference (Rejaf Language Conference) in Juba in 1928. The government leaders compared the calm among the Pajok with that of the people of Zande, found in the Western part of Southern Sudan. Most of the foreigners who came and settled in Pajok and Zande did so because of the hospitality of these two groups (Crazzolara, 1951 p.169) not all people who are in Pajok are Lwo, but all of them now speak Acholi. If we look closely, we realize that many people of Pajok came from Madi (Bar) or from Lokoyo. While other people came from Lango or Bunyoro in Uganda. Few people came from Anywak (Lokoro) and others from Lotuko.

Before we proceed, I want us to know that the name currently used in the family of Pajok is also used by Acholi of Uganda. Each of these names is also used by the Alur family (Uganda). Secondly, we need to understand the meaning of the name 'Pajok', because from time to time, if you ask children of Pajok the meaning of the name, most of them fail to answer the question. They respond that 'Pajok' is 'Pajok'. But as we shall see later in this book, the culture of Lokoro says 'Parajok' is derived from the words *para jwook*, because the people of Lokoro say that Jo Koor of Pajok used to miss their chief Ocaak, who died of an illness on mount Lofon. While Pajok culture says 'Pajok' means the people "who eat food meant for god' (Rubanga). The people call the Pajok came from Lokoro bearing the name 'Koor' but they acquired the name 'Pajok' along the way when the people of Lokoro were migrating to Acholi land. We can now say without doubt, that the people of Ywaaya, Patanga and Obwolto were the ones who brought the name 'Pajok' in Acholi Sudan. Before the coming of the Koor in Acholi land, people who lived here used to call themselves using family names like, Bobi, Bitii, Panto or Pagaya. Secondly, I think the name 'Pajok' refers to everyone who lives on this side of the land. This is because chief Keny of Ywaya wants everyone under his leadership to be called 'Pajok'.

As we shall later see in this book, everyone in Pajok came from outside, but if you ask people of Pajok the heads of the family of Pajok, some people say that the owners of Pajok are the people of Bobi, Panto, Ayu, Pagaya and Palio (pi woco ki Pocaa). But others say the owners of Pajok land are the Bittii and Kapaa, because according to the history of Pajok these two families were the first to come to Pajok, and other people of Pajok came later. According to literature, when the Bittii and Kapaa entered this land, it was unoccupied-which means the land had no owner. This is why people say Bittii and Kapaa are the owners of this land. According to the Pajok, people who came to Pajok arrived in different years. I learnt that the issue of who owns the land was not being debated by the Pajok only, but also all the Acholi of Sudan. Secondly, I also found that the clan elders of Acholi had different views on issues of who heads a particular family. This is one reason why I decided to write a book on the culture of the Acholi of Sudan, to enable people to understand everything chronologically.

Elder Ogano and Paterno Abak told me that people who came to Pajok built their houses far from each other, that during that time the other group did not know other people were near them. Each family thought they were the only ones on this land.

According to the history of Pajok, people got to know that they had neighbors because it rained heavily. So that evening, people went to harvest white ants, where they met the people of Bobii and Panto. They later asked the people of Bitii and Panto to stay with them. According to literature, the people of Bobi accepted to live together with the people who had come to harvest white ants, but the people of Panto refused to mix with the people. Some people say after a few years, the people of Panto also decided to live together with some people of Pajok because they eventully became lonely. Even though the Pajok accepted to live together with them, they did not have the heart to live as brothers. The people of Ywaya, Patanga and Obwolto were the ones who brought unity among the children of the Pajok as we shall see later.

The people of Pajok are divided into two; Pajok left and Pajok right. The clan elders divided people into groups (families) which made it easy for people talking about the Pajok to be able to differentiate between the Pajok right and Pajok Left. To better understand the family matters in Pajok, I want us to first look at Pajok left, and later we shall look at Pajok right.

There are five families surrounding the Pajok, these are; Obbo to the north, Panyikwara to the West, Palabek and Lokung in Uganda to the south and Palwar to the East. According to history of Acholi, the border of Pajok and Obbo starts from Lianga stream up to Atebi stream. Bore hunting ground where the Pajok built in Atebi stream, belongs to the Koyo (Obbo). From 1973-1984 there was a marriage agreement between the elders of Obbo and Pajok, because at that time, officials from Regional Development Cooperation (RDC) wanted land for cultivation in Pajok. When this request reached the elders of Pajok, they realized that there was no fertile land for farming in Pajok. The elders of these two families then agreed that the officials of RDC should temporarily cultivate in Oyaa hunting ground, which is also Koyo hunting ground (Obbo) found between Ayaci and Atebi streams. Later on some people of Pajok wanted the border between Pajok and Obbo to be extended around the stream of Atebi upto the regional Development Cooperation. However, the people of Obbo did not buy the idea. They said the boundary should be at Atebi stream. The boundary of Panyikwara and Pajok (Owiny-ki-Bul) is on Ayiba hill. The border of Lokung (Uganda) is in Limur River, but some people say the border of Pajok and Lokung is in Ngomoromo, while the border of Pajok and Palwar is in river Lerwa. The place called Ceng ki Dwe (Sun and Moon) is in Palwar, but the place called Bercili is in Pajok.

NORTHERN PAJOK
Pajok left has six families: (1) Bura (2) Obwolto (3) Bitti (4) Pagaya (5) Ayuu and (6) Panto.

BURA

Bura has seven small families; *Ogoya, Payako, Pamunda, Lamogi, Palyec, Paramol* and *Pakwa*.

Ogoya, Payako, Pamunda, Lamogi and Palyec all came from Cwaa (Uganda). Chief Oceng Lokwormoi led these families in Sudan when the people of Cwaa had traveled to different places, as we shall see later in this book. I realized that the debate on the people of Bura needs team work. For this reason, if we want to comprehend how Bura of Pajok reached Pajok, we should first know how the people of Cwaa migrated. Then later, we shall also look into the meaning of the name Bura. Finally, we shall see the different places that the people of Bura are living in in Acholi.

According to the history of Acholi, in the year the Pawir Bunyoro started bringing peace and development, the place gradually became small for people who had settled there. For this reason, some people left Pawir around 1870, and crossed river Aswa before entering Pajule. According to records these people were independent. Crazzolara said "The group of people who came with their chief also came from Pawir and with their regalia, to show that they were royal people. They came from across *Pawir* with the royal spear, royal drum, and royal chair   from Bunyoro these people used to be known as the leaders of Pawiir-Lwo (Crazzolara, 1950 p, 83). Onyango also attempted to talk about the regalia of the Cwaa-Bura. He said "The Palwo of Bunyoro united with the Madi of Ogako." They had their own chief. The regalia that the Palwo came with were a big drum, three small drums, spear, beads and trumpet" (Onyango, 1976, p.186).

According to literature, the day the people of Cwaa reached Pawiir, they first went to Toci stream, Oyam, Odek and later they crossed river Aswa and later went to Pajule and the chief welcomed them without any reservation. The history of Acholi says these people who came from Pawiir Bunyoro are the people of chief Cwua of Pawiir. Therefore, when they reached Pajule, they called themselves Jo-pa-Cwua, which means (people of Cwua). They did this in memory of their first chief. Gradually, they changed the name from "Pa-cwua" to "Cwua." We do not know how many years the Jo-cwua lived in Pajule, but according to literature, the people Cwua separated into three groups from Pajule. Some people went towards East, others went west, others went north and others followed the southern route. We also think that the people of Bura were one among the people of Cwua who came from Pajule and went towards the north. They then built on Guruguru Hills (the Acholi call it the hill of the animals) in Kitgum district, 20 miles from Gulu. The word *Guruguru* originated from Arabic, which means *boro* (cave).

According to Crazzolara, the Cwua left Guruguru Hills because of severe famine which killed many people that year. The Cwua went and built on Ladwong Hills among the people of Patiko. It appears as if the Cwua loved war mongering. Reports indicate that just after a few days, they fought with the people of Patiko. This is why the Patiko coined a saying "the Cwua are as bad as Lango omiru". It is true that around the year 1855, the people of Patiko chased Cwua from Ladwong Hills and they ran to Atiak. In this year, chief Lobai (who was named by the Arab as Abucala) was the leader of the people of Atiak.

From here, the Cwua started provoking the people of Atiak. This war mongering of the Cwua forced Chief Lobai to send a message to Agaala, a leader of the Arab traders in Gondokoro, to help him with foreign fighters to help him fight the Cwua. On hearing the message, Agaala immediately summoned his askaris and took them to Atiak. When they reached Atiak, chief Lobai commandeered the askaris who fought the Cwua until they fled leaving behind their animals, women and children. Chief Lobai then distributed the property of the Cwua among the leaders, and gave other to the Arabs who helped him to win the fight against the Cwua. The chief did this in line with Acholi tradition, which permits that property taken from the enemy during wars, should be shared by the family heads. It seems chief gave half of the women and children captured during the fight to the Arab, because they were slave traders. After sharing the property, chief and some of his boys escorted Agaala and his askaris to Gondokoro. But some people say it seems the askaris of Agaala remained in Atiak for almost six months. All these months, chief Lobai was leading the soldiers against Cwua and other tribes near Atiak. When the chief was still on the way to Gondokoro, the Madi came immediately after him in Atiak district. They fought with people here and many were killed. Those who escaped the spears and arrows were scattered. Others back to Ladwong Hill (Patiko). Later some people started assuming that the Madi fought them because chief Lubai had great alliance with the Arab in Gondokoro and yet the Madi did not like the way the Arabs live.

When chief Lobai came back to Atiak, he found no one but marabou storks and other birds, and he followed the others in Patiko. Records show that after this incident, the Cwua again decided to go and fight the people of Atiak (because they did not know how the people of Atiak were beaten by the Madi). Cwua sent a message to the Arabs in Obbo, so that they come and help them fight the people of Atiak. When the Arabs heard the message they immediately accepted. They knew that after winning the fight, they would get slaves, just like the Arabs of Gonokoro. The Arabs in Obbo came in a big number, but when they reached Atiak, they found that Madi had already finished what they had come for (Crazzolara, 1951pp 239-241).

The Arab traders did not like how the blacks lived. What they wanted was what made them amass more wealth. That is why the Arabs kept inciting the Acholi chiefs to keep fighting among themselves. This would allow the weaker ones to run to them for assistance, in return for slaves. According to Onyango, what the Arabs did in Acholi land in 1872 caused tension in many families, which cause unnecessary inter-family conflicts. The fights among brothers caused so much disunity among the Acholi that they could not fight their enemy, the Arabs. Because the Arabs saw that the Acholi had not weapons like guns for fighting, they kept engaging the Acholi in constant conflicts, both day and night. The Acholi history stated that the Arabs could loot whatever they felt was valuable from the Acholi each time there was a fight. These included boys, girls, women and cattle, sheep and goats. The Arabs mercilessly killed the Acholi, which made women to stop going to work in their gardens because of fear. But later, the Acholi enjoyed relative calm on 12/08/1872, when Sir Samuel Baker came to Acholi land. Baker kept on fighting the Arabs in Patiko Ajulu, until he chased the Arab leaders from Patiko. Another commendable job that Baker did was to take back 306 cattle that the Arabs had raided from the Acholi, and rescued 130 slaves. He also took 15 camels that the Arabs used for fighting the Acholi. Additionally, Baker also captured 43 security guards of the Arabs who were based in Sudan, who were working with fellow Arabs. This is why many said the coming of Baker in Acholi land resulted into some bit of peace among the people. According to Acholi history, Baker came with his wife, Mrs Baker. Acholi women loved Baker's wife very much and they called her Anya-dwe (daughter of moon, which is an equivalent of queen). The Acholi gave her this name because the Acholi believe that the moon is white and meek, of all things on earth. The moon is unlike the sun that scorches the earth in the absence of rain. The moon does not make crops withers. This also shows us why Acholi women always compare a beautiful woman, like Mrs. Baker to the moon. Unfortunately, the peace was short-lived in Acholi, because Sir Samuel Baker had to go to Egypt before peace was fully restored. Baker kept on looking for someone who could replace him in the new office he opened in Acholi. When he failed to get an Acholi, he put an Arab in charge of the office. The security guard was named Abdalla Effendi of Sudan. On 14/3/1873, Baker left Acholi and went to Egypt. As soon as Baker left Acholi for Egypt, Abdallah worked well and he was commended by many. But the Arabs who did not want the Acholi to enjoy any moment of peace were not happy with Abdallah's work. So one day the Arabs laced Abdallah's food with poison, and he suddenly died after eating the food. Many people were dumbfounded by the sudden death of Abdallah. After the death of Abdallah, the Arabs appointed two people to replace Abdallah. Fadul Mula and Salim Bey were both so ruthless, which gave the Arabs the opportunity to resume their mistreatment of the Acholi in 1888. The Acholi have a saying that "God is selfless." In 1888-1889, peace again returned in Acholi following the arrival of the British in Acholi (Onyango 1976. pp163-167).

According to Acholi history, around 1875 when the Cwua went back to Ladwong Hill, they were hit by severe famine known as "I feel the face of the woman." Many of them died due to starvation, which forced them to continue moving in search of food. In the year, chief Lamoto, son of chief Leng, was on the throne. In the same year, the Bura of Pajok was together with the Bura of Uganda (Akara Bura, Kiteng and Naam Okora). From Ladwong hill, the Cwua went in search of food in Palabek. Unfortunately, they had severe food shortage. We do not know for how long the Cwua were in Palabek since there was no food there either. But we assume that since Cwua found no food in Palabek, they could have spent only two or three nights there. According to records, while in Palabek the Cwua left and moved towards the south. They crossed river Aswa where they built on Ladwong Hills. This year, they built near the people of Palaro. It seems the people of Palaro allowed the people of Cwua to temporarily stay among them, hoping the people of Cwua would not cause conflict among them.

Before the Cwua had taken long on Ladwong hills, the people of Patiko, Paboo and Payira went to wage war against them. The people of Cwua however overpowered them. After the wars, the people of Cwua decided to teach the people of Payira a lesson they would never forget. For this reason, the elders of Cwua sent Alyaka and Loboke to the family of Lalogi to discover the secret that the people of Payira were keeping. The two went and stayed among the people of Lalogi, where they asked many questions about the people of Payiira. The people of Lalogi were cooperative and responded to all their questions. And this is how Alyaka and Loboke discovered the secrets of the people of Payira. After two or three days, Alyaka and Loboke went back home in Cwua and revealed all the secrets of the Payiira to their elders. But Acholi history does not show what secrets were discovered. Shortly, the Cwua mobilized warriors to fight the people of Payira. They fought them near river Abera near the family of Lalogi. The Cwua defeated the people of Payira and drove them to river Motongo. This also shows us that the people of Lalogi seem to have told Alyaka and his colleague that the Payira liked congregating along river Abera. They also told them the time they liked gathering along the river.

After three days, the people of Payiira gained courage and went to fight the Cwua on Ladwong Hills. Unfortunately, Cwa defeated the people of Payiira. According to Acholi history, the mother of Lalweny, the wife of Chief Lomoto of Cwua, was killed by the Payiira during this war. The death of the chief's wife angered the Cwua, much as they loved to fight.

One day, a witchdoctor advised the sons of Cwua that as the people of Payiira often passed through Cwua, even if they come across twelve Payiira's sons, they should kill only one. The Payiira used to pass through the home of the Cwua on their way to the market. The children of Cwua then took the advice of the witchdoctor in mind. After a few days, the men of Cwua came across ten people of Payiira who were going to Paboo to sell their merchandise as usual, the Cwua killed one person among the Payiira, as they were advised by the witchdoctor. They left the other nine people to go free. The Cwua later learnt that the Patiko, Paboo and Payiira had a good relationship. For this reason, the people of Patiko and Paboo also became the enemy of the Cwua. Chief Ocieng Lokwormoi of Bura Pajok realized that the Bura were always fighting. He then chose some people of Bura Pajok and started moving towards north east to Agu Hills. Here they met the people of Bobi, Bitii and Pagaya. But some people say the people of Bura of Pajok separated from the people of Cwua Bura from Pajule. The history of Acholi states that the people of Cwua Bura who remained left Ladwong Hills and went to Palabek (Crazzolara 1954, PP 522-525).

While here, the Cwua again started provoking the people of Palabek, which annoyed many. In this year, chief Tongo-moi was on the throne. When he saw that tension was brewing among the Cwua, and the people of Palabek, he relocated the Cwua to Agoro Hills. Chief Logulu of Agoro welcomed the Cwua warmly, and later literature shows that chief Logulu married the granddaughter of Alyaka of Cwua. Shortly afterwards, Okot, the son of chief Logulu slept with Adira, the wife of Abot, brother of Alyaka. According to Acholi tradition, Lakworo calls Adira his mother, and Adira calls Chief Logulu her son-in-law. As the Acholi people say, even if you fart or sleep with your mother-in-law under water, it will still be known. Surely, a few days after Chief Logulu learned of what happened between Okot and Adira. This brought shame to the chief and he ordered his people to arrest and kill his son. In Acholi, if chief gives an order like this, it must be done without question. So the people of the hill arrested Okot, speared him in the chest, but he did not die, he fled with the spear in his body. He took refuge in a cave far away from home. Okot's uncle, when he learned of the incident, concluded that his nephew must be in a cave. The following morning he found Okot in a cave where he began to treat him from.

After a week, chief Logulu inquired whether Okot was really dead or alive. The people responded that they were not sure whether Okot was still alive, and then he was stabbed, but escaped with the spear on him. The chief must have realized that Okot's uncle went to the cave, because he ordered the people to look for the two. The people heard what the chief said, but they did not go to look for Okot. At night, each of them went to their hut to sleep. Very early in the morning when the bulbul was still singing, the chief sent his messenger to go and wake people up. When everyone was awake, they gathered at the chief's. When the people had gathered, the chief again told them with a commanding voice, "Go and search for Okot and his uncle. If you find Okot, you should kill him." Immediately, that morning, the people sacrificed to go and look for Okot. They picked spears and followed the path which led to the cave. Even if the chief gave an order that they should kill his son, the people later learnt that the chief became sad why he ordered for his child to be killed. According to Acholi history, chief Logulu later conceived a plan to start fighting the Cwua because they were the ones who made him to kill his child. Unfortunately, one particular man of Logot went that night to Alyaka and told him "Get away from here immediately. Chief Logulu of Agoro wants to kill the people of Cwua in relation to his son's death." When Alyaka heard the news, he sent a messenger to the people immediately. The people of Cwua then left instantly that night, and went to a place called Okool (Crazzolara 1954, PP, 525-526).

After a few days, Chief Lomoto decided that his son should take over the throne since he was already aging. Chief Alyaka then took the people to mount Turkana, located to the East of Naamukora. From here, chief Alyaka met a slave trader named Ahmed Hussein. The slave trader was new in this family. He was from Kalongo. The history of the Acholi says, one morning, Ahmed Hussein went to hunt for ostriches in Patete desert. But as he was still walking, a man named Turukumoi of Okool stalked him from behind. Turukumoi wanted to kill Hussein, but fortunately, he saw Turukumoi before he could hurt him. Hussein picked a gun and from one of his workers and shot Turukumoi in the chest. He ran home with a bullet wound in his hand. When Hussein came back home from hunting, Turukumoi was asking other people if they knew Hussein. People responded in the affirmative. Turukumoi was the one of the children in Okool family. When Ahmed heard the news, he thought to himself, "In the past, chief Alyaka told me that he ruled over the people of Okool. So, if the people of Okool are under the leadership of chief Alyaka, why does Turukumoi want to kill me?" Hussein then sent a message to his fellow Arabs to come and arrest chief Alyaka and detain him in Odrupele cell. Later, chief Alyaka died in detention, and his brother named Lorem took over the throne. Crazzolara said, "After the death of chief Alyaka, his brother, Lorem, took over the chiefdom. That year, three small families: Imeera, Geem, and Koki united with Bura" (Crazzolara 1954, P, 526).

When Cwua left Agoro, they moved in different places and later went to the place where they live today in Uganda. The history of Acholi Uganda says Cwua Bura of Uganda has seven families. They are Naamokora, Mucwini, Umiia Anyima, Orom, Kitong, Okuti and Okool. Each family also has a chief but the sub county chief is in Naamokora. Crazzolara attempted to define the word 'Bura'. But if we look at it critically, we find that the word 'Bura' means the people of *kal*, which means the people who have the royal drum, royal spear and a royal chair. Secondly, we should bear in mind that not all the people of Bura came from Cwua Bura. Today, the people of Bura are found in Pajok,

Panyikwara, Magwi, Lokoya, Lokoro and Agoro of South Sudan. Some people of Bura are also in Patiko, Payiira and Madi Opei in Uganda. Much as they are called Bura, they are not related. However, the Bura of Pajok and the Bura in Uganda seem to have a tribal connection, because they all came from Cwua Bura in Pawiir-Bunyoro.

BURA HILL AND HUNTING GROUND
The people of Bura Pajok have neither hunting ground, nor hills.

OBWOLTO
The people of Obwolto have five small families; they are the people of P'keny, P'Okongo, P' Opiyo, P'Ogwang and Patoko.

The people of *P'keny*: the history of Pajok says P'Keny and P'Opiyo came from Lokoro around 1890. They came together with the people of Lamwoo and Patanga and P'Opiyo. Elder Opiyo was the leader of P'Opiyo family when they were coming from Lokoro. If you want to better understand the movement of P'keny and P'Opiyo people, read "The Migration of Pajok from Anywak to Acholiland".

P'Okongo people: the history of Pajok says the family of P'Okongo came from Palabek Pa Dwat. They separated into two; some people remained in Palabek (Uganda), and others came to Pajok in Sudan. According to literature, there is still a strong relationship between P'Okongo in Pajok and P'Okongo who remained in Palabek Padwat. We do not know why P'Okongo of Pajok came to Sudan, but according to Acholi history, elder Okongo was the one who brought this family from Palabek (they were known as people of Padwat. But when they arrived in Pajok, they started calling themselves "jo P'Okong," which means the people of Okongo or the group led by Okongo. Some elders of Pajok say the people of P'Okongo came and found the people of Pajok already in Ayacii, but others say P'Okongo came when the people or Pajok were still in Polila. The history of Pajok states that chief Ogwok welcomed the people of Okongo warmly and gave them land. They then built among the family of Obwolto.

P'Ogweng people: the people of Pajok do not know where the *P'Ogweng* came from. Unfortunately, when I was moving among the Acholi researching on the history for publication in this book, I did not come across any family member of the *P'Ogweng* people. But the history of Pajok tells us that elder Ogweng was the one who brought this group in Pajok. That is why they are still called the people of P'Ogweng, which means the people of or the group led by Ogweng, in memory of their first leader.

Patoko people: the history of Acholi says the people of Patoko came from Patoko Hills located in Obbo. They arrived in Pajok around 1940 when the people of Pajok were already in river Atebi. Chief Ocieng Anyoda welcomed the people of Patoko and gave them land. They built among the people of Obwolto. The History of Obbo states that Patoko moved to Pajok because they were too lazy to dig *kinyu*. That is why they were hit hard by famine and they had to relocate to Pajok in 1940. Everyone in Acholi is aware that if famine strikes, the members of that family can die of starvation, but the people of Obbo rarely die of famine because there is plenty of *kinyu* in Obbo hunting ground. The history of Acholi also tells us that whenever famine strikes, the people of Pajok, Palwar, Magwi, Omeo, Agoro, Ofirika and Panyikwara always go to collect *kinyu* in Obbo.

OBWOLTO HILLS AND HUNTING GROUNDS

The history of Pajok shows that Obwolto has only one hunting ground named Ladiki. A child from the family of P'Opiyo is responsible for taking care of the hunting ground. The people of Obwolto also have only one hill named Lagot Aluuru. They also have one god called Labot Onyom (the bachelor will marry). If you want to understand the details of this god (the bachelor will marry), read chapter three of *Jok Labot Onyom*.

BITI

The people have two small families namely; Pacwaka and Palome. All the two families came from different places as we shall see below.

Pacwaka (Biti): the history of Pajok tells us that the people of Pacwaka migrated from Bunyoro and later got their own home, and the people of Palome built amidst them later. As we saw earlier, in Pajok Left, there were four families, who own Pajok. These are Biti (Pacwaka), Pagaya (Pobuk), Panto-kera and Ayuu. All members of these four families came to Pajok in the same year, but different months. The elders of Pajok like Parteno Abak and Ogana said the people of Pagaya were the first to come to Pajok. They built on the hills of Agu, while the Biti were the second people to arrive, and built on the hills Kilak in Lokung. The people of Panto kera came third, and built among the people of Pagaya on Agu hills. The people of Ayuu were the fourth and last group to arrive. They also built in Aguu hills among the Pagaya.

Understanding the family or home in Acholi can bring a mix-up in the history of Acholi if not well examined. For instance, some people refer to Biti, as Bito or the people of Ba Bito. Crazzolara said in his book, "The Lwo Part 1 Lwo Migrations" that Jo Bitti of Pajok were called Biti or Bito, when the Lwo were still looking for a place to settle (Crazzolara, 1951, P, 108). But a detailed research into the history of Acholi and Lwo reveals that there is a family known as Bitho (Bito), Bitii and Ba-Bito. According to the history of Lwo, the Bitho family (Bito) is found in Anywak, while the family of Biti is in Pajok. The family of Bito, on the other hand, is in Pawiir (Kaberamaido). All of them separated from Cwua-Bunyoro. I do not know if the names Bitii, Ba Bito and Bito mean the same. The word Bito in Acholi means royalty, which came from Bito of Buyoro because the royal family of Cwua is in Bunyoro.

We see that after the migration of the people of Bura of Pajok from Pajule, Cwua divided into three. Some people went towards the east, others went north-wards and another group followed the western direction. It seems the people of Bitii of Pajok moved together with people of Cwua from Pajule and moved to the west till they reached Pakwac (which was formerly known as Pubungu). The history of Acholi tells us that Bitii separated from Cwua from Pakwac.

Literature also has it that Bira (Lango) of Sudan came from Bunyoro. They later separated from Bitii (Cwua) from Pakwac. Crazzolara said "Bira of Sudan seems to have been among the group that separated from Pakwac, but they went and built at Agoro Hill. From Pakwac, some people of Bitii went to Belgian-Congo and later called themselves Panyikango. From there, Bitii of Pajok left and went and built in Aguu hills in Lokung where the people of Ywaaya were settled (Crazzolara, 1954, P, 555). The Ba-Bito of Uganda split from Bitii of Pajok from Pakwac, and went and built where they live up to now.

The people of Panyikango of Congo call themselves as such because first, they want to show other people that much as they are staying in Congo, they are still under chief Nyikango of Shilluk. Secondly, they gave themselves this name to remind them of Shilluk because Acholi came from Shilluk as we saw in chapter one of this book. The word Panyikango in Acholi means the people of Nyikango.

We have now understood that the people of Bura and Biti all came from

Bunyoro. One day, when I was asking five elders of Pajok in Juba to find out if the people of Bura and Biti left Bunyoro with other groups of people, or alone, regrettably, all these elders failed to give me any response. But Crazzolara said the people of Bura and Biti left Bunyoro and went with other people. The people they left with that year came from the following families:

Jo Gaya	Jo Kwonga
Jo Cwua (Bura)	Jo Jimo
Jo Lebki	Jo Biti (Bito)
Jo Mia	Jo Senge
Jo Cobo	Jo Bobi (Bub)

We find that among all these people, the people of Cwua (Bura), Jimo, Bito (Biti) and Kwonga are the prototypical Lwo. These families are found among the Acholi of Sudan and Acholi of Uganda. But the people of Gaya, Cobo and Bobi are Madi, who earlier went to Bunyoro. However, we do not know much about the people of Lebki, Mia and Senge, because they are not found in Acholi or Alur (Crazzolara, 1954, P, 450).

Palome people: the history of Acholi says that the Palome came from Obbo (Koyo). Unfortunately, I could not trace the leader of Palome, to answer my questions on how they migrated. Secondly, I wanted to understand why the Palome left Obbo, where people never died of starvation, because *kinyu* was in abundance. It became difficult for me to get such information, but I believe in the second edition of this book, we shall get more information on the people of Palome.

BITI HILLS AND HUNTING GROUNDS

Biti has six hunting grounds; Agolo and Odoo, Yamo-Okuto, Cin-nyari, Candek, Acamo-Lango and Oder-ki-Lodongo. We do not know the names of both the old and new people who tended these hunting grounds. Another reason which made it hard to get names of people who used to tend these hunting grounds is because the soldiers of Garang made many people to flee to different places. This made it hard to get elders to get information from. The Biti also have a hill named Lagot-Lwak. However, much as the Biti are the owners of the Pajok family, they do not have a spirit/god.

PAGAYA

Jo Pagaya (or Kwac Lanyuru) has two small families: *Pubuk* family and *Paladyang*. The history of Pajok states that the people of Pabuk are the owners of the family, but the family of Pabuk and Paladyang all came from outside. According to Acholi history, the people of Pabuk came from Bunyoro, but we do not know where the people of Paladyang came from. Lwo history shows that the people of Pagaya came from Pawiir-Bunyoro (Bunyoro). Chief Ogweng took the people of Pagaya away from Pawiir-Bunyoro and they went to Agu Hill. According to literature, chief Ogweng and his people left Bunyoro because of conflict over who should be the chief. The conflict was between them and their brothers who remained in Bunyoro.

In Bunyoro, the chief always wears opilo skin (skin of rat called opilo) and sits on a royal chair when mediating over disputes. The royal drum is made of metal. In the year 1700, Ogweng campaigned because he wanted to become the chief of Bunyoro. Unluckily, people did not vote him. When he failed the elections, he immediately concluded that he was not wanted in Bunyoro. For this reason, Ogweng took the people of Pagaya and went with them to Pajule and built in Pa-twoo. The people of Pagaya lived here for a few years and later continued moving towards the north. They kept moving on the hills found between river Lirina and river Limuuru. Later on, they went and built on Guma Hill, where chief Ogweng set up Pagaya chiefdom.

Other Acholi elders say that the people of Pagaya moved together with the people of Payira. But some say the people of Pagaya move alone, and the people of Payira got them already settled at Guma Hill. However, according to Crazzolara "The first people who come to Pawiir, through Pajule, were the people of Pagaya of Pajok. And, the Payira found the people of Patiko who came from Pubungu, already living at Guma" (Crazzolara, 1950, P.83). The history of Patiko says the Payira moved separately with the people of Lira (Lango), and settled in Kweri Hill". From Kweri Hill, the Payira went and built at the foot of Guma Hill. It appears as if chief Ogweng died at Guma Hill because Crazzolara (1951) in his book "The Lwo Vo. 2" says that the Pagaya and Lamwo settled at Guma Hill without a chief (Crazzolara, 1951, P.228). After the death of chief Ogweng, Opilo took over the throne and took the people of Pagaya from Guma Hill to Agu Hill.

I found it a little hard to understand Crazzolara's book because he is talking about one family. For example, people of Lamwo. But we know very well that the Lwo are in Uganda and Sudan. In his book, he does not differentiate between the Lawmo of Sudan, or Uganda. Crazzolara said, "The people who united with the Patiko at Guma Hill are the people of Pagaya, who joined Lamwo because of family disputes" (Crazzolara, 1951, P. 230). What we do not understand here is if Crazzolara is talking about Lamwo of Sudan or that of Uganda. We very well know that the people of Lamwo of Pajok came from Lokoro/Anywak. And the history of Pajok does not say the people of Lamwo came and went to Patiko. We can now conclude that the Lamwo Crazzolara said united with the people of Pagaya over family disputes are from Uganda. These people joined the people of Pagaya of Pajok when they were still on their way to Sudan.

While at Guma hills, the people of Pagaya, who outnumbered all the other families of Lamwo united with the people of Patiko. From Gima hills the people of Pagaya continued moving towards the north east, in a hilly place. According to Acholi history, this place is found between river Lirina and river Limuuru. From here, the people of Pagaya went and built in Agu hills (Crazzolara, 1951, P.175). But some elders of Pajok like Ben Oywak told me that from Guma hills the people of Pagaya went and built in Agu hills where the people of Ywaya went and found them.

In the past, people preferred to build on hills, because it gave them a better view of impending enemies.

The Lwo, who move a lot came across the people of Pagaya the first time in Agu Hill (Pajok). As we saw in the above page, the people of Pagaya came from Bunyoro. They left Bunyoro because of fighting over who should be the chief. Majority of the people of Bunyoro remained behind, but the people of Pagaya of Pajok were the only ones who left Bunyoro under the leadership of chief Ogweng. When the people of Pagaya left Bunyoro, they moved in so many places that I can't list all here. They later on came to Agu Hill. Some people say Pagaya passed through many places. From Agu Hill, other groups went back to Patiko and others went to Paicoo, Payira, Kooro, Puranga and Pajok.

After a few years, the people of Ywaya came from Lokoro, led by chief Keny. They went to and built among the Payira at Aguu Hill. According to the history of Pajok, when the people of Ywaya arrived at Agu Hill, they met the Pagaya, Bura and the people of Palio. All these groups had their royal spear, royal drum and royal chair. Since the people of Pagaya and Ywaya each had a chief, records show that the two groups one day decided to hold a meeting regarding chiefdom. It seems during the meeting, the people of Pagaya and Ywaya resolved that Pagaya should continue being ruled by chief Ogweng, while chief Keny continued leading the people of Ywaya.

Much as the two groups each agreed to be led by different chiefs, the people of Ywaya were not happy with the resolution passed in the meeting. I am saying this because one day, the boys and men of Pagaya went hunting and left women, children and old men at home. This gave the people of Ywaya the opportunity to do whatever pleased them to the people of Pagaya. The people of Ywaya went and stabbed women, children and old men who remained at home. Chief Opilu of Pagaya was also at home, since Acholi chiefs do not hunt. The people of Ywaya also killed him. After killing all these people, they took all the pots in the home. They cut the dead bodies to pieces and put them in the pots and cooked them. According to literature, when the people of Ywaya finished committing the atrocity, they also picked the royal spear, royal drum and the royal chair belonging to chief Opilu, leaving the people of Pagaya without chiefdom.

When the people of Pagaya came back from hunting, they found the place messy and reeking of human blood, while human flesh was boiling on fire. This incident caused panic among the people of Pagaya, which forced the few survivors to flee in different directions. The history of Pajok says some people who remained in Pajok joined the people of Lamwo. But the people of Ywaya still provoked these few who remained. Afterwards, the people of Palio and Lamwo all remained under the leadership of chief Ywaya. However, some members of Pagaya fled to Palwar and built in the family of Amica. They later called themselves the people of Lobamu. Other people ran to Lokung (Uganda), while some fled to Palabek (Crazzolara, 1951, P.176). According to Tim (1985), the history of Pajok states that the people who did not immediately go under the leadership of Ywaya were the people of Bobi and Biti. Within a few years, the people of Ywaya fought with the people of Bobi for three days, and forcefully them under their chiefdom (Mr. Tim, 1985, P.39).

The people of Ywaya did this because they wanted all the people of Pajok to be led by their chief Ogwok, the father of Ocieng Lokwormoi of Ywaya. But the people of Palio, Lamwoo and Panto do not want to surrender their royal drum to chief Ogwok. This issue caused a major fight between Panto and Ywaya. The people of Ywaya defeated Panto in the fight, and took them back to be led by chief Ogwok. Fortunately, during the fight, the chief of Panto, named chief Langalanga was not killed. In memory of the war between Ywaya and Panto, the people of Ywaya composed a song:

Panto Ocelo Muduku Mwaa!	Panto fired their guns in vain!
Koc Kono!	What about Koc!
Langa-Langa Mulo ki Piny!	Langalanga crawls on the ground
Oloyi Yee!	You are defeated ho!

Even if the people of Lokoro bore the people to be led by chief Ogwok of Ywaya as we saw previously, many people did not buy the idea. The Biti, who are also the land owners of Pajok were very disappointed on seeing that chief Opilu of Pagaya, who led the people of Pajok Left, had relinquished his royal drum to Ywaya. When Biti saw that chief Opilu and his people accepted to be led by chief Ogwok, they realized there was no way out, and they also accepted to be led by chief Ogwok. Later around 1900, another war erupted between Biti and Ywaya, which lasted three days. During the war, many boys of Biti were killed. The people of Ywaya then took Biti under the leadership of chief Ogwok.

Gradually, everyone member of Pajok who was suffering under the Ywaya, temporarily united with chief Bongo-jane of Lamwo. Later, the people who united all left Agu Hill and moved to the south. As the people were still moving, chief Bongo-jane and his brother, who was his representative named Lupfunu, differed. Lupfunu wanted the people to separate, so that each group looked for a place they liked. He also wanted to take his group where they desired, but chief Bongo-jane disagreed with him. Records show that after the disagreement, everyone supported Lupfunu's idea, and immediately the people of Pajok separated, and other people went and built in Ayuu Hill (Palabek), others went and built in Padibe, while others went and built along river Pager in Kitgum. The majority who were under the leadership of Lapfunu went and settled in Polila Hill, where the people of Ywaya, who came from Agu Hill, found other people of Pajok had settled. People say chief Bongo-jane died at Polila Hill, but the history of Pajok does not talk about the death of chief Bongo-jane.

Around 09/05/1863 when the Pajok were still in Agu Hill, Samuel Baker left

Obbo with three other people and went to Pajok. When Baker reached Agu Hill, he wrote a book "I arrived at a place where people built a big family on top of hills. I met the chief of Pajok, who gave me a billygoat. His messengers later slaughtered the goat, and people ate it to cleanse my legs. The chief caught a chicken with its legs, and rotated (buko) it around my legs, and my donkey named "Filfil". The chief waved a cock on the donkey, while holding the cock. Later, the chief waved the cock around my legs. The cock was slaughtered and I shared with the people I traveled with. When the chief had finished performing the ritual, they cleansed the family in Agu Hill. I saw the family of Pajok fenced with bamboo, unfortunately, the home was so filthy compared with the family of Bar and the family of Lotuko where I lived. That month, I wanted to cross river Aswa, but the chief of Pajok told me that, it would be risky to cross the river since it was a rainy season, and the place would be flooded. Unfortunately, when we were still in Pajok, my donkey died. This made it hard for me and my messengers to travel. When I realized that it was difficult for us to travel to Patiko, we went back to Obbo (Sir Samuel Baker, 1866, vol 1 PP, 328-330).

PAGAYA HUNTING GROUNDS AND HILLS

The people of Pagaya have one hunting ground named *Akwero latin* (I have rejected/abandoned a child). The people of Pobuk are the ones who keep this hunting ground. They also have one hill named Pokec. The people of Pagaya have one god who lives on the hills of Pokec (Pakec). The son of Pagaya always offers a brown male sheep to this god, to bring good luck/blessings to the people of Pagaya and other people of Pajok. The Acholi of long ago called this male sheep "nyok oboro". We do not know the names of the former and current people who used to offer sacrifices to the god of Pokec.

AYUU

The people of Ayu have three small families; Paryemo, Panyara-bongo and Palimu.

Paryemo and Panyara-bongo: the elders of Pajok like Marcelo Ogana and Kadensyo Jada Adinya told me that the people of Paryemo and Panyara-bongo migrated from Atyak (Uganda), under the leadership of Chief Onyok. But Crazzolara said that these people of Pajok and Ayom of Panyikwara came from Lolubo-Lokoya (Crazzolara, 1954, P, 398). I also think Ayuu of Pajok (Paryemo and Panyara-bongo) truly came from Lolubo. As many people earlier migrated, I also think that these people first went to Atyak and later came to Pajok. The story surrounding the migration of Ayuu in Pajok shows us that the elders of Pajok do not know how the people of Ayuu moved during in the old days. They only know about the arrival of the people of Ayuu from Atyak in Pajok.

Chief Onyok removed the people of Paryemo and Panyara-bongo from Atyak because of the following reasons. In 1841, the people of Cwua who were in Ladwong Hill and Madi-Meto of Sudan were constantly fighting the people of Atyak. In this year, chief Abvuga was the chief of Atyak. When the chief saw that the war was intensifying, he moved away from Obvuro (the chief's compound) and went to Kalamuka. From there, chief Abvuga went to Ligee, where the Madi killed him during a fight. After the death of chief Abvuga, his son named Otira took over the throne. The history of Acholi says Otira ruled only for a few months before he was killed by a buffalo. Chief Otira had a son named Olyaa. But when chief Otira was killed by a buffalo, his son Olyaa was still a boy. For this reason, Odur, son of Jurugo, who was the brother Otira, became the interim chief, until Olyaa became an adult. According to Onyango, chief Otira of Atyak requested chief Anyala of Padibe (who ruled the people of Padibe in 1823-1850) to bring his people to help him fight against Madi-Meto. Anyala was the first female chief in the family of Padibe. According to literature, a fight erupted between the people of Atyak and Madi-Meto because a born of Madi killed chief Abvuga, the father of Otira. This is why chief Otira wanted to avenge his father on the people of Madi-meto. Chief Otira then wholeheartedly accepted to give a girl to Padibe. Chief Anyala then sent his army to help fight against the Madi-Meto. Chief Anyala listened to Chief Otira's plea and sent a large army to Atyak. When the people of chief Anyala reached Atyak, they put their chair/shield together with the fighters of chief Otira and the seriously fought the people of Madi-meto. They fought for three days and looted many cattle from the Madi. Acholi history shows that the people of Padibe were fierce fighters among all the Acholi people. For this reason, Chief Anyala did not help the people of only Atyak win their war, but they also helped chief Okeny of Lokung during a fight against an uncle of Okeny because the uncle of chief Okeny had killed Okeny's father for snatching his wife (Onyango, 1976, P, 197).

As we have earlier on seen, Cwua and Madi were always fighting the people of Atyak. Unluckily, the people of Atyak did not mind their enemies; instead, they started quarreling among themselves. Acholi elders said the relationship between Atyak-Ayago and Atyak-Pawir was so sour that they could not eat together. We now assume that the people of Atyak-Ayago and Atyak Pawir kept disagreeing because Owiny, (son of kal) of Ayago migrated with all the regalia in Pawir. In the year when Olya was to become chief, elder Opwonya the father of Agala of Atyak- Ayago (Ayuu) ordered the people to call chief Lakoo, son of P'Okec of Atyak-Pwair to come and install Olya on the throne (Crazzolara, 1951, PP, 228-229).

The people of Atyak-Ayago seconded elder Opwonya, and sent messenger to Pawiir. When the messengers arrived, the people of Pawiiir warmly welcomed them. It seems the people of Atyak Pawiir understood that the people of Ayago cursed them because of the ceremonial objects that Owiny brought to Pawiir. The people of Pawiir then accepted to give back the regalia to the people of Atyak-Ayago, so that the chief was installed in line with Acholi tradition. They organized all the ceremonial objects to be returned to Ayago. They also dressed in goat skins, leopard skin and the cob skin. According to reports, chief Lakor and his people walked 130 miles from Ayago to Pawiir. They took gifts such as *drums, a royal chair, utensils made out of the bark of tree, royal spear, and royal bead to be worn by the chief. Other gifts were cowry cells and a royal shin crafted out of different animal skins.*

When the people of Pawir arrived in Ayago, and were about to enter their home, they slaughtered a sheep as it was the norm, to unite them. Olya and his people also slaughtered a sheep. Shortly, two elders, one from the family of Pawiir and another from Ayago, took the dung of the sheep and smeared it on the forehead and chest of everyone present. This is also equivalent to prayer to the almighty God that "God the most high, cleanse our hearts, change our minds and make us one. May bad vibes depart, and may no tree stump hit the toes of any child." Later, the people of Pawiir ate their mutton, and the people of Olya also ate theirs. After the meals, Chief Lakor of Pawir gave the skull of the sheep of his people to Olya, and Olya also gave the skull of the sheep of the people of Ayago to Chief Lakor. The people kept the skull as a sign of reconciliation. Which means the people of Ayago and Pawiir could share meals without fear (Crazzolara, 1951, P, 300). The history of Atyak tells us that after reconciliation, chief Lakor installed Chief Olya on the throne and sat next to him on his royal chair. After a short while, people started eating, drinking and dancing.

It seems chief Onyok of Ayuu kept on thinking about the war the people of Cwua and Madi used to fight the people of Atyak. He later learnt that the Atyak was not a place in which to live any more, because every morning, they keep expecting that the fighters would come but didn't know which direction they would emerge from. It is because of this reason that the chief Onyok took the people of Paryamo and Panyara-bongo from Atyak and took them to Sudan (Pajok). We now know that the people of Ayuu of Pajok came from Atyak from the family of Ayuu. Acholi history says Atyak has 23 small families as listed below:

1. Lokaal (the royal family).
2. Acopele —who came from Madi.
3. Koyo (who were brought by chief Labongo from Ameny Hill and non royal).
4. Kibogi (Rapukuru) who came from Pajok.
5. P'Opwonya.
6. 6. Pa-Wiiro.
7. Pa-Mwoma.
8. P'Lokere.
9. P'Orec.
10. P'Kibo.
11. P'Rwaca.
12. P'Bono.
13. P'Rubi from Pajule.
14. Agoro from Agoro.
15. P'Lopale from Madi.
16. Lokolya from Lowi from the family of Kuku.
17. Ayuu; the group of people of Ayuu who remained while other went to Pajok.
18. Alu from Madi.
19. P'Cillo.
20. Murule from Bar.
21. P'Kwec the land owners of Atyiak.
22. P'Cware came from Madi Adrupele.
23. Ki Logobi must have migrated from Didinga (Crazzolara, 1951, PP, 301-302).

The history of Pajok states that the people of Paryemo and Payara-bongo entered Pajok in the same year with the people of Biti, Pagaya, and Panto-kera. However, they all entered the land in different months. The four families were the first to enter Pajok. This also explains why to date Ayuu are the land owners. Ben Oywak told me that when the people of Kor were coming to Pajok, they found Ayuu in Lagaya Hill and went together with the people of Kor in Agu Hill. But other people say that Kor found the people of Ayuu already settled in Agu. Elder Oywak added that the people of Ayuu were very rude, that is why the people of Kor thought that if they forcefully returned to Ayuu, it would cause deaths among them. Truly, the people of Kor used words of endearment to please the people of Ayuu. The Acholi have a saying that wisdom is better than strength. Gradually, the people of Ayuu sincerely accepted to be led by chief Ywaya.

Palimu: Elder Paterno Abak told me that the people of Palimu came from Ayuu Alali which is in Palabek (Uganda). The history of Pajok does not tell us why these people left Palabek. We also do not know the name of an elder or the chief who brought the people of Palimu in Pajok. Secondly, we also do not know if Palimu entered Pajok together with Paryemo and Panyara-bongo, or they came later and built among these people. When I was still in Sudan, I attempted to search for elders of Palimo, to tell me about this family. Unfortunately, the fight led by Garang made people scatter, which made it difficult for me to find elders of Palimu. The third area of interest was to know about Palimu among Acholi of Sudan. We got Palimu in Pajok in Magwi but we do not know if they are related. In case there is any relationship between the Palimu of Pajok and Palimu of Magwi then we shall write it in the second edition of this book.

AYUU HUNTING GROUND AND HILLS

Ayuu has only one hunting ground called Oloyo Iweny (Ayuma), meaning the giant was defeated. Long long time ago, Oloyo Iweny hunting ground belonged to the Pajombo of Obbo. The people of Pajombo later gave the hunting ground to Ayuu as a reward for helping the Pajombo fight Lango. If you want to understand more on the give-away of Oloyo Iweny hunting ground, read: Pajombo Bura of Obbo. We also find that Ayuu have only one hill named Alali Hill in Palabek Uganda. But the people of Ayuu do not have a god. I am assuming that Ayuu of Pajok call Alali as their hill because the people of Palimu who are in the family of Ayuu migrated from Palabek, and there is a deep relationship between Ayuu Palimu of Pajok and Ayuu Alali of Palabek. We learnt that during the war of Joshep Lagu (1963-1972). When the people of Ayuu of Pajok fled because of conflict in Uganda, they went and built at Ayu Alali Hill, while other people built in Akeli-kongo.

PANTO

Panto has four small families; Pajuku, Pabwoo, Pamola and Kera.

*Panto-Pajuru and Panto-Pabwoo.*Acholi history states that the people of Panto-Pajuru ki Panto-Pabwoo came from Adodi located at the border of Uganda and Sudan. According to reports, elder Opac, the father of chief Langalanga led Pajuru and Pabwo in Pajok in 1938. Other people say among these four families, the Panto-Pajuru and Panto-Pabwoo are the owners of the home. But other people say Panto-kera are the owners, as we earlier on saw in this book. But Panto-Pajuru, Panto-Pabwoo and Panto- Pamola came later and built among the people of Kera. As we read in the previous pages, when the people of Pajok were looking for a place to settle, they were so many. From Lagaya Hill, the people of Pajok continued to move until they reached Adodi Hill, where they found Panto-Pajuru and Panto-Pabwoo. According to literature, the Panto-Pajuru and Panto-Pabwoo were also very rude like the people of Ayuu. The people of Panto-Pajuru and Panto-Pabwoo built at the foot of Adodi Hill in this year because Adodi hunting ground belonged to them. Adodi hunting ground starts from Adodi Hill up to the mouth of Atebi stream. From Adodi, the people of Pajok also requested Panto to move with them, and they accepted. After one or two months, the people of Panto joined the people of Pajok and they moved in many places as seen below:

Okwero-obeno, Ongoto-Nyare (Palabek), Apul, Lagiri, Tuma-tuma and got Lotii. The Panto and some members of Pajok lived at Lotii Hill for a few months and later went to Ayuma hunting ground. When Pajok arrived in Ayuma hunting ground, Panto decided to go back to Adodi Hill, since the people of Pajok could not get a better place to settle for many years. After a few days, Panto-Pajuru and Panto-Pabwoo separated from the people of Pajok, and went and built at the foot of Adodi Hill. Around 1938, when Panto-Pajuru and Panto-Pabwoo heard that the Pajok had got a better place along Atebi stream, they left Adodi and came back to Pajok and built among Panto-kera along Atebi stream.

Pamola and Kera: The history of Acholi tells us that the people of Panto-Pamola and Panto Kera came from Labongo in Agago (Uganda). Before they came to Pajok, they went and built among the Pajuru and Pabwoo at the foot of Adodi Hill. Later, Panto kera continued with their journey and built at Agu Hill. However, the history of Acholi does not tell us if Panto-kera and Panto Pamola went to AguHill together. It seems the people of Pamola remained at Adodi Hill when Panto kera were continuing with their movement. We are assuming that the Panto-Pamola, Panto-Pajuru and Panto-Pabwoo moved together until they relocated to Atebi stream in 1983. Later the four families which were in Panto call themselves Panto. The people of Kera had their chief named chief Ayoo. Chief Ayoo was a girl who came from Labongo. Chief Ayoo later married Juku of Pajuru from Adodi Hill. After the marriage between Ayoo and Juku, god blessed them with many children, whose number we do not know. The children also gave birth to grand children, who increased the number of the family of Pajuru in Panto. This also shows us that when chief Ayoo got married Juru she widened the chiefdom. This is because it is a tradition that, if a girl elopes, the children she bears will not belong to her father, but her husband. To help you understand the movement of Panto, read, "How the Pajok dominated Lokoro chiefdom".

After a short time, he took the people of Pajok to Kiryandongo Camps in Uganda, when the SPLA/M destroyed the home of Pajok in 1987. Chief Galdino Loriang died in Kirandongo Refugee Settlement Camp (Uganda) in 2006.

PANTO HILL AND HUNTING GROUND

Panto had had one hunting ground named Adodi, and they also had one hill named Adodi. The history of Pajok states that Panto has a god named 'Adodi' which is found on Adodi Hil

CHAPTER THIRTEEN

SOUTHERN PAJOK

Pajok Right has eight small families; Ywaya, Oyere, Toro, Paitenge, Bobi, Palio Kapaa ki Patanga

YWAAYA

Ywaya has four small families namely; Ywaya Kal, Ywaya Katum, Ywaya Bolmeja and Lamwo. All the four families came from Lokoro. According to the history of Pajok, the families of Ywaya Kal, Ywaya Katum and Ywaya Bolmeja, were brought from Lokoro by chief Keny. The family of Lamwo, however, came under the leadership of Mwo, the brother of chief Keny. For many years, these four families were commonly known by the same name, "Kor" or "Lokoro". Later on, they changed their name to "Ywaya" and 'Lamwo', as we shall later see in this book. The people of Kor left Lokoro (Lofon Hill) around 1890, because of rivalry between chief Keny and his brother Mwo, over who should be the chief. The history of Lokoro says, when the conflict over the chiefdom intensified, the people of Lamwo were the first to leave Lokoro. They walked for about three days before reaching Imatong Hill. They later moved and built at Lalak Hill.

After two or three years, chief Keny again took his people from Lofon Hill and passed from Imotong Hill, and built on Agu Hill. They found Biti and Kapaa, who were also the land owners. They also met members of the Bobi, Bura, Panto-Kera, Ayuu, Pagaya and Palio families, who had already built among the Biti and Kapaa. Crazzolara said, "When the people of Ywaya reached Agu Hill, they overthrew the chief of Pagaya. In this year, the people of Lamwo of Uganda, arrived at Guma Hill where they found the people of Patiko, who also overthrew the people of Lamwo. The people of Patiko also divided into two groups. Other people moved to Pajok and built among the people of Lamwo of Pajok, and other people remained under the leadership of the chief of Patiko"(Crazzolara, 1950, P. 85). If you want to better understand the movement of the people of Kor, read: "The migration of *Pajok from Anywak to Acholi*."

However, some people of Pajok, I interacted with, like Parteno Abak, said that the people of chief Keny did not only find Bura, Palio and Pagaya at Agu Hill, but also the family of Biti and Bobi. The five families (Bura, Palio, Pagaya, Ayuu and Panto-Kera), who had settled at Agu Hill were independent. When chief Keny reached Aguu Hill, he wanted all these families to be under his chiefdom. The people of Bura, Palio, Pagaya, Bitii and Bobi, however rejected his suggestion. Some people claim that in the year the people of Ywaya built at Agu Hill, the people of Panto were still at Adodi Hill, while the people of Ayuu of Pajok were in Lagaya.

The history of Pajok tells us that since the people of Palio, Biti, Bobi, Bura and Pagaya did not want to be ruled by the chief of Ywaya, chief Keny decided to send his men to fight against the people of Palio, Biti, Bobi and Bura. Reports also show that Ywaya defeated all the five families, and put them back under the leadership of chief Keny. Sooner than later, the people of Ywaya also went to fight against the people Panto at Adodi Hill, and the people of Ayuu in Lagaya. These wars caused a lot of division among the people. According to the history of Pajok, the people of Ayuu divided into two groups after the fight.

Other people joined Ywaya chiefdom, while other people fled to Uganda and built in Palabek-Liri. They later called themselves *Ayuu-Alali*. Meanwhile, the people of Palio also separated into two groups.

One group joined chief of Ywaya, and another group fled to Panyikwara, where they called themselves the people of *Paliwa*.

Chief of Ywaya forcefully put the people of Bobi, Pagaya, Bura, Bitii and Palio under his chiefdom. So one day, chief Keny summoned the leaders of Bobi and told them,"Since you have lived in this land for long, I think it is high time you knew where other people who live on the same land are. I want you to lead people to where other people live." It seems the four families led the people of Kor and took them where other people were settled. This explains why the Kor of Pajok called themselves *"Ywaya"* meaning, people who led the way.

Since the year chief Keny entered Pajok land, till the year I was writing this book, we found that the Pajok had fourteen chiefs. "Chief Ocak, who is also known as Ocuto, brought Kor of Pajok from Anywak in Wi-Paari, and took them to Lofon Hill, where he (Ocak) later died. Below are the chiefs of Pajok:

1. Keny, son of chief Ocak, led his people from Lokoro to Agu Hill, where he died.

2. Obak, the son of chief Keny, succeeded his father, and also died at Agu Hill.

3. Atanga, son of chief Obak, succeeded his father, and he also died at Agu Hill.

4. Lagedo, son of chief Atanga, took over the chiefdom, and later relocated to Anyomo Mogeera, which neighbours Limuur River. He later died there.

5. Leng, son of chief Lagedo, succeeded his father, and died in Anyomo Mogeera.

6. Angwa, son of chief Leng, succeeded his father, and died at Apini Hill.

7. Otuke, the son of chief Angwa, succeeded his father, and died at Loremo Hill, near Apini Hill.

8. Anyoda, son of chief Otuke, succeeded his father, but he was later captured by Arab slave traders, who also killed him at Lofuu Hill near Atebi River.

9. Onek, the brother of Anyoda, succeeded the Chief, because Ocieng Lokwor-moi, the son of Anyoda was still young.

10. Ocieng Lokwor-moi, son of chief Anyoda, took over the chiefdom after chief Onek disappeared. Crazzolara said he met Oceng Lokwor-moi in 1937, but he was no longer a chief. (Crazzolara, 1951, PP. 177-178).

11. Severino Odur succeeded his father Ocieng Lokwor-moi; and around 1976, the Local Government of Torit, posted him as the chief of Magwi County.

12. Dorteo Oceng Okeny, became chief after the local government of Magwi posted Chief Severino Odur to Magwi Conty. He died in Juba in 1985.

13. Rwot Galdino Loriany, of Patanga, took over as chief in 1985, when Chief Dorteo Okeny died. Many said chief Galdino led the people of Pajok very well.

14. Vitorino Lony, of Kapaa, (many used to call him *OmwodoGwana* (meaning *he ate raw cassava*), who was the secretary of Chief Dorteo Okeny,

succeeded chief Galdino Loriany. We do not understand why the people of Pajok made Victorio Lony chief, yet Galdino Loriany, was still alive. A section of the Pajok like Victorino Adit, despised Chief Vitorino Lony very much. One day, a man named Adit told the people that, "Working with Chief Vitorino Lony is easy because he likes drinking local brew. If someone gives him local gin, and later takes a suspect before him, the complainant wins the case."

15. Chief Elpidio Omwony took over the chiefdom when the Pajok were already in Uganda. People wanted Elpidio Omwong to be their chief, because he was a son of Ywaya Bol Mega. Some elders of Pajok told me that, much as Elpidio was a native of Ywaya, he did not rule for long.

16. Galdino Loriany ruled three times. Many people claim that the Pajok always made Galdino Loriany chief, when the relationship between the people had soured. One elder told me "Chief Galdino Loriany is good at settling issues that is why the people wanted him to serve many times."

17. Chief Otoo Acokon, of Ywaya, became chief when the people of Pajok were still in Kiryandongo Camps.

18. Chief Oroma P'Locebu, of Oyere, took over power when Pajok were still in Camps- Uganda.

19. John P'Onam, of Ywaya, succeeded Chief Oroma P'Locebu in the year 2008. The history of Pajok tells us that chief Onam led the people back home from Kiryandongo in 2009.

20. The history of Pajok says, when chief Onam and his people arrived in Pajok, he found that the SPLM had appointed Chief John Abema, to lead those who were hiding in Pajok. Chief Onam was a peace loving man. That is why, when he found Chief John Obema leading, he stepped down in 2009. In 2010, when I was finishing writing my book on "The history and Expressive Cultures of Acholi of South Sudan" in Australia, Pastor Charles Okwo, of Kapaa, told me that chief John Abema was still in power.

YWAYA HUNTING GROUNDS AND HILLS

Ywaya has two hunting grounds; Oloyo-lweny (war champion) and Amoyo-tonga hunting grounds. For many years the two hunting grounds belonged to the people of Obbo, who then gave it to Ywaya. The two hunting grounds are blessed by a single person from Ywaya kal. However, the Pajok do not know the names of former and present persons who used to take care of Oloyo-lweny hunting ground. Ywaya also has four hills: *Lwoo, Ipul, Kit-aweno* and *Jale* hills. Ywaya has one god named *Lwoo*.

OYERE

The home of Pajok also has the family of Oyere. According to Acholi history, the family members of Oyere separated from the people of Ywaya, and later named themselves Oyere. We however, do not know when and where the people of Oyere separated from the people of Ywaya. But what we know is that the people of Oyere came from Lokoro under the leadership of chief Keny.

OYERE HUNTING GROUND AND HILL

The history of Pajok tells us that the people of Oyere do not have a hunting ground, hill or god. They therefore worship the god of Ywaya. To help you understand how the people of Oyere migrated, read: *"The Movement of Pajok from Anywak in Acholi land"*.

We also do not know why the people of Oyere, Toro, Paitenge and Bobi call themselves *"Lamwo"*. Some people argue that they call themselves 'Lamwo' because they are all Kor of Pajok, who came from Lokoro. In the old days, all these families used to stay together. This brings us to the question, "If the people of Lamwo and Kor were all living together, why did they separate?" Many elders of Pajok say the people of Lamwo separated from Oyere, Toro, Paitenge and Bobi, because of conflicts among the brothers. According to literature, after the conflicts, each family went and built in different places of their choice. But the people of Pajok moved in many places, that is why the children of these four families met in the land of the Pajok.

TORO

The Toro came from Nyarubanga (Bar). We do not know which year they left Bar, but we are informed that they were led by chief Anyoda to Pajok. However, some people of Toro say, they were brought from Bar to Acholiland by Chief Awarigo. According to the history of Pajok, the people of Toro have only one family- Toro. The history of Acholi says, God gave the people of Toro the talent to mold and craft different tools like hoes, tomahawks, knives, tools for digging hole, metal weeding tool, spears and arrows.

The history of Acholi says, when the people of Kor of Pajok were coming to Acholiland, they moved a lot and later arrived in Nyarubanga, where they met chief Anyoda, and his people settled there. The people of Kor wanted to take the southern direction, but unluckily, they did not know the way. For this reason, chief of Kor asked chief Anyoda to give them some people to show them the way. Chief Anyoda first contemplated over the request, and when he realized that the Nyarubanga were not friendly people, he granted chief Kor his request. For this reason, chief Anyoda sent a message to all the people that he would not only give a few people to show the people of Kor the way, but ordered all the people of Toro out of Bar. The people of Toro also knew the problems they were facing in Bar, so they decided that if they left that place, they would one day find a place to live healthily and peacefully. They then moved together with the people of Kor three days, before reaching Agoro. When they reached Agoro, some people of Toro saw that it was not easy to move with the women, children and domestic animals, so they decided to stay in Agoro, and built among the family members of Wili-Bari. This also explains why there is a strong relationship between the people of Agoro Wili-Bari, and the Toro of Pajok.

From Agoro, some group of people of Toro, together with the people of Kor, went to Adodi, where they settled for between two to four years. They reached Adodi Hill in May, the month of cultivation in Acholiland. From Adodi, the Toro and Kor built in a place called "*Lela*". It seems the place was given the name "lela" because there were many fat low rocks in this area.

According to literature, the people of Toro found the place good for them because they loved to mold tools like hoes, tomahawks, and other tools in Lela. After a short time, the people of Toro started crafting tools like hoes, tomahawks, tools for digging hole and metal weeding tool. The people of Kor did not know how to make such hand tools. The tools crafted by the people of chief Anyoda greatly helped the people of Kor during digging and weeding seasons.

Chief Anyoda was a very wise man, and wanted to know what the chief of Kor had in mind. So one day, he told chief Kor that, "I think you now know the way which can lead you to the south. So I want to inform you that from Adodi, my people will no longer continue with the journey, but go back to Bar".

The information chief Anyoda gave the chief of Kor came as a surprise, and it pained him to the bone, then he responded that, "We have seen the skills you have in making hand tools, which helps your people a lot. So we imagine that if you go back to Nyarubanga, then in future we won't find someone who can make for us those hand tools. Am suggesting that you stay with us and we become brothers." Chief Anyoda accepted to stay together with the people of Kor, but the history of Pajok tells us that some people of Toro refused to stay together with the people of Lokoro. Therefore, the people who were led by chief Anyoda, but refused to stay together with the people of Kor, separated and went and built in Palabek- Kal (Uganda). While the other group continued moving with the people of Kor up to Kilak Hill (Pajok). This explains why the people of Toro became the people of Ywaya. But the truth is, the people of Toro came from Bar.

TORO HUNTING GROUNDS AND HILLS

The history of Acholi says the people of Toro do not have a hunting ground, hill and god. They therefore worship the god of Ywaya.

PAITENGE

Paitenge has three small families namely; *Pa-Ogwang*, *Pa-Odur* and *PaKeno* (or Pa-Wokeno). The history of Acholi of Sudan tells us that majority of the family members of Paitenge came from Lokoro, and a few came from Kwenda Bar. The people who came from Lokoro moved together with the people of Ywaya (Jo-Palenga), Obwolto and Patanga. Paitenge came from Lokoro bearing the name "Kor". They got the new name "Paitenge" when they arrived in Acholi of Sudan, as we shall later see in this book.

The history of Pajok says, elder Jula, was the leader of the people of Paitenge, when the people of Kor were coming from Lokoro. There are also reports that when the people of Kor of Pajok were on their way to Acholiland, the people of Paitenge were called the people of Jula. The division among the three families came much later, when the people of *Jula* arrived in Pajok. But if the people of Paitenge came under one family known as P'Jula, why did they divide into three families? The history of Pajok says the division among the Paitenge came much later, when chief Anyoda of Ywaya, was already on the throne. There are reports that chief Anyoda married a young woman of Kapaa named Labone.

They begot two boys named Ogwang (first born) and Odur. Elders of Pajok like, Paterno Abak told me that Ogwang and his brother Odur were born in Kapaa, and grew up with kin of their mother. One day, when Ogwang had become an adult, he had sexual intercourse with his cousin. Acholi tradition prohibits a boy from marrying his cousin, and having sex with her. Some elders of Pajok said the news of Ogwang sleeping with his cousin spread among other clans. Ogwang and Odur were later summoned by the kin of their mother, who told the two brothers that, "We are not happy about what Ogwang did to his cousin sister. For this reason, we want you to go back to your father's home in Ywaya." After they were rebuked, Ogwang and his brother went to their mother, and Ogwang told his mother, Labone that, "Mother, early today, our uncle called us and expressed unhappiness why I had slept with your sister's daughter. After scorning me, he told me and my brother to go back to our father's home in Ywaya."

Labone was saddened by this news. She then went to her brothers, before them, and told them, "Very well, my brothers. My children told me that you chased them and ordered them to go back to their father's home. I do not support your decision, because I know that if they go back to Ywaya, they will be killed by the children of Ywaya because of conflict over the rain stone, and who should become chief. I suggest that if possible, you reverse your decisions."

After two or three days, the decision to chase Ogwang and his brother reached chief Anyoda in Ywaya. The history of Pajok says the people who passed the information to Chief Rwot Anyoda, also told him the fears their mother, Labone, had about her sons going back to Ywaya. Chief Anyoda understood Labone's concern and told his messengers, "Since the kin of their mother do not want my sons in Kapaa, I want Ogwang and Odur to go and stay in Paitenge."

The messenger relayed the message of chief Anyoda to the maternal relatives of his sons, who also agreed with the chief's suggestion. Shortly, the people of Kapaa sent Ogwang, Odur and their mother Labone to Paitenge as the chief had said. When Labone and her two sons reached Paitenge, chief Anyoda ordered the people of Pa-Wokeno to cultivate for his wife. The history of Pajok shows that, much as Ogwang and his brother were living in Paitenge, they still had the right to celebrate the Lagang-tie god in the family of Ywaya (Palenga). They also had the right to install the new chief of Palenga. When it was the time to celebrate the god, the people of Ywaya could go to the hunting ground and capture a live duiker and take it to Ogwang and his brother to slaughter before *Lagang-tie god*. Whenever a new chief was about to be mounted in Palenga, the two brothers would be called.

Both Ogwang and his brother Odur married from the same family of Paitenge. They then bore children, who also produced grandchildren (grandsons/daughters). The people of Ogwang gradually named themselves *Pa-Ogwang*, which means, the people of Ogwang. The people of Odur called themselves Jo Pa-Odur), which means the people of Odur. This is how the family of Pa-Ogwang and Jo Pa-Odur originated in Paitenge.

Jo Pa-Keno (Jo Pa-Wokeno): the history of Pajok says the people of Pa-keno came from Kwenda Bar around the year 1780. They moved away from Bar because of famine which killed many people that year. Clan elders of Pajok like Ben Oywak and Kadensyo Jada Adinya, told me that the Pa-Wokeno were the first to join the people of Pajok. The two families of Pa-Ogwang and Pa-Odur came later and built among the members of Pa-Wokeno. This explains why the elders of Pajok say the Pa-keno were the heads of Paitenge family.

PAITENGE HUNTING GROUND AND HILLS

The family members of Paitenge have one hunting ground named *Bur Pua*, which was later renamed Pajula hunting ground, as we shall see below. Paitenge however has two hills: Lobora and Apini Hill. The history of Acholi of Sudan says, Paitenge have one god named Lagang-tie. A child from the family of Pa-Keno (Pa-Wokeno) is responsible for taking care of its shrine. Reports also show that people who tend Lagang-tie shrine, and invite people to go hunting in Pajula hunting ground, do not eat meat of both domestic and wild animals. We do not know why the caretakers of shrines and those who bless the hunting ground of Paitenge do not eat meat from domestic and wild animals.

The history of Pajok says, elder Jula was the first man to carry the food for the god, when Lagang-tie shrine was being made. The elders also said, later, the god made elder Jula to lose his sanity, and led him to Lobora cave in Pajula hunting ground. Elder Jula stayed in the cave for three months. After three months, people who had gone to the cave found him, alive but hopeless. When those who found him recognized him, they were gripped by fear, because they thought he was already dead. In this same year, elder Ogwang was the leader of all the people of Paitenge. Those who had gone to the cave ran to him and said, "Dear, we have found your long lost brother, whose corpse you are searching, still alive in Lobora cave." The news shocked Ogwang and made him to ask again, "Where is he?" The messenger responded, "He is in Bur-Pua in Lobora cave."

When Ogwang heard this good news, he went to the kraal and picked a big, black, he-goat, and slaughtered it in front of Lobora cave. The god was very pleased with the sacrifice Ogwang offered, and shortly started eating. When the god had finished eating, he brought Jula to his brother Ogwang, and the two brothers went back home together. Ogwang was also very happy to see his brother still alive. He later ordered for the blessing of Bur-Pua hunting ground for his brother Jula. When I was still in Juba, elder Ogana told me that, "In the year Ogwang gave Bur-pua hunting ground to Jula, people started referring to the hunting as "*tim Pajula*" , which means Jula's hunting ground.

Since the year Ogwang handed over the god, Lagang-tie, to Jula until now, the shrine is taken care of by a born of Pa-Keno family. It is also that same child who invites people to hunt in Bur-Pua. Even though there is a rule stipulating who should invite people to Bur-Pua hunting ground, we find that time and time again, people could break the rule. The elders who lived long time ago cursed, that if any other person apart from a family member of Pa-Wokeno invited people to hunt in Pajula, that person should be killed by wild animals that very day, to set an example that the god of Lagang-tie gets annoyed when a traditional rule is broken. That is why the people of Pajok always say, when many people are killed on a particular hunting day in Pajula hunting ground, it means they were not invited by the true son of *PaKeno*. A good example is an incident which happened in 1820. In that year, a born of Pa-Odur, whose name we do not know, took over the role of inviting people to go hunting in Pajula from Jula. However, when people went hunting, the bush started burning, and no animal was killed on that day. Fortunately, that day, the child was near the burning bush. When the burning bush came to an end, and he saw that the hunters did not kill animals, he became frightened and ran back home. That day, everyone went back home unhappy. The history of Pajok says as this child was running back home, a buffalo, which was pursuing him found him resting in a trench. The buffalo widened its eyes in annoyance before the young man. When the young man saw the buffalo, with its red eyes wide opened before him, he ran and entered a hut next to the treanch. Reports indicate that the buffalo started by destroying the trench, and later trailed the young man and killed him in his trench hide-out. After the young man was buried, the clan elders of Paitenge held a meeting over the Pajula hunting ground. During the meeting, members resolved that, "Only the children of Pa-wokeno have the right to invite people to go hunting in Pajula."

The history of Acholi of Sudan tells us that from 1820 until 1939, a born of Pa-Wokeno was responsible for Pajula hunting ground and the god of Lagang-tie. In 1940, Okeny Oyeke, used to invite people to hunt in Pajula hunting ground. Unfortunately, the same year, an elder known as Odong Obule, father of Latansyo Lopul, violated the rule again. He took over the role of inviting people to hunt in Pajula hunting ground from Okeny Oyeke. According to reports, the elder invited people to go hunting in Pajula hunting ground, and the hunters killed many animals. The god, Lagang-tie, was upset because of this defiance. The god sent a big leopard which leapt and scratched Odong Obule's head severely. Even after seeing the big wound on Odong Obule's head, the elders of Pajok still scolded him because he broke the rule. Two to three days after the hunting, the clan elders of Paitenge again convened a meeting to discuss the issue of Pajula hunting ground. The elders continued telling Odong Obule off. They then resolved that Odong Obule should give back the role of inviting people to hunt back to Okeny Oyeke. They also strongly warned all young man from taking over the responsibility from the children Pa-Keno to invite people to the hunting ground. The history of Pajok says, the young men of Pajok took the advice of the clan elders. That is why Pajula hunting ground and the god Lagang-tie still belong to the people of Pa-Wokeno.

BOBI

Bobi has four small families; *Kiyanga, Pakeny, Paikweya* and *Paliringwen*.

Kiyanga, Pakeny and Paikweya: The history of Acholi tells us that these three families came from Shilluk, but under one name – Bobi, as we shall look at later. Reports also show that when the people of Bobi arrived in Pajok, they had three families named Pabwoc, Padera and Pakoyo. These people were led from Shilluk by elder Bobi. When the people of Bobi reached Pajok, they divided themselves into two groups. Some people remained in Pajok under the leadership of elder Aruk. These people later separated into three families;

Kiyanga, *Pakeny* and *Paikweya*. While other people continued moving under the leadership of Bobi, and went to Bira (Lango of Sudan). From here, they went to Padibe and built among the family of Pamot. In this year, the chief of Padibe, named Dera, was in a place called Atango. Records show that chief Dera succeeded his father (chief Otwal). Bobi of Uganda stayed in Atango for a few years and later went back to Bobi Hill, between Madi-Opei and Okol. According to reports, the people of Bobi did not live amicably here, because they were allegedly led into so many temptations that men and women started engaging in promiscuous sexual acts. Men could have sex with their mothers-in-law, and brothers and sisters in-laws could have sex with each other, in disregard of the cultural norm of the Lwo. The Lwo cultural norm states that a son-in-law must not have sex with his mother-in-law, and a brother in-law must also not have sex with a sister in-law, but the people of Bobi defied the norm. These immoral acts gradually caused a major conflict among the people, which forced the people of chief Dera to go back to Pamot in Atango. The people led by the chief of Bobi, however continued moving towards the south. Reports indicate that when Bobi was moving southwards, they later separated into three groups. Some people went and built in Labongo, others went to Pajule, and others went to Puranga. We do not know if the chief of Bobi built among those who went to Labongo, Pajule or if he went and built among the people of Puranga. This tells us why the people of Bobi are in Pajule, Labongo and Puranga in Uganda. Some sections of people assume that other people of Bobi of Pajok later went back to Agoro. From Agoro, another group remained, while others went to Amyel Hill, near Lira Lapono in Agago. After living in Agago for a few years, reports indicate that some people of Bobi went back to Pamot in Atango-Padibe (Onyango, 1976, P, 190).

Bobi of Pajok used to stay together with Pa-Yone, who was the original owner of Pajok. According to Crazzolara, much as Onyango says the people of Bobi are the real Lwo, he knows that the people of Bobi are Madi. As we saw earlier, the people of Bobi are in many places in Acholi of Sudan and Uganda. But what I want readers of this book to know is that much as the people of Bobi are found in many places (Sudan and Uganda), all of them originated from Bobi of Pajok. This expounds why, if you ask a born of his/her origin, they will proudly tell you that "We came from Bobi of Pajok" (Crazzolara, 1951, P, 399).

The history of Pajok says one day, the people of Palwar came to Pajok from the east and found Bobi and Pa-Yone already in Agu Hill. Unfortunately, the people of Palwar loved war mongering so much that shortly afterwards, they started grouping men to wage war against the people of Bobi. Palwar defeated Bobi during the war and took over their chiefdom. The people of Bobi later started respecting the shrine and chief of Palwar. Elder Paterno Abak told me that, "Since that year, the people of Bobi started worshiping the shrines of the Palwar."

Paliri-ngwen: Reports show that the people of Paliri-ngwen came from Obbo. They came to Pajok when the people of Obbo were still at Lotii Hill. We however do not know why the people of Palari-ngwen left Obbo and came to Pajok. Again, we do not know the name of the people who led Paliri-ngwen to Pajok. The history of Pajok tells us that when the people of Paliri-ngwen reached Pajok, they found the Pajok still at Agu Hill. The people of Paliri-ngwen came after Kiyanga, Pakeny and Paikweya and built among these three families. This explains why, later on, the people of Paliri-ngwen became the owners of this land.

BOBI HUNTING GROUNDS AND HILLS

Bobi has two hunting grounds: Bore, near Atebi River and Lanyuru Hill, where the Pajok built. But the history of Obbo has it that currently Bore is the hunting ground of Obbo. We do not understand how Bobi took over the ownership of this hunting ground. The people of Bobi also have two hills: Tul and Obwoc hills. But they have only one god named "Jok-Oyaro." We do not know the name of the person who takes care of this hunting ground, and the shrine of Oyaro god.

PALIO

Palio has three small families namely; *Pi-woco*, *Pocaa* and *Pogili*.

Pi-woco and Pocaa: The history of Pajok says the people of Pocaa are the family heads of Palio. But, the elders of Pajok I interviewed about the family of Palio did do not know where the people of Pi-woco and Pocaa came from. They also do not know why the people of Pi-woco and Pocaa left the place they settled first. Additionally, the elders of Pajok do not know which year the people of Pi-woco and Pocaa came to Pajok. They also do not know the name of the person who led these two families to Pajok. Unfortunately, the war commanded by John Garang De Mabior, divided us from Captain Paul

Loteip (commoly known as Koko) of Palio, who could have told me all about the people of Palio.

Pogili: the history of Acholi says the people of Pogili came from Logolo (Obbo). It seems they relocated to Pajok when the Pajok where already living along Atebi river in the year 1936-1940. But we do not know which family among the Obbo they came from. We also do not clearly understand why they came to Pajok. We also do not know the name of the elder who brought the people of Pogili to Pajok. I hope to find the answers to all these questions in the "Second Edition" of this book.

When the people of Pogili arrived in Pajok, they built among the Pi-woco and Pocaa. That is why the people of Pogili became one family in Palio.

PALIO HUNTING GROUNDS AND HILLS

The people of Palio do not have a hunting ground. However, some descendants of Palio claim that Pajula hunting ground belongs to them. But we saw in previous pages that Pajula hunting ground belongs to Paitenge. The people of Palio have one hill named Lakima Hill (or Ngor Hill). They have one god named *Labwor* (Lion), who lives on Lakima Hill.

KAPAA (LAWIE-ODUNY)

Kapaa has two small families; *Kapaa* and *PaibworoKapaa*. The history of Acholi says the members of Kapaa family came from Imurok, when the the some people of Paibworo and Pajok were already at the foot of Tul Hill. We do not have a clear reason why the people of Kapaa left Imurok. The people of Pajok also do not know the name of the person who led Kapaa to Pajok. The history of Pajok does not give the year when the Kapaa came to Tul Hill. Getting such information was difficult for me because I did not find an elder of Kapaa to give me information about Kapaa. I hope to find someone who will give me more information about the family of Kapaa when writing the second edition of this book. Other people of Pajok, I interacted with, told me that in the past, the family members of Kapaa and Paibworo used to intermarry. Later however, the clan elders refused the idea of intermarriage among girls and boys of these two families because much as they came from different places, they still called themselves brothers and sisters. This explains why currently, the people of Kapaa and Paibworo do not intermarry.

Pai-bworo: according to records, the people of Pai-bworo came from Anywak. They separated from the other Lwo around 1785-1800. The people of Pai-bworo were led by Chief Bong-nyero Anywak to from Tul, where they found the people of Ywaya around 1893 (?). Reports also show that the people of Paibworo were the first to come to Pajok from the family of Kapaa together with the people of Ywaya. This is why people say, Kapaa (Kapaa-Pa-ibworo) are the owners of the home. The elders of Pajok, like Adinya and Ben Oywak told me that in the year 1893, when the people of Ywaya were coming from Tul Hill, they carried along their insignia. When they reached Tul Hill, the people of Pa-ibworo, who already settled there were frightened because they thought that Ywaya would one day force them under the chief of Ywaya. The people of Paibworo also had their symbols of office, so they did not want to be led by another chief, but their own. The people of Kapaa also did not want to see another chief apart from a chief who has their roots. The people of Pa-ibworo thought the chief of Ywaya had intentions of killing chief Bong-nyero, so that he takes over the throne. This forced them to hide chief Bongnyero in a cave. Truly, when the people of Ywaya joined the people of Kapaa, they asked the people of Pa-ibworo, "Where is your chief? We want your chief and ours to agree because we are here as visitors." Unluckily, the people of Pa-ibworo did not understand why the people of Ywaya asked this question. So they responded without much thought, "We do not have a chief." The People of Ywaya were so happy to have met a group of people without a chief. The people of Ywaya immediately responded that, "Since you do not have a chief, we cannot be under your leadership, much as you are the owners of the home. We now want you to be led by our chief (Ywaya) because we have the symbols of power." The people of Ywaya did this because they wanted all people of Pajok to be led by the chief Ywaya.

KAPAA HUNTING GROUND AND HILLS
Much as the people of Kapaa are the heads of the home, the history of Acholi says they do not have a hunting ground, hill or god.

PATANGA
Patanga has four small families namely; *Pa-Obwoo, Pa-Kure, Pa-Baa* and
Pa-Abore. The history of Acholi says the family members of these four

families came from Lokoro, around the year 1890. The Patanga came together with people of Kor of Pajok, but the elders say that much as the Patanga came together with with the people of Kor, they had their own leader, named Atanga. This explains why this family later became known as "Patanga", which means, the people of Atanga. To understand how the people of Patanga migrated, read chapter fourteen of this book, *The Immigration of the Pajok from Anywak to Acholiland.*

PATANGA HUNTING GROUNDS AND HILLS

The Patanga have one hunting ground named Iyelle, and a hill named Pa-min-Acwai. The people of Patanga also have a god named *Yamo-turu*. I already stated in the previous pages that it was difficult to get elders with the knowledge about history, and this is the same thing I faced when I was searching for the history of Patanga. I experienced this same problem when I was looking for elders of Patanga. However, when we were in Juba, we could have asked elder Loyolo, but because people were afraid of the soldiers of President Omer el Bashir, I could not ask elder Loyolo to tell me the history of the people of Patanga. I hope that in the second edition of this book, we shall get more information regarding this family.

Chapter Fourteen

THE MOVEMENT OF PAJOK FROM ANYWAK TO ACHOLILAND

ANYWAK (Pajok) LEFT THE RIVER BANK

Onyango (1976) said the Lwo lived along the river bank (Lake Rudolf), in Kenya for so many years. However, many who wrote the history of Lwo said the Lwo lived for many years in the South Eastern part of Sudan, the present day "Kassala". The Lwo separated from the people of Kassala around 300 BC, and came to the present day Barh El Ghazal in *Sue River*, in southern Sudan. But according to Onyango, the first group to separate from the Lwo was "Anywak Kwedi." The people called themselves so, ("Anywak Kwedi") because of conflict over cattle between chief Odom Lopul, and Ogili Ngoleyang. Chief Odom Lopul led the whole group of people along the river in that year. The expression "anywak kwedi" is still being used by the Acholi. In Acholi, the word "Anywak Kwedi" means "Let me go with/accompany you)." The name was given to this group because when Ogili Ngoleyang was the leader of Anywak Kwedi, he decided to leave the shores of river Anywak. So the people who were in support of his decision reportedly pleaded with the chief, "Please if possible, allow me to go with you." The name was coined following the people's plea with chief Ogili to go with them. The group was subsequently referred to as "the people of let me go with you."

We do not know if the group "Anywak Kwedi" separated from Lwo when Chief Kuku Lubanga, (who was also a miracle worker) was already a chief, or they separated before Kulu Lubanga was on the throne. But we are sure that Chief Odom Lopul came after Chief Kuku Lubanga. The history of Acholi tells us that "Anywak Kwedi" separated because of failure to compromise, when chief Odom and Ogili Ngoleyang were disputing over how to divide the cattle "Anywak Kwedi" raided from cattle keepers.

(Onyango thinks believes the cattle keepers were the Masai, but I know they were the Dinka, because the history of Acholi says the Dinka lived near Lake Rudolf).

Reports say one day, as many cattle keepers were looking for pasture, reached the river bank, the children of Lwo who were hunting, saw spotted them and went back home and informed Chief Odom Lopul. When the chief heard about the many cattle keepers, he concluded that they must be the Dinka (Masai). Chief Odom had heard many tales that nomads are a very ruthless lot, who could kill people indiscriminately and mercilessly. When Chief Odom heard these stories, he became so afraid that he did not wage war against the pastoralists.

Nevertheless, Chief Ogili Ngoleyang kept convincing chief Odom to allow the people of "Anywak Kwedi" to go and fight the nomads. Chief Odom refused the idea, insisting that, "My people will not fight the nomads." Ogili, who was a warrior, then decided to fight the cattle keepers himself at night. He chose many hard-nosed men and worriors, and they went to fight the cattle keepers. The nomads lost many of their leaders during the fight. When the few surviving cattle keepers saw that the fight was intensifying, they fled and abandoned their animals. The group of chief Ogili then led the animals abandoned by the cattle keepers' home. Those who had remained at home were so excited when they saw chief Ogili coming back with more than one hundred cattle. After two days, the people of chief Ogili performed a ceremony to cleanse fighters who killed the cattle keepers. They later took all the animals and gave them to chief Odom to distribute to those who could look after the animals, as norm of the Acholi dictates. According to Acholi tradition, cattle, women and girls captured during wars are distributed among boys and men.

Chief Odom was a very dishonest man, for this reason, he took one-third of the cattle, and gave two-third to chief Ogili to distribute to those who fought the cattle keepers. The men whose children were taken to fight were saddened by chief Odoms's dishonesty. According to them, the chief should have taken only five or ten cattle, since he was not in the battle field, and leave the rest for chief Ogili and the fighters to divide among themselves. When Ogili saw the

uneven distribution of the cattle, he decided that he could not continue staying under the leadership of Chief Odom Lopul. For this reason, Ogili Ngoleyang
and his people left the river shore in search of a new place to settle. Reports
show that before Ogili left the shores of the river, his supporters requested
him to lead the people away from the river shore. The people of Ogili then left
the shores of the river and moved northwards, and later called themselves
AnywakKwedi (Onyango, 1976, PP. 49-51).

The people of Anywak Kwedi moved in multitudes, and when they reached
a new place they divided themselves into four families; *Jo-Peeno*, *Jo-Wiri*, *Jo
Thim* and *Jo-Giilo*. All these families built in the new place named "Wi-Pari", as
we shall see below.

The people of Wi-Pari moved to Lofon Hill (Lokoro)
To better understand how the people of Pari or Lokoro became the Acholi of
Pajok, it would be best for us to first look at how the Lwo separated from their
settlement in Wi-Pari in Anywak. Reports show that when the Lwo left Anywak,
they first moved along River Sobat. From there, they went to Nyangdiny River,
where other people again separated. Others followed Piboor River, while others
seem to have built along river Sobat. The people who followed river Piboor
continued moving till they reached the borders of Piboor and Peeno rivers.
The people of Peeno built along Peeno River. This group of people is currently
called Anywak North. The Lwo again separated, one group followed Peeno
River towards the East, and entered Ethiopia –these are the Anywak of Ethiopia.
The other group of people, who remained along the shores of River Piboor,
moved along the river towards the south. Before this group had moved a long
distance, they again split into two groups. One group moved along Akobo River
and reached the meeting point of river Giilo and river Peeno, where the Jo-Wiri
and Jo-Thim had settled. (Giilo and Akobo streams are tributaries that flow into
river Piboor). The Jo-Giilo on the other hand went and built along the southern
shores of Giilo River (Crazzolara, 1950. PP.51-52).

When the Jo-Wiri and Jo-Thim built near Giilo and Akobo streams, other
people later went and built along Akobo, while others continued moving
towards the south. This group then passed through different places and later
reached a desert. They later regretted and wished they had stayed back at Giilo
stream, or along Akobo River. Since the two streams, Giilo and Akobo were a

distance behind, the group continued moving till they reached a place called "Wi-Pajo" or "Wi-Pari". The words Wi-*Pari* in Acholi mean 'the end of the earth.' The Lwo settled in Wi-Pari because they wanted to decide what to do next.

Shortly, the people started asking themselves, "What shall we gain if we continue with our journey southwards?" First, Anywak is far behind us; secondly, people have passed through very fertile land for cultivation. For this reason, the people started debating whether or not to move ahead. Some people wanted to continue walking, while others did not want to, because the men, women and children were tired. Those who did not want to keep moving remained and built in "Wi-Pari". The Kor of Pajok is among those who built in wi-Pari. Meanwhile, those who wanted to continue moving went ahead, and reached Lofon Hill after three days.

The history of Lokoro says the people who left Wi-Pari for Lofon Hill moved in different groups. Crazzolara (1950) says the first group of people to leave Wi-Pari went to Lokoro, under the leadership of chief Cogo. When this group reached Lofon Hill, they settled under a big tamarind tree, which the Lokoro named "Ajubi" or "Ajobi" – the tamarind tree is remembered to date, and anyone who goes to Lokoro and asks about the tree, is shown where it used to stand. Chief Cogo and his group found *jo Pugari*, who came from Bar, already settled at Lofon Hill. After a year, or two, chief Guri again took his people from Wi-Pari to Lofon Hill. This was the second group to leave Wi-Pari that year (Crazzolara, 1950, P. 52).

Reports show that chief Omenya, of Wi-Athwoo, became the leader of all people who remained in Wi-Pari. Chief Omenya married a woman named *Abongo*, and they had a son named Libala. When Libala was only a year old, chief Omenya became so ill, and later died of the ailment. When he was already very sick, chief Omenya summoned the clan elders and told them that, "I want my son Libala to become chief of Wi- Pari if I die." The history of Lokoro has it that after the death of chief Omenya, members took his son, Libala, to be installed by Chief Dimo as instructed by his late father. Some people of *Jo Pugari* say Chief Dimo also left some cattle to chief Libala, for him to use as dowry when he grew up into an adult. Some people of Wi-Athwoo, however, dispute the claim, saying when Chief Libala became a man, he used his father's cows to marry a wife.

In the year Chief Dimo installed Chief Libala, the people of Wi-Athwoo also left Wi-Pari. They were the third group of people to follow others to Lofon Hill. This same year, Chief Libala was just one year and four months old. When the Wi-Athwoo were moving to Lofon Hill, Libala's mother, Abongo carried Chief Libala on her back and took him to Lofon Hill. Some elders of Lokoro said that the people of Wi-Athwoo moved together with the people of Pocwaa. When Chief Libala became an adult, he married a woman named Ayu, and they had a son named Okwiri. After the death of Chief Libala, his son, Okwiri became the chief. Chief Okwiri married a woman named Athoo, and the two produced a son named Jogi. After the death of chief Okwiri, his son, Jogi also became chief. Similarly, Chief Jogi married a woman named Akello, and they had a son named Otyieno. After the death of Chief Jogi, his son Otyieno, became chief. Otyieno married a woman named Apio and they produced a son named Ledo.

The people of Lokoro realized that they were so few that whenever the enemies invaded their home, they could not fight them. The people of Lokoro were informed by their elders that when they were coming to Lofon Hill, some of their brothers remained in Wi-Pari. For this reason, they decided to go back to Wi-Pari to convince those who had remained, to come to Lofon Hill. Chief Otyieno of Wi-Athwoo and Chief Gari of Pugari led the people when they were going to Wi-Pari. When Chief Otyieno reached Wi-Pari he found Chief Giilo and his son, Ranga or Amulanye, together with Chief Ocak of Kor (Pajok). Chief Otyieno kept asking Chief Giilo and Chief Ocak if they could move with their group to Lofon Hill. Reports show that Chief Giilo was the paramount chief of Wi-Pari.

Chief Giilo, Ocak and other chiefs then accepted to move together with Chief Rwot Otyieno to Lofon Hill. This explains why the people of Kor of Pajok were the last group of people to leave wi-Pari (Anywak). After the people of Kor of Pajok came to Lokoro, those who had remained in Wi-Pari gradually separated. Some people went back to Anywak, while others moved to Lofon Hill. Wi-Pari was consequently left without inhabitants (Crazzolara, 1951, PP. 157-158).

Some people claim that the Kor of Pajok was led by Chief Ajuri to Lofon Hill. I am confident that Chief Ajuri, was the son of Col, from the family of Amulanye, son of Chief Giilo. The people of Kor moved together with Chief Giilo, so I do not believe that the Kor of Pajok was led to Lofon Hill by Chief Ajuri. The history of Lokoro tells us that Chief Giilo produced a son named

Amulanye (Raanga). Amulanye also had two sons named Ajuri and Okwor, and Chief Ajuri bore a son named Ukwom. Ukwom gave begot a son named Angwee, and Okwor, brother of Ajuri, had a son named Olum. We however do not know if Amulanye had his sons when people had already come to Lokoro, or when they were still in Wi-Pari.

When the people of Kor reached Lokoro, they called themselves Utimme. The word "otime" in Acholi means, "It happened as we expected". The history of Lokoro says the people of Kor were looking for a place to settle in, so when they reached Lokoro, the people saw that the place was conducive. That is why they said, "This thing happened as we wanted." This is why the people of Kor also called themselves "Jo-Utimme".

When the people of Lokoro arrived in Lofon Hill, they split into six small families; *Wi-Athwoo, Bura, Pucwa, Pugeri, Angulumere* and *Kor*. Other people alleged that among the six families, Kor had more family members. Yet, some elders of Lokoro told me that Wi-Athwoo had more family members. In the year people arrived at Lofon Hill, the group of Chief Ocak went and built in Ajubi. The history of Lokoro has it that, that night, when chief Ocak arrived in Lofon Hill, the evil spirit attacked and killed him. Because if his death, the Kor of Pajok were subsequently left without a chief. Immediately after the death of Chief Ocak, the people of Kor of Pajok became sad over the evil spirit that killed their chief. Later on, the people of Lokoro kept teasing the Pajok saying, "The people of Kor are afraid of the evil spirit."

The history of Lokoro says this is how the Kor of Pajok became known as "Parajok". Conversely, the elders of Pajok I was talking with told me that the name "Pajok" was given to the people because they ate the food for the evil spirit, when they were going to Acholiland (Crazzolara, 1951, P.159).

Reports indicate that after the death of Chief Ocak of Pajok, elder Ajuri became the chief of Pajok. However, some people claim that chief Ajuri took over power when the people relocated near a stream in a place called Kuut or Wange kuut, about nine or ten miles to the west of Lofon Hill. It seems the people of Lokoro did not live for long in Kuut, and again went back to Lofon Hill after two or three years.

Chief Ajuri lived only for a short period with the people of Chief Otyieno, and later he fell sick and died of the ailment.

After the death of Chief Ajuri, his nephew, Olum became the chief. Chief

Olum then continued living with Chief Otyeno of Wi-Athwoo. After a few months, Chief Otyeno waged a war against his brother Oyet. He fought him so fiercely until he killed him. All the people of Lokoro condemned the chief's act and kept telling him that, "Why don't you honour your reputation? Since you have killed your innocent brother, we now want to be led by elder Alokori, but not you." Besides, the relationship between Chief Otyieno and Chief Olum was sour. When Chief Otyieno realized that he had lost support of the people, he took the women, children and his cattle and started moving towards the south till they reached Longulo Hill, in the land of the people of Loudo (Lotuko), Chief Otyieno lived here for a few days.

The history of Lokoro says one day, Otyeno's children went to water cattle at the foot of Longulo Hill. When they had reached a flat low rock at Longulo Hill, a bull that Chief Otyieno treasured so much stepped on the rock, and it left a huge print on it. The rock became soft as clay to the bull. Some people of Lokoro and Loudo claim that the mark of the hoof of the bull is still seen on the hill of Longulo.

The elders of Lokoro said from Longulo Hill, Chief Otyeno continued moving but no one knows where they went. Some people of Lokoro assume that after the death of Chief Otyieno, his son, Ledo, became the chief. He later married a woman called Yege, and they produced a son, Udyek and his brother Otyieno (the name Otyieno was given to the child in memory his grandfather, chief Otyieno).

They also added that when it became hard for Chief Ledo to live in Loudo, he later led his father's group back to Lokoro. A section of the elders of Lokoro alleged that after the death of Chief Ledo, his son, Udyek became the chief and married a woman and they produced a child called Alikori.

When chief Otyieno left Liful, members made Alikori (from the family of Boi) chief of the people of Lokoro who had remained in *Wane Kut*. After a few days, the people asked Chief Alikori if they could move away from Kut, because to them, the place was already tainted with blood. When Chief Alikori heard the request, he immediately granted them permission and they started leaving the place after five days to Lofon Hill.

The history of Lokoro says the relationship between Chief Olum and Chief Otyieno kept worsening. So, Chief Olum and his people left Wang Kut before Chief Otyieno had gone to Loudo. Chief Olum moved in many places in search of a better place for his people. According to reports, when Chief Alikori sent back the people of Lokoro to Lofon Hill, Chief Olum also passed through Lofon Hill many times.

On realizing that they had moved in so many places and yet failed to get where to settle, Chief Olum then decided to go back to live with the people of Chief Alikori. When he reached Lofon Hill, Chief Alikori warmly welcomed him and gave him a portion of land for them to build their homes. Since chief Olum had a royal spear, drum and chair, his people did not make subscription to Alikori.

A few months later, the members resolved that they wanted a county chief to oversee other chiefs in Lofon Hill. The information was passed and many people expressed willingness to contest for the position. We however do not know the names of all those who contested for the position. But people remember Olum as one of the candidates for the position. Reports indicate that many people voted Olum, and he became the first county chief in Lokoro. The election of Olum as chief gave the people of Kor more power. The county chief immediately set up tough rules that if there was any dispute to be settled, elders of the six families in Lokoro would come together, offer suggestions, but not rule over the matter. The power to pass judgment was left to the county chief and the clan elders of Kor.

During the reign of chief Olum, the people recognized that the number of people who had guns in Kor were more than any other. According to tales, the people of Kor brought the guns from Acholi and Madi. The people of Lokoro did not only raid guns from the Acholi and Madi, but in 1945, they brought some guns from Ethiopia, when the Lokoro were fighting against the people of Abas. The history of Acholi of Sudan says the people of Lokoro did not only raid guns from the Acholi, but also took a royal drum called "Jina", which means the drum which is as hard as steel. The people of Lokoro did not fight all the people of Acholi. The history of Acholi says Lokoro only fought the people of Obbo, Panyikwara and Agoro.

THE PEOPLE OF BOI ACCUSED THE PEOPLE OF KOR
One day, an unidentified child of Boi, out of jealousy, went to Torit and reported the people of Kor to the commissioner of Torit called Dr. David Owen. When he reached Torit, he went to the office of the D.C. and told him that, "Sir, I have

come to your office because I want to inform you that we have found people of Kor with very many guns, which is causing fear among the other children of Lokoro. I am now appealing to you that if possible, send your guards to Lokoro, to seize all the guns among the people of Kor."

Commissioner welcome the idea wholeheartedly and immediately sent for his guards. When the guards gathered, D.C. told them that, "Someone brought a very important piece of information from Lokoro. He said the people of Kor have many guns, which is causing panic among the people who have few guns. I am also afraid that in future if a fight starts between the people of Kor and Lokoro, many will lose their lives. I now want you to go to Lokoro and confiscate all the guns." After he had finished talking, the guards started going to Lokoro. When they reached Lofon Hill, they moved from door-to-door among the people of Kor, but they never found a single gun. Some elders of Lokoro said when the people of Kor learnt that a child of Boi had gone to Torit to report them, they hid their guns in a cave (known among the people of Lokoro as *Ababur*), in Liwayi Hill at Lofon.

Due to their unkindness towards the people of Kor, the children of Boi, directed the guards to the cave where the guns were hidden. The guards entered the cave and found so many guns, and took all of them to the D.C. of Torit.

Reports show that the guards did not only confiscate the guns, but they also captured Chief Olum and elder Kidi, the son of Owiti Alikori of Boi. The two were taken to Torit. When Mr. Owen saw the guns brought by the guards, he gave up the idea to detain Chief Olum and his friend Kidi. He instead asked Chief Olum and his friend if they could go back to Lokoro. The guards then set Chief Olum and Kidi free to go back to Lokoro.

The Kor of Lokoro had one big family, but around the year 1819, when the Palabek of Uganda engaged them in a major fight, they split into fourteen small families as seen below;
(1)   The people of Olum
(2)   Liding Right
(3)   Liding Left
(4)   The people of Pethiha
(5)   The people of Acuth
(6)   Libongi

(7)   The Pu-wandi

(8)   The Puywaa

(9)   The Ajig-ge

(10)   The people of Ajibba

(11)   The Pa Kiri-kik

(12)   The people of Pu-Ayweri

(13)   The Ligot

(14)   The Buller

Much as the people of Kor split into these small families, they were all under the leadership of Chief Olum.

KOR OF PAJOK MOVED TO ACHOLILAND

People have diverse reasons why Kor of Pajok left Lokoro. Other people Lokoro say the Pajok left Lofon because of the death of Chief Ocak (the first chief of the Pajok). While others say, the Pajok left Lokoro because of disputes over a stream where animals used to be watered. But the history of Pajok does not mention the death of Chief Ocak or conflict over a stream where cattle used to drink water from. They say the Kor left Lokoro because of conflict between Keny and his brother Mwo. We are not sure if Keny and Mwo were both sons of Chief Ocak. We also are not certain whether or not they were children of the same mother, or if they were cousins.

The history of Lokoro however says, Chief Ocak came with two boys from Wi-Pari in Lofon Hill, and they were Keny and Mwo.

To understand why Kor left Lokoro, I think we should first know what the history of Lokoro says, and later know what the history of Pajok says.

Firstly, the history of Lokoro tells us that the Pajok (Kor) left Lofon because of dispute over the stream where animals used to drink water from. The inhabitants of Lokoro claim that in the year 1819 the Wi-Athwoo all started digging the foundations of their houses in the same area. When rainy season came, it rained so much that the dug foundations were all filled up with running water, which turned the place into a big pond. Since there was always scarcity of water in Lokoro during dry season, both humans and animals could drink water from the pond. Reports show that in 1880, the people of Wi-Athwoo were unhappy to see the cattle of Kor drinking from the pond which they did not dig. The chief of Wi-Athwoo had a helper, Liyimme. He then sent for

Liyimme and told him, "I want the messengers to call everyone to go and fight the people of Kor."

The chief of Wi-Athwoo also asked the chief of Lowathia to help him in this fight. When the chief of Lowathia received the plea, he accepted and immediately gathered his people who went to help Wi-Athwoo to fight the people of Kor. The people of Wi-Athwoo and Lowathia fought the people of Kor fiercely and overpowered them. The Kor was overpowered because D.C. Mr. Owen, had in the past confiscated all the guns they had. When the people of Kor realized that they had become powerless, the broke the hind walls of thirteen huts and escaped. Only one family of Libongi, who showed courage, remained in Lokoro. There are no records indicating where those who abandoned the fight went.

Crazzolara said, "In the year the people of Kor and Wi-Athwoo were fighting, Chief Alikori was the leader of the people of Wi-Athwoo, while Olum was the chief of Kor. One day, an argument cropped up among the people of Wi-Athwoo and Kor and resulted in a fight. However, no one was killed because members of these two families used sticks to fight. After the fight, around the year 1880, Chief Olum took many people from the family of Kor to the land of the Acholi of Sudan (Pajok).

It seems after the fight, the people of Parii who had remained at Lofon Hill, got to know that some of their people were in Pajok, and they were Lwo (Crazzolara, 1951, P.159).

Secondly, the history of Pajok says the people of Kor left Lokoro over disagreement between Keny and his brother Mwo. To understand how the Pajok departed from Lokoro, I think it is good to look at how Chief Keny and his brother Mwo moved, because the movement of these two brothers is in the history of Pajok.

We however do know what triggered the dispute between these two. Some people say they were fighting over who should be the chief, but Crazzolara (1951) says chief Rwot Keny and Mwo fighting broke over the new land they had built at Lofon Hill (Crazzolara, 1951, P, 174).

After the dispute between Chief Keny and Mwo, the people of Pajok split into two. Those who were pro Keny all went back under his chiefdom, while other people who supported Mwo went back under the leadership of Mwo. According to the elders of Pajok, those who followed Mwo were more than those who supported Keny. Others argue that much as the supporters of Mwo were many, they did not have the heart of living in unity. After the fight, Mwo was the first to start taking his people away from Lofon Hill (Ajubi). They moved towards the south, unsure of where they were heading to, while Chief Keny remained in Ajubi with his group.

Crazzolara said Mwo and his group walked for almost three days before reaching Imotong Hill. From there they went and built on Lalak Hill. After two or three years, Chief Keny again took the people of Ywaya from Lokoro. They also passed from Imotong Hill, from where they went and built at the foot of Agu Hill. Chief Keny did not want to build at Lalak Hill because Mwo and his people were already there. Ywaya were also known as jo *kal* (royal people), and they later named themselves Jo pa-Lenga "they are the royal family" (Crazzolara, 1951, P, 174).

Nonetheless, when I was asking the elders of Pajok like Kadensyo Jada Adinya and Marcello Ogana, they told me that, "When Ywaya was coming to Lokoro, they did not go to Imatong Hill as some history writers of Lwo put it. The history of Pajok says the supporters of Mwo and those of Keny all moved together and passed from Okire Hill, where Kor found the clan elders of Imurok setting up their shrine. The history of Pajok says Ywaya, Lamwo, Obwolto and Patanga all moved together with the group headed by chief Keny, and Ywaya went and built at the foot of Agu Hill. The supporters of Mwo on the other hand went and built on Lalak Hill." (But we do not know if Patanga and Obwolto built at Lalak or Agu Hill). The history of Pajok says that Chief Keny and his brother Mwo all moved together, but Crazzolara said Mwo and Chief Keny moved separately.

Reports show that when Ywaya, Patanga and the group now called Obwolto were searching for a place to settle, many died of hunger. So one night, as the people were looking for where to temporarily settle, they came across lumps of bread that was arranged in order. Elders of Pajok like Adinya and Ogana said the food found on the hills of Okire by the people of Kor was left by the people of Imurok who were setting up their shrine. When the Kor of Pajok saw the food, they thought it was prepared for visitors. So they looked left and right, but did not see anyone. Since there were no people around, the people of Kor concluded that the food must have been sent by their god, just as the Almighty God dropped food for the Israelites on their way from Egypt to the Promised Land.

Elder Adinya, who also gave me much information regarding the Pajok said, "When the elders of Imurok saw many people coming, they got scared and ran and abandoned the food before the god. When the people of Kor reached the shrine, they also saw all the food and called it *"Oliya"* which means, delicious food without an owner. Since the group had walked a long distance without eating, they immediately ate the food. Obwolto family, however, refused to eat the food, thinking that the elders of Imurok laced the food with poison to kill them. Those who ate the food then kept telling those who didn't eat the food that "The stupid will die." This is how the family that refused to eat the food at Okire Hill, got the name *"Obwol-to"*, which means, stupidity is death.

But elder Ben Oywak of Obwolto said, "The fact that the people of Obwolto refused to eat the food does not mean they are stupid as other say, instead, it shows us that they are good hearted people." After eating the food, Kor became known as *"Pajok"*, because they ate food meant for a god. This also brings us to the question, "Of the fourteen families currently in Pajok, which one are the true *Pajok*?" As we saw above, not all the people who moved with Chief Keny ate the food. Secondly, other people who came from the other side and are currently in Pajok also did not eat the food meant for the god. The history of Pajok says the people who ate the food for the god were the *Ywaya* and *Patanga*. This also answers our question above. "The families of *Ywaya* and *Patanga* are the prototypical members of Pajok because they are the ones who ate the food meant for the god."

Other people who are in Pajok merely use the name Pajok, but in the real sense, they are not the people of Pajok. Gradually, everyone who lived in the north-west of Acholi of Sudan started calling themselves Pajok. The history of Pajok says the word Pajok was derived from the food for the god at Okire Hill. But according to Crazzolara, the history of Lokoro says the word "Pajok" came from evil spirit, which killed Chief Ocak of Pajok in Lofon Hill, and the people of Lokoro said the people of Kor were the people of "jok" (god) (Crazzolara, 1951, P. 159).

When the people had finished eating the food, they continued moving around Okire Hill till they reached Iyire (Obbo). From here the people of Kor moved on till they arrived at Ayuu Hill, where they found the people of Pagaya and their chief, Ogweng. A few months after the arrival of Kor in Agu Hill, Chief Ogweng made his group join the people of Kor and they moved together to Lalak Hill and later to Agu Hill. Those who lived at Lalak Hill many years ago used to call it by a different name, but when Kor of Pajok settled there temporarily, they gave the hill the name, *Lalak*. The Pajok renamed the hill Lalak because they moved in so many places. In Acholi, the word *La-lak* means one who roams a lot, or people who move in different places. The people of Lamwo, or Jo-pa-Uya, as they called themselves, then built in Lalak Hill, and Ywaya on the other hand went and built at Agu Hill. Elder Ben Oywak told me that when the people of Chief Keny reached Agu Hill, they called themselves *"Ywaya"* or *"Jo pa-Lenga"*. While the group of Mwo from Lalak Hill also called themselves *"Jo Lamwo"* or *"Jo pa-Uya"*. But according to Crazzolara, in the year Chief Keny and his brother Mwo reached Agu Hill and Lalak Hill, they found the people of Pagaya, Bura and Palio already at the foot of Agu Hill. The people of Pagaya, Bura and Palio who came from Bar had the royal spear. These are the people Crazzolara said were there when Lwo reached Gordon Hill, near Nimule. Other Lwo went towards the East and arrived in Pajok, Agu Hill and Lalak (Crazzolara, 1951, P, 57).

A section of elders of Pajok said Ywaya found Pagaya in Patworo. This also points to us that if such important history is not documented, then by year 2500-3000, if the world has not yet come to an end, the Acholi of Sudan will have no history.

The people of Pagaya came from Pawir (Bunyoro), under the leadership of Chief Ogweng. They moved ahead to Pajule (Uganda), and went up to Agu Hill. Crazzolara said, "The first groups of people to come from Pawir through Pajule were the Pagaya of Pajok, and the Payira of Uganda. The people of Patiko found the people of Pagaya and Payira at the foot of Guma Hill when the people of Patiko were coming from Pubungu (Crazzolara, 1950, P, 83).

The relationship between chief Keny and his brother Mwo was bad, so when the people of Lamwo arrived in Lalak Hill, they were independent. But when Chief Keny went and built at the foot of Agu Hill, Chief Mwo agreed that his people could unite with the people of Chief Keny. He then took all his people and placed them under the leadership of Chief Keny. Much as the people, of Lamwo went back to be led by Chief Keny, they still had the right to celebrate their god, Lacic, which is found on Lacic Hill, also known as Lamwo Hill. The people of Lamwo used to heal the sick in Lacic Hill. Whenever evil spirit related sickness broke out in Acholiland, all the people of Pajok could contribute goats and sheep and take to the people of Lamwo. The people of Lamwo would then slaughter the goats and sheep and cook for the god, Lacic so that it blessed the Pajok. The clan elders of Lamwo would gather around Lamwo Hill and sacrifice the food to the god (Lacic), once a year. Elder Ben Oywak told me that the people of Lamwo relinquished their power/chiefdom to chief Keny because they did not want to continue living in disharmony.

The Pajok lived at Agu and Lalak hills for a few years and later continued moving up to Pager River. They found the Bitti and Kapaa already around Pager River. The people of Kor found Bitti with a royal drum and a rain stone. From here, the Kor of Pajok decided to go back to Agu and Lalak hills. They also requested Bitti and Kapaa if they could move together. When the Bitii and Kapaa heard the call of Kor, they accepted the idea. After seven days, the people of Pajok, together with Bitti and Kapaa, left Pager river and moved towards north and reached Liri Palabek (Uganda).

The Pajok lived here for a short time because the hunting ground belonged to Bitti. When the members had rested, they continued moving until they reached Lagaya Hill, where the Pajok found the people of Ayuu. That year, the people of Ayuu had a chief called *Onyok*. Elder Paterno Abak told me that "The people of Ayuu were very rude. When Pajok reached Lagaya Hill, they immediately noticed that Ayuu were rude people, for this reason, they did not pay back the rudness so that they live together. When the people of Ayuu understood that the Kor of Pajok wanted to live in peace, they gradually accepted to be led by chief Keny."

From Lagaya Hill, the Pajok continued moving to Adodi Hill, where they found the Panto. Reports show that the people of Panto were also harsh, like the people of Ayuu. Panto built at the foot of Adodi Hill because Adodi hunting ground belongs to them. Adodi hunting ground stretches from Adodi Hill up to Atebi River. From Adodi the Pajok also requested Panto if they could move together and the Panto agreed. Truly, after one or two years, Panto united with the Pajok, and they moved together in different places including: *Okwero-obeno, Ongoto-Nyare (Palabek), Apul, Lagiri, Tuma-tuma* (from Tuma-tuma other people of Kor went back to their roots in Lokoro, *as we shall later see*), and at *Lotii Hill*.

Pajok lived at the foot of Lotii Hill for a few years and later left for Ayuma hunting ground (war champion). When the Pajok arrived in Ayuma hunting ground, Panto decided to go back to Adodi Hill, because the Pajok failed to get a good place where they could live for many years. After a few days, Panto separated from Pajok and went back and built at Adodi Hill.

Around 1924 the Pajok left Ayuma Hill and built in Polila Hill, where they lived for seven years. But in 1925, when sleeping sickness was claiming many lives in Acholiland, the white men took the Pajok to temporarily stay on top Lotii Hill. When the epidemic was no more, the Pajok went back to Polila Hill. And in 1932, the Pajok left Polila Hill and relocated to "Lawiny", where they lived for only a year. In 1933 Pajok again shifted from Lawiny and built in Ayacii. However, they did not stay here for long for two important reasons. First, Ayacii hunting ground where the Pajok built belonged to Obbo (Obbo did not want Pajok to continue staying in Ayacii hunting ground). Secondly, when Pajok were in Ayacii, Obbo kept insulting them that *"Pajok brag for nothing Obbo hunting ground is the one feeding you you have nothing in your name"*. In the year 1936 the Pajok could not bear the insults anymore and they left Ayacii and built at Atebi River in Bore hunting ground, which also belongs to Koyo (Obbo). Later on, the people of Koyo gave Bore hunting ground to Bobi (we do not know why the people of Koyo gave the hunting ground to the people of Bobi. Around 1938, when Panto heard that Pajok had found a better place to live at Atebi River, they left Adodi hill and went and built in Atebi, where they are living to date. Later in October, a rainy season, the Pajok realized that because the land was in Atebi River, not all of them could cultivate in the area. For this reason, the Pajok split into three groups. Some people went to farm in Oloyo lweny hunting ground, others went to cultivate in Pugee, and another group went to farm in Ladiki. This also explains why some of the Pajok left for Pugee from Atebi River.

SOME MEMBERS OF KOR WENT BACK TO LOKORO

After a few years when Chief Olum left Lokoro, the people of Lopit and Lotuko began to secretly kill the people of Lokoro. They infiltrated the people through the vacant places left by Kor in 1890 as they headed to Acholi. The people of Lopit and Lotuko continued to secretly kill the people of Lokoro. Kamure, who was also a renowned witchdoctor in Liful, was not happy over the atrocities committed by the people of Lopit and Lotuko against Lokoro. In the year 1898, Kamure was ailing, but one morning, when he saw that the people of Lopit and

Lotuko were still secretly killing Lokoro, he summoned the people of Lokoro and told them that, "People of Lokoro, I am already very weak and might die any time from now, but I still see the people of Lopit and Lotuko secretly killing our people. If the people of Kor had not left part of our land, the enemies could not have got the chance to sneak among the people in our land. I am now appealing to you that, if possible, find a way of bringing your brothers, who split from you eight years ago, (Kor of Pajok) back home. I have heard that your brothers of Kor are among the Acholi of Sudan (Pajok). If you want the people of Kor to come back home easily, I will give my messengers my shoes and feces so that they take to Pajok. When the shoes and poop reach Pajok, the food of the Pajok will go bad. If the Pajok realize that their food has got contaminated in their own mouths, they will allow the people of Kor to go back to Lokoro. If we do not do that, your brothers will not come back as we expect."

Everyone was in support of Kamure's idea, and the next morning, he called his messengers and gave them his shoes and feces wrapped in ogali leaf. He instructed them to take the shoes and feces to chief Ogwok of Ywaya. The history of Lokoro says the incident happened in October, when the Pajok were harvesting sesame. When the messengers arrived with the shoes and chief's feces in the compound of the Pajok, they took it to chief Ogwok as instructed by the witchdoctor. Truly in the morning, all the sesame and any other foodstuff became bitter. When Chief Ogwok heard that the people were complaining because all the sesame and other food had become bitter in their mouths, he called the people of Pajok and told them that, "You Pajok, there is no single day that the sesame we planted ourselves went bad like this time. You should be aware that all this was brought by Kamure of Lokoro. I now want you Pajok to allow the people of Lokoro to go back home." When the people realized that the problem was caused by Kor, they supported the chief Ogwok's suggestion.

Another morning, Chief Ogwok called the messengers of Kamure and told them that, "Very well, our people, we do not hold any grudges against Lokoro. You can go back with your brothers who left you because of a dispute." The Kor shortly gathered ready to go back home. But a few who enjoyed staying in Acholi, together with old people, refused to go back to Lokoro. The history of Pajok says those who remained gave birth to Kor (Ywaya, Obwolto and Patanga), who are presently in the land of the Pajok. The elders of Pajok and

Lokoro have the same version of Lokoro going back as I have written above, but people like Crazzolara have a different view as we shall see below.

Crazzolara (1951) said, "Chief Alikori of Wi-Athwoo, together with other people of Lokoro, were looking for reasons why Kor of Pajok left Lofon Hill. For this reason, the people of Lokoro sent their people in Pajok so that they share water with Chief Olum, after which they would then request Chief Olum and his people to go back to Lokoro. Secondly, they would also ask Chief Olum to forget about issues of the past. When the messengers of Chief Alikori reached Pajok, they reconciled with the people of Olum, and Olum later accepted to go back home.

The history of Lokoro says the people of Kor stayed in Pajok land for eight years (1890-1898), and in the ninth year, they went back to Lokoro. Reports show that within the eight years, the people of Kor used to go to Lofon to visit their brothers and sisters who remained there. Usually when going to Lokoro, the people of Kor passed through Obbo. Unfortunately, the children of Obbo teased the people of Kor a lot. The spitefulness of the children of Obbo spread later to Chief Olum. The history of Pajok says when Kor found where to settle in Pajok, they married many girls of Pajok who were also blessed with children.

In the month the people of Kor were going back, they went along with women and children they produced to Lokoro. This is one reason why the people of Lokoro learnt Acholi very fast. When they were going back to Lofon Hill, all the people of Kor knew how to speak in Acholi. In the year the people of Kor where in Pajok, Ongwe, son of Okwom, was the only one who died among the people of Kor, but the spear and royal chair remained in the family of Olum. In this year also, a big war erupted among the people of Obbo and Pajok. The history of Lokoro says when chief Olum went back to Lokoro, he did not forget about the spitefulness of Obbo, on the different days they were passing through their home. When he reached Lokoro, Chief Olum narrated to the elders of Liful the unkindness the Obbo had against the Kor of Pajok. The news angered the people of Lokoro, and they decided to revange. For this reason, the warriors wanted to fight the people of Obbo. Under the leadership of Chief Alikori, the fighters went to Obbo land at night and caught the Obbo unawares. Lokoro cut the throats of women, men, the old and young boys they came across. They did not kill girls and some boys. When the fight had stopped, they gathered the girls and cattle and took them to Lofon. During this same war, Chief Olum captured one child of Obbo, Okumu. The child must have been born around the year 1884. Since Chief Olum had only two daughters, and no sons, he decided to make the boy part of the family. Okumu was a very bright hard working boy, and he also showed his hard work to Chief Olum, and when chief Olum died, Okumu (the slave) became the chief.

The war between the Obbo and Lokoro, taught the people of Obbo so well that they never taunted the people of Lokoro who went to Pajok after the fight. The elders of Lokoro said the people of Paari had the interest of going back to fight against the Obbo, but they changed their mind because of the coming of the British to Acholi of Sudan (Crazzolara, 1951, PP. 1591562).

THE RAIN POT OF PAJOK

In Pajok, the heaviest rain is in the family of Ywaya Bolmega. They brought the rain stone from Lokoro. But much as the chief of the heaviest rain is in Ywaya Bolmeja, we find that smaller rains are in the families of Bobi, Panto and Ayuu. The elders of Pajok do not know who in the past and present used to invoke rain in Bobi, Panto and Ayuu. But the chief of Bobi, who is remembered by the people, is Aruk. And the chief of rain of Panto remembered by the people is Chief Tuke. The chief of rain of Ayu who the people remember is Chief Oling Opec.

The fact that Ywaya brought the rain stone from Lokoro shows us that the first person to invoke rain in Ywaya was Chief Ocak, who died at Lofon. After his death, the rain stone was taken care of by his son Keny, who then came with the rain stone to Pajok. When Chief Keny died, the rain remained under the care of Obak. After he died, Chief Atanga took over. When he died, Chief Lagedo became the caretaker, and when he died chief Leng took over. After the death of Chief Leng, the rain stone remained under the care of Agwa, who also died and left the stone under the guardianship of Chief Otuke. When Chief Otuke died, the stone was taken care of by Anyoda, who also died and left the stone with Chief Oceng Lokwor-moi.

But some people say chief of rain of Pajok who is remembered by the people is Lakul father of Obwoya. After he died, he left the stone with his son Obwoya, who passed over the stone to his son Gidion Ogwok before he died. To date, the rain of Ywaya is guarded by Chief Gidion Ogwok. I found that in Pajok a left handed person respects a right handed person when it comes to issues of rain making. While a right handed person respects a left handed person when it comes to matters of Labwot-Onyom god and the royal drum.

As we were seeing in Obbo, we find that the rain chief has a rain caretaker, but in Pajok, the rain chief does not have a rain caretaker. Whenever the chief wanted it to rain, he would prepare the rain pot himself. The history of Pajok says when the people found a rain stone; they would show it to an old woman or man. The elder would then take it to the chief of Ywaya. After taking the rain stone, the history of Pajok says the chief would smear it with sesame oil or shea nut butter, and then he would go back with it to his/her home.

Chapter Fifteen

PANYIKWARA

THE HOME OF PANYIKWARA

Before we continue looking at issues in the family of Panyikwara, I want us to answer a question frequently asked by many. "What does the word Panyikwara mean?" It is not easy to respond to such a question, if one does not know the history of Panyikwara. I also realized that I could not answer the question. So when I was researching on the history of Acholi of Sudan, I also asked the elders of Acholi of Sudan the same question. I found that many people did not know the meaning of the word "Panyikwara", but elder Gerelimo Mamur Odelfere, of Panyikwara, told me that people do not know the meaning of the word "Panyikwara", because they are also ill-informed about the history of Panyikwara. He (Mamur) then told me that, "The word Panyikwara means the children of Nyikwara." Chief Nyikwara came with his group from Gilo (Anywak) around the year 1603. They built in Bilinyang (Bar), where they lived for half a century 1603-1653, but Chief Nyikwara died in Bilinyang in the year 1650.

After the death of Chief Nyikwara, his son called Modi succeeded him, and took his people to Aru in the land of Lolubo. He later died in Lolubo in 1680. After the death of Chief Modi, his son, Gitala took over the throne. Chief Gitala is the one who brought the Panyikwara from Aru to Mede (Iwire Hill) around the year 1681-1682.

The Panyikwara built in Madi hunting ground, neighboring Iwire Hill. Reports show that when the Panyikwara came to Iwire Hill, the Madi were already in the hunting ground. The Madi came much earlier from Bar (Rejaf) and settled here. The history of Acholi says chief Nyikwara came from Anywak with many people including the Pacar, Pali, Palokiri and Pamunda. Since they were also searching for a place to settle, the people led by Chief Gitala then fought the Madi and defeated them.

The elders of Panyikwara said Chief Talapu did not come with the intention of usurping power from Chief Gitala. That is why Chief Talapu told the people of Chief Gitala, son of Modi that, "Bura kal, you are my brothers. Be humble as you lead and invoke the rains so that people have good crop harvests. I am a born of Pajule, and I relinquished the power to be chief to Gitala, because he is my brother." After a short while, people of Gitala gathered fighters against the people of Moli Tokuro (Madi). They fought fiercely against the Madi. According to reports, the chief of the Madi, whose name we do not know, did not die during the fight. He later gave his royal drum and spear to chief Gitala. This subsequently made Chief Gitala, son of Modi to become the chief of Acholi Panyikwara and Madi.

Since the Madi and Acholi were already being led by Chief Gitala, the office of Chief Modi gradually began using both Acholi and Madi dialects. If you went to the land of the Panyikwara, you will find that people there speak both Acholi and Madi.

Elder Palacido Langoya Yugu, of Panyikwara, told me that the other Madi who survived the attacks by the children of Panyikwara, also left Panyikwara after a short time. They went towards the West and reached a place near Juba — Nimule. After two years, the Madi Moli Tokuro again realized that this land was infertile, and they decided to go back to fight against the Panyikwara.

The Madi Moli Tokuro said the land in Mede (Iwire Hill) was fertile, but they could not stay together with the Panyikwara. The Madi immediately organized to go and fight the Panyikwara. They used bows and arrows, but unfortunately, Panyikwara did not know how to use bows or arrows. They instead used spears and shields to fight against the Madi. Before the Madi and Panyikwara started fighting against each other, the elders of Panyikwara were teaching and instructing the boys that "stab the one before me, while I also stab the one before you."

Panyikwaro were very skilled in using spears and shields when fighting. For this reason, the Madi killed many of them. But the history of Panyikwara tells us that many more Madi died during the fight. Records show that the Madi who survived, abandoned the fight and fled for safety. The Panyikwara pursued the Madi Moli Tokuro up to Kerepi. To remind the people about the war between the Panyikwara and Madi, the Panyikwara composed a song:

Nyii-ngwii Yoo Koo!

Nyi-ngwi Never Learn!

Morongolo Got Iwire nga Mailo!

Morongolo cuts Iwire Hill who raises it up!

Tong Tim Magicobo ki Nyi-ngwii Tero Dano ka Ngolo!

The wild spear which speared Nyi-ngwii Takes people to be slaughtered!

Lwiri Ma Gingeyo Con!

The spear that is known from the Stone Age!

After a few years, the members of Chief Gitala started wrangling over land. The people wanted to know the real owner of the land. The families of Goloba, Paliwa and Oyira started claiming that they were the true heads of the home, while other people maintained that Bura were the land owners.

The history of Pajok says Bura are the heads of the home, because they were the first to enter the land of the Panyikwara. The other people came and built there much later. Records also show that the family members of Goloba, Paliwa and Oyira are all cousins of Bura, but not the owners of the home.

In the year 1936, when the British had entered Acholiland, they began dividing the Acholi and Madi. The British later recognized that there was a strong bond among the Panyikwara and Madi, because the boys and girls were intermarrying. The Acholi have a saying that marriage enlarges clans (or the issue of marriages always unites people). When the white men saw this, in 1936, they picked the families of Payoko, Pajaa, Dungi, Ng-gaya and Pandiker and put them under the leadership of Madi "Local Government No 1 in Loa". Reports indicate that in that year, the families of Ng-gaya, Oloro and Palabek were being led by Chief Adiemu of Bura.

The history of Panyikwara says much as the family members of Payoko, Pajaa, Dungo, Ng-gaya and Pandiker were taken back to be led by the chief of Madi, they continued following the norms of Acholi and Madi. This also gave Panyikwara the chance to trick the people, such that whenever there was an issue of contention between the child of Panyikwara and Acholi from another family, the born of Panyikwara would speak in Madi dialect. However when there was a debate between a child of Panyikwara and a child of Madi, the born of Panyikwara could also speak in Acholi. But if there was a dispute among the children of Panyikwara, they spoke in Acholi. The history of Acholi also tells us that in the year 1936, the British took other people of Panyikwara who had remained and put them the chief of Acholi in "Local Government Centre No 2 in Magwi".

The British gathered the people of Panyikwara at the foot of Iwire Hill

Between the years 1900-1921, the Panyikwara were scattered in different places. Some people were in Iwire Hill, others in Latebe, some were in Anywang, but majority were in Awala (on the shores of Ayii River). In 1920 the people of Lokoro and Lokoya engaged the Acholi in constant battles.

In the year 1922, when the British saw that the people of lo-jur were continuing to fight the people, they gathered all the people of Panyikwara at Iwire Hill. This same year, (1922) Bura and the Paliwa were living in a place called Latebe. The British then brought the Bura and Paliwa from Latebe, and put the Bura at Ceng-ki-dwe.

The Paliwa built around a big tree sausage tree located to the East of the Ceng-ki-dwe. The British also brought other people of Goloba, and put them around Liful Hill, while others were put in Anywang.

The people lived at Iwire Hill for seven years 1922-1928, and in 1928, they started relocating. Bura shifted day and night, and went and built in Kamac, where they are up to date. The people of Goloba on the other hand moved away from Anywang and settled in Pagen, while Oyira also came and built among them. The Pamunda and Pakala however relocated to Acila.

The history of Acholi says in the year 1920, the people of Acholi were among the nine "A" Court (or the parliament of the blacks) in Panyikwara, Agoro, Omeo, Magwi, Obbo, Pajok, Palwar, Agata and Lobone. Each "A" court had a chief as listed below:

Panyikwara "A" Court	Chief Atoo Alijabu Sabuni
Agoro "A" Court	Chief Ongom
Omeo "A" Court	Chief Ogany.
Magwi "A" Court	Chief Ongee.
Obbo "A" Court	Chief Aburi Kassiba.
Pajok "A" Court	Chief Oceng-Lokwor-moi.
Palwar "A" Court	Chief Lotobe.
Agata "A" Court	Chief Ongiro.
Lobone "A" Court	Chief Oduro.

In the year 1920, the Acholi also had one "B" Court (or the parliament of the British) in Miri-onyala-Iwire. But in 1928, D.C. moved the hearing of the "B" Court to Lotii Hill in Obbo. The D.C, who was also a British, was always the chairman of the "B" Court. The British government gave the powers to handle minor cases like domestic brawls among husband and wife, disputes between brothers and clans to the chief of "A" Court. While major offences like murder and theft and robbery were handled by the chief of the "B" Court. The nine chiefs of Acholi always gathered to hear cases brought to the "B" Court in the compound of the chief in Miri-onyala, twice a year.

The ACholi chiefs also did not know English, but they knew Arabic. The D.C then got Abdalfarash Ongom of Goloba, whose command of English and Arabic was fair, to be the translator during discussions. The British chose Abdalfarash Ongom as an interpreter because he could also speak English, Arabic, Madi and Acholi. The D.C also appointed Ali Bee of Omeo, as a guard in charge of chiefs during hearings in "B" Court.

Elder Gerelimo Mamur Odelfere told me that the villages in Acholi used not to dance together, much as time and again one home could go and dance in another village. But not even a single day did the Acholi of Sudan gather to perform a traditional dance.

Reports say in the year 1927, Chief Atoo Alijabu of Panyikwara, invited all villages in Acholi of Sudan to go dancing in Miri-onyala. When the Acholi got the invitation given to every village for the first time, they accepted and came from different places to Miri-Onyala (Iwire). There were so many people dancing that space became little. But after a short time, the people of Bura and Goloba began to steal the drum-beating sticks. The dispute over the drumsticks angered the people, and forced Okwera, of Bura, to pick an ogoto reed and stabbed the Ibuc of Goloba. Ibuc bled to death, compelling many to abandon the dance. The next morning, the clan elders of Panyikwara sent a message to the D.C., telling him the violence Okwera committed against Ibuc. When the D.C got the information, he sent a guard to arrest Chief Atoo Alijabu for inviting the Acholi to go dancing, without seeking permission from his office. The guard arrested the chief and took him to Nimule, and the British took him to court. Chief Atoo was found guilty during the hearing in "B" Court, and he was sentenced to two years in prison. Chief Atoo did not serve his jail term in Nimule. He was instead taken to a jail in Kimo, located in the border of Kuku and Madi.

There are six families surrounding the home of the Panyikwara. They are Magwi and Pajok North & North West, Madi to the west, Palabek in Uganda to the South, and Agoro and Omeo to the East.

The history of Acholi states that the border of Panyikwara and Magwi is in Ing-gili stream, but other people say the border of Panykwara and Magwi is in Romo-toguli. The border of Panyikwara and Pajok is at Ayiba Hill, while the border of Panyikwara and Madi, some people say, is at Wi-Jubi stream, in Opari, but the reality is that the border of Panyikwara and Madi runs along Juba Nimule Road till it reaches River Lopai Ingwe (or River Latyieng matar); on the south part of this river Lopai Ingwe are the Madi and in the north part of this river are the Panyikwara. The border of Panyikwara and Palabek of Uganda is in River Limur (the southern bank of River Limur is Palabek-Uganda, while the norther bank of River Limur is Panyikwara-South Sudan). And the border of Panyikwara and Agoro is in River Ayii all the way till it reached Alwala hunting ground that is celebrate by family of Goloba Padegi. While the border of Panyikwara and Omeo is in the farm of Joseph Lagu, along Nimule- Juba road.

THE FAMILY OF PANYIKWARA

The home of Panyikwara is slightly different from other homes we were looking at before. Unlike Obbo and Pajok, the home of the Panyikwara is not divided into left and right. They however have nine families, with each family identified by a number. The history of Panyikwara tells us that King George William of Bura, was the one who gave the numbers to the different families in Panyikwara.

Reports show that King George William gave the numbers according to how each family entered Panyikwara. As seen below, the Bura were given the number No 1. This also shows that Bura was the first group to arrive in Panyikwara. The Goloba were given No 2, meaning they were the second family to enter the land of Panyikwara after Bura. Then Oloro were given number No 9, meaning they came much later in Panyikwara.

The Panyikwara are not only known for their distinct numbers, but for the symbol each family has, as we shall see later in "Appendix C 1 to C 2". The Panyikwara came from different places in Sudan like Lolubo (Lokiliri), Lokoyo and Tali. Other people however came all the way from Uganda in places like Alero, Lokung, Patoko and Patiko.

The families of Panyikwara and their flags here: —

Family	Number	Symbol
Bura	1	Red
Goloba	2	An elephant's head
Paliwa	3	Red top and black bottom
Oyira	4	White top, red mid and black bottom
Pamunda	5	UN —many different emblems
Ayom	6	American
Pakala	7	Seven different emblems
Palabek	8	Red
Oloro	9	Spotted

During hunting, dancing, communal farming and wars, the different families in Panyikwara are known by their numbers, but not symbol. There are two families in Panyikwara which are held in very high regard. These two families are of Bura and Oyira. People revere Bura-kot because of rain, while the Oyira family is respected because of Lori, a god. The god is very important to the Panyikwara than any other god we shall later look at in this book. Much as people respect Bura-kot because of rain, there are four families which do not honor Bura-Kot, because they have their own rain. These four families are Ayom, Pakala, Palabek and Oloro.

BURA

The history of Acholi says that Bura came from Gilo (Anywak), they went and built at Iwire Hill around 1681. Other children of Bura say they left Anywak around 1600-1602, because of dispute between Gipir and Labongo, over beads and a spear. As we saw above, Bura settled in Bilinyang for fifty years (1603-1653), and later they continued moving till they reached Aru in Lolubo.

The history of Panyikwara said Chief Nyikwara died in Bilinyang, and his son, Modi, succeeded him. In the year 1653, the Bilinyang were not treating Modi's people kindly, this made Chief Modi to lead his people away from Bilinyang. The group moved towards the East, and went to Aru in Lolubo. Chief Modi lived in Aru for thirty years 1653-1683.

Unfortunately, he fell ill from Aru and later died of the sickness. After the death of Chief Modi, his son, Gitala became the chief around 1681. Gradually, Chief Gitala realized that land of Lolubo was not suitable for farming the varieties of crops they wanted. In the year 1684, Chief Gitala took his people away from Aru, and they moved following the southern direction. And after a month or two, the group of Chief Gitala reached Iwire Hill in 1685.

The group found Madi (Moli-Tokuro) in this hunting ground, because the Madi came earlier from Rejaf (Bar) and settled in the hunting ground. Reports show that Madi did not like the idea of Gitala's group coming to the area, and they subsequently waged a war against Bura.

But the people Chief Gitala led were more than the Madi. Bura fought hard and defeated Madi, and the few who survived fled towards the West. The history of Panyikwara says the chief of the Madi did not die during the war. Later chief of Madi, and those who survived the war joined the chiefdom of Gitala. The Madi did not take long under Chief Gitala, after one year they followed their brothers in the West.

The history of Panyikwara says after a few years, Chief Talapu of Pajule (Uganda) came with his group around the year 1690, and joined the people of Chief Gitala. Chief Gitala warmly welcomed Chief Talapu and gave them land to build and grow crops.

Elder Gerelimo Mamur Odelfere told me that chief Talapu came with his regalia, including a drum named "Akenda" (or Akenda drum). Since chief Gitala, son of Modi, was a born of Anywak, he did not know the tradition of the Lwo. For this reason, when they reached Mede, they were conforming to the customs and traditions of Anywak. But a few years after the coming of chief Talapu from Pajule, the chief started introducing the traditions of Lwo among the Panyikwara.

Chief Talapu did not come with the ambition to become a chief. That is why he said, "Bura Kal, you are my brothers. Lead with humility; invoke the rains so that people's crops produce good yields. I am a born of Pajule, and I surrendered my power to Pa- Nyikwara." Chief Gitala took the rain stone belonging to Chief Talapu and added it to his.

Bura has six small families as seen below; Bura-Kot, Bura-Woroger, Bura-Pagena, Bura-Ong-goloba, Bura-Pajule and Bura-Panyamo.

The family of Bura-Ong-goloba and Bura-Pajule were the first to join the people of Bura-kot. The second family to join Bura-kot was Bura-Pagena. The Pagena came from Mundari with many cattle. When they reached Mede, they found the women of Bura-kot fetching water from a well. The boys of Pagena started helping the women of Bura-kot to fetch water. When the women saw the kind gesture and respect portrayed by the children, they sent a messenger to Chief Gitala, who told the chief that; "There are people who have come with many cattle, they were also helping us fetch water from the well. These people did not disturb us, so we were very happy". When Chief Gitala heard the news, he sent his messengers to meet the Pagena. The chief also gave a pot of brew brew Lokutu (local beer brew from leftover food) for the chief of Pagena to quench his thirst. Chief Gitala's messengers took the pot of local brew to the chief of Pagena, whose name we do not know.

The history of Panyikwaro says the chief of Pagena received the pot of wine with gladness. After receiving the brew, the chief of Pagena also picked a bull, cow and milk and gave to the messengers to take to Chief Gitala. Chief Gitala later gave the Pagena land near Bura-kot, to build and cultivate crops. This is why the Pagena became Bura-Kal and later started calling themselves "Jo Bura-Pagena". Whenever there was a dance in Panyilwara, the Bura-Pageno could hoist the flag of the Bura.

The custom also barred young boys and girls of Bura kal, Bura-Pajule and Bura Ong-goloba from intermarrying. They could however, marry boys and girls from the family of Bura-Woroger or Bura-Panyamo. Secondly, the rule also prohibited the boys and girls from the family of Bura-Panyamo and Bura-Ong-goloba from intermarrying. Among all the families of Bura, only Bura-Pagena were free to from any family in Bura.

Bura hunting ground and hill

Bura has one hunting ground called Owil-kado. This is also the hunting ground Bura live to date. Owil-kado hunting ground is not used for hunting because many people built there. But fruits like shear fruit, which are found in this hunting ground are collected and taken to the chief. Additionally, the people could also take part of the crops they have harvested to chief. If a born of Panyikwara found an animal in the hunting ground, he could also take it to the chief. The family members of Bura, who built in Owil-Kado hunting ground do not only show respect towards the chief by giving contributions, they also plant crops for the chief.

The history of Panyikwara says Bura has two hills named Ibba and Pa-womer hills. The history of Bura said Goloba are the ones who gave Ibba hunting ground to Bura, in compensation for a girl who was killed during hunting. Bura also has one god named Ibba which lives on Ibba Hill. If you want to understand more about Ibba, read chapter 24 of the book, "Traditional Religion of Acholi" (page 883).

GOLOBA
Goloba has four small families; Alero, Pajombo, Olubo and Padegi.

ALERO: The family of Alero came from Alero in Uganda. Elder Lokici led the Alero in Sudan around the year 1700. The history of Acholi says the family members of Alero left their brothers and sisters in Uganda because of famine which killed many people that year. Other elders of Panyikwara say, the family members of Alero came to Panyikwara together with the people of Padegi. They found other people already at the foot of Iwire Hill.

PAJOMBO: The family ofPajombo came from Bar around the year 1695. Chief Aramatala was the one who led the people of Pajombo to Panyikwara. They found other people of Panyikwara who came earlier, already at Iwire Hill. The Pajombo left Bar because of wrangles over cattle with their brothers, who remained behind. The history of Acholi says the Pajombo of Panyikwara moved together with Pajombo Okwee of Obbo. When they arrived at Iwire Hill, the Pajombo of Panyikwara stayed here while the Pajombo Okwee continued with their journey and built at Ayiba Hill in Obbo land. Other elders of Panyikwara say the Pajombo were the first to reach Iwire Hill before the people of Alero, Padegi and Olubo. This explains why Pajombo became the heads of Goloba family.

OLUBO: The history of Panyikwara says the people of Olubo came from Lokiliri (Lolubo). They were led by elder Wani, the grandson of chief Ambrosio, from Lolubo to Acholi (Panyikwara). This group got their name from the name,

"Lolubo". They, however, left out the letter "L", and called themselves "Olubo". They gave themselves this name to remind them of where they came from.

Elder Wani moved his people out of Lolubo, because of famine and war among the people of Lolubo. When elder Wani and his brother Lado, saw that many people were dying of hunger, and because of war among brothers, they gathered all the people of Olubo and started moving towards the south. Other elders of Goloba say Wani did not only move with his brother Lado, but with their sister Achola Latoo, and two boys named Iryem and Matidi whom he assigned to take care of their mother so that she would not fall as they were traveling.

PADEGI: The history of Panyikwara says the Padegi came from three different places and others came from Alur in Uganda. Other people came from Lopit, and others from Koyo Bira of chief Lotara. According to reports, the people of Padegi from these different places all came to Acholi of Sudan because of famine which hit the place years back.

GOLOGA HILLS AND HUNTING GROUNDS

Since time immemorial, Goloba has had three hunting grounds: Alwalaa, Wi-obur and Lomoti hunting grounds. The history of Panyikwaro says Alwalaa and Wi-obur hunting grounds belonged to Padegi. The Padegi later gave W-Obur hunting ground as compensation for a boy of Agoro-Bura, who was killed by Padegi during hunting. Lomoti hunting ground on the other hand belonged to Pajombo. The Pajombo also gave it to Olubo, to compensate for a boy of Olubo who was killed by an elephant during hunting in Lomoti hunting ground. This now proves to us that, for so long, Goloba had three hunting grounds, but now have two. They are Alwalaa, and Lomoti hunting grounds. A born of Padegi is responsible for inviting people to hunt in these hunting grounds. Goloba also has two hills: Lipul and Pa-Omer hills.

The history of Acholi says Goloba have one god named Mwonye, located in Kit. We now do not know the names of the people who used to take care of the shrine of Mwonye. But Acholi elders remember Alirinyang and Okwir as the new people who tended the shrine of Mwonye. People say elder Alirinyang was the first to take care of Mwonye's shrine. After his death, Okwir was left in charge of the shrine, a task he performs to-date.

Elder Gerelimo Mamur Odelfere told me that Mwonye's shrine is always celebrated in January of every year. Whenever it is time to tend to the shrine, three elders get a male sheep, and local brew and take it to the shrine. On reaching the shrine, the elders slaughter the sheep, cook it and eat. The left overs of the food and the utensils used for cooking are left at the shrine.

Acholi tradition prohibits the cooking or roasting of the head of a sheep sacrificed for a god. The elders leave the head of the sheep and some local brew at the shrine. After they have finished eating, they then head home. They do not take back home the utensils used for cooking that same day. The utensils are left at the shrine overnight and the next morning, an elder goes back to get them. They return the utensils home to help them in the next annual ceremony. The utensils are kept in a safe place. The elders of Goloba say when the three elders leave the shrine, huge and small snakes alike then come out to eat the left-over food and drink the local brew at the shrine.

Many descendants of Panyikwara say Mwonye is a very important god to the Goloba. So the god is not respected only by Goloba or Panyikwara. Everyone who hunts in Alwalaa must honor it. Mwonye, which is in Alwalaa hunting ground, always gives heavy punishment to those who disrespect it. For instance, Mwonye beat the people of Bar around the year 1986, when they wanted to grab Alwalaa hunting ground from Goloba. When Goloba saw that Bar were fighting over Alwalaa, they sent a message to Okwir, who was also a care taker of Mwonye's shrine, and he was the one who invites people to go hunting in Alwalaa hunting ground. When elder Okwir received the message, he was angered by the actions of Bar. He subsequently blew his hunting horn and that very night wild edible rats started eating millet from the gardens of Bar people.

In the history of Panyikwara, the edible rats did not only eat millet, but they bit the chicken of the people of Bar from their homes. This incident was to prove to Bar that Alwalaa does not belong to them. When Bar saw that wild edible rats were eating millet and biting chicken, they were embarrassed. They then started looking for ways to settle the issue. Fortunately, sir (teacher) Emeliano Lo'del of Pajombo, who was born in Jok-Okir (Ayii), and grew up with his mother's kin, was still living with his mother's kin. Emiliano Lo'del visited Goloba many times, which gave him the opportunity to learn how Goloba appeased Mwonye, when issues like this arose.

Emeliano went to Chief Koce Gumbiri, father of Loberia, who was the leader of Bar that year. Sir Emeliano then told him that, "Chief, you know very well that the people of Bar left Alwalaa hunting ground because of shortage of food and water, and the issue of children's education. Chief! Look at how the edible rats are destroying millet of your people from the gardens. The rats are also biting chicken from our compound. I know that all this is happening because of conflict over Alwalaa hunting ground. I now beg you that if possible, you settle the dispute over Alwalaa hunting ground for the sake of peace among the people of Bar and Goloba. Your people should get a male sheep and give the elders of Goloba for them to cleanse Alwalaa hunting ground."

Chief Koce Gumbiri also witnessed how the edible rats were destroying the property of Bar. When Chief Koce Gumbiri heard this message from sir Emelaino, he agreed and gave a male sheep to Okwir, as Emeliano instructed. Elder Okwir received the male sheep and slaughtered it and cleansed Alwalaa hunting ground. That very night, the edible rats stopped destroying crops and biting the chicken of Bar.

PALIWA

Paliwa have seven small families; *Oligo, Pacar, Palokiri, Paradwong, Palii, Panyijo* and *Ang-gu*. We believe that all these seven families in Paliwa, came from different places. But the history of Acholi of Sudan does not reveal where the seven families came from.

As we said in previous pages, the war led by John Garang De Mabior caused a lot of destruction, which hindered me from getting elders of Paliwa. The history of a certain family needs to be told by elders of that particular family. I am still hoping that we shall get a lot of information on the history of Paliwa in the Second Edition of The history and Impressive Cultures of the Acholi of Sudan.

PALIWA HUNTING GROUNDS AND HILLS

The elders of Panyikwaro told me that Paliwa have two hunting grounds: Ng-goyo and Okiye hunting grounds. The Palabek of Panyikwara built in Ng-goyo hunting ground but a child from the family of Palokiri is assigned to invite people to hunt in this hunting ground. We do not know the names of former and current people who used to call people to come hunting in Ng-goyo. Okiye is the second hunting ground of Paliwa, however, the history of

Panyikwara does not divulge details of people who own Okiye hunting ground. So we also do not know the names of those who invite hunters to Okiye. Every family member of Oyira built in Okiye hunting ground because they are in-laws of Paliwa. Paliwa have one hill named Iwire, and one god named Iwire. It seems a born of Palokiri is responsible for taking care of this shrine.

OYIRA

Oyira have four small families; *Gem, Pamurie, Pakwac* and *Paratik.*

Gem, Pamurie and Pakwac: The history of Acholi says the family members of Gem, Pamurie and Pakwac all came from Lamogi Gulu-Uganda. The chief of Lamogi brought these families to Panyikwara. Clan elders do not know why Lamogi of Panyikwara left Gulu. But they say when Lamogi entered Panyikwara, and found other people of Panyikwara at Iwire Hill. This year, Chief Gitala was on the throne and warmly welcomed elder Lamogi and his group and gave them a piece of land to build and grow crops. When Lamogi went to Panyikwara, they later split into three small families: Gem, Pamurie and Pakwac. They did not build at Iwire Hills, but at Ajuni Hill, which was given to them by Chief Gitala. From Ajuni Hill, Oyira relocated along a road because this year, the British constructed a road from Pageri to Torit.

According to Crazzolara, the first home of Lamogi was in Turguturu Hill in Bunyoro. From Turguturu Hill, Lamogi shifted to Agoo Hill. We also do not know where the hill is located, but we assume it is in Bunyoro. Later, they crossed River Kiir (River Nile) and came to Kilak Hill in Atyak. From here, they went and built along Ayugi Stream where Lamogi of Uganda are still living (Crazzolara, 1950, P, 87). After a short time, Lamogi split, other people went to the west, while others went northwards and others remained in Panyikwara (Madi), while other members of Lamogi continued to Pajok (Crazzolara, 1954, P, 333).

Paratik; The elders of Panyikwara told me that Paratik fell from above (from heaven). The legen of Paratik goes like this: one day, the children of Lamogi set fire on the grass in a garbage pit near the compound. When the rubbish in the pit was burning, the smoke emanating from the fire went towards heaven. The history of Panyikwara says that time, there was a man and woman who lived in heaven. When the man saw the smoke, coming from earth towards them in heaven, he wanted to know where the smoke was coming from. The man decided to pick his wife, and child who was about three to four months, and they entered the smoke, which then started pulling them towards the earth. Shortly, their feet touched the ground. When the man, his wife and child fell on the compound, the people of Lamogi who were standing near the rubbish pit where astonished, and others said, "Something which fell from above, these people can be evil spirits." The people immediately gathered to witness the miracle man and his wife who fell from heaven. The people of Lamogi gradually understood that the 'things' which fell from above are indeed humans. The elders of Panyikwara told me that the woman had a child aged between three to four months; unfortunately, she forgot and left her baby's strap in heaven. After three days, the woman cut some grass, made a big heap and set it alight. When the grass was burning, she entered the smoke that was going up, and it took her back to heaven. The history of Panyikwara says the woman went back alone, leaving her child with the father. She never returned from heaven.

Since the people of Lamogi believed that the man was a real human being, they did not chase him and his child. They gave him a piece of land to build and farm. The man built among the people of Gem, Pamurie and Pakwac. Since the people also knew that the man's wife did not return from heaven, they gave him a woman to marry, and they produced many children. When the child had become an adult, the Lamogi married for him a wife and he also produced many children. The Lamogi eventually named the family of this man "Jo Paratik," (the people of Paratik) which means, the people who fell from up. This also shows us how the family of Paratik from the home of Oyira came to be.

Some elders of Oyira also told me that for a long time, the people of Gem, Pamurie and Pakwac used not to intermarry. But when Paratik multiplied in the family of Oyira, they started marrying the girls and boys of Gem, Pamuire and Pakwac. Later, the clan elders saw that such intermarriage was indecorous among the members of Oyira, because the four families in Oyira were like brothers and sisters. For this reason, the clan elders of Oyira set a tough rule, that any young man or woman intending to marry, should get a partner from another family, but not Oyira. The rule was strictly followed. That is why, today, the descendants of Oyira do not intermarry. The members of Oyira also have one tradition they follow when celebrating the birth of a child.

Oyira hunting ground and hill

Oyira have one hunting ground called Ajuni. The hunting ground was given by Chief Gitala to Gem in the year they reached Panyikwara. They also have one god called Lori. A born of Gem is responsible for inviting people to hunt in Ajuni. He also takes care of the shrine of Lori, which is located in Ajuni hunting ground. If you want to understand more about Lori, read chapter twenty four of the book, "The Traditional Religion of Acholi."

AYOM

Ayom have three small families; Ombira, Paju and Bura.

Ombira, Paju and Bura: The history of Acholi says the family members of Ombira, Paju and Bura all came from Koyo (Obbo) around 1920. Reports say in this year, the Obbo had brought cattle to graze around Lotii Hill, because the pasture at the top of the hill was inadequate. Other elders of Obbo told me that when Obbo came under the hill, they split. Other people remained under the hill, while a few people started moving towards the west, till they arrived at Ayom Hill. The elders also told me that the people led by elder Pido-moi, son of Omini, were the ones who went to Ayom Hill. The people of Pido-moi stayed at Ayom Hill for about a decade.

But Crazzolara said the members of Ayom came from Seresere Hill, south of Lolubo (Lokoya). The place is now called "Lolubo Hills". From here, the members of Ayom of Panyikwara separated from the main group and went to Ayom Hill. But, if we ask the children of Ayom where they came from, their immediate response is that they came from Bar. It seems in the past, it was difficult to locate the borders of Bar, Lokoya and Madi because there were no boundaries. The people of Ayom left Lolubo because they wanted to be chief. Keny and his brother Obeny were the ones who led the people of Ayom to Ayom Hill. That is also where the Ayom people of live.

In the year 1931 chief Acok was the leader of Ayom. The history of Acholi says in the year 1936, the people of Ayom separated. Some people remained in Ayom Hill, while many went under the leadership of Keny and his brother Obeny. They left Ayom Hill and went eastwards, and built at Lotii Hill, in Obbo. Other members of Ayom on the other hand went to Imotong Hill (Crazzolara, 1954, PP, 398-399).

But the history of Acholi says while at Ayom Hill, Pido-moi, produced three sons; Ayom, Bira and Obalo, with different women. Around the year 1930, Madi Opari Iriwa was killing the people of Ayom, so they came down and Pido-moi went and built in Katire-Ayom, to the East of Iwire Hill. When the three boys had become adults, Pido-moi assigned them tasks. He gave Bira and his brother Obalo the task to guard the border and watch for looming enemies, while Ayom was assigned the task of grazing cattle, sheep and goats. The mothers of Bira and Obalo died barely two years after Pido-moi had finished giving the assignments to his children. So Pido-moi was left with one wife, the mother of Ayom.

One day, Bira and Obalo went very far away to check the border of their land. When they returned home, exhausted, and hungry, they found that the mother of Ayom had given all the food and milk to her son, Ayom. The two brothers were so angry with their step mother's spitefulness, yet they could not tell her. Bira and Obalo then reported the matter to their father, who became unhappy on hearing the news.

The actions of Ayom's mother put Bira and Obalo in deep thought to go back to Obbo. Early in the morning, Bira and Obalo started moving to Obbo without saying good bye to their father. When Bira and Obalo reached Koyo (Obbo), they were warmly received and they continued looking after the border. So one day, Obalo went to check the eastern side of the border, and met a family called Isore. When the members of Isore saw Obalo, they immediately thought he wanted to steal their cattle, they arrested him and told him that, "You will not go back home in Obbo."

The members of Isore also kept asking Obalo many questions. Luckily, he had not forgotten the Koyo dialect. He understood all the members of Isore were discussing among themselves. The Isore have their different language, but this time, they were speaking in Koyo dialect. They asked Obalo in koyo dialect and he did not answer even a single question. He acted like a deaf-mute, and started responding using signs and nods (body language). When the members of Isore saw this, they realized that they would not get any information from Obalo, so they said, "You will not go back to Obbo, since you cannot give us any sensible information."

The Isore then thought the best way to get information from Obalo, would be to give him a girl. So they gave him a very beautiful girl, whose name we do not know. Before she met Obalo, the elders emphasized that she should do whatever Obalo wanted from her, but not heed to his sexual advances. Whenever the elders give such orders to their girls, they would listen. The elders of Panyikwara and Obbo told me that the girl worked at Obalo's place for three months, and they used to sleep in one hut. They also told me that the girl kept telling the elders that Obalo used to ask her for sex every night, but she would refuse. The Acholi have a saying that, "A leopard cannot sleep together with a goat." Truly, in the fourth month, she could not bear Obalo's insistence, and decided to give in. The history of Acholi does not divulge if the girl slept with Obalo only once, but many people think after their first sexual encounter, the girl continued having sex with Obalo every night.

The girl did not reveal that Obalo penetrated her, but after three weeks, the elders of Isore realized that the girl was pregnant. The clan elders were shocked at the news, and some people decided that Obalo should be killed. Other elders however, refused the idea, and instead suggested that Obalo should marry the girl. One evening, the clan elders called Obalo around the bonfire, and told him that, "Child, we have noticed that the girl we put under your care is pregnant. Do you know that you impregnated the girl?" Since Obalo was acting deaf, he held his chest with both hands and lowered his head before the elders. In Acholi, when someone holds their chest and lowers their head, it means they acknowledge the information and admit that they are guilty.

Obalo then kept pointing towards Lotii Hill, to try and communicate to the elders of Isore that he has cattle at Lotii Hill. The elders understood Obalo's communication, and they chose three boys to escort Obalo to Obbo. The elders of Obbo told me that when Obalo reached home, he called his brothers and the clan elders, and told them that, "My people! Four months ago, when I went to check our land border, I met a family called Isore, who refused that I should come back home, because they thought I wanted to steal their cattle. Later they gave me a girl and I had sex with her, and she has conceived. The Isore now want me to marry the girl. I was also telling them that my paternal relatives have cattle in Koyo. This is why they allowed me to come back home to you. When Bira heard the story from his brother, he became happy, and gave fifty cows to be taken to the Isore.

The three boys from Isore led the cattle to their elders. When Obalo reached Isore with the fifty cattle, the elders became happy and they told Obalo that, "Child, we are grateful for what you have done. You can now stay with your wife, in any place of your choice." Shortly, Obalo and his wife went and built in Gicenge.

AYOM HUNTING GROUND AND HILL

The history of Panyikwara says when Ayom remained in Katire-Ayom, the chief of Panyikwara took Kata-kata hunting ground and gave it to Ayom. Ayom have one hunting ground and one hill called Ayom.

PAKALA

The Pakala have four small families; Pakala P'Akila (Lok-War), Pakala P'Ogoo, Pakala-pa-min Abwong and Pakala-Bule. The history of Acholi says the Pakala P'Akila came from Koyo (Obbo), while the other three families of Pakala P'Ogoo, Pakala-pa-min Abwong and Pakala-Bule all came from Lokung-Uganda. The history of Panyikwara also reveals that the family of Pakala P'Akila has other three smaller families: Panyuluk, Baralong and Bura P'Akila. The family of Pakala P'Ogoo also has four other small families: Bura, Panyabongo, Kwoko and Mujigi. For many years, the Pakala used not to intermarry, except the families of Bura P'Ogoo and Kwoko. But currently, the Pakala intermarry.

As we saw above, the Pakala P'Akila came from Koyo (Obbo). They relocated from Obbo because of famine which killed many people in Koyo. The elders of Obbo and Panyikwara told me that elder Lopiria, who some people call Juju, was the one who first led the Pakala P'Akila from Koyo to Lokung in Uganda. They went and settled among their brothers in Lokung. The history of Acholi says the brothers of Pakala P'Akila, who were in Lokung-Uganda, are Pakala-Bule, Pakala-pa-min-Abwong and Pakala P'Ogoo. The members of these three families warmly welcomed Pakala P'Akila and gave them land to build and farm.

Around 1910, elder Opira fell ill and he later died of the disease in Lokung. After the death of Lopiria, Akila, a born of Aru-Lolubo who grew up in the family of Pakala-Bule, became the chief. Later, the members of Lopiria named themselves Jo-*Pakala P'Akila*, which means the group of *Akila*.

Around the year 1920, the family of Pakala P'Akila, Pakala P'Ogoo and Pakala-pa-min Abwong moved away from Lokung, leaving behind the Pakala-Bule in Lokung. The history of Panyikwara says before the three families left Lokung, Chief Agwayo Nyamatira, who was fondly called Agwayo-Cwar-Nyare, of Pakala P'Ogoo, elder Akila of Pakala P'Akila and mother of Abwong of Pakala-pa-min-Abwong went to give a message to Pakala-Bule. The three told the people of Pakala-Bule that, "Very well our brothers, we are going to roam in other places, and if we get a good place then you will be notified by the sound of a drum."

Early in the morning, when the sun was rising, the members of Pakala P'Akila, Pakala P'Ogoo and Pakala-pa-min-Abwong started moving towards the West. Chief Agwayo Nyamatira was the one who gave the people directions. That evening, they reached Palabek of Uganda where they rested for a week. From here, the Pakala P'Akila and Pakala P'Ogoo continued moving towards the north, and they crossed river Atebi, in Sudan, and they settled at the shores of Atebi River. P'Akila and the group of Agwayo Nyamatira realized that the shores of river Atebi was suitable for farming, so they built there. After a short time, the members of P'Akila and Nyamatira remembered that they promised the Pakala-Bule, that if they found a good place they would sound a drum. Truly that very night, the boys sounded the drum for almost three hours. Fortunately, the wind was blowing towards the direction of Lokung. So the people of Pakala-Bule heard the sound of the drum, and they immediately understood that their brothers, who left them in Lokung have found a better place. When the people of Pakala finished building on the shores of Atebi, they named the place "Owiny-ki-bul". To date, the place is called Owiny-ki-bul. In the year 1964-1974, Owiny-ki-bul became the Headquarters of Anyanya Movement. Gen. Lt. Colonel and Commander of Anyanya Army, Joseph Lagu lived here.

The elders of Acholi told me that the P'Akila and Agwayo Nyamatira did not live long here. Around the year 1924, they relocated to Lang-gir, and stayed there for almost three years: 1924-1927. They later shifted to Mede (Iwire hills), where other people of Panyikwara where residing. The land in Mede was not suitable for growing crops that is why famine hit the area in 1932. The famine made people in Mede to scatter in different places. When the members of Pakala P'Akila saw that people were leaving Iwire Hill, they also decided that they could not move together with Pakala P'Ogoo. For this reason, the people of Pakala P'akila turned their shoes facing the opposite direction, so that the Pakala P'Ogoo could not locate them. When the Pakala P'Ogoo saw that the foot marks of the Pakala P'Akila was going backwards, they thought that Pakala

P'Akila were also going southwards, yet they were going north wards. The Pakala P'Akila went and built in Abara. When the Pakala P'Ogoo saw this, they concluded that the people of P'Akila did not want to move with them. So the Pakala P'Ogoo went back and built in Lang-gir. They stayed here until 1964, and they were displaced because of the war commanded by Joseph Lagu (Anyanya).

In the year 1964, the Pakala P'Ogoo fled to Uganda, while the Pakala P'Akila took refuge in Kit in Sudan. After the signing of the peace agreement, between the government of Sudan and Anyanya in Addisa Ababa Ethiopia in 1973, the Pakala P'Akila then continued living in Kit. This also explains why Pakala P'Akila is still in Kit.

In the year 1973, after the signing of the peace accord in Addisa Ababa, the Pakala P'Ogoo left the refugee camp in Uganda and built in Owiny-ki-bul in 1985. The war led by John Garang De Mabior later again made the people of Pakala P'Ogoo to run back to Uganda.

RAIN POT OF THE PAKALA
The history of Panyikwara says Chief Agwayo Nyamatira of Pakala, came with his rain stone. After the death of Chief Nyamatira, the rain remained in the hands of his son, Ipira. Then after the death of Chief Ipira, the rain remained under the care of Daniel Lokolong-go. Chief Daniel Lokolongo-go, still has the rain.

PAKALA HUNTING GROUNDS AND HILLS
The Pakala have four hunting grounds: Gulubu, Kiliemu, Lalworo-Odong and Cwar-nyare hunting grounds. When I was interviewing the people of Obbo and Panyikwara, I found that the Pakala and Obbo were fighting over Lalworo-odong hunting ground. Each of the two families built on either side of the hunting ground. I also think that the Obbo also know that if someone builds in another person's hunting ground, it does not mean that the person should grab the land from the owner. The history of Acholi says, Lalworo-odong hunting ground belongs to Pakala. The elders of Panyikwara, who I interviewed about the four hunting grounds of Pakala, do not know the names of the people who used to invite people to hunt in these hunting grounds. But other Acholi believe that a man from Pakala P'Akila, should be the person to invite hunters to these hunting grounds. The Pakala also have two hills; Ikwala and Pa-langu hills in Omeo. All the two belongs to the Pakala P'Akila.

NG-GAYA

The people of Ng-gaya have four small families: Pa-Lotikaru, Pa-lokecamoi, Pamea and Pa-logulu. All the four families in Ng-gaya home stead all came from Wipaco in Bar-el-Ghazel. The family members left Bar-el-Ghazel because of the division among the Lwo who were in Wi-paco. The history of Acholi of Sudan says Cakalicio and his brother Ocilo were the ones who led the people of Ng-gaya from Wipaco. Reports show that when the Ng-gaya left Bar-el-Ghazel, they first settled in Tombur in Bar (southern Bar). In this year, Chief Kenyi was the leader of the Tombur. He then welcomed Cakalicio and his groups, and gave them land to build and cultivate on.

The elders of Panyikwara told me that the group of Cakalicio and Ocilo were very hard working. They used to engage a lot in farming, hunting and fishing. The hard work of the people of Cakalicio made the people of Bar very angry. The people of Bar loved to eat mangoes and vegetables because they did not have many varieties of food crops. But when the Ng-gaya settled in Tombur, they cultivated different food crops like millet, sorghum, potatoes, and groundnuts and they had a bumper harvest.

The history of Panyikwara says the people Ng-gaya came with cattle, goats, sheep and lonaka (camels). The people of Bar then concluded that if they allowed the Ng-gaya to stay for many years in their land, they would one day take over their home/land. This imagination caused a lot of hatred among the people of Kenyi and Cakalicio.

When Cakalicio saw that the relationship between Bar and Ng-gaya was getting worse, they took their people out of Tombur. They started moving towards the south, till they reached Opari. This year, the people of Pambil were living in Opari under the leadership of chief Kenyi. The elders of Ng-gaya told me that the people of Ng-gaya did not settle in the home of Opari, but built at a distance among the Pambil. Later on, the people of Pambil located the people of Ng-gaya by emanating smoke. When Chief Kenyi saw the smoke, he sent his messengers to find out how the fire started.

The boys of Pambil then ran where the smoke was, and found the group of Cakalicio and Ocilo. The messengers of Chief Kenyi then asked Cakalicio and Ocilo that, "where did you come from?" Cakalicio, being the eldest son of Ocilo, responded that, "We came from Tombur in Bar." When the leader of the messengers heard that the Ng-gaya came from afar, he told Cakalicio, "Very well, since you are still new in the area, I want you to know that this home is not safe, because there are people who like moving in twos, and they have many times killed women, children, men and even the aged. They even raid property and take it to their homes."

Elder Cakalicio was a wise man, so he asked the Pambil man, "What do these people use to attack you? And what do you use to fight them back? The Pambil man responded that, "These people fight us using spears and shields, but we fight them using logwete (soft flexible stick that people put mud on, and thrown around, to scare birds from the fields) because we do not have spears." Elder Cakalicio again asked the Pambil that, "What time do these attackers come to fight you?" The Pambil answered that, "The attackers come any time they choose." When Cakalicio understood that the attackers came at any time to fight the Pambil, he then told the Pambil that, "If the attackers come, you inform me, and I will know what to do to them."

After a few days, the attackers who moved in twos were coming to stab the people, and then the children of Pambil quickly sent a message to Cakalicio. When the Pambil reached Cakalicio with the message, they narrated to him, "We have heard that the attackers we told you about are on their way coming,"

When Cakalicio got the message, he immediately gathered the people of Ng-gaya to go and help the Pambil to fight the impending attackers. The members of Ng-gaya picked bows and arrows and joined the Pambil. Shortly, the fighters engaged in a fierce battle at sunrise in Opari. The history of Panyikwara says the Pambil hit their enemies with logwete as they used to do in the past, but the group of Cakalicio fought the enemies using bows and arrows.

Many members of Cakalicio and Pambil died in the fight, but the enemies lost more people. The enemies thought the Pambil would continue using logwete to fight them. But when they continued fighting, they realized that the Pambil were stronger than usual. Reports indicate that the enemies did not even know what bows and arrows were, and they remarked, "What kind of bee sting makes people bleed? We fought with the Pambil several times, but there were no insects which could bite like this." When the commander of the enemies saw that his people were being killed in multitudes like bees being burned in a hive, he told the surviving warriors to stop the fight. The enemies stopped fighting and turned their backs. The fighters of Cakalicio chased them between hills. We however do not know the name of the hills. The enemies fled and left behind the people they hand captured during the fight, and the wounded.

When the people of Cakalicio came back from the hills, he instructed Katilitua (arm-forces/soldiers) to bring the prisoners of war and the wounded. Katilitua (soldiers) brought the wounded and those who were captured during the attack to Cakalicio. Cakalicio then told them that, "We were fighting you without knowing where you came from. Where do you come from?" Then one of the prisoners responded that, "We are the Ayom. We came from Katire-Ayom." The history of Panyikwara says when Cakalicio understood that the attackers were from Ayom, he tasked Katilitua to send them back to their detention cell, while those who were wounded were to be given treatment so that they get well. Katilitua took back the prisoners, and they treated those who were wounded. The elders of Panyikwara told me that some of the wounded people of Ayom recovered from their wounds, but others died.

One day, Cakalicio again summoned the prisoners (Ayom) who were in a detention cell and told them, "I want you to know that if anyone among you wants to go home, we shall allow them to go. But there are conditions that any of you who wants to go back home must fulfill. First, if one of you goes back home, I do not want to see them coming back to wage war against the Pambil. Secondly, one who has already gone back home should tell members of Ayom at home that they should abandon the idea of coming back to fight the Pambil. And thirdly, I want to tell you that if any of you wants to stay with us, they can live with us like brothers."

When the people of Ayom heard what Cakalicio said, they split into two groups. Others went back home, while others decided to live with the Pambil. Cakalicio then ordered Katilitua to release the members of Ayom who wanted to go back home. They also put those who wanted to remain behind, under the leadership of Cakalicio.

Ten months after the fight, Cakalicio and Ocilo informed the Pambil that they wanted to continue moving. When the Pambil heard that Cakalicio and Ocilo wanted to leave them, they were sad. For this reason, the Pambil told Cakalicio and Ocilo, "You cannot leave this place, because your people saved us from being killed."

The Pambil also did not know where Cakalicio and Ocilo came from. An elder of Pambil then asked Cakalicio, "Where did you come from, since you are as many as bel-ng-gaya (sorghum)?

Cakalicio responded that since you have stated it yourself that we are many like bel-ng-gaya (swarms of bees), we are the people of Ng-gaya." This is how the people who came from Barh El Ghazal or Wi-paco got the name. Reports indicate that the Ng-gaya came from Wi-paco bearing the name Lwo, and they later got the name Ng-gaya, as we have seen above.

The Pambil added that, "You people of Cakalicio and Ocilo, we will not allow you to leave us. To show our gratitude to you, we are going to give you land to build and plant crops. Additionally, we shall also give you a girl." When elder Cakalicio heard about the girl, he responded that, "If you give us a girl, she will be only for one person. If I take the girl, what shall I give to my brother, Ocilo? So I do not want a girl, but land so that we all live together."

The Pambil responded, "My brother, the members of Ayom finished our people. You are the ones who brought for us peace. Since you are in need of land, we have enough land and hunting grounds. I now give you land and Opari hunting ground." Elder Cakalicio was very happy to hear such a response and then told the Pambil that, "Since you have given me Opari hunting ground, we also want to know the boundary of the hunting ground."

The Pambil answered, "The border of Opari hunting ground ends at Langengo (Lotuturu) Stream in the north. While to the west, it ends at Kerepi, and in the south the border is at Nyako Stream, (which is at the border of Ng-gaya and Madi). To the East, the border is at Erebi in Ayom Hill (so the other side of Ayom belongs to the Ng-gaya, while the other side of the hill belongs to the Ayom).

When the two had been given land and a hunting ground, elder Cakalicio told his brother, "Well my brother, since we now have land, I want you and your people to build in the land towards the North, while my people and I will build in the south." Ocilo did not take Cakalicio's instructions in good faith, because he knew that the land to the north was hilly and unsuitable for cultivation, but the land to the south, which Cakalicio gave his people, was the fertile one. This matter caused a lot of disagreement between Ocilo and his brother.

Ocilo then told his brother, "If that is the issue, then I cannot live with you in this land. We came together from Jur in Bar-el-Ghazel; we also fought together.

Then why should we split over land dispute? My people and I will now continue moving, and we shall leave you with your land of Opari."

Cakalicio responded, "If you want to continue moving, I do not have any issue against you. Secondly, if any one wants to go with you, they are free because we are one."

The next morning elder Ocilo gathered his people and they started traveling towards the south till they reached Atiak. When the children of Atiak saw the group of Ocilo, they sent a message immediately to Chief Awic. When Chief Awic heard that some people were coming from the north, he went to meet their leader. When he reached where the people had settled, he asked them, "Elder Ocilo, where did you come from and where are you heading?"

Ocilo responded, "Am looking for a place for my people to settle."

When Chief Awic realized that Ocilo was looking for land to settle, he gave him land, from the compound of Atiak up to river Onyamo. The people of Ocilo shortly started building huts and planting crops and they later named the place *Pa-cilo*. Up to now, the people in Atiak call the place *Pa-cilo*. The people of Ocilo then produced the members in Pa-cilo in Atiak (Uganda).

When Cakalicio saw that his brother had left him, he also left Opari and went to Pakwii, where the people of Ng-gaya started multiplying. The people of Cakalicio gradually split into four small families; Pa-mea, Pa-Lokecamoi, Pa-Lotikaru and Pa-Logulu. All the four families came about when the Ng-gaya were in Pakwii. The elders of Ng-gaya told me that the four small families currently in Ng-gaya started like this: —

1. Cakalicio begot Yongo, Yongo begot Lomena, Curukunga, Mindio and Mea. And Mea begot the family of Pa-mea.
2. Mindio begot Lokecamoi, and Lokecamoi begot Pa-Lokecamoi.
3. Lomena started Iyali and Oporo-kare (Pitia); Pitia gave birth to Loti-karu, while Lotikaru begot Pa-Lotikaru.
4. Curukunga begot Logulu; and Logulu begot Pa-Logulu.

This is how the four families of Ng-gaya came into being.

While in Pakwii the Ng-gaya kept on relocating to different places in their hunting ground of Opari. They later built in the middle of Opari hunting ground that is why the Ng-gaya remained in Opari hunting ground. But if we went to Opari today, we would find two groups of people living there: the Acholi and Madi. The issue is also causing tension among the Acholi and Madi, because the Madi say Opari is their home, yet the history of Acholi states that Opari is the home of the Nga-gaya (Panyikwara).

One day, I asked an elder of Panyikwara called Mamur Odelfere, how the Madi came to live in Opari? Mamur told me that the Madi came to Opari because of marriage, because in the past, Acholi boys where marrying Madi girls and Madi boys marry Acholi girls. Eventually, the Ng-gaya girls who were married to Madi boys then built among the relatives of their mothers, and these children came as cousins of Ng-gaya. But the history of Panyikwara also says other Madi came to Opari because of a school which was built in Nyakaning-gwa or for "Rural Council", which shifted to Opari in the year 1910. The people of Ng-gaya are the land owners of Opari.

NG-GAYA HILLS AND HUNTING GROUND

The Ng-gaya have one hunting ground called *Opari*, as we saw earlier. In the past, the hunting ground belonged to the Pambil, who later gave it to Ng-gaya, for helping the Pambil to fight off their attackers from Ayom. A child of Ng-gaya is responsible for inviting people to hunt in Opari. He also blesses the hunting ground. The Ng-gaya also have eight hills; *Opari, Motoyo, Arule, Remo, Nyii, Bana, Mugo* and *Akoli Hill*. Ng-gaya have one god called *Nyii*. This god lives in Nyii Hill. The history of Panyikwara says, one day, Nyii god covered young girls of Ng-gaya who loved to banter. The fable of the girls goes like this: One day, some young girls went to fetch water from a well at the foot of Nyii Hill. Usually when Acholi girls go to fetch water, they first wash their water pots and calabashes, so that they take home clean water. Truly when the girls were scrubbing their calabashes, the god appeared to them. The god requested the girls, "Give me water to drink, I am thirsty." Majority of the girls who heard the god's request refused to give water. They thought that if they gave water to the god using their clean calabash, it would make their calabashes dirty again. But one girl among them used her clean calabash and gave water to the god. The other girls were annoyed with the girl who gave water to the god. Each of them carried their water and started telling her, "Since you have made the god to soil your calabash we will leave you at the well to clean your calabash. You will get us on the way." The girls then carried their water and started going back home, and the other girl remained, washing her calabash.

Before the girls had moved far, and before the girl who remained had finished washing her calabash, the god came and told her, "You should not follow those girls who have already gone, take another path."

When the girl finished washing her calabash, she took another path as the god had instructed her. A moment later *ajuru* (strong wind blowing in circle) came from NyiiHill and covered all the girls who refused to give him water. The girl who took another path saw what was happening to the other girls. The girl saw ajuru covering the other girls and reported the matter to elders, "Nyii has swallowed the girls I went with to fetch water."

The people of Ng-gaya respect Nyii very much. The history of Ng-gaya says the first person to take care of Nyii was elder Iyali. After the death of Iyali the god was taken care of by Logulu, and Lokecamoi took over after the death of Logulu. After the death of Lokecamoi, Mea took care of the god. After Mea died, Igeri was left in charge of the god. When Igeri died, Okec was put in charge of the god, a task he is performing to date.

PALABEK

The history of Acholi says the people of Palabek came from Tali in Mundari. When the people of Palabek where still in Mundari, they used to live in a placed called Anyumaru (Lula). The people of Mundari loved to hunt here—it seems the word *Lula* in Mundari dialect means a good hunting ground. The Palabek left Tali because of intense sunshine which scotched all the crops in the gardens.

Many people of Mundari have cattle, sheep and goats, so when famine hits the place they survive on cows' milk. But there were a few people who did not own cattle. When we were looking for information on the history of Acholi of Sudan, we found that the Palabek are among those who owned few cattle. That is why many of them were killed by famine in the year 1775, because the cows could not produce enough milk for all the women, men and children.

When Chief Combek and elder Kuki saw many people dying of starvation, they convened a meeting and Chief Combek was told the people, "Well, our people, as you have witnessed by yourselves, famine is killing many people. What do you think? Can we take the women and children where there is food?"

When the members heard the concern, they responded, "Chief we have witnessed everything with our own eyes, our people are dying of hunger. We think the issue you have raised is very important, because if we continue living in Mundari, our tribe will be wiped out. We should take the women and children to another land."

Chief Combek then told the gathering that if that was the case then, each of them should go back home and inform his wife to pack food for traveling. He then asked all of them to gather at the venue of the meeting the following morning, with the women and children, and their packed food, ready to start moving. That evening, each man went back to his family and told his wife all what the chief had instructed. In the night the women prepared food, while the men filled gourds with water to help during the journey, since there were no water sources in some places. But the people did not know where the chief wanted to take them. The people of Palabek did not tell the other members of what they had in mind, because they were afraid that if other people knew that they wanted to relocate, they would pursue them and raid their cattle.

The next morning, everyone gathered in a kraal next to the home of chief Combek. After a short time, they started moving and reached Bar after three days. They settled here temporarily for a few months, and later continued moving till they reached Aruu Hill in Lolubo. The Palabek lived here for almost two years and later realized that the land of Lolubo was not good for cultivating the varieties of crops they wanted.

The history of Panyikwara says from Aruu Hill, the Palabek split. Majority of them went to Chief Combek, while some few went to Kuki. The people who went to Chief Kuki were the Palabek of Sudan. While those who followed Chief Combek were the Palabek of Uganda. We do not know why the Palabek separated from Aruu Hill. The two groups then started moving in different routes. To better understand how these people moved, I want us to first see how the Palabek of Sudan left Aruu Hill and reached where they currently live. Later, we shall then see how Palabek of Uganda left Aruu Hill, and how they reached their location in Uganda.

Elder Kuki took the Palabek of Sudan from Aruu Hill and they started moving towards the south, for almost ten days before reaching Iwire Hill. Here they found the other members of Panyikwara already settled. In this year, Chief Gitala was the leader of the Panyikwara who were at Iwire Hill. He warmly welcomed Kuki and his group and gave them land to build and cultivate crops.

One elder of Panyikwara told me that the Palabek were devoted farmers.

When they got land, they started building and planting varieties of crops. For this reason, after only a year of planting crops, famine was no more. The Palabek then split into six small families; Miteng, Paleny, Paguta, Bura-Adiemu, Paco-Olwal and Gem, and they named themselves Bar P'Aremo. Reports say life was easy for the Palabek at Iwire Hill because they united with everyone. After a short time, the girls and boys started marrying from the family of Panyikwara. The Acholi have a proverb that, marriage multiplies tribe. Truly, the marriage solidified the relationship among other families who were not Palabek.

The other members of Palabek who remained at Aruu Hill were taken to Uganda by Chief Combek. They built in a land north west of Payiira near Acwa River. The border of the Palabek of Uganda and Sudan is in Madi-Moli and Pajok in Ngom Oromo. The history of Acholi says when the Palabek of Uganda reached the land they are in now, they found the Lango already settled on the land. This means the Lango (West Lango) are the owners of the land. After a few years, the Palabek put all the Lango under the leadership of Chief Combek. Crazzolara said, "When the Palabek reached their new place, much as they were few, they put back all the Lango under the leadership of Chief Combek. Gradually, they started intermarrying." (Crazzolara, 1954, P, 495)

When the Palabek got land for building and farming, they split into eight small families: —

Ongoto-nyare: The family members of Ongot-nyare are the royal family. Later, the family members of Pa-Uma, Pa-Dimo, Abwoc-bel pa Moaa and Palony separated from Ongoto-nyare, and they formed other small families. This explains why we have the families of Pa-Uma, Pa-Dimo, Abwoc-bel pa Moaa and Palony in the home of Ongoto-nyare. In Acholiland, if a man produces many children, he can split the families. It seems this is what the members of Ongoto- nyare did in the past. While the Pa-Koko, Ayu-alali and Lamwo built among the members of Ongoto-nyare serfs.

Abwoc-bel P'Layeng; the history of Acholi says, much as the members of Abwoc-bel P'Layeng, are one family in Palabek, they also originated from the family of Ongoto-nyare. Many Acholi elders told me that the people of Agoro who are currently in the family of Abwoc-bel P'Layeng, came from the north and built among Abwoc-bel P'Layeng serfs.

Gem-pa-wot-Gero: Reports show that in the year the Palabek entered where they are settled now, members chose Wot-Gero, who came from Mundari, as their chief, together with the Lango (the aboriginal group of Gem). Later they named themselves *Gem-pa-rwot-Gero*, which means the people of Chief Wot-Gero. Chief Wot-Gero had a brother, Loni. Later, Loni married a woman whose name we do not know, and they produced many children. Later, the children of Loni left and built in upland near the people of Gem-pa-wot-Gero serfs. This also explains why the Pa-Loni became one family in Gem-pa-wot-Gero. The history of Acholi says the Gem-pa-coto who came first in land where Gem-pa-wot-Gero built t and then came from Madi Opei. For this reason, we can now say, without doubt, that the people of Gem are the Lango, and also the land owners. The history of Acholi also says the Pakala came from (Opari) in South Sudan. They went and built among the Gem-pa-coto serfs, while the P'Abita also came from Bar. They built among the Pa-Loni serfs. This explains why currently, the Pakala in Palabek-Uganda and P'Abita became one family in Gem-pa-wot-Gero.

Labigiryam-pa-Iwon, much as the members of Labigiryam-pa-Iwon are currently the same family in Palabek, we find that all of them originated from Ongoto-nyare. Reports show that the pa-Lagoto or P'Atanga and P'Owila all came from Logwar in the south. They built among the Labigiryam-pa-Iwon serfs. While the Larubi came from Palaro and built among the Labigiryam-pa-Iwon serfs. This explains why the P'Atanga, P'Owil and Larubi became a family in Labigiryam-pa-Iwon, which is in Palabek.

Logwar-Pa-Ayote: The members of Logwar-Pa-Ayote also split from the people of Ongoto-nyare, because Ayote also saw that his people had become many. They therefore wanted to increase their families. When Ayote split from Ongoto-nyare, members then chose him to become chief, and they called themselves Logwar-Pa-Ayote.

The history of Acholi says when Chief Combek brought the Palabek in this land, they found the Orogo already settled here. When the members had chosen Chief Ayote, later, Chief Combek took the people of Orogo and put them under the leadership of chief Ayote. The people later called themselves Logwar P'Orogo. It seems Chief Combek also found the Pa-Iloo already settled in this land. Reports show that he also put them under the leadership of Chief Ayote. This is why people say the Pa-Iloo are the land owners. But the Madi-Pokony came much later from Bar and built among the Logwar serfs. This is why the family members of Logwar P'Orogo, Pa-Iloo and Madi-Pokony have become family members in Logwar-Pa-ayote in Palabek.

Ayu-Palabek or Ayu-Labooro: Shortly, the people of Chief Combek entered Palabek, since the people who came from Tali were many, people chose Ayu as chief to lead other people of Palabek together with Labooro. Later, this group called themselves Ayu-Palabek or Ayu-Labooro -which means the group of Chief Ayu. Labooro has a brother named Ladyang. Ladyang produced almost six sons; one of them was called Lema. LObboro's children also produced children, and named themselves Ladyang – which means the group of Ladyang. The people of Ladyang built among the people of Ayu-Palabek (Labooro). Later, people insulted the people of Lodyang that they were witches and wizards, because of the insults; they gradually changed their name to "Polojok", which means people who have magical powers, or sorcerers. In the year 1942, the people of Cobbo built among the Ayu-Labooro. This also proves to us how the Ladyang, (Polojok) and Cobbo became one family of Ayu-Palabek.

Pa-Dwat: The Pa-Dwat came from Madi. They were led by Chief Dwat to Palabek where they now live. The history of Acholi does not tell why the Pa-Dwat left Madi, but we assume that they left their land because of hunger. As we earlier saw in this book, many people left their land because of famine.

Paracelle: The Paracelle came later to Palabek, they came from Lokai (Madi). If we went to Paracelle, we would find that, much as they speak Acholi, they also speak Madi (Crazzolara, 1954 PP.)

PALABEK HILL AND HUNTING GROUNDS

The Palabek have two hunting grounds. They are Kugi and Maria hunting grounds. They also have one hill called Lokwenya. The Palabek have one god called Lokwenya which lives in Lokwenya Hill. The Palabek do not know the name of those who in the past invited hunters in these two hunting grounds. But people remember elder Edwardi, son of Adiemo. If you want to understand more about the Lokwenya, read chapter twenty four of the book, "Acholi Traditional Religion — Lokwenya god" page 404.

OLORO

The Oloro have nine small families: Bura, Cubo, Kilio, Pamulu, Monoteng, Cung-gura, Monoja, Kurula and Ogura (Lomberi).

Bura

The people of Bura came from Aruu (Lolubo). They were taken to the land of Acholi of Sudan by Chief Gac. The history of Panyikwara said Bura was the largest family in Lolubo. The Bura remember Chief Mogga as the first chief. Chief Mogga produced two sons, with two different mothers. One son is named Gac. We however, do not know the name of the other son.

One day, chief Mogga called the two boys to the house of the junior wife and told them that, "Very well children, the Acholi said no one knows when death will strike. if I die tomorrow, the rain stone will remain with you. The rain invoking power is selective. Whoever the rain stone fall in front of, should know that that is his rain. He should not disclose or show it to his mate. I want the person who will find this stone to keep it very well because that is his rain."

Chief Mogga died after a few years, and his son, Gac took over the throne. Sir Bernard Oring, of Oloro, told me that, a few months after the death of Chief Mogga, one rain stone fell in front of Chief Gac, and another rain stone also fell before his brother. Chief Gac and his brother were invoking rain for the people of Lolubo. Gradually, the people realized that it would rain more if Chief Gac invoked the rain, and their crops would yield better than when the rains were invoked by his brother. Later, all the people of Lolubo started respecting Chief Gac. When the brother of Chief Gac saw that everyone was showing respect to Chief Gac, he became sad. Many times when Chief Gac met his brother, they would exchange words. When Chief Gac saw the souring relationship between him and his brother, he called him and said, "Well my brother, you and I can no longer live in the same place. For this reason, I have concluded that we cannot stay with you, because, if we continue living together, then tomorrow death might occur among us. I don't want death to occur because we are children of the same man. So, I will leave you in my father's land and go to roam elsewhere. If the god that my father adores is powerful, then I will find a place to settle."

The next morning, Chief Gac left Lolubo with a few people and entered Acholi land. Reports show that Chief Gac left Lolubo around 1921. The history of Acholi says the people of Chief Gac found other people of Panyikwara still in Medee (Iwire Hill). Chief Gitala, of Panyikwara, warmly welcomed the people of Chief Gac and gave them land to settle and cultivate. The brother of Chief Gac remained in Lolubo with many people. Much as there was a disagreement between Chief Gac and his brother, the Bura who remained behind and those who went to Panyikwara still call themselves brothers and sisters.

The history of Oloro says the Bura were the first to come to Panyikwara among the other people of Oloro. The other families in the home of Oloro came later, and built among the Bura serfs.

Ogura

The people of Ogura came from two different places. Others came from Aruu (Lolubo), these where brothers and sisters of the people of Bura who had remained in Lolubo. While other people were brought by elder Ogwee, father of Yocam. They became cousins in Bar. They all built among the people of Bura. But other people claim that the Ogura were the first to come to Panyikwara. Others say it was the Oloro, and others say some members of Oloro came later and joined the Lomberi. The Ogura built among the Bura in Medee.

Some people however, say no one knows where the Ogura came from. While others think the Ogura fell from the sky on their tails, and that is why many people had fractured waist. The people who lived here then gathered those with fractured waist, and gave them land for building and farming. Later, the group named themselves Ogura, which means people who were gathered.

Pumulu

The family members of Pumulu came from Bar, under the leadership of elder Otoo. They joined the Oloro as slaves. Some Acholi elders told me that the Pumulu came to Acholi land around 1922-1923, and built among the Bura in Medee.

Cubo

The members of Cubo family came from Bar-Nyarubanga to Panyikwara, led by elder Ogeno Odire. Some people say the Cubo are cousins of Ogura who came to their maternal relatives. There is a strong bond between the Cubo and Ogura. That is why the girls and boys of Cubo and Ogura do not intermarry.

The history of Panyikwara says when the people of Oloro where in Medee, all of them were under the leadership of chief Otokare.

Kilio

The members of Kilio came from Lokayi (Madi), but they did not come from

Madi, the same way other members of Oloro or Panyikwara did. Reports show that many years ago, the children of the chief could marry the children of another chief, just like these days, the children of the rich also marry from the rich. The history of Panyikwara says one day, Chief Modu of Lokayi went to dance. Then he admired Luri, the daughter of Chief Otokare of Oloro. Acholi tradition says if a chief admired a girl, the girl should not turn him down. After a short time, Chief Modu married Luri with at least twenty or more heads of cattle. Chief Modu also had another wife, who was a Madi. God blessed the wives of Chief Modu with many children, and the children also produced many children.

In Acholi, if a man sees that a woman does not know how to take care of her home, he concentrates on the one who knows how to keep her home well. In Acholi, taking care of the home means cooking good food, and welcoming visitors in an acceptable manner (like welcoming visitors with smiles). This is why the Acholi also have a saying that, "A man is won with the cooking pot."

Many Acholi elders told me that Luri was hard working like her mother, because a girl learns how to do domestic chores from her mother's house. Luri then went and worked hard in Madi, just as she used to work hard while at her mother's house. Acholi, women, unlike the women of Madi, always like to cook varieties of food, so that the man can choose which one he likes most. Acholi women also like cooking dishes like malakwang, and food mixed with sesame or groundnut paste, ground pea sauce with shea oil, fried meat, pumpkin leave sauce and many other that I cannot write all here. They do not pour salt anyhow as women from other tribes do. This reminds me of what Chief Aburi of Obbo used to say whenever he tasted a well prepared meal, he would say, "This food as tasty as Ayany's mother's"– meaning, this woman knows how to cook, just like my wife, the mother of Ayany. Unfortunately, the eldest wife of Chief Modu did not know how to prepare tasty meals, and taking care of the home, so Chief Modu concentrated on his second wife, Luri.

When the eldest wife of Chief Modu saw that her husband was concentrating on her co-wife, she became envious and started killing her co-wife's children with poison. An elder of Oloro told me that after only one year, the eldest wife of Chief Modu had killed all the children of her co-wife.

When Luri saw that her co-wife had killed all her children, she also decided to revenge. Unfortunately, Luri did not have the poison, so she decided to stab her co-wife's children with a knife. One day, Luri picked a knife and stabbed her co-wife's child in the chest. Reports show that the mother of the child nursed her son's wound for three days, but the child died. When Luri realized that she had committed an offence, she was terrified and left her husband's home and went to her father's home in Oloro. That month, Luri was three months pregnant. After nine months, Luri gave birth to a boy in her father's home and named her son "Becu". When Chief Modu heard that Luri had given birth, he came to her father's home to reconcile with her. The history of Acholi and Madi say when a women runs back to her father's or brother's place, the husband should go after her, so that they discuss their contention. The clan elders always wished to know why a woman ran away from her husband's home.

When Chief Modu reached the compound of Oloro, he found boys and men thatching the granary of Chief Otokare. The children warmly welcomed Chief Modu. They made him sit under a granary shade which was next to the one they were thatching, and gave him water to drink.

Shortly, Luri who was in her mother's house abruptly saw her husband sitting under the granary shade. She shouted in a loud voice, "You children of Oloro, why do you allow this man to enter this home? Don't you remember that this man maltreated me when I was with him? Luri then fell down crying:

An Dooo, Coo Peke!	Poor me, there are no men!
An Dooo, Coo Peke!	Poor me, there are no men!
An Dooo, Coo Peke!	Poor me, there are no men!

When the boys heard their sister's cry, they became angry and each of them picked a stick (twigs of half dried opobo tree), which they were using to make the granary, and started beating Chief Modu.

When chief realized that he had had enough of the canes, he dashed looking for a hiding place. He ran to three different huts, but he could not enter them. The boys did not spare him and continued beating him. When the chief reached the fourth hut, he had had enough strokes of the cane, so he forced himself into the hut, which was also the hut of Luri's mother (Modu's mother-in-law's hut). Because he forced himself to enter the hut, he broke a chest bone.

When the boys saw that Chief Modu had entered his mother-in-laws hut, they did not follow him. But we do not know how the chief came out.

The next morning, a messenger, whose name we do not know sent a message to the people of Chief Modu saying, "The boys of Oloro fought your chief." When the elders of Madi heard the message, they convened a meeting and resolved, "The Madi must take three cattle to soothe chief Otokare." The Madi chose ten boys so that they take the fine to chief Otokare. Because according to Acholi tradition, if people annoy the chief, they must pay a fine to him with cattle or goats. The clan elders of Madi also instructed the boys, "As you go to the home of Oloro, if any child from that home wants to fight you, we do not want to hear that any one among you lifted a finger to fight back. If you finish giving the offering to the chief, we want you to ask him if he can give you Chief Modu".

Shortly, the boys of Madi walked to Panyikwara and took three cows as offering. When they reached the home of the Oloro, they were welcomed and given seats, and water to drink. When the boys had rested, they sent a message to Chief Otokare, requesting him to allow them see Chief Modu. When Chief Otokare got the information, he sent his messenger to call the boys. The messenger went and called the Madi boys, and the boy gave three cows Chief Otokare. Later on the boys asked Chief Otokare if he could give them their chief (Modu). Chief Otokare was happy to receive the gifts and told one of his messengers to give Chief Modu to the Madi boys. The messenger went and released Chief Modu from detention, where elderly women were nursing his wounds till he healed. The messenger gave the chief to the Madi boys as instructed by Chief Otokare. The boys received their chief and then went back home.

In Acholi and Madi, the royal chair is not assumed by just anyone. Reports show that when Chief Modu was released from the detention cell of Chief Otokare, he was observing from among his children's wife if he could get one child who would in future become the chief.

Later the chief realized that there was no child among the children of the eldest wife who could become a chief. So he sent a message to the people of Oloro that they should allow his son, Becu, to return home, because after his death Becu would become the chief of the Lokayi.

When Chief Otokare received the message, he called the clan elders of Oloro for a meeting and told them, "I received a message from Chief Modu, requesting Becu to return home." The clan elders were not happy when they heard the message. They then answered Chief Otokare, "Becu cannot go back to Madi, because he will be a child messenger in the home of Oloro, since he is a cousin of Oloro.

Truly, Becu did not return to Madi as his father wanted. Reports show that when Becu became an adult, he married a woman and they produced many children. On the other hand, Luri, Becu's mother had eloped and produced other children. Later, Becu and Luri's children also produced children and they named themselves "Jo Kilio". This issue now brings us to another question, "Why do the Panyikwara say the people of Kilio came from Madi, and yet the family members of Kilio were children of Becu and Luri, who were also born in Oloro?"

Today, people say the people of Kilio came from Madi, because Becu was the child of Chief Modu of Madi. Much as Becu married and produced in his mother's kin home, the history of Acholi stresses that children take after the family linage of their father. This explains why people say the children of Becu are also Madi. Secondly, Luri gave birth to other children much as she was married to chief Modu. According to tradition, even if a married woman goes and produces children with another man, the man who married her will have rights over those children. Because we saw earlier on that Chief Modu married Luri with many heads of cattle. So when Luri went back to her mother's home, the people of Oloro did not return the dowry of the Madi. For this reason, all the children Luri had with her new husband are the children of the Madi. The new man was a merely billy goat for mating. This also proves why people say the people of Kilio came from Madi.

Kurula

The family members of Kurula came from Bar to Acholiland, under the leadership of elder Okwera. The history of Acholi does not tell how the members of Kurula moved till they reached Panyikwara. But some elders of Panyikwara told me that the members of Kurula left Bar because of conflicts and deaths that were common among the people. Reports show that when elder Okwera saw that his people were dying in multitude, he took them to Acholi land (Panyikwara). They built among the people of Bura. This explains why the Kurula became the family members of Oloro.

Monoteng

The history of Acholi does not state where the Monoteng came from. But to date, we find that Monoteng are the same family in Oloro. I think we shall talk more about the Monoteng in the second edition of this book.

Cung-Gura

When I was moving among the Acholi of Sudan, I did not find anyone who could give me information about the people of Cung-gura. For this reason, we do not know where the people of Cung-gura came from, and which year they entered Panyikwara. This is one issue we shall research about in the second Edition of this book.

OLORO HILLS AND HUNTING GROUNDS

The family members of Oloro have two hunting grounds: Deyo and Koto-koto hunting grounds. The history of Panyikwara says for time immemorial, Deyo hunting ground belonged to the Pakala. Later the Pakala used the hunting ground to marry a girl of Bura. Reports show that later, the Bura also gave the hunting ground to the people of Ogura, who came as cousins (as we saw earlier). This explains why to-date, a born of Ogura invite hunters to Deyo hunting ground.

The elders of Oloro told me that elder Acega was the first person to invite hunters to Deyo hunting ground. After he died, the hunting ground was taken care of by Kenyi. When Kenyi died, the hunting ground was left under the care of elder Orom. After the death of Orom the hunting ground was guarded by elder Mugeni. When Mugeni died, Yocero took care of the hunting ground (a task he is performing to-date).

The history of Panyikwara says from 1982-1983, the people of Bar were wrangling over Deyo hunting ground with the members of Oloro, because other members of Bar built in Deyo hunting ground, so they claimed that Deyo hunting ground belongs to them.

One day, the members of Bar were in a meeting and when elder Mugeni realized that the Bar were for a meeting, he blew his horn, and after a short time, a leopard came from Deyo hunting ground and stood before the hunters of Bar. When the people who were attending the meeting saw the leopard, they immediately agreed that Deyo hunting ground belonged to the Oloro (Panyikwara).

Elder Mugeni did this to prove to the Bar that no one in Bar can invite people to go hunting in Deyo hunting ground, except a born of Oloro. This means that no one should fight over a hunting ground, because all hunting grounds have owners. Secondly, the horn to call people to the hunting ground is not blown by just anybody. On the day of hunting, the owner of the hunting ground is the one who invites the hunters, so that they are not injured, or attacked by wild animals. If the invitation horn is blown anyhow, it causes serious punishment to the people. A perfect example of this was in 1979, when an elder called Orom blew the horn for Deyo hunting ground. When people went to hunt, the hunters were hit by hail stones and everyone was annoyed why the hunting ground invoked rain and hailstones. The people gradually discovered that the person who blew the horn was an elder Orom, who was not the owner of the hunting ground. So the members were very angry with Orom, that he became blind.

Tim Koto-koto is an isolated bush between Layoyo of Nga-gaya and Maria hunting ground, an isolated bush that has become a hunting ground for the members of Oloro because it has many wild animals. The history of Panyikwara says long ago, Koto-koto had no owner, but in 1950, when elder Nataniel left Kamuli (Amee), he went and built in Caiyuni. Later Nataniel saw that Koto-koto had no owner, yet it had many animals, he then started inviting people to hunt in Koto-koto. Nataniel blew the horn for Koto-koto hunting ground for five years, and later died during the war of Cala, in 1955. After the death of Nataniel, no one thought of taking over Koto-Koto hunting ground. Reports show that much as no one inherited the hunting ground, in 1957 the people of Panykwara continued hunting there. We do not know if in this year, any one could blow the horn of Kotokoto hunting ground.

The people of Oloro have one hill called Logura, which also belongs to the Ogura. Majority of the Acholi of Sudan are Christians, they also know very well that all things on earth were created by God. He also put each thing in its place. But other elders of Oloro were telling me that Logura Hill fell from the sky. The people of Ogura also fell from the sky, as we earlier on saw. The people kept saying that the Ogura fell from the sky together with a stone, which gradually grew and became a hill that is now referred to as Logura Hill.

The people of Oloro have a god called Nywandi, which sits in Logura Hill. The god is taken care of by a born of Ogura family. The elders of Oloro told me that people remember Acega as the first caretaker of Nywandi shrine. After Acega died, the shrine was attended to by Kenyi, and Orom took over after

Keny died. When Orom died, Mugeni took care of the shrine. When Mugeni died, Yacero was left in charge of the shrine, till now. This also shows us that the blower of the horn of Deyo hunting ground is also the one who takes care of Nywandi shrine.

The history of Panyikwara says Nywandi helps the people of Oloro in three different ways: —

First, when a woman of Oloro elopes with another man, her first husband goes to the owner of Nywandi god and tells it about the incident. The owner of the god would then get water and leaves of olwedo tree and curses the women before the god. After the owner of the god has finished cursing the woman, he would then tell the first husband to go back home. The next morning, if the woman goes to fetch water in the well, she would fetch water and put it on her head with ease, but when she reaches her compound, the water pot would get stuck on her head. When the home people witness such an occurrence, they would immediately know that the owner of Nywandi god has cursed the woman.

The clan elders would, that very moment, send two or three people to the clan members of the woman's first husband. When the messengers reach the home of the man, they would sit to debate the matter. The messengers of the second husband would then tell the relatives of the old husband, "Every person makes mistakes. We realized that one of our brothers made a mistake and eloped with your wife. We now ask for your forgiveness. If possible have mercy because our brother is not the first person to make such a mistake. We also know very well that if such a thing happens, the offender would give the woman's first husband shells, leopard skin and a male sheep. For this reason, we have also brought these three things as the Acholi tradition demands."

Most times, when such offerings are brought, the clan elders do not reject them. Truly, after the discussion, the first husband accepted the offerings. They then sent a boy who was ten years old to the home of the second husband. Before the boy went, the clan elders instructed him, "If you reach the compound of those people, go straight to the woman with a water pot on her head, and tell her to put the pot down. If the woman puts the water pot down, you should come back to us immediately." The boy started going, when he reached there, he went to the woman who had a water pot on her head and told her, "Well, woman, put the water pot on your head down." When she carried the water pot, she realized that the pot also accepted to come down. The boy returned home as he was instructed.

Secondly, Nywandi helps boys of Oloro during marriage ceremony. The elders of Oloro told me that much as Nywandi helps boys of Oloro, it does not help all the boys of Oloro. Nywandi helps only boys from the family of Ogura. Marriage ceremony is always planned by the father of the boy and the father of the girl. Acholi elders say if the boy's father admired a girl, and the girl refuses his advances, the father of the boy would then go to the owner of the god so that he curses the girl before the shrine. When the owner of the god receives such a message, he gets *olwedo* leaves and water in a small calabash, and curses the girl before Nywandi. Acholi girls always bring water for cooking, bathing and water for drinking from a well, which are sometimes a mile away from home.

Reports show that when the cursed girl goes back to fetch water in the morning, she fetches water and puts it on her head with ease. But later, when she reaches home with the water, she can no longer put the water pot down, because the water pot would have got stuck on her head. When the father of the girl sees that the water pot has gotten stuck on her daughter's head. He immediately knows that his daughter has been cursed by some boy before the god. For this reason, the father of the girl tells his daughter to take the water to the home of the boy's father she thinks had interest in her. The girl then takes the water to the home of the boy's father. When the girl reaches the home of the boy, she would then put the water pot down without problems. When such a thing happens, the girl would not go back to her father's home; she would become the wife of the boy. For this reason, many people of Panyikwara, upon seeing an elder of wooing a girl from the family of another member of Panyikwara would immediately asked "Which family in Oloro do you come from?" If the man says he is from the family of Ogura, they would instantly tell the girl, "Eee! Child, take care of yourself because tomorrow the head pad will get stuck on your head."

Thirdly, Nywandi god also helps the people of Oloro during the period of hunting. If the period for hunting approaches, the owner of the hunting ground, who is also the owner of Nywandi god, immediately blows so that the hunters are not injured, or attacked by wild animals.

THE RAIN POT OF THE OLORO

The history of Panyikwara says the rain pot is in the family of Bura. The first rain chief remembered by many was chief Mogga. The elders of Panyikwara said chief Mogga came with his rain stone from Aru (Lolubo). This is also one thing why the group of Mogga did not give their contributions to the Bura of Panyikwara when they entered Acholi land.

After the death of chief Mogga, the rain stone remained with his son Gac. After Gac died, the rain stone was left in the hands of chief Ayela-meri, who also died and Ismail Omakoyat took care of the rain stone. When Ismail Omakoyat died, the rain stone remained under the care of Chief Lomena. Chief Lomena also died and chief Aluka took care of the rain stone. Andrea took care of the rain stone when chief Aluka died. Andrea died in Juba on 2/12/1999. Reports say after the death of Chief Andrea, the Oloro do not know where the rain stone remained. This is how the rain of Oloro got lost. To-date, no one knows where the rain stone is.

The Oloro have two shrines, the first shrine is in the family of Ogura. The members of Ogura (Lombari) also celebrate the shrine. The second shrine, which is also the biggest, is in the family of Kilio. A child of Kilio is also the one who celebrates the shrine. The shrine comprises the families of Kurula, Cubo Bura and Pamulu. The children from these four families do not marry among themselves, but they can marry girls from the families of Ogura, Monoteng, Cung-gura and Monoja. The history of Panyikwara says the families of Monoteng, Cung-gura and Monoja do not intermarry, but the boys and girls can marry from the family of Kurula, Cubo, Bura and Pamulu.

PAJAA

The home of Pajaa has two small families; Pajaa Bura and Pajaa Palee.

Pajaa Bura: The members of Pajaa Bura seem to have come from Madi. They were led by elder Wod-Nyarie to Acholiland. The history of Acholi says the Bura came and built in Bucili, which is a far distance from Iwire Hill, where other members of the Panyikwara where. When I was asking the elders of Panyikwara why the Bura left Madi, they told me that they also do not know why the Bura left Madi. But they know that the Bura came to Bucili around the year 1845-1850. The Bura are the land owners of Pajaa, because they were the first who started coming from the members of Pajaa Palee.

Bura were dedicated farmers, who loved to open up large farmlands. But they did not cut trees from the gardens because they didn't have axes. Bura also loved slaughtering animals like goats and sheep on farming days. Since the Bura did not have axes, they could only skin the animals and not cut the bones.

Phillip Okoo, a man of Pajaa, told me, "The Pajaa Palee came later and built near the Bura. However, the people of Bura did not know that some other people had built near them. The Palee came with axes, and shortly, they entered the farms of the Bura, and found that the Bura had not cut trees from their gardens. When the Palee saw all these, they cut all the trees from the gardens of Bura. They also cut the bones left behind by the Bura, cooked and ate it. After they had eaten, the Palee went back to their temporary settlement. They also took some food for those who remained in the settlement.

The next morning, the Bura came back to farm and were surprised to find all the trees in the garden cut down, and the bones all taken. On this day, the Bura continued digging and they ate and went back home. When the Palee timed that the Bura had left, they went back and found that the Bura had dug the garden but not cut the trees. They had also left so many meaty bones. Palee cut the trees from the garden, and cut the bones and cooked. After eating, they went back to their settlement.

The following morning, when the Bura came back to the garden, they found all the trees in the gardens cut and all the bones taken. This happened about five or six times and Bura finally asked themselves, "Who always cuts the trees from our garden? We want to see these people, because good people like these should be taken home. But what should we do to get them?"

One man came up with an idea and told his brothers, "If we want to catch these people, I think it would be good if some people among us hide near the garden after digging. If these people come, and they are already cutting the trees from the garden, those who are hiding near the garden should let them finish cutting the trees, and later surround, capture and take them home." All the members of Bura supported the idea the man came up with.

One day, Bura gathered after they had finished digging. They chose energetic boys and men to hide near the garden. The chosen boys and men hid all round the garden. Before they had gone back home, the clan elders instructed the chosen boys and men that if the kind hearted people enter the garden, the children of Bura should make sure they are not seen by the Palee. The elders thought that if the Palee saw the Bura hiding, they would run away with their axes. The children of Bura heeded the instruction.

That evening, the Palee came to the garden and started cutting the trees as they usually did, while other people were cutting the bones and cooking. The Bura then witnessed from the bushes what the people of Palee were doing. When food was ready, the Palee sat down to eat. After a short time, the Bura started emerging one by one from the bushes.

Phillip Okoo told me that when the Palee saw Bura emerging from the bushes, they sat still and did not run, because they wanted to see what the Bura were going to do to them. Bura surrounded the Palee, caught them and took them home to elder Wod-Nyarie. The history of Panyikwara says elder Nam-moi, the grandchild of Mercede, wife of Chief Mathia Aburi Lolori of Obbo, who was also the leader of Palee, was also among those who were caught in the garden.

When elder Wod-Nyarie saw Nam-moi, he became very happy. The Bura were also happy upon seeing the Palee. Elder Wod-Nyarie warmly welcomed the Palee and told them, "I want all the members of Palee to stay among the Bura. For this reason, I want Nam-moi to send a message to the Palee at the settlement to come and build among the Bura."

Elder Nam-moi was also happy to hear such a message from Wod-Nyarie. He sent his messengers to the Palee who had remained in the settlement to come home. The messengers went and brought the Palee home. Elder Wod-Nyarie then gave them land to build and farm. The Palee built among the Bura as instructed by Wod-Nyarie. In the land of Acholi of Sudan, people usually start to open farm lands in August. They start by opening up gardens for planting sesame. So we are assuming that the Palee came in Bucili between April and June. The Palee built huts and also planted different varieties of corps. The elders of Panyikwara told me that elder Nam-moi came with a rain stone, later chief Nam-moi gave his rain stone to Wod-Nyarie as a sign of gratitude for what the Bura did for them. The history of Acholi says Bura did not have rain. The rains stone of the Palee has made the Bura to become the chiefs of rain in Pajaa.

Reports show that later, elder Nam-moi asked chief Wod-Nyarie if he could change the name of the home from "Bucili" to "Bwola". Nam-moi and his people wanted to change the name of the home to Bwola because they wanted those who would come later to know that Palee people were deceived by Bura. This is why they (Palee) came home. All the people of Pajaa seconded the idea of Nam-moi, and they changed the name "Bucili" to "Bwola". In memory of this, the Pajaa composed a song:-

Iyaa, Eyaa Wic Pa Nam-moi Ma Ogero Bucili!	O, O the Nam-mois who built in Bucili!
Wic Pa Namu Ma Ogero Bucili!	The Nam-mois who built in Bucili!
Wic Pa Nam-moi Gero Bwola!	The Nam-mois builds in Bwola!
Lotino Lee Gitemo Kit-gi Kwe!	Young animals try them in vain!
Anyamu Ma Odong i Munu!	Anyamu who grew up n modernity!
Wic Pa Nam-moi!	The Nam-mois!

Chief Wod-Nyarie did not keep the rain stone for long. Some elders of Panyikwara told me that chief Wod-Nyarie gave the rain stone to his elder brother, whose name we do not know.

PAJAA-PALEE

The members of Pajaa Palee came from Cwua in Uganda to the land of Acholi of Sudan, under the leadership of chief Nam-moi. The Palee came to Panyikwara around the year 1885. The history of Acholi Sudan of says the people of Palee left Cwua because of hunger which was killing many of them in Cwua in 1885.

From Cwua the people of Palee came to Gulu, and they continued moving up to Atiak. The people of Palee did not settle in Atyiak. They continued moving up to Nimule, at the border of Sudan and Uganda. Reports indicate that the members of chief Nam-moi did not also settle in Nimule. They continued moving till they reached Bucili (Daka), near Moli Andro, to the West of Opari Hill. The people of Palee found Bura already in the land. Since the people of Palee were not social, they built far away from people of Bura. As we were seeing in the previous page, Bura did not know that other people were settled near them. After a short time, the members of Palee found the gardens of

Bura, and started cutting trees in the midst of it. Later, Bura brought them home. But some people say members of Dungo were the ones who brought members of Palee and took them to Chief Wod Nyarie. Later, Chief Wod Nyarie got a girl of Bura and gave to chief Nam-moi to show gratitude towards Bura for coming to them.

Around 1930, the people of Pajaa left Bwola and went to Iwire Hill, where other members of Panyikwara were living. The chief of Panyikwara welcomed members of Pajaa and gave them land to build and farm near Atebi River, in a place called Omboloci, near Owiny-ki-bul on the route to Madi. Members of Pajaa then built near the members of Dungo, Ng-gaya and the Patoko. This also explains why the members of Pajaa became brothers of Dungo, Ng-gaya and Patoko.

Other elders of Pajaa-Palee told me that after the death of chief Wod-nyarie, members installed another person on the throne. Unfortunately, no one remembers the names of the different chiefs who succeeded Chief Rwot Wod-nyarie. They kept saying the only chief members of Pajaa Palee remember is Chief Olam Firu.

DUNGO

Members of Dungo have only one family called "Dungo". The members all came from Bar Nyony-kir. The history of Acholi does not state why the members of Dungo left Bar Nyony-kir, and the year they entered Acholi land. Acholi elders told me that from Bar, members of Dungo came and settled in Moli Tokuro, and they came without a chief. So when Wod-Nyarie heard that members of Dungo had reached Moli Tokuro, he sent messengers, who brought them to live under the leadership of Medee.

Members of Dungo built among the Bura, and this later led to a good relationship between Pajaa and Dungo. This made elders of Dungo to later set a rule that girls and boys from the two families could intermarry, but a man could not marry a woman who already has a husband. The elders of Dungo Bura also set another rule that the children of Dungo should not marry the children of Palee. We do not understand why the elders set such a rule.

DUNGO HILLS AND HUNTING GROUNDS

Members of Dungo have one hunting ground named Dungo. The hunting ground stretches from Moli Tokuro road up to Kiir River (River Nile). Elder Nyango-rac is the one who blows the horn of Dungo hunting ground. Tradition prohibited anyone from cutting trees in this hunting ground without seeking permission from the owner of the hunting ground. For this reason, if anyone cuts a tree from Dungo hunting ground without permission from the owner, he would be severely punished. A good example of this is the incident which happened to a child of Moli Tokuro. One day, a man from Moli Tokuro cut a mahogany tree from Dungo hunting ground without asking for permission from Nyango-rac. He used the wood to build a fishing boat. Dungo elders told me that when the man finished making his boat, he went fishing. When he reached the river, he threw his net and he did not catch even a single fish. After sometime, the man remembered what he did. When he returned home, he told his brothers, "Today I went to the river to catch fish using my new boat, but I did not catch even a single fish. I don't know what is wrong."

When the children of Moli Tokuro heard this, they asked the man, "From where did you cut the tree you used to build the boat? The man answered, "I cut the tree from Dungo hunting ground." The children of Moli again asked him, "When you went to cut the tree from the hunting ground, did you ask the owner of the hunting ground?" The man answered, "I did not ask the owner of the hunting ground". The children of Moli then told him, "If you did not ask the owner of the hunting ground, you should know very well that, the owner of the hunting ground is the one who was angry with you. If you want the owner of the hunting ground to become happy, take an offering to him."

The man then picked a ram and money and took to Nyango-rac. When Nyango-rac got the offering, he picked an *olwedo* branch and water, and sprinkled a blessing on him, and the man went back home. The next morning, the man picked the boat and went back to the river to fish. When he reached the river, he caught many fish.

Other elders of Panyikwara told me that members of Dungo do not have a rain stone, hill or god.

THE RAIN POT OF PANYIKWARA

In Panyikwara, the biggest rain is with the Bura, but as we were seeing in this book, some members of smaller families in Panyikwara also have a rain stone. Chief Beli A. Lukweramoi was the first person responsible for invoking rain in Bura. Some people say the brothers of Chief Lokwera-moi, were not happy with the chief. So we do not know why people were unhappy. Acura, the brother of chief Lokwera-moi, stole one rain stone and went and sold it in Lokoya, because of a dispute that was between them. When the members of Panyikwara understood that Acura stole the rain stone and sold it in Lokoya, they sent messengers to the chief of Lokoya. When the messengers of chief Lokweramoi reached Lokoya, they went to the chief and told him, "Chief, we have come to you because we were sent by Chief Lokwera-moi, because of the rain stone that was sold by a born of Panyikwara in Lokoya." The chief also knew that he bought a rain stone from Acura. So he picked the rain stone and gave to the messengers of Chief Lokwera-moi, who took it to the chief of Panyikwara. When Chief Lokwera-moi got the rain stone, he later picked the rain stone and other rain stones and gave them to his nephews who were in Goloba, Paliwa and in Oyira. The elders of Panyikwara told me that in Goloba, the chief gave the rain stone to his nephew, Aramatala, and gave another rain stone to Koka in Paliwa family. He also gave another rain stone to Ocito, in the family of Oyira. This also proves to us why the family members of Paliwa, Goloba and Oyira respect the Bura. But the big rain stone remained with Chief Bali Lokwera-moi. After the death of Chief Beli Lokwera-moi, the rain stone remained with his son, Franko Beli. After Chief Rwot Franko Beli died, the rain stone remained with Petero, who has it up to now.

Chapter Sixteen

PALWAR

THE HOME OF PALWAR

There are four families surrounding the home of Palwar. These families are Obbo to the north Pajok to the West, Lokung to the South and Katire to the East. The history of Acholi says the border of Palwar and Obbo is in Lianga river. The border of Pajok and Palwar on the other hand, is in Lerwa River, in a place called Ceng-kidwe (sun and moon) in Pawar. But a place called Bercili is in Pajok. The border of Palwar and Lokung is in ?? While the border of Palwar and Katire is in ??

What is the meaning of Palwar? Palwar means children or descendants or grandchildren of Chief Olwar. In short, Palwar means the people of Chief Olwar. The Palwar have eight small families: — Palwar, Amica, Koyo P'Abee, Lomarati, Agata, Omere, Lobone and Isore.

PALWAR

The families of Palwar came from different places such as: Lango Teretenya (Logire), Agoro, Madi-Opei, Padibe and Lokung in Uganda. Other people came from Katire Imila and Obbo. Crazzolara in his book said that, "chief Obeere, of Lango Teretenye, produced three sons: Abanya, Logu and Olwar Rama. Chief Obeere's sons later split into three groups. Logu and his group remained in Lango Teretenye, Abanya took his group to Pader, and Olwar Rama went with his is people to Palwar (Sudan).

According to R. Oywak, the first home of the Palwar was in Lokoro. They moved from Lokoro to Logir, and headed to Kekerek. They later proceeded up to Obeere Hill in Agoro South. From there, the Palwar went to Utika which is in Lala Hill, near Aringa River.

Reports show that other people of Utika joined the Palwar, and they went to a place called Palwar in Sudan. Obeere and Utika are well known places in Palwar (Crazzolara, 1954, PP, 532-533).

The history of Palwar says Chief Olwar Rama took his people from Lango Teretenye to Agoro. From here, other people of Agoro joined his group, and they moved on up to Lala hills. At Lala Hill, they found the people of Utika. Records show that from Lala Hill, some people of Utika again joined chief Olwar and his group, and they continued moving up to Madi-Opei.

A section of Palwar elders told me that, when Chief Olwar Rama arrived in Madi-Opei, some people of Madi-Opei also joined his group and they went with them to Padibe. The group of Chief Olwar Rama lived only a short time in Padibe, and headed to Lokung, and built in Ceng-ki-dwe near Atebi River — the first settlement of the Palwar. Ceng-ki-dwe is on the other side of River Atebi, which is towards the East, while the people of Bobi of Pajok are on the western side of River Atebi.

According to Crazzolara the first chief of the Palwar was Rama (Olwar). After chief Rama died, his son, Oyoo took over the crown. When chief Oyoo passed way, his son Ongom succeeded him. And when chief Ongom died, his son Ating became the chief, whose son, Lamwak also succeeded him after he died. After the death of Chief Lamwak, his son Okec-Otome became the chief around 1947. After the death of Chief Okec-Otome, his son Paulu Otoo became chief (Crazzolara, 1954, P, 533).

The year the Palwar were in Ceng-ki-dwe, they split into four small families as follows. Those who came from Lango Teretenye called themselves "Jo Abong" and"Pa-woko (Pa'lodak)". Those who came from Agoro named themselves "Jo Agonga". People who migrated from Madi-opei named themselves "Jo Pa-Owoo (Pawodak)", and those from Lokung called themselves"Jo Pa-Otika (Potika)".

After a few months, when elder Daudi Obwonyo, saw that there was growing disagreement between him and his brothers, he left Padibe and built among the Palwar. He subsequently became a cousin, because his father was from Lamogi.

A son of Lamogi married a girl of Abong when the people of Chief Olwar

314

settled in Padibe. The women later gave birth to a son, Daudi Obwonyo. When Daudi Obwonyo became an adult, one day, his mother told him, "Child! I am a girl of Abong, my brothers left me in Padibe when I married your father. Your uncles are in the home of Abong in Palwar-Sudan. I want you to know where your maternal relatives are, because we do not know what the future holds." When Daudi saw that there was a dispute between him and his brothers, he remembered what his mother told him. On this basis, he left Padibe, because he thought of searching for his uncles.

The history of Palwar says Daudi Obwonyo came to Palwar without a wife. Later, his maternal relatives married for him a wife. They produced children, who later called themselves "Jo Lamogi". This is why when you ask any born of Lamogi of Palwar, "Where did you come from? They will immediately say "We came from Padibe" —because Obwonyo is a child of Padibe, so, he is a cousin of Abong (Palwar).

After a short time, other people came from Iwala Hill in Katire, and later built among the Palwar. For long, they called themselves "Jo Pa-Lodaka" – the word *lodaka* in Acholi means, *people who have been rejected by others*. It seems those who came from Katire called themselves so, because they loved to secretly kill others. But their brothers who remained in Katire did not like indulging in atrocities like the Pa-Lodaka. A few months after the coming of Pa-Lodaka, other people came from Koyo P'Lopiribok in Obbo. They later built among the Palwar, and later called themselves "Jo Koyole". We assume that these people called themselves "jo Koyole", because they, wanted the children, who would came later to remember where their grandparents came from (Koyo Obbo).

Julius Okeny told me that when the Koyole left Kicenge, they first settled in Ngabara. From here, other people refused to move further and remained in Ngabara. Other willing members continued moving ahead till they reached Ceng-ki-dwe (Palwar). This also tells us why there is a strong relationship between the Koyole and the people of Ngabara of Obbo.

The history of Acholi says the people of Rwot Olwar came and found the people of Koyo P'Atany already in Ceng-ki-dwe. As we saw in the previous pages in this book, the people of Koyo P'Atany separated from their brothers in Obbo, and built in Ceng-ki-dwe. Reports also show that when chief Olwar entered Ceng-ki dwe, he was leading his people, and chief Atany was also had his people.

The people of Abong later became land owners, which also brings us to the question, "If chief Olwar found the people of Koyo already in this hunting ground, why did the people of Abong become the land owners? Aren't the people of Koyo the land owners?" We shall answer this question later. First, let us see how members of other families came to Palwar.

Chief Olwar had stayed for only a few years among the Koyo, when the family members of Amica, Koyo P'Abee, Lomarati, Agata, Omere, Lobone and Isore, also started coming to the land of Palwar. They found the Abong still in Ceng-ki-dwe. Each family came with their leader. They also had a royal drum and spear. Later, these people gave their royal drum and spear to chief Olwar, as we shall see below.

Reports show that the people, who came later, arrived in Palwar in different months. I cannot therefore write all the years and months these people entered Palwar, because there is no literature which shows how they arrived in Palwar. But we know that these people are the ones who brought the eight families that are in Palwar; as we saw earlier.

Chief Olwar died when the Palwar where still in Ceng-ki-dwe. After the death of chief Olwar, his son Lotome took over the throne. When Lotome became chief, he thought it improper for people living in the same area to be led by different chiefs. One day, chief Lotome called a meeting of clan elders, and told them, "Well, my people, I am very disappointed that we are still under different chiefs, yet all of us live together. If you want us to be strong, we should unite under one chief, and have one voice. You can now choose from between the reigning chiefs, who can unite the people of Palwar. If such a person becomes our chief, in case a fight erupts, we shall stand united." All the clan elders seconded the idea of Chief Lotome. They immediately chose chief Lotome as the chief of Palwara.

Julius Okeny told me that after chief Lotome was elected, other chiefs who had royal drums and spears, gave them to their new chief- this is why the Abong became the home owners.

Chief Lotome led the people of Palwar with humility. If we see the history of Acholi, we find that the Palwar were the only people, among the Acholi, that did not fight with another family in Acholi land. This is because they were peaceful, loving, and united people. Nevertheless, we find that the family of Amica is the only one which fought with the Koyo Lokomini (Koyo P'Atany) of Obbo. The Acholi elders said the Amica fought against the Koyo P'Atany because the boys of Koyo P'Atany killed a girl of Amica when she was traveling from Katire to Palwar. The Amica then compensated for the death of the girl.

The history of Palwar says, if there was an important message to be passed, people did not blow whistles or sound drums as we saw earlier on with some people. They instead sound ululation. Among the Pajok and Obbo when ululation was sounded they know that wild animals surrounded people during hunting. Or, hunters had gotten lost in the hunting ground. On many occasions however, the Acholi ululate when enemies come to attack their homes. Whenever ululation was sounded, all the boys and men would pick spears and shields and run quickly where ululation had been heard. When the Palwar heard ululation, they also immediately knew that there was a problem.

PALWAR HILLS AND HUNTING GROUNDS

The Palwar have only two hunting grounds, Akwero and Iliwa hunting grounds. But they have four hills: Oluko Hill in Akwero hunting grounds, Iwala, Acen and Loboki hills. The Palwar respect only two of the four hills, because they give whatever the people ask for. The two hills are Oluko and Loboki.

The blowers of horns for Palwar hunting ground celebrate the hill at least once a year. The celebration is always done during dry season, between the month of November and December. In Acholi, hunting normally takes place from January to March. An elder prepares these two hills ahead of hunting for three important reasons. First, so that dry grass does not cut men. Secondly, to bring good health among the people, and thirdly, so that birds do not eat millet during farming.

Reports show that on the day the elders are celebrating this hills, the law prohibits women from hitting their grinding stones to make them sharp for grinding. Secondly, the law also bars people from moving aimlessly on this day, and elders station the boys on all the routes that lead to Palwar, so that they ensure that everyone is obeying the rule.

The elders then give the boys the authority to arrest anyone found breaking the rule. Those arrested for breaking the law pay a fine equivalent to a goat, chicken or money. If the offender does not have any of the items listed here, the boys remove his shoes or spear. If the arrested person is a family member, and they do not have a goat, chicken or money, they pay the fine with a basket of millet.

Because of this, on the day of celebration, every one would stay at home, till the elders return home from the celebration. The history of Acholi says, the people would collectively agree on a date to gather and eat the items collected as fine during the celebration. Tradition states that the goats, chicken and money collected as fine should not be given to only a few people, but all the clan elders should eat them together.

The Palwar also have one god named Oluko. We do not know the person who the horn of Palwa hunting ground. Secondly, we also do not know the name of the person who takes care of Oluko shrine.

AMICA

The people of Amica have five small families. They are Icar (Iryok), Ikwari (Irumi), Pa-longoku, Pa-lobamu and Lotiiri.

Icar and Ikwari (Iryok and Irumi)

All the family members of Icar and Ikwari came from Iwala (Katire). The history of Palwar says the Katire chased the people of Icar and Ikwari, because they were secretly killing people of Katire. The story of Icar and Ikwari goes like this. Time and again, the Icar and Ikwari loved to secretly kill people. So the people of Katire did not know who were secretly killing people.

One day, a girl of Katire was walking along a path. That time, there were also some two boys who had hidden themselves along the path. One boy was an Icar, and the other was from Ikwari. When the boys saw the girl, they immediately developed the urge to kill. They killed the girl and went back to Iwala Hill. Fortunately, an elder of Katire who was nearby saw the atrocity committed by the boys. The elder relayed the news of the killing of the girl to the clan members and told them, "Well, my people, we are tired of deaths. I think those who are killing us here are the people of Icar and Ikwari. I witnessed what they did to the girl. What should we do?" When the clan elders heard the message, they thought it was needless to fight or avenge the death of the girl. They then sent a message to the people of Katire, and later they sent the same message to the British, so that they determine how best to deal with the Icar and Ikwari.

Before long romour the message reached the people of Icar and Ikwari.

When they heard that the Katire wanted to send the British to them, they were terrified. So they moved to the top of Iwala Hill, thinking that no one would follow them.

After a few days, the people of Katire sent three messengers to the British. When the messengers reached the office of the British, they told him, "Sir, the people of Katire sent us to you with one important message. Members have discovered that the boys of Icar and Ikwari killed one of their girls. Not only this, incidences of secret killings are on the increase among the people. Members have sent us to you, so that you find a way to reduce such killings."

The British was thankful to the members of Katire for sending him such a message, as it made him know what was happening among the people. The British told the people, "I think to reduce the secret killings among you, all the people of Icar and Ikwari should relocate to the foot of the hills. If they shift, then it will be easy to control them."

The British chose ten guards and gave them guns, and they went and met chief Lotome. When the British reached Iwala Hill, they found that all the boys and men had gone on the hill to hunt for bats and ticks. Only women, children, the aged, and chief Lotome of Lwala had remained home. The chief welcomed the British and his guards and gave them a skin to sit on and water to drink.

The chief did not know why the British and his guards went to them on the hills of Iwala. When the British had rested, he moved closer to chief Lotome and told him, "Chief, we came to your home today because we have got a message from the Katire that the children of Icar and Ikwari like to secretly kill people. Secondly, ten days ago, the children of Icar and Ikwari also killed one of their girls, who was walking on the path. Later the boys ran to the top of this hill. When I heard the news, I was saddened, because I want peace to prevail among you. So, one way of restoring peace among the people is for them to shift beneath the hills."

When the British had finished giving the information, Chief Lotome was terrified and responded in a scared voice, "Sir, if you want my people to shift at the foot of the hills, and if you listen to me, you should order your guards to shoot at all the people who have remained in this home, but they should not kill me. Because if the boys and men come back from hunting, and they find that the guards have killed those who had remained home, they will be scared. If the people ask me who killed all these people, I will tell them, "The guards of the white man are the ones who killed the children, women and the aged because the British wants all the people of Icar and Ikwari to move to the foot of the hill. The British also instructed that if anyone refused to relocate down the hill, the guards kill them. Because I know very well that even if I tell my people that the British want the people to move to the foot of the hill, and I do not say they killed people, they will not accept to go and settle there."

The British then bought the idea of Chief Lotome, and called ten guards and instructed them, "I have given you the authority to shoot anyone you see on this hill, except chief Lotome."

Without wasting time, the guards started shooting the women, children and the aged. When those who remained home heard gun shots in the area, the wise ones fled and hid at the foot of the hill. But the stupid ones were lifting their faces up, and were killed by the guards.

In the evening, when the men and boys were returning from hunting, they found home was in a sad atmosphere. Dead bodies were lying in disarray with their legs crossed over the others'. Some bodies were still bleeding. They found chief Lotome seated and dumbfounded. He also said he was so sad for what the British did to the people.

Shortly, those who were hiding at the foot of the hill came out, and they also knew that it was Chief Lotome who gave the bad advice to the British. So they did not reveal the truth to their brothers who returned from hunting.

The hunters asked chief Lotome, "Who killed our people like this? How did you survive the killings?" The chief responded, "The British came with a lot of force. He wants all the people of Icar and Ikwari to relocate at the foot of the hill. When the British killed the women, children and the aged, he wanted to prove to us that if we refuse to relocate below the hills, he will continue killing till the people heed his order. So if the people relocate at the foot of the hill, such secret killings will cease. The god of my forefather is the one who rescued me; I would have also been killed."

The people of Icar and Ikwari, were very frightened when they heard the information. They then spoke in one voice, "All of us should shift down the hills, because if we do not shift as the British wants, more people will be killed in future." After eight days, everyone shifted to the foot of the hill, and the Icar and Ikwari moved away the foot of Iwala hill. They went and built in Ceng-ki-dwe (Palwar). Later, the messengers of chief Lotome sent a message to the

British to inform him that the people had relocated from Palwar. The British was very thankful to chief Lotome, for the good advice he gave, and he was also happy to hear that the people of Icar and Ikwari had shifted to Palwar.

The history of Palwar states that the Icar and Ikwari were the first to introduce the idea of hunting bats and ticks in Palwar. This is also why the people of Amica love to hunt bats and ticks. In the home of Amica, bat meat and ticks are important when welcoming a guest of honour, just as chicken is important to welcome some visitors in Acholi.

Pa-Longoku

The people of Pa-Longoku came from Agoro south, under the leadership of Elder Agura to Palwar. The history of Acholi of Sudan does not mention why these people left Agoro. We also do not know which year they entered Palwar.

Pa-Lobamu

The people of Pa-Lobamu came from Pagaya of Pajok, as we were seeing on the culture of the Pagaya. The history of Pajok says, one day, the boys and men of Pagaya went hunting. Women, children and the aged remained at home. This gave the people of Ywaya an opportunity to do whatever they wanted with the Pagaya. Ywaya then went and stabbed the women, children and the aged. Chief Opilu of Pagaya was also at home, because Acholi chiefs do not go hunting. The Ywaaya also killed him.

After killing all these people, the Ywaya picked all the pots in the home and chopped the human flesh, put it in the pots and cooked it. Reports indicate that when Ywaya were done with their atrocities, they also removed the royal spear, drum and chair of Chief Opilu – this made the Pagaya to remain without a chiefdom.

When the Pagaya came back from hunting, they found the place in a mess, and the smell of blood reeking all over. This incident caused a lot of panic among the Pagaya, and it made those who survived the attacks of the Ywaya to scatter. Other people remained in Pajok, while others fled to Palwar. They went and built among the people of Amica, and later called themselves "jo Pa-Lobamu." (The people of Lobamu)

Lotiri

The people of Lotiri also came from Katire-Lango (Crazzolara, 1951, P.173). But we do not know if they moved together with the other people who came from Katire. If you want to deeply understand the history of the people of Lotiiri, read the *Second Edition* of this book.

AMICA HILLS AND HUNTING GROUND

The people of Amica have one hunting ground called Iliwa. They also have two hills, Iwala and Acen hills. The people of Amica also have a god called Ilai.

KOYO P'ABEE

The members of Koyo P'Abee came from Agoro North (Uganda). They were brought to Sudan by Chief Abee, who was also the rain chief. They came because of famine which was killing many in Agoro. But the history of Palwar does not state how the people of Koyo P'Abee migrated. I think we shall write more about the Koyo P'abee, in the second edition of this book.

HUNTING GROUND AND HILL OF KOYO P'ABEE

The members of Koyo P'Abee have one hill, Laboki, but they do not have a hunting ground or god.

LOMARATI

The history of Acholi of Sudan says the family people of Lomarati came from Koyo Obbo. But we do not know why they left Obbo. We also do not know which year they left Obbo, and the name of the person who led them to Palwar. Some people, however say, that the people of Lomarati came from Isore. However, according to Crazzolara (1951), the people of Lomarati came from Lango in Katire (Crazzolara, 1951, P.173). I think we shall get more on the history of Lomarati in the second edition of this book.

LOMARATI HILLS AND HUNTING GROUNDS

The people of Lomarati do not have a hunting ground, hill or a god.

AGATA

The history of Acholi of Sudan says the people of Agata came from three different places. Some people came from Agoro North, others from Lokung, and some from Labati-olwonga (all in Uganda). The people of Agata left Uganda because of famine which was killing many people that year. When I was interviewing Acholi elders, some of them told me that the people of Agata came from Koyo (Obbo). To better understand the history of the Agata, you should read the second edition of this book.

AGATA HILL AND HUNTING GROUND
The people of Agata have one hunting ground named Agata, but they do not have a hill or god.

OMERE
The history of Acholi of Sudan says the people of Omere also came from Agoro North, Lokung and Labati-olwonga. They moved together with the people of Agata, and later separated from the people of Agata. However, much as the people of Omere split from Agata, we find that there is still a strong blood relationship between them. The people of Omere left Uganda because of famine which was killing many people that year. When I was asking Acholi elders, others told me that some of the people of Omere came from Koyo (Obbo). Read the second edition of this book to better understand the history of the people of Omere.

OMERE HILL AND HUNTING GROUND
The people of Omere have no hunting grounds, hill or god.

LOBONE
The history of Acholi says the people of Agata, Omere and Lobone all came from Uganda, as we saw above. Other people came from Agoro North, others from Lokung, and some came from Labati-olwonga. The people of Lobone left Uganda because of famine which killed many people that year. To understand the history of the people of Lobone well, you should read the second edition of this book.

THE HUNTING GROUND AND HILL OF LOBONE
The people of Lobone have no hunting ground, hill or god.

ISORE

The history of Acholi of Sudan does not state where the people of Isore came from. But when I was interviewing Acholi elders, who are not from Isore, they told me that the Isore seem to have come from Katire. For this reason, we cannot clearly state where the Isore came from. But if you want to understand better the history of Isore, read the *Second Edition* of this book.

ISORE HUNTING GROUND AND HILL

The Isore do not have a hunting ground, hill or god.

Chapter Seventeen

MAGWI

THE HOME OF MAGWI

There are five homes surrounding the land of Magwi. They are Panyikwara and Omeo to the west, Obbo to the East, Imurok and Ofirika to the north and north-west. The history of Acholi of Sudan states that the border of Magwi and Panyikwara is in the valley of Romo-toguli. But some people say the border of Magwi and Panyikwara is at Ing-gili River. The border of Magwi and Omeo is at Kigoya River. The border of Magwi and Imurok (Ifwotu) is at River Koli, on the way to Torit, while the border of Magwi and Obbo is at the hill of P'Loyo-moi (Licari).

The people of Magwi have eight small families; *Orak, Bura, Amika, Lobu're, Afufuru* (Ijula), *Palonganyi, Palimu* and *Kilio.*

ORAK

Before we explore into the history of the the different families in the word Magwi, I want us to first answer this question: "What does Magwi mean?" When I was still in Juba, I asked each of the fifteen elders of Magwi this same question, "What does Magwi mean?" Ten elders told me, "Magwi means, we do not know where we came from." They told me that the name "Magwi" was derived from a word of Ofirika "Omagwi", which means, we do not know where we came from.

The elders of Magwi also told me that, when the people of Orak came to Magwi, they first settled in a place called "Edikoyi", which is near Okire Hill in the home of Ofirika. The people of Orak lived in Edikoyi for almost a decade.

Reports show that when the people of Orak had just entered Ofirika, the people of Ofirika asked them, "Where did you come from?" It seems the people of Orak knew a bit of Ofirika language. So they responded in Ofirika dialect that "Omagwi". The word "Omagwi" in Ofirika means "We do not know where we came from." The people of Ofirika then said, "Look at these people of Omagwi!" (Look at people who do not know where they came from). The people of Orak then started telling each other that, "Let's see if the people of Ofirika call us *Omagwi*". Truly, the members of Ofirika, then called the people of Orak, Omagwi. Gradually, the people of Orak removed the "O" at the beginning of the word "Omagwi", and then called themselves "Jo Magwi" (the people of Magwi).

But other five elders of Magwi told me, "Magwi means "*I will wait for he who will come to disturb me.*" It seems the people of Orak called themselves so because they left their first settlement because of disputes and fights between them and their brothers who remained behind. Because of this, the people of Orak kept thinking that, maybe, because of this, those who remained behind were following them. In Acholi land, when a man has accepted to fight, he tells himself, "Anyone who follows me here must surely be looking for trouble." In short, the man would say, "I will wait for he who looks for me." I later met people like Santo Oyet Ongin, son of Magwi, who lives in Brisbane (Australia) hesaid the word "Magwi" was derived from the word "Makwi" in Lotuko language, which means "oyado dish".

As we saw in the previous page, the history of Acholi says the people of Orak built at the foot of Okire Hill. We do not know the name of the elder who led the people of Orak to Magwi. But the second group of people who followed Orak were the Bura Palonganyi (or Bura Palonyung). The people of Bura Palonganyi were led by Chief Awiya from Koyo of Imurok. They came and built on Okire Hill.

Reports show that the Bura Padyeri came after Bura Palonganyi, and built among the people of Orak much later. The history of Magwi says the people of Orak and Bura lived in Edikoyi for almost ten years. And in the 1930, the people of Orak relocated and built in Lobela hunting grounds (Lobela hunting ground belongs to the people of Ijula). The people of Bura Palonganyi, and Bura Padyeri, however, left Edikoyi, and built near the Bilal's Road, which runs from Torit to Opari.

As we were seeing earlier in this book, the people of Orak were the first to

326

come to Okire hills, followed by the people of Bura Palonganyi. This is why the people of Orak became the home owners of Magwi. If you want to know more about the history of the people of Orak, read the *Second Edition of this book*.

The history of Magwi says, before the people of Magwi built in Lobela hunting grounds, they migrated in many places like; Acila and Magwi Meri hunting grounds, Ogwar and Reke hunting ground. Later, they cam and built in Lobela hunting grounds, the present day Magwi. Lobela hunting ground is very conducive for farming. People say Lobela hunting ground starts from the West of Kimoru River, up to the south of Aduce stream, from here, Lobela hunting grounds entered into the north of Ayii River.

ORAK HILL AND HUNTING GROUND

The people of Orak do not have a hunting ground. They also do not have a hill or god.

BURA

The people of Bura have two small families. They are Bura Palonganyi (Bura P'Onyunga) and Bura Padyeri (Bura P'Diko). The history of Magwi states that Bura Palonganyi and Bura Padyeri both came from Koyo of Imurok.

Crazzolara then said the people of Bura Palonganyi came from Kidonge, which is in Lotuko land (Crazzolara, 1951, P, 173). Other people said the people of Bura Palonganyi were the first to come among the people of Magwi, and the Bura Padyeri followed. The elders of Magwi told me that elder Auya was the one who brought the Bura Palonganyi from Imurok in the land of Acholi of Sudan. They left Imurok because of a disease which was killing many people that year.

But Crazzolara, in his book, "The Lwo Part 11, Lwo Traditions" wrote, "The people of Bura-Palonganyi came from Kidonge which is in Lotuko. They are also the owners of the rain stone. The first chief of Bura was called Rukunyang. Later, Chief Rukunyang produced a son named Cokale. After the death of Chief Rukunyang, his son Cokale succeeded him. Chief Cokale also married a wife, and they produced a son named Ongee. When Chief Cokale died, his son Ongee became the chief. Chief Ongee was the one who brought the people of Bura Palonganyi from Kidonge in the land of Acholi of Sudan (Crazzolara, 1951, P, 173)".

The people of Bura Palonganyi came and built between Okire Hills. They found the people of Orak already settled in Edikoyi -at the foot of Okire Hill. In the year the people of Bura Palonganyi reached Okire Hill, it seems the the people of Orak had lived in Edikoyi for about two years. Gradually, the people of Orak and Bura Palonganyi started intermarrying.

The history of Magwi says chief Auya of Bura Palonganyi came with a rain stone. So, when he shifted below Okire Hill, he bought another rain stone from Chief Awiya of Orak.

After staying at Okire Hill for eight years, the people of Bura Palonganyi later realized that the land between the hills was not good for farming. So they shifted at the foot of the hills among the people of Orak. Other elders of Magwi told me that, the year the people of Bura Palonganyi shifted at the foot of Okire Hill, is the year when the people of Bura Padyeri came from Koyo of Imurok. They built among the people of Orak later. Reports show that the people of Bura Padyeri did not shift from Imurok because of hunger, but they followed their brothers (of Bura Palonganyi) because of the blood relationship between them.

The people of Orak and Bura lived at the foot of Okire Hill for many years, and in 1930, the people of Orak relocated from Edikoyi, and built in their hunting ground named Lobela. The Bura Palonganyi and Bura Padyeri, on the other hand, shifted from Edikoyi and went and built close to Bilal's road that runs from Torit to Opari.

But Santo Ongin, son of Magwi, who lives in Brisbane Australia, of Magwi said before the relocation of the people of Magwi in Lobela hunting grounds, they stayed in Acila and Meri hunting grounds, and Magwi, in a place named Ogwar. Later, they shifted to Lobela hunting ground, where the people of Magwi are living to-date. The people of Magwi shifted from Lobela hunting grounds, because the land is good for cultivating crops.

The history of Magwi say, the land of Lobela hunting grounds starts from the West of Kimoru River to the south of Aduce River, up to the north of Ayii River (Santo Ongin, 2005, P, 2).

BURA HILL AND HUNTING GROUND
The people of Bura do not have a hunting ground, hill or god.

AMIKA

The people of Amika have five small families, namely: *Logwar, Onyang, Lokomiji, Imurok* and *Ongero*. The history of Amika says that the people of these five families all came from different places.

Logwar

The members of Logwar family came from Lokoro, but the elders of Amika do not know the name of the elder who led the people of Logwar in Magwi. They also do not know why the people of Logwar left Lokoro. If you want to know much about the history of the people of Logwar read the *Second Edition* of this book.

Onyang

Some people of Onyang family came from Koyo of Obbo, while others came from Omeo. But the history of Acholi does not state which year the people of Onyang entered Magwi. So, we think the people of Onyang entered Magwi after 1930, because this is also when other families in Magwi, entered the land of Magwi. We do not know why Onyang family left Obbo. Secondly, we do not know the name of the elder who led Onyang family from Obbo to Amika. If you want to comprehend the history of Onyang, read the second *Edition* of this book.

Lokomiji

The clan elders of Amika told me that the members of Lokomiji family came from three different places. Some members of Lokomiji family came from Oyere of Obbo, others came from Omeo, and some came from Ofirika. They all built in the place where they live today. But the elders of Amika did not tell me the name of the elders who brought the members of Lokomiji from the different places. They also do not know which year the members of Lokomiji entered Magwi. If you want to understand more about the history of Lokomiji, read the second edition of this book.

Imurok

The members of Imurok family came from Imurok. The history of Magwi does not tell which year the people of Imurok of Amika arrived in the land of the Acholi of Sudan. But the history of Magwi says, before the members of

Imurok relocated to Acholiland, there was intermarriage between them and the people of Onyang.

The elders of Amika told me that the marriage between the members and Onyang was one-sided, which means the boys of Imurok were the ones who were marrying the girls of Onyang. For many years, the culture of Acholi has had it that when a boy marries from another place, he should go and build among his in-laws. This is why the people of Imurok moved to Amika, and built among the members of Onyang (brother-in-laws or sister-in-laws). The children they produced then started their own family of Imurok, which is in Amika.

The war led by John Garang barred me from getting much information from the elders of Magwi/Amika. If you want to understand more about the history of the members of Imurok of Amika, read the second edition of this book.

Ongero

The history of Magwi says, in a certain year, elder Lokaria relocated from Amika, and went and built in Meri Magwi hunting ground, in a land between Panyikwara and Magwi. He later named his home as "Ongera meda" (meaning, monkeys add to my population). Lokaria named his home such because, sincerely, there were no people in this land, but many monkeys were living in Meri Magwi hunting ground. This is why the people of Lokaria said, "Since there are no people here, you monkeys should increase my population. Later, the people named the home of Lokaria, "Ongero". This explains why the home of Ongero became part of Magwi. We can now say that members of Ongero are the members of Imurok who were the first to build in Amica. If you want to know more about the history of Ongero, read the second edition of this book.

AMIKA HILL AND HUNTING GROUNDS

The people of Amika have one hunting ground named Meri-Magwi. A man of Logwar family is responsible for blowing the horn of Meri-Magwi hunting ground. They have one hill named Bome. The people of Amika also have one god named Aliri-nyakal. The history of Magwi says, a child of Ongero is the one who celebrates Aliri-nyakal god. Unfortunately, the elders of Amika did not the names of the elders who used to celebrate the god in the past years. But the one whom the people remember, is Elder Okil. He died and Justo Oryem, was left in charge of the god, to date.

330

LOB'URE

The members of Lob'ure have two small families. These families are P'Iyelle (Jinge), who came from Bar, led by won Kwac Iyelle to Magwi. And P'Ocen Ogwom (Ogom), came from Lokoro, after P'Iyelle. The Lob'ure did not migrate because of famine or war as we previously saw with other Acholi.

The elders of Magwi told me that one time there was war between the Acholi of Sudan and Bar. But we do not know which home in Acholi went for that war. Reports show that after the war, the people of Acholi captured the people of Bar who survived the war, and made them prisoners of war. Later, the people resolved that all the prisoners of war should be put under the leadership of the chief of Magwi. The chief of Magwi received the prisoners and gave them land to build and grow crops. Later, these people called themselves "Jo Lob'ure". They then lived under the leadership of their elder named Igelle. But some people say, other members of the two families in Lob'ure, came from Lokoro and entered Magwi after 1930.

Reports show that the members of Lobu're who came from Lokoro, left Lokoro because of famine which was killing many people that year. The elders of Magwi told me that the members of Lobu're found other people of Magwi already stationed where they are now.

LOB'URE HUNTING GROUND AND HILL

The people of Lob'ure have only one hunting ground named Acila. They do not have a hill or god. We also do not know the name of the people who blow the horn of this hunting ground.

AFUFURU or IJULA

Unfortunately, when I was in Juba (Sudan), I did not get any elder of Afufuru to give me information on the history of Ijula. Secondly, when I was interviewing the elders of other families in Magwi to give me information on the history of Ijula, all of them told me, "Anyone who wants to know the history of Ijula, should ask a born of Ijula. This issue made writing the history of Afufuru difficult for me. But if you want to understand more about the history of Ijula, read the *SecondEdition* of this book.

AFUFURU HILL AND HUNTING GROUND

The members of Afufuru do not have a hunting ground, hill or god.

PALONGANYI

The home of Palonganyi have four small families; *Orak, Imurok, Pa-Wii* and *Marari*.

Orak

The history of Magwi does not state where the members of Orak of Palonganyi came from. But many elders of Acholi say the members of Orak who are currently in Palonganyi, split from the members of Ijula/Afufuru (Orak). We do not know why the Afufuru split, but the history of Acholi says elder Lagul was the one who took his people to Palonganyi. The members of Orak were also the first to start building in the land of Palonganyi. For this reason, they became the owners of the home.

Imurok

The members of Imurok family of Palonganyi came from Imurok. Some people think the members of Imurok of Palonganyi migrated together with the Imurok of Amika.

Pa-Wii

The history of Magwi also says the members of Pa-Wii also came from Imurok. They left Imurok because of famine and war. It seems they were brought to Magwi by Elder Awii. This explains why they called themselves "Jo Pa-Wii" -which means, the people of *Awii*.

Marari

The family members of Marari came from Pa-lwoo (Uganda). They left Uganda because of famine, but we do not know which elder brought them to Magwi. The history of Magwi states that the members of Marari found other members of Magwi already settled where they are now.

PALONGANYI HILLS AND HUNTING GROUNDS

The members of Palonganyi have four hunting grounds namely, Lobela (as we saw earlier in this book, Lobela hunting ground belongs to the people of Ijula. Acholi elders told me that Lobela hunting grounds also belongs to the members of Orak of Palonganyi. This is why some elders say, the members of Orak of Palonganyi separated from the Orak of Afufuru. This is why the members of Orak of Palonganyi and Orak of Afufuru, became the owners of Lobela hunting ground), Ogongo, Odume and Ondire hunting grounds. A child from the family of Orak is the one who blows the horn of all the four hunting grounds. The members of Palonganyi have two hills, Kina-nuka and Ondire hills. They also have two gods namely, Lwoo and Iboro-konya. The elders of Acholi of Sudan told me that a born of Orak is also the one who celebrates the gods (Lwoo and Iboro-konya).

PALIMU

The home of Palimu has one family named "Palimu". All the family members of Palimu came from Bilinyang (Bar). Reports show that the members of Palimu left the land of Bar due to famine. Around 1898, Bar was hit by severe famine, and many people lost their lives due to lack of food. Elder Koji, who was also blind, on realizing that many people where dying of hunger picked his three daughters, Akec (Jore) the eldest, the second born was Laloku, and the third born (whose name people do not know) and they started moving. Elder Koji was searching for people to buy his daughters with millet (food). Elder Koji and his three daughters followed the east and reached "Ogabu" — which is in the land of Lokoya.

In 1898, Chief Kajami Liciri-kwat, the father of Arinya-kono, who was also the grandchild of chief Lolik of Lokoya was on the throne. He welcomed elder Koji well and gave them where to sleep. Koji stayed at Chief Kajami Liciri-kwat's place for seven days. After seven days, Koji's daughters asked their father, "Can we continue moving or not?" The history of Magwi says all these days Koji stayed in Lokoya, Chief Kajami showed him much respect. He kept giving him varieties of food and waragi to Koji (local whisky). Chief Kajami also gave the three girls varieties of food, since they did not drink alcohol. Chief Kajami also told them interesting stories, and all the girls became happy. Unfortunately, Koji did not understand why Chief Kajami was showing him that much respect. Gradually, Koji realised that Chief Kajami was regarding him highly because he had interest in his daughter, Jore (Akec).

Reports show that one day, chief Kajami went and knelt before Koji, and told him, "Elder, your are now old, you cannot walk a long distance since you have been made week by starvation. Secondly, I want to tell you that, if your daughter, Laloku and her younger sister want to continue moving, they can go ahead. But I want you and Jore to remain here with me. I will take care of you without any doubt."

Parmount Cheif Lolik Lado

When elder Koji heard what Chief Kalami told him, and the good things he was doing for them, he agreed with him. Later Koji went and told Laloku and her sister, "God be with you. I want you to go to that hill towards the south." The hill that elder was pointing to his two daughters was Okire Hill. The next morning, Laloku and her sister followed the path towards Acholi, leaving their father and sister, Jore in the compound of Ogabu.

The girls went and settled in "Bege Nyaa" which is at Okire Hill. Later, Laloku married a man and they produced many children, and the children later called themselves "Jo Palimu", as we shall later see in this book. The history of Magwi does not state whether or not Laloku's sister married. Other people say the sister of Laloku, left Laloku in Magwi, and she went and entered the family of Abong in Obbo. But I understood that, it seems, the members of Magwi are confusing the information about the sister of Laloku, with the issue of marriage of Akono, who went and married Anyaker, the sister of Chief Aburi of Obbo.

After a few months, a message was sent from Magwi from Ogabu, that chief Lolik had married Jore. God thereafter blessed Jore with six boys. The first born was named Alimu, second born named Dik, the third born was called Oyat. But elders of Magwi do not know the names of the three children who followed Oyat. Elder Koji stayed with his in-law for four years, 1898-1902, and in the year 1902, he died of an illness.

Chief Kajami Liciri-kwat then buried his in-law, Koji, in Lokoya, and organized a funeral rite as the custom of Lokoya and Acholi demands.

The history of Magwi says chief Kajami, the grandchild of Chief Kajami Licir-kwat, also had another wife from Lokoya. The wife, a daughter of Lokoya, gave birth to girls, and later produced a son, who she named "Okeny", because he was the only boy among girls. Since the mother of Okeny was a queen, the custom of Lokoya, just like the custom of Acholi, stipulates that a son of the queen is the one who becomes chief, upon the death of his father.

The brothers and clan elders of Ogabu then told Akec (Jore), "Our wife, you also know that your co-wife produced only girls, and only one boy named Okeny. The custom of of Lokoya states that, the son of a queen is the one who becomes chief if his father dies. As our brother is now weak with illness, Okeny should succeed him. But we the clan elders have realized that Okeny was still very young- he could not succeed his father. We have realized that you are the only one who has grown up sons. The clan elders have proposed that if chief dies, one of Ajore's sons should become chief. But we realized that if this proposition is effected, then in future it will cause death among the children of Jore and her co-wife's children. The clan elders then told Jore, "When we were discussing among ourselves, we found that other people of Ogabu and the clan mates of your co-wife do not want your son to become chief. But some people among us were saying that if one of your children assumes the throne, then in future he will be killed. Since the issue of the chiefdom is so complex, we now want you to take your children to the land of Acholi, before the chief dies." The news terrified Jore; and she went to her husband and told him the good heart the clan elders have towards her and her child. Jore's husband also saw that the elders' advice was good, because he told Jore, "Woman! Thank you for heeding to the advice of the clan elders. I now want you to take the six children to that hill with forked peak (Okire Hill). I also hope that you will find your two sisters who went there before." After he had finished talking, Chief Kajami entered his hut and picked a rain stone, gave it to Jore, and told her,

"If you feel that the temperature is high when you are walking, sprinkle water on the rain stone, and the the temperature will cool down. Keep doing this till you arrive in Okire hills." The chief continued telling his wife, "Our children, "Alimu" and "Diko," both know how to craft hand hoes, tomahawks and excavation tools very well. If you find a place to settle, the rain stone I have given you should help you in farming".

Then the next day at dawn, Jore (Akec) put the six sons before her, and they started moving towards Acholiland. As Akec and her sons were walking, the sun shone very bright and it became very hot. Jore then remembered what her husband told her. She got water and sprinkled on the rain stone. Immediately, it rained for Jore and her children. Jore and her children walked for two days and they later reached Okire Hill. The elders of Magwi told me that, when Jore and her children reached the foot of Okire Hill, they settled in a place near "Bege Nyaa" where Laloku live, (Akec's sister, Laloku, came before as we saw earlier).

Jore came to Bege Nyaa during rainy season, probably around April or June. The children of Jore immediately opened up large farmlands. When the crops had yielded, the brothers of Alimu were scaring away the birds from the gardens. The members of Amika did not even know that other people had settled near them. Later on, the members of Amika saw the children of Akec because of the rising smoke. In this year, the members of Amika were in Meri-Magwi hunting ground.

Reports show that the members of Amika thought of killing Jore and all her children, since other people of Magwi were unaware of their entry in Bege Nyaa. The members of Amika, then consulted Chief Awata-Leme, who was also the chief of Amika that year, if they could kill Jore and her children. Chief Awata-Leme objected to the idea. He asked his brother Onyang, who came from Imurok, to go and find out how Jore and her children were doing. The chief also instructed Onyang to bring Jore and her children among the people.

Elder Onyang did not defy the orders of the chief. He went to Bege Nyaa, and found that the children of Jore had produced good crop yields and asked them, "Where did you come from?" Other children did not answer Onyang's question. But their elder brother, Alimu, responded, "We came from Ogabu land, which is in Lokoya." Onyang again asked Alimu, "In whose hunting ground have you planted your crops?" Alimu answered, "We do not know the owner of the hunting ground." Later, Onyang asked Jore and her son Alimu if they could go with them home. Since Alimu was also looking for a place to settle, they accepted to go with Onyang. He told his other brothers to pack enough food for the journey only- and leave others in Bege Nyaa. In Acholi custom, if a man dies or goes to work far from home, his eldest son takes care of the family. This also explains why Alimu took care of his father's children.

When Alimu reached home (in Magwi hunting ground) with his father's children, elder Onyang immediately took them to chief Awata-Leme. The chief was very happy to see Alimu, and he gave him land and he built near her sister Laloku. Since Alimu was from a royal family, he also married a royal woman. While his brother, Diko on the other hand married from the family of Imbaro (Omeo). Diko produced a boy with his wife, and they named him Akono. The history of Magwi says, when Akono became an adult, he married Anyaker, the sister of Chief Aburi of Obbo. Later, Chief Awata-Leme gave the people of Alimu, Mulaya Hill, which explains why the members of Palimu got Mulaya Hill.

As we were seeing above, much as the children of Laloku produced children with the people of Magwi, they did not have a family. The elders of Magwi told me that when Alimu and his brothers entered the chiefdom of Magwi, they married girls and produced many children. Later, the people of Alimu and the children of Laloku named themselves "the people of Alimu" or "the people of Palimu".

Other people said Jore came with her children to the people of Amika, around the year 1923. This year, there was severe famine among the people of Amika, because the land of Meri-Magwi was not good for growing crops. Jore, Alimu, and his brothers therefore survived on *mbo'yee* and wild yams. When Alimu realised that eating *mbo'yee* and wild yams was not giving her satisfaction, she went to Obbo in search of *bel aluk caa* a species of sorghum in Sudan). When Alimu reached Obbo, Chief Aburi warmly welcomed him and asked him, "Where did you come from? What brought you here?" Alimu responded to chief, "I came from Bege Nyaa. Famine has driven me to Obbo." When chief Aburi heard Alimu's response, he told his messenger to get six bags of millet and gave to Alimu, to take with him to Magwi. The messenger of Chief Aburi filled six bags of millet and gave to Alimu who went with them back to Magwi.

In the year 1930, as we were seeing above, the people of Magwi shifted from Okire Hill. The people of Palimu shifted and built in "Nyalopure", which is near

Palonganyi. Immediately that year, when the members of Palimu shifted to Nyalopure, a certain man came and buried a charm in a bonfire, where the children of Palimu liked to converge in the evening. The history of Magwi says that the charm the man buried in the bonfire place of the people of Palimu, was a miracle charm used to change people's minds and conduct. The charm changed the minds of the children of Palimu, and they began to hate one another.

Years ago, the children of Palimu loved each other so much, but when the charm entered their hearts, they started quarreling among themselves and this made them to later spit into two groups: Palimu Right and Palimu Left. The people of Palimu Left went and built far in Nyalopure, while th people of Palimu Right remained in Nyalopure. This is how the members of Palimu split into *Palimu Right and Palimu Left.*

PALIMU HILL AND HUNTING GROUND
The members of Palimu do not have hunting ground, hill or god.

KILIYO
The members of Kiliyo split into two small families. They are *Ogitana* and *Ocak*. The history of Acholi says the members of the two families all came from Hiliu which is in Torit. Elder Lokidi was the one who brought the people of Kiliyo to Magwi, because between 1932-38, famine was killing many people in Hiliu (Torit). The members of Kiliyo found the members of Magwi already in their current settlement. If you want to understand more about the history of the people of Kiliyo, read the second edition of this book.

KILIYO HILLS AND HUNTING GROUNDS
The people of Kiliyo have one hunting ground called Lokore-longutu (which means human flesh). But the people of Kiliyo do not have a hill or god.

THE RAIN POT OF MAGWI
There are two rains in the home of Magwi. A big rains stone is in the family of Bura, while a small rain pot is in the family of Logwar in Amika. The elders of Magwi told me that the first rain chief of Bura was chief Auya. They also said chief Auya came with a rain stone. But when the members of Magwi were

still at the foot of Ondire Hill, Chief Auya bought another rain stone from the members of Ijula. Reports say, after the death of Chief Auya, the rain remained with chief Ongee. After Chief Ongee died, the rain remained with Chief Owau. When chief Owau died, the rain remained with Amadeyo, who also died and the rain stone was taken care of by Chief Wurubano Anyam, who is keeping the rain stone up to today.

The elders of Magwi do not know the name of the past chiefs of rain of Logwar (Amika). But they told me that chief of rain of Amika, who many remember, was Chief Laborio Abore. Chief Abore does not have a rain care taker. For this reason, he set tough rules to his people that if anyone in Amika finds a rain stone, they should bring it themselves to him.

As we were seeing the issue of the rain pot of Obbo, we found that the chief of rain of Magwi also has two rain pots, with each pot containing ten rains. If the chief of the rain wants to invoke rain, he sends a rain caretaker to smear the rain stone with oil. Later, the rain caretaker would also pour water in the rain pot. He would then stir the rain stones in the pot with his hands. After a few minutes, rain would fall for the people.

CHAPTER EIGHTEEN

AGORO

THE HOME OF AGORO

There are five homes surrounding the land of Agoro. They are Panyikwara to the South, Omeo and Ofirika to the East, Aru to the West and Lolubo (Lowai) to the North West. The history of Acholi of South Sudan says the northern border of Agoro and Panyikwara, and to the south is River Ayii. The border of Agoro and Ofirika is in Ngulek hunting ground (Ofirika hunting ground) and Kituru hunting ground (the hunting ground of the people of Agoro). The border of Agoro and Aru is in wiobur and Kituru hunting grounds (both are Agoro hunting grounds), while the border of Agoro and Lolubo is under a big tamarind tree, in a place called "Abutuki in nyong", or "Ageronyong". The people of Agoro called the place "Ageronyong"to cover up/coat the vulgarity of the expression "Abutuki in nyong". They then named the place "Abutuki in nyong" or "Ageronyong", in memory of the incident where a son of Agoro had sex with a girl of Lowoi under the tamarind tree. The people of Agoro have nine small families namely: Wili Bari, Orimi, Patoko, Bura, Opara'ba, Ogura, Pawili, Okareng and Kicari.

Agoro, just like Obbo, is divided into left and right. The people of Agoro left have three small families. They are Willi-Bari, Orimi and Patoko, while the people of Agoro right have six small families: Bura, Opara'ba, Ogura, Pawili, Okareng and Kicari.

Before we deeply examine the history of the different families in Agoro, I want us to answer this question, "What does the word Agoro mean?" When I was moving among the clan of Acholi of Sudan, I found that many people do not understand the meaning of the word "Agoro". I hope this book will help many people to understand its meaning. Unfortunately, I found that people attach different meanings to the word "Agoro".

People like Crazzolara say, "Agoro" stands for the the name of Agoro Hill. He said, "The name *Agoro*, among the Acholi and Madi, stands for the hill which is 10,000 feet high. This hill separates Acholi land and Lango. The people of Lotuho are situated to the north of this hill. They call the side of the hill which is in the land of the Lotuho, Imotong. The name Agoro came much later. Many years back, the people who are now called Agoro where called Lango. The people of Agoro who are living at the foot of Agoro Hill in Uganda call themselves "Southern Agoro, while the other people of Agoro are staying in Agoro land in Sudan. The Agoro who are in Sudan call themselves Northern Agoro. Northern Agoro and southern Agoro are separated by Longitol Hill and Lokung. So the name of Agoro tribe is found among the Acholi, Alur, Jo-Lwo (Kavirondo). The name is also found among the Lango-Omiru (Crazzolara, 1954, P, 508)".

But other elders of Agoro, like Mario Wani Atanga, and Jacob Oryem, told me, "Agoro means people who split because of disputes over white-ants" as we shall see below. In the primitive days, the people of Agoro used to call themselves brothers and sisters, but they were moving a lot. Reports indicate that much as the people of Agoro were moving a lot, their first settlements were Agoro and Imotong Hill. The people of Agoro also used to call themselves "Jo Logot" or "Ngaaro". The people of Agoro, known as "Ngaaro", had lived along Ngaaro Stream. They got the name "Ngaaro" from this stream.

The history of Acholi does not state where the Ngaaro came from. However, the people of Ngaaro said the people of Lokaforok split from them and went to Lango Teretenye. This explains why the people of Lokaforok are in Teretenye. They still speak Ngaaro language (Crazzolara, 1954, PP, 508-509).

In the olden days, the people of Agoro-Ngaaro had seven small families as noted here: *Agula-Ngaaro* (Logot and Lokaforok). *Irumo* are in Sudan and Uganda, *Long-gorone* (or Lakole to the north of Imotong Hill), *Lolo'bai* (in Uganda and Sudan),

Lobokai (are in Sudan and Uganda), *Lokudukai* (are in Lokaforok) while *Lo'dimarak* (are in Lamwo of Sudan). All these people used to live in one place. Then around 1916, the British set a tough rule that all the people of Agoro should relocate to the south-highlands, up to Palogaa.

The history of Acholi of Sudan says the members of the other six families accepted the idea of the British to relocate. But the family members of Lodimarak, who were under the leadership of Chief Lopwonya, refused the idea of the British, and went to Agoro Hill to Katire (Sudan). In 1924, the British again set a condition that the people of Agoro, who relocated to the South from Palogaa, should return to Agoro Hill. Reports show that the people of Agoro who went to the south of Palogaa came back, but the people of Agoro who went to Katire (Sudan) did not return to Agoro Hill (Crazzolara, 1954, P, 510).

AGORO LEFT
The people of Agoro left have three small families; *Wili-Bari, Omiri* and *Patoko*.

WILI-BARI
The people of Wili-Bari also split into three small families, they are; *Panyulu, Imude* and *Kuku*. The history of Agoro says the families of *Panyulu* and *Imude* both came from Rumbek around 1700. It seems the people of Imude were the first to step on Agoro land, and the people of Panyulu came later. Elder Nyamoyo was the one who brought the people of Imude from Rumbek, but the elders of Acholi do not know the name of the elder who brought the people of Panyulu. Elder Nyamoyo came with his people and built in Agoro, while the people of Panyulu came and built among them later.

Kuku
The family members of Kuku came from Kaji-kaji around 1850, and later they also called themselves "Kuku". This was to remind them about their brothers who remained in Kaji-kaji. Reports show that the people of Kuku later went and built among the people of Imude and Panyulu later. Gradually, the members of the three families joined into one big home, which is now called *Wili-Bari*.

WILI-BARI HILLS AND HUNTING GROUND
The members of Wili-Bari have one hunting ground named Botolo. The people of Panyulu are the ones who blow the horn of Botolo hunting grounds. But the elders of Agoro do not know the name of the former and current people who were/are blowing the horn of Botolo hunting ground. The members of Wili-Bari also have two hills named Botolo and Pika hills. The history of Agoro

says that both hills belong to the people of Panyulu. The people of Wili-Bari have one god named Kurumunda.

ORIMI

The history of Acholi says the people of Orimi came from five different places. Some came from i *Bar-Nyakenyi*, others from *Lowai* in Lokoya, *Aruu* in Lolubo. Other people came from Lokoro, while other groups came from *Loudo* in Obbo. Later, all these people who came to the family of Orimi, also split into four small families; *Owiria, Pawele, Gem* ki *Kur-laa*. The history of Agoro says some people of Owiria and Pawele came from Bar-Nyakenyi, and others came from Lowai. A section of Agoro elders told me that the people who came from Bar-Nyakenyi were led by elder Merok, and those who came from Lowai were brought by elder Okwer.

The people of Orimi arrived in the land of Agoro between 1885 — 1886. When they reached Agoro, they immediately built at the foot of Pika Hill. There were no people at Pika Hill, for this reason, the people of Orimi became the land owners. They lived at Pika Hill for almost four decades (1886 — 1926). In 1926, the British took all the people of Orimi to Acila River which is in Panyikwara. They lived at Acila for almost ten years (1926 — 1934).

Around 1935, the British again took all the people of Agoro along the road which runs from Opari to Torit. The people of Agoro lived there for five years. And in 1940, they relocated to Ayii River, where they are now.

The elders of Agoro told me that other people of Kur-laa came from Aruu, and some came from Lokoro. The elders of Agoro told me that they do not remember the name of the elder who led the people from Aruu.

The family of Gem came from Loudo in Obbo, but the elders of Agoro did not tell me why the people of Gem left Obbo. They also did not tell me the name of the elder who took the people to Agoro.

ORIMI HILLS AND HUNTING GROUND

The people of Orimi do not have a hunting ground or god.

PATOKO

The people of Patoko have two small families. They are *Paguur* and *Panyimo*. *They both came from* Patoko Hill in Pajok. Elder Olem-Cigira was the one who brought the people of Paguur and Panyimo in Agoro. The history of Acholi says in the year 1890, there was a dispute between the people of Paguur and Panyimo and other which made them leave Pajok. Elder Olem-Cigira, of Paguur, after seeing the souring relationship, took the people of Paguur together with the Panyimo to Agoro. The peole of Agoro welcomed the people of Olem-Cigira well and gave them a place to settle. Later, the people of Paguur and Panyimo called themselves "Jo Patoko", in memory of their old place of settlement. Up to now, there is still a strong bond between the people of Patoko of Agoro and the Patoko of Pajok. This is also one reason the people of Patoko of Agoro still worship Patoko Hill.

AGORO RIGHT

Agoro right has six small families namely: *Bura, Oparaba, Ogura, Pawili, Okareng*, and *Kicari*.

BURA

Bura has three small families: *Mikito, Palyiec* and *Pa-Amiti*. The history of Agoro says all these three families came from different places. The members of PaAmiti came from Bar-Nyakenyi. They left Bar because of famine. Chief Amiti was the one who led these people to Agoro. They later called themselves P'Amiti -which means "the people of Amiti". Chief Amiti came with rain stone, royal spear and drum. We do not know where the rain stone remained after the death of Chief Amiti.

But much as the history of Agoro says the three families of Bura came from different places, I found that the people of Agoro still don't know where the people of Mikito and the Palyec came from. But others think, the members of these three families all came from Bar-Nyakenyi. I am assuming that many elders of Agoro think so because many Acholi came from Bar-Nyakenyi.

We were seeing above that during the olden days the people of Agoro, all lived together. Later, the British divided them, which made other people to come to Katire (Sudan). Much as the history of Acholi does not state the migration of the people of Agoro from Katire, to Bar-Nyakenyi, I think the first group of Agoro lived in Katire, and later shifted to Bar-Nyakenyi. From there, they came to Acholiland. This explains why people say the people of Agoro Bura came from Bar-Nyakenyi. But if we follow the history closely, we find that the people of Agoro Bura came from Katire. Other people say that the people of Cwua Bura, of Agoro Uganda moved together with the people of Agoro Bura of Sudan. Because the history of Acholi says Cwua Bura of Uganda came from Bar of Chief Meela. They were brought to the land of Acholi of Sudan by Chief Waka.

Elder Jacob Oryem and Sir Alexander Oyet, of Agoro of Sudan, told me that the people of Agoro Bura came from Bar-Nyakenyi, which is in Rajaf (Juba). They also told me that in the year famine hit Bar, many died of starvation, forcing many people to leave Bar. When the people of Bura where in Bar, they lived under the leadership of two people, Amiti and Opoko. Elder Ajur produced his son, Awaac, and Awaac produced a son, Opoko (Crazzolara, 1954, P, 511).

When elder Amiti and Opoko saw that many people where dying of famine, they got a group of people, and started moving towards the south.

Many elders were telling me that the people of Cwua Bura and Agoro Bura of Sudan moved a lot in the hunting ground, without knowing where they were heading to. Gradually, the people of Agoro Bura and Cwua Bura came to a place called "Oburi". After two or three days, when they where still resting, it rained cats and dogs, and it became hard for them to continue with their journey, because of flood. It became very difficult to move with the women and children. For this reason, the people of Agoro stayed in Oburi for a short time so that the floods could subside. When the rain stopped, the sun shone that very evening and people harvested white ants (Agoro). The history of Agoro says the members of Amiti caught a lot of white ants, but the people of Opoko and Cwua Bura, who are in Uganda, caught few white ants.

When the group of Amiti saw that there was a lot of food, they told the people of Opoko that they would not continue with the journey. They wanted to stay in Oburi until the group ate the white ants to completion, before proceeding with their movement.

When the members of Cwua Bura and the group of Opoko heard the information, they left the group of Amiti in Oburi. They went and later built among the people of Agula-Ngaaro, at Agoro Hill in Uganda. Later, the group of Opoko called themselves "Agoro P'Opoko" or "Logot Agoro". While the Agoro who remained in Sudan called themselves "Agoro P'Bar. Reports show that some members of Agoro P'Opoko later came back to the land of the Acholi of Sudan, but they did not stay for long in Sudan. They went back to Uganda (Crazzolara, 1954, P, 511).

The history of Acholi says that Chief Waka, of Cwua Bura, took his people from Oburi to Atyiak. They settled in Okago where the people of Pagara used to live. Some people say the brother of Chief Waka and his wife who had a new born baby remained in Oburi (Sudan). From Atyiak, Rwot Waka took the people of Cwua Bura to Agoro Hill. Other people built on the hill, while others built in Madi Opei. The members of Cwua Bura, who built in Madi Opei, settled there for a few months, and later found that land in Madi Opei was clay soil, and it could not produce good crop yields and could crack the feet of the chief. For this reason, the people of Cwua Bur did not take long in Madi Opei. They relocated to Ogoya -which is at the foot of Okool Hill.

Chief Waka died in Ogoya and his son Labeel succeeded him, and also died in Ogoya. After the death of Chief Labeel, his son Odur became the chief. Reports show that Chief Odur was the one who took the people of Cwua Bura to Okong-lela (Ikolong), which connects to Okool Hill. Gradually, the people of Cwua Bura of Okool called themselves *Lwak P'Leeng* (Crazzolara, 1954, P, 523).

Some people said not all the people of Agoro of Uganda came from Sudan. Others came from different places. Later, the people of Agoro who came from Sudan, and those who came from other places split into ten small families: *Wili-Bari* (Panyulu), *Ariimi, Patoko, Irenge, Ogoora, Bura, Opara'ba, Koyo* (Kicari), *Okaari* and *Imurok*. The members of the nine families in Agoro, Uganda speak Ngaaro, Acholi, Madi and Lokoya dialects. But the people of Panyulu speak only Acholi.

OPARA'BA

Opara'ba has two small families, *Pakwal* and *Won-cuk*. The members of these two families came from Bar-Nyakenyi around 1886. We do not know if the Opara'ba came together with the people of Cwua Bura. Other elders of Agoro told me that elder Cwaka Meringiro was the one who brought the members of Pakwal, while elder Won-cuk brought the members of Won-cuk. When the members of Opara'ba reached the land of Acholi of Sudan they built their first settlement at the foot of Oboto Hill in Wi-Obur hunting grounds. The people of Opara'ba realized that Oboto Hill was good because of two reasons. First, the land around the hill is conducive for farming. And secondly, there were flat low rocks on which women could dry their millet and fermented and toasted flour for making kwete alcohol.

Unfortunately, before the people of Opara'ba had settled, the people of Lokoro started killing the people of Cwaka and Won-cuk. When Cwaka

Maringiro and Won-cuk, saw that the people of Lokoro were killing many people, they took the people of Opara'ba and relocated to Logura Hill, which is in Deyo —Deyo hunting ground belongs to the people of Opara'ba. The history of Agoro says the people of Opara'ba lived at Logura Hill for almost forty years (1886-1926). In 1926, the British took the people of Opara'ba to the bank of Acila Stream in Panyikwara. The people of Opara'ba lived in Acila for ten years (1926-1934). Later, they they realized that Acila was not a good place, because of scarcity of water for drinking. During rainy season, people could fetch water for drinking and cooking from Acila Stream. But in dry season, women went about five miles away looking for water.

In 1935, because of scarcity of water, the people of Opara'ba left Acila. They relocated to Ayii River, where they lived for five years 1935-1940. In 1940, the people of Opara'ba shifted near Captain Cook Road, where they built and are living today.

OPARA'BA HILLS AND HUNTING GROUNDS

The members of Opara'ba have one hunting ground called Wi-Obur. The history of Agoro says years ago, the hunting ground belonged to the people of Goloba. In the year 1900, the people of Goloba gave the hunting ground in compensation of a girl of Won-cuk, who they killed. This is why Wi-Obur huntng ground became the property of the people of Opara'ba. Reports show that the first horn blower of Wiobur hunting ground was Won-cuk. After the death of Won-cuk, the hunting ground remained under the care of his son, Koria. When Koria died, Atanga Kengo Moi took over, and when he died Jajur Wang-kwany was left in charge. When Jajur Wang-kwany passed on, the hunting ground was taken care of by his son, Lokuta. In the year 1986, when I started writing this book, elder Lokuta was the one who was blowing the horn of Wi-Oburi hunting ground.

The history of Acholi says the people of Opara'ba have one hill called Oboto (the word *Oboto* in Agoro dialect means *people of the hill*). However, the people of Opara'ba do not have a god.

OGURA

The people of Ogura have two small families. They are *Wur-ber* and *Nyamuto-kori*. Some elders of Agoro told me that other people of Wur-ber came from Aruu (Lolubo), while others came from Rumbek. Reports show that the members of Wur-ber, who came from Aruu, were the first to step on Agoroland (Acholi Sudan). They came around the year, 1685-1700 (?), and the people of Wur-ber, who came from Rumbek, entered the land of Acholi of Sudan around 1700-1886 (?). They built among the people of Wur-ber who came from Aruu later on. Other people think when the people of Wur-ber came from Rumbek to Acholi land, other people of Agoro where already in the place near Pika Hill. Later, the people who came from Aruu, and those who came from Rumbek, settled together in the one family, now called Wur-ber, which is in Agoro-Sudan.

The family of Nyamuto-kori also came from Rumbek around 1700-1886 (?). We do not know whether or not the members of Nyamuto-kori and Wur-ber, who came from Rumbek, moved together. The history of Acholi of Sudan says that elder Nyamutokori was the one who led the members of Nyamuto-kori family from Rumbek. The members of Nyamutokori found the members of Wur-ber, who came from Aruu, already settled on the land of Acholi-Sudan. It seems when the group of Nyamuto-kori, reached the land of the Acholi of Sudan, they found the people of Agoro at the foot of Oboto of Lagura Hill. The group of Nyamuto-kori went and built among the people of Wur-ber. The people of elder Nyamuto-kori gradually called themselves "the people of *Nyamuto-kori*".

Some say the people of Nyamuto-kori, Panyulu, Imude and a section of the people of Wur-ber moved together with the people of Cwua Bura (Agoro) who passed through to Uganda, while the people of Nyamuto-kori remained because of white-ants as we saw earlier.

OGURA HIlLS AND HUNTING GROUND

The people of Ogura have one hunting ground, Logura. A born of Wur-ber is responsible for blowing the horn of the hunting ground. The elders of Agoro told me that they do not know the name of the first person to blow the horn of the hunting ground. But the one whose name people remember was elder Gambuye. The elders of Agoro also do not know the name of the people who blew the horn after the death of Gambuye. All these happened because no one documented the history of Agoro, all information was passed from elders to their young ones orally. Always when an elders tells the history of a place to a wise child, they will get more knowledge and memorise it. But if elders give such information to a dull child, they always forget much of the information.

The people of Ogura have one hill called Nyar-kenyi. This hill belongs to the people of Wur-ber. The people of Ogura also have a god called Wor-bura. A child of Wur-ber is the one tasked with the responsibility of taking care of the shrine. The elders of Agoro do not know the names of the people who were taking care of Wor-bura shrine. They told me that the care taker of the shrine, whose name the people remember is Ambrose Bara. After Ambrose Bara died, his son, Paul Okot Ambrose, should have taken care of the shrine. Unfortunately, the war commanded by John Garang De Mabior, which started in 1983, made the people of Agoro scattered. Some people I was talking to assume that if peace returns in Sudan, Sir Paul Okot Ambrose will take care of Wobura shrine.

PAWILI

The people of Pawili have one family called *Pawili*. The history of Acholi says all the members of Pawili came from Imurok (Katika) around 1700. Records show that around 1700, the members of Imurok-Katika realized that elder Wili and his group could turn into leopards anytime they wanted. Most times, the members of Pawili could turn into leopards whenever they wanted to eat human flesh. The history of Agoro says the people of Wili were biting many people in the land of Imurok.

One day, the elders of Imurok-Katika were discussing some issues around a bonfire. They were saying in one voice, "We do not want Wili and his group to continue staying among us, because if they continue living with us, then they will finish our children." The next morning, the clan elders of Imurok sent messengers to Wili with a message that he (Willi) should leave Imurok. When elder Wili learnt that the people of Imurok did not want them, he took his people to Okwaa —which is near Okaru (Lokoya). The people of Lokoya gave the people of Wili a warm welcome and gave them a place to settle.

The people of Wili had also moved with cattle. The history of Agoro says later on, the people of Lokoya also started stealing the cattle belonging to the people of Wili. Unfortunately, the group of Wili did not leave the habit of eating children. They continued eating children when they settled in Okwaa. Gradually, the people of Lokoya realized that many children were disappearing, but did not know what/who was making the children disappear. After a short time, the people of Lokoya learnt that the people of Wili were the ones eating their children. For this reason, in the year, 1705 the people of Lokoya chased Willi and his group from their land.

Since the people of Lokoya did not want the members of Wili to continue staying on their land, Wili took them and they started moving towards Acholi land. They walked for about three days and later arrived in Agoro, and built among the people of Agoro Right. The members of Wili entered the land of Agoro bearing the name Imurok (they used to call themselves the people of Imurok (jo Imurok). They produced many children and later called themselves "Jo Pawili" -which means, the people of *Wili*.

Some elders of Agoro told me that the Pawilli left Okwaa (Lokoya), because of four reasons. First, it was because of famine which was killing many people. Secondly, they left Lokoya because of theft of their cattle. And thirdly, they left because of constant fight between them and their brothers who remained behind. And fourthly, the Pawili left the land of Lokoya because the people of Lokoya chased them due to their habit of eating children.

As we saw in the previous page, the Pawili built among the members of Agoro Right. This is also one reason why the people of Pawili have become one family in the home of Agoro of Sudan.

Much as the Pawili left Lokoya, we find that they still worship the god of Okwaa, which is in Okwaa Hill in Lokoya. Okwaa god and Okwaa Hill are the uniting factors of the Pawili and their brothers in Lokoya. The Pawili still worship the god of Okwaa, because in1705, when the members of Wili were still in the land of Lokoya, elder Wili ate Lokirwanga at the time of circumcision of the people of Lokoya men. According to the custom of the Lokoya, if anyone eats orwanga meat, it means he has been circumcised, so such a person, even if he moves to another land, he must continue to worship Okwaa. This is the reason the Pawili still worship Okwaa of Lokoya till this day.

Acholi elders told me that much as the people of Imurok and Lokoya chased the members of Wili from their land because of eating human flesh, the Pawili themselves did not understand this habit. Reports show that when the Pawili entered the land of the Acholi of Sudan, they continued eating children, because it was their nature. Since the Pawili were cannibals, they set one tough rule that no child of Pawili should eat *ocuka* and *malakwang* vegetable dishes. The reason was that if anyone ate the dishes, their teeth would go blunt, and they would not be able to bite a human being, even if they had turned into a leopard.

The history of Agoro says the person who was very popular among the Pawili, when they were in Acholiland was Lobaya. One day Lobaya wanted to kill a person. Always when Lobaya wanted to change into a leopard, he did not want his wife to see him morph into a leopard. That night, Lobaya and his wife were sleeping at the fireplace. Lobaya then asked his wife to enter the house, but she objected and continued sleeping at the bonfire. When Lobaya saw that his wife was not going to budge, he then told her, "Well, sleep! Then you will soon see what you want to see." The woman did not understand why her husband told her such thing. Truly, she continued sleeping at the fireplace. After a short time, Lobaya turned into a leopard, he bit his wife to death. This shows that Lobaya's wife did not know that her husband could change into a leopard. If she did, she would have listened to him. When Lobaya had killed his wife, he did not eat her flesh, but went to the village to look for children as always.

Around 1890 the girls of Pawili realized that it was not good to be killing the children of their friends. For this reason, women started beating the children with mingling stick. The custom of people who can change says that a child should not be beaten with a mingling stick, lest they should be unable to turn/change into a leopard. All the women of Pawili knew this rule. This is why they started beating the children with mingling stick, because they wanted the habit of biting people to discontinue.

From 1890, when the women started beating the children with mingling stick, the power to turn into a leopard, ceased among the members of Pawili – the mingling stick spoiled the celebration. Later, the Pawili started eating *ocuka* and *malakwang* dishes freely.

Even if we saw in the previous pages that the people of Agoro split into Left and Right, we still find that during the olden days, they were under the leadership of Amiti of Bura. Later, chief Amiti married a girl from the family of Agoro left. They produced a son named Lokici, which made Chief Amiti to become the chief of Agoro Left. In the year the members of Agoro left saw that Lokici had become an adult, they asked Chief Amiti to give part of his chiefdom to him. This means that Lokici would become the Chief of Agoro Left. Since

Chief Amiti, was also an in-law of Agoro Left, he did not object to the idea. Chief Amiti then installed his son Lokici chief of Agoro Left. Chief Amiti then ruled over the members of Agoro Right. This also shows us how the people of Agoro Left, left the rule of Bura.

Reports show that gradually, the people of Agoro Pawili lost their chiefdom to the people of Magwi. There is no proof why the people of Agoro went back under the leadership of the chief of Magwi. But some people assume that it must have been because of the British who took the people of Agoro and their sovereignty and put them under the leadership of the chief of Magwi. We also do not know whether or not the people of Agoro immediately went back under the leadership of the chief of Magwi after the death of Chief Amiti. Even if the Pawili respected Chief Amiti, the chief also wanted them to respect the clan elders in the home of Pawili.

OKARENG

Okareng has two small families, *Pa-cobono* and *Agilimiang*.

Pa-cobono: The history of Acholi says some people of Pa-cobono came from Lowai, in Lokoya. While others say some members of Pa-cobono came from Locurak, in Ofirika.

Reports say the people of Pa-cobon who came from Lowai, left the land of Lokoya because of famine. But the history of Acholi does not state which year they entered the land of the Acholi of Sudan. The elders of Agoro told me that the members of Pa-cobono were brought by elder Cobon from Lowai. Other members of Pa-cobono came from Locurak in Ofirika, bearing the name Locurak. Reports show that the people of Locurak left the land of Ofirika, because of war and constant fights which erupted among them each time there was a dance. If you want to understand more about the fights, read "Locurak under Ofirika". Later the people who came from Lowai together with those who came from Ofirika called themselves "Jo Pa-Cobono" –which means the people of *Cobono.*

Agilimiang: The history of Acholi says some members of Agilimiang came from Langairo, and others came from Locurak in Ofirika. It seems when those who came from Locurak, reached Agoro, they split into two. Other people entered the family of Pa-Cobono, and some joined the family of Agilimiang. The elders of Agoro told me that elder Lotodo was the one who brought the people who came from Longairo. They left the land of Longairo because of famine and fighting. All the people of Pa-cobono and Agilimiang came and built in Agoro-Wai. They found other people already settled in Agoro. Chief Amiti, of Agoro Bura, welcomed the people of Pa-cobono and the people of Agilimiang and gave them a place to settle.

OKARENG HILLS AND HUNTING GROUNDS

The people of Okareng have one hunting ground called Kituru. Other elders say the people of Okareng shared Kituru hunting ground with the people of Iyere. But we do not know very well how the people of Okareng shared Kituru hunting ground with the people of Iyire. What we know is that a born of Okareng is the one who blows the horn of this hunting ground. The people of Okareng also have a god called Okwaa. This god is at Okwaa Hill. We also find that Okwaa Hill, which also belongs to the people of Okareng, is in the hunting ground of the people of Kicari.

KICARI

Kicari has only one family, Kicari. All the members of this family came from Lowai (Lokoya), under the leadership of elder Nyagum to the land of Acholi of Sudan.

KICARI HUNTING GROUND AND HILL

The members of Kicari have one hunting ground called Kicari. They also have one hill called Kicari. But they do not have a god.

Chapter Nineteen

OFIRIKA

THE HOME OF OFIRIKA

There are three families surrounding the home of Ofirika. They are Lokoya to the north, Omeo to the west, and Magwi to the south, runs up to the south and south east. The history of Acholi says the boundary of Ofirika and Lokoya (Lowai) is in Ngulek and Cukayo hunting grounds (both are hunting grounds of Ofirika). The border of Ofirika and Omeo is in Ikola and Kilaba hunting grounds (both are hunting grounds of Omeo). While the border of Ofirika and Magwi is in Itele, Kobwari and Cukayo hunting grounds (all hunting grounds belong to the members of Ofirika).

As we saw earlier, we find that the names of other homes have meanings. Before we even proceed to look at the history of the people of Ofirika, I want us to answer one question, "What does the word Ofirika mean?" Justine Oboma and Abraham Paulino Atari, of Ofirika, who also gave me a lot of information said, "Ofirika means, people who lived between two hills." We also think this is true, because the people of Ofirika live between Fuka and Okulu hills. Many Acholi elders told me that, Ofirika was a small family among other families in Acholi County. The number of tax payers among them, that time, was less than five hundred (500). According to rules, if the number of taxpayers in any place does not exceed five hundred people, the British would not give them a chief. Since the number of taxpayers in Ofirika was less than five hundred, between 1900-1923, the British put them under the leadership of Chief Joseph Olaa, of Magwi.

One year, the people of Ofirika sat in a meeting and resolved that the people of Ofirika could not continue being ruled by the chief of Magwi, as if they did not have people who could be leaders. After the meeting, the people of Ofirika chose Chief Lokwat Patige. They also elected five people from each family to help the chief during court hearings. These people were Labilo Lobone, Barat Lokide, Apire, Gregorio Lacivilo and Lotiri-jil. By bad luck, the people later realized that Chief Lokwat Patige did not have full authority, unlike the other Acholi chiefs.

Under the Local Government Act, if a chief collects taxes from the people, he uses the money to pay his workers, and takes part of it to the County Chief or Sub County Chief. However, Chief Lokwat was not capable of paying his workers, because the British told him to give all the money he collected as taxes to Chief Joseph Olaa. In short, we can say, the role of Chief Lokwat, was just to collect taxes from the people of Ofirika. Even if his role was just that, I realized that making Lokwat chief gave the people of Ofirika a lot of confidence. Reports show that Joseph Olaa, a born of Omeo, was also the first chief of Magwi.

Chief Lokwat led the people of Ofirika very well. And in 1926, when the British government took the people of Ofirika, together with a section of the people of Omeo and Agoro to settle at the road side. That time, Chief Lokwat Patige was on the throne. After the death of Chief Lokwat, the people of Ofirika did not elect anyone to take over the chiefdom. When the British saw this, they took back the people of Ofirika under the leadership of chief of Magwi as it was before. It seems the British put back the people of Ofirika under the chief of Magwi, in the year Chief Marino was leader. After the death of Chief Marino, elder Loliya-moi of Ofirika became the chief.

Chief Loliya-moi was the first member of Ofirika to touch the chief's throne in Magwi. Chief Loliya-moi led all the people of Magwi, Omeo, Agoro and Ofirika. This also proves to us that the people of Ofirika were the only ones who were not under the leadership of the chief of Magwi. The people of Omeo and Agoro were under the leadership of the chief of Magwi.

Much as Ofirika is a small home in Acholi, we still find that they have six small families: *Lomiling, Lodulang, Tabwor, Locurak, Romorok,* and *Iyere.*

LOMILING

The people of Lomiling have four small families. They are *Lohelengi, Ijuhok, Ibore* and *Imolongoi.* Then members of all these families came from different places as we shall see here below.

355

Lohelengi: The history of Acholi says the members of Lohelengi came from Iyire (Obbo). Elder Odire Hohofir was the one who brought them from Iyire to Ofirika. Reports show that these people left Iyire because of two important reasons. First, because of diseases and deaths which were disturbing the people. Secondly, they left Iyire because life in Iyire had become very difficult, because the people of Iyire loved clandestine war. So the members of Lohelengi saw that if they kept staying there, it would in future cause many deaths among the people. The people of Lohelengi built at the foot of Habulo Hill, where they are living up now. The leaders of Ofirika, such as Abraham Paulino Atari, said the people of Lohelengi came and found the people of Romerok already settled at Habulo Hill. Reports show that the elder who led the outsiders (Romerok), welcomed the people of Lohelengi well and gave them land to build and plant crops.

Ijuhok and Ibore: The members of Ijuhok family and Ibore came from Imurok. Elder Dalaha was the one who brought the people of Ijuhok, while elder Lwala brought the people of Ibore to Ofirika (Acholi Sudan).

Many Acholi elders told me that, the people of Ijuhok left the land of Imurok because of diseases that was killing many people that year. When elders Dalaha and Lwala saw that many people were dying, they gathered the members of Ijuhok and Ibore, and told that them, "We should look for a place where we can live in peace."

Reports show that these two groups of people settled among the group of Lohelengi. It seems the people of Ijuhok and Ibore were related. This is also why people say that Iwala and Dalaha should have been brothers. But we do not know who of the two brothers is older. But what we know is that since Justin Oboma said, "Dalaha was a shabby man, with mob, long unkempt hair. While elder Iwala was always smart, and had many cattle. Some people say, when the members of Iwala were still in Imurok, elder Iwaca separated with his brother, Dalaha, because of his inhygiene.

Imolongoi: The history of Ofirika says the members of Imolongoi family came from Igara. Elder Abiliwac was the one who brought the members of Imolongoi to the land of the Acholi of Sudan. Other elders of Ofirika told me that the members of Imolongoi were the last people to join Lomiling family.

LOMILING HILL AND HUNTING GROUND

The members of Lomiling have one hunting ground, Cukayo (Aliha). Some elders say the people of Lohelengi came and found that the hunting ground had no owner. Lohelengi were the first to draw the border of Cukayo hunting ground, which also explains why they became the owners of the hunting ground. A born of Lohelengi is responsible for blowing the horn of Cukayo hunting ground. Unfortunately, I did not get time to ask the names of those who blew the horn of this hunting ground. I think we shall write the name of the past and present people who blew the horn in the *Second Edition* of this book.

The members of Lomiling also have one hill called Habuho. They also have one god called "Ituhoh", which resides on Habuho Hill. A born of Lohelengi is the one who celebrates Habuho god. People say the first priest of Ituhoh shrine was elder Langa-bolo. After the death of Langa-bolo, the shrine was left under elder Irwangi. After the death of Irwangi, Ituhoh was taken care of by Peter Langa-bolo. When Peter Langa-bolo died, Ituhoh god was taken care of by his wife named Anita. Anita is taking care of the shrine up to now.

LODULANG

Lodulang has only one family which is also called Lodulang. All the people of this family were brought from Loudo (Latuko) by elder Lokwat Patige. The history of Acholi says the members of Lodulang left Loudo, because of a bad relationship between Lokwat Patige and his brothers who remained behind. When Lokwat Patige saw that disputes and fights were intensifying among the people, he gathered his people and brought them to Acholi, so that they would live in peace.

According to reports, when the members of Chief Lokwat Patige arrived in Ofirika, they found the members of Ofirika who came earlier already settled at Habulo Hill. The people of Ofirika are still at Habulo Hill. The elder who was leader of the outsiders (Romorok), who are also the land owners, welcomed the people of Lokwat well and gave them land to build and grow crops. Later, other people of Lodulang went and built in Igara.

LODULANG HILL AND HUNTING GROUND

The members of Lodulang have one hunting ground named *Mulek*. Elder Lajafa was the first person to blow the horn of Mulek hunting ground. After the death of Lajafa, the hunting ground was taken care of by his son; Icalang. When Icalang died, Lobira took over the hunting ground. Lobira also died and Aburujo took care of the hunting ground. Elder Aburujo died in 1999. Since people scattered because of war, the people of Lodulang (Ofirika) do not know very well who was left in charge of Mulek hunting ground.

The members of Lodulang have one hill called Omala. They also have one god called Omala. The god is found on Omala Hill. The history of Ofirika says elder Lajafa was the first person to take care of the shrine. Reports show that on the day celebrating the shrine, the owner of the god would take unfiltered kwete alcohol (angaci) to the shrine. When he reached the entrance of the cave, he would, stump the ground, so that all the snakes in the cave could be alerted that he had brought for them food. Later, he would sit at the entrance of the cave, and pick a vase of local brew and pour more *angaci* on the ground. After a short time, big snakes and small ones would emerge one by one and lick the alcohol. On the day of celebrating the shrine, the owner of the god would sit at the entrance of the cave until all the god's snakes drunk the alcohol to satisfaction.

When elder Lajafa saw that the snakes had not had enough alcohol to drink, he would pour *angaci* for them to lick. After this, elder Lajafa would get water, wash his feet before the shrine and go back home. We do not know for how many years elder Lajafa took care of the shrine. But one thing we are sure of is after the death of Lajafa, the shrine remained with his son, Icalang. After the death of Icalang, he god remained with Lobira. After Lobira died, Aburujo was left in charge of the god. Elder Aburujo died in the 1999, since many were scattered because of fighting, the people of Lodulang (Ofifika) do not know who was left in charge of Omala god.

TABWOR

The people of Tabwor have only one family also known as Tabwor. All the people of this family came from different places. The history of Ofirika says other members came from Lafon (Lokoro), and other came from Loudo (Lotuko).

Some elders of Ofrika told me that the people of Tabwor who came from Loudo were led by elder Ijong. But other elders told me that elder Barat Lohide was the one who brought this group from Loudo.

We do not know very well if Ijong and Barat Lohide were brothers or not. We

358

are well aware that all these happened because the history of the members of Ofirika was not documented. Reports show that the members of Tabwor, who came from Loudo, were the first to enter the land of the Acholi, followed by the people who came from Lokoro. All the people came from Loudo and immediately built in Habuko Hill. The history of Ofirika tells us that the people of Tabwor who came from Lafon, were brought by elder Cokili to Acholi land. Elder Cokili and his group left Lokoro because of quarrels and fighting with their brothers who remained behind. The elders of Ofirika told me that the members of Tabwor, usually loved to quarrel whenever the boys were eating *monyomiji*'s food.

Reports show that one day, the people of Tabwor prepared food for all boys in the group of monyomiji. The boys under the leadership of Cokili were also in the group of this monyomiji. But when the boys were eating, the leader of the monyomiji invited other people to eat, but not boys who were under the leadership of Cokili. This issue caused a very serious dispute and fighting among the boys. Cokili also understood that that was not the first time his boys were being denied food. For this reason, Cokili took his people away from Lafon, because he thought that if they continued living in Lafon, then in future death would occur among the people.

Cokili gathered his people and told them, "My people, I want to inform you that our brothers do not have good heart towards us. This issue was brought to light on the day the boys in the group of Monyomiji were eating. I think if we continue living together; in future there will be death among us. I now appeal to everyone under my leadership to prepare so that we continue roaming."

All the people of Tabwor supported the idea of elder Cokili. Truely the next morning, they began moving towards Acholiland. They walked for almost five days and later reached Habuko Hhill, where they found their brothers who came from Loudo. The elder of Romorok welcomed the people who came from Lokoro warmly and gave them a place to settle. They built among their brothers who came from Loudo.

TABWOR HILL AND HUNTING GROUND

The people of Tabwor have one hunting ground called Ifakulang. They also have one hill called Tinyara. But they do not have a god. The elders of Ofirika did not tell me the names the owners (past and present) of the hunting ground.

I think we shall get the names of the past and present owners of the hunting ground in the second *Edition* of this book.

LOCURAK

Locurak have only one family, Locurak. The history of Acholi says all the members of Locurak came from Loudo (Lotuko). They left Lotuko land because of famine, but we do not know the year they entered Acholiland. Some people say the people of Locurak are related to the people of (Ramorok). This is why they moved together when they were coming from Loudo. Reports indicate that elder Imoyi was the leader of the people of Locurak when they were coming from Lotuko. The history of Ofirika say, when the people of Locurak reached Acholiland (Ofirika), they built together with the people of (Ramorok) at the foot of Ramorok Hill.

One day, Locurak and Ramorok were dancing. After a short time, Locurak started quarreling with the boys of (Ramorok) because of the evil-eye who were killing people. The boys continued arguing and later it led to a serious fight between the boys of Locurak and the boys of Ramorok who were dancing. The elders of Ofirika told me that the fight did not end at the dance arena, but it spread all over the homes and people continued fighting for three days. Many boys and men lost their lives in the fight. When Chief Imoyi saw that the fighting was escalating, on the third day, he went and stopped the fighters.

Acholi tradition states that when a chief stops the people fighting, they should listen. Truly, when Chief Imoyi told the boys and men to stop fighting, the boys and men listened to him and put their spears and shields down. Reports say immediately after the fighting, other members of Locurak shifted and built among the members of Tabwor, while others went and built in Okareng (Agoro). Few people remained in the home of Locurak (Ofirika).

LOCURAK HILLS AND HUNTING GROUNDS

Locurak have one hunting ground called Mulek. The history of Ofirika states that the members of Locurak shared this hunting ground with the people of Lodulang. We however do not know why the people of Locurak shared Mulek hunting ground with Lodulang. But the elders of Ofirika say much as the members of Locurak shared Malek hunting ground with Lodulang, on the day of hunting, a born of Lodulang is the one to blow the horn of this hunting ground. This also shows us that the owners of Mulek hunting ground are the people of Lodulang.

RAMOROK

The people of Ramorok have one family known as Ramoro. All the members of this family came from Loudo (Lotuko) because of famine. But we do not know which year they entered the land of the Acholi of Sudan. As we saw above, the members of Ramorok moved together with the members of Locurak, because they are related. Elder Imoyi is the man who brought the people of Ramorok and Locurak to the land of Ofirika.

However, some elders of Ofirika like Abraham Paulino Atari said the members of Ramorok were the first to arrive in the land of Ofirika, and members of Lodulang were the second group after them.

The people of Locurak came much later. They followed their relatives. This explains why the members of Ramoko have become the owners of the land of Ofirika. Other people came and built among them much later. Many years back, the present day Ramorok, where known as "the people of Loudo' or "the Loudo". But they later acquired the new name from Ramorok Hill. This is why the people of Loudo currently call themselves, *Ramorok*.

RAMOROK HILL AND HUNTING GROUND

The people Ramurok of have one hunting ground, Ifil. Unfortunately, the elders I interviewed on the history of Ofirika didn't know the names of the former and current people who blew the horn of Ifil hunting ground. The history of Acholi says, the members of Ramorok do not have a hill, but they have a god named Ajilimit. The elders of Ofirika I was interviewing also do not know the names of the people responsible for taking care of Ajilimit shrine. I suggest you read the second edition of this book, if you want to understand more about the god and hunting grounds of Ramorok.

IYERE

Iyere have one family also known as Iyere. The history of Acholi says Iyere came from Lowai (Lokoya). They left Lokoya because of famine and fighting which killed many people that year. But we do not know the name of the elder who brought them from Lowai to the land of the Acholi of Sudan. The members of Iyere came and found other members of Ofirika already settled at the foot of Ramorok Hill, and built among these people much later. I also hope that we shall understand more about the members of Iyere in the *Second Edition* of this book.

IYERE HILL AND HUNTING GROUND

The members of Iyere have one hunting ground named Kituru. The elders of Ofirika, I talked to, told me that they do not know the name of the first person who was the blower of the horn of Kituru hunting ground. But they told me that after the death of this man (whose name is not known) the hunting ground remained under the care of Lotirigil. After the death of Lotirigil the hunting ground remained under the guardianship of his wife, Lotiri. After the death of Lotiri (the wife of Lotirigil) the hunting ground remained with the son, Lomuke. Up to the time I was writing this book, Lomuke was the one blessing and inviting the people to hunt in Kituru hunting ground. The people of Iyere do not have a hill or god.

THE RAIN POT OF OFIRIKA

In the home of Ofirika there is a rain pot in the family of Lodulang, also called Kabwore by some people. Another rain stone is in the family of Ramorok. In the land of Acholi, when the rain stone is in two families, it always causes confusion among the people. I think that for this issue not to cause confusion among people, first, we should see how the rain stones came to these two families.

First, I want us to consider the issue of the rain stone of the people of Lodulang, and later we look at the issue of the rain stone of the family of Ramorok. This is the best way for us to understand how the rain stones came to the families of Lodulang and Ramorok.

The rain stone of Lodulang: The elders of Ofirika told me that when the members of Lodulang were coming from Loudo, the father of Lokori was in possession of the rain stone, which has remained in the family of Lodulang. We saw in the previous page that Lokwat Patige was the one who brought the Lodulang from the land of Lotuko. Later, he also became the chief of the people of Lodulang. As we saw in the previous chapters, the history of Acholi says the chief of rain should lead the people. We do not know very well why the father of Lokori did not become chief, yet he had a rain stone.

The history of the people of Ofirika says after the death of the father of Lokori, the rain stone remained with his son, Lokori. After Chief Lokori, died, his wife, Lotibai took over the rain stone. After the death of Chief Lotibai, the rain stone remained with her son, Cibiriano Lokori. The rain stone was still with Cibiriano, even when I was writing this book. The first care taker of the rain stone or Ehejek, (as the people of Ofirika referred to him) from the family of Lodulang was Fidele. After the death of Fidele, elder Masimo Lomojong became the caretaker. After the death of Masimo, elder Firmo Ikare became the rain caretaker. When Firmo Ikare died, elder Labaka became the caretaker of the rain stone, and when he passed on, elder Karlo Masimo became the caretaker of the rain stone.

Elder Karlo Masimo died around 1999. Due to fighting in Sudan, people do not know with whom he left the rain stone of Lodulang. The role of the rain care taker of the people of Lodulang is the same as the role of other rain care takers in other places.

The rain stone of Ramorok: The history of Ofirika says the second rain stone is in the family of Ramorok. Reports show that Chief Ajafa was the first chief in the family of Ramorok. He also brought the rain stone from Loudo. The elders of Ofirika told me that much as Chief Ajafa had the rain stone, by bad luck he had no rain care taker as we saw with the family of Lodulang. The elders of Ofirika told me that gradually, many people were taking rain stones they found to chief of the rain of Lodulang, while a few took theirs to the chief Ramorok.

It seems people did this to the chief of Lodulang, so that they produce good crop yields. They also found that chief of the rain of Ramorok did not invoke enough rain as the chief of Lodulang during planting season. In Acholi, if a chief wanted to please his subjects, he should satisfy both their hearts and their stomachs. Reports show that, truly, the chief of Lodulang always pleased the people by invoking enough rain to produce good crop yields. When I was asking the name of the person who succeeded Chief Ajafa, I found that no elder of Ofirika knew who the person was.

Chapter Twenty

OMEO

THE OMEO HOME

There are three other settlements that surround Omeo. They include Ofirika on the (north), Agoro on the (west), and Magwi on he South and South-East. The history of Acholi states that the boundary between Omeo and Ofirika between Ikola and

Kilaba (both are Omeo hunting grounds), the boundary between Omeo and Agoro is between Ikola and Kimunu, and the boundary between Omeo and Magwi is in Lodunu, Ogongo Lobela hunting grounds (all are Magwi hunting grounds).

However, according to Fr. Justin O. Bongomin, the son of Omeo, who lives in Portland (Maine) United Stated of America, Omeo history begins with the coming of Ikwaka sub clan of Omeo Morwari. Omeo Morwari is composed of four sub-clans; these are Ikwaka, Igara, Kilyo and Ohobok. Ikwaka clan is the first group of Acholi to settle in Omeo. Historically, Ikwaka did not come concurrent with the mass movement of the Lwo immigration. In about 1800 AD, an Anywak family headed by Ocido, Nyakaba, and Nyakicer decided to move from Upper Nile southwards. They came with all their belongings family and cattle to Omeo. They probably penetrated Omeo between Okaru, Lowai and Lagabu hills.

From Lagabu, they then turned eastwards till they reached Ibanyak hills where they settled. At that time, Ibanyak hills and the surrounding land was empty. There were no human beings inhabiting the land it was no man's land. This Anywak family, (which later came to be) known as Ikwaka, did not claim the ownership of the land. Perhaps the reason why they did not claim the land was that it was mountainous and not suitable for permanent habitation. Another reason is that, these people were still on the move, they had not yet reached their destination; hence, there was no need to lay claim yet on anything.

The Ikwaka lived in Ibanyak for many years, and then afterward they abandoned the land. The reasons for abandoning Ibanyak were based on superstitions. The Ikwaka elders say that one day some Ikwaka young men were building a granary on mount Ibanyak. They made up the frame and began to tie the bottom part of the granary. The next thing was to thatch the granary.

Suddenly, the string that held the granary got cut and the granary began to roll down from the mountain. When the news reached the elders that the granary has rolled down the mountain, they were all alarmed. They said that it was a bad omen and theretofore people should descend from the mountain. They abandoned the place and moved southeast of it to Ihola.

When the Ikwaka moved from mount Ibanayak, they came and settled in the land called Ihola. That was the place where the founder of Ikwaka, Ocido, Nyakaba, and Nyakicer and their family members dwelled. They had always talked about their land Ihola. When Ikwaka arrived in the land, Ihola was no man's land there were no people living in the area.

After living in Ihola for many years, the Ikwaka again moved away from Ihola and went southeast-wards. They moved into a new land which they called Kimuno. In Kimuno, they settled first on mount Kilijok and then in Imolongo. Years later an unknown group of people who came from Lokoya took Ihola and settle in the land. This Lokoya group later came to be known as Mokoi. They were headed by a man named Apak Nyatugwo from the sub-clan of Ilany.

Since then, the Ikwaka have lived in Kimuno and built their shrine in Imolongo. Kimuno is the second land that Ikwaka owned. The other clans of Omeo live on these lands up to this day. Until recently, the new Ikwaka generation did not know much about their land, some even did not know that the land belonged to them. Since their founders moved away from Omeo, they left the new generation with very little knowledge about the land.

In the past, during the tribal wars, the Omeo people lived on mount Kilijok. Some elders reported that even some people from the neighboring Agoro and Panyikwara came and took shelter in the caves and on this mountain during the wars. The mountain was well fortified on all sides to prevent the enemies from climbing. That is why in the later days the cave was known as "Oteny pa

Nyekomwoi" or simply the cave of Nyekomwoi because Nyekomwoi was the first person to settle on Mount Kilijok and people also took refuge in the cave.

Around the year 1870, the founding father of Omeo, Ocido and Nyakaba left Omeo for Pajok. No reason is given as to why they left Omeo for Pajok. When they arrive in Pajok, they went and settled with the father of Licebo Agari of Pajok Oyere where they got assimilated. There has never been any blood relationship between Omeo Ikwaka and Pajok Oyere.

The children of Ocido and Nyakaba that were left in Omeo were Okwir Lidek Lomeri and Okwer Nyekomwoi Nyakaba; other cousins were Loguca Anyang Nyakaba and Okwang Lolu Nyakaba. Their generation continued to live in Omeo up to this date.

Towards the end of the 19thcentury, Ikwaka started to disperse from Omeo. Other groups of Ikwaka migrated to Panyikwra and settled in Goloba, among the Padeggi sub clan. Others moved into Agoro and form the clan of Agoro Patoko. In 1920, another group of Ikwak migrated in to Aruu, and settled among the Lolubo. The last group of Ikwaka moved into Opirka, and settled among the Omiling sub clan known as Lopulang.

Before we dig deep into the history of Omeo, let us answer this question, "What does Omeo mean?" I asked many Omeo elders this question when I was in Juba, but I discovered that there was nobody who could answer the question. Therefore, I ask any Acholi who reads this book to give me the answer if he knows, so that I can include it in the second edition of this book.

According to Crazzalara, there is a strong relationship between Omeo and Agoro because they used to intermarry, especially when Omoeo was at Kilijok Hill, which is near Pika Hill where Agoro people were. Omeo are kins of Imurok, Ofirika and Igaraa because they all came from Lango (Crazzalaro, 1951, P, 173).

The Omeo people lived at Kilijok Hill between 1919 and 1926. The British Government in Opari sent their security men, Suleiman Ali, an Alur man from Ombasi-Uganda, together with an elder, Olam to Chief Oyokobeli, to tell him to release some Omeo young men to work in the road construction project between Nimule and Juba. Simplicio Obwoya, an Omeo elder, told me that at the time Sudan Government was looking for young men to help in road construction, some Omeo men were already working in the road construction project between Nimule and Juba. People say the security men, Ali and Olam, arrived in Omeo when people were passing time at the evening fire on the compound. They welcomed Ali and his friend very warmly. The people offered the visitors seats and water to drink. They allowed Ali to take a brief rest before he could tell the people what took him to Omeo. After a while, three Omeo elders asked Ali, "What issue brought you to our home?" Ali answered, "I came from Opari. The government representative at Opari sent me with a message to Chief Oyokobeli. The government wants the chief to send some boys to work on the road. That is what the government sent me to tell your chief."

Omeo elders told Ali, "Alright, security man. We are grateful to receive your message, but it is now dark. We would like you and your friend to sleep here and we will take you to Chief Oyokobeli in the morning. Ali and his friend did not object to the elders' advice. Unfortunately, Ali did not know what was going to happen to him the next morning. The elders went back to the people at the bond fire on the compound and reported, "We met Ali and his friend and they told us that it is the government representative at Operi who sent them to Chief Oyokobeli. The white man wants some boys to work on Nimule Juba road. Since it is already dark, we asked Ali and his colleague, Olam to spend a night with us and we will take them to the chief tomorrow in the morning. They accepted to sleep here, so we gave them space to rest."

That evening, the chief received a message that a white man's security men had beaten Omor Leka-moi of Omeo to death; Omor Leka-mio was working on the road construction project. Omor Leka-moi was Chief Oyokobeli's nephew. The chief was greatly hurt when he heard about the death of his nephew. He was annoyed with the white man. That night, Oyokobeli sent a word about the death of Omor to the people of Murwari, in Omeo South. Chief Oyokobeli had not known that some security men of the white man was at his place.

In the morning, some girls gave Ali and Olam water for washing their face. After this, Omeo elders took Ali to a goat pen and assigned two elders to watch over him. They took Olam in a different house. They then reported to their chief, "Chief, there is a visitor from Operi. He spent a night with us. His name is Suleiman Ali. He said that the white man sent him to you so that you send some boys to work on Nimule Juba road. Can we bring him to you now?"

Chief Oyokobeli told the elders that, "I cannot meet Ali because I have just received a message that the white man has just killed Omor Leka-moi. I do not want to send other boys to work on the road because the white man may kill them as he has killed their brother, Leka-moi".

As we have seen above, Chief Oyokobeli immediately sent a word for the people of Murwari in Omeo South. Murwari ululated and a multitude of people gathered at the place.

On hearing the ululation, Suleiman Ali asked the two elders who were with him, "What is wrong that ululation is sounded?" The elders sensed that there was something wrong and that could be a secret that did not need to be released to a visitor or a stranger. So they could not tell him what the problem was. The elders also knew that if Suleuman Ali learned the reason why ululation was sounded, he would run away. So, they told him, "Security officer, do not mind. The sun is burning people's crops in the garden. They are ululating because they want to meet the rain maker." Ali calmed down when the elders explained the situation to him.

People assembled in Murwai dance ground where they discussed what should be done to avenge the death of their brother, Omor Leka-moi, who had been killed by the white man. The oral source says that these people unanimously agreed that they should kill Suleiman Ali to pay back the killing of their brother. They selected five strong boys, among them was Lodeker's brother of Kilo, who were charged with killing Suleiman Ali. The five boys wasted no time to take weapons like axes and made straight for the goat pen where Ali was. Ali thought the boys brought for him important message from Chief Oyokobeli. The boys held Ali by his neck, pressed him down before they strangled him. They hit his head with axe about four times until he died.

The Omeo elders, Chief Anthony Onek and Simplicio Obwoya told me that Olam who came together with Suleiman Ali, was in a hut near the goat pen. He saw everything that the Omeo boys did to Ali. That freighted him so much that he got out of the hut and began to run back to Opari. Simplicio Obwoya told me that Olam roamed the Omeo wilderness because he did not know the place well. As he was running in the wilderness, he bumped into Ayau, the grand father of Alex Oringa, of Omeo. Ayau held Olam by the hand and asked him, "Why are you running wildly like this?"

Olam responded that, "The white man sent my friend Suleiman and I to Chief Oyokobeli because he wants more boys for the Nimule Juba road construction. When we reached Omeo, they welcomed us and offered us space to sleep. My friend Ali slept in a goat pen and I slept in a hut next to the goat pen. Early in the morning, five boys went to the goat pen where Ali was and hit him with axe to death. The death of my friend scared me. That is why I am running to find my way back to Opari.

Ayau was not pleased by the brutal killing of Ali. If Ayau had had the same sentiment with other Omeo people, he would have killed Omal. Fortunately, Ayau did not have the feeling to avenge the death of Omor, so he took Olam up to Operi in the hands of the white man and he returned to Omoe.

Immediately, that morning, Omeo people took the body of Suleiman Ali and dumped it near Mayi-mayi Hill; they did not bury Ali because they feared that if they buried him, his blood would follow them. They wanted his body to be eaten by vultures and lions. A few days after, the five boys went back to Mayi-mayi hill to check if vultures and lions had eaten Ali's body, but to their dismay, nothing had touched the body. They were mesmerised by what they saw; why vultures, not even lions ate the body. They reported to elders that, "We went back to the hill to check if lions or vultures had eaten the body of the vicious man, but we found the body intact, no lion or vulture touched it." In the culture of Acholi, if someone was killed, his body was thrown in the wilderness and wild animals would eat his body immediately if he was at fault. But if he was innocent, his body would lie there, no animal would eat it.

When Omeo elders received this report they said, "Omeo, you have killed Ali for nothing. If he were not innocent, wild animals would eat up his body."

Simplicio Obwoya told me that Olam reported to the white man everything that happened to Suleiman Ali. The white man received the report with great displeasure. So, he sent his security men to fight the people of Omeo. When the white man's soldiers entered Omeo, they opened fire on everybody, men, women, children and the elderly alike. The oral source says that immediately after this fight, the soldiers took the Omeo people who survived the gun, together with the people of Agoro and Ofirika and made them to settle by the road side. The white man did this for two significant reasons. First, to make it easy for him to find out the criminals among the people of Omeo, Agoro and Ofirika, and second was to control the people so that this kind of atrocity did not happen again. It is also said that after taking the people at the road side, the white man took Lodeker, the brother of the killer, to Opari where the killer was hanged.

At the road side, the white man place Omeo on the land that spreads from Kweyo-pa-Jaka-Jaka, near Magwi School, up to Ing-gili Stream, at the border of Panyikwara and Magwi. However, Santo Oyet Ongin, in his essay about Magwi, maintains says "The white man took the people of Omeo to a place called *I Tye Meri*. Agoro were taken to a place called *Yaa Nimira Tamania*, which begins from Ing-gili Stream and ends in Rum-tukuli, which is at the boundary of the land of Panyikwara. The people of Ofirika were taken to the foot of Fuka Hill and Okulu Hill.

The history of Acholi says that Omeo and Agoro lived at the road side from 1919 to 1941, before the government allowed them to go back and settle on their ancestral land, because the land at Magwi was not fertile. The people of Murwari migrated to Kilabak, Pino-pino migrated to Kimuno, Hohoi migrated to their ancestral land, (in the hunting ground called Ikola), the people of Imbaro settled in the hunting ground of Palonganyi and the people of Ikoo settled in their hunting ground, Ikoo.

However, a Magwi man, Santo Oyet Ongin believes that the people of Omeo settled at the foot of Kilijok Hill and they had their headquarters at Imologno, and the people of Agoro settled at a place called Wai, with their headquarters at Dabur.

The history of Omeo states that during throng hunting, the Pino-pino hunters stood together with Mohoi (which Omeo called *cope*) and Imbaro hunters stood together with Ikoo hunters. Omeo are a peace-loving people. That is why they did not fight with other settlements in Acholi, as Obbo fought Pajok. But Acholi elders said that even if Omeo did not fight other Acholi people, they fought Ofirika because Ofirika people were clandestinely killing their people. Other Acholi elders told me that in 1963, in Anya-nya One war, Sudan government put the people of Omeo, Agoro and Ofirika under the chief of Magwi. A large government army barracks was at Magwi (near Kumaru Stream).

Omeo is one small house in Acholi, which is why the Sudan government did not make Omeo independent, but put them under the leadership of the chief of Magwi. As we have seen before, it was the policy of the Sudan government that any group of people whose population of tax payers did not reach five hundred were not given chiefdom. The government gave chiefdom to people whose taxpayers were five hundred and above. Acholi elders told me that the government found that the tax payers of Omeo were less than five hundred, so they were assigned to the chief of Magwi.

Omeo, just like other homes we have looked at in this book, was also divided into South and North. I want to handle the history of Omeo North first, and eventually I will look at the history of Omeo South.

OMEO NORTH

Around 1500 -1650 Omeo North clan was already formed although some of the sub clans came later. The Omeo North has four large families: *Pino-pino*, *Imbaro*, *Ikoo* and *Mohoi*

PINO-PINO

The Pino-pino family has three smaller families which include *Ilukamii*, *Okurak* and *Igara*.

The Acholi history tells us that the people of *Ilukamiri* and *Okurak* came from Lafon (Lokoro); Kijaba led them to Acholi Sudan from Lokoro, but the history of Omeo does not explain the reason why Ilukamiri and Okurak migrated from Lokoro.

However, some oral sources say the people of Ilukamiri came from Igara, which is in Imurok, and it was Chief Nyakori who led them to Acholiland. They settled at the foot of Kilijok Hill. Other Omeo people who came later found the people of Chief Nyakori already at the foot of Kilijok. Chief Nyakori headed Ilukamiri well, and when he died, the chiefdom was left in the hands of Togo's daughter. Togo was the brother of Chief Nyakori. During the reign of this woman some Ilany (Mohoi) people joined them without their chief. Some Omeo elders told me that Ilany people came with a lot of authority. The female chief was scared when she saw the authority that these people came with. Consequently, she handed over her chiefdom to Ilany. That is how Ilany became the owners of the place.

According to oral sources, Igara people came from Igara which is in Imurok. It was an elder called Ogala who led them to Omeo. We do not know why they moved away from Imurok.

PINO-PINO 'S HUNTING GROUNDS AND HILL

Pino-pino has two hunting grounds: *Kimuno* and *Ayei*. The history of Omeo states that Kimuno and Ayei hunting grounds belonged to the people of Ilukamiri. The first caretaker of Kimuno and Ayei was Kijaba. When Kijaba died, Aleda (Kijaba's wife) took over the authority. Aleda died in 1998??

after which the people of Omeo do not know who took up the responsibility of both Kimuno and Ayei.

According to Fr. Justine Bongomin, a son of Omeo, from Ikwaka sub-clan, Kimuno hunting ground belongs to the people of Ikwaka. Kimuno land is a small land but has a big mountain known as Kilijok (*kidijok*) or the stone of the gods. Decades ago, there was an Ikwaka man named Nyekomoi who lived on it. He builds his homestead on top of the mountain. And the mountain has an enormous cave known as (*oteny pa nyekomwoi*), or the cave of Nyekomwoi.

Pino-pino has a hill called Pino-pino, and it is the people of Ilukamiri who own the hill. Pino-pino has a god called Pino-pino, which is on Pino-pino Hill.

IMBARO

Imbaro has five smaller families which include *Igara, Iwala, Biakiri, Okobok* and *Bura-kal*.

Igara: Acholi history tells us that Igara came in two groups from Igara of Imurok, led by Ayau and the other group was led by Riama Lobiong. It seems they moved together with the Igrar which is in the family of Pino-Pino and other Igara who are in the house of Ikoo. Igara were the first people to enter Imbaro, and it seems they split up after reaching Acholiland (Omeo). Many people say that Ayau Aluka and his brother Riama Lobiong and their people left Imurok in 1900 and settled in Imbaro. Omeo says that when Aluka and his people came to Omeo (Imbaro), there was no one on the land; they therefore claimed the ownership of the land.

Iwala: According to Fr Justine Bongoimin, the people of "Iwala" came from Pari Lokoro), they were led by elder Lomokotiro Lonya. However, many elders of Omeo reported that the people of Iwala came from Pakala-pa-Akila in Panyikwara, they were brought to Omeo by their leader called Lonyung, when they reached Imbaro, and they camped with Igara, chief less. Omeo history has it that Iwala were the second group of people to enter Imbaro – they came after the people of Igara. The history of Omeo tells how Lonyung and his subjects split from Pakala-pa-Akila, but it seems Iwala split from Pakala-pa-Akila, when Pakala-pa-Akila returned to Owiny-ki-bul. Other people say that Iwala split from Pakala-pa-Akila when they were still at the foot of Iwire Hill, and Pakala-pa-Akila moved to Owiny-ki-bul, leaving Iwala at the foot of Iwire, and Iwala later broke away when they were at Panyikwara when famine broke out in Mede. Then Iwala went to Omeo and settled with the people of Imbaro.

Bura-kal: The family of Biakiri came from Pari (Lokoro), they were lead to Acholiland by Ngole Itunyo. The Acoli history states that some of the people of Bura-kal came from NyaRubaanga (Bar) and others came from Imurok. An elder called Atuya was the one who led the people of Bura-kal from Nya-Rubanga. Atuya came together with his brother, Murungole and Biyakiri who led part of the people of Bura-kal who came from Imurok to Acholi. We do not know why Bura-kal left both Bar and Imurok.

IMBARO'S HUNTING GROUND AND HILL
Imbaro people do not have hill, hunting ground, neither do they have a god.

IKOO
The people of Ikoo have four smaller families: Ohobok, Igara, Lobilit, Onyameil and Ongulu.

Igara and Ohobok: The families of Igara and Ohobok came to Omeo because of the famine that attacked them in their places of origin. The family of Igara, of Ikoo, came from Imurok (Lotuko) they were led to Acholi land by elder Iki Pere; while the people of Ohobok came to Omeo from Ofirika, they were led by elder Okot Aliwa. They all came and settled in Ikoo. They settled in the hunting ground that was not owned by anybody, so the land became theirs.

Onyiamiel: The Onyamiel family came from Lopit, but Acholi history does not tell us why Onyamiel people left Lopit. They were brought to Omeo by elder Ocorobar Awangole.

Lobilit: The history of Acholi did not tell us where the people of Lobilit, who settled in Omeo today, came from. And the name of the man who led them to Omeo remains a mystery.

Ongulu: The family of Ongulu came from Ongulu of Imurok (Lotuko), the Omeo elders do not know the name of the leader who led them to Acholi land. We also do not know the year in which the people of Ongulu left Imurok.

IKOO'S HUNTING GROUNDS AND HILL
The people of Ikoo have two hunting grounds which include Ikoo and Magero. Unfortunately, Omeo elders do not know the person who took care of the

hunting grounds neither do they know anyone who takes care of it now. Ikoo have a god called Ikoo which is on Ikoo Hill, the only hill they own.

MOHOI

Mohoi comprises three smaller houses. They are *Ilany, Liria* and *Ongario,* but some people say they have six families: *Ilany, Liria, Ongario, O'boko, Marari* and *Pa-carigol.* But some people say they have "seven" families: Ilany, Liria, Ongario, O'boko, Marari, Pa-carigol and Omiling. I want to leave this to the readers of this book to tell if Mohoi really has seven families as the elders said. If it is true, I will reaffirm it in the second edition of this book, but for the meantime, I say Mohoi has three families: *Ilany, Liria* and *Ongario.*

There is a lot of disagreement among elders of Omeo about the belonging-ness of the families of O'boko, Marari and Pa-carigol to Mohoi. Others contend that O'boko, Pa-carigol and Marari descended from Ilangy, Liria and Ongario which are in Mohoi. But some elders maintain that these three houses came from elsewhere and joined the people of Ilany, Liria and Ongario. According to the history of Omeo, three young men founded O'boko in Omeo; the three young men were Okot Iliwa, Wani Imorok and Odak, all of whom came from Igara in Imurok. They married and got children and grandchildren, but they resolved not to build their own clan in Mohoi. This indicates that it is not right to say that Mohoi comprises six families. According to Fr. Justine Bongomin, Omiling forms part of the Mohoi families. The family of Omiling came from Ofirika but he does not know why they left Ofirika and who led them into Omeo land. But in my opinion Rev Fr. Justine is somehow confusing Omiling and Pa-caragol, who came from Omiling in Ofirika.

However, some people argue that if the families of Paratik of Oyira and Ogura of Oloro (in Panyikwara) formed own families in Panyikwara, why is it not possible for O'boko, Marari and Pa-carigol to form their own family in Mohoi? Oral sources say that the three boys, Okot Iliwa, Wani Imorok and Odak, who founded O'boko had come and stayed in the homestead of Akere of Ilany. Marari people came from Palonganyi in Magwi, and it was an elder called Akere Lokilacong who led the people of Marari from Palonganyi to Omeo around 1910. Some people say that Akere Lokilacong came alone and settled with his brother-in-law, Lobeyuk. He later begot children. Omeo elders told me that Lobeyuk hailed from Ongario because in the old day, the people of Palonganyi and

Ongario used to intermarry. Pa-carigol, on the other hand came from Lomiling which is in Ofirika. Some people said that Carigol came to Ofirika alone and he settled in the hands of his brother-in-law, Kijaba of Liria?? Kijaba gave Carigol space to settle in, and he later married a woman from the house of Ilukamii of Pino-pino. Their offspring are the current people of Pa-carigol in Omeo.

Ilany people came from Ifwotu. They were led by Lorim to Omeo. They moved away from Ifwotu around 1901. But Acholi history does not tell us why Lorim moved his people to Omeo. Omeo elders told me that when Lorim's people came to Omeo, they settled at Mohoi. Some Omeo elders told me that Lorim was the first person to enter Mohoi, followed by the people of Liria and Ongario.

Liria, according to Omeo history, came from Liria in Lokoya,, and they were led to Omeo by an elder called Lakol around 1902. But Omeo history tells us nothing about why Lakol moved his people from Lokoya to Acholi. Some people think that they left Liria because of an outbreak of famine, but some people contend that they left the place because of frequent fights they had with their brothers who remained behind in Lokoya. So, they were looking for a peaceful place. They later found a place in Omeo and they called themselves Liria in memory of the place that hosted them after the trouble.

Ongario came from Longario which is between Juba and Liria. Oral sources maintain that Abeten and his brother Lorwang were the ones who brought the people of Ongario to Acholi of Sudan around 1904. Lorim of Ilany welcomed them and gave them a place to settle in.

MOHOI'S HUNTING GROUND AND HILL

Mohoi has one hunting ground called Ikola. It is Ilany who celebrates the hunting ground, but Mohoi elders do not know the first owner of the hunting ground though some of them say that the person they could remember as the first owner of the ground was Lalongo. When Lalongo died, his wife, Aleda took over the management of the ground. It is Ikola hunting ground that the people of Omeo and Mohoi respect very much. Elders told me that to show respect, when hunters speared an animal and the animal ran to Ekewayi deity, thus, Omeo custom refuses that when someone spears an animal he should not shout his praise name, or ululate, it has to be respected. If, by bad lack, the hunter shouted his praise name or ululated on the animal he speared, if by mistake a person shouted his praise name, the animal, with the power of the god, would get up and run away.

Omeo elders also told me that when hunters found the white bee comb full of honey, in the wilderness (Ikola), no one should express surprise about it. If one of the hunters did that, for example, if he said, Mmmm, the comb is full of honey!" — then the honey turned into worms. Therefore, when Acholi hunters went to hunt in Ikola, they did everything with respect without shouting praise names, ululating or blowing horns and without making noise.

According to Fr Justine Bongomin, a son of Omeo, he argues that as Ikwaka claimed authenticity and ownership of Kimuno, they lost claims over Ihola. It is believed that Ikwaka lost ownership of Ihola to Mohoi because of the following three reasons.

First, while Ikwaka were still living on mount Ibanyak, a daughter was also marriage to a Mohoi. She asked if Ocido could allow her to cut grass for thatching her hut from the land of Ihola. It is reported that instead of allowing her to cut only grass, the Ikwaka allowed their daughter to bring her husband to build a house in Ihola. This means that the Ikwaka have allowed her to live in Ihola and take care of the land. So the people from Lokoya followed them and found a place to live in Ihola.

Secondly, it is because of a second marriage between Ikwaka and Mohoi. That, another beautiful Ikwaka girl got married again to a young man from Mohoi. This marriage happened when the founder of Ikwaka Ocido was still alive and they were at Imolongo. Because of these marriages, the Ikwaka allowed Mohoi to continue living in Ihola.

Thirdly, when Ocido realized that there was nobody among the Ikwaka to rule the land, he temporary allowed the people of Moki to live in Ihola (this reason is disputable). But when the daughter of Ikwaka that was married to a Mohoi, Ilany sub-clan was about to die, she gave the responsibility of the land to her son, who was, of course, from Mohoi and an Ilany. During this time, Ocido was no longer in Omeo; he had already left Omeo for Pajok.

The people of Mohoi have one important god called Ekewayi on Mohoi Hill. According to the people of Omeo, the person who celebrates the god is the one who cooks for the god. The elders told me that if someone hears ululation in Ikola and he does not see the person ululating, he should just know that it is the god making the ululation.

OMEO SOUTH
Omeo South has only one family called *Murwari*.

MURWARI
From the seven families in Omeo, it is said that the first family to come to Omeo South is Kilio. They came and settled where they are today. Other families of Murwari came after them. They found Kilio people already on the land. As we have seen before, land conflict is a headache to Acholi elders. Most of the time, nobody knows the owner of the land in question, or the owners of the land because there is no written record that would objectively guide young people to the truth.

Murwari comprises four houses as *Kilio*, *Igara*, *Okobok* and *Ikwaka*.

The Omeo history contends that Kilio people came from Hiliu at Torit, where Norwegian Church Aid (NCA) built their offices in 1977. Two elders, Onyir and Ocak were the ones who brought the people of Kilio to Omeo around 1896. But according to people like Rev. Justin Bongomin, the family of Kilio were led from Heliu in Torit to Omeo by elder Iribu Ibariahaliang. Oral sources told me that Onyir was Ocak's elder brother. The followers of Onyir and Ocak left Hiliu because there was animal raiding conflict between them and their other brothers who remained in Hiliu. It is said that when Kilio reached the place called Murwari, they found the land vacant. There was nobody occupying it. They settled on the land and became its owners. Ocak, because he found the land infertile, took some of the people with who they came with his brother, and led them to Jok Hill, which is along the road from Magwi to Panyikwara.

The people of Igara migrated from Igara in Imurok. They were led by an elder called Kanera Gumaci to Acholi in Sudan, around 1897. It is said that the Igara families who are today found in Omeo Right and Omeo Left, all of them left Imurok because of power conflict. They settled in the hands of Onir of Kilio who gave them a place to settle in.

Okobok: The family of Ohobok came from Imurok (Lotuko), the Igara families who are today found in Omeo Right and Omeo Left, all of them were led into Acholiland by elder Igwe. Some Ohobok came from Bilinyang (Bar) and others came from Imurok. The history of Acholi states that Riya-moi is the one who brought the people of Ohobok from Imurok; but some people said the family of Ohobok were brought from Imurok to Omeo by elder Lowala Awok and his brother Lungamwoi. The history of Omeo does not tell us the name of the person who led the Ohobok people who came from Bilinyang. The Okobok from Bar and those from Imurok settled in Murwari (Omeo) around 1898. They came after Igara. Some of the people of Lowala settled together with Kilio and others settled with Igara. It is aid that one man, whose name we do not know, went and settled in Obbo in the family of Palyec. This is one reason why there is strong kinship code between Palyec of Obbo and Okobok of Omeo.

The Ikwaka people all came from Lutuko around 1899. It was Pido-mio who led them to Acholiland in Sudan. They settled with Riya-moi while others were hosted by Lowala of Okobok. Riya-moi and Lowala gave these people space not only for settlement, but also for cultivation. But as we have seen before, to some people, like Fr. Justine Bongomin, the family of Ikwaka came from Anyuak. They were brought intoAcholi land in South Sudan by Ocido and Nyakaba.

MURWARI 'S HILLS, HUNTING GROUND AND GOD

Murwari has a hunting ground called *Kilabak*. A Kilio man is the main celebrant of Kilabak hunting ground because the hunting ground belongs to Kilio. The Omeo history says that the first celebrant of Kilabak was Iribo. After the death of Iribo, Kilabak was left in the hands of Itilang. By the time I was writing this book, it was Layoo who was the main celebrant of the hunting ground. He was also the priest of the god, Okobicak. This brings us to the question, "Why did the elders of Kilio remove the authority of celebrating hunting ground and priesthood from young men? Why was the same authority left in the hands of a woman or a girl?"

Some elders told me that the authority was removed from young men not only because they lacked respect for the god, but they did not also respect the royal clan elders. The girls were more respectful to both the god and elders. So, elders gave girls the authority to celebrate the hunting ground and to have the priesthood of the god. Some elders said that if the boys did not change their ways of life, girls would have that authority over them for a long time.

Murwari people have three hills: *Kilijok, O'deki* and *Ocee*. All the three hills are said to be Kilio's, but Murwari are the legitimate owners. Murwari has only one god called Okobicak.

THE RAIN POT OF OMEO

Long ago, in Omeo, rainmakers came from the house of Bura (Imbaro) only, but in 1925, the rain stone became two. One went to Omeo South and the other remained with Bura in Omeo North. This brings us to the question, "Why does the rain making of Bura splits into two?" Bura people say that Chief Nyayumasi was the first chief in Bura. She was a female chief. She made rain for both Omeo South and Omeo North. After the death of Chief Nyayumasi, the rain making power remained with Nyangori — also a woman. Around 1925, an elder called Oyokobeli told Chief Nyangori, "I have eloped with a girl from Murwari and she came with a rain stone. I am quite aware that she cannot make rain here without your permission. Some people said that the woman did not want the chief to know that she had a rain stone, but because her opinion violated Acholi customs, her husband had to consult the chief.

To Chief Nyangori, it was not possible to have two rain makers in Omeo. She then gave one of her stones to Oyokobeli's wife of Murwari. It is said that the chief did not give all the stones to Omeo South, she remained with some stones. She continued to make rain fro the people of Pino-pino, Mohoi and Ikoo in Omeo North. The three families subscribed to Chief Nyangori.

Oyokobeli's wife later gave all her stones to her husband. That made Oyokobeli the first chief of Omeo South. Chief Oyokobeli also made rain for Igara, Okobok and Ikwaka in Omeo South. All the three families subscribed to Oyokobeli. That is how the rain-making power of Omeo was split between Omeo North and Omeo South.

When Oyokobeli died, the power was left to his son, Ogany. After the death of Ongany, it was left with Okunu Ongolo-ngwen. When Chief Ongolo-ngwen died, Ibrahim Loburan (the son of Chief Ogany) became the next chief after whose death, the stone went to Tekilia's mother. When Tekilia's mother died, the stone was given to Regina, Ibrahim Lobura's wife. She is still keeping it up to today.

The history of Acholi states that the first care-taker of the rain stone of Murwari (Kilio) was Kanera, after whose death Olweny became the next care-taker. Oriya took it over after the death of Olweny. Omeo elders told me that Kanera, Olweny and Oriya were all from the house of Igara.

The history of Omeo states that when Chief Nyangori was about to die, she gave her stone to Itunyo, and Itunyo became the next Chief of Omeo North who died and left the chiefdom to Got-moi. When Got-moi died it remained with Omoi who died and left it with Chief Ogok. Chief Ogok died and Aye took over. When Adye died, the next chief was Kayol's mother, Chief Omio's wife. The Omeo elders with whom I lived in Juba told me that in 1986, Kayol's mother still had the stone and she was making rain for Omeo North.

Chapter Twenty One

RELIGION IN ACHOLI

Before we look at different religions or the state of traditional African religion in Acholiland, I would like us to critically scrutinise the way of life of the old-day Christians. However, we are not going back to the time of creation or the time of Abraham and Moses, but we should look at the life of Christians from the time Christ was born (not before Christ). To better understand this, we need to answer some of these questions. "Was there differences between the traditional Christian? If there were differences, what did religious leaders do to settle such disputes? How did modern Christianity come to Sudan? How did Christianity come to Acholiland? Did the Acholi people have their own religion in the old days? Or I could ask, did Acholi know God or not? What made them to abandon their religion if they knew God and had their own religion?" We will try to answer these questions, one by one, in this chapter. First, let us look at disputes among Christians after the death of Jesus Christ.

DISPUTES AMONG THE OLD DAY CHRISTIANS

Long ago, Christians in Europe, Asia, and America were just one body known as CHRISTIANS IN COMMUNION. After the death of Jesus Christ in 33A.D. disputes erupted immediately among Christians. They split up into four groups: *East, West, Roman* and *Churches of Reformation*. Although they were in these smaller groups, Christians worship one God in the name of our Lord Jesus Christ.

This also brings us to one other question: "What brought this dispute among Christians?" What brought problems is what the apostles wrote in 2Thessalonian 2:3. Some of the differences occurred when some of the twelve apostles were still alive. One of the apostles, Paul in his letter to Thessalonian stated very clearly that there were differences between Christians (2Thessalonian 2:7). When Jesus was still alive, he led Christians very well. But when he died, Jesus had left Christians and his apostles without a leader. Although Jesus appointed Peter, Peter did not work as he promised Jesus to take care of Christians and apostles. This made disputes to arise among Christians.

A French man once said, " in every group of people in this world, there are always two groups. First are those who give orders to those who are loyal, and the second is the group of people who oppress the loyal. This is found among peoples of the world."

Around 1945-1960, leading and uniting Christians became very hard because leaders like Alexander the Great and Emperors of Roma, claimed that they were God, and inflicted severe punishment on those who opposed the government.

Between 306 and 337 A.D. (C.E.), Constantino gave Christians freedom to manage their affairs as written in the Holy Book. Although they had the freedom, Christians did not follow the word of God. Their leaders continued to do bad things and causing disputes. Later they thought of uniting all Christians. Around 1850 they started programme called 'ECUMENICAL' in Greek. This means Christians should be united. Disputes were not only among lay Christians, but it was also among Reverend Fathers (Pastors).

THE ATTEMPT TO UNITE CHRISTIANS

In 1910 leaders of Christians organised a conference in Edinburgh-Scotland. They called it First World Missionary Conference. In 1919 religious leaders in Roma called a meeting in Rome. They discussed faith and righteousness of Christians. They resolved that each Christian prayer should touch at least a message from the Bible. Pope Benedict XV objected to Catholics attending the conference. In 1921, religious leaders formed International Missionary Council whose work was to teach the word of God in the right way, and to reduce conflicts among Christians (Awake, 1991, PP, 3-4).

In 1927, religious leaders had another meeting at Lausanne in Switzerland. They wanted to review what they had discussed in 1910 (about Christians' faith and doing the right thing). They also wanted to find out what was impeding unity among Christians. Other religious leaders from Protestant, Orthodox attended this meeting, Pope Pious X1, did not allow Catholics to attend the meeting. In 1928 Pope Pious X1 wrote a letter which, in Latin, is called Mortalium animos — where he opposed the idea of ECUMENICAL MOVEMENT. He also warned Catholics not to give any assistance to Ecumenism (Awake, 1991, P, 4).

In 1948, anther religious body, World Council of Churches (WCC) opened with one hundred and fifty members. Out of the one hundred and fifty members, 60% were Protestants. Pope Pious X11 (1948) did not allow Catholics to to join WCC. Pope Benedict, Pious X1 and Pious X11 did not tell people why they objected to Catholics joining those religious groups and attending their meetings. Because of the respect Christians had for the popes, they obeyed the without question (Awake, 1991, P, 5).

In 1958, when Pope John XX111 entered the pupal office, he brought many changes in the Catholic Church. Pope John was 77 years of age. He started by calling a meeting for all the bishops in the world. The meeting was held in Rome where they discussed 'how Christians could unite as one people, Jesus Christ's disciples.' all Bishops agreed that all Christians should unite as one people (Awake, 1991, P, 5).

In 1960 Pope John X111 opened office of Secretariat in Vatican to unite Christians, and in the same year, Catholics accepted to join WCC. In 1962 Pope John X111 called Vatican II. He did not live long enough to see the impact of Vatican II. He died in 1963. In 1963 Pope Paulo V1 entered office and furthered Pope John X111's ideology of unity. On 21/11/1964, he denounced the Catholic objection to joining Ecumenism. He said, 'The restoration of unity among all Christians is one of the principal concerns of second Vatican Council (Awake, 1991, P, 6).

One of the things that hampered unification of Christians was Pope's opposition to it because Pope wanted to be the supreme power over all Christian, but Protestants did not subscribe to it.

Dr Samuel McCrea Cavert was one of those who were preparing the laws of WCC — he said, "The Pope's acceptance to join Ecumenical did not bring any unity among Christians because Roman Catholic Church leaders think that their church is the only true church" (Awake, 1991, P,8).

THE COMING OF MODERN RELIGION TO SUDAN

In 1848 Pope Gregory XV1 opened the Apostolic Vicariate of Central Africa and had his office in Khartoum. The work of Apostilic Vicariate of Central Africa, was mainly evangelizing everybody. In 1848 many religious leaders came to Sudan to find where they could begin their evangelisation work. Christianity was the first religion to enter Sudan in 1846. The missionaries built their first church in Khartoum which later developed into the headquarters of the Apostolic Vicariate of Central Africa.

In 1898, when Mahdi's rule ended, there were fewer Christians in Northern Sudan. Those were Christians who were baptised between 1850 and 1881. The Reverend Fathers left Sudan around 1882 because of the Mahdi's oppression of religious leaders. In 1899, the British government appointed F. R. Wingate Governor General of Sudan. Wingate liked religious leaders and allowed them to go out and teach people. In October of 1899 two Comboni fathers, Fr. J. Ohrwalder and Fr. W. Banholzer came back to Sudan to take care of the buildings they had left behind.

A government representative called Kitchener ordered that all the church houses should be demolished and the government should take over the land from the missionaries. All the church houses were demolished. When these two fathers came back, they did not find the houses. Sador Kitchener gave the missionaries another piece of land along the River Nile where they built St. Mathew's Cathedral and Sisters' Schools.

On 4/1/1900, Bishop Antonio Roveggio (1894-1902) took the Comboni community to Omdurman. He found some other religious leaders other than Catholic in Sudan. All of them continued with their missions of evangelisation. To the Arabs, it seems Islam brought more teachers than other religions did. As a result, "New people –special issue January 2000" show the population of the different religious groups in Sudan at that time:

Catholic	8%
Other Christians	7%
Islam	65%
Traditionalism	20%

But in reality, there are relatively more Christian than Muslims in Southern Sudan. The population of the religious groups in Southern Sudan is as follows.

Catholics	40%
Other Christians	30%
Islam	10%
Traditionalism	20%

MODERN RELIGION IN SOUTHERN SUDAN

In 1850-1889 modern religion did not send deep roots in Southern Sudan because of three reasons:

(1) People did not like the whites and religious leaders because religious leaders and local administration were actually one.

(2) Some religious leaders died because the new environment did not

suit them. Many died of diseases. Those who survived the diseases had to leave Southern Sudan.

(3)   The people of Turky, Egyptian and Arab who moved from Northern Sudan to South Sudan advised leaders like Baker, Gordon and others not to allow missionaries to teach people the word of God. The leaders also heeded to their advice.

Christian Missionaries reached Sudan in 1840, because Mohammed Ali (the viceroy of Ottoman Egypt) had allowed religious leaders to teach the word of God to the people in Sudan. In 1848 propaganda Fide sent four Reverend Fathers to Sudan. The four Fathers included Fr. Knoblecher Slovene, Padre Fr. Anjelo Vinco (of Don Nicola Mazza Verono School in Italy), Fr. Pedemonte (of Jesuit) and Fr. Rayllo (of Jesuit). Fr. Pedemonte was the leader of the four fathers. They first temporarily settled in Khartoum (1848-1851). Then in 1851 they left Khatoum and moved to Southern Sudan where they built the first Catholic Church in Gondokoro (1851).

In 1853 the religious leaders left Gondokoro because Bar people were unfriendly to them. Secondly, they left because many of their priests were dying of some sicknesses. So, they all went back to Khartoum. In 1885 Mahdia sent away all Christian leaders out of Sudan. However, taking over Mahadi's government in 1898 paved the way for Christian missionaries to continue teaching in Sudan. Islam leaders moved together with the Christian missionaries continued to do their teaching. The British government had low opinion of Southern Sudanese. They did not want to develop the place, and they did not want to give them formal education.

Cromer, a British government representative based in Egypt, said that the government said that if they allowed missionaries to go to Southern Sudan, it would cause conflict between government workers and missionaries. Cromer was quite aware that the Church Mission Society (CMS), were very negative about Islam. He also knew that Fr. Daniel Comboni, of the Catholic Church, did not like the British government. So, Cromer did not allow them in Southern Sudan.

The religious leaders abroad were following keenly what was happening in Southern Sudan. They did not give time to the British government in London to have a say. Secondly, in a meeting which was held in Cairo, Austrian Emperor (the Mission's patron) condemned the government's treatment of the missionaries. When the government had received a lot of pressure, they eventually allowed missionaries in Southern Sudan in 1905. The missionary groups allowed in Southern Sudan included:- (1) CMS (2) American Presbyterian Mission(APM) (3) and Catholic. The government ordered that religious teaching must be accompanied by formal education because that was a way of bringing development to the people. The government also cherished peace for development and there was no one other than Sudanese themselves. The government sent some soldiers from Northern Sudan to Southern Sudan. Those soldiers were all Muslim Arabs. They began to teach Islam to the local people with whom they lived.

Many British D. Cs, in different parts of Sudan, were very happy to hear that the soldiers called Mamur and Jallaba were teaching Islam. But the British government in London was not impressed by this development. He said that most British were Christians. It was not good to have Islam teaching going on among Christians and traditionalists of Southern Sudan. The missionaries abroad supported the government's argument. But Sir Reginald Wingate, Governor General of Sudan, differed with the British government in London. He wanted Islam to be taught in Southern Sudan.

The Sudan Government Leaders from 1956-2010 (Figure No18)

Before the British government came to Southern Sudan, it was Belgium that ruled the southern part of Sudan. They were Christians, so they told people to rest on Sunday only, but the British government and their soldiers ordered people to rest on Friday. People were not pleased with this change. They followed the teaching because they had no voice.

EQUATORIAL BATTALION
When R.C.R Owen, Governor of Mangalla, realised that their security was at stake, he ordered for recruitment of soldiers to form Equatorial Battalion, and

the recruits must be black people and all of them must use English language. Secondly, he ordered that everybody must rest on Sunday as Belgians had put it before. People unanimously agreed with Owen.

Many boys, including Acholi boys, were recruited in the Equatorial Battalion. Seven years after, the black soldiers took up army leadership from Arab soldiers. They then changed the name Equatorial Battalion to Corps, and they were ready to protect their people against their enemies.

Every clan that joined the force was assigned a number because it was hard to understand soldiers. People understand what is in the hearts of the soldiers only when they sing it out.E.T.N. Grove said it clearly, "The song of Acholi soldiers No.7 Coy Equatorial Battalion was:

Dodinga is like a government

The real government is behind, it is on the way

Landowners run away from the white government

The government of the black is just at the gate (3)

BRITISH DIVIDED LAND AMONG RELIGIOUS LEADERS

Between 1903 and 1905, the Sudan government gave out land to religious leaders as follows:

► Northern Sudan was given to Muslim. Muslim had 99% of the land against 10% given to Christians.

► Upper Nile Province (up to the border of Ethiopia and Sudan) was given to American Mission called United Presbyterian Church of America.

► The land on the West of River Nile, up to a place called Luul together with Barh El Ghazel Province (excluding Rumbek) was given to Catholic.

► Equatorial (on the West of River Nile:- Yei, Muru, Yambio and Rumbek) was given to Church of England, which was later called Episcopal Church of Sudan.

► On the East of River Nile (in Equatorial where Acholi, Madi, Lotuko, and Langi are), the government did not give to any Christian denomination because all these people were, in 1903, under the government of Uganda.

In 1901 Bishop A.M. Roveggio of the Catholic Church left Omdurman for Acholiland and Lotukoland. He found it hard to enter the place when he reached

Gondokoro because to reach Acholi and Lotuko, he needed to obtain permission from the government of Uganda. Consequently, he returned to Omdurman.

In 1905, when the government had finished giving out land, CMS did not have land in Southern Sudan. They came to the place in 1906 and they built their first church in Bor (which is close to the border of Malakal and Juba).

The Catholics soon came to the land government had given to them immediately after the government had given them, but they did not begin to build immediately. The Catholics built their first church in Rajaf in 1919. The first Sudanese to become a Reverend Father was Fr. Deng Surur, a Dinka Abyei. Arab traders arrested Deng Sorur and his mother in 1871 and jailed them in Khartoum. In 1875 Surur Daniel Ferim Deng escaped from prison and took refuge in a Catholic Church in El Obeid. That year, Bishop Comboni was in El Obeid Mission. He welcomed the man and baptised him and later took him to Rome where he studied Seminary (1877-83).

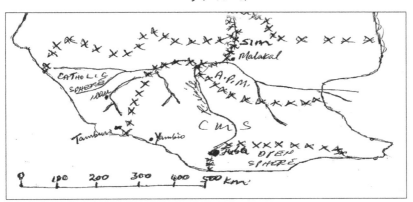

Figure 19: British divided land to religious leaders.

After finishing the theology course from Beyrut Seminary, Deng was given the sacrament of Ordination by Bishop Francis Xavier Sogaro from Cairo on 8/5/1887. He died in Cairo on 11/1/1900.

In 1919, the religious leaders in Southern Sudan continued to divide the land in Southern Sudan among themselves.

- ► Western Equatorial was given to Catholic Church.
- ► Eastern Equatorial was given to Protestants.
- ► The whole of Barh El Ghazal was given to Catholic.
- ► Malakal (Upper Nile) was given to Catholic, CMS and APM.

As we have seen above, Catholic got the largest portion of the land. This also shows us why up to 40% of Christians here are Catholics.

THE COMING OF MODERN RELIGION IN ACHOLI

Religion was not a new phenomenon; it was there even in the old traditional days. Acholi worship the Creator very much. They call Him Jok. Jok is the being that does not have flesh and is immortal. He lives eternally and no one can see Him, but He can see us. He knows everything, good or bad. He created everything we see in this world. Jok is the one who gives us health and He is the one who brings us death. Jok gives rain to the rain-maker chiefs when they ask for it. The main home of Jok is in heaven. He has small resting places such as cave, the foot of big trees, at the bank of rivers/along streams /at the side of lakes and wells, under pots in the houses of different clan leaders and many other places that we cannot count in this book.

The spirit of a dead person does not go to heaven but to a place that Jok has assigned to them. Such spirits usually do not go far away from their clans so that when they are called upon, they come very fast. This explains to us why when someone dies in the wilderness, elders say his spirit should be taken home. Traditional religion has strong rules that tell people how to live together. Unfortunately, all these rules were not written down. Children learn the rules from their parents. For example, one evening when I was taking a walk in Alia (Obbo), I overheard a man, how he was teaching his children with the tradition of his people as follows:

a. "My child, there are problems in this world. Everybody should take care of themselves. If your brother or sister wrongs you, you forgive them. Just as elders said it, clan matters are soaked with water behind the door shutter, but you pour sand in the eyes of a stranger who offences you. You do this to protect your life because when an enemy wants to kill you, he will truly kill you."

b. "But it is prohibited for you to sleep with the wife of another man. If he catches you, or hears about it, he will kill you. Sleeping with a girl who has consented to you is not an offence, as long as you have the wealth to pay what her people ask for. If someone sleeps with your wife, kill him, but if someone sleeps with your daughter, do not kill him; just see if he has wealth (money, sheep, goats, cattle). If he does not have any wealth, let him pay fine (luk) and mother's breasts, then let him go. You daughter will find a wealthy man."

Jok is not evil; neither is He a Satan as foreigners have been saying. This brings us to two questions. First is, "If the old time Acholi called God Jok, then from where and when did Jok get the name Rubanga?" Secondly, "How did Jok, the Creator of heaven and hearth and the omniscient became Satan?"

When the Catholic missionaries entered Uganda, they built a big church in Rubaga in the land of Baganda. As we have seen before, all Acholi of Sudan, Madi, Lotuko, Langi were initially under the government of Uganda. That means if there was a meeting, they gathered in the main Church in Rubaga or Rubaka. The white fathers who came from overseas did not want people to worship God using the name Jok. They said since Rubaga was the main church, the Creator should get His name from there. They changed the 'k' in Rubaka to 'ng' and called Him Rubanga. That is how Jok got a new name. Catechists began to use the name Rubanga everywhere.

Acholi people believe that women and children have spirit, and their spirits have no where to go after their death. People do not respect the spirits of women and children because the spirits do not have the power to chase evil spirit from among the people and to bless their posterity. The end of world, purgatory and the coming of the messiah are new things to Acholi. To Acholi, the end of the world is death. A dead person does not come back to life but continues life in a place Jok has selected for him. All spirits live for ever. Why does the end of the world come when all spirits are in peace?

When Jok wants to talk to someone, He comes to him in a dream. Jok's dream does not come anyhow. It comes to clan elders only, when He wants something (when he is hungry). When an elder has had this kind of dream, in the morning, he says it out immediately, '   thespiritofmyfather came to me today. He said he is hungry.' The elder then looks for a sheep to pacify the shrine. We will look at how the shrine is pacified later in this chapter.

The spirits of men are not the same. Their powers are as follows:

(1)   The spirit of a grand father (shrine) has the power to unite the clan. It also chases evil spirit and provides health to everyone.

Acholi have shrines which are dug on the compound of a senior elder of a clan.

(2)   The spirit of a father (or Auma) has less authority. If children have

headache they ask the help of the spirit of the father. It can releave the headache. The spirit of a father is usually kept under a pot in the house. We will discuss Auma later in this chapter.

Many people in this world did not know about the coming of the messiah because his coming was announced to Israelites who were very distant from Acholi. Other people, apart from Israelites, did not know about the coming of the messiah. When Jesus Christ was born in Nazareth his tribes mates did not accept that he was the the messiah whose coming was prophesied. They saw that he led a life that was not worthy of that he was the one prophesied about. The bad life that Jesus' brothers talked about was not written down in the Bible. The Bible only talks about people's skepticism about Jesus being the messiah. Israelites believed that the messiah would come from the house of King David as written in (2 Samuel 7:12-13).

This brings us to another question, 'If the Israelites who are the tribesmates of Jesus did not accept that he was the messiah, then why did Acholi believe in him?' When missionaries taught about the coming of the savior, people welcomed the teaching. However, some people accepted the teaching to please the missionaries, while others believed that everybody would resurrect from death when the savior came to judge people.

Chapter Twenty Two

MISSION IN ACHOLI OF SUDAN

LERWA MISSION

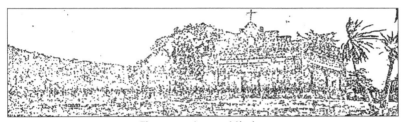

Figure 20: Lerwa Mission

On 21/6/1923, Pope instructed the missionaries to build many churches among the people of Northern Uganda and Southern Sudan.

The first foreign religion to come to Acholi of South Sudan was the Catholic. In 1925 Fr. Cereda and Fr. Cardani left Kitgum (Uganda) for Lerwa. They were the first Fathers to enter Acholi of South Sudan. They built three grass thatched houses in Lerwa. They used one of the houses as a church. The church we see at Lerwa today was built much later in 1945.

A few months later, Fartelo Egidio came to Lerwa from Rejaf (Juba), and Fr. Rinaldo came from Gulu. Fr. Ghiotto followed Fr. Rinaldo also came from Gulu to be the leader in Lerwa. In 1925 when Fr. Cereda and Fr. Cardani came to Acholiland in Sudan, the people of Pajok were in Oloyo-lweny hunting ground, and Obbo were in Logolo hunting ground. At that time small pox and sleeping sickness were killing many people. Fr. Cardani and Fr. Cereda moved the people of Obbo to Loti Hill, and the people of Pajok were moved to Polila because of the two diseases that had attacked them.

The missionaries faced hardship in reaching the church which they built on Lerwa. The hill was far away from people and climbing it was not an easy task. However, the three priests struggled to teach the word of God. Fr. Ghiotto died of malaria in 1926. Acholi did not receive the foreign religion with one heart. In 1926, seventeen people were baptised.

In 1925 the white man asked Pajok, Obbo, Omeo and Agoro to settle at the foot of Lotii Hill. Then in 1932 the white man asked everybody to return to their former homes since the diseases were contained. The Fathers followed people to their former places, and they moved to Palotaka. The Fathers did not forget about Lerwa, they went back time and again to pray with the people of Lerwa. The church in Lerwa was built by the Fathers themselves in 1945 when they were taking refuge from the Second World War. They named this church Queen of Peace.

PALOTAKA MISSION

The history of Obbo states that Palotaka Mission was built in Logolo hunting ground, the land which is on the left side of the road from Loudo to Pajok, and extends to Ayii Stream, where Iyire are today. In 1920, when Chief Aburi gave this land to the people of Iyire to settle in, at Nyara, it is said that some of the Iyire people decided to leave the place and settle with the people of Kitaka, and they called themselves Kitaka Kwenda. That is why the history of Obbo contends that Kitaka Kwenda came from Iyire. Long time ago, the land of Palotaka and Alia was one piece. Some people were in Alia and the place which we call Palotaka today was a grazing ground for Chief Aburi's cattle, goats and sheep. In 1920, Chief Aburi brought Lotaka, a mna of Iyire, to be his cattle keeper. Domestic animals at that time, were kept in the grazing ground. For this reason, Chief Aburi asked Lotaka to erect his kraal close to home so that it would be easy for him to take care of the animals. Lotaka did as he was instructed and looked after the animals. That time people called the ground Aburi's grazing ground. Pa-Lotaka in Acholi, means Lotaka's place, or the place where Lotaka settled. Obbo called the place Lotaka's because Lotaka actually lived there. One thing that some people do not know is that calling a place somebody's does not necessarily means the person owns the land. In 1933, when Fartelo Egidio wanted to build a Mission in Obbo, the people of Obbo gave him the land where Lotaka was (Chief Aburi's grazing ground).

Figure 21: Palotaka Mission

Fartelo Egidio began to clear the building site at Palotaka in November, 1933 when he came back from his holidays in Italy. In 1934 Fr. Cardani and a Sister left Lerwa and moved to Palotaka. It was at that time that Fartelo Vergani began to build the church we see at Palotaka today. Unfortunately, Fartelo Vergani died of malaria before he finished building the church. After the death of Brother Vergani, Fr. Fartelo Egidio finished building the church in 1935, and they called the church Palotaka Mission. That is how the name of the big church in Acholi was named.

During the 1940s war, the priests of Loa, Juba, Rejaf and Torit all sought sanctuary in Palotaka and Lerwa. During this time of refuge, Fr. Fartelo Colussi built Palotaka Teachers' College. Immediately after the war, Father Began to build schools for the local people. Boys embraced the new formal education, but girls were relatively reluctant to join it. Since Palotaka had many big trees, especially at the foot of the hill, the place was cool. The Fathers therefore shifted to Okaru in Palotaka.

Very few Acholi children, at that time, went to the school built in the place. The priest recruited the literate children as catechists. Among them were Genisyo Okoli of Pajok and Okwer Munu of Obbo. The priest asked for more catechists from Kitgum and Gulu because the catechists at Palotaka were over-whelmed by the large number of catechumens. They sent enough catechists in Sudan. Some of the Ugandan catechists were sent to teach in Lotuko. One Lotuko (Illieu) man called Valleriano Oreggi said, "Between 1925 and 1926 there was an Acholi catechist called Emmanuelle. He knew Lotuko language very well. He called the Creator, Rubanga. So, the Lotuko people who received catechism from Acholi catechists called the Creator Rubanga. The name 'Ajok' came later."

The first Acholi of Sudan to receive modern religious message were the people of Obbo and Pajok. Religion later went to Palwar, Magwi, Panyikwara, Omeo, Agoro and Ofirika. Religion spread in other places when the priests began to work in Palotaka. Acholi did not want the new religion, but the missionaries forced them into joining it, thinking that that was the only way of bringing peace among the people. Secondly, the missionaries told people that it was through religion that development could come to them faster.

Palotaka is 70 km south of Torit. The *Patron Saint* of Palotaka is *Holy Family or Guardian Angels*. They built twenty chapels in different places to help Christians whose homes were far away from Palotaka. There are eight chapels on the west: — Agoro Wai, Agoro South, Omeo, Panyikwara (Abara), Owiny-ki-bul, Magwi, Kit and Ame; and twelve of them are on the east:- Alia, Loudo, Iyire, Lerwa, Pajok, Palwar, Kicenge, Lobone, Upper Talanga, Poger, Omere, and Agata.

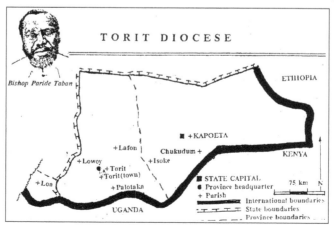

Figure 22: Map of Torit Diocese

Although Acholi Christians go to church, they have not forgotten their traditional religion. This brought conflict between the Christians and religious leaders. The Fathers said shrine was a bad thing and Christians should abandon it, but the old Christians continued to practise Acholi traditional religion. For that matter, today Acholi has three religions: (1) The traditional shrine: — this is the first and most important religion to Acholi. This is because when people ask for something before the shrine, Jok usually provides it. If someone angers his clan and he is cursed before the shrine, he dies. Inherited religion may not be very helpful. It is a shield of the white man to fight the black people. (2) The Catholic Church — this is the second important religion in Acholi. (3) Protestant — this is the third religion among the people. Acholi people do not like the teaching of Protestant. That is why there are fewer Protestants in the Acholi community.

In the world, every ethnic group has the name of the Creator in their own language. Why do the foreign religions reject the name of the Creator, called by people who know Him? For a better understanding, let us first look at how different people call the Creator. The British call the Creator God; Bari call Him Ngun; Shulluk call Him Jok; Arabs call Him Alah; Swahili call Him Mungu; Lotuko call Him Ajok; and Acholi call Him Jok or Rubanga. If Lotuko, Acholi and Shulluk call the Creator Jok or Ajok, why do the white people stop Acholi from calling the Creator Jok? Is it because Jok is Satan? The whites do not know the meaning of Jok. To the Nilotics, Jok means God or Holy Spirit (B. A. Ogot, 1967, P, 143).

MISSIONARIES OPENED SCHOOLS

As we have seen before, when the government permitted missionaries to enter Southern Sudan, they instructed them that evangelisation should go together with formal education. Because that was one of the fastest ways the government could bring development to the people. Among the missionaries that came to Southern Sudan, it was the Protestants whose teaching was good. The Catholic schools were weak. This is why most of the pupils who studied in Catholic schools did not go to university, unlike the Protestant schools.

The Catholic Church opened the biggest school in the whole Acholi area in Palotaka in 1923. They opened a primary school — Primary 1-2' (in the Mission). However, for other children in other parts of Acholi, they built what they called Bush Schools. The bush schools had only two classes – P1 and P2.

All the Primary two pupils would do their examinations from Palotaka. The pupils from different bush schools were selected to join P3 in Palotaka. It took the missionaries and the government a long time to open Primary Three and Primary Four in the bush schools.

Mr. Bimbashi Grove, who was in Opari (Madi) that time, categorised schools into two: the first category were schools which were to prepare children to become Secretaries to the Chief's Court. The second category was to prepare children to become interpreters/translators of Acholi and English to the chiefs and other Acholi people. The children being prepared for interpretation and translation were taken to Vernacular Schools. Another category of school was for the children of chiefs and very bright pupils selected from Vernacular Schools. After completing the education, these children were to be recruited as Local Government Administrators. The government also opened their own schools, but their schools were not good as the missionaries'.

In 1925 Elementary Schools were in every part of Acholi, Madi and Didinga. In these schools, children were taught vocational skills such as carpentry and building. These schools were opened in the following years.

- ▸ In 1921 they opened in Loa/Madi;
- ▸ In 1923 they opened in Palotaka/Acholi;
- ▸ In 1924 they opened in Nagishot/Didinga.

In 1925, up to twenty children completed their studies from these schools. Most of the graduates became secretaries in the courts. The interest to open Intermediate Schools came in 1929. In the same year Intermediate Schools were shifted from Rajaf to Okaru. Most of the children who went to study in Okaru ran back home because life was difficult there. The pupils would study in the morning and go to fetch firewood in the afternoon. They ground millet, paste and cooked by themselves. To Acholi boys, grinding and cooking was the work of women and girls. The Lotuko and Madi children also had the same opinion about cooking. So, many Acholi, Madi, Lotuko and other pupils ran away from Okaru. As many pupils were running away from Okaru, Fr. Frederici and Fr. Todesco wrote to the police in different parts of Acholi, Madi and Lotuko. In their letter to the police, they instructed the police to arrest and take back any child who escaped from Okaru. The children who had not yet escaped from school, when they heard of the police arrest, the boys decided to remain at schools so that they got in no trouble with police.

Between 1935-36, Mr. C.W. William, who was in charge of all schools in Sudan, came from Britain to see the sate of education in the country. Mr. William witnessed and understood the kind of maltreatment teachers subjected pupils to and reported it to his supervisors when he returned to Britain. Mr William was not impressed by the Catholic teachers because they were not teaching the right curriculum to the children. The Catholic communities abroad were not happy with Mr. William because of what he reported about the Catholics in Sudan. The Catholic priests claimed that Mr. William gave a bad report about them because they were Italians. Teachers were also not well trained to teach. Fr. Karl Johan Lundstrom said, '.in 1944 there were only thirty well trained teachers. All these qualified teachers were deployed in bush schools.

SEMINARY SCHOOL
Between 1928 and 1965 Italian missionaries opened a seminary school in Okaru. Okaru Minor Seminary, which is in Torit District, is the first seminary school that the Catholic missionaries opened in Southern Sudan. They opened this school for the children of Juba, Torit and Yei. In 1933 the missionaries built the second seminary school in Bussere-Wau. This school was for the children of Wau, Rumbek and Yambio. In 1974 Bussere became a Major Seminary for the seminarians who returned from Uganda and Zaire. Porkele, on Yei Meridi Road, is a Minor Seminary, which is the third Minor Seminary opened in (1959).

From 1930 to 1940, the students who completed minor Seminary in Sudan went to study in Lacor Major Seminary -Gulu (Uganda). However, in 1956, the Catholic priests opened a Major Seminary in Tore, and it was run very well up to 1964 when the government of Sudan sent away all the white Fathers out of the country. Bishop Ireneo Dud, on hearing this order, did not want the seminarians at Okarru Minor Seminary to be left uncared for. For that matter, on 24/5/1964, the Bishop ordained Fr. Paride Taban though he was left with one year to complete his studies in Theology.

When the white Fathers left Sudan, all seminarians converged at Kit (1964 to 1965). In July 1965, they went to Uganda to continue with their studies. In 1973, the Bishop of Sudan called back all the Major Seminarians to Sudan where they continued to study at Palica Juba (1973 — 1975). In 1975, Major Seminarians were ordained moved from Palica in Juba to Bussere, Wau. In the 1978 conference of Bishops of Sudan held in Khartoum, it was resolved that Major seminarians should return to Juba (Munuki). Between 1984 and 1987 all seminarians returned to Juba and in 1990, and because of Garang De Mabior's rebel activities, the missionaries shifted the Major Seminary to Kobar (Khartoum).

The first Acholi child to join seminary and studied up to the level of theology was Oreste Oyet of Panyikwara-Pajaa (1947). Unfortunately, he was not ordained. In Fr. Dellagiacoma's book, *Sudanese Catholic Clergy and Major Seminarians* written in 1992, states that the Acholi children who made it to major seminary were forty two, out of which only nineteen were ordained priests. The first Acholi child to be ordained a priest was Leopoldo Anywar of Magwi in 1960. The second person was Agustino Oboma of Pajok in 1961. Fom 1947 to 2000, the Acholi children who were ordained were eighteen. See below.

THE ACHOLI CHILDREN ORDAINED PRIESTS BETWEEN 1947 AND 2000.

No.	Father	Origin	Ordained by Bishop in the month of	He is in the community of .	Retired or died?
1	Leopoldo Anywar	Magwi 1942	S. Mazzoldi (Tore) 17-12-1960	Diocese — Juba.	Died in Palabek 9-4-68 (Uganda.)
2	Augusti on Oboma	Pajok 1946	S. Mazzoldi (Palotaka) 17-12-1961	Diocese — Juba.	Left work in 1974.
3	Mark Lotang	Obbo 1947	(Rome) 27-4-1971	Diocese — Juba	Left work in 1977
4	Akim Dario	Panyikw ara 1957	Paride Taban (Palotaka) 12-1-1986	Diocese — Torit	
5	Albino Adot Oryem	Pajok 1956	Arch. Bishop Paulino Lukudu Loro — Juba 13-12-1987	Comboni Fahers	
6	Oyet James Latansio	Pajok 1962 (Yei)	Arch. Bishop Paulino Lukudu Loro — Juba 18-12-1988	Diocese — Yei	

7	John Ocaya	Pajok 1963	Arch Bishop Paulino Iokudu Loro — Juba 10-12-1989	Diocese — Juba.	
8	Marcel Olal	Pajok 1964 (Soroti)	Arch Bishop Gabriel Zubeir (Khartoum) 21-4-1991	Diocese — Torit	
9	Justine Oyet	Omeo 1964?		Apos. of Jesus	
10	Paul Sebit	Pajok 1967	Arch G. Zubeir (Khartoum)	Dioc-Torit	
11	Michael Okello	Obbo 1968	Arch.G.Zubeir (Khartoum) 7.5.1995	Dioc-Torit	
12	Kalisto Lokwiya	Pajok 1969	Arch.G. Zubeir (Khartoum) .4.1996	Dioc-Torit	
13	Joseph Sunday	Pajok 1968	Bish. Paride Taban Kiriandongo	Dioc-Torit	
14	Nelson Mwaka	Pajok 1968	13.12.1997	Apost. of Jesus	
15	John Oryem	Obbo 1969?	B. Antonio Menegazzo (El Obeid) 29.11.1998	Dioc-El Obeid	
16	Joseph Ocan Obote	Obbo 1964	Bish.Daniel Adwok K. (Atbara) 15.2.1998	Dioc-Torit	
17	Joseph Apwoya	Pajok 1967	Arch. Paulino Lokudu (Juba) 25.4.1999	Dioc-Torit	
18	Mark Nyeko	Panyikwara 1969?	(Uganda)	Apost.of Jesus	
19	Martin Ocaya	Pajok 1968?	Arch. Paulino Lokudu (Juba) 7.1.2001	Dioc. Torit	

WHITE FATHERS IN ACHOLI 1900-1964

According to Fr. Dellagicoma, in his book about the Fathers who worked in Southern Sudan, there are twenty nine priests who worked in Lerwa and Palotaka. Here are the names of the fathers who worked in Acholi:

1. **Baj Giuseppe** (1903-), born in Gaggiano-Milan, ordained in 1926, and worked in Southern Sudan from 1929 to 1953, in Lao, Palotaka and Juba.

(2) **Bertnazzo Giuseppe** (1916), born in Vicenza-Italy, ordained in 1949, and worked in Palotaka between 1951 and 1952.

(3) **Calegari Gluseppe** (1896-1963), born in Vernate-Milan, and worked in Palotaka between 1953 and 1954.

(4) **Cardani Umberto** (1879-1966), born in Lerego-Verese. He worked in both Sudan and Uganda. At first he worked in the land of Madi of Palaro in Uganda (1915-1917), then in Moyo 1917-21. In 1923-33, he worked in Loa, between 1933 and 1936, he worked in Lerwa, and he worked in Palotaka from 1937 to 1949.

(5) **Cereda Paolo** (1897-1984), born in Albavilla-Como, and worked in Lerwa and Palotaka between 1932 and 1958.

(6) **Deberto Aleardo** (1898-1969), was born in Roverchiara-Verona. He worked in Uganda and Sudan. He took only one year in Palotaka (1947-48?)

(7) **Della Piazza Alberto** (1913-), was born in Primiero-Trento, and he worked in Torit, Palotaka and Loa between 1946-1951. After this, he went to Uganda (1958-60).

(8) **Del Zotto Erminio** (1912-), was born in Cordenons-Pordenone. He worked in Equatoria for 21 years (i. e. 1938-59) at Okaru, Torit, Palotaka and Juba.

(9) **Di Fabio Pasquale** (1929-), was born in San Velentino- Pescara. He worked in Juba, Isoke, Kit, Lerwa, Palotaka and Kadule, between 1957 and 1964.

(10) **Fornasa Giovanni Battista** (1883-1951), was born in Selico-Vicenza, and he worked in both Sudan and Uganda. In Sudan, he worked at Kodok, Malakal and Lerwa from 1929 to 1933.

(11) **Galli Giuseppe** (1907-), was born in Vavzago-Milan. He worked in

Sudan between 1931 and 1962 at Khartoum, Juba, Kapoeta, Okura, Issoke and Palotaka. In 1971, he was transferred to Uganda.

(12)   **Gambaretto Cesare** (1888-1967), was born in San Giovanni Ilarione-Verona. He worked in Palotaka at different times as shown here. Between 1939 and 42, 1946 and 51, 1956 and 1960. In 1964, the government of Sudan chased away all the white priests from Sudan. Fr. Casare lived in Italy for a few years and came back to Africa. That time, he did not return to Sudan. He went to Padibe in Uganda where he buried Fr. Saturnino Lohure (Lotuko, a Lotuko man) in January 1967.

(13)   **Giuliani Quirino** (1915-), was born in Marienkirchen-Austria. He worked in Palotaka, Okaru and Juba between 1950 and 1954.

(14)   **Grotto Francesco** (1919-), was born in Malo-Vicenza, and he worked in Torit, Kapoeta and Palotaka between 1952 and 19663.

(15)   **Mazzocco Igino** (1913-) was born in Chiampo-Vicenza, he worked in Torit, Okaru, Isoke, Lowai and Palotaka between 1939 and 1955.

(16)   **Molinaro Luigi** (1888-1985), was born in Volpino-Verona, he first worked in Uganda in 1913, and between 1920 and 1931, he worked in Torit, Loa, Nagishot and Lerwa.

(17)   **Montemanni Giorgio** (1915-1964), was born in Alessandria, he worked in Okaru, Torit, Palotaka and Lirya between 1946 and 1957.

(18)   **Muratori Carlo** (1902-1959), was born in Creda-Bologna around 1926-9136 and 1939-48. He worked in Rejaf, Torit, Isoke and Lerwa. He wrote Acholi- *Bari- Lotuko English Dictionary*.

(19)   **Nani Giuseppe** (1909), was born in Lanza-Como, he worked in Sudan twice. That is from 1937 to 1948 and from 1951 to 1955 in Tonga, Comboni College Khartoum, Okaru, Palotaka, Lafon and Lawai.

(20)   **Negrini Paolo** (1910), was born in Caspoggioc-Como, and he worked in Okaru, Palotaka, Torit, Lafon and Loa between 1936 and 1962.

(21)   **Pasquali Carlo** (1925), was born in Verona, around 1952-1960, and he worked in Palotaka, Lafon, Tali and Kworijik.

(22)   **Rinaldo Giuseppe** (1885-1973), was born in Piazza Armerina-Anna, he worked in Acholi for 24 years at Lerwa and Palotaka (1929-1954). He left priesthood in 1954 when he was 70 years of age, and he later died in Italy.

(23) **Simeoni Antonio** (1923-), was born in Cassacco-Udine, around 1950-64, and he worked in Okaru, Lafon, Isoke, Loa and Palotaka.

(24) **Simonelli Giuseppe** (1907-), was born in Lumezzane-Brescia, and he worked in Sudan between 1932-43, 1952-61 in places such as Loa, Isoke, Torit, Rejaf, Palotaka and Lerwa.

(25) **Soriani Elio** (1918-), was born in Piazzola sul Brenta-Padua, around 1946-55. He worked in Palotaka, Lafon and Khartoum.

(26) **Spagnolo Lino** (1910-), was born in Recoaro-Vicenza, he worked in Sudan for thirty years (1934-64) at Kapoeta, Torit, Isoke, Palotaka, Loa, Kator (Juba) and Okaru.

(27) **Vergani Dionigi** (1900-1938), was born in Cavenago-Milan, he worked in Lerwa and Palotaka between 1929 and 1938. He died of black fever from Palotaka.

(28) **Vitalini Dino** (1916-1977), was born in Rome, and he spent the most of his life in Palotaka (1947-1963), he worked in Isoke for just a few months and came back to Palotaka. The government of Sudan refused to give a Stay permit in January 963. He then proceeded to Brazil in 1964. In 1970, he went to Uganda and worked at Kalongo (Acholi-Uganda). He fell sick with cancer from Kalongo and died from Verona where he was taken for medical attention.

(29) **Zambonardi Giuseppe** (1884-1970), was born in Gardone-Brescia, Mukwongo. He worked in Arua-Uganda (1911-1920), and then he worked in Rajaf between 1920 and 1923.

(30) Paride Taban, was born in Loa, Madi around 1912, he worked in Palotaka between 1973 and 1977. He was ordained a priest in 1964 when the white priest had run away from Okaru Seminary.

(31) John Baptist Lohitu, was born in---??, he worked in Palotaka between 1977 and 1983.

(32) Fr. Gary, was born in Italy in -??--, he worked in Palotaka between 1984 and 1986.

(33) Fr. Julius Igaa, born in Madi, he worked in Palotaka between 1984 and 1986.

In 1927 when Eastern Equatorial became autonomous Prefecture Apostolic, the Catholic missionaries appointed Fr. Zambonardi a Perfect. With all the authorities he had, he developed the missions in Rejaf, Torit and Isoke. He later opened missions in Palotaka, Okaru, Kapoeta, Lafon and Yei. In 1935, the land on the west of River Kiir (River Nile) was given by the government to Protestants. However, he negotiated with the government and he was allowed to build a mission in Yei. There were many white Brothers and Fathers who worked in Acholiland, but the ones whom most Acholi people should remember most is Zordani Giuseppe (1907-) who was born in Vicentina-Vicenza. He liked Agrculture. He worked in Juba Vicariate between 1931 and 1939, and from 1946 to 1962, he worked in Okaru, Isoke, Torit and Palotaka. He was the one who opened the farm we see in Palotaka today. He also added more buildings. The farm did not only help the priest of Loa, Torit, Isoke, Lafon and Juba, but also Acholi people at times of famine. The farm also provided job opportunities to Acholi people since all the work was now in Torit, and Torit is 36 miles away from Acholi.

Figure 23: a Catholic Bishop.

Chapter Twenty Three

ISLAM

Most Acholi did not want to follow the Islamic teaching. I think this is not correct because, most of the time, Islam liked pulling rope with Christians. What usually gives a party a better ground to win an argument? It is a deeper understanding of Quran and the Bible that provided that strength. That means it is worthless to engage in religious argument if you do not have good knowledge of the two books.

To understand Islam, let us first answer the following questions, "What does Islam mean? Who is Prophet Muhammad? When was Muhammad born? Where did he live? What is the name of his father? What is the name of his mother? Who exposed Muhammad to religion? Was religion in Arab world before Muhammad was born or not? If there was religion, then what kind of religion was it? Did Muhammad know the Bible, or not?" If we answer all these questions well then we can understand the difference between Muhammad and Jesus Christ. All the answers are found in in *Islam and Christianity Ninety questions and Answers,* written by Abdul-Masih from Nigeria in 1970/71. I will answer all these questions from Abdul-Masih's book without adding anything to it so that no confusion arises.

Although it is said that Islam came from the Arab word, "Aslamia," which means a believer in Islam, Aslamia has two meanings to Arabs. The first meaning is anyone who believes in God (Allah). The second meaning is followers of Prophet Muhammad. Muhammad was a Semite who lived in Arabia. Oral sources state that Muhammad was a medium height man, and was a very bold person. His beards were long and his feet were cracked and rough. He did not smile or laugh anyhow. His eyes were black and usually wrapped his head with henna. He was born around 570 A.D. in Mecca.

Who were the parents of Muhammad? Prophet Muhammad hailed from a house called Quraish (Bame Hashim). His father was called Abdullah, son of Abd-al-Muttalib. Muhammad's mother was called Amina, daughter of Wahib. Both Muhammad's parents died when he was only two months old. His grand father, Abd-al-Muttalib, fed him on goat's milk until he was six months of age, and Abd-al-Muttalib gave him to Abdullah — Abdullah was Abd-al-Muttalib's younger brother.

When Muhammad was twenty five years old, he went to live with his aunt called Ali. A few years after, Muhammad left his aunt and began to work with Khadija, a widow. Khadija's husband was a very rich man with many large shops. All these shops and wealth were left to Kadhija when her husband died. Muhammad was a hard working man and Khadija liked him very much. Khadija often sent Muhammad on sales missions to Palestine and Jerusalem.

It did not take long; Khadija fell in love with Muhammad. Muhammad also acknowledged her love – they got married. Prophet Muhammad lived with his wife for twenty six years. Khadija was older than Muhammad by fifteen years. After the death of Khadija, Muhammad married many wives with whom he begot many children. Among the children, he loved his daughter, Ayeshad most.

Muhammad learnt the Bible from Waraqa ibn Naufal, Khadija's cousin. Waraqa knew the Bible very well, when Quran was not yet there. When Muhammad was forty years old, he began to teach together with Waraqa. Religion eventually touched Muhammad's heart. Later, Muhammad said he could not live with adulterous people because, in the town he lived, adultery was a common practice. He went to live in a cave in Mount Hira, far away from the town.

Quaran claims that, one day, Angel Gabriel (Jibril) appeared to Muhammad and told him, "I want you teach the word of God who created Heaven and earth" (96 Alaq 1-5). Angel Gabriel appeared to Muhammad in 610 A.D. Muhammad accepted the angel's instruction and began to teach Quaran for twelve years in Mecca and he attracted sixty disciples to help him in teaching. For three years from the time Muhammad began his teaching, people in Mecca did not want to listen to his teaching. He continued to teach the word of God to women and his friends. The first person to embrace Muhammad's teaching was his wife

Khadija followed by his aunt Ali. The third convert was Zeyd who was Khadija's servant, and the forth covert was his friend, Abu Bakr.

Muhammad taught his followers that, "Jesus Christ is the Messiah – a person chosen by God to redeem mankind from sin." When people understood that Jesus Christ was the Messiah, they welcomed Muhammad's teaching whole heartedly. Muhammad later told people that Jesus would come to prepare the way for him because he was the true and last Messiah. On 24/09/622 A.D., Muhammad and his disciples left Mecca for Yathrib, 280 miles north of Mecca. He lived in Yathrib until his death, which occurred on 8/6/632 A.D. Yathrib was later named Medina. The people of Yathrib liked Muhammad' teaching, and he said such people were Ansar, those who could help, but some people did not want to listen to his teaching and called him "Manafigun," which means a liar.

Muhammad fought and defeated Mecca. He fought them because most people in Mecca did not support his religious ideology. He burnt all the altars of the traditionalists in Mecca. From then forth, his religion became deep rooted in Mecca. In 632 A.D. Muhammad went on a pilgrimage to Mecca; when he returned to Medina, he died of severe malaria. Early in the morning before his death, Muhammad prayed together with a congregation in the Mosque. The prayer was led by Abu Bakr. After the prayer, he went back to his house where he died during the day. His disciples were informed of his death immediately.

A man called Omar, when he heard of the death of Muhammad, strongly advised Muhammad's disciples, "No one should report that Muhammad has died because he is a Messiah. For that reason, he should not have died." The disciples tried to conceal the information in vein. It was later known that Muhammad was dead.

The disciples took Muhammad's body to his daughter, Ayeshad. When Abu Bakr confirmed the death, he objected to Omar's idea of concealing the death. Omar did not relent from telling people that Muhammad was not dead. Abu Bakr, on the other hand, openly told people, "Muhammad has died."

All Christians know that Jesus Christ died and resurrected on the third day and went back to heaven, but Muhammad did not rise from death, he will resurrect on the day of the end of the world when all the dead rise from death. This shows us that Jesus Christ has the power to triumph over death, but Muhammad does not have even a drop of that power. This brings us to the question "Who did God send, between Jesus and Muhammad, to save mankind?" Muhammad was buried in Medina. That is why many Muslims go to Mecca yearly to pray on Muhammad's grave.

Therefore, Jesus Christ was sent by God to save mankind. John 3: 16-18 reads, "For God so loved the world that is why he gave his only Son, that whoever believes in him should not perish but have eternal life. For God did not send his Son into the world, to condemn the world, but in order that the world might be saved through him

DIVISION AMONG MUSLIMS

Islam, just like Christianity, is divided into many denominations. Before his death, Muhammad indicated that his followers were going to be divided into seventy three groups. Muhamad said, "From the seventy three groups, only one will go to hell, but the rest will go to heaven."

After forty years of the death of Muhammad, Islam split into two groups, Sunni and Shia. Sunni think they are the true followers of Muhamaad, not Shia. Shia also think they are the owner of Islam. Most Muslims are in the group of Sunni with 90%, and Shia are 10%. Most Shia are found in Iran and Iraq.

Chapter Twenty Four

TRADITIONAL RELIGION IN ACHOLI

THE SHRINE

Shrine is very important in Acholi. Acholi people dug their shrines on the compound of an elder, but in a royal house, the shrine is erected in front of the rain-maker chief's house. The shrine is not constructed with any tree species but *olwedo* tree only. If *olwedo* tree was already on the compound, the shrine would be constructed under it. But if *olwedo* is not on the compound, they cut it branches from the bush and used them for constructing the shrine. The back of *olwedo* to be used for erecting the shrine must be removed.

A clan elder built a shrine on a boulder in front of which they built two small fetishes, one on the right and the other on the left. The roof of the fetish is usually thatched with spear grass. The fetish on the right stands for the senior wife and her children and the left one stands for the junior wife and her children. This does not mean that only men with two wives are the ones to build a shrine, a man with one wife can also build it. The Acholi culture demands that the main celebrant at the shrine must be a man. The main celebrant should be the chief elder in the family. If the man has only one wife, the two fetishes both stand for the one wife and her children. If the elder has more than two wives, he does not build three or four fetishes because the culture wants only two fetishes. The third and other wives do not have fetish though they are members of the family.

Figure 24: The Acholi Shrine

In Acholi, rituals are performed at the shrines in November or December when people have finished harvest and stored food in the granary. November and December are also the months of hunting, and on the first week of either months, elders invoke the spirits of the ancestors before the shrine for two important reasons. First, they ask the ancestors to open the way for the hunters and keep them safe in the wilderness. They also seek cleansing so that they are protected against the attack of evil spirits.

A few days before the day of grand rituals at the shrine, elders send words to all aunts, uncles, nephews, nieces, brothers and sisters under this shrine to come for the ritual at the shrine. This celebration does not need only the daughters who are at home, but also those who are already married. When everybody is already there before the shrine, a white billy goat or a black one is slaughtered in front of the shrine. This makes us ask the question, "Why do we use only black or white billy goat to be slaughtered at the shrine?" In the culture of Acholi, the colour of the goat used at the shrine is very important because the colours have meanings. Black is chosen to obscure the evil intention of a dark hearted person to bring ailment in the family. White is to clean the ill feeling from the heart of an adversary.

Early in the morning, elders bring the chosen billy goat before the shrine. One of the elders open the month of the goat and spit in it saying, " .ourfore-fathers, open the eyes of your children who have gathered here today, open the eyes of other children who are away (in town). Bless them and give them health. Let no grass cut the legs of the boys and men who are preparing to go for a hunting expedition." When this elder ends his prayer, another gets up and spits in the mouth of the billy goat and repeats the prayer said by the first elder, "our forefathers, open the eyes of your children who have gathered here today, open the eyes of other children who are away (in town). Bless them and give them health. Let no grass cut the legs of the boys and men who are preparing to go for a hunting expedition."

The prayer is repeated by the consecutive elders, but even if there are many elders at the shrine, it is the tradition that only three or four elders say the prayer before the shrine. After the three or four prayers to the ancestors, they then lay the goat in front of the shrine, and one elder kills it by hitting the back of its head. The goat for this kind of ritual is not skinned by anybody other than a nephew of the family. After skinning the goat, the nephew put the carcase on a door shutter, and one elder pierces its stomach with a knife. He then removes the dung from the intestine and puts it in a small calabash and puts it at the shrine. The elder calls everybody one by one and smears the dung on their feet and chest. After he has done this on everybody, the elder solemnly throws the dung on the shrine. It is said that if elders prayed at the shrine to curse someone who annoyed them, the person usually dies.

After this ritual, the nephew continues with cutting the carcase and gives it to women to cook. The neck and the head of the goat is the nephew's. That is why elders say " the head of a goat is nephew's food." But when I moved among the Acholi of today, I discovered that the modern Acholi do not respect the culture. Even some elders do not mind about this aspect of the culture where a nephew takes the head. If you attend any Acholi celebration or ritual, you find that a nephew skins the goat, but when it comes to eating, anybody can eat the head. This shows that Acholi people are not following their culture. The head of goat slaughtered at an occasion like this is not eaten by anybody else but a nephew.

Most of the time, the elders who come when the dung is already put on the shrine, take the calabash of dung and throw it on the shrine saying their prayer, "our forefathers, open the eyes of your children who have gathered here today, open the eyes of other children who are away (in town). Bless them and give them health. Let no grass cut the legs of the boys and men who are preparing to go for a hunting expedition."

One important thing I want readers of this book to know is that nobody should quarrel or fight on the day of celebrating the shrine so that God can listen to the prayer of His children. If anybody quarrels or fights on this day, the clan elders gives him a very heavy punishment, or they may curse him before the shrine, which may cause him severe illness or death. As we have seen before, if elders curse somebody, the person may die.

In the evening, when the sun is about to set, elders begin to eat in groups of age mates. After eating, everybody washes their hands in one calabash, and the head of the family carries the water calabash in his left hand. He then dips olwedo leaves in the water with his right hand and sprinkles the water on the people who are before the shrine. He then pours the remaining water to the east saying, "Let the good things come from the east." He pours the rest of the water to west as he says, "Let the bad things go to the west." This man now implants the olwedo leaves on the shrine and places the calabash upside down at the shrine. Acholi believe that all good things come from the east. That is why an elder pours water to the east and and asks for blessings. The Acholi people also believe that bad thing usually come from the west, and that is why the elders say the evil should go to the west. That means they are dispelling death from the house whose members have gathered together before the shrine. Olwedo leave, to the Acholi people, is a symbol of peace. That is why during rituals or blessing, Acholi use olwedo leaves to sprinkle water on people. Elders told me that after this meal, people drink kwete (millet/shorgum beer) before they retire to their homes.

If a hunter kills a leopard, he places the skin of the animal on the shrine because it is his father's shrine that kept him safe, and it is the same shrine that enabled him to kill the leopard. As he places the leopard skin on the shrine, the hunter silently says " Thank you my grand father. The God of my father, I thank you for what you have given me. I give you this leopard skin to wear. Lie face up and open the eyes of your children who are in darkness." This skin is kept on the shrine for one day. The following morning, the elder whom the shrine stands in front of his house, takes the skin and keeps.

AUMA

What is Auma? Auma is the spirit of a father covered under a pot in the house of a first born son in a particular house or family. In Acholi, spirits are divided into two: the spirit of a father and the spirit of a grand father. According to Acholi culture, the spirit of a father has less authority than the spirit of a grand father. The spirit of grand father is called before the shrine, but the spirit of a father is called under a pot. If the spirit of grand father wants something to eat, it normally comes to people in dreams. Acholi people know that, when the spirit of a father is annoyed, it brings headache and illnesses to children. The spirit of a father does not get annoyed anyhow, except when it is hungry. This annoyance does not show up in a clan leader's dream like that of a grand father. If the annoyance of the father's spirit is not shown in dreams, then how do the clan leaders know that it is hungry? When people are attacked by cough, headache, fever or other illnesses, clan elders go consult diviner priests to find out the causes of the ailments. The diviner priest talks to the spirit of the father of the family, "Alright, the spirit of we want you to tell us if you are aggrieved or you want food." The spirit will tell whether he is aggrieved by his people or he wants food. The people who are with the priest cannot hear the discussion of the spirit and the priest. It is the priest who reports to them what the spirit says. The spirit of the father often does not specify the food he wants, clan elders know that the spirit of the father usually eats the lower back meat, or the heart of an antelope or duiker are the parts of an animal that are prepared for auma.

When the day for Auma draws closer, the person at whose home Auma is celebrated sends a word for all brothers and sisters to attend the ceremony. All these people assemble at the main celebrant's home. Very early in the morning, at the first cock crow, the elder puts on fire the food that the diviner priest told him, but if the priest did not tell him, then he puts smoked lower back meat or heart of the animal. Men are the ones who cook in Auma ceremony. The food for the father is not cooked on the compound but in the house, and it is not cooked with onion. It is pasted with groundnut paste or sesame paste. When food is ready, the cook puts water on fire to make bread for all the invited people. Acholi culture allows daughters of the home to attend this ceremony, but they are not allowed to eat the food offered to the spirit of the father because they come to only witness what their brothers are doing.

When the water has boiled, the cook pours flour in it and mingles the bread. He serves the bread and covers it with a new basket. If there is no new basket, he can use an old one to do the same. Auma bread is not covered with linen or a plate. This food is not eaten in the morning neither is it eating in the afternoon. When the sun is setting, the elder who prepared the food and his brothers enter the house to mend Auma. The elders wash their hands, pinch off bread and mix with the source, and kneeling down, they put their hands together and stick the bread at the bottom of the pot. After this, the elders sit down to eat.

The elders wash their hands in a calabash after eating. The head of the family then carries the water calabash in his left hand, and he holds *olwedo* leaves in his right hand and dips in in the water in the calabash, while praying, "My father, we have given you food. I implore you to grant health on the children at home and unto those who are in foreign land." After his prayer, the head of the family takes a soft broom, which stands for the children in the foreign land, and puts it standing upright on the floor. He silently pours the water in which hands were washed on the broom. He is not supposed to pour out all the water on the broom. He leaves some little water in the calabash, and he pours the remaining water to the east as he prays, " let good people come from the east." The elder later pours the remaining water to the west saying, "let bad people go to the west." He takes the leaf of *olwedo* with which he was supplicating, fixes in the outside front roof. Putting the leaf on the roof implies the wish of the people for peace to prevail in the house.

OMARA *god*

What is Omara god? Omara god is the god of girls and women. It is the god that denies women fertility. In Sudan, especially among Acholi, if a woman realises that she does not have ova – the ability to conceive, she asks clan elders to take her to Omara god so that he gives her fertility. Acholi people believe that God does not create all women in the same way. He creates some women with hot pot (fertility), which means that when such a woman sleeps with a man, she easily conceives. There are also women who are created with cold pot, which means even if such a woman sleeps with a man for months or years, she cannot conceive. In Acholi, clan elders take women with cold pot before Omara god.

When a girl elopes with a boy and she takes one year or more without conception, she asks her father to take her before Omara god. Conception is very important among the Acholi of Sudan. Therefore, if a father hears that his daughter's pot is cold, he calls all the daughters of the family to his home. All the girls turn up in the home of the father of the girl. Very early in the morning, the man presents his daughter before Omara god. The father of the girl, together with the other invited daughters of the family, present their prayer before God. Some people believe that such a girl will never conceive even if she is taken to Omara god. But Acholi people believe that Omara god usually grant fertility to women whose pots are cold. One ting that I want readers of this book to understand that, it is not necessarily true that women with cold pot cannot conceive. They can, but it may take a long time before they do.

On the day this girl is presented before god, all the other girls invited sit on their feet in front of Omara god. Each of the girls silently pray in their hearts, " Lord, we have come before you for our sister (they call her name). We implore you to grant her fertility. We also ask you to have mercy on her." On finishing their prayer, the girls assemble at the side of a granary.

The clan elders pierce the stomach of a billy goat in front of Omara god. A nephew skins the goat and gives the meat to the girls to cook. I do not know if the nephew is the one to eat the head of this goat as we have seen before. The Acholi culture demands that when the girls finish cooking the food, they do not test even a drop of it. They give it whole to clan elders. The girls are only allowed to test how much salt is in the food, but they should not swallow it. Clan elders eat the food before Omara god. If they fail to finish the food, they each carry their shares home.

After eating, elders call the girls back to sit before Omara god, and one elder uses olwedo leaf to sprinkles the water with which they washed their hands on the girls. This includes the girl whom they have come to pray for. Every elder sprinkles water on them while saying, " the spirit of our grand father (Chief), your girls have given you food today. Clean their hearts. Grant (calls the name of the girl) fertility. You who left your blessing with us, allow us to continue blessing your children. We implore you to grant health to other children who are not here." After this prayer, one elder inerts the olwedo leaf on the roof from outside. The girls sit by the side of a granary, or under a platform, and later retire to their homes. I know that no statistics has been taken on Acholi women, I believe that 3/5 of the women presented before Omara god, later conceived and bore children. A baby girl born after this prayer is named Alur, but if it is a baby boy he is named Olur.

LABOT ONYOM god

Although elders say that there are only smaller gods in Pajok, I discovered that the biggest god that all Acholi people of Pajok worship is Labot-onyom god, because this god unites all the people of Pajok. Labot Onyom, is Pajok's principal jok. O'Byrne, R. J. (2015) observes that to understand the role of Labot-onyom in Pajok, one must first understand what is meant by "jok". Jogi (the plural of jok) are best understood as powerful non-human spiritual forces, are deeply predictable, have the power to posse people, and thus can be both helpful and dangerous. Associated with deeper cultural logics of productivity and destruction, they are connected with giving and taking productivity of all kinds, agricultural and social as well as biological. A fundamental structuring principle among most Nilotic communities, jok and jogi are central in Acholi understandings of the world" P.21).

Essentially, what this means is that Labot-Onyom will protect and defend all Pajok community members as long as the jok's good will is maintained with the annual sacrifice of a large male sheep. This is unlike fixed jogi who only protect members of a particular sub-clan.

Majority of Pajok elders claimed that during and after the last civil wars in South Sudan, Labot-Onyom protects Pajok people in many different ways: firstly it brings wind which confuses or destroys enemies. This is linked to the sending of an *ajuro* (whirl-wind) that disorients them, leaving them vulnerable; secondly, by removing sickness or disease, specially airborne diseases like measles; thirdly by guiding someone lost in the bush back to their home; and lastly, by protecting citizens of Pajok who are fighting elsewhere. But the last role of Labot-onyom for protecting citizens of Pajok who are in the army seems to more confusing, because Pajok men hardly join military although they like joining police and prison forces.

It is said that the first owners of Labot-onyom god were the people of Paibworo. But they later gave out the god to the people of Obwolto. The oral source has it that Paibworo gave the god to Obwolto in appreciation to Obwolto. Long ago, the people called this god Lapii pa Paibworo (Paibworo's

Blessing). It was later given the name, Labot-onyom. Pajok elders told me that Pajok brought the god from Paibworo around 1948-1950, because at that time a severe famine called "abongo wang dako" (I feel the face of the woman) had broken out among Acholi of Sudan. In the same year, there was abundance of foodstuff in Uganda. So, the Acholi of Sudan from the villages of Obbo, Pajok, Panyikwara, Palwar and Magwi went to look for food in Uganda. The people did not go to only one place like Patongo or Palabek. So the Sudanese divided themselves as shown below.

- ▶ Some of Obbo, Magwi and Panyikwara people went to Palabek and others went to Atyak.
- ▶ Some of the people of Palwar went to Lokung while others went to Padibe.
- ▶ Some Pajok went to Pajule (Cwua).

The people of Pajule did not like visitors, so they were not pleased by the people of Pajok's visit though Pajok also helped them a lot with garden work. Pajok people worked for the people of Pajule for about a month. When garden work was almost ending, the people of Pajule killed a Pajok boy. They boy was a nephew of Obwolto, and he had gone to his mother's kin during the time of search for food. One evening, the people of Pajok found that one of their boys was missing. They asked themselves, "Where is the boy?" One Pajok person said, "You, the people of Pajok, do not look for the missing boy because the people of Pajule have killed him. I saw them kill him with my own eyes."

The people of Pajok were not happy to hear the sad news of the death of the nephew of Obwolto. They resolved that all the people of Pajok who were in Pajule should return to Sudan immediately. The following morning, before sun rise, the people of Pajok set off from Pajule and eventually came to Atebi. They told people who remained at home in Sudan what the people of Uganda did to their nephew. They sent a word for Obwolto elder who was enraged by the news. The Obwolto elder ordered his horn-blower to blow the horn so that all the people of Pajok could assemble. The horn-blower wasted no time to execute the order. He sounded the horn and the people of Pajok immediately learned that there was something wrong. So, each of them picked their spears and rushed to where the horn was blown. This attracted very large crowd.

The Obwolto elder stood up and told the gathering that, "My people, I have called you to tell you about the death that killed our nephew. The boy had gone to Pajule as other people also went to search for food. Unfortunately, the people of Pajule killed him for no apparent reason. I am not pleased with this news. I believe that you are all not pleased with it too. I have called you here because I want you to go to Pajule and avenge the death of our nephew."

In Acholi of Sudan, if an atrocity like this is committed, people come together. When the Obwolto elder talked to them, Pajok people agreed to avenge the death of the boy. The Obwolto elder then made his petition, "There is nothing wrong we have done to our brothers in Pajule. It is the blood of our brother that the people of Pajule killed that should look at them. There, the people of Pajok, go and avenge this death. I pray that you go safely. No tree stump should hit their feet. Lord, the God of our grandfather, widely open the way and clean it for your people."

After his petition, the elder told the warriors, "There you are boys and unmarried men; I want you to get women in the war you are going for. If you find women, children and cattle in Pajule, don't kill them. Bring them home. The women and girls you will bring will eventually become your wives." Thus, the word Labot-Onyom means a bachelor can now get married.

After the elder's address, the Pajok warriors ran to Uganda. In two day's time, they were in Pajule. The warriors besieged a Pajule village called Agago. They reached Agago when the people were still sleeping. At day break, Pajok began to spear the people of Pajule in their sleep. Oral sources maintain that many people of Pajule died in this war, and the rest ran away from their homes. Women and girls also wanted to run away, but as their elder ordered, the warriors of Pajok did not give them time. They captured the women and girls. Any Pajok warrior, who captured a Pajule girl or woman, took her home for a wife. The men who did not find women in this war, went back with heads of cattle, and later married from home with the animals they brought from Pajule. This shows that god listened to the elder of Obwolto and everything happened as he said.

The people of Pajok showed their appreciation to the Obwolto by giving him a big ram and hoe. The elder buried the hoe in front of the house to be a blessing to Pajok. Whenever the people of Pajok are going to war, or want to do something important, an Obwolto man prays for them. Secondly, it is also an Obwolto man who celebrates the Labot-onyom god. Just like other gods in Acholi, this god is celebrated in December. The god is celebrated for four reasons. Firstly, they do it so that the grass does not cut the hunters in the wilderness. Secondly, it is to provide safety to warriors going to war. Thirdly, to grant health to the people, and fourthly, they do it so that the god provides them food in abundance. As we have seen above, that is how the blessing of the Paibworo of Pajule got the name, Labot Onyom.

JIKILOTI *god*

Jikiloti is the god that the people of Obbo worship. It is the god of Koyo Omini. It is said that before the coming of Abong in Obbo, it was a Koyo man who celebrated the god. The history of Obbo contends that Koyo gave the god to the father of Lokuro, a nephew of Koyo Omini, in the family of Gari (Loudo). As we have seen before, the Gari people came from Abong Kure (Obbo). Opio Lonyor-moi, the father of Kalaudio, is the one who led them to Loudo, and they settled in Ijula. The elders of Obbo told me that Koyo gave Jikiloti god to the father of Lokuro. They said that after the death of Lokuro, the god was left to the mother of Lokuro. When Lokuro's mother died, the god was left to Micci, the grand child of Lokuro of Abong. When Micii died, he left the god to his son, Ojok. To date, the power of celebrating Jikiloti god lies in the hands of the people of Gari. Although the people of Obbo worship Jikiloti, they also have many smaller gods. See Appendix A1-2. Obbo elders told me that the second god that Obbo worship is Lwoo god, which is also the god of Pajombo people.

The people of Obbo worship Jikiloti god very much because it gives them five things. Firstly, when it is celebrated well, the god grants the people of Obbo health. Secondly, the god stops evil spirits from attacking the people. Thirdly, the god gives the people of Obbo abundance of rain and good harvest. Fourthly, it protects the Obbo hunters against all odds in the hunting ground, and fifthly, it clears the way for Obbo warriors during wars.

How Obbo Celebrate Jikiloti god

As we have seen before, Acholi celebrate their gods in November or December, but Jikiloti of Gari is celebrated in April. I was told that a few days to the day of celebration of the god, Gari elders select some boys to collect food contributions from every household in Obbo. They boys collect flour, fermented millet flour for beer, smoked meat, sesame and groundnuts. They bring all they collected to the god's priest.

Two days to the day of celebration of Jikiloti, the priest sends for everyone to attend the ceremony. People are forbidden from moving around anyhow on the day of the celebration. Secondly, foreigners are not allowed in Obbo on that day. The neighbours of Obbo such as Pajok, Palwar, Magwi and Owiny-ki-bul usually know if Obbo is celebrating their god, so they do not go there. If a foreigner enters Obbo on that day, the youths of Obbo levy a fine on him, and he pays in terms of money. An Obbo person who breaks the custom by walking around anyhow is also fined. He pays money, millet, chicken or goat.

On the day of the celebration of Jikiloti, the priest sends a man in the grazing ground to bring a big white ram. In the past, even now, people keep their goats and sheep in one grazing ground. The man sent in the grazing ground will take any ram that he finds good enough for the occasion and brings it home. The owner of the ram does not get annoyed that his ram has been taken, but some people do not want theirs to be taken. If the owner of the ram wants his ram to be paid for, the elders of Gari raise money and pay to him.

Early in the morning, the priest takes the ram towards Ayii Stream, where Jikilioti god is. On the way, he cuts the testicles of the ram and leaves it to go to the house of the god, under oywelo tree, which is one kilometre away from Ayii Bridge. The priest of the god, his wife and three elders follow the ram slowly. When it reaches the house of the god, the ram lies down and dies instantly. The wife of the priest carries a vase of beer for the god. When the entourage of the priest reaches the house of the god, one elder pours the kwete beer from the vase into a ditch which is on a flat rock. Obbo elders told me that, in this place there are pot-like ditches that God made when he was creating the earth. All the three pots are filled with kwete, when two other elders are skinning the ram. Four big snakes emerge from the cave when they smell the kwete. The small snakes remain in the cave. After drinking the alcohol, the big snakes get back into the cave. The small snakes then come out to drink the alcohol. It is said that when the snakes are drinking kwete, the three elders and the priest praise them and call them, "Chief, Chief, Chief."

When the ram is skinned, it is cooked in one pot. The whole food is given to the chief because this food is not eaten even by the elders who accompany the priest. They go back home and eat the food which was prepared for them – kept under the pot of the priest of the god. The people who go for this ritual must be strong hearted because during the ceremony, snakes just move freely among people. In Acholi culture, killing god's snake is prohibited. Obbo elders told me that sometimes the snakes do not go to eat from the ditch, but come to eat from home. They do not eat the mutton because it is all left at the ritual place. So they come to drink kwete which is under the pot in the pot in the house. No one picks a stick to hit the snakes when they see them enter the house – as we have seen above, the god's snakes are not killed. If someone kills one, it brings sickness, death and other problems to the people of Obbo. Obbo elders also know that the snakes that crawl on the compound, or enter the house that day have come to eat. So, when a snake is entering a house, they tell the snake with great respect that, "Chief, it is good you have come. Enter the house and eat." The snakes enter the house, and it is strong hearted elders who sit at the doorway. They sit there until the three elders and the priest return from the god's house. The snakes go back to their place after finishing eating. They say that the snake that come home to eat do not bite anybody, but it is also said if god's snake bites someone, the person dies.

After giving the food to Chief, the priest of the god and the three elders return home and sit together with the elder waiting for them at the doorway. The god usually makes rain drizzles, before people begin to eat, so that the people who have come for the celebration are not dirtied by dust. Immediately after the drizzle, the sun shines very hot. Within a short time, the soil is completely dry. People now settle down to eat and drink.

On the day of celebrating Jikiloti god, the priest of the god does not open chicken cage. The chickens remain in the cage until people finish eating. The priest then calls the nephews who are around and he instruct one of the nephews to take chickens from the cage and give to all the nephews who are there. In Acholi culture, on the day of celebrating the god, all the chickens in the cage are given out to nephews of the family, but they leave only one cock and a hen in the cage.

LWOO god

The people of Obbo praise the god and call him Chief Lwoo. This god belongs to the people of Pajombo. The god is celebrated by man from Okwee in the family of Pajombo. In the previous chapters, we have seen migration of Okwee, where we are told that when the people of Olwedo reached Obbo, they settled at the foot of Pakwa Hill in Cama. It was from here that they got Lwoo god. Although the place belonged to Koyo people, the Lwoo god did not belong to them. That is how the people of Okwee took up the ownership of the Lwoo god.

Like other gods, Lwoo god is celebrated once a year, and Lwoo god is celebrated in February. Obbo elders told me that Olwedo is the main celebrant of Lwoo god. After the death of Olwedo, over ten people relayed the priesthood of Lwoo. Unfortunately, the people of Pajombo do not remember the names of those previous priests. But the leaders of Obbo today know that, after the ten or so priests, Ongom Ociti took up the priesthood of Lwoo. When Ociti died his son, Itingo-wii took up the priesthood from 1960 to 1979. In 1979 when Otingo-wii died, his son, Lopit became the next priest of Lwoo. I do not know if in 1986, when I began to write this book, Lopit was still the priest of Lwoo. However, between 1988 and 1991 most people of Pajombo (Okwee) proposed that if Lopit died, Benjamin Lotoo who was a teacher should take over the priesthood, but Benjamin was not interested in it. Some people agreed with Bejamin because Benjamin was a formally educated person, and secondly, he was the Principal of Loka Senior Secondary School. Unfortunately, Benjamin used to drink and laugh maniacally. This made some people to think that it was Lwoo god that was making him insane. But there was nothing that showed that Benjamin was insane.

A few days to the day of celebration of Lwoo, as the oral sources say, Okwee elder inform people in three day's time not to move around anyhow. The celebration of Lwoo god usually takes three days, and in the three days people are restricted from unnecessary movement. If the youth find you breaking the custom, you pay a fine with a billy goat, or chicken, or money and they take you to the priest's home. The custom of the Pajombo people is that a person caught breaking this decree, remains at the priest's home until the celebration is over.

Pajombo also ordered that everybody who cultivates in Ongol-kor, should contribute to Okwee. The contribution can be in terms of millet, sesame, groundnuts or peas. This contribution from people who cultivate in Ongol-kor is kept pending the rite in Ongol-kor the following year. On the day of the rite, women brew kwete, which five or seven selected men take together with a ram to the god. The clan elders take an old woman who has never given birth to a child to sleep in the house of god. The old woman lies down and an elder covers her with the skin of antelope or the skin of ngir. The old woman remains lying there until the men who have taken the offers to god come back home. The old woman, according to elders, does not stay there alone. Clan elders chose five women who sit by her side. The old woman is not supposed to go for a call (urinate or defecate), or drink water until the five men have returned home.

The elders of Obbo told me that at the time that the old woman is lying in the house of god, snakes and tortoises freely move about her. The woman is not afraid of the snakes because, as we have said before, the snakes of god do not bite people anyhow.

When they reach the house of god, they leave the billy goat to go by itself into the cave in the god's home. The billy goat lies at the mouth of the cave and dies there on its own. Before they do anything, the elders pour kwete in the ditch at the mouth of the cave for the snakes and hares which are there to drink. The god immediately sends a guinea fowl to wave a blessing to the elders. It flies over the elders flapping blessing on them, after which it falls down and dies immediately. After the guinea fowl, all the snakes in trees and from the cave come out to drink the alcohol given unto them. A short while after this, some white animals appear on Lwoo Hill. When they see these animals, the elders are not supposed to show surprise of what they have seen. If one of the elders does so, it completely ruins the celebration that has brought them there.

At this moment, two or three men begin to skin the billy goat and two of them go to gather *oduko* firewood. Lwoo god's meat is not cooked with any other firewood apart from *oduku*. The elders cook the meat in a three edged hearth made of three stones, close to the mouth of the cave. No one should walk over the firewood which is in the hearth because it ruins the celebration. If an elder forgets and strides over the firewood, they remove all the firewood in the hearth and replace them with new ones.

When the food is ready, two or three elders, clad in antelope skin, go to mend the god's house in the cave after which they begin to eat. The custom says that no one should bite the bone. They should only eat the meat. If one elder bites the bone, the celebration is ruined. They have to take another billy goat so that the celebration begins afresh. The people of Pajombo and Obbo know this custom very well, and they observe it so that the celebration is complete without any mishap.

The elders return home after eating, but before they reach home, the god sends for them antelope, buffalo or water-back. The animals will just die in front of the elders. The god does this to show his pleasure for the offer that the people gave him. That is why the people of Acholi say "Lwoo god is not dark-hearted, selfish or corrupt." The elders skin the animals and take the meat home. Before they enter home, one of them blows the horn. On hearing the horn, the women who are with the old woman loudly sound yodel. When they hear a yodel, the Pajombo people know that the god has accepted their offer.

Back at home, a billy goat and a cock are slaughtered before the shrine. They cook the liver, heart and lungs of the previous year. The heart, lungs, liver and eggs are all cooked in different pots. The people who remained at home prepare the foods named above and wait for those who went to the cave. The food is usually pasted or spiced with mushroom. The shrine is fenced with animal net to prevent chickens and other animals from entering the celebration area.

Some Obbo elders told me that the people of Okwee usually eat at the celebration of Lwoo together with the people of Bura. The people of Okwee do not eat in the house, neither do they eat at the platform within the net fence, but they eat before the shrine, the Bura eat outside the net fence.

The meal is followed by drinking. The Acholi alcohol is bitterer than any other people's in Torit District. When alcohol has got into their blood, men and women get up to dance. There are seven songs with which people usually praise Lwoo god, but the most popular of all the songs is this one:

Ee! Ee, Palwo
Lwo people chiefs
Have turned the shoes and going back
Have cast shoes which become small like vase's mouth
O! Have cast shoes Yee
The boys of Padiru will enjoy moi
On the hill, they are moving backward
The Lowar-mois leaders are going back

The masses dance until the next morning. That morning, women cook the remaining meat from what the god offered the elders. The remaining meat is shared by elderly women. Young women are not allowed to take the meat home. This is how the Pajombo people celebrate their god in Obbo.

The Acholi culture demands that the elders who went to the cave of the god must leave all the meat god gave them at the shrine before they settle to eat. The old woman lying in the house now gets up and picks the liver, lungs and heart of the animals the elders have put before the shrine, sticks them on a stake and pushes it in base salt ash to preserve it from going bad. The stake meat is later smoked and preserved for the next year's celebration of the god.

IWIRE god

There are three gods worshiped in Panyikwara, but among the three gods, Iwire is the the most adored and it is the one that belongs to the people of Paliwa. The three gods are Iwire, Ibba and Lori. The people of Panyikwara also adore other smaller gods like Lokwenya, the god of Oloro people. To better understand the gods of Panyikwara, it is useful to look at them one by one. Let us first look at Iwire god and others will follow.

To have good understanding of Iwire, there are three significant questions. The first one is, "How did Iwire god began?" The second question is, "What is the name, or what are the names of the Paliwa celebrant of the god?" The third question is, "How do the people of Paliwa celebrate their god?"

At the time when the people of Panyikwara migrated at the foot of Iwire Hill, there was a man called Adyer, from the house of Paliwa. It is said that Adyer was a very proud man. On Iwire Hill was a flat rock on which, all the people of Panyikwara knew that, nobody should whet his spear. Adyer also knew very well that no one was allowed to whet his spear or knife on the rock, but he usually whetted his spear and knife there. But immediately after whetting his spear and knife, Adyer blew his horn – he never went away from the rock without blowing his horn. It is said that Adyer's horn was very loud, so loud that almost everybody at the foot of the hill knew it. He would blow the horn for four or five minutes and slop down the hill.

Iwire Hill was not happy with Adyer because Adyer's horn always gave her headache. One day when Adyer was whetting his spear as usual on the flat rock, Iwire swallowed him. The people of Paliwa waited for their brother in vein. One day, Adyer came to his brother in a dream. He told his brother, "My brother, do not look for where I am. It is Iwire Hill that swallowed me. I want you to tell our brothers that the god want a ram. You move round the hill with the ram, but do not kill it. Leave the ram alive at the foot of Iwire Hill. If you have done all these, I will later appear to you."

The following morning, Adyer's brother who had this dream told his elder brother, "My brothers, our brother, Adyer, came to me in a dream. He told me that we should not look for him. It is Iwire god that swallowed him. The god wants a ram which we should move round the rock with, and we should leave the ram alive at the foot of the hill. If we have done this, he will show up to us. This is why I have called you here this morning, so that you know that our brother is still alive."

These people wasted no time to do as instructed in the dream. They took the ram, followed all the instructions and left the ram alive at the foot of Iwire Hill. Oral source has it that the ram remained grazing at the foot of Iwire for five days. On the fifth day, Adyer was seen on Iwire Hill and the people of Paliwa and Panyikwara, who saw him, were surprised to see him after many days from his disappearance.

When the ram saw Adyer, it ran up to him, lied down and died instantly. Adyer immediately disappeared from the sight of those who were seeing him. Long time ago, this hill was not called Iwire, but it got this name to mean that it was moved round with a ram. The information is in the Acholi word "wir".

The history of Panyikwara contends that when Adyer wanted to eat, he would appear to his elder brother in a dream. The man would then call his brothers as we have seen above and tell them what Adyer wanted. A Paliwa elder gives a ram to be taken at the foot of Iwire Hill. The ram is left there for Adyer to eat. The Panyikwara elders told me that a man who has children cannot celebrate Iwire because the custom of Paliwa is that it is a barren man or a man who has not yet had a child that should celebrate the god. But we can see that there are very few barren men in the house of Paliwa. It is said that the first man to celebrate this god was Kilen Amwoda. We do not know the next celebrant after the death of Kilen Amwoda. For more information about Iwire god, read the second edition of this book.

IBBA god

The Acholi history tells us that, though Bura people were the owner of the place, they did not have a god. The god Ibba god came much later. This brings us to the question, "How did Bura get Ibba god?" A Panyikwara elder told me that they got the god when the people of Panyikwara were already at the foot of Iwire Hill. This is how they got the god: Bura had a girl who was as beautiful as crested crane. She was called Ibba. Many people told me that dust did not stick to Ibba's feet even when she walked on a dusty place. Her feet would look like she walked on cement. The cleanlinesses of this girl made Panyikwara boys to fear courting her. Ibba was very famous in Acholiland.

At this time, there was also a boy in Magwi (I do not know his name). The boy was also very famous in Acholi. When he heard about Ibba, the boy dressed in shorts and white surab (socks) which is a little long. The boy set out for Panyikwara to court Ibba. It is said that the boy kept going to Panyikwara for about six months to woo Ibba. Because the boy was also very handsome, Ibba acknowledged his love.

One day, the boy asked Ibba, "Beloved, I know my hut is up to Magwi, and your love for me is also very profound. Now I ask you to go with me to my hut in Magwi. What do you think?"

Ibba was aware that, Acholi girl who had boyfriends would usually visit the boys in their sleeping huts for sex. So, Ibba did not object to her boyfriend's proposal. She went to Magwi at least two or three times to visit her boyfriend. There was a small hill which Ibba passed by on her way from Panyikwara to Magwi. People said that it did not take many months; the hill was angered by Ibba when she was going to Magwi. The boy waited for his beloved for many days. He thought perhaps Ibba had changed her mind about him, or she was dead. The parents of Ibba, on the other hand, thought that she might have eloped with a man.

The people of Panyikwara used to pass from this hill many times. So one day when some Panyikwara people were passing from there, Ibba appeared to them. They recognised her as Ibba. They reported to Ibba's father that they saw her on the hill. Ibba's father just knew that it was god that swallowed his daughter. He also knew the Acholi custom that a person who is swallowed by god is asked for by a ram. He took a ram a vase of kwete to the hill to appease the god. When he reached the cave, he slaughtered the ram and cooked it. He gave the whole food to god, and he put the vase of kwete besides the food. Eventually, the nameless hill got a new name, Ibba Hill.

As Iwire Hill and Ibba Hill are close to each other, Adyer who was swallowed by Iwire began to go to woo Ibba. Having seen that there was no way she could find her old boyfriend, Ibba accepted Adyer's advance. The elders of Panyikwara told me that Adyer married Ibba and they begot many children. To date, the people of Panyikwara think that Adyer and Ibba are still alive. People think that Adyer, Ibba and their children will not die. The Bible says that God took Mary and Jesus to heaven alive. The people of Panyikwara also thin that God took Adyer and Ibba to an eternal home.

The history of Panyikwara contends that Ibba, unlike her husband, when hungry, she shows up on Ibba Hill, and the clan elders just know that she wants something to eat. So the priest of the god slaughters a ram for her at Ibba Hill. If the priest does not have a ram, the people of Bura raise money to buy one. At least three or four men usually go to celebrate Ibba god. When they are about to reach the cave on the hill, the man untie the ram. The ram runs into the cave and take a short time there and comes back and lies before the ditch that God made in front of the cave. I was told that this ditch has three "pots". The middle pot is larger than the other two. A saucepan of kwete does not even fill it.

The elders then slaughter the ram and let its blood flows into the three pots which are close to one another. It is said that if the god wants to eat only blood, the men do not pour kwete in the pots. It is the god to choose what it wants to eat. The elders of Panyikwara did not tell me how the god chooses what he wants. Panyikwara elders told me that Ibba goddess does not eat the whole ram. She usually eats only the liver or the head. I was told that the liver and the head of the ram is always not cooked. They give it raw to Ibba. So, when she wants liver or the head of the ram, it is given to her, but sometimes an elder forgets and pours kwete in the ditch. If this happens, the goddess sends strong wind with pebbles.

After elders have finished offering food to Ibba, a male snake and a female snake come to them. They say, the male snake stands for Adyer and the female one stands for Ibba. Elders of Panyikwara told me that the female snake has two horns, two eyes, two ears and two bridges of nose. But the male snake has one horn, one eye, one ear and one bridge of nose. The two snakes drink the alcohol or eat the mutton or lick the blood in the pot and go back to the cave when they are satisfied. The children of the snakes come immediately to eat or to drink what their parents left.

The elders take home the parts of the mutton that the goddess does not want. The culture of Paliwa prohibits the elders who are going back home after the celebration, from looking back. On reaching home, the elders enter the sacred house straight away. At that time, other elders are also waiting for them. One of the elders waiting for them at the doorway closes them in the house, and one of the later scoops water in a calabash, drinks it, rinses his mouth with it and spits it backwards to appease the goddess. The elders then share the meat they came back with and open the door so that others can assemble to drink.

LORI god

Lori god is the people of Oyira's. Acholi history has it that Lori god was born by a daughter of Magwi, whose name I do not know. When the woman conceived, every Oyira person expected her to give birth to a a normal human baby as other women did. Unfortunately, when her time to deliver the child came, she gave birth to a small stone, and everybody was astounded. The Oyira women did not throw away this stone. They performed rituals on the mother and named the stone Lori. We will see Acholi celebration later in this book. It is said that after the ceremony, a small hut was built for the stone. I do not know the name of the first priest of this god, but elders told me that an Oyira Pakwac man is the one to celebrate the god. As I have said above, nobody remembers the name of the first celebrant, but they remember Ocito who, after his death, was succeeded by Ogula Nicomia.

Every year, when Lori wants something to eat, he shows people different strange things. Sometimes he fires a gun, or drives a car and everybody hears the sound, or brings strong wind. He does this to show his priest that he is hungry. So, if people see one of the signs I named above, the priest takes a white ram for the god. If the priest does not have a white ram, people raise money to buy one to be offered to Lori. The priest always gives food to Lori between November and December. The gods are celebrated in these months because Acholi people realised that these are the months that the gods ask for what to eat. We can also say that Acholi give their offers to gods within this time because that is the time when Acholi people must have completed harvest and foodstuff is already stored in the granary in abundance.

LOKWENYA god

The people of Lokwenya have Lokwenya god. The history of Acholi tells us that. Lokwenya is the god of the people of Palabek. They say Lokwenya god is a big tortoise which is imortal, but we do not know how this tortoise came about. The people of Palabek do not know the first priest of Lokwenya, but the one who people can remember is Edwardi, son of Adiemo. Just like other gods, Lokwenya is celebrated around November and December when fresh foodstuff from the garden is in abundance. Secondly, Lokwenya is celebrated at this time because that is the time of hunting expedition in Acholi. When hunters want to get to the hunting ground, they celebrate the god. The priest of the god is also the owner of the hunting ground. He celebrates Lokwenya to grant safety to the hunters. It is Edwardi who celebrates the god and he also owns the hunting ground. To celebrate Lokwenya, he makes every house-hold in Palabek contributes goda (sorghum). After collecting the contributions, Edwardi prepares food under ogali tree which is at the home of the god. Lokwenya does not eat just anything; it eats duiker and pasted ground pea.

Edwardi does not go alone to celebrate the god. He goes with two or three other elders. They take with them duiker meat and a vase of kwete alcohol. I was not told whether it is women or men who carry the kwete and meat. When these elders return from the celebration, each of them enters his house without talking to the people who remained at home. They do this so that the spirit of the god peacefully settles down. The following morning, men, boys and women set out for a hunting expedition in Lokwenya hunting ground. Since the god has just been fed, he brings to the people of Palabek animals to kill and no one gets hurt during the hunt. The Lukwenya god is very important to the people of Palabek.

THE BELIEFS OF ACHOLI

When the white people came to Acholiland they thought the people of Acholi did not have a belief in God because they saw that, in Acholi, when someone died, people go to sorcerers to find out the cause of the disease or death. They did not know that Acholi did not belief in sorcerers as their God, but taken as doctors who could administer medicines to the sick (the same as Medical Doctor).

The sorcerer does not examine diseases with machine as medical doctors do. They use shells. Acholi people, just like other ethnic groups, are aware that there are deaths or diseases that can cause more death. There are diseases that are caused by mosquito and germs, but there are deaths that are caused by the spirits of ancestor. This always happen when clan elders have not given food to the spirits. The food is offered to the spirit in front of a family shrine. Many elders often in front of whose house the shrine is, migrates to a new home and leaves the shrine in the old homestead. This act angers the spirit of the grandfather because they have left him in the wilderness. This act usually causes death. However, those who do not know Acholi culture well believe that disease and death come from God.

Some Acholi people think consulting sorcerer often causes conflict among people because sometimes the sorcerer says somebody has done something even when such a person has not. The bereaved often believe that that is the truth. Such confusion afflicts many people whose dear ones are in agony or have died. Elders told me that, often times, the house of the deceased try to find ways of killing the person alleged to have caused death in their family.

POISON

Acholi people do not drink poison for no good reason. Drinking poison is done when, for example, a man is caught sleeping with another man's wife, and he denies doing it. The accused and the complainant drink poison which is prepared by a diviner priest, or a sorcerer. The sorcerer puts water in two calabashes and dips royal spear in both calabashes. The royal spear is dipped in the water so that whoever drinks the water yet he is telling lie, the power of the spear causes him stomach upset. At least one of the two would be found guilty or telling lie. Acholi elders told me that the guilty party always falls sick (inflammation on the skin) instantly after drinking the poison, but the innocent party remains healthy. If the accused falls sick, it indicates that he is actually guilty of adultery. If the complaint (the husband of the woman) falls sick, it means he falsely accused the other man. Clan elders slaughter a sheep and smear its dung on the person who falls sick after drinking the poison to cleanse him from the dreadful outcome of his vow of innocence. If the victim is the person who was accused of sleeping with another man's wife, after he is healed, he is asked to pay fine to the husband of the woman. In the past, whoever was guilty of sleeping with a man's wife paid a fine with two to five goats, but today the fine to be paid is already agreed upon by the people (read "Paying bride wealth," and "paying elopement fine'). But if the accused was proved innocent, the husband of the woman paid him two or five goats. If he did not have goats, he would pay the amount of money clan elders asked him to pay. This payment cleaned the soiled name of the innocent.

I was told by Acholi elders that sometimes the two conflicting parties did not drink the poison. They would make two chickens to drink it on their behalf.

In this case, each party would bring his own chicken. The chicken of the person who was found guilty would fall sick, while the chicken of the innocent would remain healthy. What I described in the previous paragraph, about the guilty party, is what happened to a guilty person in this scenario.

VOW

Acoli people always take vows only when parties have failed to resolve an issue or to agree on one thing. When a party is doubtful of the state of affairs in which they disagree with the other party, he declines from making a vow because of the heavy gravity of vow. So, one has to deeply consider the truthfulness of his proclamation before taking a vow.

Acholi people chose spear, knife and gun to be their objects of vow. This choice was based on the fact that all the three objects are fiery. In Acholi culture, the spear, or knife, or gun used for vowing must be one that one time killed a person. If there was no such spear, or knife or gun, they would make the parties lick the chief's royal spear. Elders told me that only the spear, knife or gun that killed, were used in vows because they were the only ones that could cause sickness to the guilty party.

The interest to vow is usually one person's. He picks a spear and solemnly proclaims in a high tone, "If I truly did what I am accused of, I lick the pear to cause me stomach upset, or to prick my chest." Others would say, "If I did it, let lighting strike me."

After this, the two parties lick a spear or a gun or a knife three times. If one of the two vow-takers did what led to vow, he would fall sick in one day or a month, and in most cases, such a person dies. People would now say the knife, or spear, or gun had struck the guilty. The offender often paid fifteen goats or the amount of money levied on him. This would be followed by slaughtering a ram. Elders pierce the stomach of the sheep ram with knife or spear with which the two took vow and the ram would be slaughtered at the scene of the vow. The sick person is then smeared with the dung of the ram. This is one of the ways Acholi people vow. Other ways of doing the same is by lay down a door shutter and the conflicting parties jump over it, or they lay a child on the ground and the conflicting parties jump over the child.

ANYA-NYA

Before we delve into the discussion of anya-nya, let us answer the question, "What is any-nya?" It seems anya-nya came from the Acholi word "naya-nya" which means something that burns. "Won" means the owner or father of. So, "won anya-nya" means he who has poison or herb that kills people. The poison corrodes the body of the victim until he dies. Acholi people lived in isolated homesteads, so it was difficult for killers to poison someone with whom they did not live on the same compound. Acholi people did not kill people indiscriminately. They often killed people from a particular family.

The owner of anya-nya has many ways of killing people. One method is to put the herb or poison on the grass. As he spits the herb, he calls the name of his intended victim and points to the direction of the home of the victim. He does this so that anya-nya does not attack anybody else, but the person he wants to die. In deed, the charm attacks nobody, but the moment the intended victim passes from there, he is attacked immediately. Most of the time, the anya-nya killer traps his victims by putting the anya-nya on the pathway, or by burying it at the doorway when people are away, or in the garden, and children are away playing. Sometimes he does it when people are sleeping in the night. At times he dusts the medicine in the air, and it flows to the person the killer wants to die. Or, he puts it in the victim's food. Most people killed with anya-nya, either ate it in food, or drank it in kwete alcohol.

Elders told me that, if God does not want some one to die, He sends lightning and strikes out the medicine out the ground. The moment such lighting occurs, people just know that someone had buried medicine on their compound. A house immediately got burnt. The fire caused by lighting cannot be put out with water. It is put off with fire. So, when a house is being burnt by lightning, a grass torch is lit and thrown in the flame gutting the house, and it immediately dies out.

It is said that lightning contains a very big cock, and some people say lightning's cock is as big as crested crane. The cock alights on the house after lightning has struck the homestead. I do not know whether people really see the cock or not.

EVIL SPIRIT (CEN)

There are three different ways by which evil spirit comes to a family. One is when a person dies of hunger when someone refused to give him food, it brings evil spirit in the family because the person died angry. A person who dies of hunger like this may have cursed the person who refused to give him food, and said, "The death of hunger should not end with me. Let it go on." In Acholi, when a person is cursed, he should do what he was cursed for not doing to others. If he is cursed for refusing to feed a hungry person, he should not give food to another person in the same condition. If he does the contrary, he causes deaths in his family (i. e. himself, his children and wife). Some elders told me that if the the spirit of the person who died because he was not helped is not appeased immediately, the deaths continue even to the grand children of the cursed.

Secondly, evil spirit can attack a family when a person refuses to house another person who is running for his life. In Acholi, a person who sends away a person fleeing from danger should send away any other person who needs the same help in future. If he allows another person to take refuge in his house, it invites evil spirit in his family.

The third thing that brings evil spirit in a family is killing a person. In Acholi people used to kill others because they must have stolen their hat or cap. Killing a person like this brings evil spirit in the family. When elders realise that there is evil spirit in the family, they tie an evil spirit-goat to revert the death from humans. It is the goat that will die in this case. This will block the evil spirit from the family. If this is not done, the death spreads to other families in the clan. Killing an innocent person is the fourth thing that brings evil spirit in a family.

EVIL-EYE

Acholi elders told me that there are not many evil-eye people in Acholi because it is an inheritance from parents. Although some people say evil-eye is God-sent, we see that it is genetically transmitted. I do not know if everybody from a house where the evilness is, is evil-eye. Most of the time people call members of the family evil-eye. Some people say it is naturally left to one member of the family from a dead evil-eye person. The power remains with one of the children (a daughter or a son). That means not everybody in the family of an evil-eye person does not have the same power.

Acholi people say it is usually a son who gets the power from his parent.

If the evilness goes to a daughter, it will be very hard for her to get a man to marry because no man wants to marry an evil-eye woman.

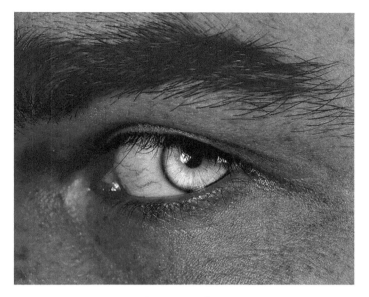

Figure 25: Evil-Eye

Even if Acholi people prefer a man to have evil-eye, such a man also finds it hard to find a marriage partner. This does not mean that girls always refuse evil-eye men, but it is the parents of the girls who will levy so heavy a bride price on the man that the boy cannot pay. Elders told me that people levy higher bride price to men who come from evil-eye families and less to those who come from non evil-eye families. So a rich evil-eye man just pays the bride price levied on him, no matter how much. The bride does not become an evil-eye because she is from a different family.

The evil-eye people do not want others to know that they are, even if they live in the same home, but they do not know that it is very hard to hide it. It will come out even after very many years. People will always tell what you are as time passes by.

It is hard to differentiate the evil-eye from other people because it is not seen in their eyes. To some people, it is easy because, to them, the pupil of the eye of an evil-eye is small and the lens is large. Others have red eyes.

How do the evil-eyes cause pain to others? Acholi people say that if an evil-eye person wants to cause problem to somebody, he sadly and sternly looks at the eyes of the person, and poison enters the eyes of the victim. The people of Acholi therefore, do not want someone to look into their eyes too much. If somebody does it, he receives scolding from the person he looks at, "Why do you look at me like that? Do you want to poison my eyes? If there is anything bad on me, take a leaf and remove it."

There are six parts of the body that the evil-eye people like poisoning: (1) ear (2) throat (3) stomach (4) liver (5) legs and (6) heart. If the poison is directed to the ear, the victim may end up being deaf. If it is directed to the throat, food choke or gets stuck in the Vitim's throat. To the stomach, it causes diarrhea. To the liver it causes a serious liver disease whose medicine is not found in Acholi. Some people say that it is the evil-eye who causes a particular sickness is the only person who can cure it, but elders told me that if the evil-eye causes liver disease, no one, not even the evil-eye himself can cure it. If the evil-eye sees a fast runner, he makes his legs swell so big that he cannot run anymore. He can also cause a mysterious miscarriage of a one month or two month pregnancy, but he can reverse the situation when a diviner priest causes temporary blindness to the evil-eye. The worst pain an evil-eye can cause is the disease of the heart because the sickness can kill the victim in a day.

Acholi people like Shilluk know very well that the evil-eye does not attack humans only. Rev. D.S. Oyler in his book, "*The Shilluk's Belief In The Evil Eye*, asserts that, "Evil-eye attack does not happen on human beings only, but also on domestic animals such as cow, goat, sheep and dog." If someone drinks the milk of a cow which the evil-eye has bewitched, it causes him stomach upset, and swells the stomach. This is an indication that the cow has been bewitched. Therefore, most Acholi people hide well bred animals so that the evil-eye does not see them.

In Acholi, a victim of evil-eye is not taken to the hospital; instead he is taken to a diviner priest or a sorcerer. Before working on the patient, a divine priest asks the family of the patient for a black ram or a billy goat. When the animal is brought, the diviner priest puts a big nail on fire and heats it red-hot. He burns the eye of the animal with this nail. He does this to shift the sickness to the evil-eye himself. After burning the eye of the ram, the priest turns to the patient and tells him, "My friend, the sickness has fled." The priest usually does two important things to a patient. First, he cures the patient. After he is cured, the patient buys a protective herb from the priest and wears round his neck to protect himself from the evil-eye. In the old days, when a diviner priest cured a patient, the clan members of the patient paid the priest with a bull, but now that most people do not have animals, they pay the priest any amount of money.

Acholi people, most of the time, do not keep quiet about a patient's visit to a diviner priest. Even the evil-eye who caused him the problem will have a chance to know that the patient is consulting a priest. This causes the evil-eye serious worries. The same evening, the evil-eye goes to the priest and asks for forgiveness. The priest forgives him, but with a punishment. He tells the evil-eye, "I have forgiven you, but bring for me a ewe or a hoe." Just like any other person, the diviner priest also fears death. So, after receiving a ewe from the evil-eye, he reprimands the evil-eye, "Alright, I have helped you. Next time, I do not want to hear that you have caused problem to another person. If I hear that you do it again, I will kill you."

It is said that the evil-eye does not afflict the poor because they do not have money, foodstuff or domestic animals. He looks at the rich. Therefore, those who have money and many domestic animals should be careful with evil-eye. People put herbs in the garden and wear protective charm on their arms (read about protective charm) the evil-eye usually inflicts pain on people for meat, groundnuts, sesame, fish and alcohol. Acholi people believe that, to avoid the wrath of the evil-eye, one should throw a bit of food to a dog or chicken before he himself eats it. So, even if the evil-eye finds the person eating, he cannot inflict any pain on him.

ABOMINATION (KIR)

Before we say much about abomination, let us answer the question, "What is abomination?" Many people are not able to differentiate between vow and abomination because abomination and vow are closely related in meaning, though they mean different things. It is said that if two brothers, for example, quarrel and one of them refuses to eat food from his brother's house because he is still annoyed with him, and another day he accepts to share food with his brother from the same house before a cleansing ritual is performed, he becomes sick. If they don't slaughter a goat immediately, he dies. So, if there is abomination, clan elders should cleanse it before the parties involve themselves in an act that sparks the adverse consequence.

GARDEN CHARM (DUBO)

What is protective charm? This is a herb or an object that a person puts in his garden to protect his garden from thieves. It also protects the crops in the garden against evil-eye. There are types of garden charm that an Acholi person can put in his garden. Firstly, the protective charm can be the head of a chicken, wrapped together with fingers of millet and buried in the garden. Secondly, it can be a seed of sodom apple (solanum incanum), pierced with thorn, and hung on a tree together with fingers of millet, or peas. The garden charm to be put in a millet garden comprises sodom apple fruit and millet finger. If it is to be put in a garden of peas, it is a combination of sodom apple and peas.

A garden charm can also be a fishnet which the owner of the garden ties on a tree stump or on a tree branch in the garden.

In the old days, people believed that when a garden charm attacked a person, it caused him leprosy. Today people say the charm does not cause leprosy, but infertility. It can also cause running stomach, headache and swelling disease. Modern Acholi believe that hitting a person with mingling stick (for making bread), stirring stick (for stirring soup), or a burning firewood that cause leprosy. They also believe that removing food from in front of a person angrily is another cause of leprosy.

HUNTER'S CHARM

This charm protects hunters in the wilderness. It is said that a hunter who has strong charm does not often meet fierce wild animals. Secondly, such a hunter does not often come back home from a hunting expedition without killing an animal. Thirdly, those who have this charm cannot be bewitched by evil-eye. They usually use an overgrowth from a tamarind tree and *olwedo, ogali, oduko, babu or larueco* trees. They say, the charm from *pabu* make a person a swift and mobile walker, so troubles do not get him easily. The problem with *pabu* charm is that it may not give the owner time to eat because he is always up and down, and may leave even when food is almost ready. Paterno Abak told me, "A man who has this charm is propelled by the charm to leave home though he sees his wife preparing food for him."

440

Chapter Twenty Five

TRADITIONAL INITIATION RITE

In my research on initiation rite, I discovered that some Acholi clans of Sudan do not have initiation rite as we will see in this chapter. To those who have it, the rite is very important because it is one of the ways of instilling discipline in the youths and make them respect elders and their colleagues. The Acholi people who have initiation rite are disciplined than those who do not have it.

In the Acholi tradition, there are two types of initiation rite. The first is traditional rite and the second is modern rite, which came much later. The traditional rite is more honoured among Acholi people than the modern one. In this chapter, we will see how the two rites work in Acholi. We will start with traditional rite and turn to modern rite. The oral sources maintain that, long ago, there was no initiation rite in Acholi. But the people who were assimilated by Acholi were the ones who brought the practice in Acholi. The tradition of rite came from two sources. The first was from Lotuko (Imurok) and the second was from Lolubo. Those who came from Lokoro, Cwua (Uganda) also learned to practise initiation rite from the people of Lotuko and Lolubo. Although different Acholi people named their rites differently, the rules that govern the practice of initiation is still the same to all. This is why Kevin D.Philip Howard and William J. House, maintain that, "Acholi has no age sets or age groups".

There are groups into which boys are initiated. When a person is initiated in one group, it takes him three or four years to move to the next two groups above (see Figure 1). For a better understanding of initiation in different Acholi settings, let us look at what it is in every clan.

INITIATION IN PANYIKWARA

Of all the eleven clans in Panyikwara, it is only Goloba that has initiation rite. Elders told me that, in the past, Goloba did not have the rite. It came much later, brought by the people of Olubo who cam from Lokiliri (Lolubo).

How did the practice of initiation right enter Goloba? Long ago, famine broke out in Lolubo, so Wani and his brother, Lado found that they could not live in Lolubo any longer. So, they moved towards Acholiland. This happened when Wani's mother, Achola Latoo, was still alive. Wani chose two boys, Iryem and Matidi, to take care of his mother on the way.

A few days, Wani and his people reach Iwire Hill, where some Panyikwara people had settled. The people of Panyikwara welcomed Wani and his people and gave them land for both settlement and cultivation among the Goloba people. This is why Olubo became one of the clans in Goloba.

One day, Achola Latoo went to market and bought so many items that she could not easily carry by herself. Fortunately, she was a very strong woman. She carried some of the items on her head and others in her hands. A Goloba boy called Mato-Nam was riding a bicycle behind her. Mato-Nam found Achola very tired, but he did not help her to carry the load. He left her struggling with it on the way.

Achola was annoyed with Mato-Nam for leaving without helping her. She took him for a bad boy; he did not show her respect. In Lokoya, if you people find elders with load like that of Achola, they often helped them. That was one ways the youths of Lolubo showed respect to elders. When Achola saw Mato-Nam rode past her, she just shook her head and continued trudging.

When she reached home, Latoo called the elders of Goloba and told them, "My people, I want to tell you that I am annoyed with Mato-Nam because he showed me no respect when I was returning from the market. He rode his bicycle past me, and he saw how I was struggling with luggage in my hands and on my head. He never thought of stopping to help me. He just passed. This has been the first time for me to see a boy showing no respect to an old woman like me. In Lolubo, children like Mato-Nam would be punished by his age group members if he does not respect elders. I therefore request you to embrace age group system in Goloba so that it disciplines wayward people."

The Goloba elders were equally not pleased by the story because the Acholi children were not to respect their parents only, they were to respect any elders around and those they meet on the way. The gathering accepted Achola's proposal and they began the practice of initiation. Wani showed the people of Goloba the different roles and responsibilities of different age groups. A few months later, the people of Goloba were grouped in different age groups as we will see later. That is how initiation rite got into Panyikwara (Goloba).

In the Panyikwara tradition, initiation is divided into five groups, *Koyoo, Nyeme-Nyeme, Kaburu, Japan* and *Kalang* – see Figure 25.

It is said that the people of Goloba do their circumcision after every four years. This happens when the Koyo group is to hand over authority to Nyeme-Nyeme. At the same time, the boys in different groups such as Kaburu, Japan and Kalang are initiated in higher groups as those below them take over the position they left. This is done after every three years so that it gives time for boys and men to fill the different groups. On the day of circumcision, Nyeme-Nyeme, Kaburu, Japan and Kalang make a drum. They do this from a stream or at a well, not far away from home. Not every group member participates in making the drum. Each group sends three skillful members to do the work with others. When they finish the work, this team chooses two or three members to take the drum to Koyoo – the Koyoo members assemble together on this day. The head of Koyoo stands up and receives the drum from the boys and inspects if the boys of Nyeme-Nyeme, Kaburu, Japan and Kalang made the drum well. If this elder is satisfied with the work, he gives it to two or three other elders to inspect if it is well made. If the elders are satisfied with work, they tell the boys who brought the drum to go back to their groups. As the elders inspect the drum, others would be making platform for drying the drum. They put the drum to dry on the platform after elders have finished their inspection.

As the drum dries on the platform, the different age groups draw nearer to Koyoo. A selected member of Koyoo gets up, fixes a flag on the ground and talks to the Nyeme-Nyeme group, "Good, boys! This year, we leave for you the chair. We also give you a drum and our flag today."

Although Koyoo hands over their flag to Nyeme-Nyeme, they do not just simply give them the drum. So, in the night, when everything is silent, Nyeme-Nyeme sends the Japan group to steal the flag from Koyoo. If Japan finds Koyoo still awake, they take the drum by force. If Japan fails to take the drum, then Koyoo will not leave the chair for Nyeme-Nyeme. Once that happens, Koyoo has to extend their term to keep the chair by four more years.

Most of the time, if the Kaburu and Kalang groups realise that Koyoo is defeating the Japan group in the fight, they join Japan so that they remove the drum. If the Japan group manages to raid the flag, one of them runs rounds the dance arena three times. Some of the Koyoo men also run after the boy who is rounding the arena. If the Koyoo men do not catch him, the boy finally runs to the camp of Nyeme-Nyeme, Kaburu, Japan and Kalang. This boy now implants the flag in the ground, and the groups of Nyeme-Nyeme, Japan, Kaburu and Kalang dance traditional dance around it to show their happiness, as they have successfully raided the flag from Koyoo. That means Nyeme-Nyeme now has power and authority. This also gives opportunity to all other age groups to be promoted to the next level. People dance for four or so hours before Japan finally hands over the drum and flag to Kaburu, and the Kaburu group passes the same to Nyeme-Nyeme. That is the tradition to be followed during the initiation rite in Acholi. However, there is one important thing that I want the readers of this book to understand. That is, it is the Japan group who must always be on the forefront in war.

After Nyeme-Nyeme have received the drum, the Koyoo group ask them again, "You the members of Nyeme-Nyeme, we want to know the name of your new flag. What do you call it?" Naming a flag is very important among the people of Goloba. All the previous groups had names for their flags. So, one of the members of Nyeme-Nyeme gets up and tells the Kooyoo group, "Our people, we are very happy because we have got power today. Yesterday, the people of Panyikwara called us Nyeme-Nyeme, but from today onwards, we are called Koyoo. Our new flag and drum are called (he gives the new name of the drum and flag)." Later the new and the old holders of flag each take a brown cock and wave it on the drum. When ther finish the waving, the outgoing Koyoo group, with respect, hands over the drum to the incoming Koyoo.

Figure No 26 : Initiation of Goloba-Panyikwara

INITIATION IN OMEO

We have seen in chapter twenty that Omeo has five main clans. The five clans have initiation rite and age group system which unite them because they have only one main rite (Lang-gara). Although they have only one central rite, other smaller clans also have their own rites. There are three categories of rites in Omeo, which are in both central and smaller rites. They are Elders' Council, Lowaki and Langara. These three groups are the heads of clans and authority is in their hands. If Omeo goes to war with other people, it is Lowaki to be in forefront, followed by Lang-gara group. In Murwari clan, Molo-molo and Mangala immediately follow Langa-gara. In Imbaro clan, Boro and Lokiti groups are the ones to follow Langa-gara in war. Other age groups do not go to the battle field. They remain to take care of home.

The Omeo initiation is slightly different from those of other Acholi of Sudan. I say so because the people of Omeo usually know how many boys should be initiated into German, Kilangi, Kuru-kak, Leme (Atanya) or Iruu, but in Goloba, for example, they do not know how many boys are to join Kalang group (see Figure 1). Even the people of Pajok do not know how many children should join Pajok or Nyig-kic (see Figure 3). When the day of initiation draws closer, they sent for four boys from every clan to enter the age group system. The elders of Omeo told me that the twenty boys selected from different clans also elect their leader from among themselves. The group of boys joining German, Kilangi, Kuru-kak, Leme and Iruu is called "Oliemu". This name was given to this group because they are still children growing like luxuriant oliemu grass. They are young thriving belligerents and healthy boys who are instrumental in war.

As we have seen above, at the time of initiation rite, every Omeo clan sends four boys to join Royal Oliemu. I was told that if there is a dance in Omeo, the twenty oliemu boys dance round the arena together. On the day of the dance, the leader of oliemu implants a spear in front of the shrine in the arena. In Acholi tradition, the leader of oliemu usually goes with six or seven spears in the dance arena. So, when he arrives at an arena, he fixes one spear there, and when he goes to another arena, he does the same, and so forth. In Panyikwara, if the leader of oliemu has fixed his spear in the arena, nobody should remove it because that is a sign that the leader of youths has arrived.

Omeo boys are initiated after every twenty five years. How is the initiation rite done? What is required of Lowaki group to be promoted to the Council of Elders? How do the lower groups promoted to the next group? If we answer all these questions well, we will understand how the initiation rite is done in Omeo.

In about three days to the initiation day, Lowaki and Lang-gara call their meetings. In these meeting, each of the groups selects four or five strong members. The eight or ten selected boys are sent in the wilderness to make fire. The boys spin a stick in a small hole in another stick producing a hot powder from the friction between the two sticks. This hot powder eventually burst into fire. These boys light the fire on a grass torch.

Other Lowaki and Lang-gara members go to fetch firewood in the bush. They then pile the firewood on the path that the boys who have gone to make fire will return through. Others will be making a drum. The drum is dried with fire and is later hung on a tree on the compound where people who have come to attend the initiation rite will assemble. Before the twenty boys arrive, elders fence the compound with branches of *lango* thorn tree and *lacaro* thorn tree. The twenty boys also make big fire on the path through which the boys who have gone to make fire will return so that they jump over it as they come back home.

At the wee hour, the boys making fire in the bush select two fast runners from their group. They are to run very fast and jump over the fire made on the way, remove the thorn fence and hit the drum which is on the tree on the compound.

Everybody becomes very happy when they hear the drum because this shows that authority has been handed over to a new Lowaki age group. On the same day, Lang-gara also hands over authority to a new group, and Molo-molo, Boro and Lokondulo take over from Lang-gara. It is only Pinno-pinno and Ikoo that do not have boys to sen to Lang-gara, but some elders told me that, on the day of initiation of Pinno-pinno and Ikoo they select some boys from the group of Leme [Atanga] Kikilangi to join Lang-gara. It is also on this day that Lwaki become Council of Elders. The children who are not yet in age group system are initiated in the groups of German, Kilangi, Kurukak, Leme and Iruu. This is how the initiation rite of Omeo is done. The different groups in the initiation rite of Omeo are these:

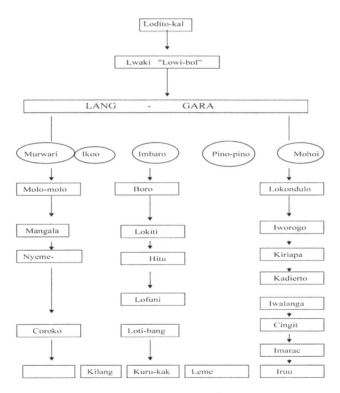

Figure No 27: Initiation of Omeo

INITIATION IN PAJOK

Pajok has fourteen main clans, and they are all under the main initiation rite system. The people of Pajok used to like initiation rite very much, but from 1973, the practice began to die down though others still talk about it. Therefore, elders of Pajok cannot clearly explain how Pajok boys are initiated. But they still know the different age groups in Pajok. That is why I am also unable to tell how Pajok boys are initiated. Pajok people say they have eleven age groups as follows:

1. Rwot-kot

2. Lapidi-kot

3. Lodito-kaka

4. L acer

5. M eritiko

6. Amelwedo

7. Kalang

8. Lokwic i buru

9. Ogwal "nyo" Mworo

10. Bwonyo

11. Pajok

Figure 28: Initiation of Pajok

INITIATION IN OBBO

Figure No 29: Initiation of Obbo

Obbo has fourteen main clans, and all of them have one central initiation rite. Elders told me that, in the past, the people of Obbo respected initiation rite very much, but when the white man came to Acholi, many Obbo people began to take initiation lightly. Most people of Obbo do not know the names of the different age groups in Obbo. Only one elder, out of twenty, knows the tradition and practice of initiation rite well. I discovered that the different age groups in Obbo are as follows.

INITIATION IN AGORO

Just like Obbo and Pajok, Agoro also has only one initiation rite, which brings together the nine clans of Agoro. The children of Agoro, like the children of Obbo, do not want the practice of initiation rite. However, some few people of Agoro are still interested in preserving their initiation culture. Research reveals to us that Agoro has seven age groups as shown below.

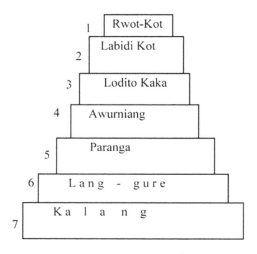

Figure No 30: Initiation of Agoro

INITIATION IN MAGWI

The Magwi history tells us that initiation rite like those of other Acholi clans we have seen before. The rite is done in Palongany clan, and all other Magwi people respect it. Oral sources maintain that Magwi boys are initiated after every four years. In Magwi, the young people who commit offence are publicly punished on the day of initiation. Elders ask the offenders to bring sheep, cow, or flour. Elders take all these to Palonganyi, and people gather to eat at the rite. Read *Second Edition* of this book. Magwi initiation has five groups as shown below:

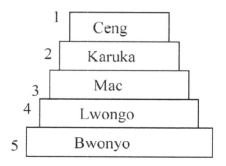

Figure No 31; Initiation of Magwi

INITIATION IN OFIRIKA

We have seen in some previous chapters that Ofirika comprises six clans. Three of the six clans practice initiation rite. They are Tabwor, Lodulang and Lomiling.

Boys and girls in these clans are initiated after every fourteen years. It is during the initiation that girls and boys receive lessons from elders. Boys are taught on a different day from the girls. Youth offenders are punished by clan elders during the rite. The punishment that young people are normally given in Acholi is that they bring to elders a sheep, a cow and fermented flour, which they eat before the next initiation rite. The different age groups in Ofirika are:

Figure No 32 Initiation of Ofirika

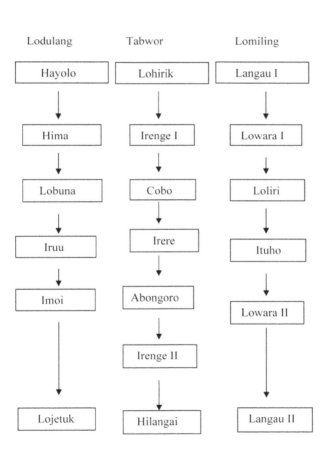

RESPONSIBILITIES OF THE AGE GROUPS

In this chapter, we realise that among the Acholi of Sudan, there are seven initiation rites. They include Panyikwara, Omeo, Pajok, Obbo, Agoro, Magwi and Ofirika. People in the different rites have their specific responsibilities as we see below. Although each group has their role, this also shows us that Acholi people, though they live in different places, are actually one people. Let us look at the role of each group in initiation rite. The history and culture of Acholi tell us the roles of different groups in initiation rite are as given below.

Rain Chief

Looking at initiation rite, only Pajok, Obbo, Agoro, Panyikwara and Omeo are the Acholi clans that have Rain Chief. But Magwi and Ofirika do not have Rain Chief. No elder told me why these two clans do not have rain chief in their initiation system. Some people told me that the idea of rain chief came to Goloba (Panyikwara) much later. They had initiation rite but without a rain chief. I do not know how the people of Goloba began to use the idea of rain chief.

In the initiation rite system among the Acholi of Sudan, Rain Chief is a very respectable person. In developed countries, it is weather specialists who can tell when it is likely to rain, but in Acholi, it is the rain chief who knows the day and time when it is going to rain. This power has made rain chiefs very respectable people in Acholi. The people of Acholi believe that this power comes from God. As we have seen before, when God is annoyed, he can punish people for one person's sin. This fills people with fear and they respect the rain chief. Food crops grow well when there is rain, so no one should anger the rain chief because his anger brings famine. Acholi people fear famine like death.

The people of Acholi do not only respect the rain chief, but they also like pleasing him. They please the chief when they have just had fresh harvest, and they give him the food crops before they have tested it. Every household under a particular rain chief contributes food staff to be given to the rain chief. For easy collection of the contributions, the rain chief has his representative in every clan to whom members of the clan collect their contribution. The representative of the chief then chooses eight or ten people to carry the food staff collected to the home of the chief. The rain chief receives the offer and gives back some to the person who raised the contribution from the people. The chief also gives some food staff back to the people who helped to carry it to him. The remaining food is kept in the chief's barn or granary. If the chief has more than one wife, he shares the food staff equally among the women. The chief does this because his visitors can be hosted in the house of any of his wives. So, every wife's granary or barn should be well stocked with food staff. The chief distributes his wives in different villages, not only for the purpose of hosting visitors but also for his own security. When the chief is moving around in the villages, he sleeps in the home of the wife in whose village darkness finds him. The chief does not sleep just in anyone's home.

Even if the chief has many wives, he does not keep his rain stones in all the houses of the wives, but he only keeps it in the house of the senior wife (the queen), as we have seen with the chief of Obbo. If the senior wife dies, the chief shifts the rain stone to the house of a junior wife. The rain stone is not kept by anybody.

The rain chiefs often have more than one wife. Some of them may have as many wives as the number of settlements in their villages. Each wife settles in a settlement. If there are ten settlements in the village, the chief will have ten wives, and so forth. For example, chief Aburi of Obbo had sixteen wives because Obbo comprises sixteen settlements. Chief Aburi placed these wives each in one settlement. A chief cannot take care of everybody when he has only one wife. In Acholi, it is the home of the chief that visitors are hosted. For that matter, a visitor, or foreigner who darkness gets anywhere, asks for the house of the wife of the chief. Acholi people are well known for their hospitality to visitors. In Acholi culture, when one receives a visitor, he should provide water for bath, food and drink (kwete alcohol) to the visitor. A visitor is hosted by any of the chief's wives even if the chief is not in that home that day.

In Acholi, foreign visitors are hosted in the house of the rain chief. It is a usual practice that the rain chief slaughters a sheep or a cow for visitors of this kind. The Acholi people rate their chiefs in terms of their hospitality. They do not like a spiteful chief.

Another role of a rain chief is to settle disputes among the people and uniting them. When the white man had just come to Acholi, they would speak to the people through the rain chief. They would say everything they wanted to communicate to the people to the chief and the chief would interpret to the people. The white man did not talk to the people of Acholi people face to face. The people listened to the chiefs so much that none of them would dispute whatever he said. When the white man realised that the people listened to the chiefs, they used the chiefs for a long time because that is one of the ways they could also punish offenders – they did it through the chiefs. Eventually, the white man discovered that, it was through initiation rite system that they could do whatever they wanted. The white man thought it was not good to use the chiefs all the time as if they were the only ones who had the brain to help people develop. It did not take long before the white man initiated a modern initiation rite system, which in this book, I have called "orwanga gala" in Acholi. However, the white man is very wise. They did not abandon the rain chiefs immediately after initiating a modern rite system. They gave the rain chiefs the authority to settle minor disputes among their clan members. Major disputes were to be settled by Sub-County Chief. The sub county chief would corporally punish minor offenders. For major offenders, he asked them to pay money, or animals like sheep, goats and cattle. The sub county chief and his assistant take all the payments to the government. The white man used some of the money to buy kwete or waragi to the chief and his assistant as their allowance. Eventually, the white man began to pay sub county chief some money. It did not take many years, the white man removed the authority to settle minor dispute from the rain chiefs and gave it to sub county chiefs. The rain chiefs remained with the authority to make rain only because that was one thing the white man could remove from them. The power to make rain is hereditary, so no one can remove it from a person.

Rain Chief's Attendant

All the Acholi rain chefs have their attendants. The role of the attendant is to go on errand for the chief on the day of rain-making. Another thing the chief's attendant does is to collect rain stone that he sees around as we will see below. The chief's attendant can be a person from his family or any other person from outside his family. Most of the time, the chief chooses one of his children to be his attendant.

If the chief finds that there is no child of his own, or children from his people, then he will have no choice but to bring a person from outside his family. The outsider must be a child whose father came with him from outside but grew up in the chief's place. The best example is Chief Aburi of Obbo, who chose David (Daudi) of Imurok to be his attendant because David grew up in his place. David's parents came with him to Obbo running away from famine that broke out in Imurok. It is said that after the death of David, Chief Aburi replaced him with Opiny of Lokoro, who also grew up in his place. However, the Acholi culture demands that the chief's attendant should be from the house of the chief. They thought so because a foreign attendant could steal the rain stone away from the chief. It is said that, among all the Acholi chiefs, it is only the chief of Panyikwara who did not bring a foreign attendant. When he wants to make rain, the chief instruct his attendant to stir the rain stones in the vase or bowl. The rain chief's vase or bowl is usually kept under a big tree at the stream or well. It does not take long, after the attendant has stirred the rain stones that it begins to rain.

The Council of Elders

The Council of Elders comprises men of 45 to 100 years of age. Their main role is to assist the chief in settling minor disputes among the people, especially disputes between men and women. The Acholi people said, "Domestic affairs are multiple." Most of the time, there are disputes between a woman and a man. Often times, such conflict arises because a man does not want to work in his wife's garden, or a man has slept with the wife of another man, or a woman slept with another man. Another source of conflict is a girl's conception outside wedlock. Other causes of conflict in the house could also be theft of domestic animals such as goats, sheep and cattle, or stealing some one's foodstuff. One other cause of conflict in the house is when a woman slaps her private part before her husband. There are many issues that I cannot list all down here, but the ones I have mentioned above are the major causes of conflict between men and women.

Council of Elders does not only help the chief in settling disputes, but they are also a body of advisors to the rain chief and his subjects because they are knowledgeable about the good ways of life of the people. Oral sources say that, in some parts of Acholi, the Council of Elders has a leader. Some people say it is only the Council of Elders of Obbo that has a leader. Obbo South's Council of Elders is led by Orundi, and Obbo North is led by Akayii. We have seen before that when a chief wants to talk to his subjects, he orders his messenger to sound a drum or blow a horn. This messenger is usually chosen from the embers of council of elders.

The group of Mac, Lacer, Meritiko, Nyeme-nyeme, Awurniang, Lowak and Lowii bol are very important groups in the initiation rite system of Acholi. These groups have the roles of keeping peace and taking care of homes.

If an enemy attacks Acholi, the groups of Mac from Obbo and Magwi, Lacer and Meritiko from Pajok, Nyeme-nyeme from Panyikwara, Awuriang from Agoro, Lowara 1 of Lomiling, Irenge 1 of Tabwor and Hima of Lodulang, from Ofirika and Molo-molo of Murwari, Boro of Imbaro and Lokondulo of Mohoi (in short, the people of Omeo call this group "Lowii-bol") from Omeo are the ones to lead the warriors of Acholi. The people of Omeo named these groups Lowii-bol rightly because the members are men of the age of 50-60, they are at the age of hot blood and the age of less fear of death. The men in this age group eat well and do not often fall sick.

Figure No. 33: A leader of Acholi warriors

The group of Abic, *Amelwedo, Kalang, Mangala, Nyem-nyem, Lokiti, Hitu, Iworogo, Kiriapa, Kaburu, Paranga, Lobuna, Iruu, Cobo, Irere, Loliri, Ituho*

The group of Abic in Obbo, Amelwedo and Kalang from Pajok, Mangala and Nyem-nyem of Murwari, Lokiti and Hitu of Imbaro, Iworogo and Kiriapa of Mohoi from Omeo, Kaburu from Goloba (Panyikwara), Paranga from Agoro, Lobuna and Iruu of Lodulang, Cobo and Irere of Tabwor, Loliri and Ituho of Lomiling from Ofirika are the immediate line of defence behind Mac, Lacer, Meritiko, Awuriang, Lowara 1, Irenge 1 and Hima in the battle field. The men in this age group are people of 40-49 years of age. Acholi people do not want people of this age to die. But in hunting expedition, it is this group that is in the foreground. They position themselves at the fire in the wilderness. Acholi elders decided that this age group should lead hunters because they are very good marksmen. When they spear an animal, the animal does not run far; it just falls down and dies.

The group of *Goda, Lokwic* from *Buru, Ogwal, Japan, Lang-gure Coroko, Lofuni, Loti-bang, Kadierto, Iwalanga, Cingit.*

This group comprises young men of 15-39 years of age. They take instructions from the groups of Abic, Amelwedo, Kalang, Mangala, Nyem-nyem, Lokiti, Hitu, Iworogo, Kiriapa, Kaburu, Paranga, Lobuna, Iruu, Cobo, Irere, Loliri and Ituho. This age group does not go to the battle field. They remain at home to take care of women and children. If enemies attack them at home, this age group fights to protect children, women and the elderly.

The groups of *Ngini-ngini, Bwonyo, Pajok (Nyig kic), Kalang, German, Kilangi, Kuru-kak, Leme (Atanya), Imarac, Iruu, Imoi, Lojetuk, Abongoro, Irene 2, Hilangai, Lowara 2* and *Langau 2*

Members of this group are boys of the age of age 0-14 years old. The primary role of this group is to take elders' errands. Acholi elders often lie under a big tamarind tree or any other big tree near home. If any of them wants water or fire, they send a boy in this age group to fetch it for them. Elders used to lie face up in a ditch and would ask a boy in this age group to shave his pubic hair. The boy would then dust the pubic region with ashes and begin to pluck the pubes one by one. The Acholi culture demands that a child who disobeys elders would be brought froward and punished on the day of initiation. Such a child may be caned or asked to bring a ram for elders to eat. If the culprits brought a ram, elders would ask other disobedient children to roast the meat for them. The boys who roast the meat must not test it at all. This is the initiation rite practice in Acholi of Sudan. If you want profound knowledge of the initiation rite system of Acholi, read the second edition of this book. Let us now turn to modern initiation rite system.

Chapter Twenty Six

THE MOCK OR MODERN INITIATION RITE

When the British had fully taken roots in Acholiland, with the ambition to lead the Acholi, they started their own initiation rite, which was different from the one of the native Acholi. During all the years that the British were dealing with the rain chief, they understood all the tasks performed by each group in the traditional initiation system very well.

The British became unhappy when they found that the Acholi respected the rain chiefs more than them. They then looked for ways of making the people love them instead of the rain chief. They realized that the only way they could convince the natives to abandon their rain chief was to start their own mock initiation rite, or modern initiation rite. Besides, the white men also reasoned that dealing with the Acholi in their modern initiation system would be easier than working with the rain chief, because everyone would listen to them, and do only what they (the British) wanted.

We shall see later here that unmarried boys and men were not in the mock initiation system. Only men who had wives and owners of the home were in the mock initiation system.

In the mock initiation system, the views of the rain chief are not very important, though the British agreed that the rain chief had powers over the people included in the mock initiation system. The history of Acholi says many times the chief appointed by the white man could seek advice from the rain chiefs, especially about relationship between men and women.

The mock initiation system has nine groups: Rain Chiefs, Sub-County Chiefs, Parish Chiefs, Clan Leaders, Village Chiefs, council of royal elders, council of ordinary elders, Heads of Homes and Heads of Families. The Rain Chief and the Sub Parish Chiefs are not very relevant in the white man's initiation rite system.

See Figure 8: Modern initiation below

Sub-County Chief

In 1932, the British took over the power to settle disputes among the people from the rain chief and gave it to the Sub-County Chief. He appointed the Sub-County Chief to fullfill the desires and interests of the British.

As we were seeing here, even if the Sub-County Chief was settling disputes between a husband and wife, he still sought advice from the rain chief on how to settle the matter. This was because in Acholiland, the rain chief had wide experience in dealing with marital woes. Much as the British gave the power to settle disputes among the people to the Sub-County Chief, reports state that many Acholi were not happy about it. The Acholi elders I was talking to told me that even if the British did not want the people to show respect towards the rain chief, later the Acholi continued showing respect towards the rain chief. The sub county chiefs appointed by the British strictly enforced the laws of the British. Gradually, the British appointed four chiefs in Acholiland. They were: Chief Aburi in Obbo, Chief Onek P'Anyoda in Pajok, Chief Lotone in Palwar and Chief Ango in Magwi. The British put the members of the four homes of Omeo, Panyikwara, Agoro and Ofirika under the leadership of the chief of Magwi.

Before county chief came to Acholiland, the civil servants of the government of Sudan gave the locals the power to elect the Sub-County Chief. The people could choose whoever they wanted and forward their names to the D.C. or Chief Executive Officer in Opari. This was done because the locals realized that the Sub-County Chiefs they elected in the past could sell their ideas for the love of money, which caused many problems and confusion among the Acholi. But when the British gave the people the power to elect who they wanted to lead them, it brought peace and happiness among the people.

But between the years 1974-1976, when Severino Odur was elected county chief of Magwi, the people could forward names of people they want to be their chiefs to the county chief, who would then forward to the DC or Chief Executive Officer in Torit. The role of the Sub-County Chief was very important to the people, so the people did not choose just anyone to become a chief. There are eight things the people also considered before electing as chief.

First, one who contended to be a chief must be able to read and write in Acholi. The ability of the candidate to write English and Arabic would be an added advantage.

Secondly, a person who wanted to become chief must have the heart to unite the people.

Thirdly, anyone interested in becoming a chief must be well versed with the culture and tradition of the Acholi.

Fourthly, anyone lobbying for the position of chief must not be money-minded or greedy for the wealth of the land.

Fifth, anyone interested in becoming chief must be hospitable to visitors. Sixth, a contending chief must listen to the ideas and views of the people, without selling it to outsiders. Seventh, anyone intending to be chief should be courageous, and able to represent the people to the government on any issue affecting them in that particular home. And eighth, a person who wanted to become chief should be morally upright, and not court other people's wives.

If the people saw that a candidate fulfilled all the above requirements, they would forward their name to the county chief, and he would later become the village chief. But if a candidate did not fulfill one or two of the above requirements, they were considered unfit to become the chief.

County Chief

In 1976 when the Local Government of Torit saw that the chiefs were overwhelmed with work, they installed a county chief in Magwi as a paramount chief of the Acholi. Fortunately, that year, the British gave the power of electing the chief to the natives. For this reason, the people elected Severino Odur of Pajok as the first county chief in Acholiland. The elders of Acholi of Sudan told me that Chief Odur led the people very well and later the British appointed him as the head of the "B" Court, while the other small chiefs were put in charge of "A" Court. The British established the "C" Court in Torit.

The local government set tough rules that all matters that needed mediation, should first be taken to "A" Court. If the chief of this court found that he could not handle the case, he would forward it to "B" Court.

The county chief had nine people who assisted him on the day of settling disputes. If the chief of the "B" Court also realized that he could not settle the case, he would forward it to the (Magistrate) in the "C" Court in Torit. But most times, many cases were settled in "A" Court and "B" Court. Cases that were always taken to "C" Court were cases of murder, because the chiefs of "A" Court and "B" Court did not have the power to handle murder cases.

The county chief was the representative of the Central Government of Sudan, which was among the Acholi. All information from the civil servants went through the county chief. Not only this, if the people had complaints on the government, they sent it to the county chief. In 1979 when Chief Severino Odur died, the Acholi chose Otaviano Oyat Akut of Magwi as chief – he became the second county chief in Acholiland. Chief Oyat Otaviano led the Acholi well, much as the war commanded by John Garang De Mabior almost shook his chiefdom. This also shows us how the county chiefs originated in the land of the Acholi of Sudan.

Rain Chief

The history of South Acholi Sudan states that some rain chiefs had two rain pots, while others had three. Reports indicate that other rain pots contained ten rain stones, while others had twenty rain stones. On the day the rain chief wanted to invoke rains, he would send the rain caretaker to smear the rain stones in the pot with oil. After this, he would fetch water and pour in the rain spot and stir it with his hand. When the rain caretaker had finished his task, he would return home. After a short time, rain would fall.

If the chief was annoyed with the people, and wanted the sun to shine such that people's crops were scotched, he could also send the rain caretaker to go and pick the rain pot and put it in the sun, so that it is heated by the sun. Or sometimes, he could tell the rain caretaker to bring the rain pot and hang it at the fire place in the house. If the rain care taker hanged the rain pot on a tree or at the fireplace as ordered by the chief, the sun could shine so much that all crops in the gardens would dry up.

Reports also show that among the Acholi, there were some people who tried to imitate the skill of the chief in invoking and barring rain. Such people also did not want the people to respect the rain chief. The Acholi elders, I was talking to from South Sudan, told me that whenever such people wanted to stop rain from falling in someone's garden, they would pick millet fingers and bury in the ground. They made sure the head of the millet finger faced where they do not want it to rain. If the rain chief wanted to invoke rain in such a place, all his attempts would fail. The people in that area would be unhappy with the rain chief, thinking he didn't want to invoke rain in their area.

If such a thing happened among the people, they would start investigating why the chief did not invoke rain in their area. Since people knew that there were some ill-intentioned individuals that could stop rain from falling, they could search the surrounding of every home, to find out if any one truly buried millet fingers near their house, or in any other place. If the people found millet fingers buried in the ground, they would remove it and slaughter a sheep, and the blood would be used to cleanse the place. One man would then take the finger of millet and throw it in a well. If all this was done, the rain chief would then summon the rains with ease.

The history of Acholi states that the rain chief helped the British a lot when they had just entered Acholiland. But the British were so stone-hearted and ungrateful that they did not appreciate the rain chief even once. After some-time, the British started advising the people against respecting the rain chief, saying rain was a gift from God. When some people heard that rain was a gift from God, they started disrespecting the rain chief. Shortly, the people started respecting the British because of their skin color, thinking they were the second God in the land.

The history of Acholi of Sudan also states that much as few people took the advice of the British, many people did not. They continued showing respect to the rain chief as their culture dictated.

In those years, when the rain chief was angry, the sun would shine so much that all crops in the gardens would dry up or get scotched. A good example of this happened in1982, when chief Ochilo, son of chief Aburi, was angry with the people of Obbo. The sun destroyed all crops in the garden, which irritated the people of Obbo very much. In 1982 Ochilo Aburi and his brother Vitto Aburi were debating over the issue of rain, with each claiming that the rain was in his custody. Unfortunately, the people of Obbo also did not know who of the two had the rain.

Since the people of Obbo did not know which of the two brothers had the rain, early in the morning, they gathered and set a big fire in the compound of Loudo. The people then sent strong boys to arrest Vitto and his brother Ochilo. The boys arrested Vito and Ochilo, tied them with strong sisal ropes and took them near the fire set in Loudo compound. Before the two were placed near the fire, the people asked, "Who between the two of you has the rain stone? The sun has destroyed all our crops in the garden. If you do not tell us who has the rain stone, then we shall throw both of you in the raging fire before you." The two were speechless. Only tears flew from their eyes.

When people nearby saw that the people of Obbo truly wanted to burn Vito and Ochilo, they reported the matter to police. The Police came and saved Vito and Ochilo from being put to death because of the rain stone. This also shows us that much as the people were under the British rule, they were still very interested in their culture. Many people in Acholi knew that rain comes from God, but God gave the power to invoke rain or stop it to the rain chief.

Parish Chief

In the year the British started working with Sub-County Chief in Acholiland, they gave each Sub-County Chief the authority to choose anyone among the people to act as his Parish Chief. The Parish Chief had two important roles.

First, together with the leaders of the chiefdom, the Parish Chief assisted the chief during mediation. Secondly, he together with the guards collected taxes from the people.

The culture of Acholi therefore permitted each Sub-County Chief to have five or fifteen Parish Chiefs. This depended on the number of people under the leadership of the Sub-County Chief. The history of Acholi says if the Sub-County died before another Sub-County Chief was elected to replace him, the people could appoint one of the Parish Chiefs to be the interim Sub-County Chief, until the people elect a new Sub-County Chief. Culture allowed this because the Parish Chief, having been working with the Sub-County Chief, got experience in presiding over meetings or parliament.

As we saw above, there are eight requirements that anyone who intended to become a sub county must meet. If the people wanted to choose a Parish Chief to act as the Sub-County Chief, they were supposed to ensure that the contender met all the eight requirements. First, the acting Sub-County Chief should know how to read and write Acholi language. If the candidate knew how to write English and Arabic, it would be even better. Secondly, the candidate should have the spirit of uniting the people. Thirdly, the candidate should know the culture of the Acholi. Fourthly, he should not be greedy for money or material wealth. Fifth, he should be hospitable. Sixth, he should be someone who follows the ideas of the people without selling the interests of the people to outsiders. Seventh, he should be courageous and able represent the people to the government on any issue affecting the people in the home. And eighth, he should be morally upright and not court other people's wives. If the people found that one person among the Parish Chief fulfilled all the eight requirements, they could then choose him to become an interim Sub-County Chief, until a new Sub-County Chief was elected. But if the people realised that two or three Parish Chief met the eight requirements, they would sit down to debate, and later choose one to become an acting Sub-County Chief.

Clan Leader

Every worker needs an assistant so that work becomes easy, and is done effectively. As we were seeing above, Parish Chief is an assistant of the chief. The role of the Parish Chief was also very important to the people. This was why the Acholi culture stipulated that he should have an assistant, Clan Leader.

In Acholiland, the Parish Chief had one or more Clan leader, depending on the number of people in his area. Culture allowed a Parish Chief with many people to appoint three or four to assist him in working with the people. The history of the Acholi of Sudan states that people could report small matters of contention to the clan leader. If the clan leader found that he could not solve the matter, because of its complication, he would then take the matter before the Parish Chief. But on many occasions, the clan leader could easily settle small disagreements among the people.

Village Chief)

The role of the village chief was introduced much later in the land of the Acholi of Sudan. They learned the tasks of the parish chief when they fled to Uganda. Before this, the Acholi of Sudan could farm without the village chief. But the Acholi of Sudan had farmers' groups that could bring them together from door-to-door or from home -to-home. And before the Acholi of Sudan had fled to Uganda, they used to portion a part to dig without measuring it with a stick. They used *keyo*. Later, the people of Acholi of Sudan realized that the *keyo* system encouraged laziness. Many times, the elders could sit down smoking, yet the boys and men who did not smoke continued digging. Yet again, when it came to the time of drinking alcohol, everyone would take equal quantity. The young ones then discovered the tricks of the elders and the smokers. Therefore, whenever the boys saw that the elders had sat to smoke, they would pick their bows and arrows or go to see where the vultures alight, and *keyo* would remain there. The boys did this because they understood that their culture prohibited them from telling or stopping the elders from smoking when people were digging. If by bad luck any child mistakenly told an elder off when he was smoking, such a child would be caned at the initiation rite ceremony.

From 1948-1950 Sudan was hit by severe famine, forcing many Sudanese to go looking for odd jobs in exchange for food in Uganda. The history of the Acholi of Sudan says after working for food in Uganda, some people returned to Sudan, but others remained in Uganda.

The story of Acholi states that in 1964, 70% of the Acholi of Sudan fled the Anya-nya One war in Uganda, and 30% remained in hiding in Sudan. The Sudanese saw that the Ugandans farmed under the Parish Chief or Company. In 1964, the refugee camp was only in Acol-pii (Agagu). So the number of refugees was very high, and the refugees recognized that Agagu Refugee Camps could not accommodate all of them. Many of them subsequently fled and built in Palabek, Lokung, Padibe, Patongo, Kitgum and Gulu.

In this year, I was still very young, but could talk. Our parents took me and my two sisters to a place called Akeli-kongo, which is near Palabek Kal. Later my father introduced me to Benadino, my clansman, who came to Uganda around 1948-1950 and established a big shop in Palabek. Besides, other refugees also found their relatives who went to Uganda between 1948-1950 and built among them. When it came to a period of cultivation, the Sudanese refugees started cultivating together with their relatives who had settled there. When the Acholi of Sudan went to their gardens, they found that their brothers did not use keyo system as they used to do from Sudan, but each person was given a portion (measured in feet) depending on the quantity of alcohol of the owner of the garden. If the owner of the alcohol has one or two gallons of kwete, each person digs 25 (5x5) portion of the garden. If the farm owner had three or five gallons of kwete each person would clear 50 (5x10) portions of land. But if the garden owner had six and more gallons of kwete each, person would clear 75 (5x15) portion of land. The Acholi of Sudan gradually realized that this was the best way to do communal farming. If an elder went to smoke, no one would clear his portion. This method of farming taught elders a lesson, which made everyone to start working hard during communal farming.

In 1973, when the Sudanese were coming back home, they brought the idea of giving a portion to each farmer. Reports show that when the refugees came back home with the new skill they learnt in Uganda, their brothers who remained in Sudan, embraced their simple style of farming in groups, which were referred to as "company". Most times, people say wars are bad, but we found that sometimes wars are good. On close examination, we realized that the system of leadership of village chief or "katala" was one thing that was introduced to the Acholi of Sudan because of the war of the Anya-nya. Wars are bad sometimes, but are sometimes advantageous because it makes refugees to learn new skills. This also explains what some people say, "A man who likes staying in the kitchen always says his wife prepares the best meals." Because he does not know that there are other women who cook better than his wife.

Much as the British put the village chief in their initiation system, we find that he is also in the group of the traditional initiation system (see Figure 32 above).

Council of Royal Elders

The role of the council of royal elders is to mediate over small issues like disputes, fights and theft among the people in the chiefdom.

Council of Ordinary Elders

The role of the council of ordinary elders was also to settle small issues among the people. If such issues arose among the people, they could take the matter to the council of royal elders, who would then summon the clan elders to help discuss the matter. The clan elders could also mediate over some issues without forwarding it to the council of royal elders.

In Acholiland, there are many small issues which were forwarded to the people in the different groups in the initiation system. Always when the elders in a particular home saw that they could not handle an issue of contention among the locals, they would forward the matter to the council of ordinary elders.

Heads of Households

The heads of households are those who had deep knowledge and understanding about the relationship between men and women. It should be noted that most male group members of the heads of households had wives. To better understand the issues affecting men and women, a person is to have a wife, so that during meetings, he speaks among the people not from abstracts but from reality of life based on his personal experience. If you were an unmarried man, how would you then know the causes of conflicts among husbands and wives? If we examine closely, we learn that married men know issues relating to the lives of the married people better than unmarried men. For this reason, the Acholi did not invite an unmarried man to mediate over disputes between a husband and wife. The heads of the home in Acholi liked to build their huts in close quarters, such that all the men would eat around the same bonfire.

As we saw above, we find that minor issues were very many in families and among the Acholi. There was no single family without an issue of contention. The small issues were always related to quarrels, fights, curses, if a woman thumped her genitalia before her husband (or hit the mother drum as the Acholi describe it), or if a man lifted his penis before his child, and incest leading to pregnancy between boys and girls, etc.

Other important role of heads of households was to lead the groom while taking money to the home of mother-in-law during marriage. On the side of the bride, there were also heads of the households that took charge during the marriage, and discussed the marriage details with the head of household from the groom's side. During marriage ceremonies, other people like boys and girls, women and children in the different groups did not speak on matters of marriage. The culture of Acholi wants this group of people to only listen to whatever the elders were discussing.

Among the Acholi of Sudan, matters of marriage are left to heads of households, because they are courageous, are forgiving, soft spoken and know how to mediate over issues. Most marriages initiated without the involvement of heads of households always ended in quarrels and fights. This also explains why people did not want boys to get involved in marriage negotiations, because they are short tempered. They always do not speak calmly, they are quick to get angry and many times their meetings end in fighting. Not just anyone got involved in family matters anyhow. A person who mediated over a family issue should be a member of that family. This is why many times, if you move among many Acholi, you hear people saying, " .this issue affects the family of Oloro, Goloba, Kitaka, Amika, Ywaya, Amica, Pino-pino, Abong or Orimi". Culture states that if, however, they realized that they could not settle the matter; they would then forward it to the council of ordinary elders of sub parish chief.

The history of Acholi states that the third and equally important role of heads of households was to take care of Auma shrine.

Owners of Homes

Home owners are newly married boys, who have only one, two or three children. The history of Acholi states that boys that were in the group of home owners did not have the right in the initiation rite, so they followed instructions from heads of homes. According to tradition, during cultivation period a boy, who completed his portion (*katala*) earlier, was expected to help a head of a home if the head of the home had not yet finished digging his portion.

As we saw in the initiation rite of the British, we found that among the groups of initiations, there were also groups called village chief. Let us see how the government of farmers works as given below.

Chapter Twenty Seven

THE FARMERS' GOVERNMENT

Farming

Every family member in the land of the Acholi of Sudan survives on produce from garden. Although the land of the Acholi in the south and north is not fertile, yet they grow different types of crops. The Acholi are well known among the Nilotics, because of their concentration on farming. I remember in 1962, when I was just eleven years, the Dinka were passing through a sesame group field and the people had planted on both sides of the road. When the Dinka saw the large gardens, they thought the gardens were opened using tractors. But they later learned that the Acholi used hand hoes to open the farm land. The Dinka were therefore surprised at how the Acholi were such committed farmers, because there were no large farms like group gardens in the land of the Dinka. It was the first time the Dinka saw such a large farm.

Secondly, we find that the Acholi in the north received more rain than the Acholi in the south. This allowed people to plant different varieties of crops from April to August. This is why, Mr. Grove said, "Acholi from the north and around the hills harvested crops three times a year, while the Acholi from the south, (also the same as the Madi) harvested crops only twice a year. In 1918, during rainy season, the different varieties of crops planted by the Acholi in one garden were as below:

Acholi from the North

1   A newly opened garden would be used to plant peas during rainy season.

2   In July, the people would harvest peas and plant millet and sorghum for the dry season in this same garden. Millet would be harvested around November, and sorghum would be harvested around April of the following year.

3   In the same garden, people would again plant millet and sesame. These crops would be harvested in July, referred to as wet season millet and sesame.

4   After this, the people could plant sesame and dry season peas. These crops would be harvested in November- after this the owner of the garden would leave the garden, because it would have been over used. He would then shift and start farming in another land.

5   The Acholi from the north also planted groundnuts, but ground nuts were usually planted in another way. If the groundnuts were planted behind the home, they would also plant cassava in the same field. Later, the groundnuts would be harvested and the cassava would remain. Cassava takes longer to mature, between six to nine months. After nine months, the cassava would be eaten.

Acholi from the South

The digging and planting season of the Acholi from the South is as below:

i.   A newly opened garden is tilled and peas, groundnuts and sesame would be planted in it. The crops were harvested in July.

ii.   If the garden was bare, they would again plant millet of different varieties. Among these varieties of millet, sorghum would get ready for harvest first in November, and other varieties would be harvested in June of the following year.

iii. After this, they would again plant different varieties of millet, but in the same field, they would also sow sesame. The sesame would be harvested in November. This sesame and millet were called *"dry season millet and sesame."*

iv.   The important crops among all the Acholi are those harvested in November (these are millet, sesame and peas). "In Acholiland, men are in charge of digging, while women collect rubbish from the gardens and weed the crops."

I realized that the digging and planting season in Acholiland has not changed, much as the Norwegians brought new seeds to the Acholi. The new millet varieties brought by the Norwegian in Acholi are Serena, red groundnuts, etc.

Farmers' Government

Farmers' government is a group of people gathered under the same village chief, and they are found in every family in Acholi. We find that in Acholiland, a single home can have as many as six to fifteen farmers' governments, depending on the number of farmers in the area. We also find that all the governments of the farmers in all the different homes in Acholi have six different groups seen below:

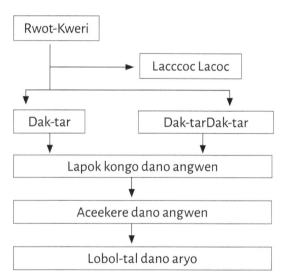

Figure No 34: Government of the farmers

If we want to better understand how the government of the farmers is, we should look at the responsibilities and rights of each group in the government of the farmers.

Village Chief

In 1973 when people returned from Uganda, they started the system of leadership of the village chief and farming based on portion division. The village chief was always chosen by the farmers. So in Acholiland, we find that each parish chief had between 45-60 farmers. The people did not choose just anyone to become village chief. There were qualifications the contenders of village chief were expected to fulfill. The rules of the farmers stipulated that anyone chosen to become a village chief must have the three qualifications below: —

i. He must be a diligent farmer.
ii. He must also be someone with the heart to unite the people.
iii. He must be person who does not love to quarrel or fight with the people.

The rules of the farmers also stipulated that the village chief must be elected after every four years. A village chief could be re-elected for another four-year term, if he had a good work record. But after the second term, the chief is prohibited by law from standing again for the same office, even if he is still hard working. But if the people saw that the village chief did not perform in his first term in office, they would elect another in his position.

As I said earlier, the people held the village chief in a very high regard. The law therefore prohibited anyone from insulting, or deriding the village chief. If by bad luck anyone insulted the chief, such a person would always be punished. He would get a cock and give to the chief as a fine. If the same person insulted the village chief for the second time, they would be punished and immediately fined thirty pounds (LS 30.00). If the same person insulted or disparaged the chief for the third time, the members of the farmers group would take the person before the sub parish chief. Many times when such a case was taken before the sub parish chief, he would sentence the person to one or three months in jail.

Secretary

The farmers set a rule that that all the farmer's governments should put in writing, all the things happening during the meeting of the farmers. For this reason, members chose one boy who knew how to write Acholi language, to be the secretary of the village chief. One of the issues that were supposed to be documented was when, a woman, whose garden had been cultivated, prepared sour local brew or put too much water in the alcohol. The secretary was also expected to record all the punishments given to a wrongdoer. The role of the secretary is as seen below:

1. Writing all the resolutions made during a meeting.
2. Keeping the book of the members clean and safe (so that it is not stolen).
3. Registering all farmers under a particular village chief.
4. Recording names of wrong doers and the punishments given to them by farmers.
5. Keeping money paid by women who brew alcohol badly, or money paid as fine by a farmer who didn't go to the garden.
6. Moving among people during all the farming days, except when he is sick.

Beer Doctor

A doctor is someone chosen to taste whether alcohol is bitter, sour or had a lot of water, when people were cultivating. A doctor is supposed to be someone who could distinguish between sour and sweet alcohol. The people also chose two people to act as doctors, because when people are cultivating the garden of one doctor, the alcohol would be tested by his colleague, and vice versa. The farmers would do like this to avoid subjectivity. If the doctor found that the alcohol was sour or watery, he would tell the people who would then sit under a tree shade. The members would then warn the owner of the garden against making poor quality alcohol in future.

They would then ask the owner of the garden to bring two or five bottles of alcohol, depending on how bad the alcohol was and the number of farmers in the garden. If the owner of the garden did not have alcohol, his wife would give money equivalent to the number of bottles of alcohol she had been asked to give.

If a doctor lied that the alcohol was tasty even if it was sour, the owner of the garden would not be punished. As human beings, we always favour ourselves and our own tribe, but if two doctors were appointed to ascertain the quality of alcohol, it would eliminate such favoritism. But time and time again, the doctor could also say the alcohol was nice, even when it was sour, so the people would punish or fine the doctor (LS 30.00). The people would also tell him to be impartial.

Alcohol Distributors

Whenever women took alcohol in the garden, the rule dictated that not everyone could dip their finger in the brew. For this reason, the farmers under each village chief chose four people to be distributors of alcohol. These people were chosen so that work was done faster. As we saw above, after a doctor had finished tasting the alcohol, and the members had concluded their debate, the four people would start distributing alcohol.

The alcohol taken from the gardens were normally distributed using gallons or calabashes, depending on the number of people in each group. The farmers sat according to age groups. Those in the same age bracket sat together. For this reason, farmers' groups in the land of the Acholi of Sudan were grouped as below:

- ▶ *Boy's groups* – were males from the age of 12 to 25.
- ▶ *Men's group*- comprised of males from the age of 26-45.
- ▶ *Elders' group*- these were a group of people from the age of 46-70.

After the four people had finished serving the farmers with alcohol, they called a person from each group, to take the alcohol to their other members who would be seated under tree.

Other role of the alcohol distributors was to serve food to those who opened farm land. But most times, people assigned boys who did not distribute alcohol, to serve food. The rules of the farmers stipulated that the food for people who opened farm lands should be accompanied with water, meaning, one or two gallons of local brew.

In the past, when people had finished digging, they returned home to drink remains of *kwete*, but in 1973 when the Acholi of Sudan who had fled the war to Uganda came back home, they abandoned the habit of drinking the remains of *kwete*. This was because many times people would fight during such gatherings.

The women started filtering the remains, called Katanga. Members then resolved that *Katanga* should be taken from the garden. Whenever the four people had finished serving drinks, they also distributed *katanga* to the members.

Security Guard

As we saw in the previous page, most times if people were drinking kwete or its remains, they liked engaging in banters that lead to quarrels and fights. The farmers' government then resolved that two or four people should be appointed as security guards to maintain peace. The security guards were always appointed based on their strength and physique. The four people were called the guards of the village chief. The roles of the security guards were as follow:

First, during meetings, they ensured that no one interrupted someone who was making a point. Secondly, they ensured that there were no unnecessary movements during meetings. Thirdly, if a new member wanted to join farmers in the garden, they would first get permission from the guard. The guard would then inform the village chief about the new member(s) intending to join the farmers' group. If the village chief agreed, the new member would then join the group which had someone they were interested in. Before the new member sat down with the group, the guard would search him. If the guard finds that he has a knife or a stick, the guard would remove all these things, before allowing him to go and sit in a tree shed.

The rule of the farmers was against anyone carrying a stick or knife, because if a fight erupted, the fighters could take the knife or stick from the new member and hurt the others. But if the village chief disagreed, the new person would be requested to go back immediately. Fourthly, the role of the guard was to stop members who wanted to start quarreling or fighting in the garden. The fifth and equally important role of the guard was to give permission to anyone who intended to answer nature's call, when people were still eating and drinking.

Portion Measurer

As we saw earlier on, many years back, the Acholi of Sudan used *keyo* system of digging. But when the refugees of Sudan (Acholi), came back from Uganda in 1973, they brought new farming methods that they learnt from Uganda. This method was called, *katala*, or portion division system. Before the *katala* system was introduced in the land of the Acholi of Sudan, the role of *katala* measures was to estimate portion. So when members started using the *katala* system, those who used to estimate portions began to measure portion/*katala* to each farmer.

As we also saw earlier, *katala* was not used anyhow; the farmers clear numbers of portions depending on the quantity of alcohol/ *kwete* that the owner of the garden had given to those he had called to dig in his garden.

Each village chief in Acholi always had two people to measure portion. If one of the two fell sick during cultivation, the village chief would appoint one boy to replace him. The rule of the farmers stated that if farmers were going to cultivate another persons' garden the following morning, each person's portion was to be measured the day before the day of cultivation, so that they find the portions already clearly demarcated when they start cultivation.

In the morning when the farmers had gone to start cultivation, those who measured the portions only showed each of the farmers their portion. If, however they did not apportion the entire garden on that day, they continued demarcation the portions as other people went on cultivating.

This is how the government of farmers worked in the land of the Acholi of Sudan. If the government workers of Sudan wanted to know the number of people eligible to pay taxes, they would go to the village chief, because he had the names of all the farmers in his jurisdiction. Boys qualified to pay tax when they were 21 or 25 years old. If a man had two boys, who were suitable to pay taxes the village chief then removed the man from the list of tax payers. In Acholiland, anyone aged 51 years did not pay taxes to the government, because they had grown up children, who would also be paying taxes to the government.

Chapter Twenty Eight

CORONATION OF THE CHIEF

In the past, the throne of the chief was not fought over, but left for the rightful successor. But gradually, people started installing other people to become chief, even if they were not members of the royal family. Such people could have come from outside and entered the family, or someone from a different clan chosen by the people to become chief. This always happened when the people saw that such a person was well mannered, and could unite the people. One thing I want us to understand before we proceed to state how the Acholi installed their chief is that the children of the rain chief, who were chosen by the rain stone, were not installed the way we shall see below.

The installation of an outsider as a chief in Acholiland is as seen below. If people wanted someone to become chief, they sent the clan elders to him around 7:00 pm, when it was already dark. They captured the man and took him to the home of an old woman, who couldn't bear children. The Acholi elders I was interviewing told me that there were different ways in which the Acholi coroneted chiefs. In this book, I will not write all these methods.

Reports show that if the clan elders took the captured man in the house of the old woman, they later removed his skin/dress from his waist and bathed him from inside the house, which had a hold dug to allow water to sink. After the clan elders finished bathing the man, they would put back the skin to his waist, and take him to a place prepared for him by the old woman.

People say the Acholi have a herb, whose name I don't know, that the elders put in the mouth of the chief on the day of his coronation. I was asking many people, because I wanted to know the name of the herb (roots) that they give to the chief on the day he is being installed. Unfortunately, all these elders did not know the name of the herb. They said there was only one herb that was given to the new chief. When it was one or two days to the day of coronation, the clan elders would choose a few people to go and dig out the roots of the herb, so that the sap was given to the new chief.

The next morning, on the first day people would prepare to coronate the chief. The women who kept the chief in her house would pea food known as *laputa*. She would cook the food without putting salt in it. At sunrise, the elders would bring the chief and he sat with his back facing the East. One of the elders would give the chief a drop of the root sap (herb) using a small calabash. The chief would swallow the sap and later eat the food prepared by the old woman. He would also eat the food while basking in the morning sun. This is one of the things that happened when a chief was being installed on the royal chair.

On the second day, the elders would slaughter a black billy goat in the morning. The skin would be dried and later given to the chief to wear around on his waist. The elders would give the goat's meat to the old woman hosting the chief to cook for the chief. She would then prepare the meal without putting salt in it. If the chief failed to eat all the food prepared for him, the old woman hosting him, together with other old women at the coronation ceremony, would eat the remaining food. These are the things that happened on the second day of installing the chief.

On the third day, the old woman would again cook goat's meat and the chief would eat only that meal that day. While on the fourth day, very early in the morning, at exactly 7:00am, the elders would tie the goat's skin round the chief's waist and take him back to his home, where other people would be waiting for him. The people waiting for him at his home would prepare a royal chair for him, so that when he arrived home, he would sit on it. When the chief arrived home, the people waiting for him would immediately seat him on the royal chair. On the other hand, the people would have chosen for him a woman they considered well mannered and able to keep the people. The people waiting for the chief also prepared a chair for the chief's wife for her to sit near her husband. The chair the queen sat on was not called a royal chair, but the chair of the queen. The people also chose two men to sit near the chief and the queen. The queen sat on the right side of the chief, while one man sat on the right hand side of the queen, and the other would sit on the left side of the chief and another man would stand behind the chief, while holding a shield. At the time, the elders would have placed a spear before the chief's chair.

This celebration usually takes three days, starting from the day the chief was inaugurated and reached his home, till the day the celebration ended. In all these three days, the chief and the queen together with three people would be sitting before the royal spear as I have described above.

The history of Acholi says that during these three days, when people are for the coronation of the chief, the three men chosen by the people would sleep in one house together with the chief and the queen. During all these three days, the chief would not get time to have sex with his wife. On the fourth day, the elders would take the chief to take a bath in a well. They would take him in the bath point, and one person among them would hold the chief on both hands and pushed the hand of the chief towards the water and withdrew the hands from it twice. And the third time, the elder would take the chief in the bath point. The chief would then take a bath in the bath point. After he had finished bathing, he would wear the skin and go back home. Before he reached home, the people at home would be spreading cow hide, where he would sit. When the chief reached home, he would sit on the hide spread for him.

The people would let the chief rest for a while and later tell him to stand up. They would then take the royal chair and put on the cow hide, for the chief to sit on. After the chief had sat on his chair, the elder who took the chief in water, would pick a piece of broken clay pot, and shave the chief's head. Shortly, five gray haired women would go to the chief holding sticks. They would go one after the other, and each of them would spit on the chief's head, points him in the face while saying, "We do not want you to be a glutton. You should be a jolly person. Give water and food without favoritism. You should cater for the people." When all the five women had finished spitting on the chief's head, they would go back and sit.

The chief would also get up and go to his place. The following morning, the people and clan elders would take the chief to see all the families under his jurisdiction. Reports show that in every family that the chief visited, people slaughtered for him a bull or billy goat. They also gave him *kwete* and *waragi* to drink. Everyone would eat and drink together with the chief. Later they would dance before the chief, to show their happiness to him. After the chief had finished moving in all the families, the elders took him back home, with the women making ululations, while saying, "We have got our chief." When the chief arrived home, he would give five cows to the people who coroneted him. The five cows are not slaughtered but the elders would take them to their homes.

On the day of the chief's coronation, if he had children, they would all be hidden so that they did not witness how their father was being installed on the throne. After the elders had finished installing the chief, they would then give him rules to use. Some of the rules stated what he should not eat. The things that the chief was not supposed to eat were the meat of animals like hippopotamus, antelope, elephant, mud fish and pork. But if the people under the chief's leadership killed an elephant, the law stated that they should take the ivory to the chief. If a person killed a giraffe, he should also take the tail to the chief. Later, the chief would divide the giraffe's tail into two. Half of it remained with him, while the hunter took half of the tail. This was one of the ways Acholi coroneted or showed respects to their chief.

Chapter Twenty Nine

COURTSHIP AND MARRIAGE
IN THE ANCIENT TIME

ANCIENT COURTSHIP OF THE ACHOLI

To understand Acholi courtship issues well, I think it is good for us to answer questions like: What is courtship? How does a boy court a girl? How does a boy start wooing a girl? Where does the boy start his courtship from? What shows that a boy or a girl is interested in the other? What does a girl want to see in a boy? What does a boy wants to see in a girl? Why do men think of what they want to do? How does a girl know whether a boy wants to marry her or not? What does the mother of the girl do when a suitor of her daughter comes home to woo her? At what time do Acholi boys go for courtship; at night or during the day?

If we answer all these questions, one by one, we can understand Acholi courtship. Unfortunately, even when we ask Acholi people that "What is the meaning of courtship?", many of them cannot explain it. One elder told me courtship (*cuna*) originated from the word "*cuno*" (that is, to court), like court-ing white ants, courting a rat hole, or courting corridor between hills. Why do Acholi people do all the above? All the Acholi people know that people do that so that white ants do not fly away, so that rats do not enter their holes.

In Acholi, wooing a girl is to convince a girl with sweet talks. A boy would convince a girl with sweet words so that she does not listen to any other boy. The issue of courtship is not only for boys, even men can woo women — a man convinces a woman not to listen to any deceitful messages of other men.

If we look at the meaning of the word courtship, we shall find that, this are

481

lies which girls usually like to hear. Girls do not know that courtship is a lie that is nice to listen to. In this book, I will not write all the details of how boys woo girls, but this is what boys are usually fond of telling girls whom they love. When a boy has seen a girl whom he loves, he moves nearer and talks to her:

Boy: Excuse me; it seems I saw you somewhere. Don't you remember me? I have a very deep interest in you that I want you to be my wife.

Girl: I don't know you. You also don't know me.

Despite that response, the boy does not give up since he is interested in marrying her. He goes ahead wooing the girl. The boy confirms if the girl is not interested in him by looking straight into her eyes. As we shall discuss later in this book, a girl does not usually show her love for a boy immediately, even when she loves him. Later, the boy would think of a different strategy of approaching the girl. This can be at home, in the market, in a dancing arena or where the girl likes going to grind millet.

Boy: Oh! The Chief's daughter! You look very nice to me. If you fall in water, I can still drink the water because of the love I have for you. I think about you daily, night and day, I love you more than my mother.

Girl: Eh! You boy, leave those nonsensical talks. I don't want to listen to you. I hate you like sesame which is hated by elephant.

Boy: There is no girl on earth, whom I love like you.

Girl: Ok, son of a bull, I have heard what you have said, but you should know that people do not dig a garden in a day. Give me time to think over it. Some girls like saying that "I have a man." A boy who is not determined, after hearing such statements, might withdraw eventually, but an experienced boy would not.

Boy: Good, God be with you, and let Him give you good thoughts until we meet in future.

Girl: Alright, thank you. Let Him protect you as well.

These are the main issues about courtship, but when you look at it deeply, you find that there are a lot of lies in them. For example, "I think about you day and night" and "I hate you like the elephant that has refuse sesame." Listening to such words is very interesting to boys and girls. There is no body on earth who thinks about his friend day and night. We have different thoughts in our minds, each of which comes and goes, and another one comes and goes, and days pass like that. As I have been saying earlier on, an Acholi girl normally doesn't show her love immediately to the boy. She pretends that she does not love the boy so that tomorrow the man doesn't insult her. When we look at the answers of the girl, a person who is not an Acholi would think that this girl does not love the boy. But we also know that many times girls make this kind of statement when they are actually interested in the suitors.

Figure 35: A boy courts a girl at the roadside

When we look at the boy's statement, we find that it is full of lies because there is nobody on earth who loves his wife more than his mother. This still takes us to what I have been saying that courtship is full of lies.

Long time ago, courtship between boys and girls in Acholi would take between three to six years. Courtship is usually initiated by men. Girls did not court boys. If unfortunately, a girl initiated the courtship, people would tell her that she was a prostitute or a lecherous. Even when a girl is interested in a boy, she does not show it immediately because she wants to know the boy. She would want to know what the boy is thinking about her. Mr. Harvey said it very well that there are many things that girls would like to know to find out whether the boy she loves has those qualities she likes or not. The first thing they would want to understand is if, truly this boy has given himself for her. Secondly, girls want to know the future plans of the boys. Thirdly, they want to know whether this boy is hard working and like smartness or not. When a girl finds that the boy has all these three things that she cherishes, she now looks for a way of maintaining the interest the boy (Harvey, 2009, P, 2).

Acholi men do think that women listen to other people, especially friends and elderly women who do not know what is in the hearts of men. All the women here on earth, whether in Australia, America, Europe, Africa, Canada or Asia, think that if a man loves them, then they can influence the man's thinking. This is false. Women cannot change the mindset of a man. Some people may ask, "Why is this not true?" This is not a true statement, because even when women listen to advice from outside or from elderly women or from the radio, all these can't change the mindset of a man. For this reason, even if a girl loves and respect a boy very much, this respect alone is useless if the girl has not understood and ascertained that the boy has truly given himself with all his heart to the her before she accepts and gives him all her heart and love (Harvey,2009,pp 3-7).

There are three things that a man usually likes doing to help him ascertain his manly qualities. First is, a man would want to show that he is a man. He does not want to be taken for a woman. This is why boys and men in Acholi always say, "Just be a man; don't be a woman." This means a man should heed to a man's advice, not a woman's. For this reason, we usually find that, in Acholi, men do not think alike with women. A man considers himself a man when he (1) looks at himself as a man, (2) does what men's work, not women's, (3) what he does should bring peace in his family. He starts to learn men's work just at the time of his birth; a boy falls down in labour blood with a man's mindset immediately. All the years that a boy is growing, he learns men's roles and activities like war, climbing trees, being strong hearted and courageous even when he is hurt, he should not cry. Others are herding cattle, sheep and goats, harvesting honey, setting trap for wild animals, broadcasting seeds in the garden and hunting as well. A boy also learns how to keep lives and peace from his mother, sisters and brothers. These are the reasons why boys don't want anybody to play with their mothers or sisters. He wants to see that everything goes on smoothly in the family. When he is a grown up, a young man does not change his manly mind set. God has created, in the blood of men the spirit of keeping the lives women and children; a man always wants to be number one in front of the public. This shows us why men normally don't stay at home. He goes around looking for money and food. He works day and night to make sure there is peace in his family. Men do this because in Acholi, people differentiate between a man and a woman by what a person does and the person's sharpness. Unfortunately, women don't understand why men don't like staying at home. Many women tell their husbands, "You like roaming about so much. What are you looking for?" (Harvey, 2009, pp11-15).

This is one way we have seen earlier on, boys initiate courtship, but I want to tell you, readers that there are so many ways a boy can initiate courtship. Some are here:

Boy: Eh! Slender, God has really created you. As if I have seen you somewhere, but cannot remember.

Girl: I don't know.

Boy: Don't you remember me?

Girl: I can't remember.

Boy: What's your name?

Girl: My name is _____ (If the girl has interest in the boy she tells the boy her name, but if she does not have interest in him she will not tell the boy her name)

Boy: What is there at home?

The girl would think of why the boy is asking her many questions? The girl bends her head down in respect the way tradition wants, then ponder silently on why the boy asked her so many questions? "What does he want from me?" After some few seconds, she will raise her eyes up and look at the boy in the face directly and respond to him this way:

The girl: there is nothing and our home is Okay.

Boy: Where do you live? Many Acholi girls always don not like hiding their homes from boys.

Girl: I live (she shows where their home is).

Boy: the boy inspects the girl with his eyes from the head up to the legs, then from the legs to the head. He then later says, "Alright, girl, I will come to your place tomorrow evening to see you." Just in a moment, the boy moves closer to the girl with a lot of smiles, shakes hands with her and goes.

Before the boy goes far, he looks back to see the girl, all this shows that he has great interest in the girl. On the other side, the girl also looks back to see the boy. This is also to show she is interested in the boy.

That night the boy and the girl's minds reel with a number of thoughts. The boy wishes day could brake quickly so that he could go to the home of the girl. When the day finally comes, in early evening about, the boy washes his face, the arms and cleans his heels very neatly, then smear the body with toilet soap (Lux) to make his body smell nice. He combs his hair and wears khaki shorts and a short sleeve shirt. He then wears a pair of shoes and a long pair of socks that stretches up to the knees. But in the ancient time, the boy would bathe and throw the cloth on his shoulder, or wear a free wear, pick his spear set out for the girl's home. Traditionally, it is not allowed for a boy to go for courtship on the first day alone. He should move with two or three of his friends. Traditionally, when a girl has finally committed herself to a boy, the boy can visit the girl's home alone.

When going to the girl's home, many times, boys discuss what they should go and say that would capture the girl's interest. Secondly, when they are asked, how should they respond to the question? In a short while, the boys would arrive at the girl's home. When they find the girl alone at home, they don't just enter straight in the house. Most of the times Acholi boys go for courtship, they get the mothers of the girls at home. The boy would stand at the shade of the granary or the shade of any tree that in the courtyard. The girl would also be looking at the boys with the edge of her eye. If the mother of the girl was inside the house, at this time she would get out leaving room for the boys. She picks the skin of a wild animal, goes and sits on it in the shade of the granary or under a tree in the courtyard. The mother of the girl would sit turning her back towards the door so that she would not see what the boys do to the girl. Some Acholi boys are fond of touching the breasts of girls or her flank when they are for courtship. This is one thing that many mothers-in-laws do not want to see. When the mother of the girl has gone out, the girl would put a smart clean skin for the boys to sit on, and she invites the boys to enter the house. The new generations who live in the cities do not use skin for sitting. They take the boys straight to their sitting room where there are good modern chairs.

The boys would enter the house one by one, and the suitor of the girl enters. They sit down, and girl picks a clean water calabash and serves them with water to drink while kneeling down. At this time that the girl is serving water, her suitor would be would be looking at the sharpness of the girl. Many times boys often get to learn the good traits and the bad traits of their loved ones right from their home.

After the boys have drunk the water, the girl takes back the calabash back to where it was, and washes it later when the boys have gone back. The girl sits down on one skin put aside, leaning against the central pole in the house. She sits with her legs folded one on top of the other, She picks one piece of soft broom and attentively listens to what the boys have gone to tell her.

Just a few moments the boys would begin asking her different questions. A girl that many boys like courting knows how to respond to questions unlike girls who are not wooed very often, and do not know how to respond to boys' questions. Boys learn courtship from their friends, but a girl learns how to respond to questions at courtship when there are many boys talking to her. Sometimes girls learn how to respond to courtship questions from friends. But even when some girls have learnt how to respond to boys from their friends, you will still find that to respond to some questions is still a challenge to them. Difficult questions usually bring some small sweat on the forehead of the girl. When a girl finds that to respond to such a question is difficult, she begins breaking the soft broom in to smaller pieces.

Acholi tradition refuses the boys from taking too long in courtship at the home of the girl; they should take a minimum of 30 to 45 minutes. They do like this so that the mother of the girl does not get tired sitting under the tree or in the shade of the granary. Most of the time, the mother of the girl would have some work to do in the house. When the boys take about one hour or more, it interrupts the work in the home.

Before the boys go back to their home, they agree together with the girl which day they visit her next. If this was their first day of courtship, before the boys get out, the girl asks the name of the father of her suitor, "What is your father's name?" She also asks the clan of the boy, "Which clan are you from?" The boy tells his father's name and the clan where he comes from, like (Abong, Oyere, Obwolto, Kapa, Bura, Goloba, Amica, Palonganyi etc.). Later the boys get out and go back to their home.

When the boys are getting out from the house, the mother of the girl would be looking at the boy from where she is. She checks on the dressing of the boy and the appearance of the boy. Women of the olden day knew how responsible boys walk and how those irresponsible ones walk. As the boys are used to moving in a group of three or four, the mother of the girl may not know who exactly among the boys has interest in her daughter. When the boys have disappeared, the mother of the girl would enter the house and ask her daughter immediately:

"Atuktuk."

Mama, whose son is that who has come to visit you today? What is the name of the boy?"

The girl would answer her mother with respect, "Mama, did you see the boy who is medium height (or the tall one or the short one), or the one with long hair or short hair, the one who wore a striped shirt or a red shirt, is the boy I am interested in. The boy told me he is the son of (Dikomoi, Lokwormoi, Dermoi, or Lyekamoi)." They are from the clan of (Paitenge, Orak, Padyeri etc.). As I have been saying earlier on, elderly people in Acholiland would know a boy well by the name of his father. This is also the reason why the mother of the girl was asking the name of the father of the boy.

And if the mother of the girl finds that the father of the boy has poison for killing people, or he is a sorcerer, the mother of the girl would tell her daughter in a tactfully, "Okay my daughter, why do you want to spoil our clan? The boy who came is from a family of your father's clan. This marriage is impossible because we do not want to disrepute the clan. For this reason, I am telling you that you should forget about this boy. Throw your net elsewhere. There are many boys out there." This is a peaceful and respectable way to show the girl that the family of the boy is not good. The clan issue here does not mean that the boy and the girl are true clan mates, but it is just a wise way to show the girl that, that family is not good. They have poison for killing people, or they are sorcerers. Traditionally, it is not allowed for a girl from a reputable family to get married to a family with such a background. A girl whose family practices witchcraft should not get married to a boy, whose family does not, because when such a woman is brought home, may begin to kill the family members and other people. Sometimes such a woman would also kill her husband.

When a girl listens to this from her mother, she knows that this boy is coming from a bad family or they are sorcerers. When such a boy comes back another time, the mother of the girl would immediately rush to take her daughter to the innermost part of the house, and she just sits at the doorway. The girl would sit inside without getting time to welcome the visitors. The boys remain standing, and the mother of the girl just looks at them from the edge of her eye, as she mumbles: "Mmmm mmmm mmmm." The boys would stand until they are tired and go back home complaining, "Why did the mother of the girl block for us the door? We should understand that she does not like this courtship. If that is so, there is no need for us to waste our time visiting this girl."

Figure 36: The mother of the girl has blocked the doorway

If the mother of the girl knows that the boy interested in her daughter comes from a good family clan, she just keeps quiet. She will not talk much because that family of the boy is clean. When she does not say anything, the girl would immediately know that her mother is in support of their affair. When the boy comes back another time, the mother of the girl gives them time. She sits at the granary or goes to the neighborhood. When the boy has seen the mother of the girl has given them time, they also immediately understand that the mother of the girl is in support of the love. The only issue would be remaining the girl herself. The girl then welcomes the boys in their house.

The girl serves the visitors with water to drink and then he suitor starts to ask questions, "'Okay, last time, I know we did not conclude our discussion, we stopped on the way. As you told us, we also know that a garden is not completed in one day. But I have a feeling that, in the past few days you were thinking about what I told you. As I told you truly that day, I truly love you.

My love is bigger than the head of an elephant, if you could only see what is in my heart; you would see how big my love for you is. But it is not bad as we have come today; we want to find out from you, where your stand point is on this issue. What is important in marriage is that, both the boy and the girl must have deep roots of their love, to avoid having suspicion in the future" (Harvey, 2009, P, 17). The girl would answer the boy while bending her head down, she only looks at the boy with the edge of her eyes as she says, "I thank you for coming back, I want to make you know that, I was thinking about what you told me recently, but I realise that the issue is not yet fully in my mind." When the boys listen to such answers, they continue talking to convince the girl. As I wrote earlier on in this book, courtship usually takes about three to six months before the girl accepts and begins to show her love for the boy. During these months, the girl would be seeking for advices from her friends or from her mother.

Even when the girl says, this boy's interest has not yet touched her heart, the boy does not give up. He continues asking questions, it is okay, I have heard your response, but I want to understand whether you have any barrier?" After learning that the boy's family is a good one, the girl would respond, "There is no barrier." The boy would still continue asking the girl, 'What does 'no barrier' mean? Does it mean you love me?" Many Acholi girls normally do not answer this kind of question immediately, they keeps quiet until the boy leaves their compound. The boy would then greet the girl then go back home. Before the boys disappear from the courtyard, the mother of the girl would enter the house and talk to her daughter, It's good if courtship is taken this way, I want to tell you something sweet, "Good Atuk-tuk, I want to say that, with this boy, the issue of clan relationship between you is not there, his father is a very hard working man. I do feel the boy would also be a hard working boy like his father. The boy is really a son of a man. I know his parents very well. He is also hard working like his father. The mother of the girl would talks like this because if her daughter has interest in the boy, she should know that her parents have no objection. Secondly, the woman wants her daughter to know that if she gets married to this boy, they will not have any problem in future in their house.

Another day, when the boy pays a courtship visit again, he would ask the girl, "Recently, I asked you two questions, "What does 'no barrier' mean?" Does it show that you have interest in me?" But unfortunately, you did not answer it that day. Before we go further with any discussion, I want you to respond to my two questions." After this, the girl would keep quiet for about two or three seconds then answer the boy in a simple way, "It is okay. It is okay; it means there is nothing that should make me turn you down. I also love you the way you love me. When the boy listen to this response, turns the head sideways looking at the wall, smiles a bit, then turns to look into the eyes of the girl. Some girls may also say to the boy, "It is okay, all these days, I have been thinking about your proposal so much, then later I found out that, you truly love me. Today I want you to know that I don't have anything else about the proposal." The issue of *I don't have anything else to say* is the same with *I have love you* the way you love me. Acholi tradition does not allow girls to tell boys openly, "I love you."

And if the mother of the girl knows that the boy who wants the daughter is from a bad family or clan, when the boys are coming out from the house, she silently watches the boys from the side of the granary where she is seated. She looks at how the boy walks, and she asks herself, "Whose son could this be, who is proposing to my daughter?" She would wait when the boys have gone, and ask her daughter, "Atuk-tuk, mama, whose son have come to you today?" The girl would answer her mother, "That is the son of   (calls the name of the father of the boy)." In Acholiland, elders know boys by their father's name. When the mother of the girl has learnt that the boys' father has vice like local poison for killing people, she would tell her daughter "Why do you want to spoil our clan? You should forget completely about this boy. Throw your net elsewhere. There are other good animals there in the bush." The issue of clan relation in Acholiland means the family of the boy is bad. They have poison for killing people. The question of clan here doesn't mean that the boy and the girl truly come from the same clan. As the boy also does not know whether the mother of the girl has interest in their love, they would come back another time to meet the girl. On the day that the boys are coming, when they reach the compound, the mother of the girl would tell the girl to go inside the house while she sits and block the door. She does not give the visitors anything to sit on. They will just stand until they are tired. She does not give any opportunity for her daughter to meet the visitors. The boys stand until their legs are tired while the mother of the girl would look at them from the edge of her eyes, and mumbles, "Mmmm Mmmm." When the boys have waited in vain, they go back talking to one another, "The mother of the girl seems not interested in this affair. Therefore, it would be good for us not to waste our time going back to her home. You should stop talking to this girl, she will waste our time."

If the suitor was in the first group which we saw earlier on, then courtship is now over because the girl loves the boy. What remains is getting the date for showing up oneself or the day for the actual marriage where the boy would take the bride wealth as we shall look at later in this chapter.

There is nothing here on earth that we can compare with the love of a woman or a girl. When a woman tells a man, "I love you" it is true that she loves the man from the bottom of her heart. For this reason, first, when the girl has loved the boy, when is asked to walk on water, she can walk on water, because she has much love for the man. Secondly when the girl has already given her heart to the boy, even other men were also courting her, she will not accept any of them. This is because everything that the boy is telling her sounds very nice in her ears, and would also see everything that the boy does as good to her. Thirdly when a girl has already loved a boy, she can walk in a dark forest near their home without fear, even when on that hill is there is a lion or leopard. Fourthly, when a girl has loved you, she will be open to you and tell you all that is in her mind and heart. In addition to that, a woman who loves her husband would not want any problem to occur to him. She can easily lick the body of her husband with her lips. The madness of love that is in women sometimes would make them not be able to differentiate between bad and god things said by the man. In the beginning of their love, even when the man quarrels with the woman, she would try to contain and hold her love for the man. This is the behavior of women to men (Harvey, 2009, PP, 20-21).

What shows that a man loves a woman?

In Acholi there are many things that can prove if the boy really wants the girl for marriage, but I am not going to say all of them in this book. What I want the readers of this book to understand is that, a researcher on love affairs discovered that women say that the much they love men is the same way they feel men should love them. If you ask a black woman, a white woman, a coloured woman, "What is love?" she will tell you that I do not want my husband to be flimsy lover. My husband should not be hard with money. I want a man who can say in public that *this is my wife whom I love with all my heart.*

However, a researcher on love relationship between men and women says that men cannot love women the way women love them because the kind of love women have is different from men's. Research revealed that even if a man loves a woman, he cannot keep calling her after every half an hour. This does not mean the man does not love the woman, he does. Even if a man does do things as his lover expects, he still loves her. There are three things that when a man does, shows that he loves a woman. First the man who wants to marry a woman should tell his friends and his clan members about is relationship with the woman. This is what the white man calls introduction.

Secondly, in the olden days, a man who wanted to marry a woman would buy for her a bungle for the woman's hand, but today a man buys a ring for the woman's finger of the left hand. The man also brings foodstuff and gives money and other things to the woman. The money helps the woman to buy things she wants in the house. The Acholi culture has it that it is the work of the man to bring everything the woman wants in the house. A man who takes care of his home is usually proud In Acholi, we call this kind of responsibility, helping the woman when she has problems so that famine does not enter the house. Therefore the work of Acholi men who are at home is to cultivate crops, hunt for animals, gather bee honey and buy clothes for his wife and children. However, the work of Acholi men who are in foreign lands is to look for jobs in factories and offices so that he gets money to feed his family, rent a house, pay school fees, buy medicine if one member of the family is sick. A responsible Acholi man, who can take care of his family, does not handle money carelessly. He does not waste money on lecherous woman outside his marriage. He does not waste money on alcohol. A man can go to drink in a bar when he knows the condition at home is okay. A responsible man uses his money to make sure that his wife and children do not suffer and they do not sleep hungry.

A man who loves his wife, protects her and their children against the attack by fierce wild animals. Hence, one of the demands of Acholi culture is that a man should protect his family against danger. There is no Acholi man who allows anybody to play with his mother or his wife. If anybody tries to do that, the man will fight him instantly. Acholi elders say that a man learns the responsibility of protecting life and family right from the time he suckles. Most of the time, boys do not think that their mothers can make mistakes. That is why they pick a bone with anyone who disturbs their mothers. Some people say a male child learns to protect life when he is still in the womb. Fourthly, if a man receives a woman's phone number and fails to call her for one or two day, it can be concluded that he wants to just sleep with the woman. However, if a man receives the phone number of a woman and calls her in one or two day, it means he really wants to marry the woman. He is looking for a woman who could help him look after his home or family (Harvey, 2009, PP, 80-82).

A man does this to please his wife because the four factors we have looked at above are the things that bring happiness and good life in marriage. To add on to that, readers need to know that Acholi men are not the same. There are men who are responsible and there are those who are not. Similarly, there are women who can take care of their marriage very well, and there are those who cannot. Those who cannot are the women who love the man because of his material wealth. A woman who 'loves' a man because of his money or material wealth can be referred to as *sugar mammy* or *gold diggers*. In Arabic they are called *dul barit* and in Acholi they are called "*ka jony*" or "*dako abal kari*". A man who marries a sugar mummy should know that when he loses money from his hands, the woman will definitely live him and go to another man who has money. In Acholi culture, the man is to provide everything his wife needs in the house. This usually happens with the Acholi who are at home, but to those who are in the foreign lands, it may be hard to provide everything in the house because life in those places is different from the life led at home. At home people drink free water, but in the foreign land water is bought, even responding for calls of nature are paid for. The only free thing in the foreign land is the air that God provides. So, I want to advise the Acholi women and other African women who are in foreign lands that they should not think that it is only the work of a man to bring food and money in the house. The world in which we live today is different from the world of the past. The tradition may not hold today because things are changing. Today a woman can get office job and earn money that can bring money and food in the house. The Acholi said it rightly, "One hand cannot open the anus." At this time, a man may not protect his wife from adversaries only, but he can also help her by advising her, helping her in coking and carrying a child. I am an Acholi who is aware that the Acholi culture does not allow Acholi boys and men to cook, but I see that there is nothing an Acholi man loses when he has engaged in cooking or preparing tea. It will never change him into a woman. He will remain a man as

God created him. Most Acholi men do not like taking their wives to shops to buy for the party wears or wears for other occasions, but a man can go together with his wife for a public meeting (Harvey, 2009, PP, 25-27)

What shows that a woman loves a man?

There are three things that show that a woman loves a man. The first is supporting the man at times of problem. Secondly, the woman opens up to the man so that he knows everything in the mind of the woman. Thirdly, she offers the man her body. There is no man on earth who does not like sex. There is nothing in this world that is better than sex. A man can walk together with a woman, holding her hand, he can touch the woman when they are together, but what makes a man feels very close to a woman is sexual intercourse. A man who says sex is not important in marriage tells a lie. Men love to sleep with women just as they like inhaling air for life. For this reason, if a woman refuses to sleep with her husband for many day will find that her husband has gone to look for other women outside the home (Harvey, 2009, PP 41-44).

Some Acholi men would begin having sexual intercourse with their wives, two weeks after delivery. Other things that show that a woman is in love with a man is that she gives the waist beads to the man she loves, and the man would use the beads for hanging his horn on his neck. But modern girls and women now a day give a handkerchief that is properly designed, with perfume properly sprayed on it to men. Why do women and girls give handkerchief to men? The word "handkerchief" in Acholi means "think about me." A girl or a woman gives a handkerchief to a boy or a man to make him remember her or to make him think about her.

When a girl or a woman has already acknowledged the boy's love, they will come to marriage. Courtship does not end simply because a man lives with his wife under the same roof. Courtship is done every day because the man does not want to hurt his wife. The woman also does not want to annoy her husband. Before the day of marriage is appointed, the girl prepares *kwete* and invites the boy to their home. When the boy receives this invitation, he becomes as happy as a sheep that has given birth to female. This is one way of strengthening love. Sometimes there would be no ample space for the girl to relax with her boyfriend at her father's home. She then takes the brew to the boy's house in the evening at around 3:00pm or 4:00pm. Aware that his girlfriend is bringing *kwete* in his house, the boy invites his friends whom they used to go together for courtship at the girl's home. After that good time, the friends would go back while the girl sleeps there at the boy's place and goes back at dawn. She begins visit the boy to have good time as they have premarital sex without the knowledge of the parents, but one of her close friends may know what is going on between them. Acholi girls usually sleep together with elderly women in their house. She tells her friend about her visit so that when she is coming back at dawn, her friend would open for her the door. When a girl comes back from the visit and found her friend is dead asleep, she enters through the narrow gap left next to the door shutter. When the girls in the house lean that one of them is going for such visit, they do not tell their brothers or the parents. Girls do it that way because all of them are the same. They do it that way because they find it useless to expose your friend out, when you will also do the same mistake because if you exposed your friend today, tomorrow she will also expose you outside.

How can a man differentiate between a marriageable woman and unmarriageable woman?

Searching for a woman who can keep her house is not a simple work to men, because women are of two kinds: those who want to get married, and those who do not want to get married, or want or do not want to take care of the children if they have children. Acholi men search for women who want to be settled in their house. This does not mean that some men do not also search for women for passing time. When a man wants to get a woman who wants to settle in her house, he should also know how to look for such women. When we see in the western world, we find that there are some people we go at the river side fishing as a game, when he hooks one, later he will throw it back to the river or water. Such people are called "sport fishing people", in English. But when we look at Africa and other developing countries, we shall find that people who are there don't go fishing for sports, they go to fish for food (Harvey, 2009, PP, 71-72). What is important to us here is "keeping". There are some women and girls who give themselves to men or boys because they want to see how much they love them. A woman or a girl who gives her body in order to experience how love is, is the same with a man who has gone fishing, and after a catch, throws it back to the water, and doesn't keep it for food.

A woman or a girl who has this kind of life, the Acholi people say they are just for enjoyment of life only. They do not want to get married. Fortunately Acholi women who are at home (in South Sudan) cannot tell the man, "I want to stay with you temporarily," but when we look at Acholi ladies who are abroad in America, Australia, Canada, Europe, Britain and Norway, there is no shame in them, they can easily say I want to stay with you temporarily. In Acholiland there is nothing like temporal marriage. That is the life style of the whites that some Acholi want to adopt and make it theirs. There are some Acholi men who are not morally upright. When a woman tells such a man that she wants to live for him on contract, he will not refuse because that suits his interest.

But I want to tell readers that, in Acholi land there are some women who give their love and trust completely to a man because such women or girls are interested in marriage. So, it is a bit simple to differentiate between a woman who wants to be properly married and those who just want to enjoy life. First a woman who wants to be married usually does not easily declare her love for a man. For this reason, a woman usually knows better if she really wants to get married or not. A man may not know what is in a woman's heart. A woman, who gets the telephone of a man and doesn't give hers, usually is taken to be a woman who wants to be married, but women who get the telephone contact of a man and she also gives hers would be one of those who want to enjoy life. We can say, in short, that she is a woman hunting for men, not ready for marriage (Harvey2009, PP, 79).

Secondly a woman who wants to be married tells the man everything in her heart, but a woman who does not, often tells the man the contrary of what is in her heart. Thirdly, a woman who hopes for marriage, time and again, asks the man about their future life, but a woman who is not interested in marriage does not think about the future, she only minds of what to eat, and tomorrow finds its level.

How can a woman differentiate between a man who wants to marry and the one who does not?

There are so many things that can show a woman that the man truly wants to marry her or not. For this reason, I am not going to write everything in this book, but I am going to help our future Acholi children and state four things that could help a woman tells whether the man is interested in marriage or not.

a. A man, who tells the truth to a woman, is a man who is interested in marriage, but a man who is fond of telling lies to a woman is not interested in marriage.

b. A man who likes listening to his woman's advice and uses it is interested in marriage, but a man who is fond of refusing advices of the woman, is not interested in marriage. The man may only be interested in sexual relationship.

c. A man, who deceives his wife that he is going to buy something from the shop yet he is going to sleep with another woman, is not a good man who wants to get married. But when a man says he is going to a friend, and he truly goes there, that is a man who loves the woman and wants to get married. This is the type of men worth marrying.

d. A man who ask the woman, time and again, when he should be introduced to the parents of the woman, loves the woman and wants to marry her, not a man who tells the woman to forgive him because there is no time to introduce himself to the parents or the clan members of the woman (Harvey,2009,PP, 81-83)

It is very simple to handle men. When a woman asks the man to do for her everything that she likes, the man tries his best to do it because he wants to make the woman happy. What Acholi women, like other women, want is that the man should tell her the truth, and should not like sleeping with prostitutes. Harvey in his book "Act like a Lady, Think like a Man" says in Europe, a man can ask the woman whether he can have sex with another woman (Harvey, 2009, PP, 121), but in Acholi, such ideology does not exist. A man cannot ask his wife to have sex with another woman. What is it that this woman does not have? When a man says such things to his wife, it would also means that he is despising his wife. All women have the same vagina. There are very few Acholi women who usually push for their marriage. I got many women who also do not want to know, from men before marriage, what they would do for them in future. Many Acholi women do not asked such questions because they fear asking such a difficult question to a man. Some women think that when they ask questions, their marriage might break. This brings us to one question, "What should a woman do to remove fear from the heart?" A woman who wants good life should not fear to ask the man she intends to marry. There are four questions that a woman can ask before their marriage, and these are:

(1) *Young Boy, what do you want to do in the next one month, or year?*

Such a woman asks such a question after they have been in love for at least three or six months. This question means the woman wants to know if the boy is going to introduce her to his parents. The man's response can show to the girl if the man is interested in marriage or not. A man who does not know what to do in one month or one year of relationship, is not a good man for marriage. A good man usually introduces himself and shows what he intends to do for his future.

(2) *What are you doing after the three or five years?*

In the next three or five years, a good man thinks of what he will do to avoid hunger from shaking up their marriage. Acholi boys who are in the village will say he will dig hard to get good yields that may bring him money. A boy, who lives in town, would say he would likes to study hard so that tomorrow he can get good job that earns him some money. Acholi elders used to say that a man who does not think of what he should do to get money after three or five years, may not be able to keep his family well. He may make his family members suffer hunger. A woman who wants to get settle, like other women, should look for a man with good bright future plans. Every time a girl or a woman asked her man this kind of questions, and he does not respond to, means the boy may have an ill-feeling that he does not want the girl to know. Elders usually say, you can trap a person by what he says. Acholi boys learn how to keep their homes from the arena where they used to play as we have seen earlier on. But people like Harvey (2009) say, a boy starts to learn about women from his mother. A boy who loves his mother will also love his mother when he gets married. On the other hand, a boy also learns how to take care of his family from his father. A boy who likes staying near his father learns many things (Harvey, 2009, P, 139). This is one thing that the Acholi people say, a hard working man would also produce a hard working boy or child, but if a man is lazy, his son would also be a lazy boy. This is not for boys only, it is also happens to girls. If a girl whose mother is hard working keeps her house well, Acholi elders say that a daughter of a hard working woman will also be hard working and will take care of he own house. But if a girl whose mother is lazy, she would also be lazy and unable to take care of her house. This is the reason why some men despise some women and say "Your mother has not taught you well. Why do you bring the laziness of your mother here?" or they say, "Leave the laziness of your mother back at your home." All this is said because of the irresponsibility of the mother of the girl.

(3) *What do you think about me?*

This is a question that a woman should ask before their relationship has taken six months. The answer to this question is very important because it tells the woman whether the man is interested in marriage or not. A responsible girl can chart with her beloved, but the most important thing she wants to know from the boy is, "What does the boy think about her?" The boy, on the other hand, is interested in finding out if the girl is responsible enough to take care of a family.

(4) *What do you feel about me?*

In this question, I do not want readers to use thought and feeling interchange-ably because there are two different words. If a boy cannot tell the girl what he feels about her after two months, it indicates how he treats the girl. He does not want to take the girl serious. He only wants to fulfill his body desire. We may say the boy does not love the girl – he is not interested in marriage. The answer the girl wants to hear is "   I am always unhappy if I do not see you. I wonder what you do at father's home. When I see you like this, I am happy like and ewe that has given birth to a female – you are the kind of woman I have been looking for." All these show the girl that the boy is interested in marriage and he loves her. Secondly, this kind of response usually causes happiness and smile to the girl.

If a boy cannot answer these four questions, the girl should change her mind about him because he is not interested in marriage – he is just wasting the girl's time for nothing. I want to say that a girl should ask these four questions before she is fully in love with the boy, or before going to bed with the man. A girl who accepts to sleep with a boy within the first one to five weeks of their courtship, yet she has not yet understood the stand point of the boy, is at fault. This is because there is nothing that proves that the boy wants to marry her. The boy can desert her any time. For this reason, a woman who sleeps with a man without proving his intention should not blame anyone else but herself. I do not want to say that all women who accept to have sex with men in the first week of their relationship are not married by the men. It can happen, but very few people among Acholi can do that. What I want to tell our girls is that they should have enough time to know each other, so that if it comes to elopement or payment of bride price, everyone should say, "This is the woman or man I have been looking for." I want to tell the girls of today that they should be careful with their body because men like a woman who respects her body. A girl who respects her body often finds a responsible man. A girl offers her body to a man when she has found out that the man is interested in marriage. However, there are girls who think that if a boy does not sleep with a girl, the boy will look for another girl to sleep with. That is why some women offer their body to a man in the first week of their relationship. The secret that most girls and women do not know is that, if a girl refuses to sleep with a boy, the boy will consider her a responsible woman – a girl whose mother properly educated. If women knew this, they would not sleep with men before knowing their intension in the relationship. Secondly, the possibility of sex is in the hands of the woman. If she refuses, the man cannot force her. Acholi call that action a raid. The Acholi culture does not allow raid.

Sometimes some women think narrowly that if they sleep with a man, wash their clothes, if she bares a child or cooks for the man, the man will not leave her, neither will he tell her lies. This is not true because all men tell their wives lies in different ways. Some men sleep with other women even if they have wives at home. Some men also do not tell their wives how much they earn at work. However, not many Acholi women sleep with men other than their husbands. Very few of them do so, and most of them are women who are not given enough money in the house. Women are always aware that sex comes with conception, but men do not think the same way. A man sleeps with a woman and washes his body, and it cannot be told that he has done anything. Sleeping with a woman, to some men, is like just purging their sexual lust. So, it does not mean that when a man sleeps with a woman then he loves her and wants to marry her. A man can love his wife, children and the kind of life his wife has brought in the house, but such a man still goes to sleep with other women outside. This does not mean anything to man.

The secrets of boys and girls

After six months or a year, a girl reveals her relationship with a boy to her mother. The Acholi culture prohibits a girl from telling her father about her love life. It is her mother who tells her father about it. When it is ripe for the mother of the girl to tell her husband about the love life of their daughter, in the evening when people have gone to bed, and the man is now eating his special meal, the mother of the girl draws close to him and tells him, "Father, there is something I want to tell you. We know that all Acholi girls shine on the other side of the river (meaning girl can get married in any village, region or country). I think it is proper for a girl to find a place where she can settle. What I want to tell you is that, last week my daughter told me that she is in a relationship with the son of _____ (gives the name of the father of the boy). As the father of the girl, you should also know this. I have also been asking people and I found out that the family of the boy does not have poison to kill people, and they are not night dancers. I do not know, what do you think about the issue?"

Acholi culture tells us that when a woman talks to her husband in this way, the man listens to her. He briefly responds to his wife, "It is okay, Min Otoo. I have heard what you have told me. I am grateful to my daughter for revealing her secret to you. As you have said, I also know that the family of this boy does not have anything bad. There is nothing more I can say. We will wait to hear from the boy's father if the boy is interested in marrying our daughter. I am glad for the information."

The boy, on the other hand, tells his father about his relationship with the girl. Acholi culture does not allow a boy to reveal his relationship to his mother. It is to his father that the boy gives the information, and the father, in turn, tells his mother about it. In the evening, after his bed room meal, the father of the boy tells his wife, "Alright Min Atuk-tuk, Acholi said that it is very bad if a boy kills a person, but if he elopes with a girl, or asks for the hands of a girl, it is not bad. We do not know where boys usually go, and we do not know what takes them there. What I want to tell you is that, yesterday when I was resting at the bonfire on the compound, my son _____ (he calls the name of the boy) told me that he is asking for the hands of _____ (calls the name of the father of the girl). I think this girl can take care of her house. When I heard of this relationship, I asked myself if their house has poison for killing people, or if they are night dancers or evil-eye people. We also know that when a boy is fully grown, he needs to find a house. I do not know, as the mother of the boy, what you think about it?" In Acholi tradition, when a man tells his wife about this, she does not object to it because she knows that her husband has already accepted it.

The woman then respectfully responds to her husband, "Thank you my husband. I am glad for the information. I do not have any other opinion apart from yours." Parents usually discuss this kind of topic in their sleeping house.

The traditional Acholi liked elopement. Payment of bride price is a recent phenomenon as we will look at below here. Before we look at elopement and payment of bride price, let us first look at what they desire in the life of each other. These are the things a boy wants in the life of the girl:

1   A girl should love the work such as weeding, grinding millet and sorghum, cooking, washing clothes and keeping the house clean.
2   A girl should love the boy and his clan without any discrimination.
3   A girl who comes from a family without poison, night dance, evil-eye and theft.
4   A girl who does not like quarreling with people and her husband.
5   A girl should not be an adulterous.
6   A girl should be free of sicknesses such as tuberculosis, evil spirit, leprosy and other strong chronic diseases.
7   A girl should not be a drunkard.

A girl also wants to lead a good life. What she wants to see in the boy's life are these:

▶   A boy who like work such as digging, building, timber work, repairing bicycle, hunting and others.
▶   A boy whose family does not have poison, are not night dancers, evil-eye and thieves.
▶   A boy who does not discriminate the girl's clan from his.
▶   A boy with the strength to fight (to take care of the family) – a boy who is not a coward.
▶   A boy who respects his mother-in-law, father-in-law and other elders.
▶   A man who does not waste money on alcohol and other women outside, but one who dresses his wife and children and takes care of the family.
▶   A boy who minds about treating his wife and children.
▶   A man who minds about paying school fees of his children as demanded in the new generation.

As we have seen before, the boy courts the girl from the house of mother of the girl. Acholi culture does not allow courtship on the pathway or outside. But some Acholi boys violate this rule and they do their courtship on the way to water points, at grinding places on low rocks, on the way to the market, in the garden when chasing birds from crops and so on, and so on.

There are three kinds of marriage in Acholi (elopement, parents' agreement and payment of bride price). Before I explain the three kinds of marriage, let us first look at how the rain chief does his courtship. How does a rain chief court a girl?

THE RAIN CHIEF'S COURTSHIP

The courtship of the rain chief is different from the courtship between ordinary boys and girls. The chief does not court the girl he has admired face to face. Secondly, the chief does not court a girl from her father's home as Acholi tradition demands. In Acholi culture, the chief tells his guards, "You take that girl to my home because I want her to be my wife." That is what Acholi refer to as "ngato anyaka" (booking a girl). The guards now take the girl to the chief's home, and the girl does not resist or refuse the chief. This is also a source of pride to the girl, that the chief saw that she is a good woman. More importantly, she is more beautiful to the chief than other girls in the dance arena. Booking a girl by a rain chief does not only bring pride to the girl, but also to her parents, because they think their daughter has been chosen by the chief because of her beauty.

Figure 37: The rain chief books a woman in the dance arena

There are four ways for a chief to book a woman. They are:

First, if the rain chief feels love for a girl in the dance arena or in the market, he put a bangle on the hand of the girl. No boy now opens his mouth to court this girl who has a bangle on her hand. If a man begins to court the girl, it brings problem to all the subjects of the chief. If the chief learns that another man is wooing the woman he had already booked, he gets annoyed and makes the sun shine and dries crops in the gardens. When the sun shines, people will just know that someone has annoyed the rain chief. Maybe someone has insulted him or is courting his wife. People then ask, "What is wrong that the chief make it shines like this?" If people learn that someone is wooing a girl whom the chief has already booked, they send four or six people to the man. These men will quarrel with the man and later tell him to leave alone the girl whom the chief booked. When the chief has realised that the man has stopped courting the girl he booked, he immediately make it rain. If the man who is courting the girl does not listen to the men who were sent to him, the chief leaves the sun to shine until all the crops in the garden are withered. People do not support this kind of disrespect.

The second way a rain chief can book a woman is done at the dance arena, because in the olden days the chiefs liked visiting the arena where girls and boys danced. If he likes any of the girls, he immediately books the girl, and he tells his guards to take the girl to his home. Immediately after that, the rain chief sends his guards to the father of the girl to inform him that he has already booked his daughter. The Acholi culture has it that the girl that the chief books from the dance arena is the one who will be the queen.

The third way is where the chief does not meet the girl face to face. It is his subjects who book for him a responsible and hard working girl. The clan usually wants a woman who can host the chief's visitors even when the chief is not around. Later, the subjects inform the chief, "Chief, we have found one woman who can unite your people. We want this woman to be yours." When he receives this information from his people, the chief does not decline it. He welcomes the woman wholeheartedly.

The fourth way by which a chief books a woman is to choose a woman from another royal family. The woman then would be accompanied to the house of the rain chief, after which he pays dowry as required by Acholi traditional law that when a rain chief has a son and another rain chief from a different clan has a daughter, the father of the daughter may offer her daughter to the son of the other chief. This happens when there is friendship between the two chief parents. The Acholi history states that, in the olden days, children of chiefs married among them. The marriage is an arrangement between the father of the girl and the father of the boy, each father keeps reminding his child about the marriage as they grow up. These are the four ways by which a chief can book a woman in Acholi.

Elopement

Elopement is an arrangement between a girl and a boy who want to live in the house as husband and wife. This kind of marriage is ancient because most Acholi boys now like to pay bride price to the parents of the girl as we will see later. When the day for elopement has come, the suitor of the girl and three of his friends come close to the sleeping hut of the girls. The girl is also aware that the boy is coming for her today. If they have bicycles, the boys go on two bicycles to bring the girl home. One bicycle is used to carry the girl. If they do not have a bicycle, the boys go on foot to get the girl. The Acholi culture says that when the day for elopement comes, the girls also tell her close friend about it. Both the girl and the boys know where and what time they are supposed to meet. Most boys like stealing girls around 11:00 pm to 12:00 mid night. This is the time when many people are deeply asleep. The girl now picks two bed sheets, two tablet of toilet soap, shoes and two or three dresses and she makes for the boy's home. When it is time to go, the girl tells her friend to escort her on the way, and she leaves the house bare handed. It is the escorting friends who carry her luggage.

The boys, on the other hand, are eagerly waiting for the girl, and they keep looking at the road if the girl is coming at the appointed time. When the girls arrive; the boys greet them and thank the escort for accompanying her friend to the meeting point. Within a short time, the girl is on the bicycle carrier, and her suitor is carried on another bicycle. At this time, the girl who escorted her friend does not go back to the house immediately. She delays a little so that other girls in the house and the old woman (the owner of the house) think that she is still easing herself. Acholi elders told me that at this time of elopement, many a times, the boys of this home would be charting with their village girl near the girls' sleeping hut. So, the escort does not go to where they are. She goes straight to their sleeping hut. The other girls, although they have seen the girl return alone, they do not ask this girl where she has left her friend.

In the morning, the father of the girl waits for her daughter in vein. He does not say a word, but he thinks to himself, "It seems somebody's son has stolen my daughter. My daughter usually does not take this long in bed. She often comes out early to sweep the compound. It is okay; let us wait for what the sun will bring today."

After two or three day, the father of the boy sends a messenger to the father of the girl, and the messenger says, "Elder, I have come to deliver to you important piece of information. I would not like you to be afraid. If you have lost your little nanny goat, know that it has entered my goat pen." The father of the girl informs his brothers of the messenger's message. A few days after, they appoint the day they should follow their daughter. Before the appointed date, the father of the girl sends his messenger to the father of the boy with the information. At the girl's home, they select two boys and three clan elders to follow the girl.

When the father of the boy receives information from his friend (father of the girl) he informs his brother and they wait for the visitors with food, drinks and money to pay the fine for taking away the girl. In Acholi culture, on the first day when the family of the girl follows her, her father does not receive payments except a few which we will look at here. In the past, the fine levied for elopement was uniform for everybody. So, there was no negotiation at the time of payment of the fine.

Marriage affair was not discussed during the day or early in the morning, but it was done in the evening. The payment of elopement fine is not discussed in the house, but in front of the house. If it is raining, then they can do it in the house. Two boys and three elders enter the compound of the mother-in-law at 5:00 pm, but sometimes something may cause a delay. If that happens, they send one person ahead so that the appointed time is kept. Keeping time in marriage arrangement is very important. If the team of the groom does not keep time, they may be asked to pay fine. Most of the time the fine ranges from SL 500.00 to SL 1,000.00.

When the team family of the girl arrives, two or three girls receive them and spread for them animal skins to sit on. Acholi people like discussing elopement while sitting on antelope skin. Each of these people removes their shoes and left at the doorway as they go to sit down. Removing shoes from the feet is a show of respect. If the team of the boy enters with their shoes on in the house of the mother-in-law, the girls fine them SL 1,000.00 or more. Discussion does not begin immediately when the visitors have arrived. They are given time to take water. After a rest, the speaker of the boy's team sits next to the visitors, clearing his throat, Mmm mmm mmm, and asks the messengers, "Alright, our people. What brings you to our home? Is there an issue?"

An elder on the girl's side responds, "Yes, elder. We are your visitors. We learnt that our lost little nanny goat is with you here. We would like to see the nanny goat if it is with you."

The boy's team calls the girl, and she sits down. One of the elders asks her, "Where is the man who has corrupted your mind?" The girl just points at him without saying a word. Then the clan elders ask her to draw closer to see what her suitor will pay. The speaker of the boy now pulls out everything required for the fine and puts it before the messengers. Acholi history has it that the payments for elopement are as shown below:

·	Premarital sex fine	Ls 0.60.
·	A hoe (in kind)	Ls 0.00.
·	A ram (in kind)	Ls 0.00.
·	Mother's breast milk	Ls 5.00.
·	A bungle for the girl	Ls 0.00.
·	Acknowledgement of the marriage	Ls 5.00 or Ls 10.00.
·	A lump of pounded tobacco (in kind)	Ls 0.00.
·	Total	Ls 10.60 or Ls 20.60.

The money for elopement fine is not just given to anybody, it is for her parents. If both parents of the girl are dead, the brother of her father and his wife will take the money, as instructed by the father of the girl. Usually, the mother of the girl shares the LS 5.00 "breast milk" fine with her co-wife. If she does not have a co-wife, she uses the money alone. If the mother of the girl died and left her co-wife, the co-wife uses the money.

After paying the elopement fine, people now get to drink. Small calabashes swim in *kwete* like boats in the water. The team of the girl and the boy's are not allowed to mix easily with each other. For that matter the girl's team sits in one house while the team of the boy sits in another. The hosts select beautiful girls to serve the visitors food and alcohol. This is also a good opportunity for the boys who followed the girl to get girls for marriage.

When people are now tipsy with *kwete* and *waragi*, they begin to dance, and they dance until morning. As people dance, it is not allowed for the messengers of the boy to sleep. If one or two of them sleeps, the girls will dust them with millet flour or flour for making alcohol. The girls do this so that whoever sleeps will not deny it in the morning. In the morning the girls ask the man who slept at night to pay them some money. If he pays the money, the girls will bring for him water to wash his face. Acholi boys know this practice very well; so many people do not want to sleep during the marriage ceremony. If nobody from the boy's team sleeps, the girls will look for alternative way of getting money from them. So, they hide all the shoes that are left at the side of the house. When the time of departure for the team of the boy's side has come, everyone pays for his shoes. In the past, the payment for the shoes ranged from Ls 2.00 to Ls 5.00. But today it ranges from Ls 20.00 to Ls 50.00 – it is girls who charge these fees. Whoever does not pay for his shoes, goes back home bare footed. But Acholi men usually help one another. They raise money for whoever does not have it because they want to avoid insults and spitefulness.

At sun rise, before the people of the girl have not yet set out for home, they would instruct the girl to first go back home for blessing. After this, the girl will then return to her father's house after blessing. Shortly, the girl's team put billy goat in front of them and start marching towards their home, while the girl return to her father's home.

Before seven day, the girl asks her husband to allow her to go home for blessing ceremony. The moment she arrives at her father's home, the following morning elders slaughter the ram. The meat is prepared and eaten by both men and women. The water with which they washed their hands is sprinkled on the girl by elders so that God widely opens her way (this means, so that God bless her with fertility). This ceremony is very important to Acholi. If it is not done, the culture says, she will not bear children, and yet child production is very important in marriage. Two days after the ceremony, the girl goes back to her husband.

There are some Acholi who demand that on the day of paying elopement fine, the bride price should also be clearly stated, but other people are opposed to the method. They say bride price is given when the boy is ready to pay it. This is because elopement is paid in the boy's home, but bride price must be paid in the girl's father's home. This is done one year after the girl has gone back to her husband. Acholi people give one year for the boy and her wife to find out if his wife can conceive. Secondly, it gives the boy time to assess if this girl is responsible or lazy. It is the father of the boy to inform the father of the girl that they want to bring the bride price, and he suggests the day that his people will bring the payment. If the father of the girl has waited for the report of the father of the boy for long, he can remind him about the marriage, but he does not give them the day they should come to the home of their mother-in-law. This is because the father of the girl does not know whether the father of the boy has the bride price or not.

On the day of the marriage ceremony, both the clan of the girl and that of the boy converge on the compound of the mother of the girl. In the old days, bride price was not high. It was between pounds/LS 20.00 and 25.00. In Acholi tradition, chiefs pay slightly higher bride price than the ordinary people do. The chief pays between Ls 30.00 and Ls 50.00. There are men who can pay all the bride price at once, but there are also those who cannot. The father of the girl receives any amount of money brought on that day, and the father of the boy pays what is left later. What will be paid later is put in writing, and both the father of the girl and the father of the boy receive a copy of the document.

Some men may not be able to pay all that has been asked for. As the Acholi people say, marriage is a rubbish pit. If this man has a daughter, and when the daughter is married later on, he can use the bride price to finish paying the bride rice of the mother of the girl, because the girl's mother was not fully married. This is where Acholi people say, "A girl marries her mother."

Even if he has completed marriage, the boy can still take firewood to his in-laws when his mother-in-law or father-in-law is sick. He also buys all the medicine prescribed by doctor, all this goes on account of marriage.

The Acholi culture says that the bride price should not be rendered useless; it should also bring a woman in the house. This means the brother of the girl should use his sister's bride price to pay the bride price of his wife. This is why the Acholi culture says, "A girl marries a girl."

Long ago, Acholi girls did not get pregnant before they were married. The practice of girls getting pregnant from the house of their parents is a recent development in Acholiland. The Acholi people looked at pregnancy outside marriage as a source of insults to the family and the whole clan. This is one thing that all Acholi of Sudan do not want to hear. This does not mean that no Acholi girls get pregnant from the house of their parents. When I asked some Acholi elders, they told me that some Acholi girls also get pregnant from home, but this earns their parents insults. The moment a girl is impregnated outside marriage, she is sent to live in the home of the person responsible for the pregnancy until she delivers. The tradition also has it that no bride price should be paid when the girl is still pregnant, but some Acholi people go against this customary law and receive elopement fine because they say elopement fine is not bride price. After the girl has delivered, she is to be returned to her father's home, and she remains at home until her husband pays her bride price. When the boy is ready with the bride price, he has to follow his wife and arrange for the payment of the bride price. But if the boy is not interested in marrying the girl, the tradition sets the girl free to look for another man.

Courting divorced women is a problem in Acholiland. The boys who are not skillful in courtship usually go for divorced women because they are easy to court. The tradition wants a married man, not a boy, to marry a divorced woman because she is already mixed up with the teaching of another man whom she divorced. Boys should marry girls because teaching girls is easier since they have not yet listened to the teaching of another man. This is one reason why Acholi men who marries divorced women find life in the house hard. They do not know why the first or the second man left the woman. This experience is in keeping with the Acholi proverb, "If you carry a log that some-one dropped, you may drop it soon because it may be infested with ants." If you marry a divorced woman, it may not take long before you divorce her, unless death comes to one of you before divorce. The woman will do what she did to her first or second husband to her new husband. Some men marry women based on their beauty not because of her moral uprightness – this is bad. In Acholi, some men do not want elopement, they are interested in parents arranged; let us now look at how parents arranged marriage is done.

Parents arranged Marriage
The history of Acholi states that, long ago, other ethnic groups such as Lotuko, Imuruk, Lokoro and Lango of Uganda fought Acholi. Acholi people also had

internal fights among themselves. These internal and external conflicts made it difficult for boys to go far away from home to look for girls to marry. Acholi culture condemns bachelorhood. So, if the father of the boys realises that finding a girl to marry is now difficult for his son, he looks for a girl from among the daughters of friends. When he finds one, he tells his friend, "Well my friend, I thank the Creator for giving you a girl child. Since we are good friends, I request you to spare this girl for my son." Because of the good friendship, the father of the girl does not object to this request.

The father of the girl then reports to the mother of the girl, "Well, my wife, my friend _____ (he calls the name of his friend) requested for the hands of our daughter for his son. We are well aware that, in Acholi tradition, a girl is not booked twice." This usually happens in Acholiland, especially when the children are grown ups, and they had been playing together during childhood. *Otong-kak* (marriage arrangement) is done by parents of the boy and parents of the girl, and they keep it a secret.

When he sees that his daughter is now plump, the father of the girl sends his daughter with *kwete* to the father of the boy. Long ago, a girl would not refuse her father's errand. She delivers the *kwete* to the father of the boy. The homes of the two parties were often close to each other.

Figure 38: Girl sent with kwete

At this time, the boy is ripe for marriage but has no interest in the girl because he does not know the arrangement going on between their parents. His father receives *kwete* from the girl, drinks it and the girl returns to her father's the home. The girl takes *kwete* to the man four or six times. After this, the father of the boy talks to his son, "Child, you have seen the girl who has been bring for me *kwete* the last four or six months?" The boy responds, "I saw her, father." His father now reveals to him the secret arrangement he has with the parents of the girl, "Yes, child, that is your wife."

The boy bows to his father to show respect to his father – he does not say a word. Bowing, in Acholi, does not mean a show of respect, but also shows that the boy has accepted his father and the father of the girl. The woman who grew up in the locality and is married in this manner is referred to as *"Daa-kac"* (a woman of the place). The father of the boy has to meet all the payments required in the marriage of *Daa-kac*. The Acholi culture does not prohibit a boy from marrying another woman if he wants to, because in Acholi, a man can marry two or more women as we have seen with Chief Kassiba of Obbo. But it is the boy himself to pay the bride prices of the subsequent women after the first. That is one thing that makes Acholi boys to seriously take to digging to get bride price.

After talking to his son, and he is sure of the availability of the bride price, the father of the boy informs the father of the girl of when they want to pay the bride price. When he receives this information, the father of the girl prepares *kwete*, *waragi* and food for the visitors. He also invites his brothers to come and attend the marriage ceremony. In addition, the man instructs his daughter not to go far away from home that day.

MARRIAGE CEREMONY

On the marriage ceremony, the father of the girl gives the messengers a young billy goat and a *lojili* hoe. In Acholi culture, the team of the messengers comprises six to eight men and seven women. The team of the boy enters the compound of the mother-in-law at around 6:00 pm. They do not enter straight to the compound. They stand at the edge of the compound and the girl to be married receives the goat and the hoe from their hands, and ties the goat at the side of her mother's house. She puts the hoe under the spiritual pot of her mother. This is how the girl shows her clan that she acknowledges this marriage.

Figure 39: A girl tying a goat at the side of the granary

One man eventually invites the team of the boy to get seated. In Acholi of Sudan, if the girl has already taken the goat and the hoe, it means there is no problem, since the hoe and the goat have now entered the mother-in-law's house. After this, people begin to eat and drink. This is followed by dancing, especially when people are now tipsy. They dance up to morning. In the morning the girls serve the visitors with water to wash their face, and more alcohol to drink. After the merry making, the team of the boy returns home.

TAKING THE GIRL TO HER HUSBAND

In the Acholi tradition, the girl does not go to her new home immediately after the marriage ceremony, she first remains in her mother's house. After one month, her mother prepares four bundles of cleaved firewood, two bundles of grass for making fire, one tin of flour for brad, a cock, and two kilograms of salt, three bottles of cooking oil and other things necessary for her daughter. She then selects thirty girls to escort her daughter to her husband. The escorts are not just chosen anyhow, they must be hard working girls.

The mother of the girl now informs the father of the boy of the day her daughter and her escorts will go home. When the day finally comes, the thirty girls set out for the journey at 9:00 pm. The team travels at night because no one should see the girl who is being escorted to her husband.

The father of the boy, on the other hand, informs his son of the day his wife is coming. The boy now invites his friends and girls to come to welcome his wife, and they converge on the compound of the boy; the escorts arrives carrying firewood, grass, flour and cooking oil on their heads. One girl from the team of the boy receives the escorts and shows them where to put their luggage. After this, the girl also seats the escorts; they usually sit next to the hosting girls and boy's friends. On this day the bride does not sit among the friends of her husband. She chooses three or four girls with whom they go to the sleeping hut of her husband where the bed is dressed in white bed sheet. The bride and three girls don't sit alone in the sleeping hut. There are usually three or four boys in the hut.

The friends of the boy then begin to drink alcohol, and they begin to play with the escorts of the girl. They remain here up to cock crow before they retire to their sleeping houses. Before they retire home, they first distribute the visitors to where they will sleep. It is the tradition that the girls are given sleeping places close to the sleeping house of the boy (the groom). The following morning, the escorts are assigned some chores to do at the home of the mother of the boy. Some of them go to fetch water, others remain to grind millet and prepare food. The tradition does not allow the newly married girl to work when the girls who have escorted her are still at the boy's home. She just looks at things being done. The escorts do not use foodstuff from the boy's mother's house, they use what they have brought. They also use the firewood and grass they came with to make fire.

Boys again converge on the compound of the father of the boy the next evening, and the girls boil for them bath water, and they invite each of the boys to bathe. This goes on for three days or a week. This also offers the boys' opportunity to court the girls who are visitors. Elders told me that skillful speaker can find a marriage partner from among the visitors. After seven days, other girls go back home, and they leave behind one or two girls to help the married girl with work. These girls remain here for a month and go back home.

Payments for Marriage
Four or five months after, when the father of the boy has ascertaining that the woman is responsible, arranges for payment of the remaining marriage items as follows:-

1.	Premarital sex fee	Ls.00.60pt.
2.	A ram	Ls03.00pt (usually taken in kind).
3.	Mother's breast milk	Ls.05.00pt.
4.	Bride price	Ls.20.00pt.
5.	A lump of pounded tobacco leaves	Ls00.80pt (often given in kind).
6	Total	Ls.29,40pt.

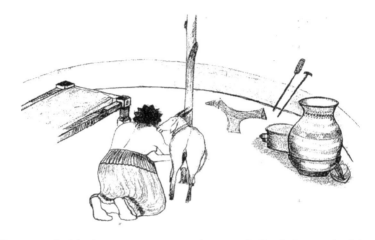

Figure 40: A girl tying a nanny goat on the central pillar in her mother's house

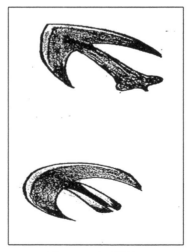

Figure 41: Lojili Hoe

516

The payment from the opening of the meeting used not to be there in Acholi. It came from the people of Madi and Bar. However, this is how Acholi, in the past, used to marry. Moreover, the marriage of rain chiefs was different from the ordinary marriage as I have described above. What payment does a rain chief make for the bride price of his wife?

THE MARRIAGE OF RAIN CHIEF

We have seen how a rain chief books a woman. This brings us to the question that how does the rain chief pay bride price after booking the woman? After booking the woman, the chief informs the father of the woman of the day he will send his messengers to him. On the day of the marriage, the chief selects two or three elders and two or three women to take the payments to the father of the girl. The payment by the chief is a little higher than that of ordinary people. They are as given below:

- ▸ Premarital sex fine.   Ls.00.60pt.
- ▸ A blood ram .Ls03.00pt (usually taken in kind).
- ▸ Mother's breast milk   Ls.05.00pt.
- ▸ Pounded tobacco leaves. Ls01.00pt (usually taken in kind).
- ▸ Bride price   Ls.40.00pt
- ▸ Total   Ls.49.60pt.

It is the woman who teachers her daughter

Marriage is an instrument of pride and show of wealth for the father of the boy. It is also shows the girl's sense of responsibility and the social life of her parents, because Acholi men do not want a careless and lazy girl. In Acholi tradition, a boy from a poor family finds it hard to get a woman to marry, just as it is to a lazy girl or a girl whose family has poison for killing people.

Acholi boys do not court girls who are too far away from their place. They look for girls whose parents they also know. They do this so that they do not face difficulty on the day of the marriage ceremony. As we have seen before, a girl does not marry a boy whose parents do not know her parents. How does a boy or a girl know the life of his or her beloved? I think we have answered this question before, but for the importance of the matter, let us revisit the question.

As we have seen before, Acholi boys like girls because of their being responsible. Girls also like boys who can take care of them. Even if a girl likes smartness, if she is not responsible, she finds it hard to find a man to marry.

Acholi girls listen to the teaching of their mothers. Most of the time, when the mother of the girl is together with her daughter, she gives her daughter different teaching about courtship, love and marriage life. Some women want their daughters to marry wealthy men, because when a girl is married by a wealthy man, part of the wealth may spill over to his mother-in-law to help her. However, if the girl marries a poor man, her family may also remain poor. To remember this phenomenon, one Acholi man from a poor family sang this song:

Anongo dako mo pwonyo nyare	I found a woman teaching her daughter
Ni pe iyee lacan	Don't marry a poor man
Anongo dako mo pwonyo nyare	I found a woman teaching her daughter
Ni pe iyee lacan	Don't marry a poor man
Lacan bene dano	The poor is also a human being
Lalonyo bene dano	The rich is also a human being
Dano ducu dano pa Rubanga	All humans are God's creatures
Pe iyee lacan.	Do not marry a poor man

This singer wants to tell Acholi woman who hold this view to change their view of life because all humans are created by God, and poverty is given by God. He also wants to say that Acholi people should not discriminate against the poor during marriage. The intent to marry should come from the heart of the boy and the girl who want to marry each other (because of love).

If we critically analyse the view of the women of Acholi of Sudan, we realise that they think that it is only the rich who are humans, and the poor aren't. They do not know why people are called man. It is not because of status of being poor or rich person. That is why the singer says, "The poor is also a human, the rich is also a human, and everybody is God's." In Acholiland people say, "A poor man is not a human being" because he does not take care of his house – this is a man who does not dress his wife and children well, does not feed them well, does not take them for medical attention and above all, he makes it easy for famine to enter the family's space.

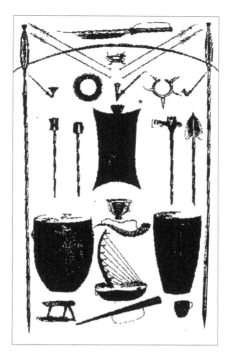

Figure 42: The Acholi Regalia

Chapter Thirty

MODERN COURTSHIP AND MARRIAGE

MODERN MARRIAGE

Handling marriage is confusing to the modern Acholi people because there is no unified rule to guide everybody in marriage process, unlike it was during the olden days. Bride price and other marriage related payments are different in different Acholi clans. For this matter, the father of the girl asks for as much bride price as he wants. I have discovered that there is no uniform bride price and other marriage payments in modern Acholi marriage. Every parent asks for any amount for the bride price of his daughter's bride price. I will not write all the differences in charging bride price in this book because that needs one full book of its own because every Acholi clan has its own charge. Otherwise, I will talk about the general charge which is the tradition of the whole Acholi of Sudan.

Traditional Acholi marriage and modern Acholi marriage can be categorised into four as follows:

(1) The marriage of a girl who stopped in Primary or Junior
(2) The marriage of a girl who stopped in Senior/University
(3) The marriage of a housewife.
(4) The marriage of a girl to a foreigner.

The bride price and other charges in the four types of marriages are different as we will look at them later in this chapter. The parent arranged marriage is absent in the modern marriage system, but boys still elope with girls as it used to be in the traditional time. However, today, we have discovered that man who wants to marry usually deliver dowry directly into bride's mother's house, nevertheless. It is important to note that both traditional and modern marriage starts with courtship and end with marriage ceremony. The boys of today do their courtship through letters though some of them physically go for courtship.

There are not many differences between the courtship of the modern boys and the traditional ones. As we have seen before, a girl tells her mother about her relationship with a boy after six months or one year. Traditionally, a girl is not supposed to tell her father about her relationship with a boy. She tells her mother and her mother tells her father about it. When it is time to tell the father of the girl about her love life, her mother waits until people have gone to sleep and her husband is eating the bed side meal (commonly known as *ogony-laa*), she draws close to him and says, "Father, I have something little to share with you. We all know that all girls in Acholiland get married overseas –that is getting married to another family. Even if that is what the tradition says, I think it is good if a girl finds where to settle. What I want to tell you is that, last week my daughter told me that she is in a relationship with the son of _____ (mentions the name of the father of the boy). As the father of the girl, you should know about this. I have been asking people and I discovered that the family of the boy does not have killer poison, night dancing or evil-eye. I do not know, what do you think about the matter?"

In Acholi tradition, when a woman tells her husband such issue, he listens to her. The man then responses, "Alright, Min Ageno, I have heard what you have said, and I thank my daughter for revealing her secret to you. As you have said, I am also aware that the family of the boy is clean. I do not have much to say, but we shall wait for information from the father of the boy if the boy is interested in marrying our daughter. Thank you for the information."

The boy, on the other hand, tells his father about his relationship with the girl. Acholi culture does not allow a boy to reveal his relationship to his mother. It is to his father that he gives the information, and his father, in turn, tells his mother about it. In the evening, after his bed room meal, the father of the boy tells his wife, "Alright Min Atuk-tuk, Acholi said that it is very bad if a boy kills a person, but if he elopes with a girl, or asks for the hands of a girl, it is not bad. We do not know where boys go, and we do not know what takes them there. What I want to tell you is that, yesterday when I was resting at the bonfire on the compound, my son _____ (he calls the name of the boy) told me that he is asking for the hands of_____ (calls the name of the father of the girl). I think this girl can take care of her house. When I heard of this relationship, I asked myself if their house has poison for killing people, or if they are night dancers or evil-eye people. We also know that when a boy is fully grown, he needs to find a house. I do not know, as the mother of the boy, "What do you think about it?" In Acholi tradition, when a man tells his wife about this, she does not object to it because she knows that her husband has already accepted it. The woman would then respectfully respond to her husband, "Thank you my husband. I am glad for the information. I do not have any other opinion apart from yours." As mentioned before, parents usually discuss this kind of topic in their sleeping house.

Other boys, who are raised by their mother's kin, reveal the secret of relationship with girls to their maternal uncles. When is now ready with everything required for marriage, the father or uncle of the boy sends a messenger to the father of the girl with a letter that indicates the day and time when they will go for the marriage ceremony. When he receives the message, the father of the girl calls his brothers and some clan members to discuss the message. In the meeting, they look at various things which include what is necessary for taking care of the visitors, and which girls should cook. The things that are required on the day of the marriage are food, *kwete* and *waragi*. They also establish who should chair the marriage ceremony, and the amount of money to be paid for the marriage.

On the day of the marriage, the boy's team enters the compound of the mother-in-law at the exact time they appointed. Before the team enters the compound, three or four girls then block for them at the door, they ask for money for opening the entrance – that is money for the door. The door would not be opened unless money is paid. It is the girls who charge the money for opening the door, which is between Ls.50,000 and Ls.100,000 (Australian dollar $500 or $1,000). The girls charge the amount for opening the gate according to the level of the wealth of the father of the boy. A boy whose father is poor may pay Ls50,000 ($500), but a boys whose father is rich can pay Ls 100,000 ($ 1,000). As I have said before, the practice of paying for the opening of the door was not in Acholi tradition; it later came into Acholi tradition from the people of Madi and Bar. It is said that the Acholi boys who intermarried with Madi and Bar were the ones who brought the practice into Acholi culture.

The boy and his father accompany the messengers to marriage ceremony to witness and listen to everything by themselves. When the team of the boy has completed the payment to open the door, the girls allow them to enter the compound. An aunt then shows the visitors to their seats which have been set apart from the hosting team's. The marriage ceremony in Acholi is usually held in the house of the mother of the girl. But elopement fine is usually paid in front of the bride's mother's house.

In Acholi, marriage ceremony is not discussed when people are siting on chairs, but they sit on animal skins (mat or papyrus mat if the are in foreign land like town or city). After the visitors have had a short rest, the messengers of the girl invite the girl to be near the team of the boy. The clan of the girl then selects two or three people who will act as messengers and they stay away from the negotiation group.

One messenger on the side of the girl tells the leader of the team of the boy, "Mmm Mmm! What brings you to our home? We are grateful for your coming." The leader of the boy's team responds, "Alright, elder. Today we are your visitors. We received the information you sent for us. That is why we are here."

Before they go far, a messenger of the father of the girl asks the girl, "Who is the one, among the people seated here, who has won your heart? The girl raises her head a little and points at the boy with her finger as she says, "He is there in _____" She indicates the boy with colour of his shirt or trousers the boy is wearing at the time.

The messenger of the father of the girl asks the boy, "Son of the elder from where did you meet our child?" The boy responds, "I got her from the house of her mother." This response is very important to the parents of the girl because if the boy says "I met the girl on the way," it is treated as contempt to the parents of the girl. This means this girl is a useless and she is a prostitute. Secondly, this response would also mean that the girl does not have both parents.

The messenger of the father of the girl continues to ask the boy, "Do you really want this girl to be your wife?" The boy answers, "I do." When they finish asking the boy, one clan elders asks the girl similar questions, "Where did you meet this boy?" The girl respectfully responds, "This boy found me at my mother's house here." The elder further probes, "Do you really want this boy to be your husband?" The girl answers, "I do."

The people in the audience carefully listen to the boy and the girl. When the elder has completed his question session, he turns to the audience and tells them, "There you are. You have heard everything that these two children have said with your own ears. We should all be grateful for this. Marriage is a traditional matter which unites people. We the people of the girl, have no objection for a girl who brings a man at home like this gives us pride. Not to waste time, you, our visitors show us everything you have come with on the animal skin (or on linen). We will look at other issues after seeing what you have brought. Thank you." The messenger then sits down.

A messenger of the father of the boy takes linen which is four or eight metres long and spreads on the floor. He counts the money on the linen or animal skin one by one. When counting this money, the notes or coins are not piled on top of the other. The money is counted when it is already dark and the lump of the mother of the girl is used to light up the house. But before the messenger finishes counting the money, one of the women on the side of the girl teasingly puts off the lump. She then tells the messenger, "It is dark, and how do you count the money? Bring your lump so that people can see the money you have brought."

Since all Acholi people know this kind of teasing, the messengers of the boy must have carried their own lump and paraffin. He then lights his lump immediately and continues to count the money. After finishing counting the money, he says, "Alright, our in-laws! These are the things we have brought." He then sits down.

If the messenger of the father of the boy forgets to carry their own lump, the messengers of the father of the girl ask them to pay for the lump, and it is usually not more than Ls150 ($ 50) before they continue counting the money. The light is not only for counting the money, but it has to be on until morning. The issue of lump was not there in Acholi tradition of marriage. People used to count money with the light of the fire in the hearth. The idea of lump and paraffin was copied from the people of Madi.

The two parties now discuss the money presented before them. If the boy, one time, insulted his mother-in-law, he pays a fine which is deducted from the money presented in the house. The fine of contempt to a mother-in-law is LS 1,000 – LS 2,000 or $ 250 – 500. If they deduct the money which is on the linen, they ask the leader of the boy's party to add more money. When people go for marriage ceremony, not only one person keeps the money. They distribute the money between two or three people to keep in their pocket. So, when a question of this kind arises, they know where to get the money from.

After levying the fine, the leader of the team of the girl's father is asked by the leader of the messengers of the father of the boy for permission to get out for a short time – they want to borrow money. Their leader calls one of the members who has the money to go with him on the way. The leader then asks his friend to give him the money that can replace the deduction made. He gives the leader the amount of money needed and they get back to the house. The leader then adds the money on the money on the linen and says, "Alright our people! I ran around and got something little. That is all I have."

The host checks how much money has been added and takes it if it is considered enough, but if they think it is not enough, they ask the head of the boy's team to add more money. If they ask them to add more money, the leader goes out together with one of his members who will pull out some money and give the head of the team. When the messengers of the father of the girl are satisfied with the money on the floor, they ask the girl to carry the money and put under her mother's pot. This indicates that the marriage has been accepted. The moment this is done, the aunt of the girl sounds yodel, and people outside just know that the marriage has been acknowledged.

Sometimes, some people may not be able to pay as much as the father of the girl wants. So, the messengers of the father of the girl tell the visitors to go back and top up the money. This often happens because different people have different views and interest in money. But there are parents who are not very mindful of money. Even if the money is little, they receive it and ask the boy to bring more later. This kind of parent usually thinks of the welfare of their daughter. However, some parents are money minded, and they are the kind of parents who chase away the visitors if the money is little. Refusing to receive the little money usually leads to the girl's pregnancy before she is married. When the money is rejected, the girl begins to visit her boyfriend so that she is impregnated. When she becomes pregnant, traditionally, she has to go to and live with her boyfriend.

When I was still in Sudan, many people grumbled about the rate of bride price among the Acholi people. As a result, Chief Otaviano Oyat Akut, who was a County Chief of Acholi, at that time, called a clan elders' meeting on 13/4/1991. The clan elders were from Magwi, Panyikwara, Obbo, Pajok, Omeo, Agoro, and Palwar -the meeting was held at Lologo Displaced People's Camp (Juba), and I also attended the meeting. The people who missed this meeting were the Ofirika. The meeting took five months. It ended on 18/10/1991. In the meeting, people agreed on different rates to be paid in marriage:

Girls who stopped in Primary/Junior

Members agreed that the marriage payment of a girl who stopped in Primary or Junior should be:

1.	Unwanted pregnancy fine	Ls.01,500.
2.	Mother's breast milk	Ls.00,500.
3.	Messengers' allowance	Ls0.0,150.
4.	The cost of interruption of education	Ls.03,000.
5.	Bride price	Ls.05,000.
6.	Total	Ls.10,150 .

It was also agreed that the bride price of girls who have not gone to school should be the same with that of those who stopped in Primary or Junior, but without interruption of education. Therefore, the total dowry for a girl who has gone to school has come to LS 7,150 as the LS 3,000 for interruption of education is excluded.

Girls who reached Secondary or University

Acholi elders take girls who have completed Senior Secondary, College and University to be mature enough for marriage. For that reason, they reduced the payment for school drop out for such girls. The bride price of the girls is also reduced. So, it was agrees in the meeting that the marriage related payment for the girls who have completed secondary education and university education be as follows:

1. Premarital sex fine   Ls.1,500.
2. Mother's breast milk   Ls.0,500.
3. Messengers' allowance   Ls.0,150.
4. Interruption of education Ls.1,000.
5. Bride price   Ls.5,000.
6. Total   Ls.8,150.

Housewife

In this meeting, the elders of Acholi of Sudan agreed that if a man asks for the hands of a woman who was married but has divorced her husband, the new man can marry her by meeting the following payments:

1.	Premarital sex fine	Ls.2,500.
2.	Wasting the time of the mother-in-law	Ls.0,500.
3.	Messengers' allowance	Ls.0,150.
4.	Bride price	Ls.5,000.
5.	A billy goat for blessing girls	Ls 0,025 (usually in kind).
6.	Total	Ls.8,175.

The meeting affirmed that if the divorced man had or had not completed paying the bride price, and then they share what the new man is paying with his father-in-law. But if the former husband had not paid anything, the money that the new man will pay all goes to the father of the woman.

The three kinds of payment we have seen above, the Juba meeting agreed that it should only apply to marriages between Acholi people only. Some Acholi children were also intermarrying with other ethnic groups, so the meeting set a different payment for marriage between Acholi children and other ethnic groups. When an Acholi daughter bares children with a foreign man, her children are not considered Acholi children, but nephews and nieces of Acholi. For example, if a boy from Madi, Loa marries a girl from Pajok in the house of Kapaa, their child calls Pajok her mother's kin and Madi his tribe. He does not call himself an Acholi. This is why we say a family tree may get distorted in this way. To Acholi people, though intermarriage with other ethnic group promotes unity, it also distorts the family tree. One other agreement reached in the Juba meeting was that when an Acholi girl, formally educated or not, gets married to a foreign man, the marriage payments should be as below:

The marriage of a foreigner and the marriage of uneducated girls

1. Premarital sex fine   Ls.10,000.
2. Mother's breast milk   Ls.00,500.
3. Messengers' allowance   Ls.00,150.
4. Bride price   Ls.35,350.
5. A sheep (for a housewife)   Ls.00,025 (usually in kind).
6. Total   Ls.46,025.

After the Juba meeting, people waited to see if the rules set would be put into practice, but nobody did. A man whose daughter is to be married, whose daughter's elopement fine is to be paid charges any amount of money that he wants. Eventually people began to take those who cannot pay the marriage or elopement charge before the chief. Acholi elders found out that the prices agreed on in the Juba meeting can only work before the chief. The father of the girl can charge any amount as he wants, and if the boy cannot pay it, the father of the girl now takes him before the chief so that he pays the amount the chief will ask him to pay according to the Juba agreement. The man then pays that amount as agreed in the 1991 agreement. I do not know why Acholi elders made these rules and later decided to make only work before the chief.

Parents find the amount of money paid before the chief very little, so in 1995 elders held a meeting to review the marriage rules set in 1991.

The 1995 Juba meeting was held under the chairmanship of Chief Otaviano Oyat Akut, and the members agreed that the marriage related payments should be as below:

The marriage of a foreigner and the marriage of a girl who stopped in Primary or Junior

1.	Premarital sex fine	Ls.30,000.
2.	Mother's breast milk	Ls.00,500.
3.	Messengers' allowance	Ls.00,150.
4.	Interruption of education (Primary – University)	Ls.20,000.
5.	Bride price (and ten goats)	Ls.150,000.
6.	Total	Ls.200,650.

The marriage of a foreigner and a girl who stopped in Senior/University

1. Premarital sex fine — Ls.30,000.
2. Wasting time of mother-in-law — Ls.00,500.
3. Messengers' allowance — Ls.00,150.
4. Interruption of education — Ls.20,000.
5. Bride price (and ten goats) — Ls.150,000.
6. Total — Ls.200,650.

The marriage of a foreigner and a housewife

1.	Premarital sex fine	Ls.30,000.
2.	Wasting time of mother-in-law	Ls.00,500.
3.	Messengers' allowance	Ls.00,150.
4.	Bride price (and ten goats)	Ls.150,000.
5.	Total	Ls.180,650.

In the 1995 meeting held in Juba, members emphasised that bride price, elopement fine, interruption of education of a girl should be uniformly charged. Members looked at the issue from the perspective of God and argued that, whether educated or not, a woman is a woman.

As time go by, we realise that members did not put the rules they agreed on in 1995 into practice. Like the 1991 rule, these were also practised only before the chief. This shows us that the Acholi of South Sudan cannot set rules that govern charging marriage related payments because every man looks at his daughter as his wealth; no one should play around with her.

However, a man who really wants to marry a girl will just do it in the house of the father of the girl without any doubt. But the boys who do not want to pay high bride rice, or is not interested in marrying the girl, usually takes the matter before the chief.

The Acholi tradition demands a man not to spend the bride price of his daughter anyhow. He can use some of the money, but should give out part of it as shown below:

- If the girl was raised by her uncle Ls.1, 500.00 for her upbringing will be paid to her uncle.
- If the girl was conceived outside marriage (and her mother was not yet married) her grandfather takes all the payments and he (grandfather) would give to the father of the girl Ls.1,500.
- If the woman was a housewife whose bride price was not fully paid, her father takes all the money and pays back what the former husband had paid.
- If the woman was fully married, her father receives the money and gives it to the man who had married her (It is usually the man to follow the case of his wife when she elopes with another man). If she had a

child or children with her former husband, her father gives some of the money to her former husband to pay for the children.

Acholi parents, as we have seen before, charge the bride price of their daughters and other marriage related payment the way they want. However, in Acholi customs, the following are things the father of the girl usually asks for:

1. Premarital sex fine.
2. Mother's breast milk.
3. Pregnancy fine (if the girl conceives from her mother's house).
4. Opening the door of the mother-in-law.
5. Messengers' fine.
6. Interruption of education (for educated girls).
7. Mother-in-law's dress or a table linen, without any red spot.
8. A lamp,
9. Paraffin for lighting the lamp
10. Laundry soap
11. A lump of pounded tobacco.
12. Match box.
13. Arrows (only for the people of Panyikwara).
14. A family goat (if the woman elopes when she has a child).
15. Bride price in terms of 10 – 15 goats (in kind.
16. Other goats for bride price 5 – 8 (in terms of money Ls.2,500).
17. Aunt's goat (either in king or in shillings).
18. And the total amount.

The total money the father of the girls would ask was Ls.21,882, but this time the total amount of money required is Ls.3,000,000 – tis is what chiefs and other Acholi elders do not support because the amount charged scares the boy. To better understand the difference between the olden day marriage and modern marriage, let us turn to how marriage has successively changed from 1900 – 1995. The changes are as follows:

THE MARRIAGE CHARGE IN ACHOLILAND.		
1900 — 1932	1933 — 1963	1964 — 1995
1-Premarital sex fine	Premarital sex fine --	Illegal ex with a married
Ls.0.10 – 60	Ls.0.60 – 3.000 Opening	woman--- Ls.3,00
2-	the door-- Ls.0.02	Pregnancy fine Ls.3,00
A billy goat	– 1.000 Wasting time----	– 50,000 Clan ----Ls.1,00
-----------	Ls.0.03 – 5.000	— 10,000 Wasting time-----
3-	The sitting skin —	Ls.5,00 — 15,000
Wasting time Ls.0.01	Ls.0.01 –	Messengers'--Ls.1,00 — 10,000
.03	1.000	Interruption of education
4-	Soap---- Ls.0.00 – 0.010	Ls.2,50 -150,000 Linen------ Ls.
Bride price Ls.5.00 –	Arrows----- -----------	500-5,000
20.00	Goats (10 – 25) -------	Lamp------Ls.0,50 — 3,000
5-		Paraffin--Ls.0,20 -1,000
Tobacco -	Aunt's goat---- ----------	Soap 2---Ls.0,01 — 0,250
----------	Tobacco ---- ----------	match box----Ls.0,01 -0,060
Premarital sex fine	Bride price Ls.20,00	Arrows------- -----------
Ls.5.11 – 20.90	– 100.010	Goats-Ls.0,16 — 225,000
	Total -Ls.21,20– 110,010	Aunt's goat Ls.0,02 -8,000
		Family goat--------------
		Bride price- Ls.100,00-300,00
		Total Ls.124,00 – 794,810

A table showing changes in marriage in Acholiland

The amount of money charged on marriage is on the increase. It is increasing by at least 20% after every decade. This brings us to the end of courtship and marriage in Acholiland. However, there are other Acholi marriage traditions. Fortunately, this does not deal with money. That is why I have not said anything about them. This does not mean they are not important. This is mainly concerned with marriage between clans-mates, the marriage of a bustard girl, the marriage of twin girls and how to cleanse children. I cannot conclude my writing, in this book, without writing something about this issue. Let us look at marriage between clans-mates, marriage of a bustard girl, marriage of twins and cleansing children.

Marriage between clans-mates

Acholi tradition prohibits marriage between members of the same clan, but because of little knowledge of the tradition, some Acholi girls and boys marry members of their own clans. Most of the time, this kind of marriage happens when elopement and pregnancy happens when parents have not been consulted about the relationship. When this happens, it is recommended that the parents of the two parties discuss how to separate them. Unfortunately, today girls and boys do not mind much about clan and tradition. They are more particular about beauty. That is what influences the love of a boy or a girl toward the other. Secondly, this removes the power of their parents to separate them. When the parents of the two parties realise that they cannot separate them, they leave them to go ahead and marry.

If the boy and the girl agree to go ahead with the marriage, elders then have to appease the ancestors and please the clan elders who are still alive. The father of the boy provides a sheep to cleanse the boy and the girl. Thus, for the success of the marriage the father of the boy gives the ram to two elders in the family to kill and skin. After skinning the sheep, the elders put the raw liver of the ram in a small tray and place it before the boy and the girl. One of the elder instruct the girl to put the liver into the mouth of the groom and the same elder also instructs the boy to put liver into the mouth of the bride. Customarily, it is the girl that starts this process and after they have finished, they both take their seats.

The women in the clan quickly cook the mutton for the clan elders. Traditionally, it is the nephew who eats the head and legs of the ram slaughtered for the traditional rituals. Other clans do not eat this food, but women prepare for them alternative dishes such as antelope meat.

After eating and washing their hands, the elders call the boy and the girl to sit down in front of the house of the boy's mother. The elders then sprinkle the water in which they washed their hands on the two. The water is the elders' blessing on the children against the wrath of the tradition on them – to also unite them as husband and wife. The clan elders allow them to consider their kinship distant. The elders cut the neck of a vase and put on the pinnacle of the house of the mother of the boy to unite the boy and the girl. This indicates that clan elders have endorsed the marriage. The father of the boy now makes the marriage payments as levied on him. However, if the elders see that the kinship between these two people is too close, then after eating, they separate them – no marriage.

The marriage of a bastard girl

A child who is conceived before his father has properly married his mother is called a bastard in Acholi. A child of this kind, by tradition, belongs to his mother's kin, and it is their mother's kin who take their bride price. The father of such a girl can take the premarital sex fine because the payment is related to raising the child. The rest of the payment goes to the girl's mother's kin. This payment does not belong to the girl's father, but her mother because the father of the girl did not marry the girl's mother.

If a man has two or three bastard girls, he takes the bride price of the other two daughters because the bride price of the first one marries their mother. The Acholi tradition says that the girls' mother's kin take only the first girl and the rest are their father's. If all the three girls are raised by their mother's kin and they get married from the hands of the mother's kin, their father does not get anything from the bride price. But if the girls' mother's kin are good people, they give the father of the girl premarital sex fine and the bride price of one of the girls.

Acholi tradition recognises the fact that a girl brings wealth home and a boy takes wealth away from home. In Acholi, it is not only girls who are considered bastards but also boy. This means when a boy is old enough for marriage, it is his father who marries for him. But a boy who grows at his mother's kin will get bride price his uncles. The Acholi say, "Whoever is raised by his mother's kin will marry for him."

The marriage of twins

Most often, twins are born a boy and a girl, but sometimes they may be both of the same sex. When the twins are of the same sex, it is said that the first boy or girl to be born is the one to get married first or be married first. Even if the second of the twins has got someone to marry, he or she cannot go ahead to marry her if the first of the twins has not yet married.

If the first of the twins (Opiyo) has got a girlfriend, he reports to his father and his father presents the twins with a white or black billy goat before the god. On the day the father of the twins is performing the rituals on them, clan elders converge in his home. In the morning, Opiyo and Ocen sit in front of the family shrine, and their father moves round them two or three times, with the billy goat in his hand. As he does this, he says, "There Chief! I have brought your children before you. Bless them. Open the future of this child who wants to get married, and let his future be bright."

On the other hand, if the child who wants to get married is a girl (Apiyo), she tells her mother about it, and her mother tells her father about it. It is not the father of the girl to provide the goat for the rituals. He sent a word to the father of the boy to bring either a white or a black billy goat for the rituals. Apiyo's father invites clan elders to the blessing ritual of his daughters. The man moves round the twin girls with the billy goat in his hands. After this, Apiyo and Acen sit in front of family shrine, and their father moves round the twin girls 2-3 times with the billy goat_____.and let her future be bright."

The Acholi people say that if the twins are not presented before the god, the boy may become mad, or he becomes barren, or the god prevents the girl from conceiving. It is the tradition that the girl twins are presented before the god with a female goat, but if that cannot be found, a billy goat may be used. The father of the twins keeps the female goat so that it multiplies – and the goat is called sacrificial goat. When they multiply, the goats cannot be used by any other person without asking the permission of the twins.

All other payments for marriage of the twins are the same with those of other girls as we have seen above.

Cleansing ceremony for children

We have seen above that when a man elopes with a married woman who has children or a child, he must provide a goat for cleansing the children. The billy goat has many names. Some people call it a family goat, others call it blood goat, while others call it bedding goat. Cleansing a woman who elopes with children in her hands to a man is not done the same way in every part of Acholi. The Acholi of the north such as Obbo, Pajok, and Palwar, used not to cleanse children with billy goat, but with a white cock. However, the Acholi from the south like Magwi, Omeo, Agoro, Ofirika and Panyikwara use billy goat. Using a billy goat or a ram for cleansing children has just come to the Acholi on the north around 1965-1973.

It is allowed, in Acholi tradition, to take the bedding goat to the mother of the woman unaccompanied by other things like flour, slat, firewood, cooking oil, onion, paste and alcohol because these things are provided by the kin of the mother of the girl. On the day of taking the goat, the suitor of the girl goes with three or four people. The team of the girl assembles in the morning, and the suitor takes the goat in the house of his mother-in-law (or the house in which he found the woman). The women then comes together with her children and sit in the house, and the man holds the goat by the rope tied round its neck and moves round the woman and her children as he supplicates, "Chief! This practice has not started with me; I implore you to grant health to the children and their mother."

After his prayer, he strangles the goat and pierces its stomach with the spear that he has carried from his home. He picks the dung from the stomach of the goat and smears on the chest of the woman and her children's so that they live a calm life. The man again takes the dung and smear on the forehead of the woman and her children's – so that they have no headache. Lastly, he smears the dung on the back of the hands and feet of the woman and her children's – so that they get good yields of crops, and their feet take them to good places. He smears the remaining dung on the door so that those who are not in this gathering also get married. This implies that he has also smeared the feet of those who are absent.

When the goat is skinned, clan elders give its liver to women to cook for her and her new husband. Eating the liver together signifies that the woman and the man are now one. If the child experiences any problem in future, it is not blamed on the man, but possibly, on evil-eye people. If a man does not cleanse the children, and one of them later dies, the kin of their mother of the children will blame him. After eating the liver, the man takes his seat and the clan of the woman gives him *kwete* to drink together with his friends before they return to their homes. Meanwhile the clan of the woman remains there chatting and waiting for food. After eating, elders bless the woman and her children. The woman sleeps in her father's home on that day and returns to her home the following day.

GOOD LIFE IS A GOOD EXAMPLE

> *"Nothing is more important than good life in this world" (David Stars)*

As we have seen, there are issues that can cause quarrels and fight in the house among Acholi people. Unfortunately, Acholi men do not understand what women want from them. Dunas says, "*The thing I cannot answer in my life is that what does a woman wants from a man?*" What we should all know is that every woman wants god life because it brings happiness.

There are many things that bring conflict in the house. It may be the husband or his wife who triggers conflict. This is what men should tell women who do not know, that the following are the causes of unhappiness:

1. Do not attend women's meeting.
2. Do not go to church.
3. I do not want you to befriend a divorced woman, or go to the house of women of bad influence.
4. Why do you bear only girls?
5. I do not want you to go chatting at your friend, and I do not want your friends to visit you.
6. Our marriage has turned into something else; there is no love between us anymore.

Women, on the other hand, say the following to men without knowing that they make men unhappy:

1. I am tired of your wax.
2. I am tired of your talks.
3. You move out too much.
4. You like sleeping with other men's wives.
5. You do not mind about me.
6. I do not see the money you work.
7. All your money goes to prostitutes.
8. You do not want to help my parents; you only help yours.
9. You do not want to support me in times of problem.
10. You take care of other people's children only.
11. You are as foolish as your mother.
12. You come back home late every day. Where do you stay?

All these expressions can bring conflict and fight in the house. An elder told me that the reason why some men do not want their wives to go to church or for a meeting is because when they are there, the women only gossip about the life of a man and a woman in the house. Therefore, this is one way a woman can learn bad habits and conducts.

Many Acholi people try to make good life in the house, but many find it hard because the man and his wife do not think alike. The man's perception of life is different from the woman's. Stephen says, "A man does not have the same view as a woman because they do not know that it is their opinions" that bring good life in the house. If a man and his wife want to have *the same perception (which is usually difficult if not impossible) they should change their ways of looking at life and their conduct — if they do this*, eventually, they find that life is good and no one judges each other (Stephen, 2004, P, 17).

A woman or a man who wants peace to be in the house by showing love and happiness to each other, and yet he or she has not changed their ways of life, we can say without hesitation that good life will never come in the house. As Stephen asserts, "When you shout too much in my ears, I cannot hear what you are telling me" a cultivator knows when to plant crops; good cultivators usually follows cultures of farming (Stephen, 2004, PP, 21-22). William George also contends that God has given the choice to lead a good life or to lead a bad life in the hands of everybody — that is how we are as human beings" (Girlbert, 2009, P, 2).

There is a map in the head of every person, and it can be for showing the realities and values in this world. So, there are people who say they are the only people who hold the truth and other people have to use their opinion. This stems from what people believe is the truth. Before we begin to look at our good life can show us the way, I want a woman and her husband, now reading this book, to study the picture below for two or three minutes.

Figure: 43: Horse's head and Frog

The man should now ask the woman, "What have you seen in this picture?" The woman answers him, "I have seen a frog." Then the woman should also ask the man, "What about you, what have you seen in the picture?" The man answers, "I have seen the picture of the head of a horse." I want everybody to ask themselves, "Who, between the two of us, said the truth?" the woman can say to herself that she is the one who said the truth and the man also thinks the same way. But we may find that neither the woman nor the man told a lie because of them said the truth – the woman actually saw a frog, and the man saw the head of a horse.

Secondly, both the man and the woman should hold the picture from a different angle and the man should ask the woman, "What have you seen in this picture?" The woman answers, "I have seen the picture of the head of a horse." If the woman asks her husband, "What have you seen?" He says, "I have seen a frog." If we study the picture well, we realise that it is two in one. One picture is of the head of a donkey and the other is of a frog. A person who sees this picture for the first time may not see both figures at the same time. But he can see both pictures at once when he gives it a second look.

I now give the partners a few minutes to discuss what they have been studying in this picture. The man will actually agree that at first sight the woman saw a frog and in the second sight she saw the head of a horse. The woman will also agree that at first sight the man saw the head of a horse, and the second time he saw a frog. This tells us that in this world, a woman does not look at things the same way with a man. This does not mean somebody is at fault, but many times this causes quarrel and fight between the woman and her husband because they do not know that they are both looking at issues in different ways. The man tells the truth and his wife also tells the truth, but because of little knowledge one thinks that the other is telling a lie. This is what often happens between men and women (Stephen, 2004, PP, 25-27).

As we have seen above, if the man and the woman did not sit down to discuss the picture, they would not agree that there are two pictures – the picture of a frog and that of the head of a horse. It is because they discussed the picture that they were able to tell that there are two picture on the paper. If you only see a frog, you cannot agree that there is a picture of the head of a horse on the page. This is what causes quarrel and fight in the house because everyone looks at things differently. A woman looks at marriage life in her own way and the man looks at it in his own way. This does not mean there is no truth in this world – truth exists. Mr. Partick Murra contends, "There are two secrets in marriage which show us how to take care of marriage. First, when the woman or the man realises that he or she is at fault, he should admit. Secondly, if the woman or the man knows that he or she is not at fault, he or she should keep quiet – as the Acholi say an issue becomes bigger by response (Gilbert, 2009, P, 2).

SETTLING DISPUTES BETWEEN A MAN AND A WOMAN

When an issue of this kind is in the house, it causes conflict between the man and his wife. Family Mediation Centre of Australia reports, "Quarrels occur between a man and his wife because of children, money, feeding the family and the man's love affairs with other women (FMC Relationship Services, 2005, P, 16). Life in the house is difficult if the man does not listen to his wife or the woman does not listen to her husband. It is humans who settle dispute between human. When there is a dispute between a man and a woman, they can settle it if the follow what the tradition demands them to do. If they do not, quarrel and fight erupt, and most often that leads to family breakdown.

When there is conflict in the house, no one listens to the other because every one finds it useless to listen to the other. There are people who desire settling their dispute while others do not like to settle their disputes settled – this depends on how our parents taught us.

When there is conflict between a man and a woman, clan elders give them time to calm down. The tradition of Acholi does not allow settling disputes when the conflicting parties are still boiling with anger because anger does not allow one to talk peace as the Acholi proverb says, "Fire is put out by water," or "Hot water is not cooled by hot water."

1. If a man and his wife accept that the clan can settle their difference, all good results will benefit them. The elder who chairs the meeting has to cross examine the man and his wife. The chairperson of the meeting is chosen based on people's trust in him and his age. The dispute settled is the secret of the family, and it must not get out to non members, because if it is told to non members, it soils the name of the clan. This is in keeping with the rules of Family Relationship Centre of Australia, which say, "The mediator in family dispute first talks to the man and the woman

separately and later brings them together. He also tells the couple that their talk is confidential. This may make the husband or the wife reveal everything without fear" (FMC Relationship Services, 2005, P, 21).

The dispute between couples is settled at the home of the husband. If the woman has run to one of the relatives of the man, she is taken back to her husband on the day of settling the dispute. In Acholi, one or two people may not be able to settle family dispute, just as we have seen in Australia. So, it is a collective mediation – it is done in the presence of the husband's clan members and his wife's.

In Acholi tradition, when there is conflict in the house, it is said that the husband and his wife should first try to settle it by themselves. If they find that they cannot do it, they call the brothers of the husband to help them to settle it. If the brothers of the husband fail to handle the case, they involve the bride's brothers, and if the brothers of the wife fail to handle the case, they take it before the husband and the wife's clan elders. Most of the time family dispute is properly settled in this forum. Sometimes clan elders also find it hard to settle some disputes, so they forward them to the chief. Acholi chiefs have elders' council which comprises elders from different clans. These elders are experienced in family disputes settlement.

Acholi people have ground rules that people have to follow when they are settling family disputes. The rules are given below:

1. No one should interrupt a person who is speaking.
2. Everybody should listen attentively, and understand everything said.
3. Everybody in the meeting must speak with respect — do not speak carelessly or interrupt a speaker.
4. Whoever wants to speak must wait until the present speaker has finished his deliberation, and he will not speak until the chair has allowed him to.
5. A dispute handled by clan elders is a secret, and no one should talk about it outside the meeting.

Here we can contend that Acholi tradition is similar to that of Australia, though we still find some difference between them. In Australia, it is allowed for a woman to chair a meeting to settle dispute between a man and his wife, but in Acholi a woman cannot be the chair because it is a man who is the founder of the family and is more knowledgeable in family matters.

The chair asks the man or his wife to tell members what caused conflict between them. Some women and men know how to logically present issues while others do not. If the chair realises that the wife or the husband cannot present his or her case well, he gives them by saying and asking the following questions:

- Tell us how the conflict started between you and what causes it.
- What do you want the people who are here to do so that the matter is settled satisfactorily?
- Do you thing a red-chest sun bird is between you – if it is, who could that be?
- What do want a woman or woman to do so that this conflict does not continue?
- Did the man throw things from the house, or did the woman squeeze her husband's testicles?

From the responses to these questions, clan elders can make out a lot of information from the man or his wife. If the couple has a child or children, the chair tells them that the most important people in the house are the children. After the presentation of the couple, the chair asks members to ask questions about things they have not understood well. After this, they begin to point out where the husband or the wife went wrong. The elders also give useful pieces of advice to the man and his wife. The power of judgment is in the hands of the members in the meeting. Even if the man or his wife does not accept some of the rulings, with the authority of the elders, he or she has to accept it. Secondly, during the settlement of the dispute, the woman's kin usually side with her, while the husband's kin also side with him. It is the judgment that tells where the husband or wife erred, and they are warned not to repeat it. As Acholi people say, they condemn bad acts but not the people who did it.

The chair then asks the husband or his wife if there is any other issue. If there is any, members will listen to and discuss it. If there is nothing more, the issue concluded. After the issue is settled, the chair asks the husband and his wife to shake hands. Hand shake, in Acholi, signifies unity, forgiveness and peace. As Rodney Dangerrfield asserts, "A good woman forgives her husband when he wrongs her" (Gilbrt, 2009, P, 2).

Before the couple go back to do other things, elders strongly warn them that they do not want to hear any conflict after this. Each of them should reform.

UNITY IS BETTER THAN CONFLICT

God created people differently. A man has a brain; a woman also has a brain. So, a woman can think, read and do everything as a man does. But in Acholi, men say women cannot perform men's tasks. This is a lies, which I can also say is primitive. When I was in Sudan (Africa), I thought a woman could not drive a car, build an iron roofed house, be a pilot, be a doctor, and be a manager or director. When I came to Australia, I discovered that Acholi of South Sudan are wrong – because I found Australian women driving, working in hospitals, piloting planes and many women hold offices – if I don't fear telling lie, 75% of officers in community services in Australia are women. While in South Sudan, 90% of the government officials are men although in principle it was agreed that women should occupy 25% of positions in public offices. Having said this, we could conclude that whether in Australia or in South Sudan, men suppress women. A woman with a university degree does not earn the same salary with a man with the same qualification. Her salary is a little lower than their male counterparts'.

In Acholi a man thinks he is everything: head of the family, he is the one to look for money, to feed the family and he holds the power and authority for everything. Acholi people do not know that things are changing. What people used to do to women in the past are not applicable today – unity is better than conflict. We cannot emphasise that the Acohli men like defending themselves. Egoistic thinking all the time does not develop the family. If there is no unity between the husband and his wife, things will not move as required. Before I go further, I would like you to study the following pictures of horse:

Figure 44: The picture of horse
Source Woody J: Unity is better that conflict

542

"Two pathways confused hyena"

In the first picture, each horse wants to eat the grass before it without minding about the rope round its neck. In the second and third pictures each of the horse is struggling to reach the grass, but they learnt that is impossible. So, in the fourth picture, when the two horses realised that both of them could not reach the grass, they sat down to talk about it. They asked, "Why are we unable to reach the grass before us?" They discovered that they could not reach the grass because there was no unity between them – they are to be united because unity is better than conflict. In the fifth and sixth pictures, the two horses are eating the grass without any conflict. This happened because of the listening and unity between them. If a man and his husband continue to live bad life, family life becomes hard, and it may lead to family breakdown. This is why Acholi elders want a couple to settle their dispute by themselves. This is also why Sacha Guitry says, "After marriage, a man and a woman will be like a coin which has two sides, they cannot see each other, but they live together (Gilbert, 2009, P, 2).

Chapter Thirty One

BIRTH AND ITS CELEBRATION

BIRTH

Production of children is very important in Acholi. So, after marriage a woman is not to take many months without conceiving. If a woman gets married, or she elopes and lives with her husband for six to twelve months without conception, people begin to grumble about her and her husband's fertility. If the groom already has a child, elders now grumble about the bride because the groom has already proved his fertility. If clan members learned that the bride one time committed abortion, clan elders advise the boy to look for another woman so that he could get a child.

When women from the family of the woman learn that the family of the man is urging him to look for another woman, they also tell their daughter to try to prove her fertility outside her marriage – she should sleep with another man whom she thinks is fertile. Since a man sleeps with his wife at night, he cannot tell if his wife slept with another man. If she is impregnated by another man, her husband cannot know. This is happening many times among Acholi people. However, there are some Acholi men who can hold their patience when their wives take a little long without conception. They do not hurry to sleep with other women outside their marriages. Some Acholi believe that even if a woman takes a year without conception, at least one day God will grant her fertility. Her husband continues to live with her, but he is allowed, by the tradition, to look for another woman. Sometime when a woman takes too long to conceive, elders take her before Omara god as we have seen before in this book.

Acholi women, just like other women, take eight to nine month to deliver, but there are women whose delivery takes longer than usual. Acholi women used to deliver from home because there were no hospitals around. The closest hospital in Acholiland was Torit, which is 50 miles away from Acholiland. Fortunately, there are some very experienced female traditional birth attendants. On the day of delivery, women in the family of the husband of the expectant mother, call a traditional birth attendant who remains with the expectant mother until she delivers.

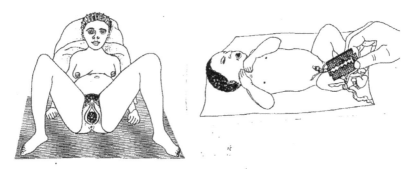

Figure 45: A woman is delivering

Some women deliver without problem, while others have complicated delivery — they may take one or two days. The women attending to the woman in labour ask her if, one time, a boy took something from her because such a thing may cause her trouble during labour time. At times the women do not even consult elders when the birth delays, they just tap the woman's waist with her husband's shoe three times. So, this is to tell us that if the child is not coming out because its father moves a lot, after taping her mother's waist with the shoe, the baby should come out. Not long after this, the child falls in the hands of the attendant who has been waiting for it. She receives the child with both hands. The attendant then ties the baby's navel with a string and cuts it. Before the child is washed, women inspect its body to find out if it is healthy and nothing is missing. A healthy child should be as described below:

1. If the baby girl has one vagina/if a baby boy has one penis and two testicles.
2. Does the baby has human nose and arms?
3. Does it have human finger nails and toe nails?

4. Does it have two arms?
5. Does it have one anus?

There are children who do not have to live because they will become source of mishaps in the family. So, an abnormal baby is killed by women attending to its mother, immediately after birth. However, some of them usually survive, especially when their mothers deliver them without the help of attendance. A woman may find it hard to kill her own child even if God has created it without some parts of the body. The children who are killed immediately after birth have the following description:

1. A child who does not have vagina or penis.
2. A baby boy with only one testicle, which Achol people call "Long-gelere/ lalwee".
3. A baby whose forehead or nose resembles elephant's.
4. A baby who is missing some fingers or toes, or conjoined twins.
5. A baby with one eye.
6. A baby who has vagina, penis and testicles.

There are many other factors that I cannot write them all here. Sometime when people learn that a baby has died at birth, where woman say the baby has sucked blood, or air has entered its chest, the child is in the category of abnormal births. As stated above, when women see an abnormal baby, they kill it instantly so that other people are convinced that it sucked blood or air has gone to its chest. Acholi tradition does not want abnormal child to be kept alive because it is hard to take care of it. If a normal child dies at birth, it is God's plan because Acholi women do not kill normal babies.

A baby normally when born, is washed and covered with a clean bed sheet and placed on bedding skin or on a bed. Women begin to celebrate the birth of the child the same day. The celebration is not done the same way among different groups of Acholi. Every clan has its own way of doing it. In this book, I will not talk about all the different celebrations that are there in Acholi clans because celebration of birth needs a book of its own. However, I will talk about the general celebration used by most Acholi women.

Celebrating a newly born baby

Acholi have different ways of celebrating birth, but in most cases we find that many aspects of the celebration are similar or the same. This helps us to understand Acholi celebration and rites. Let us look at one way which Acholi women use. A baby girl's celebration is different from a baby boy's. A baby boy spends three days in the house, from birth, but a baby girl spends four days. Within the three or four days, the baby must not get out. The same applies to its mother except when she wants to go for a call or bath. If the mother gets out to bathe or to respond to nature's call, she does not leave the baby alone in the house. She leaves a woman or a girl in the house to sit next to the baby so that the spirits of the ancestors do not descend on the baby. The main food of the mother of the bay, within the three or four days, is porridge. After bath in the morning and in the evening, the woman takes porridge prepared with sesame or ground nut paste.

Before the day of bringing the mother of the baby out, the family of her husband sends a word for all clan members to attend the celebration. The mother of the woman is also invited, and she prepares paste for her daughter. The relatives of the baby's father come with *kwete, waragi*, flour, smoked bush meat, ground pea sauce and vegetable.

On the day of bringing the mother of the baby out, when women have not yet started cooking, the mother of her husband or his sister bring her outside. The woman's mother-in-law carries the baby in her left hand, hooks one of her right fingers to the mother of the baby's left finger and pulls her out with it. The mother of the husband of the woman seats her on a log or animal skin in front of the house. Before the woman sits down, her mother-in-law taps her waist three ties if the bay is a boy, or four times if the bay is a girl. The woman then sits down and receives the baby from the hands of her mother-in-law.

The mother-in-law puts a mingling stick or a stirring stick in a saucepan and the mother of the bay hold them in her right hand. The mother-in-law brings peas and pours in the hand of the mother of the baby four times if the baby is a boy, or three times if the baby is a girl. If one seed of peas falls at the time she is pouring them in the hand of her daughter-in-law, the mother-in-law picks it and puts it in a container. After this, aunts and girls in the family sound loud yodels. Aunts pour sesame or ground nuts in the hand of the mother of the bay three times if the baby is a boy, or four times if the baby is a girl. If sesame or ground nuts fall at this time, the mother-in-law picks hem and puts them in a container. After this, a girl or an aunt sounds a loud yodel.

The ground nuts and sesame that dropped in the saucepan is eaten by the mother-in-law and she takes the saucepan home. The mother-in-law of the mother of the baby holds her by the hand and takes her into the house. A short while later, women divide foodstuff among themselves to cook. They then prepare different dishes. In the evening, before eating, a sister of the husband, of the mother of the baby takes her to bathe, walking with their fingers interlocked. The mother-in-law of the mother of the baby is not supposed to bathe her, but she remains in the house bathing the baby.

After the bathe, the sister-in-law of the mother of the baby and the mother of the bay interlock their fingers and walk back into the house to smear oil on her body. After this, the mother of the baby is led out of the house by her mother-in-law, with two of their fingers of both left and right hands interlocked. As they move out of the house, the mother-in-law moves backward and the mother of the baby sits on a log. Before she sits down, her mother-in-law tries to seat her down and pulls her up three times if the baby is a boy, and four times if the baby is a girl.

Before eating and cleansing the woman, her husband fakes going to the garden to dig, if the baby is a boy. But if the baby is a girl, the man fakes going to the garden to check his animal traps, or to track animals in isolated bushes. This is because women are not cultivators. When the man has gone to cultivate, his wife has to prepare food and take it after him in the garden. As he waits for the food, the man sometimes grumbles, "Mmm! What kind of woman is that, that cannot bring food on time? I am very hungry. I will beat her when she comes."

The man complain not knowing that the woman is doing her best to prepare food for him, and before he finishes what he is saying, his wife appears in the garden. On seeing the woman, the man begins to scream, "Is this the time to bring food to the garden? If you do not want to bring food here, you better remain at home instead of provoking me." He picks a stick and goes to fight the woman and he hits her with it. The woman throws food to the ground and runs back home. If the baby is a boy, its mother takes food in the garden three times, and when the baby is a girl, her mother takes food to the garden four times, and her husband keeps saying the same thing.

The mother-in-law takes different dishes, bread and paste and tries to feed the mother of the baby with, pulling it back and pushing it to her mouth three times if the baby is a boy, or four times if the baby is a girl. (See Figure No 44).

Later, the mother of the baby bites the food and spits it on the ground three times if the baby is a boy, or four times if the baby is a girl. Later, her mother-in-law pushes the remaining food into her mouth, and she gently chews it and swallows. Other women now serve food to all clan members who have come to attend the ceremony. The food of the mother of the baby is served separate from others'. She eats together with her husband's sister. The mother-in-law eats from the cooking pot together with other elderly women.

After eating, the sister of the husband of the mother of the baby takes her by the hand and leads her into the house, and lies the baby down on an animal kin smeared with sesame oil. It is said sesame oil is good because it makes the baby feels cool. Later, the sister of the husband of the woman fills a small calabash, or a medium size one with water, and she puts a leaf of *olwedo* leaf in it. She also puts two small stones by the head of the baby. The aunt of the baby and other women names the child. The women and men, who are outside, now enter the house in pairs, and each of them gives the child a name he or she wants the child to be called. Each person giving the child a name dips the *olwedo* leaf in the calabash and sprinkles the water on the baby as he or she calls the name they are giving the child. As an Acholi, I know that on the day of naming the child, people give the baby very many names, but only one of them will be familiarised. An old woman told me, "It is the mother of the baby who makes the name popular; a name that has pleased her."

There are Acholi names that even if people do not propose, they come by themselves because they are traditional circumstantial names. For instance, a male first born child is named "Lokang", and a female first born child is named "Lakang." Even if people give many names, later we find that the circumstantial name is popularised.

The people of Omeo and Agoro give the first born child different names from those that other Acholi people use. A male first born child is named "Lokang", and a female first born child is named "Adye." A child who follows the first born is named "Loboi," if he is a boy or "Laboi if she is a girl.

THE BIRTH OF TWINS

The Acholi tradition considers twins godly, and they are born in specific families. That means if your uncle or your father has had twins, you will, most likely, have it too, and vice versa. This inheritance may come from the family of the husband or from the family of the wife. In Acholi, the names of twins are predetermined. If the first of the twins is a boy, he is named "Opiyo" or "Apiyo for a girl. The follower of Opiyo or Apiyo is named "Ocen" or "Acen" respectively.

Celebrating the birth of twins differs from the celebration of ordinary birth. When a woman gives birth to twins, she remains in the house with her husband for four days if the first of the twins is a girl, or three day if the first of the twins is a boy. On the fourth or third day, the parents of the twins, if the mother of twins wants to go out for a call, she gives Apiyo or Opiyo to her husband to carry. Some Acholi women told me that when the father of the twins wants to go out for a call, he puts a broom next to the baby who is lying down – the mother of twins usually remains with one of the children in her hands.

Figure 46: A man carrying a broom in place of a baby

During the three days when the parents of the twins stay indoors, the clan of the man sends a word for the clan of his wife to inform them that their daughter has given birth to twins, and secondly, to invite them for the celebration of the birth of the twins. The clan of the woman prepares to come for the celebration, and the mother of the woman has to provide the requirements for the celebration. The rule of the Acholi tradition, if the twins are a baby girl and a baby boy, the family of their mother should bring:

► A young ewe and a young white hen [the ewe is kept for the twins].
► *Kwete* [any quantity].

550

- *Waragi* [no definite number of bottles].
- Smoked meat sauce.
- Cooking oil.
- Flour.
- Firewood or charcoal.

If the twins are both boys, then the family of their mother should bring the following for the celebration of their birth:

- A ram and a white cock [the ram is slaughtered for people who come for the celebration].
- *Kwete* [unspecified quantity].
- *Waragi* [unspecified number of bottle].
- Smoked meat sauce.
- Cooking oil.
- Flour.
- Firewood or charcoal.

Acholi tradition also demands that the family of the father of the twins should provide the following items:

- A ram and a young hen [or a white cock, and the white hen is kept for blessing the twins, and the ram is slaughtered to feed celebrants].
- *Kwete*.
- *Waragi*.
- Smoked meat sauce.
- Sesame paste or ground nuts paste.
- Cooking oil.
- Flour.
- Firewood or charcoal.

On the day of the celebration, the families of the parents of the twins assemble in one place, and the family of the father of twins gives a *canga* to the mother of the twins and one *canga* to the first of the twins, Opiyo or Apiyo. It is not the family of the man alone that brings *canga*, but the family of the woman also does, they give one to the father of the twins and the other to the second of the twins, Ocen or Acen. *Canga* is to show that the man belongs to a clan and the woman too.

In the morning, the grandfather of the twins clads his son and his daughter-in-law in *canga* and *okengo* and presents the couple before god, and an aunt shaves the heads of the couple. At this time, the clan of the man also clad themselves in *okengo*, but the tradition does not allow the clan of the woman to be in *okengo*. They do this so that it is easy to distinguish between the kin of the mother of the twins from the kin of the father of the twins.

A short while after, clan elders slaughter the ram that the paternal grandfather of the twins brought and divide it into halves. One half is given to the kin of the mother of the twins and the other to the kin of the father of the twins to cook. The two groups do not cook in the same heath. The kin of the mother of the twins serve what they have cooked to the kin of the father of the twins, and vice versa. Before eating, an elderly woman places a man and a woman before the god. The woman hands one of the twins to the man and the man hands the other twin to her. After this, people go in pairs to mend the god. One person in the pair must come from the clan of the man and the other from the family of the woman. The tradition allows only eight people to do this. They mend the god in front of the shrine erected at the side of the house of the mother of the twins (see the picture of the shrine below).

Figure 47: Celebration of the birth of twins

Some elders told me that they put a small calabash of unfiltered *kwete* in the shrine. They also mend the house of the god in pairs while the person from the clan of the man sits before the right house of god and the person from the clan of the woman sits in front of the one on the left. Each person does the mending as they say in a low solemn tone, "Here I give you food, be happy." When the eight people complete this ritual, the rest of the celebrants assemble to eat and drink.

After eating, if one of the twins is a girl, the clan of their father prays, "Lord we ask you to bless this ewe with health. We also ask you to tell us where these twins have come from. If they came from the family of their father, let the ewe bear a ram, but if they came from the family of the mother's kin, let the ewe bear a ewe.

After the blessing from the family of the father of the twins, one person tethers the ewe in the grazing ground among other sheep. This is then followed by entertainment, and they perform twin dance. This is a lustful kind of dance; a man dance while shaking his waist on a woman, and the woman also shakes her waist on the man. The grandparents of the twins also do it the same way without any fear. No one shows respect on this day – everybody shakes their waist sexually without any fear. In this dance one aims at throwing their dance mate to the ground. If a man throws a woman to the grown, he lies on top of her and shakes his waist as if he is sleeping with her. When a woman throws a man to the ground, she also does the same. Both men and women dust their face with flour on this day.

Acholi women told me that there are many songs for twin dance, but I am going to write only one of them which is very important and common to the people of Acholi, and here it is:

Dok Tere Ma Giyer (2)	Her vulva is hairy (2)
Dok Tere (2)	Her vulva (2)
Dok Nyare Ma Giyer (2)	Her pubis is hairy (2)
Dok Nyare (2)	Her pubis (2)

It is at this time of the dance that people give their gifts to the twins, and the gift should be the same for each twin so that one does not get annoyed with the other. This is why the Acholi people buy the same dress, shoes and other things for the twins. If a person cannot give equitably divide the gift, the tradition allows him to place it before the twins. After dancing and gifts, people continue with drinking and conversations before they each retire to their homes.

If the ewe bears a a female sheep, they wait until it bears a male one, but if it first bears a female, they also wait until it bears a male before it is slaughtered. Later, the clan of the man and that of the woman converge to eat it. They eat this sheep to separate the twins. As mentioned above, if the ewe first bears a ewe, after the ram has been eaten, the clan of the man takes the ewe, and the clan of the woman takes its mother. If the ewe first bears a lamb, the clan of the woman takes its mother. This brings us to the end of women's celebration of twins in Acholi.

Performing rituals on a woman

Presenting a woman for ritual and returning a woman for rituals are two different things as we will see later. In Acholi, a woman is presented for ritual when there is disagreement between her and her husband. This kind of this agreement can crop up when a woman claims that she was impregnated by her husband and her husband claims that she was impregnated by another man. There are many such complaints among Acholi young women and young men. When the parents of the woman find it hard to settle the issue, they take the woman to the home of the man. The family of the man also welcomes her and wait when it is one month to her time of delivery, then the women in the family of the man presents her for rituals. This brings us to four questions, "How do women present this woman for rituals? Who performs the rituals on her? Why do the women present her for rituals? What happens after the rituals?"

On the day of the rituals, women from the clan of the boy converge on the compound of the mother of her husband. Early in the morning before the woman has got out of the house, her mother-in-law places a log in front of the house. Then a woman enters the house, interlocks two of her fingers with those of the pregnant woman, and she begins to walk backward, pulling the pregnant woman out of the house. On getting out, the woman seats the pregnant woman on the log, and she interlocks her fingers on those of the pregnant woman and pulls her up, and lets her sit again. The performer of the rituals should try to seat the woman and pulls her up again three times if it is a man's ritual, or four times if it is a woman's. If they do not know the sex of the child, they pull her up and push her down four times — a woman's ritual.

At the time one woman is performing the rituals; other women are busy preparing different dishes. Later, the mother-in-law of the pregnant woman puts a bit of every dish on a lump of bread and pushes it four times, forth and back at the mouth of the woman. She later pushes the lump of bread in the mouth of the woman, who chews it slowly and swallows. Her mother-in-law spears oil mixed with red ochre on the chest and neck of the woman asking, "Why do women perform rituals on a woman? Acholi women perform rituals on a woman when there is serious disagreement between her and her husband, when her husband complains that the pregnancy is not his, but the woman claims it is the man who impregnated her. Acholi tradition has it that performing a ritual on a woman reveals the truth of who is responsible for the pregnancy. If the woman is impregnated by the man she claims is responsible for the pregnancy, she will deliver well, but if the pregnancy is not the man's and the woman is presented for rituals, the baby usually dies at birth. The tradition says the baby dies because the blood on which the ritual was performed was not the man's. Sometime such babies do not die, but will experience serious ailments in her life. It is said that the ailment can paralyse the hands or legs of the child.

Blood Ram

Most Acholi of today cannot answer you if you ask, "Why does a man take the blood goat to be slaughtered in the house of his mother-in-law if his wife delivers from the house of her mother?" This is because they do not know their culture well. Who take the blood goat? If a girl finds a man to marry her and she conceives, it is believed that the blood is the man's, not the woman's. Acholi culture does not allow a man's blood to be at his mother-in-law's. If it happens, the man has to provide a goat for cleanse the house of his mother-in-law because blood is hot. In Acholi, a woman does not deliver from the house of her mother, but sometimes it happens due to some factors.

This often happens when a woman has run back from her home to her mother because her husband has fought her—she must have been pregnant at that time. If the time of delivery comes before the dispute between the woman and her husband is not yet settled, the woman can deliver from the house of her father. Here, her father asks for blood goat, which they pierce in the stomach to cleanse the blood that pours in the house of her mother.

In Acholi culture, it is women who eat the blood goat, but I have discovered that the Acholi men of today eat blood goat freely. They do this because of the little knowledge they have about their culture. The family of the girl cannot perform a ritual on her, but they call the family of her husband to come and cleanse their wife, and they bring the following items for the ritual:

1. A billy goat
2. Flour
3. Ground nuts paste or sesame paste
4. Two tablets of soap for washing hands
5. Smoked fish (for women who do not eat goat's meat).
6. A hoe for removing blood from the house of the mother of the woman. If the hoe is not there, the man pays Ls.10.
7. The man also pays Ls. 50 for water to wash the mouth of the women after eating the goat.

Some Acholi elders told me that in the past, there was nothing like blood goat, and when the practice came to Aholi, other things to prepare the goat's meat was not brought by the man, they were provided by the family of the woman. This practice, in Acholi, is recent.

Chapter Thirty Two

CULTURAL NORM REGARDING DEATH

Death in Acholi

Death is a matter of importance in Acholi, which explains why the Acholi highly respect the dead. The death of persons between one to 60 years is more painful, than the death of persons who are 61 to 100 years. One day when I was still in Juba, I asked three Acholi elders who were seated under a mango tree, "If people respect death, then why do some people quarrel or fight during funeral rites?" The elders responded that, there are many reasons that explain the cause of quarrels and fights. But later I realized that there are two main reasons why people always quarrel or fight among themselves during funeral rites. First, people do not understand that Satan is the cause of death on earth, much as the Acholi always say during burials, "It is God who gives and takes away." Secondly, the Acholi think death befalls a person because of actions of a fellow man. Hence, even if one dies during hunting, the Acholi still say he was killed intentionally.

According to the history of Acholi, death takes two forms. The first is referred to as *skin death* (natural death). The second one is known as *hand death or wilderness death*. To better understand the two forms of death, I want us to look at each of them separately. We shall start by looking at *hand death or death in the wilderness*, and later handle natural *death*.

Hand death and death in the wilderness

Before we proceed to look at what entails the two forms of death, I want us to first attempt to answer this question. "What is hand death?" "What is death in the wilderness?" In Acholi language, hand death is when one is killed using hand-held weapons like spear, knife, a gun or an arrow. When such a person dies, it is said that the person died of hand death. Cases of death by stabbing with a spear normally occur during hunting, or during domestic fights. This is what the Acholi refer to as, "the wind blew/deflected the spear, arrow or the bullet on a hunter".

Death in the wilderness, on the other hand, is death caused by attacks on a person by wild animals during hunting. When a person goes hunting and is killed by a wild animal, it is said that he died wilderness death or that he was devoured by the wilderness. They do not say that he was killed by wild animals, because saying so makes it hard to moan the dead. But the Acholi understand that many people are killed during hunting by wild animals such as elephants, loin, leopards and buffaloes. When a person is killed by a wild animal, the body is brought home, but not kept in the house. According to Acholi culture, when a person is killed by wild animals, the body must be kept in the field and covered with the roof of a small (lakodo) granary. The dead body then kept there and is buried immediately when the grave is dug.

Acholi tradition has it that even though a person is killed by wild animals, the clan members investigate the cause of his death. How do they investigate the cause of death? Acholi elders told me that people use different ways of finding out the cause of death. When the grave is being dug, the kin of the mother and the kin of the father of the deceased make incantations. The maternal relatives could stand up and say, "If this death came from us, we want diggers to find the root of a tree". Shortly, the paternal relatives also get up and, and supplicate, "But if this death was caused by us, we want diggers to find a hole." When the grave diggers have finished sinking the grave, elders then bury the dead. Investigating the cause of death does not stop during the incantations. Afterwards, the maternal and paternal relatives mourn the death. At dusk, the maternal and paternal relatives get the wood of a rat trap and chant again. The maternal relatives' chants go like this, "If this death came from our side, this trap should ensnare a female rat." The paternal relatives on the other hand pray, "If this death was caused by us, this trap should catch a male rat." After the incantations, if the grave diggers found a tree root while digging the grave, the clan members conclude that the death was caused by the maternal relatives. But if they found a hole, the clan elders would say the death was caused by paternal relatives. Secondly, if the people found that the trap caught a female rat, it would mean the death was caused by paternal relatives. But if the trap enmeshed a male rat, the clan members would say the death was caused by maternal relatives.

In the past, when a person died hand death, the clan would give a girl in compensation. A good example of such an incident happened between the people of Obbo and Koyo. As we saw earlier, one day, Onyala, the son of Otoo Ibrahim, unintentionally killed a woman of Koyo, and a girl was given in compensation (Lalum).

The people of Koyo were ready to fight the Obbo, but the people of Obbo were not willing to fight, because they understood very well that it was not just for them to fight the war. This is why the elders of Obbo resolved that the people of Abong should compensate the woman with a girl to prevent further deaths.

When the people of Obbo were handing over Lalum as compensation, they supplicated, "If this death really came from the family of Abong (Obbo), the first born of Lalum should be a boy." Reports say after a few months, Lalum conceived and gave birth to a baby boy and named him Okwor. This proved that the death was caused by the family of Abong (Obbo). After Lalum gave birth, Abong brought a male sheep and speared it at the river bank of Lerwa, to unite Obbo and Koyo. This is how the Acholi compensated someone who died hand death.

On the other hand, if a man accidentally hurts or kills someone during hunting, the clan of the man brings a big male sheep or billy goat to the owner of the hunting ground. The owner of the hunting ground then spears the male sheep to cleanse the hunting ground, to avert more occurrence of such incidence. The people who killed also got another billy goat and take to the bereaved family, for them to cleanse those who participated in burying the dead. These are the things that are needed for hand death. For a better understanding of the payment for hand death, see the payment for hand death. It is not different.

Natural Death

Before we proceed to look at natural death, I want us to first answer this question, "What is natural death?" The history of Acholi says that, natural death is death bought by illness. The illness can take five minutes, six days, one month or two months. It can also be one or two years. People who die natural death always die indoors or from a health facility.

Natural death could befall any normal person, a leper, a chief, and twins or first born. I learnt that there are different customs regarding different forms of death, as I earlier wrote in this book. We shall therefore revisit these customs later in this chapter.

Anyone could die natural death regardless of age. It could happen to an old person, or a baby. What does an old person do when they realises that they are about to die? When an elder dies, to whom does he leave his blessing?

According to Acholi tradition, when an elder, who has children, realises that he is bedridden, he calls his most favored child and tells him, "Alright my child, it seems my days are numbered. Before I die, I want to inform you that, you should hold the *olwedo*/blessing of your grandfather— look after your brothers and sisters. If there is any issue in my father's family you should be responsible. Take this *olwedo* leaf and supplicate- bring me your hand**."**

The child gives his hands to his father, who holds both hands and spits on them saying, "My grandfather left his spit with my father. Before his death, my father also spit in my hands; so today, I also leave my blessing in your hands. As an elder, I have noticed that you are the only one who can take care of your siblings." After these words, the elder takes olwedo leaf and hands it over to his son. This also shows that all the powers of their father remain with the boy-child. The elder later tells the child to go back and play with other children. After a short time, the elder calls the child and his brothers, who would come and sit close to him. When the children are seated, he tells them, "Alright children, it seems I am about to be eaten by the soil. While am still breathing, I want to inform all of you seated here that, each of you should change for the best. I want you to live in unity, as you share the same parents. No one should segregate against the other, because I treated you without favoritism. Secondly, I want all of you to watch over your brother (he points at him and says his name). Obey what he tells you. If anyone disobeys him, he would have disobeyed me."

At that moment, the elder shows the children that he spat in the hands of the son he mentioned. But even though he does not say this, his children would infer from his communication that he spat on their brother's hands.

The elder would die after a few days. Upon his death, an elderly woman from this family folds his legs and puts his hands across his chest. The woman covers his mouth with a small calabash. During the olden days, the dead were buried with the cloth they were wearing, or even naked. Only Acholi who lived in town were buried in coffins. Besides, a person who died in an urban setting was brought back home in a coffin, and buried in the same coffin. Gradually, the Acholi who lived in towns outgrew the habit of folding the legs of dead people and covering their mouth with a small calabash. The dead lies on their back in the coffin, with both hands placed over their genitalia, and their head covered with a white cloth.

When the children hear of the death of their father, they dig a grave on the right side of the house. Other people sit near the dead to condole with the orphans and his clan members. The history of Acholi tells us that prior to the digging of the grave, an elder first measure the length of the dead, so that the body fits in the grave. Before the boys start digging the grave, the bereaved family makes incantations using spears, and the stick used to measure the grave and spear or knife. A member of the bereaved family who made the first incantation picked the stick and measures the length of the grave and made a mark on the ground three times (if the dead was a man) or four times (if the dead was a woman), while saying, "There! If the death which befell this person came from our family, it should meet a hole." He or she throws down the sick. And another maternal family member takes the stick and marks the ground three times (man) or four times (woman) while praying, "There! If this death came from our family, it should meet a root." He throws the stick down.

The people of Panyikwara did not mark their graves with stick, spear, knife or arrow as we saw earlier. But they scratch the ground where the grave would be dug, with twigs of *oryang* thorn or *owak* tree as the maternal and paternal relatives make incantations, as we saw in the previous pages.

In Acholiland, the dead are buried at the doorway. If the deceased was a man, he would be buried on the right, but if she was a female, the body would be laid to rest on the left side of the doorway. However, those who lived in town are buried in the cemetery.

Shortly, the men would start digging the grave. Digging a grave takes a short time because boys and men take turns to do it, till they realised the exact measurement. The Acholi do not bury the dead in a shallow grave. The grave is sunk about one and a half to two meters. Since in Acholi, a dead person is buried by the door, the grave is dug deep so that the stench did not come out.

If the cause of death originated from the paternal relatives, they will find a hole in the grave as they asked in their prayer. But if the cause of death came from the maternal relatives, then they find a tree root as they had prayed for. Sometimes, people find both roots and a hole in the grave. This means the cause of dead is from both the maternal and paternal relatives. Most times, people find roots or a hole only when digging a grave. Sometimes, they do not find either roots or a hole. If this happens, it proves to the clan elders that the death was caused by outsiders. Much as the death is proved to have been caused by a foreign element, as I was saying below (see page 538), the clan members of the deceased still investigate the cause of death by setting a trap, or scattering sorghum for the chicken. If a hen is the first to start eating the sorghum, it proves that the death was caused by a woman. But if a cock starts eating the sorghum first, it means a man caused the death. We shall see later in this chapter how the clan members investigate the causes of death using different means. The history of Acholi says if the grave diggers do not find either the root of a tree or a hole, they may find stones, which signifies that an evil-eye is responsible for the death of the person. This is because a stone in Acholi culture stands for evil-eye.

After the boys and men have finished digging the grave, they inform the elderly men and women seated near the dead body. According to Acholi culture, if the deceased was male, aged between 30 to 100, his body is cleaned by aged men. But if the deceased was a boy, aged between one day and 29 years, elderly women are in charge of cleaning the body. If, however, the deceased was a girl or woman, elderly women would are the ones to clean the body. Men are not supposed to clean the body of a dead woman or girl. Unfortunately, the Acholi elders did not tell me why Acholi culture prohibits men from cleaning the body of a dead woman or girl. After the dead body has been cleaned, the men or women smear the body with shea nut oil.

In the past, after the corpse was cleaned, it would be smeared with shea nut oil, but the body would be placed in ash spread on the floor. The ash that was spread over the dead body was not picked from the fire-place, but from the rubbish pit. Nowadays, the Acholi also wash the body of the dead. They also smear the body using oil. But the practice of placing the dead in ash has been abandoned. Prior to burying the dead, the girls ask for their money for taking the dead body out of the house (see payment for death). The person who lost his dear one would pick money and give to the girls. If he does not give money for taking the dead body out of the house, the girls stop the burial and sit firmly at the door. Such incidences always caused quarrels and fights during burials among the maternal and paternal relatives. This was because those asking for money for taking the dead body out of the house feel despised. May people pay the money to the girls, but other people who do not want to pay the money, especially if the deceased woman married from another tribe other the Acholi, like the Dinka, Nuer, Lotuko or Kakwa. This is what causes conflict among the people. The family members rarely refuse paying money to remove a dead body out of the house.

One day I asked four Acholi elders, "Why do people clean dead bodies? And why do they smear the body with shea nut oil? These elders told me that there are three important reasons why the Acholi clean a dead body and smear with shea nut oil. The three reasons are: one, the dead have already separated from their clan. Everyone is aware that the dead is already on the way to a place prepared for him by the god of his ancestors. Custom dictates that when a dead person is on their journey to the spirit world, the body should be cleaned and smeared with shea nut oil or perfumed soap. Since a dead person cannot bathe, they are cleaned by elderly men or women. Secondly, the Acholi are very religious people. The Acholi know that the spirit of a dead person goes to heaven (to God). That is why they clean the body, so that the spirit that leaves the body reaches heaven before God when it is clean- because God does not entertain filth. Thirdly, shea nut oil appeases the dead, as it walks to its father's home. In Acholi land, if a person is going on a journey, they carry a water jar (gourd), but since a dead person can no longer carry a water jar, old men or women smear shea nut oil on its chest–to cool its chest during the journey to heaven. The Acholi believe that the journey to heaven is very long, and there is no water on the way. So shea nut oil can quench the thirst.

After smearing the body of the dead, an elder would instruct three men to enter the grave to receive the dead body. He also chooses three or four other men to lower the body to the grave.

Figure 48: Clan members pouring soil on the dead

After the girls have received the money, they hand over the dead body to those responsible for its burial. The history of Acholi states that if the deceased was an old person, the body is put straight in the grave without performing any ritual. But if the deceased was a young person, two elders lift the body and move it round the grave three times (for a boy) or four time (if the dead was female). Later, the elders put the body in the grave. Unfortunately, no elder told me why old people are buried immediately, while the young ones are first rotated around the grave before burial. I think it was because of the conflicts that affected the people of Sudan, which gave the people little time to investigate why the old where buried without any ritual. When the dead body is already in the grave, a man would be placed with his head over his left hand, while the right hand remained up – this is for holding the spear. But if the dead was a female, the head would be placed on her right hand, while the left hand would remain up for her to make ululations and hold the man's waist. The above norm applied even to those who died in *town*. However, one impor-tant thing when burying one who died in town is that, the head is made to face the home of the Acholi where the Acholi home is located from that town.

When the body has been put in the grave, one man gets out of the grave, leaving two people in. One person should be a maternal relative, and the other a paternal relative. The two then pour soil on the dead body using a logule (elbows) backwards. See figure 49. If the dead was a man, the soil is poured, using elbows, three times, but if the dead was a woman, the soil was poured four times. After pouring soil on the dead, the two persons would then get out of the grave and people continue with the burial. As the grave is about to be filled up with soil, one of the elders stops people from throwing soil. He calls clan members of the deceased – so that they throw soil on the dead. If the dead had children, each of them would throw soil on the father's or mother's corpse. But if the children of the deceased was absent during burial, the brother's child present would pour soil in their place. If the dead is a woman, and her child is not around during burial, her daughter's child would throw soil on her grave.

Those who pour soil on the deceased stay close to the grave, with their backs turned to the grave. An elder picks two balls of soil, and closes one in the right hand, and one in the left hand. He then throws both balls of soil in the grave. An elder gives him soil three times if the dead was a man, and four times if the deceased was a woman. Any child who threw soil on the grave headed back home without looking back. Tradition has it that, any child who looks back after throwing soil in the grave would be haunted by the spirit of the dead. According to culture, if the dead was a boy or a girl, his or her parents would be the ones to pour soil on their grave.

When I was still in Juba, I asked some Acholi elders, "Why do people throw soil on the dead?" The elders told me that it proves to the dead that much as they no longer see, God has already separated them from the living. Secondly, to let the dead know that much as they have been separated from the living by God, they should have one heart. Thirdly, to inform the dead that as the Bible says, all of us come from dust and will therefore return to dust. So those throwing soil on the dead would silently say, "You have gone ahead, we shall follow you tomorrow if our time comes."

After this, people continue pouring soil on the dead and later compress the soil. Acholi tradition says after the burial has been completed, the grave diggers and those who took part in the burial, would together put their hand on the tools used to dig the grave, which will by this time be placed straight on the grave. One person then pours water on the hands of the grave diggers three times, if the deceased was a man. If the dead was a woman, he would pour water on the people four times. When one of them is pouring water, they would be twisting their hands on the tool used for digging the grave three times or four times, depending on the sex of the dead.

Tradition has it that no one is expected to cry when the dead is being placed in the grave. Crying when a dead person is being lowered in the grave is an abomination. It means the person crying expects another person to die. In other words, crying at this time brings bad spirits on the living. After all the rituals have been performed, and the dead has been buried, those who took part in the burial moved a distance away to wash their hands. At this time, the women, men and the children then start crying. After the burial, everyone sits under the granary or tree in the compound. Those who performed the burial put the tools used in digging the grave on the verandah (or near the grave, if it was near the door way). However, if the burial takes place in town, people go to the home of the deceased, to take the spirit of the dead home. These tools would remain on the verandah until the day of performing the funeral rite. Acholi custom says if the deceased was male, people mourned for three days, but if the dead was a female, people mourn for four days. The days are counted starting on the day the dead was buried. Tradition also says on the first day of burial, the clan members do not hold any meeting until the evening of the second day, that is when the maternal and paternal relatives of the deceased would seated around the fire place, to discuss issues relating to the death.

The Acholi take issue of death quite seriously and in an orderly manner. Before the maternal relatives ask what could have caused the death of nephew or niece, they first investigate the form of death that befell their nephew or niece. As people gathered around a fire place an elder from the side of the deceased, would tell the maternal relatives the cause of death of their sister's child. He narrates how the illness started, the number of days or months the sickness lasted, until the death. After the people have listened to the elder and understood what he narrated, the kin of the mother of the deceased then asks for payment for the death. (See payment for death). If however, they realized that no hole, roots or stones were found when the grave is being dug, the maternal and paternal relatives would immediately agree on how to perform *teka*. As I said earlier, when a person dies and no hole, roots or stones are found his or her grave, clan members still insist on performing *teka*. The maternal relatives always do this performance after the dead had taken two days in the grave – the relatives perform *teka* in three different ways as we shall see below.

The matters of death are not only discussed by the maternal and paternal relatives alone, but mediators also attended. The history of Acholi states that mediators did not take part in the discussions, but only listen to what has been agreed upon or rejected by either party. They however intervene and give their opinions, when the meeting turns rowdy. But the maternal relatives preside over the entire meeting. If tensions begin to flare among the maternal and paternal relatives, then the people shake leaves – which means the meeting would be adjourned and resumed the following evening. In some cases, such meetings take two days, especially if the maternal and paternal relatives are in disagreement. If the maternal relatives are dissatisfied with the discussions, they table the matter before all, on the final day of the funeral rite. Before everyone has eaten or started drinking alcohol, they first discuss the matter that is unresolved between the maternal and paternal relatives. If the issues are resolved well, the mourners would then start indulging.

Performing *Teka*

On the second day of burial, the maternal relatives perform *teka* in three different ways as seen below:

(1) *Cucumber Ritual*: the maternal relatives take three cucumbers, one for them, one for the paternal relatives and the other for the witness. They then make incantations, "There! If this death that befell our sister came from our side, let the rats eat the cucumber you put in our name. However, if this death came from the paternal side, a rat should eat the cucumber put in their name. But if the death came from an evil-eye, we also pray that a rat should eat the cucumber put in their name. After his incantation, the maternal relatives take the three cucumbers and put each of them in a different location in the bush near the home. Very early the next morning, one of the elders would go to check the cucumbers. According to Acholi elders, if cucumbers are prayed over like this, a rat would not eat any at all. If there was an issue, the rat eats only one cucumber, which also points where the death originated. According to Acholi culture, if the death was not caused by the maternal relatives, paternal relatives or the witness, a rat would not eat any of the cucumbers. Other tribes think this is a false belief, but the Acholi know very well that this is possible, because it is the same as praying to the Almighty God.

Pouring sorghum or sesame to chickens: On the second performance of *teka*, the maternal relatives get sorghum or sesame, and pray, "The people of my ancestors! If this death was really caused by us, then a hen must be the first to eat the sesame or sorghum poured out here. But if it was caused by paternal relatives, we pray that a cock should be the first to eat the sorghum and sesame poured down here." A paternal relative would then pour the sesame or sorghum on the compound, before resuming their seat. The elders take their seats in a shelter, or by a granary, watching whether a cock or hen would be the first to eat the sorghum or sesame.

Acholi history states that if the death was caused by maternal relatives, a hen would come first to eat the sorghum poured on the compound. Conversely, if the death was caused by paternal relatives, a cock would come first to eat the sesame or sorghum. If a hen ate the sesame or sorghum first, the clan members would conclude right away, "The maternal relatives were the ones who brought death upon their own person." Yet, if a cock ate the sesame or sorghum first, the clan members would also say, "This death came from the family of the husband." Shortly, the family members would be blamed for the death. As we can see from Figure 50, it is a cock that starts eating the sesame or sorghum; this indicates that the death has come from the side of the husband's family.

Figure 49: Clan elders are watching a cock or hen that would be the first to eat the sorghum

(b)　*Trapping a rat*: the third method the maternal relatives use to know who killed their sister's child is by ensnaring a rat. In the evening when people are outside conversing, one of the maternal relatives sets a rat trap under a pot where house rats frequently pass from. If people are aware that there are no rats in that house, the maternal relatives would set the trap in the bush, near the home of the deceased. The Acholi who do not have rat traps, set nets in rat corridors near the home of the dead. Before the maternal relative go to set the rat trap or net, one of the paternal relatives would pray, "If this death was caused by the paternal relatives, the trap should ensnare a male rat." While another elder from the maternal side would pray, "If this death truly was caused by the maternal relatives, this trap or net should enmesh a female rat." After the maternal and paternal relatives have finished praying, they would pick the trap or net and give to one person to set it.

If the trap hits a female rat, it means the death was caused by maternal relatives. On the contrary, if the trap hits a male rat, it proves to the clan members that the death was caused by the paternal relatives. In Acholi performing *teka* is very important because it is one way the clan members know the cause of death.

After three or four days, the clan members gather to perform a funeral rite. On this day, the father of the deceased slaughters a billy goat on the grave, to cleanse the hands of those who buried the dead. The goat is slaughtered and skinned by a nephew, and no one else. After finishing his work, the nephew gives the meat to women to cook. The nephew takes the head and neck of the goat and cooks it by himself and eats it all alone, if there are no other nephews around.

One of the elders takes the dung of the slaughtered goat and smears it on the hands of those who buried the dead, and sprinkle some on the tools used for digging the grave. He puts some of the dung on the chests and legs of members of the bereaved family. One day, when I went to Obbo for a burial, and a goat was slaughtered to cleanse those who buried the dead, I asked a few elders, "Why do the Acholi put the dung of the goat on people's chest and legs? What function does putting dung on people's legs and chest perform to the people who buried the dead and the bereaved family?" The elders responded, "If the people who buried the dead are not cleansed, they would realise very poor crop yields — blood would destroy all their crops. Secondly, the goat's dung is put on the chest of the bereaved family to bring blessing — and good health. Thirdly, the dung is put on people's legs and chests so that no other person dies in a similar manner, or by the same cause, during the time of mourning, or immediately after burial."

In the evening when food is already prepared, people gather to eat and drink. If the dead was an old person, a married man, or a married woman, after eating and drinking, people would start dancing funeral dance. The Acholi love funeral dance very much and usually enjoyed it till morning. In the morning, while other people leave the burial place, the maternal and paternal relatives remain behind. They wait till evening, and then the maternal relatives ask for a funeral goat—a hen and cock to wave on the grave. The bereaved family hands over all these items to the maternal relatives, so that the spirit of dead is appeased wherever it would be. The maternal relatives slaughter the funeral billy goat and cook it that very night. The next morning, after the third cock crow, the maternal relatives get up to eat. They eat the whole goat, but leave the head. They hide the head of the billy goat, and after eating, one of the elders waves the cock on everybody on the compound, while silently saying, "God, we want to go back home. We pray that you pour your blessings upon the members of this family. Give the dead a cool heart in his grave."

After this, the maternal relatives do not go back to sit, but pick the head of the billy goat they had kept together with the bones left after eating, and a billy goat, and head home. Acholi culture states that whenever the maternal relatives are going back from a burial, they are not supposed to look back. Secondly, Acholi culture prohibited a man holding the sacrificial cock from stopping to urinate on the way, even if the urge is strong. If by bad luck the man urinates on the way, the chicken he is holding dies. Acholi culture also states that if the sacrificial cock dies, it indicates that the cultural norm has not been observed, and may lead to bad omen on women, children and men from the maternal side.

After the maternal relatives have moved a distance from the burial home, and reached the first stream, they sit by the side of the stream and eat the head of the billy goat here. After eating the head of the billy goat, they leave the skull and bones in the stream. Reports show that the maternal relatives also leave the utensils they used for eating in the stream. This is a rule that applies whether the deceased was an elder or a child.

The Death of a Leper

From time immemorial, when a leper died, the body would be washed, smeared with shea nut oil, and later taken into the bush and hanged on a tamarind tree. Leprosy is among the diseases detested by everyone in Acholi. Due to ignorance, some people believe that if a leper dies and is buried by the door way like any other dead body, another person would suffer from the same disease. Much as people regard leprosy as a terrible disease, they fondly called it "sanitation disease". Leprosy should have been hygiene related disease in its real sense, but I found that those who suffered from the disease were impoverished. The disease also made them unable to maintain cleanliness at public gatherings. Some people don't like sharing meals with a leper.

Before we delve more into issues of leprosy, I want us to answer this question, "Why do people hang the body of a leper on a tamarind tree? Why don't they bury the body of a leper by the door-way, as other bodies? According to Acholi culture, hanging the body of a leper on a tamarind tree is a pact between the dead and the other clan members still alive. Many think that leprosy is caused by a curse or something hot. The body of a leper was first hang on a tamarind tree, so that the disease did not spread to other family members.

Figure 50: In Acholi, when a leper dies, his body is hanged on a tamarind tree.

When I was interacting with the Acholi of Sudan, I realized that the current Acholi no longer dangle bodies of lepers on tamarind trees, because the new Acholi are Christians. And they believe that a leper possesses a holy spirit, which is inherent. The new Acholi therefore know that lepers have the same spirit as people without leprosy. The Acholi agree that leprosy is a disease which is only skin-deep, so it does not affect one's spirit. This means, both lepers and those who don't have the disease are equal before God. Thirdly, the Acholi know that the spirit of a person never dies, so if a person dies, their spirit continued living. For this reason, the Acholi say the spirits of the dead watch over everything being done by their clan-mates on earth. This means, if the body of a leper is hanged on a tamarind tree, the spirit would be upset. Some people believe that if the spirit of a leper is displeased, it would cause bad omen on the surviving clan members. For this reason, the new Acholi resolved that the body of a leper must be buried in the ground, so that it is not eaten by vultures. Much as the current Acholi agree that the body of a leper should be buried, we still find that the body of a leper is buried behind the house, but not at the door-way as like other bodies. If a leper dies in a town like Juba or Torit, the clan members bury the body in a cemetery among other bodies buried years ago, or even recently. What remains a mystery to me is why a dead leper of today are buried behind the house instead of door-way. As people of God we should treat the dead equally.

The payment for the death of a leper is the same as for the other dead people. Secondly, the funeral rites of a person who dies of leprosy are the same as the rituals performed over any other dead person as we saw in the previous pages. These are the traditions that relate to the death of a leper.

The death of the rain-chief

For many years, the Acholi have been holding the rain-chief in a very high regard, and no one disagreed with him. The Acholi also have a saying that death does not know a chief, because he is also human as any of us. After the death of a rain chief, men clean his body and smeared it with shea nut oil, cover his mouth with a new basket. They laid him on a hide, and covered his head with leopard skin. If the family does not have a leopard skin, the family members borrow from friends. If, however friends also do not have it, they are forced to buy from the market. Sometimes, people fail to get a big leopard skin to cover the head of the rain-chief. The family members then get the skin of a young leopard, cut it and tie it around his wrist. The rest of his body would be covered with a white sheet.

As we saw earlier, if a person dies, the maternal relatives receive the death requirements. In the same way, if a rain-chief dies the maternal relatives receive the requirements just as we saw earlier in this chapter (see payment for death).

The burial of a rain- chief also takes three days, but custom dictated that the children of a chief should carry the spirit of their father after a year. The phrase "carrying the spirit" of the chief means exhuming his skull. The children carry the skull of their father and put it in a pot, and keep it under a big tree near a stream. If the chief's home is far away from a big stream, the children would put the skull in a small steam near his home. Sometimes, a chief would die from a town or in a foreign land, just like chief Aburi of Obbo who died and was buried in Lokung – Uganda. (His children have not yet brought his skull home). They put it in a pot and take it under a big tree near a stream, because it is what their custom demands. In Acholi, matters relating to death are handled in the same way. However, the custom relating to the death of twins is slightly different. What is the custom relating to the death of twins?

The Death of Twins

Acholi history states that, when a twin dies, the body is also cleaned and smeared with shea nut oil, just like it is done with any other dead body. In the same way, when a twin dies, his or her grave is also cleansed as we saw earlier. When the grave is of the required depth, and the body is about to be lowered in, the body is first put in a pot, which is then put in the grave–this happens when the twin dies at a very tender age. However, if the twin dies as an adult, custom requires that the body should be put in a metal tank. But if the twin dies at a young age and is buried in town, the skull would be disinterred, as required by custom. The skull would be draped in a sheet, and one small stone would be placed beside it –this happens when the skull is being taken home. When the people taking the skull arrive home, the clan members would dig a grave and the skull would be buried afresh. Custom requires that even if the grave is cleansed during the time of burial in town, the maternal and paternal relatives again make incantations around the grave. After the men had finished digging the grave, the elders would take the skull and the stone beside the body, and put them in a pot and bury them. The skull spends three or four days in the grave, then the father of the deceased gets a billy goat to cleanse the hands of those who participated in the burial, as we saw earlier. On this same day, food and alcohol would be prepared. After a short time, people would start eating and drinking. If however, the dead was an adult, the mourners would dance after the drinking. But if the dead was still young, the mourners dispersed after eating and drinking. Tradition prohibits people from dancing during burial, if the deceased was still a young.

One day, I asked some Acholi elders from Lologo camp (Juba), "Why don't people leave the bones of a young twin in town?" They said it was because of two reasons: first, everyone in Acholi says twins are children of spirit– which means they are a gift from God. So the skeleton of a child believed to be a gift from God to the parents should not be far from home. Secondly, the skeleton of a twin is not left in town because many Acholi believe that twins have powers given to them by God. So if their skeletons are far from home, especially if the deceased was still young, it would make their mother infertile. But if the dead was already an adult, leaving the skull in the cemetery could bring bad spells on the elders and the young ones.

Acholi tradition states that payment for death of twins is the same as for other people. This is the norm regarding the death of twins.

The Death of a First born

A first born is highly respected in a family. When the Acholi talk about the death of a first born, they do not refer to the death of a child that was born first in the family, but rather, the child that dies first in the family. Reports show that if a family has four, six, or more children, and none among them had yet died, the first child to die would be called the first born or the death of a first born. The death can befall the first born, the third or even the sixth born. If the first born dies first, the Acholi refer to it as the death of a first born. If the third born dies first, they also called it death of the first born. If the first born dies, women clean the body and smear it with shea nut oil. During grave digging, the maternal and paternal relatives also pray, as I mentioned earlier in this chapter. The girls also ask for money for taking the dead body out of the house. Acholi culture barred people from talking a lot when the first born child dies. Custom also prohibits people from crying too much when the first child dies. I know that some Acholi women like crying a lot during burials. When such women begin to cry, the elders allow them to cry only for a few minutes and they are stopped.

One day, I asked some Acholi elders, "Why does custom prohibit people from crying too much when a first born dies?" The elders responded that people are prohibited from crying a lot when the first child dies because it is the same as asking God, "God, why did you take away this child alone?" This was the same as asking God why he took only one child. Which could be interpreted as the mourner was asking God to take away another brother or sister of the deceased, so that they give company to the deceased in their new world. Such statements are similar to sorcery or curses, so people do not want to listen to them. Secondly, I continued asking the elders, "How does mourning become sorcery?" Crying a lot becomes wizardry because that is still the first case of death in the family, and if anyone continues crying, it means they want another person in the family to die. If this was the second death in the family, no one would say crying a lot is bad, and brings bad luck in the family, so it is not regarded as sorcery.

When the boys and men have finished digging the grave, the clan members would then take the body for burial. According to Acholi culture, the first born child was not laid in the grave sideways, but in a sitting posture. Later, one of the elders takes the small left finger of the dead, and puts it in its mouth. He covers the head of the deceased with a sheet. All burials are done in the same manner as we saw earlier in this chapter (see burial pg. 535).

Payments for Death

In the past, the Acholi of South South and Acholi of the north agreed on one payment for death. This rule was well implemented and people chose only five things to pay for death. The maternal relatives asked for five things as I will discuss below:

i.	*Lango*	Ls.00.05.
ii.	Knife, a spear (in kind –or money)	Ls.00.10.
iii.	Fire billy goat (in kind)	Ls03.00.
iv.	A sacrificial cock and pot	Ls.00.25.
v.	A lump of pounded tobacco (in kind or money)	Ls00.10.
vi.	Grand total	Ls.3.50.

This norm was well executed among the Acholi north and Acholi south from the year 1900 – 1964. But due to intermarriages between Acholi and Madi, the Acholi south copied other rules from the Madi. They then added these rules to the traditional rules of the Acholi —on the five items to pay for death. The first cultural rule the Acholi borrowed from the Madi was getting a dead body out of the house (or the money for girls). The second was money for the grave. These two rules were not among the Acholi. Acholi elders told me that the rule of getting a dead body from the house, and things for the grave initially worked only among the Acholi in the south. Gradually, because of intermarriages between the Acholi south and north, the issue of getting a dead body from the house, and paying money for the grave was introduced in Acholi north.

Reports show that if cousin of Acholi south die, and the deceased had married an Acholi north, they would ask for money for the girls immediately at the grave side. This rule caused chaos among the people, because the Acholi in the north disagreed that the two rules were not theirs. Consequently, other people refused to implement it. Much as the Acholi in the north refused to use this rule, the maternal relatives later out-spoke them. In the land of the Acholi of Sudan, the maternal relatives have the authority to ask for item for the death of their sister's child. This explains why Acholi have a saying that, "The voice pressed the ring pad."

Unfortunately, when the Acholi south brought this rule from Madi, people did not agree on a specific amount to be paid for getting a dead body out of the house, and for the grave. Anyone charged any amount of money for taking a dead body from the house, and for the grave.

Acholi tradition states that the rule brought by Acholi south was forever rejected by some people such as Pajok. Reports show that the Pajok were the only ones who maintained the five items (1964 – 1989).

Much as the Pajok refused to obey the rule of the Madi, some Acholi later on realized that they had also introduced giving a billy goat for the girls, which was not practiced by Acholi. Many Acholi elders told me, "The issue of billy goat for the ladies started from the family of the Obwolto, and later spread among the Pajok and other Acholi." I then asked the elders, "Why did the issue of a billy goat for the girls start in Obwolto?" Unfortunately, there was no elder from Obwolto who could answer my question. When Chief Otaviano Oyat Akut realized that the matter was becoming contentious among the people, he convened a meeting of all the Acholi in Juba. This meeting was held for five months. It started on 13/4/1991 and ended in 18/10/1991. It was held in Lologo

Displaced Camp. I also attended the meeting – this gave me the chance to get important information to write in this book. During this meeting, people discussed many issues regarding payment for death. During the meeting some Acholi realized that working with the Panyikwara became difficult, because the Panyikwara did not share their ideas with other Acholi. Members realized that the charges of the Panyikwara were so high (Ls 6.46). Other Acholi stipulated that all charges for payment for death should be Ls 3.85. After this meeting, which took six months members then specified the payments as below:

No.	Payment for death	Palwar, Pajok, Obbo, Magwi, Omeo, Agoro and Offirka.	Panyikwara
1-	The grave	Ls.00.10	Ls.00.10
2-	Skull	02.50	02.50
3-	taking the body out of the	00.50	00.50
4-	house (for girls) A hen (in kind)	00.05	00.05
5-	Digging rod	00.10	00.10
6-	A spear or knife	00.10	00.10
7-	Nanny goat (or money)	00.50	00.50
8-	Three to five arrows	—	02.50
9-	A billy goat (in kind)	—	—
10-	Two carton of cigarettes (in	—	—
11-	kind)	—	—
12-	Two cartons of matches (in	—	00.11
13-	kind)	—	
	Leopard skin (or money if it is not there) Ground nuts (in kind in Panyikwara). Payment for death =		
		Ls.03.85 ==============	06.46 ========

N.B. If the deceased was an unmarried woman then the husband pays all the money for death to the maternal relatives, then married the dead body on charges set by the people at Ls.150,000.

Inheriting a Widow

The culture of the Acholi of Sudan states that if a man dies and leaves behind a widow and children, the widow is not allowed to re-marry a man from outside. Tradition allowed her to choose a boy or man among her late husband's brothers. Acholi culture says if a woman has interest in her late husband's brother, the man does not enter into a sexual relationship with her immediately. The woman would first mourn her husband for a year or two. This is also the time people evaluate who among the brothers can take care of the widow and her children. The woman would then silently watch the man she has interest in – she watches whatever the man does to her. Acholi tradition says a man who is interested in a widow is always the first to prove his hard work to the woman. How does the man show that he can work hard?

The Acholi have a saying that, a house without a man is always cold, with no food and clothes for the woman and children. Besides when the wind blew the roof top, no one would repair it. This made the rain fall in the house, in addition to other problems that I cannot list here.

A man who is interested in taking care of his brother's widow always repairs the roof of the widow's hut that was blown off by wind–the widow watches quietly. A man who wants to inherit his brother's widow always brings home game meat for the widow–the woman would watch quietly. A man who wants to take care of his brother's widow asks for seeds from the widow during planting season and plants for her – the woman watches silently. The woman would then see all that her late husband's brother is doing, while saying silently, "Eh, This is a person who can take care of my children?" Acholi culture states that, a man who repairs the roof of a widow's hut, cultivates her garden and brings her game meat after hunting, does all those these quietly without saying anything to the widow – all these good deeds are what the Acholi termed as "courting without words." When a man is doing all these, he quietly watches the widow, to see if she has facial expression of love or mood – a man who is experienced in courtship can detect a face full of love.

Other brothers on seeing what their sibling is doing to the widow back down/not interfere. The clan members also see what the man is doing and not say anything. But they would be asking themselves, "Does this man want to inherit the widow? We thank God! Our orphans cannot be taken away to a foreigner?"

On the other hand, the clan members also watch what the man does for the widow. The women in the clan would then start gossiping to the widow. Acording to Acholi tradition, the moment the women see one man doing some chores for the widow two or three of the women would go to converse with the widow in the evening. In their conversation, one of the women would tell the widow, "Ah! Woman, it seems this man _____(mentions the name) will take care of you and the children. We want you to think over it for some time." When the widow hears such statements, she does not respond immediately, but ponder over it. The two or three women keep coming to converse with her. All these days the women come to the widow, they would also hint on the different things her late husband's brother was doing for her.

After one or two years, the widow would stops mourning her husband. One morning, the clan elders call all the brothers of the deceased together with the widow. They sit in front of the eldest brother's, or the widow's hut. The clan elders ask the widow, "Very well woman, you have already untied your mourning string, secondly, your blood is still warm – you are still fertile. Today we want to know from you, among the brothers of your late husband, who are present here, who do you want to take care of your children?" The woman, based on the good things one of the brothers has been doing for her, points at the man she desires, "I want that one, and because I know very well that he can take care of me and my children." The woman responds like this because of the good work the man has done for her. Besides, all this time he has been helping her, he has not attempt to forcefully open her door at night.

When the elders have heard from the widow, they again turn to the man and ask him, "Have you heard what your sister-in-law has said?" The man answers, "Yes, I have heard all that she has said. I don't have anything to say. The children she has are my brother's children. I have accepted to take care of them together with their mother." The elders would continue talking to the man, "Well child, thank you for your responses. Before you start to live in your in-law's house, we want you to bring a billy goat, to cleanse the children."

The following morning, the man gets a billy goat from the grazing ground, spears it and smears the dung on the chest of the widow and her children's. The meat is cooked and eaten by the clan elders. That very evening, the man asks for bathing water from the widow, and she will immediately concludes that the man will sleep in her house that night. The woman takes bathing water behind the house, and comes back in the house to lay the bed. If the woman used to sleep together with the children, that night, she would take the children's bed to the kitchen. After bathing, the man would enter the bedroom. This is how inheritance of widow is done in Acholi.

But sometimes, the widow could see that no one among her late husband's brothers could take care of her and the children. Such cases always arose because of two reasons: one, when the woman saw that her in-laws were bad mannered, so she would turn all of them down. Inheriting one would mean piling more problems. Secondly, such issues cropped up when the brothers in-law had seen that the widow behaved inappropriately, so none of them would want to associate with her. If however, the clan elders saw that the men are ill-mannered, they would ask the widow to look for another man from the late husband's clan.

According to Acholi culture, a nephew can inherit the wife of his dead maternal uncle. So if the widow realises that there is a nephew who can take care of her and her children, she forwards his name to clan elders. The clan elders later call the nephew and the widow, and tell the nephew, "Child, Acholi have a saying that *a nephew inherits his uncle's wife.* Today, it is your turn. Your uncle's wife wants you to inherit her. We now want you to get a billy goat and spear it to cleanse the children." The nephew does not turn down the widow. Shortly, he brings a billy goat, spears it and smears the dung on the chest of the children and the widow.

That evening, the nephew asks for bathing water from the widow. It is from here that the widow knows that, that night the nephew will take the place of her dead husband. The woman takes for him bathing water behind the house, and prepares the bed. If the woman used to sleep in the same room with the children, this time she takes their bed to the kitchen. After bathing, the nephew enters the house to sleep. This is how a nephew inherits his uncle's wife in Acholi.

The history of Acholi also says if the widow realises that there is no man among her late husband's brothers or nephews to take care of her and her children, she searches for a man outside the family. Tradition does not allow elders to force a man on a woman against her will. The widow then lives here while searching for a good man outside the family. According to Acholi tradition, this man is also required to bring a billy goat and slaughter to cleanse the children of the deceased. Secondly, the bereaved family asks the new man to pay back the bride price that was paid by the deceased. The man pays the amount charged by the family of the deceased, before taking the widow. The children, however, remain with the bereaved family. If the widow is still breast-feeding, culture does not allow her to go with the baby to her new husband's home. If she goes with child, the brothers of the deceased will bring the child back home when the child has grown up.

Sometimes, some women would go to their new husband's home before their bride price is paid. If this happens, the children she produces from with her new husband will be claimed by the family of her dead husband.

This brings us to the end of the different ways that men in Acholi used to inherit widows.

Chapter Thirty Three

ACHOLI PROVERBS

Acholi have many proverbs that cannot all be written in this book. Since many proverbs are being forgotten, I think I will write 189 most important ones here. The Acholi always use proverbs, when they do not want foreigners who learned Acholi language to understand the meaning of their conversation. Very few people who know Acholi language know Acholi proverbs. But majority do not understand proverbs at all.

Below are the Acholi Proverbs:

S/No	Proverb	S/No	Meaning
1	A duiker is not tracked with one rain	1	If you do not detect his fault today, you may do it tomorrow.
2	It is a visiting dove that is trapped.	2	If you go where there is death, it is a visitor who dies.
3	A hard calabash is managed by fire.	3	He met a person stronger than himself.
4	Imitation killed hare	4	Do not compare your wit with others' because it may cause you death.
5	One of the legs of "I wish I knew" is behind.	5	You may regret your action in future.
6	I eat my death.	6	I have to eat anything and die with.
7	A red-chest sun bird.	7	A person who likes causing confusion.
8	Agoro white ants do not eat across the stream.	8	Take your share and leave your friend's.

9	A water pot breaks at the doorway.	9	Failure may come when you are about to finish the work.
10	A fart is smells stronger than feces.	10	A serious famine.
11	Trouble causing is good for birds.	11	Conflict is a vice.
12	The water pot presses upon the ring pad.	12	The voice of the majority suppressed Pilate/me.
13	A monkey laughs at the tail of the one in front of it.	13	The problem your friend experiences today may be yours tomorrow.
14	The head of the hind monkey is blood-stained.	14	Being the last person may cause you death.
15	Calabashes jostle with each other.	15	Let people also use your property.
16	A duiker and a dog	16	He will run and catch the prey.
17	Maize do well where there are no teeth.	17	Barren people usually have good harvest, yet there are no children to feed.
18	It was burnt because of comparing its footprint with elephant's.	18	Do not compare yourself with the rich.
19	A guinea fowl bears its traits.	19	A bad woman bears bad children.
20	A duiker dies at langol's.	20	Do not compare yourself with the rich.
21	Calmness made billy goat fatty.	21	It is not good to use force, be calm.
22	Living at the anthill made antelope brown.	22	If you live with bad people, you well eventually become bad.
23	Take cover at the hunting net.	23	Wait patiently.
24	It has the beauty of lalaa vegetable.	24	A person may look good, but he or she is actually bad.
25	Live with your heart and do not live with your lung.	25	All words that come from my mouth are bad in your ears.
26	The wound of the back	26	Be careful, otherwise, you will displease him again.
27	Giving the clan's hand.	27	Helping people.
28	A wet stalk	28	He slept with her.
29	Argument made chicken toothless.	29	Too much argument can cause death.
30	Poverty does not go with foolishness.	30	Do not waste what you have, be wise.

31	They eat themselves like fish.	31	They accuse each other.
32	Eat like rats.	32	You eat little by little and you will eat more at your place.
33	One hand does not open the anus.	33	He is without an assistant – unity is strength.
34	He has long finger nails.	34	He is a thief.
35	He eats like the heel.	35	He uses people's property but does not give his.
36	Should I die for food, I will return it.	36	Do not. Disown your brother or sister for food.
37	Even if you fart under water, it will come out.	37	Even if you keep your misdeed a secret, people will still know.
38	He is too prepared.	38	Adequate preparation.
39	Returning often to the same place made antelope to carry the stalk of spear.	39	It is bad to continue doing wrong things, it will cause you problems.
40	A playful kid breaks the granary.	40	Heed to advice so that you do not fall into problems.
41	Sweet tongue.	41	He entices people with sweet words.
42	A goat stares at he who skins it.	42	A person who stops conflicting parties often finds problems.
43	Little sauce finishes the bread.	43	Do not despise a small bodied person, he can throw you to the ground (or can settle serious dispute).
44	Chickens run with the intestine of their dead friend,	44	Do not criticise others for the fault you share with them.
45	What touched your anus also touched mine.	45	The problem you experienced yesterday, I experienced today.
46	He removed wax from koga's vent.	46	Letting out the secret of your friend.
47	It is mountains that do not meet, but humans do.	47	We will meet in future.
48	A dog goes where it is given bones.	48	People go where they are helped.
49	Kinship gifts are supplemented with laughter.	49	You will get more tomorrow.

50	You are flogging feces.	50	You are wasting time.
51	Brandish a leaf after a dispute is settled.	51	Maintain the blessing.
52	What defeats an axe, a hewing hoe cannot manage.	52	An ardent offender does not listen to anybody.
53	Dry season eggs do not hatch all.	53	You cannot please everybody in a gathering.
54	Borrowed things do not form crust.	54	Your own property is better that others'.
55	You laugh with blood on your teeth.	55	Wait for your time; you will also be in trouble.
56	Smoke rises from fire	56	Everything has a cause.
57	The ear does not grow beyond the head.	57	Be respectful and listen to elders.
58	You will be accountable, holding millet of Magwi people.	58	If it becomes a problem, you will be responsible.
59	Pitch camp	59	A brief stop (in the hunting ground)
60	I *boole*	60	Let us go ahead (in the hunting ground)
61	In bira and separation	61	They cannot be separated, they like each other a lot.
62	A dog bites the finger that feeds it.	62	The one you help may turn out your killer or enemy.
63	You will see what monkey saw in the pea garden.	63	You will be in trouble if you continue doing this, or you get into the problems you have never been in.
64	You will see what prevents sleep.	64	Moving around too much can caused you trouble.
65	The ear and the eye.	65	The clan's relationship.
66	A bath place is not a place to dry oneself.	66	Assistance is not given every day.
67	Adequate salt in the food.	67	I am tired of disputes; the canes have rocked my body.
68	Putting dung in people's mouth.	68	Putting words in people's mouth.

69	A man and a man	69	Both of them are strong.
70	Warthog will kick the hair	70	Take care.
71	Cry at the smoke.	71	Worried about the past.
72	When two elephants fight, it is the grass that suffers.	72	When two leaders rival for power, it is the local people who suffer.
73	Castrating a dog.	73	Settling a difficult dispute.
74	Waiting for the last, you spear a dog.	74	Do what is at hand, you will regret leaving it.
75	Do not uproot the pumpkin on the old homestead.	75	Do not reject your friend, you will still meet tomorrow.
76	Akica's offspring.	76	A good person.
77	A clan is not strapped on the back with baby strap.	77	Love for one's clan is proved at the time of problem, not at meal.
78	A haughty person eats dewy vegetable.	78	A haughty person is often starved, he does not get anything.
79	Shyness makes you eat poison.	79	Doing thing shyly causes you death.
80	The white hyena skirts the arena.	80	A man who sleeps with another man's wife cannot enter her house when her husband is around.
81	Conflict builds on exchange of words.	81	Be quiet.
82	The white teeth stink.	82	A person who appears good, but he is actually bad.
83	The head of the warthog that remains behind is blood-stained.	83	Move together with others so that nothing happens to you.
84	The nose of the beauty stinks.	84	The person appears good, but he or she is bad (adulterous, a thief, etc).
85	A friend fermented blood.	85	Kinship is deeper than friendship.
86	He who roasts the egg knows the position of the albumen.	86	An offender knows what he or she has done.
87	Thieves met on *kira*	87	People of two extremities have met today.

88	We do not inspect the teeth of he who takes care of the garden.	88	The person who takes care of the garden usually eats first, because he takes a little from the garden before the owner.
89	The lizard protects itself yet nobody eats it.	89	Cowardliness saves life.
90	The lion resorted to sausage fruit.	90	You refused it in the past, but it has become nice today.
91	Nice words settle debt.	91	Good speech purges one's offence.
92	I slept hungry over the matter.	92	I never heard anything about the matter.
93	A hunter sees the water gourd with his own eyes.	93	Be prepared all the time.
94	Elephant broke *oryang* branches to roast its meat.	94	He was beaten with the stick that he brought (or a child has brought the cane for caning himself).
95	Fight while seated.	95	Handle issues humbly.
96	The dead man lost the case.	96	He cannot know the case against him, neither can he know anything good that came later.
97	His puppy is a fast runner.	97	He is a liar.
98	*Lakul* is seen with the hair line on his fore head.	98	Do not despise a small person; he can pour sand into your eyes.
99	A puppy does not play with the milk in the stomach of another.	99	Do not disturb me because I am hungry, or do not disturb me because I have problems.
100	The water of clan dispute is poured behind a door shutter.	100	Even if your clan member wrongs you, you still have to join hands – forgive your clan members.
101	The small round headed creature.	101	A human being.
102	The falling off of one thatch does not make the roof leak.	102	A bad character should be isolated, it does not disunite people.
103	Moving slowly kept the white man from falling.	103	Do things slowly, and you will manage.
104	Small gift leads to the big one.	104	Do not turn down what you have been given just because it is little.

105	Fire begets ashes.	105	Children who do not help their parents.
106	The fire blazes yonder.	106	A girl is married in a foreign land.
107	Slowly with the birth of Ongoro	107	He will meet you in future.
108	Swallowing words is a virtue.	108	It is good to be patient.
109	Hare's sleep.	109	Faking sleep.
110	Put off the fire.	110	Be calm.
111	Ocen is a human and Apiyo is also a human.	111	Today we eat at mine, tomorrow we eat at yours.
112	One frog surged the water.	112	One person can spoil many people.
113	Joke put a fetus in the womb.	113	Extraordinary play with brothers-in-law can lead to pregnancy.
114	Errand is a nanny goat.	114	An obedient child often finds food where he is sent, or an elder gives him s reward when he comes back.
115	The rats in Akech's mother's house.	115	They are the same, or they are all bad people.
116	A distant stick does not hit a snake.	116	What is far away does not help.
117	A male tortoise is proved by it testicle, or A male tortoise is proved on fire.	117	A person's sense of responsibility is seen at the time of difficulty, or a strong person is seen during a fight.
118	It pulled my upper and lower ear.	118	It has become too much for me.
119	The house covers many issues.	119	Every marriage has issues; do not let out your marriage problems.
120	You can back up the chicken; you can back up the wild cat.	120	Both are at fault.
121	It has become *amida*	121	What you once rejected has become good.
122	White ants flew out after chicken have gone to roost.	122	The offender came after the owner of the home, or the issue came when I had already gone.
123	Cucumber is brought together by its seeds.	123	A girl marries her mother if she was not yet married.
124	The axe fell in water.	124	A barren man.

125	When you dip fishing basket in water, it catches anything.	125	Eat and add to yours.
126	He died in the battle field.	126	To drink or eat something and not pay for.
127	A cutter of a wire.	127	A woman who eloped with a man and returned home, or has separated with her husband.
128	Obbo looked down upon son of Acaya.	128	Do not look down upon small bodied person. He can beat you.
129	Many rats cannot make a hole.	129	Too many people doing the same work causes laziness.
130	A cold house.	130	The food that a woman serves to please clan members (a woman who had run away).
131	Fee for interruption of work	131	Alcohol or money paid for attending a meeting.
132	Eagle turned its back to the sky.	132	I used to help him, but now he does not want to help me.
133	A dead house.	133	A house without a woman.
134	He came with his bow scratching the ground.	134	He came when he was very ready.
135	Do not drink porridge from its middle lest it should burn your lips.	135	Investigate patiently and you will find out the truth.
136	Borrowing is better than stealing.	136	He who begs is not at fault.
137	A stream is supplied by its tributaries.	137	Unity is power.
138	Do not carry a log that is dropped on the way.	138	Do not marry a divorced woman because she will also divorce you.
139	He is alerted by the last white ants.	139	Being absent minded when others are talking, and getting involved at the last moment.
140	Do not equate sleep to death.	140	The rich is not comparable to the poor.
141	Do not scare eagle with death.	141	Patiently wait and you will catch the offender.

142	When water pours, it cannot be gathered.	142	When a mistake is made, it is irreversible.
143	Do not hit the drum in the mid of the air.	143	Do not accept anything you have not understood; or do not respond when it is not your turn to speak.
144	Do not laugh at the mother of rainy season.	144	Do not be deceived by your eyes, it can rain anytime it pleases.
145	Unity is strength.	145	No one can live without others.
146	Wear shoes on thorn pricked feet.	146	The wrong has been done, and it is too late.
147	Wisdom is better than strength	147	Use your brain so that you can eat.
148	Does a fox ask a dog?	148	I also do not know.
149	Slowness turned words into stones.	149	Do things at the right time, or else you miss them.
150	The spear has weakened the elephant.	150	He has got what he wanted; or he has been seriously caned.
151	A snake in the hole.	151	He only looks good, he is actually very bad.
152	The death of millet on the grinding stone	152	Endless love.
153	A cock does not crow on the compound of the other.	153	Even if you are very strong, do not provoke someone to fight on his compound, or do not respond to a matter that is outside your zone.
154	A worker deserves a pay.	154	Do things that can bring you profits.
155	Playing with fire makes you get burnt.	155	Do not associate with offence for it may become yours.
156	Strong eye	156	Wisdom.
157	Greed is better than theft.	157	Ask and they will give you.
158	If you walk at night, you tread on a broken calabash.	158	Walking too much can make you meet trouble.
159	Listens with the back of his head.	159	A naughty and stubborn person.
160	Do not push people back like women's urine.	160	Do not keep repeating things that have already been understood.

161	We will meet on the anthill.	161	We will see who people will choose between the two of us.
162	You are the next one.	162	You will be in trouble at the end.
163	Move around with people's arms.	163	Do not confuse people for it may cause death.
164	He has forgotten like a person gathering white ants.	164	He is not worried about anything.
165	His eyes are strong like *okweko's*.	165	A person who cannot be deceived.
166	Night obscured the white cow.	166	Darkness covers bad thing (adulterous acts); or do not talk anyhow in darkness for your enemies may listen.
167	A tree is not climbed from the top.	167	Things need to be handled orderly.
168	Two pathways confused hyena.	168	Do one thing at a time. Do not be corrupt.
169	A bent tree cannot be straightened.	169	A spoiled person cannot be corrected.
170	Opening people's eyes.	170	Deceiving people with sweet words.
171	Accept things with the thunder.	171	Accepting something you have well understood.
172	White ants on the small anthill.	172	A dirty woman bears many children.
173	Everyone eats where he or she works.	173	Every worker is a thief of money.
174	No one pricks his own eyes.	174	No one can kill his brother or sister.
175	White ants fly out from its hole.	175	Every matter has a cause.
176	Do not blame the wind when white ants are not flying out	176	Problems are God given, but some people still blame it on the clan.
177	The skin of *worole* (ngec) looks smarter with horn to be blown.	177	Living miserable life; or someone who is a parasite to others.
178	Making a baby strap for an unborn child.	178	You cannot tell the future.
179	A sharp-eye person	179	A lecherous person.
180	No one has been hued from a tree.	180	Everybody has parents and a clan.

181	Vomit cannot be licked.	181	Once a mistake made, it is not reversible.
182	Whoever denies you white ants saves you from diarrhea.	182	If somebody refuses to deliver bad information to you, he saves you from getting involved in it.
183	Marriage is rubbish pit.	183	Payment of bride price is not done only once.
184	Walks with the heels	184	A proud person.
185	A meek ram	185	A person who does not know how to quarrel or fight, but if you provoke him he will not spare you.
186	Laziness took monkey to the bush	186	Laziness makes you unable to take care of your family.
188	The nose and the eye	188	Blood relations.
189	The nose cannot detect smell.	189	No one knows what will happen tomorrow.

Chapter Thirty Four

INTERNAL WAR

In the past all the Acholi of Sudan regarded themselves as brothers and sisters. Even as I write this book, everyone comes together when there is any problem with one group of Acholi. But I also learnt that, much as the Acholi of Sudan lived together as brothers and sisters, minor conflicts still occurred among them. I then asked the elders of Acholi what caused such conflicts. We learnt that in the past there were wars between brothers in Acholi. "So what caused this fights?" The elders responded, "There are many things that caused fights among brothers, but there are always four main causes of fights among brothers, and these are:

  i.   Hypocrites.
  ii.   Wicked/ stone-hearted chiefs
  iii. Acholi like reparation, they do not want to feel defeated.
  iv.   Narrow-mindedness and disunity among brothers (people)

When I was moving among the elders of Acholi of Sudan, I gradually realized that some elders had evil hearts, and did not want the children to know their history. Other elders told me that it was not right for children to know that bad records of the past, because it would make them seek revenge. According to the elders, vengeance would complicate conflict resolution among the Acholi. But such viewpoints are wrong, because history informs and shapes people's directions and actions. Ignorance of history in most cases cause conflicts among people. A close examination shows that internal conflicts did not happen among all the Acholi. For instance, families like Panyikwara and Palwar did not fight each other. Hence, the Panyikwara and Palwar are only peaceful people among the Acholi. According to history the Acholi of Sudan who engaged in fights with their brothers were the Obbo, who conflicted with the Pajok. The Obbo also fought with the people of Magwi. The people of Agoro fought with the Ofirika, while the Agoro also conflicted with the people of Magwi.

To better understand the internal conflicts in Acholi, I think it is better if we answer these questions: When did these fights happen? What were the causes of fight between the brothers? What do the Acholi remember about the conflicts? Is there any song or anything that the olden people left to remind the new generation? Were there any changes among the people after the fights?

All clan elders who fought among themselves should be asked these questions. Let us examine the issues relating to brotherly fights in Acholi one by one.

Conflict between Obbo and Pajok

Secret warfare happened between the Obbo and Pajok for many years, and no one documented them. As we saw earlier, history disappears when not put on paper. I met some clan elders, who remembered some of the internal conflicts, but many could not give the chronology of their history. The history of Acholi says that there have been many conflicts between between Obbo and Pajok, but the most prominent one is the "Pep' war". Pep was a son of Pajok, from the family of Kapaa. The history of Pajok says Chief Ocieng had twelve messengers, and Pep was one of them. Other Acholi elders told me, "All messengers of the chief are hypocrites" – that is what caused fights between the Obbo and Pajok.

Both the Obbo and Pajok have different versions of what caused Pep's war. The conflicting versions are a result of lack of documentation of history. Had the history been written, such differences would not have arisen. Someone might ask, "What do the people of Obbo and Pajok say about the conflict of Pep?"

According to the people of Obbo, the conflict started because of a girl called "Launa" – a born of Pajok. Reports show that Launa was a very beautiful girl, and most men fell in love with her at first sight. Chief Ocieng Lokwor-moi, of Ywaya-Pajok wanted Launa to be his wife. On the other hand, chief Aburi of Obbo also wanted Launa to be his wife. Hence, the two chiefs had to compete for her. The history of Obbo and Pajok says, much as Launa knew that the two chiefs admired her, she did not show her interest in either of them. Although Launa had not shown interest in the two chiefs, neither of them told the other about his interest in Launa.

One day, Chief Ocieng gave his messenger, Pep a knife, to take to chief Aburi.

In Acholi, this is an insult. Chief Ocieng did this to discourage Chief Aburi from pursuing Launa. Before Pep left Pajok, Chief Ocieng told him, "If you reach Obbo, tell Chief Aburi that, Chief Ocieng wants to see you. I also want Chief Aburi to come here in Pajok". Shortly, Pep set out for Obbo. When he walked for about two hours, he entered the compound of Chief Aburi. In the past, it was not easy for a visitor to meet the chief. For this reason, Pep did not meet Chief Aburi. Pep called one person who was at the chief's home and told him, "Chief Ocieng Lokwor-moi sent me with an important message to Chief Aburi. Tell him that a visitor from Pajok is outside."

The man sent the message to Chief Aburi, who told him, "Chief, there is a man outside who said Chief Ocieng of Pajok sent him with an important message." At that time Chief Aburi was conversing with his friend Teda, of Pajombo. Chief Aburi told his messenger, "Well, go back to him and let him give you the message from Chief Ocieng."

The messenger of Chief Aburi went back to Pep, and told him, "What has Chief Ocieng sent you to do?" Pep responded, "Chief Ocieng sent me to bring this knife to chief Aburi —while showing the knife to the messenger." Pep gave the knife to the messenger of Chief Aburi, who then took it to Chief Aburi. Chief Aburi was upset on seeing that Chief Ocieng Lokwor-moi sent him a knife. Chief Aburi immediately said, "I do not want to hear what Chief Ocieng has to say, I also do not want to see Pep in my compound." Shortly, Chief Aburi turned to his friend Teda and asked, "What does Chief Ocieng want from me?" Teda responded, "Aburi, you are a man; Ocieng is also a man. Whatever it is, just prepare yourself to fight Pajok."

Later, Chief Aburi called his guards and told them, "I don't want Pep to go back to Chief Ocieng in Pajok. I want you to arrest him and tie him with a rope. I also want you to whip with and dump in a rubbish pit. Chief Ocieng should come to me if he is strong." The guards hurried where Pep was, and immediately put him down and tied him with a sisal rope. He was flogged till he was unconscious. The guards thought he was already dead. They then took his body to the rubbish pit as they were ordered by Chief Aburi.

As we saw earlier that the messengers of the chiefs were hypocrites, chief Aburi also had such hypocrites among his guards. When one of the guards saw what the guards of Chief Aburi did to Pep, he ran immediately to Chief Ocieng. When he reached Pajok, he told Chief Ocieng Lokwor-moi, "Chief, much as you are calmly seated, Chief Aburi has already killed the messenger you sent to him with an important message." When Chief Ocieng heard the news, he summoned his army to go and fight the people of Obbo to avenge Pep's death.

However, according to the Pajok, the conflict of Pep did not start with the issue of Launa, but because of a rain stone. The Pajok say Pep was a true born of Kaapa. So he loved staying at his friend's home (whose name they do not know) in Obbo Obbo. That month, Pep was at his friend's in Obbo. One day, as the two friends were walking along a pathway, Pep found a rain stone. He picked the rain stone and showed it to his friend who advised him to take the rain stone to Chief Aburi. At that time, when foreigners found a rain stone, they were required to take it to Chief Aburi. The issue of taking a rain stone to the chief was not only practiced by the Obbo, but other chiefs as well. Unfortunately, Pep refused his friend's advice, and instead took the rain stone to Chief Ocieng in Pajok. Pep's friend was unhappy with what he did- this was against their cultural norm. Pep's friend decided to report the matter to Chief Aburi and said, "Chief, yesterday, as we were walking along the road with my friend Pep, he found a rain stone. When I told him to bring it to you, he refused. Today he has taken the rain stone to Chief Ocieng in Pajok." When Chief Aburi heard the news, he told this man, "If this child (Pep) comes back, you bring him to me."

When Pep came back, after a few days, to his friend in Obbo, his friend immediately sent a message to Chief Aburi. Chief Aburi on hearing the news of Pep's return to Obbo, called him (Pep). Pep also obeyed, because he did not know why Chief Aburi was calling him. He immediately went to Chief Aburi, who asked him, "Pep, I was told that you found my rain stone. I want to know where you have put it. I don't want to talk much; all I want is my rain stone." Pep replied, "Chief, I did not find any rain stone. Secondly, I don't understand what you are saying."

Chief Aburi was angry with Pep's response. So he called his guards and told them, "I do not want to see this man called Pep. I want you to arrest him and tie him with a rope, flog him and throw him in a rubbish pit. Chief Ocieng should come to me if he is powerful. Pep acted spitefully by taking my rain stone to Chief Ocieng."

Instantaneously, the guards took away Pep, who was before Chief Aburi, and pinned his neck to the ground. They tied Pep with a rope and whipped him to unconsciousness, and the guards thought Pep had died. So they dragged his body and dumped it in a rubbish pit.

Reports show that Pep regained consciousness because of the early morning chill. When he opened his eyes, he realized that he was in a rubbish pit. He struggled to get up, and immediately concluded that Obbo was not a good place to stay. At once, Pep began to move back to Pajok. When he reached Pajok, he told Chief Ocieng how Chief Aburi mistreated him. That day, Chief Ochieng was down because of an injury he sustained when he stepped on burnt grass stem.

When Chief Ocieng heard the news, he concluded that Obbo was truly in competition with Pajok. He later selected six boys to secretly go to Obbo. Prior to the boys' travel to Obbo, Chief Ocieng cautioned them, "There! When you reach Obbo, I want you to throw leaves at the door of the people of Logolo and Opokomere, because these people are ours. If in future the Pajok go to fight the people of Obbo, I do not want any child of Pajok to fight any member of Logolo and Opokomere. Besides, I have already sent three of my messengers to take a spear with one side of its blade smeared, and a knife to Chief Aburi."

In the evening, the Pajok from four families: Bura, Ayu, Panto and Kapaa gathered (all of the Pajok left). Chief Oceng instructed, "You are going to fight the people of Obbo. I don't want any born of Pajok to lay a finger on people who are living in huts with leaves thrown on their doorway, because they are our clan mates. But people living in houses not marked by leaves at the doorway should all be killed, women and children alike."

On the other hand, the Obbo also knew that a major fight was about to be waged on them, so the Obbo waited for the Pajok. At around 12:00 mid night, when it was dead quiet, the Pajok entered the homestead of Obbo. Shortly, the men occupied a field called "Kinyeye". Kinyeye is in Logolo hunting ground. In this fight of Pep, some members of Obbo did not stand with the Abong. According to the history of Obbo, the Padyeri were the only ones who supported the Abong.

The men engaged in a fierce fight in "Kinyeye", and so many people of Pajok and Obbo died. Some Acholi elders said the number of the people of Obbo who died during the fight exceeded those of Pajok. When the Obbo realized that they had become weak, they escaped from behind the homestead– the Obbo turned their backs to the Pajok (fled). Abong ran and scattered all over,

597

but the Padyeri gathered and hid in Logolo hunting ground, and the Pajok set fire after them. Many people were burned like monkeys in the hunting ground. But those who could run fast escaped without injuries.

Reports show that after the fight, the Pajok left Kinyeye and went to nearby villages. The women who saw the Pajok coming escaped, leaving behind their children who were asleep. The Pajok then started picking the sleeping children, made big fire and cooked the children in a pot. According to reports, older children were cut into two, so that their bodies could easily fit into the cooking pot. The newborns were however put whole in the cooking pot.

The history of Obbo states that much as some members of Obbo did not want to help the Abong, they immediately sounded ululations when they saw the cruelty of the Pajok towards the people of Abong. The Obbo all gathered and went to fight the Pajok. They fought until they chased the Pajok from Obbo. Later, Chief Aburi came home with the few members of Abong clan who survived the fight. The Pajok later composed this song in memory of the war:

Panto ki Ayuu tyeko lotinno!	Panto and Ayo will finish the children!
Koc Kono Pajok Obino Roman!	Koc Pajok could have come to Roman!
Langure Aburi Coko Lwak Pere Terokany!	Langure Aburi takes his people here!
Lokot Ogoyo I Yang Waii!	Lokot once defeated you!
Parajok Obino Ningning?	How did the Pajok come?
Munu Kany!	The white man here!
Lokot Goyo Langure!	Lokot defeats Langure!

The Conflict Between Obbo and Magwi

Acholi history shows that there were few conflicts among the Obbo and Magwi. The accounts of the Obbo, state that the Obbo did not fight all the families in Magwi, except the family of Palimu. One day, I asked some Acholi elders, "How did the war between Obbo and Palimu start?" The Acholi elders told me that the fight was started by Chief Aburi. Due to his war-mongering traits, one day, Chief Aburi sent his guards with a knife handle, to Chief Obwona of Palimu.

Chief Obwona is the father of Lodya. When the guards of the chief reached chief Obwona's compound, they found his guards guarding the palace. Chief Aburi's guards instantly picked the knife handle, and gave it to Chief Obwona's guards to take to their master. Before taking the knife handle to the chief, the guard asked the messengers, "If Chief Obwona asks who sent the knife handle, what should I tell him?" Chief Aburi's guard replied, "If your master asks you, tell him that Chief Aburi sent the knife handle. He (Aburi) also wants chief Obwona to come and visit him in Obbo." The guard then took the knife handle took to chief Obwona. When chief Obwona saw the guard coming towards him with a knife handle, he became petrified, and immediately asked the guard, "Who sent that knife handle you are holding?" The guard responded, "Chief Aburi of Obbo sent it to you. He also wants you to go and visit him in Obbo."

When Chief Obwona got the message, he immediately prepared himself and called five of his guards to escort him. After a short time, Chief Obwona reached Obbo, and found chief Aburi waiting for him. The history of Acholi states that when Chief Obwona arrived in Obbo, Chief Aburi did not give him water for drinking, or a seat. Chief Aburi started asking Chief Obwona before he had rested, "Get up, you man! There are no visits! What has brought you to Obbo?"

Before chief Obwona could answer, Chief Aburi picked a gun and shot Obwona in the chest. According to reports, Chief Obwona was a strong man, so he did not fall instantly after he was shot. He escaped with his gun-shot wounds, while bleeding profusely. Chief Obwona attempted to run with his injury up to Palimu, but he became weak after losing a lot of blood. He died on reaching Logoro Hill.

The history of Magwi tells us that Chief Obwona died on the hill, and his guards left him there, and later sent a message home. When the Palimu heard that their chief had died, they immediately asked the guards, "Who killed our chief?" The guards answered, "Chief Aburi shot him in the chest with a gun." Afterwards, the people of Palimu asked themselves, "Is chief Obwona really dead?" They did not believe that Chief Obwona had truly died. For this reason, they started moving towards the hill where the body of Chief Obwona was. They also thought the injury that chief Obwona sustained was minor, so he could still be alive.

But Lo'dya Rokomoi, the eldest son of Chief Obwona, stopped the people from going where his father's body lay. He asked them to stay home, and he went by himself to see his father's injury. He also wanted to prove whether his father was still alive or dead. The people of Palimu heeded to Rokomoi advice and remained at home. As directed by the guards, Rokomoi went where his father's body rested. When he arrived at the hill, he proved that his father had indeed died. He then picked a hand knife from his arm, and cut off his father's neck. He took only his father's head back home.

The history of Magwi states that before Chief Obwona died, he had sternly instructed his children against burying his body at the doorway upon his death. He instead willed his body to be put in a cave in Okire Hill. When Rokomoi brought his father's head home, the people of Palimu gathered and asked Chief Obwona's children, "What shall we do with your father's head?" The chief's children replied, "When our father was still alive, he instructed us to bury his body in a cave in Okire Hill after his death." When the clan elders of Palimu, heard this, they took the chief's head to a cave in Okire Hill as he instructed.

On returning from Okire Hill, people convened a meeting to discuss what should be done to Chief Aburi to avenge the death Chief Obwona. After hours of discussions, they resolved that the Palimu should fight the Obbo, to death because the murder of Chief Obwona was an insult by the Obbo on the people of Palimu (Magwi).

The history of Acholi says after a few months, the Palimu prepared and went to fight Obbo. Unfortunately, they were very weak and the Obbo killed so many of them that the whole place was overflowing with blood. Many people of Palimu died in the fight. Some people commented that the Palimu took themselves to be slaughtered by the Obbo. The few survivors fled back to Magwi.

The War between Agoro and Ofirika

The conflict between the Agoro and Ofirika happened when shea nuts were ripening in Acholi. One day, the women of Agoro went to collect shea nuts from the bush. At that time, one man of Ofirika was watching the women of Agoro collect shea nuts. He right away, informed the people of Ofirika, "My people, the women of Agoro have gathered to collect shea nuts." When the boys of Ofirika heard the message, many gathered and went to stab the women of Agoro.

One day, I asked the elders of Agoro, "Why did the boys of Ofirika decide to stab the women of Agoro?" Unfortunately, there was no elder who could answer my question. This is another issue I will research on and publish in the *Second Edition* of this book.

According to illustrations, when the boys of Ofirika reached the bush, they found the women of Agoro busy collecting shea nuts. The boys immediately started stabbing the women with spears, amid screams from the women. The history of Agoro states that many women died that fateful day. The women who survived the spears ran home to tell Chief Dermoi. Chief Dermoi was very angry when he heard the news, and immediately thought of avenging the death of the women.

On the other hand, the boys of Ofirika went back home and narrated everything they did to the women of Agoro. Chief Lopula of Ofirika was elated when he heard what his boys did. Some people say when Chief Lopula heard the news, asked everyone to be vigilant and ready for anything the people of Agoro would do to Ofirika. In fact, the men of Ofirika sharpened their spears, and waited for any impending fight from the people of Agoro.

Around the year 1940, Chief Dermoi of Agoro waged a war on the people of Ofirika. The elders of Agoro told me that the warriors of Agoro Right and Agoro Left all went for this war. Many Acholi elders said the Agoro warriors out-numbered the people of Ofirika. Because of the large number and might of the warriors of Agoro, they fought until they defeated Ofirika. Many women, men and children of Ofirika died during the conflict. Other reports indicate that the fight ended draw, which means both sides lost the same number of people. Other people say Chief Dermoi was injured during the fight by the Ofirika. Luckily, he did not die. Reports show that when Chief Dermoi reached home Agoro, he stitched a calabash over his wound, and it healed. Reports also indicate that when Chief Dermoi was injured, he thought so much of his wives, and he would always cry that, "Eee! Eee! I will die, people will enjoy my wives. God of my father! Why do you treat me so badly?"

Later, Chief Dermoi of Agoro brought the people Ofirika under his chiefdom, and settled them on Kilijok Hill. This explains how Chief Lopula lost his chiefdom – because Chief Lopula, together with his people, went back under the leadership of Chief Dermoi.

The history of Acholi states that Ofirika lived under the leadership of chief of Agoro from 1940 — 1990. In 1990, when the government of Sudan established the Magwi Rural Council, the government representative called Marko Aluma of Madi (Moli- Andro), took the people of Ofirika and put them under the leadership of Omeo. In 1992 Ofirika became independent from Omeo.

The Conflict between Agoro and Magwi

The Acholi like going hunting as a family, but sometimes, one family could go with another family. History has it that the Magwi loved to go hunting with the people of Agoro. The people of Agoro could stand on the right, while the people of Magwi would stand on the left. When it was time to go hunting, the people of Magwi and Agoro would assemble in one place, and go together in the hunting ground.

One month in 1930, the people of Magwi and Agoro heard about hunting. But before they set out for the hunting, the hunters of Agoro and Magwi unanimously agreed to meet in a place called Duma-lalor, located in the territory of the chief of Agoro. On this day, everybody gathered before time for burning the bush. When the people of Agoro and Magwi were waiting for the time to burn the bush, one Magwi person brought a haughty conversation. He said, "If a reed rat emerges, people will scatter in different directions." And one child of Agoro responded, "If the edible rat comes here, we shall be the ones to kill it."

When the born of Magwi heard the response of the born of Agoro, he again asked that, "What will come, O*pilia (edible rat)* or *Obiliok (edible rat)*?" Much as the Acholi speak the same language, there are certain things that are called or pronounced differently in different villages. For instance, the Pajok, Obbo, Magwi and Agoro all call edible rat in a differently. If we go to Magwi, we find that they call edible rat, *opilia*. But Agoro call it *obiliok*. The debate on how to pronounce a reed rat caused chaos among the Magwi and Agoro. The people of Magwi said that the people of Agoro did not know how to pronounce edible rat, and called it *Obiliok*. The people of Agoro, on the other hand, claimed that the people of Magwi did not know how to pronounce edible rat, and called it *opilia*. This exchange continued, and it became a big fight among the Magwi and Agoro. Many people from Agoro and Magwi lost their lives. People stabbed themselves, and the plan to go hunting was foiled.

Chapter Thirty Five

THE CONFLICT BETWEEN OBBO AND LOKORO

People have different versions of the war between Obbo and Lokoro. The Obbo have a different version, while the Lokoro also have another narrative. But one thing that the two groups agree on is that there was a fight between them.

To better understand these contradictions, I want us to hear what the people of Obbo have to say, and later we have look at the version the people of Logolo have.

(a) What do Obbo say about the fight between Obbo and Lokoro?

The people of Logolo are famed among the Acholi as fish mongers. The people of Logolo sold fish to their friends and neighbours such as Lotuko, Lopit, Acholi and the people of Bar. The history of Acholi states that around1890, the people of Kor relocated from Lafon Hill and settleed among the Acholi of Pajok. Some brothers of Kor who remained at the foot of Lafon Hill, also did not forget about their brothers who went to Acholiland. For this reason, in 1901 the people of Kor who remained in Lafon always went to Pajok to visit their brothers and sisters who lived in Pajok. Since the people of Lokoro were renowned fish mongers, they went to Acholiland daily to visit their bothers. During such visits, they would always carry fish and sell to the people of Agoro, Magwi and Obbo.

Reports show that in 1901 ten people of Lokoro were going to Pajok. When they reached Obbo, they came across the children of Logolo. That year the people of Logolo had built in Owil. When fifteen children of Logolo saw ten people of Lokoro coming, they (Lokoro) started fighting the people of Kor. The history of Obbo states that during this fight, the children of Logolo killed two children of Lokoro. Reports also show that the children of Lokoro who survived, fled back to Liful.

In this year, Chief Ranga, was the leader of the people of Lokoro. When the eight surviving children reached Liful, they went straight to Chief Ranga and narrated what the children of Obbo did to them, as they were going to visit their brothers and sisters in Pajok. One of the children told Chief Rang, "Chief, we came to inform you that the children of Obbo fought us and killed two of us. They even took our fish."

The history of Obbo states that in 1901, Chief Ibrahim Otoo of Abong, was the leader of the people of Obbo. In that same year, the people were still settled at the foot of Lotii Hill. According to reports, when Chief Ranga received this news, he did not immediately send messengers to Chief Otoo in Obbo. This does not mean Chief Ranga was afraid of Chief Otoo, rather, Chief Ranga wanted to seek advice from the elders of Lokoro, on what should be done to Obbo to avenge the death of the two children.

After two days, Chief Ranga summoned all the elders of Lokoro and told them what the children of Obbo did to the children of Lokoro, as they were passing through Obbo. Later the elders resolved that since the people of Obbo killed their children, the Obbo should give two girls as compensation. The elders of Lokoro added that the issue of compensating lost lives with girls is also practiced in Lokoro.

In 1902, Chief Ranga sent messengers to Chief Ibrahim. Reports show that before the messengers left Lokoro, the chief instructed them, "If you reach Obbo, I want the people of Chief Otoo to compensate my people they killed last year. If he has anythings for the compensation, he should give them to you so that you bring them to me." The messengers reached the compound of Chief Otoo, and they told his guard, "We are children from Lokoro. Our chief sent us to Chief Otoo with an important message." Chief Otoo's guard then relayed the message to their master. When Chief Otoo heard the message, he asked the guard to send the messengers to him because he wanted to hear the message from them. The guards went and called the children of Lokoro. When the messengers came before Chief Otoo, he immediately asked them, "What brings you to my compound today?" One of the messengers answered, "Chief, we have brought for you an important message from our chief. A year ago, when ten children of Lokoro were passing from your territory, the children of Obbo killed two of them. Chief Ranga has therefore sent us with a message that if you have items to compensate the death of the two children, you should give and we take to him as the traditions of Acholi and Lokoro stipulate." Chief Otoo responded that if such compensation is to be made, then it should be done by the people of Logolo because they were the ones who killed the children."

Later, Chief Otoo asked his guards to take the children of Lokoro to Logolo. In this year, elder Olak was the leader of Logolo. When the messengers of Lokoro reached the home of Logolo in Owil, Olak sent a message to the people to come and hear what the people of Lokoro had to say. The children of Logolo assembled to listen to the message brought by the children of Lokoro. When all the people of Logolo assembled, one elder from the side of Chief Otoo, got up and talked to the gathering, "Very well my clan mates, you have understood that your children killed two children of Lokoro, last year when the children of Lokoro were going to Pajok. Today, the chief of Lokoro has sent his people to take from us the items to pay for the death of the children of Obbo. Chief Ranga, of Lokoro, wants us to give two girls in compensation of the two children."

When the children of Logolo heard about the compensation, they started mumbling. The people of Logolo responded in chorus, "What kind of teeth do the people that we are supposed to give as compensation have? Do they have teeth that lookNg-gacaa ng-gacaa? The people of Lokoro have muddy-brain (useless-brain); we are not going to pay anything to them." When the children of Lokoro heard this response, they quietly got up and went back to Liful. The messengers of Chief Otoo were also speechless on hearing the response. They went back to Chief Otoo to inform him about what transpired at Logolo. Chief Otoo was so saddened with the response he got from the children of Logolo through his messengers. But there was nothing he could do to resolve the matter. When the children of Lokoro reached home, they told Chief Ranga, "Chief, we took your message to Obbo as you instructed us. But when we reached, they refused to compensate the death of the two children they killed." When Chief Ranga heard this, he commanded his people to go and fight the people of Obbo, because they displeased him.

That year, the people of Obbo all built together at Lotii Hill, but the home of chief and other children of Abong were a bit far from other members'. The history of Acholi says about five hundred Lokoro people came to fight the people of Obbo. The people of Lokoro sieged Obbo at around 3:00 am, and immediately started spearing the Obbo at exactly 5:00 am, which is the best time for sleeping. The people of Lokoro fought Obbo for five hours till 10:00 pm. The fight started from Boru and ended in a small stream, which is presently called Obbo-bil- which means since Obbo refused to compensate the people of Lokoro, they should also feel the pain of losing dear ones. Reports indicate that the Obbo lost more than one hundred people in this fight. But majority of people who died were from Logolo, Kitaka and Loudo. Acholi elders say that at least fifty people of Lokoro also died in the fight.

Reports show that the only home which the Lokoro did not reach was Chief Otoo's. In the past, custom was against killing women and children during conflicts. For this reason, the people of Lokoro captured women and children of Obbo, and took them to Liful. The history of Acholi and Lokoro state that when the people of Lokoro reached Liful, men who had no wives, got wives from among those who were brought from Obbo, while men who did not have children got from among those captured from Obbo. Other elders of Acholi told me that during this conflict, some women were taken when they were pregnant. The history of Obbo states that many expectant mothers were captured during the fight. However, the children who were born in Lokoro, by expectant mothers who the Obbo remember are Ayora Longirodel, Owinyo and William Olweny of Loudo (Abong) and Dyiang and Akwai of Kitaka. Some of the children of Obbo who were still in their mother's womb and born in Lokoro did not return. But the five of the children namely, Ayora Longirodel, Owinyo, William Olweny, Dyang and Akwai later went back to Obbo around the year 1940.

The Obbo composed a song in memory of the fight between Lokoro and Obbo:

Obbo Nya-kicum!	Obbo nya-kicum!
Lokoro Otum i Ngom Boru!	Lokoro were finished in Bour!
Obbo Nya-kicum!	Obbo nya-kicum!
Tong pa Logot pe ngeyo Agoro!	Logot's spears don't know Agoro!
Obbo Nya-kicum!	Obbo Nya-kicum!

(b) What the people of Lokoro say about the fight between Obbo and Lokoro.
The people of Kor of Pajok left Lokoro in 1890 because of the fight between them
and the people of Wiatwoo. When they left Lokoro, they moved and passed near
Lotuko. In the same year, the people of Lotuko and Lopit repeatedly taunted the
people of Lokoro. Reports show that the people of Kor passed through Lokoya,
Agoro, Magwi and Obbo before reaching Pajok. The history of Acholi and Lokoro
state that, when people of Kor where traveling, the children of Agoro, Magwi
and Obbo stabbed them along the way, and many people lost their lives.

In (1890) Chief Olum was traveling with his people of Kor. Chief Olum was
not happy with what happened. Some elders of Lokoro and Acholi say, much
as the people of Magwi and Agoro stabbed the people of Kor, the people of
Olak of Logolo (Obbo), killed more children of Lokoro. The history of Acholi
states that in the year the people of Kor were in Pajok, the children of Obbo
attempted to build a relationship with them. But much as there was a relationship between the children of Kor and Obbo, we find that the children of
Lokoro still harboured the intention of revenging the atrocities committed
against them by Obbo. Reports state that the people of Kor deceived Obbo
with smiles, but their hearts remained dark.

In 1898, Chief Ranga asked Kamure to bewitch the people of Pajok so that
his people return home. Kamure obeyed the chief and picked his feces and
shoes and gave to the messengers to take to Pajok. The following morning
after the messengers of Kamure arrived in Pajok, all food in Pajok smelt of
feces. When Chief Olum saw this, he told the people of Kor, "It is Chief Lokoro
who wants you to go back home." Olum said this because he was well versed
with Kamure's deeds.

The following morning, the people of Kor gathered to go back to Liful
(Lafone). After a short time, the aged, and those who were living peacefully in
Acholi refused to go back to Lokoro. Reports indicate that when the people of
Olum were going back to Liful, they also passed through Obbo, Magwi, Agoro
and Lokoya. According to the elders of Lokoro, the month the people of Olum
were going back to Lokoro, they were not attacked by the people of Obbo,
Magwi, Agoro and Lokoya. When the people of Kor arrived in Liful, Chief Ranga
(father of Limungiro) welcomed them warmly and told them to build among
their brothers who remained in Lafone years back. The people of Olum who
returned home from Pajok built among their brothers.

In the year (1898) Limungiro also took over the chiefdom of Lokoro, and was the leader of the people of the people of Lafone (Liful). The people of Kor, who returned from Pajok, narrated to the chief the problems they encountered on their way to Pajok. They told him how the people of Lokoya, Agoro, Obbo and Magwi killed many of them. But the children of Obbo killed the children of Lokoro the most. When Limungiro heard this, he responded, "You children of Lokoro, take my animal net to Obbo." This means the children of Lokoro should prepare to go and fight the Obbo. He then cursed the Obbo so that nothing wrong would happen to the children of Lokoro. Much as Chief Limungiro said this, reports show that the people of Kor did not come immediately to retaliate on the people of Obbo. They stayed for about four years (1898 -1902), when the people of Obbo had already forgotten the atrocities they had committed on the people of Kor.

In 1902, the people of Kor estimated at five hundred siege the people of Obbo at around 3:00 am. A fight erupted at exactly 5:00 am, and it lasted for five hours. The fight started from Boru and ended at a small stream, the present-day Obbo-bil. The people of Kor gave this name because the Obbo killed their people years back, so they wanted them to also feel if death is good. The children of Obbo were almost wiped out in Obbo-bil.

The Obbo who died in the fight, outnumbered the people of Lokoro.The history of Lokoro says they fought three families: Logolo, Kitaka and Loudo. In the past, women and children were not killed during wars. For this reason, the people of Lokoro captured the women and children of Obbo, and took them to Liful. When they reached Liful, the clan elders distributed the women to the men who had no wives. The children were given to couples who did not have children —because they wanted children. In the same year, (1902) the people of Lokoro also fought the people of Magwi and Agoro.

Chapter Thirty Six

FAMILY TREE

Acholi is a people, in the whole of Africa, that like family tree very much. When Acholi people talk of family tree, they mean blood relations, not a relation based on money or food. Knowing relatives is very important because it helps young people from marrying relatives. As we have seen before some boys and girls who are related get married to each other simply because they do not know that they are relatives. Even if such a case is reported to elders, it is the same as wearing a she on a thorn-pricked foot. If such boys and girls knew that they were blood relatives, they would not engage in love affairs with each other. That nothing was written about Acholi clans and tribe, their origins are only known to the point where elders can remember. Most elders remember only two past generations. Anything beyond that may not be remembered. That is where problem comes from. Most elders do not know the grand fathers of their grand fathers. Very few people in Acholi can remember 5 to 15 grand fathers of the family. However, most of them cannot name the children of those grand fathers one by one. They can only talk about one grandfather.

People do not remember names of the siblings of a grandfather they talk about. This is one of the reasons why young related people can marry each other. If there is a grandfather of both a boy and a girl, whose name can be remember, that is where the two cannot marry each other. The best example is Abong. The history of Acholi tells us that the people of Abong came from Tirangore (Lotuko) or Toposa (in Kapoeta). When I was sharing with Abong elders, I discovered that they could remember Loberete, which means their family lineage ends with Loberete and together with the people of Bura-Kitaka where he first settled with his people when they left Kapoeta. I discovered that Loberete did not beget only Moronyo, but also other children. However, because of tracing family lineage, the people of Abong could remember only Muronyo. When we examine very closely, we shall find that elders who want to trace family lineage would choose only one boy child like Loberete and Moronyo to keep record of the family descent.

The knowledge of family lineage is usually transmitted to the next generation by word of mouth. An elder tells his child and his child tell his, and on and on. If we take the people of Obbo, for example, the Abong clan is known because of Kassiba and his son, Otto Ibrahim. Very few children of Abong know their family descent that exists between Agunya and other Abong children who live in Obbo today.

To proper identify a clan, people have names that denote blood relations. Acholi people do not have only one name for identification of kinship. To better understand the family/clan names, let us look at three different clan naming among Acholi of Sudan: —

1. From the eight clans in Acholi, seven of them call a husband of their sister, Oraa, but one of them, Agoro , call husband of a sister, "Liwota".
2. Other Acholi people call the brother of a woman's father-in-law, "Oraa," but the people of Pajok call him "kwara."
3. Thirdly, the Northern Acholi call husband's sister, "waya" or "Ayena", but Southern Acholi, for example, Agoro, call husband's sister, "ywera."

To avoid disparities, in this book, we will use one name to show the family lineage, but where I cannot, I will use two or three from different clans.

Here are names that can be used to identify lineage: —

S/NO	What do you call him or her?	If you are a woman	If you are a man
	The husband of your aunt	My father	My father/my friend
	The husband of your sister	My husband	My brother-in-law/my friend
	The husband of your daughter	My son-in-law (oraa)	My son-in-law (oraa)
	The husband of your mother	My father	My father

S/NO	What do you call him or her?	If you are a woman	If you are a man
	The husband of your grandmother	My grandfather	My grandfather
	The husband of your niece	My brother-in-law (oraa)	My brother-in-law (oraa)
	The husband of your sister	My husband	My brother-in-law
	The grandmother of your wife	My grandmother	My grand mother
	The grandmother of your husband	My grandmother	My grandmother
	The grand mother of your father	My grandmother	My grandfather
	The grandmother of your father	My grandmother	My grandmother
	The grandmother of your grandfather	My grandmother	My grandmother
	The grandmother of your grandmother	My grandmother	My grandmother
	The the wife of your son	My daughter-in-law	My wife
	The wife of your paternal uncle	My uncle's wife	My uncle's wife
	The wife of your brother (ywera/ayena)	My sister-in-law (ywera/ayena)	My sister-in-law/my wife (ywera/ayena)
	The wife of your cousin	My sister-in-law (ywera)	My sister-in-law (ywera)
	The wife of your father	My father's wife/my mother	My father's wife/my mother
	The wife of your grandfather	My grandmother	My grandmother
	Wife of your nephew	My niece (ywera)	My wife (ywera)

S/NO	What do you call him or her?	If you are a woman	If you are a man
	The grandfather of your wife		My father/my grandfather
	The grandfather of your husband	My grandfather/my father	My grandfather
	The grandfather of your father	My grandfather	My grandfather
	The grandfather of your mother	My grandfather	My grandfather
	The grandfather of your niece	My father-in-law	My father-in-law
	The grandfather of your nephew	My brother-in-law	My brother-in-law
	Maternal uncle of your wife	My uncle	My brother-in-law
	Maternal uncle of your husband	My brother-in-law	My uncle
	Maternal uncle of your father	My grandfather	My grandfather
	Maternal uncle of your mother	My uncle/my grandfather	My uncle/my grandfather
	Maternal uncle of your son/daughter	My brother-in-law	My brother-in-law
	Maternal uncle of your nephew/niece	My brother-in-law	My brother-in-law
	Maternal uncle of your grandfather	My grandfather	My grandfather
	Maternal uncle of your grandmother	My grandfather/my uncle	My grandfather/my uncle
	The mother-in-law of your father	My grandmother	My grandmother

S/NO	What do you call him or her?	If you are a woman	If you are a man
	The mother-in-law of your mother	My grandmother	My grandmother
	The mother-in-law of your sister	My mother-in-law	My mother-in-law
	The mother-in-law of your brother	My mother-in-law	My mother-in-law
	The mother-in-law of your maternal uncle	My grandmother	My grandmother
	The mother-in-law of your aunt	My grandmother	My grandmother
	The mother-in-law of your niece	My mother-in-law	My mother-in-law
	The mother-in-law of your nephew	My mother-in-law	My mother-in-law
	The mother-in-law of your grandfather	My grandmother	My grandmother
	The mother of your wife	My mother	My mother-in-law
	The mother of your husband	My mother-in-law	My mother
	The mother of your mother	My grandmother	My grandmother
	The mother of your father	My grandmother	My grandmother
	The mother of your nephew	My sister	My sister
	The mother of your niece	My sister	My sister
	The mother of your grandfather	My grandmother	My grandmother
	The brother of your husband	My brother-in-law/my husband	My brother-in-law
	The brother of your wife	My brother	My brother-in-law

S/NO	What do you call him or her?	If you are a woman	If you are a man
	The brother of the father of your wife	My father	My father
	The brother of the father of your husband	My father-in-law/my grandfather	My uncle
	The brother of your mother	My uncle	My uncle
	The brother of your father	My father	My father
	The daughter of the brother of your father	Owora	Lawora
	The son of the brother of your father	My nephew	My nephew
	The son of your father's sister	My nephew	My niece
	The daughter of the sister of your father	My niece	My uncle?
	The son of your mother's brother	My uncle	My mother?
	The daughter of your mother's brother	My niece	My nephew?
	The son of your mother's sister	My brother	My cousin?
	The dughter of your mother's sister	My cousin	My nephew?
	The son of your sister	My nephew	My niece
	The daughter of your sister	My niece	My brother-in-law
	The son of the maternal aunt of your wife	My nephew	My nephew/my brother-in-law
	The daughter of the maternal aut of your wife	My niece	My niece

S/NO	What do you call him or her?	If you are a woman	If you are a man
	The son of the maternal aunt of your husband	My brother-in-law	My son
	The daughter of the maternal aunt of your husband	My sister-in-law	My sister
	Your brother's child	My brother?	My -in-law/my wife?
	Your husband's sister	My aunt	My aunt
	The sister of your wife	My sister	My mother/my wife
	The sister of your father	My aunt	My aunt
	The sister of your mother	My mother	My grandmother
	The sister of your grandfather	My aunt	My grandmother
	The sister of your grandmother	My grandmother	My mother-in-law
	The -in-law of your aunt	My grandfather	My -in-laaw
	The -in-law of your brother	My -in-law	My grandfather
	The -in-law of your sister	My -in-law	My grandfather
	The -in-law of your grandfather	My grandfather	My -in-law
	The father-in-law of your grandmother	My grandfather	My father-in-law
	The father-in-law of your daughter	My father-in-law	My grandmother
	The father-in-law of your son	My father-in-law	My grandfather
	The aunt of your father	My grandfather	My father-in-law
	The aunt of your father	My grandmother	My grandmother
	The aunt of your wife	My aunt	My aunt

S/NO	What do you call him or her?	If you are a woman	If you are a man
	The aunt of your husband	My mother-in-law	My grandmother
	The aunt of your grandfather	My mother-in-law	My father-in-law
	The aunt of your grandmother	My grandmother	My grandmother
	Your wife's father	My father-in-law	My father-in-law
	Your husband's father	My -in-law	My father-in-law

Bibliography:

Ahmed Bayoum, 1979, The History of Sudan Health Services, Kenya Literacy Bureau, Nairobi.

Akena p'ojok London, 2008, The Eastern Axis of the Great Lwo Migration, Cambrige University Press, London. Awake, can the Churches Unite? February 1991.

B.A. Ogot, 1967, History of the Southern Luo, Vol. 2 Migration and Settlement 1500-1900, University of East Africa Press, Nairobi Kenya.

Bethwell A. Ogot, 1967, History of the Southern Lwo, Vol.1 Imigration an Settlement 1500-1900. University College of Nairobi, Kenya

Crazzolara F.S.C.F, 1950, The Lwoo Part I Lwoo Migrations, Missioni Africane – Verona, Italy.

Crazzolara F.S.C.F, 1951, The Lwoo Part 11 Lwoo Traditions, Missioni Africane – Verona, Italy.

Crazzolara F.S.C.F, 1954, The Lwoo Part 111 Clans, Missioni Africane – Verona, Italy.

Directorate of Catholic Church Volv.I 1995.

Islam and Christianity, Ninety Questions and Answers by Abdul-Masih, Daystar Press, Ibadan, Nigeria 1970-71.

Gilbert Cruz-Carreon, 2009, Marriage Quote, Queenland University of Technology, International Accredited Business School, Australia.

Family Mediation Centre, Relationship Services, 2006, Melbourne, Australia.

Minutes of Obbo/Iyire Conferrence, 23-24th December 2007, Loudo Obbo.

Ministry of Foreing Affairs, 1973, Peace and Unity in the Sudan, Khartoum University Press, Khartoum.

New People Special issue Jan. 2000.

Onyango-ku-Odongo J.B. Webster, 1976, The Central Lwo During the Aconya, East African Literature Bureau, Nairobi Kenya.

Rev. Vittorino dellagiacoma, 1992, Sudanese Catholic Clergy and Major Seminarians, Edition V1, Khartoum, Sudan.

Rev. Vittorino dellagiacoma, 1986, Missioneries in Southern Sudan 1900-1964, National Major Seminary Khartoum, Sudan.

Richard Layard, 2006, Happiness: Lessons from a New Science, There is a Paradox at the heart of our live, Penguin, London, UK.

Robert O. Collins, 2008, A History of Modern Sudan, Cambridge University Press, UK.

Samuel Baker, 1866, The Albert N'yanza Greate Basin of the Nile, and Exploration of the Nile Sources, Volume 1, London Macmillan and Co, UK.

Samuel Baker, 1866, The Albert N'yanza Greate Basin of the Nile, and Exploration of the Nile Santo Ongin, 2005, Lobo me Magwi, Australia, Brisbane Sources, Volume 11, London Macmillan and Co, UK.

Sudan Notes and Records, Volume 11, Acholi Customs by Capt.E T N Grove, Printed in German, 1918-1920.

Steve Harvey, 2009, Act Like A Lady, Think Like A Man, First Edition, 10 East 53rd Street, New York, USA.

Stephen R. Covey, 2004, The 7 Habits Of Highly Effective People, Powerfull Lessons in Personal Change, New York, USA.

Sudan notes and records, Volume 24, The Shilluk Tribe by M.E.C. Pumphrey, Printed in German, 1941-45.

Tim, 1985, Acholi decision making: A paper for the Norwegian Church Aid Sudan Programme: Torit, Sudan.

The Watch Tower. A Divided Church Can it Survive? July 1st 1994.

William J. House and Kevin D. Philip Howard, 1995, Social Survey among the Acholi, University of Juba, Sudan.

Appendix

No	Wii Gang	Gibino ki	Opoke i dog ot	Lotela megi	Tim megi	Got megi	Jok megi
1-	Abong	Tirangore (Kafurere)	1- Abong pa Rwot 2- Abong Kure	Imayi	-Amalac -Lokile	Pe	Jikiloti
2-	Kitaka	Iyire-Kalamoro Logolo-pa-Okuka Imila-Katire Ifwotu	1- Kwenda Tingili 2- Abolyero 3- Lokomini 4- Lokowor 5- Irwangi	 Adat-Jakwor Rwot Omini " " Gira Idyeku	-Lohile -Holok	Lomolong Lomakwa	
3-	Loudo	-Abong Kure -Ngabara Imurok -Ikolong Gunyoro " Omeo	Gari Ijula-pa-Lowala Ijula-pa-Loremoi Orak Mararii Irwangi Mohi	Won Lonyormoi Lowala Loremoi Agwinya Lowic-Cilmoi	 Bong-won Ladeng-deng Ayoko Agongara	Koyoro (i Magwi)	
4-	Koyo	Wegi paco	- Bira (Rwot) - Patany - Obalo - Ayom	Atany	-Ciri -Oyaa (RDC) -Abiri -Lobano-Ayi -Alyebi -Igoli -Lotii -Apala -ALai	- Abiri - Lotii - Coko - Layuru - Iloii - Ciri	Nya-Rubanga (i got Abiri
5-	Tingili	Loudo-Torit Loudo-Torit Loudo-Torit	Ileregi Logoti Pagwee		Balbal Lohilim Bukbuk Iluki		
6-	Ngabara	Ifwotu Imila	Iriok Palo-pali Lotiri		Aliebi	Lotii Gumia	
7-	Iyire	Ifwotu	1- Iyire pa Lomunya (Kal) 2- Iyire pa Igele (bong)	- Lomunya - Igele	Kapai Bokoro	Nil	Nil

619

Obbo Left Appendix "A

No	Home	Came from	Smaller clans	Leader	Hunting ground	Hill	God
8	Logolo	Kor (Lokoro) ""	1- Pawino 2- Pakuka	1- Owino }Omego 2- Okuka	Logolo		Agore
9	Padyeri	Duk-pa-dyer Ngabara	1-Pa-tyeno 2-Bwola	Girokon	Abar		
10	Opokomere Duk-padyer (Dinka)	Karamoro (Iyire)	1-Opoke-mere (kal) 2-Okano-Mere	Mr. Oyat (brother of Girokon split because of a fight between them)			Nya-Rubanga
11	Lokide	Imurok Bar (Bilinyang from Nya-Rubanga	1-Lokide Bura 2-Lokide Kurukak (Bong)	1-Oboyo 2- Aliya Kec	1- Meri-Lokide 2- Lohube	Lohube	Muul in Meri hunting ground)
12	Pajombo	Lango in Agoro North Bar	1-Bura 2-Okwee (bong)	(a) Agoro (ii) Wino Lakaba (Olwedo)	-Okony-kor -Ongol-kor -Amoyo-tonga -Pakwa	Pakwa -Lwoo (Rwot)	Lwoo (i Cama)
13	Oyere	Imurok Imurok Odiya (Ikotos) Mado Opei (Lango)	Panyibila Wor-Obwoli Palyec Game	1-Kobu Kwar Icunga	Oloyo-tiko	Inapua Nil	1- Odik-piny
14	Pokongo	Ayom Bura-Woroge Oyere(Obbo) Ayom ki Agoro (Bura)	Pokong-Kal Pajanggi Lokomini Omili	Ariko	-Gili-gili -Lalworoodong -]om -Akidi	Pokongo	Nya-Pido.

Pajok Left Appendix "B1"

No	Home	Came from	Smaller clans	Leader		Hunting ground	Hill	God
15	Obwolto	Lokoro	i- Opio ii- Okongo iii- Patoko	Lakau		Ladiki	Lagot-Aluru	Labot-Onyom
16	Bura	Cwaa (Uganda) Pakwa (Obbo) Pajombo	1 Ogoya 2 Payako 3 Pamunda 4 Lamoki 5 Palyec 1 Paramol 2 Pakwa	1- 2-	Oceng Lokwor-Moi ?			
17	Bitti	-Wegi Paco - Koyo	i- Pacwaka ii- Palome			-Agolo ki-Odo Yamo-Okuto -Cin Nyari -Can dek -Acamo Lango -Oder-ki-Lodongo	Lagot-Lwak	
18	Pagaya "Kwac-Lanyuru"	Wegi Paco	i- Pobuk ii-Paladyang	Ogweng		Akwero	Pokec	
19	Ayuu (Wegi gang)	Atiak Palabek (Uganda)	1- Paryemo 2- Panyara-Bongo 1- Palimu			Tim Oloyolweny	Alali	
20	Panto (Kera)	Wegi paco Labongo (Uganga)	i)Pojoku ii) Pabwoo i)Pamola ii)Kera	Opac (rwot Langa-Langa)		Adodi	Adodi	Adodi

Pajok Right Appendix "B2"

No	Home	Came from	Smaller clans	Leader	Hunting ground	Hill	God
21	Ywaya	Lokoro	1-Ywaya Katung 2-Ywaya Bolmeja 3- Ywaaya Kal 3-Lamwoo	Keny Mwoo	Oloyo-Lweny Amoyotonga	Ipul Kit-aweno Jale Lwoo	Lwoo
22	Oyere	Lokoro					
23	Toro (Ywaya)	Nyarubanga (Bar)	Toro	Rwot Anyoda			
24	Paitenge	Lokoro	a- Pa Ogwang b- Pa Odur c)Pa Keno	Jula	Pajula (Bur Pua)	Lobora	Lagang-t
25	Bobi	a-Wegi paco b-Got-Lotii (Obbo)	1-Kiyanga 2-Pakeny 3-Paikweya 1- Paliri-gwen		- Bore — Lanyuru	- Tul - Obwoc	Oyaro
26	Palio	)iWegi Paco ii)Obbo (Logolo)	i)Pi woco ii)Pocaa a- Paliri-gwen		Pajula	Lakima Nyo Got-Ngor	Labwor
27	Kapaa	i)Imurok ii)Palabek (Uganda)	Nine) Kapaa ii) Paibworo		Pe	Pe	
28	Patanga	Lokoro	1-Pa Obwoo}				
			2-Pa Kure 3-Pa Baa 4- Pa Abore	Atanga (Pa Keny)	Iyelle	Pa min-Acwai	Yamo-Tu

Panyikwara Appendix "C1"

No	Home	Came from	Smaller clans	Leader	Hunting ground	Hill	God
29	Goloba	Lokiliri Koyo Bira Lopit ki Alur Alero (Uganda) Bar	1-Olubo 2-Padegi 3-Alero 3-Pajombo	Wani Kwar Ambrozio Lokici 2) Aramtala	Alwala	Pa-Omer Lipul	Mwonye
30	Paliwa		1-Oligo 2-Pacar				
			3-Palokiri 4-Paradwo 5-Palii	Koga	Ong-goyo	Iwire	Iwire
31	Pakala	Lokung Koyo (Obbo)	Pakala-pa-Ogoo Pakala-pa-Akila	Agwayo Cwar Nyare Lopiria	-Gulubu -Kuliemo -Lalworo-Odong (Tim Lalworo-Odong Panyikwarivaling over it with Obbo -Cwar Nyare	-Ikwala -Pa Lanyu (is in Omeo	
32	Oyira	Lamogi (Gulu) fell from the sky	1-Gem 2-Pamurie 3-Pakwac 4-Paratik	Lamogi (Orugo) Paratik	Ajuni	Ajuni	Lori
33	Palabek	Tali	1-Miteng 2-Paleny				
			3-Paguta 4-Bura Adiemu 5-Paco-Olwal 6-Gem	Kuki	Kugi and Maria	Lokwenya	
34	Oloro	Bar/ Lolubo Bar Aru Lolubo Bar Madi	1- Ogura 2- Pamurlu 3- Bura 4- Cubo 5- Kilio 6- Monoteng 7- Cung-gura 8- Kurula	Ogwee Otoo Mogga Ogeno O. Becu Giricon Logoti Okwera	Deyo Koto-koto	Logura	Nywandi

35	Bura	Wegi paco (Anywak) Pajule(Uganda) Mundari	1-Bura Kot 2-Woroger 3-Panyamo 4-Ong-goloba Pajule Pagena	Rwot-Nyikwara	Owil-kado Panya-moo	Ibba (Goloba gave her in palce of a girl the killed)	Ibb'a
36	Ayom	Koyo (Obbo)	1- Ombira				
			2- Paju 3- Bura	Pido-moi	Kata-Kata	Ayom	
37	Ng-gaya	Bar-el-Ghazel	Pa-Lotikaru Pa-Lokecamoi Pa-Mea Pa-Logulu	Cakilicio and Ocilo	Opari	Mugo Opari Motoyo Arule Remo Nyii Bana	Nyii
38	Pajaa	Wegi paco Cwaa(Uganda)	1-Bura 2-Palee	Wod-Nyarie Nam-moi			
39	Dungo	Bar-Nyongkir	Dungo				
40	Payoko						

Palwar Appendix

No	Home	Came from	Smaller clans	Leader	Hunting ground	Hill	God
41	Palwar	Lango (Uganda) Padibe "Madi Opei" Lokung Agoro Katire Obbo	1-Pa-Wojok 2-Lamogi 3-Abong (head of home). 4-Pa-Owoo 5-Pa-Otika 6-Agonya 7-Pa-lodaka 8-Koyole	Daudi Obwonyo	Akwero	Oluke	Oluk
42	Amica	Katire Katire Agoro South Pagaya-Pajok	Icar Ikwari Palongoku Pa-Lobamu	rwot Lotome	Iliwa	Iliwa Acen	Ilai
43	Koyo p'Abee	Agoro North		Abbe (Rain chief)		Laboki	
44	Lomarati	Isore					

45	Agata	One-Agoro North Two- Lokung Three- Labati- Olwonga						
46	Omere	1 Agoro ma malo 2 Lokung 3 Labati- Olwonga						
47	Lobone	i)Agoro North ii)Lokung iii)Labati- Olwonga						
48	Isore							

Magwi Appendix

No	Home	Came from	Smaller clans	Leader	Hunting ground	Hill	God
49	Bura		-Bura Palonyung				
			-Bura Padyeri.	Auya	Pe	Pe	Pe
50	Amika	1-Lokoro 2-Imurok 3-Koyo and Omeo 4-Obbo and Omeo Imurok	1- Logwar 2-Imurok 3-Onyang 4-Lokomiji 5-Ongero		Meri-Magwi	Bome	Aliri-nyakal
51	Labure	1-Bar 2-Lokoro		Igelle			
52	Afufuru (Ijula)	1- Imurok					
53	Palonganyi	1-Imurok Nine- Wegi paco 1)Imurok 1)Pa-Iwo	1-Imurok 2-Orak 3-Pa-wii 1) Marari	Lagul	-Lobela -Ogongo -Odume -Ondire	Kinanuko Ondire	-Lowoo -Iboro- Konya
54	Palimu		-Palimu North -Palimu South				
55	Kiliyo	Hiliu (Lotuko)	1-Ogitana 2-Ocak	Lokidiman	1-Lokore Longutu		
					2-Tim Got-jok 3-Maji.	Got-Jok	Ipuruheny

625

Agoro Right Appendix "**F1**"

No	Home	Came from	Smaller clans	Leader	Hunting ground	Hill	God
56	Bura	Bar-Nyarkenyi	1-Mikitoo 2-Palyec 3-Pa-Amiti	Amiti	Wi-Obor	Nyar-kenyi	—
57	Opara'ba	Bar-nyakenyi Bar-nyakenyi	Pakwal Won-cuk	Cwaka Won-cuk	Wi-Obor	Lagot Oboto	
58	Ogura	Aru ki Rumbek Rumbek	1-Wur-ber 2- Nyamuto-kori	Nyamuto-kori	Ogura	Nyarkenyi	Worbura
59	Pawilli	Okwaa (Okaru)	1-Pawili 2-? 3-	Lobaya	— Okwaa		Okwaa
60	Okareng	Lokoya and Ofirika Longairo and Ofirika	1-Pa-cobono 2-Agilimiang	Cobono Lotodo	Kituru	Okwaa	Okwaa
61	Kicari	Koyo (Lowai)	1-				
			2- Kicari 3-	Nyagura	Kicari	Kicari	?

Agoro Left Appendix **F2**

	Home	They came from	Smaller clans	Their leaders	Hunting ground(s)	Hill(s)	]god(s)
62	Wili-Bari	Rumbek Rumbek Kajo-Kaji	1-Panyulu 2-Imude 3-Kuku	Nyamoyo	Botolo	Botolo Pika	Kurumunda
63	Orimi	Bar-nyakenyi ki Lowai Bar-nyakenyi and Lowai Loudo (Obbo) Aru and Lokoro	1-Owiria 2-Pawele 3-Gem 4-Kur-laa	Merok and Okwer Merok and Okwer Merok	— —		—
64	Patoko	Pajok Pajok	1-Paguur 2-Panyimo	Olem-cigira Olem-cigira	Wii-Obor	Patoko	-

Omeo Left Appendix "G1"

No	Home	Came from		Smaller clans	Leader	Hunting ground	Hill	God
64	Murwari	Igara Bilinyang and Imurok Hiliu (Torit) Lotuko	1- 2- 3- 4-	Igara Okobok Kilio Ikwaka	Kanera Riyamoi and Lowala Onyir and Ocak Pidomoi	-Kilabak -Kilijok -Odeki	Kilijok O'deki Ocee	Okobicak (at Kilijok).

Omeo Right Appendix "G2"

No	Home	Came from	Smaller clans	Leader	Hunting ground	Hill	God
65	Pino-Pino	Lokoro " Igara	Ilukamii Okurak Igara	Kijaba Kijaba Logala	Kimuno Ayei	Pino-pino	Pino-pino
66	Imbaro	Igara(Imurok) Nyarubanga and Imurok Pakala-pa-Akila	Igara Bura-Kal Ikwala	Aluka Atuya and Biyakiri Lonyung	Not there	not there	Not there
67	Ikoo	Igara (Imurok) " Lopit	Oboko Igara Nyemel	Awangole Awangole	-Ikoo (Ocamari) -Mangero	Ikoo	Ikoo
68	Mohoi (Mokoi)	Ifwotu Liria (Lokoya) Longario Ikoo(Igara) Palonganyi	1 Ilany 2 Liria 3 Ongaro 4 Oboko 5 Marari 6 Pa-Carigol	Lorim - Lakol Abeten and Lorwang Okot Iliwa Akere-lokilacong Carigol	Ikola	Mokoi - Ibanyak	Ekewayi Mokoi

Offirika Appendix "K"

No	Home	Came from	Smaller clans	Leader	Hunting ground	Hill	God
69	Lomiling	Imurok Imurok Iyire Igara	Ijuhok Ibore Lohelengi Imolongoi	Dalaha "Ondire Hohofir Abiliwac	Cukayo	Habuho	Ituhok
70	Lodulang	Loudo (Lotuko)	Lodulang	Lokwat-Patige	Mulek	Omala	Omala
71	Tabwor	Lokoro Loudo (Lotuko)	Tabwor	Rwot Ijong Barat-Lohide	Ifakulang	Habuko	Ikoo
72	Locurak	Loudo (Lotuko)	Locurak	Imoyi	Mulek		
73	Ramorok (Kicika)	The owners of home are Loudo	Ramorok		- Ifil		Ajilimit
74	Iyere	Lowai Lokoya)	Iyere		Kituru		